The Wiley Bicentennial–Knowledge for Generations

Each generation has its unique needs and aspirations. When Charles Wiley first opened his small printing shop in lower Manhattan in 1807, it was a generation of boundless potential searching for an identity. And we were there, helping to define a new American literary tradition. Over half a century later, in the midst of the Second Industrial Revolution, it was a generation focused on building the future. Once again, we were there, supplying the critical scientific, technical, and engineering knowledge that helped frame the world. Throughout the 20th Century, and into the new millennium, nations began to reach out beyond their own borders and a new international community was born. Wiley was there, expanding its operations around the world to enable a global exchange of ideas, opinions, and know-how.

For 200 years, Wiley has been an integral part of each generation's journey, enabling the flow of information and understanding necessary to meet their needs and fulfill their aspirations. Today, bold new technologies are changing the way we live and learn. Wiley will be there, providing you the must-have knowledge you need to imagine new worlds, new possibilities, and new opportunities.

Generations come and go, but you can always count on Wiley to provide you the knowledge you need, when and where you need it!

William J. Pesce
President and Chief Executive Officer

Peter Booth Wiley
Chairman of the Board

www.wiley.com/college/microsoft ***or***
call the MOAC Toll-Free Number: 1+(888) 764-7001 (U.S. & Canada only)

Microsoft® Official Academic Course

Supporting and Troubleshooting Applications on a Windows Vista® Client for Enterprise Support Technicians

Microsoft® Certified IT Professional Exam 70-622

Owen Fowler

Credits

EXECUTIVE EDITOR	John Kane
SENIOR EDITOR	Gary Schwartz
DIRECTOR OF MARKETING AND SALES	Mitchell Beaton
MICROSOFT STRATEGIC RELATIONSHIPS MANAGER	Merrick Van Dongen of Microsoft Learning
GLOBAL MOAC MANAGER	Laura McKenna
DEVELOPMENT AND PRODUCTION	Custom Editorial Productions, Inc
EDITORIAL ASSISTANT	Jennifer Lartz
PRODUCTION MANAGER	Micheline Frederick
CREATIVE DIRECTOR/COVER DESIGNER	Harry Nolan
TECHNOLOGY AND MEDIA	Lauren Sapira/Elena Santa Maria
COVER PHOTO	Corbis

Wiley 200th Anniversary logo designed by: Richard J. Pacifico
Lesson 13 written by: Russell Smith

This book was set in Garamond by Aptara, Inc. and printed and bound by Bind Rite Graphics. The covers were printed by Phoenix Color.

ISBN 978-0-470-11591-6

Printed in the United States of America

10 9 8 7 6 5 4 3 2 1

www.wiley.com/college/microsoft *or*
call the MOAC Toll-Free Number: 1+(888) 764-7001 (U.S. & Canada only)

Foreword from the Publisher

Wiley's publishing vision for the Microsoft Official Academic Course series is to provide students and instructors with the skills and knowledge they need to use Microsoft technology effectively in all aspects of their personal and professional lives. Quality instruction is required to help both educators and students get the most from Microsoft's software tools and to become more productive. Thus our mission is to make our instructional programs trusted educational companions for life.

To accomplish this mission, Wiley and Microsoft have partnered to develop the highest quality educational programs for Information Workers, IT Professionals, and Developers. Materials created by this partnership carry the brand name "Microsoft Official Academic Course," assuring instructors and students alike that the content of these textbooks is fully endorsed by Microsoft, and that they provide the highest quality information and instruction on Microsoft products. The Microsoft Official Academic Course textbooks are "Official" in still one more way—they are the officially sanctioned courseware for Microsoft IT Academy members.

The Microsoft Official Academic Course series focuses on *workforce development*. These programs are aimed at those students seeking to enter the workforce, change jobs, or embark on new careers as information workers, IT professionals, and developers. Microsoft Official Academic Course programs address their needs by emphasizing authentic workplace scenarios with an abundance of projects, exercises, cases, and assessments.

The Microsoft Official Academic Courses are mapped to Microsoft's extensive research and job-task analysis, the same research and analysis used to create the Microsoft Certified Information Technology Professional (MCITP) exam. The textbooks focus on real skills for real jobs. As students work through the projects and exercises in the textbooks they enhance their level of knowledge and their ability to apply the latest Microsoft technology to everyday tasks. These students also gain resume-building credentials that can assist them in finding a job, keeping their current job, or in furthering their education.

The concept of life-long learning is today an utmost necessity. Job roles, and even whole job categories, are changing so quickly that none of us can stay competitive and productive without continuously updating our skills and capabilities. The Microsoft Official Academic Course offerings, and their focus on Microsoft certification exam preparation, provide a means for people to acquire and effectively update their skills and knowledge. Wiley supports students in this endeavor through the development and distribution of these courses as Microsoft's official academic publisher.

Today educational publishing requires attention to providing quality print and robust electronic content. By integrating Microsoft Official Academic Course products, Wiley*PLUS*, and Microsoft certifications, we are better able to deliver efficient learning solutions for students and teachers alike.

Bonnie Lieberman
General Manager and Senior Vice President

Preface

Welcome to the Microsoft Official Academic Course (MOAC) program for Microsoft Windows Vista. MOAC represents the collaboration between Microsoft Learning and John Wiley & Sons, Inc. publishing company. Microsoft and Wiley teamed up to produce a series of textbooks that deliver compelling and innovative teaching solutions to instructors and superior learning experiences for students. Infused and informed by in-depth knowledge from the creators of Microsoft Office and Windows Vista™, and crafted by a publisher known worldwide for the pedagogical quality of its products, these textbooks maximize skills transfer in minimum time. With MOAC, students are hands on right away—there are no superfluous text passages to get in the way of learning and using the software. Students are challenged to reach their potential by using their new technical skills as highly productive members of the workforce.

Because this knowledgebase comes directly from Microsoft, architect of the Windows Vista operating system and creator of the MCITP exams, you are sure to receive the topical coverage that is most relevant to students' personal and professional success. Microsoft's direct participation not only assures you that MOAC textbook content is accurate and current; it also means that students will receive the best instruction possible to enable their success on certification exams and in the workplace.

■ The Microsoft Official Academic Course Program

The *Microsoft Official Academic Course* series is a complete program for instructors and institutions to prepare and deliver great courses on Microsoft software technologies. With MOAC, we recognize that, because of the rapid pace of change in the technology and curriculum developed by Microsoft, there is an ongoing set of needs beyond classroom instruction tools for an instructor to be ready to teach the course. The MOAC program endeavors to provide solutions for all these needs in a systematic manner in order to ensure a successful and rewarding course experience for both instructor and student—technical and curriculum training for instructor readiness with new software releases; the software itself for student use at home for building hands-on skills, assessment, and validation of skill development; and a great set of tools for delivering instruction in the classroom and lab. All are important to the smooth delivery of an interesting course on Microsoft software, and all are provided with the MOAC program. We think about the model below as a gauge for ensuring that we completely support you in your goal of teaching a great course. As you evaluate your instructional materials options, you may wish to use the model for comparison purposes with available products.

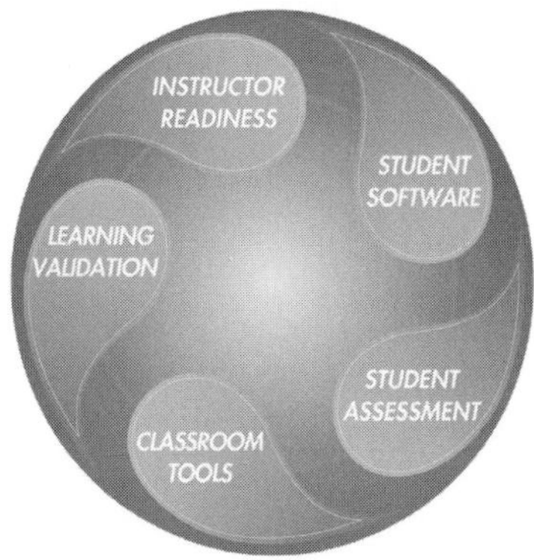

Illustrated Book Tour

Pedagogical Features

The MOAC textbook for Windows Vista is designed to cover all the learning objectives for that MCITP exam, which is referred to as its "objective domain." The Microsoft Certified Information Technology Professional (MCITP) exam objectives are highlighted throughout the textbook. Many pedagogical features have been developed specifically for *Microsoft Official Academic Course* programs.

Presenting the extensive procedural information and technical concepts woven throughout the textbook raises challenges for the student and instructor alike. The Illustrated Book Tour that follows provides a guide to the rich features contributing to *Microsoft Official Academic Course* program's pedagogical plan. Following is a list of key features in each lesson designed to prepare students for success on the certification exams and in the workplace:

- Each lesson begins with an **Objective Domain Matrix.** More than a standard list of learning objectives, the Domain Matrix correlates each software skill covered in the lesson to the specific MCTS "objective domain."
- Concise and frequent **Step-by-Step** instructions teach students new features and provide an opportunity for hands-on practice. Numbered steps give detailed, step-by-step instructions to help students learn software skills. The steps also show results and screen images to match what students should see on their computer screens.
- **Illustrations:** Screen images provide visual feedback as students work through the exercises. The images reinforce key concepts, provide visual clues about the steps, and allow students to check their progress.
- **Key Terms:** Important technical vocabulary is listed at the beginning of the lesson. When these terms are used later in the lesson, they appear in bold italic type and are defined. The Glossary contains all of the key terms and their definitions.
- Engaging point-of-use **Reader aids,** located throughout the lessons, tell students why this topic is relevant (*The Bottom Line*), provide students with helpful hints (*Take Note*), direct them to useful downloads (*Downloads*), or show alternate ways to accomplish tasks (*Another Way*). Reader aids also provide additional relevant or background information that adds value to the lesson.
- **Certification Ready?** features throughout the text signal students where a specific certification objective is covered. They provide students with a chance to check their understanding of that particular MCTS objective and, if necessary, review the section of the lesson where it is covered. MOAC offers complete preparation for MCITP certification.
- **Knowledge Assessments** provide three progressively more challenging lesson-ending activities.
- **Student CD:** The companion CD contains the worksheets that accompany each lesson.

www.wiley.com/college/microsoft *or*
call the MOAC Toll-Free Number: 1+(888) 764-7001 (U.S. & Canada only)

Lesson Features

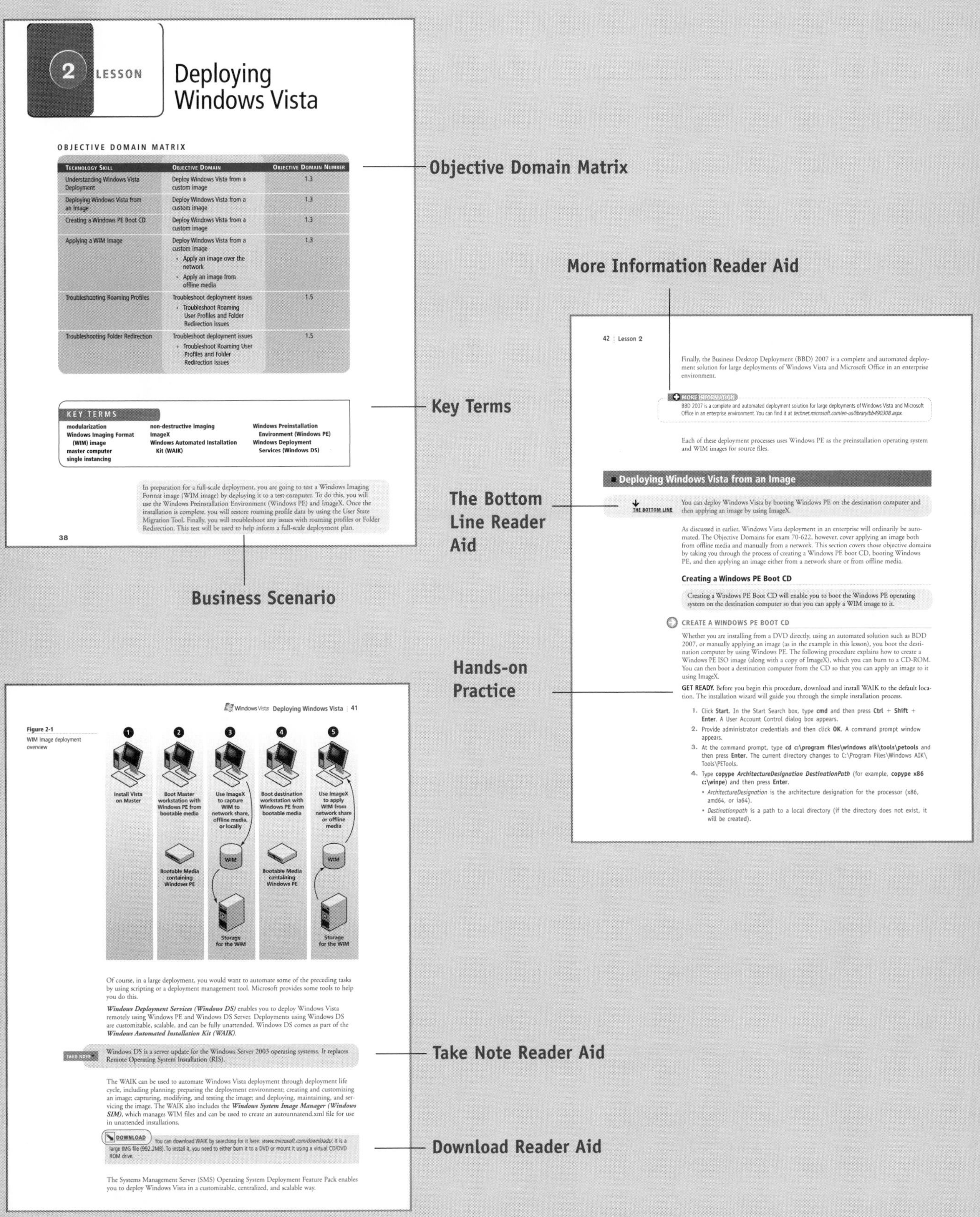

www.wiley.com/college/microsoft *or*
call the MOAC Toll-Free Number: 1+(888) 764-7001 (U.S. & Canada only)

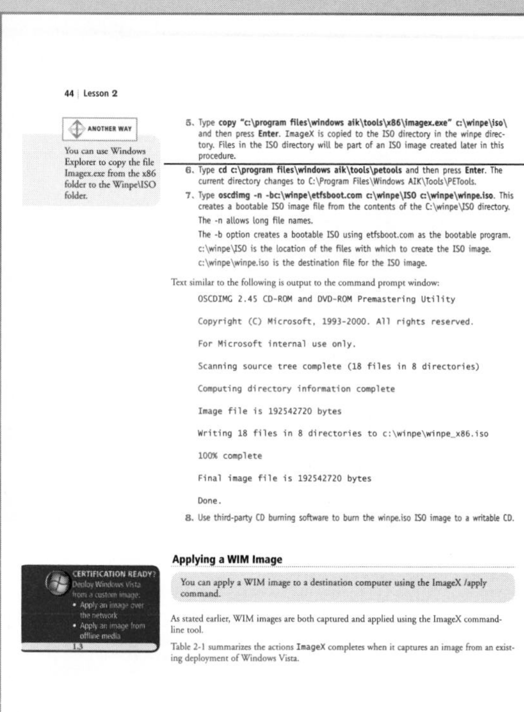

44 | Lesson 2

ANOTHER WAY

You can use Windows Explorer to copy the file Imagex.exe from the x86 folder to the Winpe\ISO folder.

5. Type **copy "c:\program files\windows aik\tools\x86\imagex.exe" c:\winpe\iso** and then press **Enter**. ImageX is copied to the ISO directory in the winpe directory. Files in the ISO directory will be part of an ISO image created later in this procedure.
6. Type **cd c:\program files\windows aik\tools\petools** and then press **Enter**. The current directory changes to C:\Program Files\Windows AIK\Tools\PETools.
7. Type **oscdimg -n -bc:\winpe\etfsboot.com c:\winpe\ISO c:\winpe\winpe.iso**. This creates a bootable ISO image file from the contents of the C:\winpe\ISO directory.
   The -n allows long file names.
   The -b option creates a bootable ISO using etfsboot.com as the bootable program.
   c:\winpe\ISO is the location of the files with which to create the ISO image.
   c:\winpe\winpe.iso is the destination file for the ISO image.

Text similar to the following is output to the command prompt window:

```
OSCDIMG 2.45 CD-ROM and DVD-ROM Premastering Utility

Copyright (C) Microsoft, 1993-2000. All rights reserved.

For Microsoft internal use only.

Scanning source tree complete (18 files in 8 directories)

Computing directory information complete

Image file is 192542720 bytes

Writing 18 files in 8 directories to c:\winpe\winpe_x86.iso

100% complete

Final image file is 192542720 bytes

Done.
```

8. Use third-party CD burning software to burn the winpe.iso ISO image to a writable CD.

CERTIFICATION READY?
Deploy Windows Vista from a custom image.
- Apply an image over the network
- Apply an image from offline media

1.3

Applying a WIM Image

You can apply a WIM image to a destination computer using the ImageX /apply command.

As stated earlier, WIM images are both captured and applied using the ImageX command-line tool.

Table 2-1 summarizes the actions ImageX completes when it captures an image from an existing deployment of Windows Vista.

Another Way Reader Aid

X Ref Reader Aid

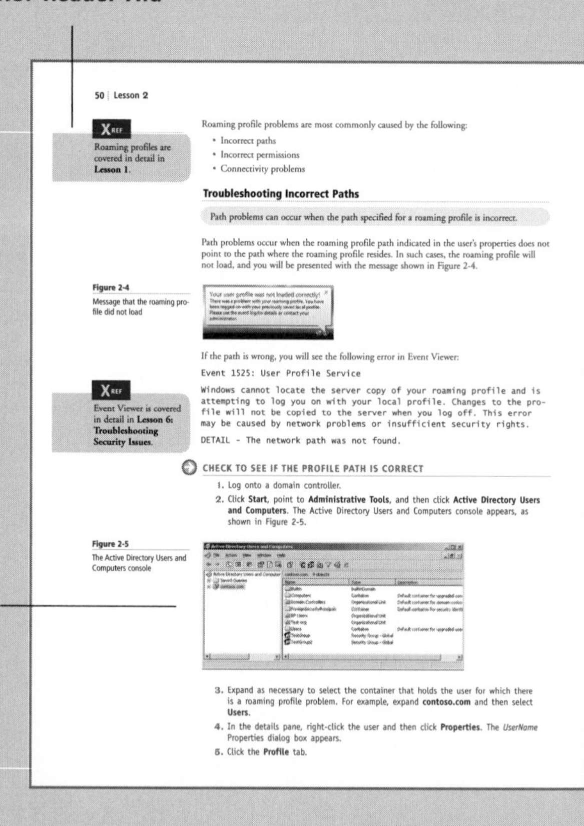

50 | Lesson 2

X REF

Roaming profiles are covered in detail in **Lesson 1**.

Roaming profile problems are most commonly caused by the following:

- Incorrect paths
- Incorrect permissions
- Connectivity problems

Troubleshooting Incorrect Paths

Path problems can occur when the path specified for a roaming profile is incorrect.

Path problems occur when the roaming profile path indicated in the user's properties does not point to the path where the roaming profile resides. In such cases, the roaming profile will not load, and you will be presented with the message shown in Figure 2-4.

Figure 2-4
Message that the roaming profile did not load

If the path is wrong, you will see the following error in Event Viewer:

```
Event 1525: User Profile Service

Windows cannot locate the server copy of your roaming profile and is attempting to log you on with your local profile. Changes to the profile will not be copied to the server when you log off. This error may be caused by network problems or insufficient security rights.

DETAIL - The network path was not found.
```

X REF

Event Viewer is covered in detail in **Lesson 6: Troubleshooting Security Issues.**

CHECK TO SEE IF THE PROFILE PATH IS CORRECT

1. Log onto a domain controller.
2. Click **Start**, point to **Administrative Tools**, and then click **Active Directory Users and Computers**. The Active Directory Users and Computers console appears, as shown in Figure 2-5.

Figure 2-5
The Active Directory Users and Computers console

3. Expand as necessary to select the container that holds the user for which there is a roaming profile problem. For example, expand **contoso.com** and then select **Users**.
4. In the details pane, right-click the user and then click **Properties**. The *UserName* Properties dialog box appears.
5. Click the **Profile** tab.

Screen Images

Easy-to-Read Tables

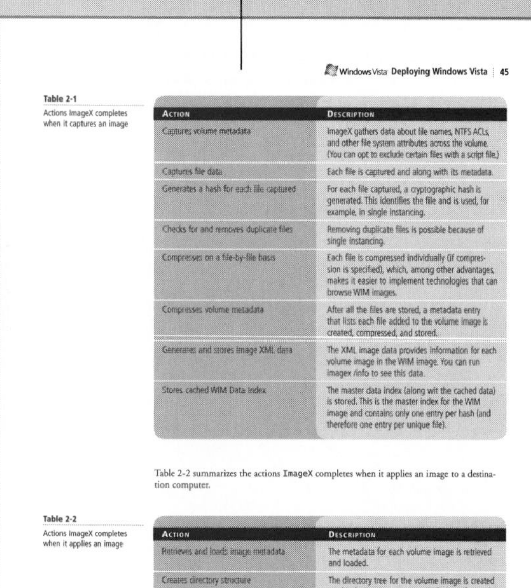

Windows Vista Deploying Windows Vista | 45

Table 2-1
Actions ImageX completes when it captures an image

Action	Description
Captures volume metadata	ImageX gathers data about file names, NTFS ACLs, and other file system attributes across the volume. (You can opt to exclude certain files with a script file.)
Captures file data	Each file is captured and along with its metadata.
Generates a hash for each file captured	For each file captured, a cryptographic hash is generated. This identifies the file and is used, for example, in single instancing.
Checks for and removes duplicate files	Removing duplicate files is possible because of single instancing.
Compresses on a file-by-file basis	Each file is compressed individually (if compression is specified), which, among other advantages, makes it easier to implement technologies that can browse WIM images.
Compresses volume metadata	After all the files are stored, a metadata entry that lists each file added to the volume image is created, compressed, and stored.
Generates and stores Image XML data	The XML image data provides information for each volume image in the WIM image. You can run imagex /info to see this data.
Stores cached WIM Data Index	The master data index (along wit the cached data) is stored. This is the master index for the WIM image and contains only one entry per hash (and therefore one entry per unique file).

Table 2-2 summarizes the actions ImageX completes when it applies an image to a destination computer.

Table 2-2
Actions ImageX completes when it applies an image

Action	Description
Retrieves and loads image metadata	The metadata for each volume image is retrieved and loaded.
Creates directory structure	The directory tree for the volume image is created on the destination computer in the specified path.
Extracts file data	Each file is extracted from the image in the same order in which the file was stored.
Applies files	The extracted files are loaded, decompressed if necessary, and copied into their place on the destination computer. The metadata for each file is applied.
Applies directory metadata	This step is completed last so that permissions on directories don't interfere with applying files.

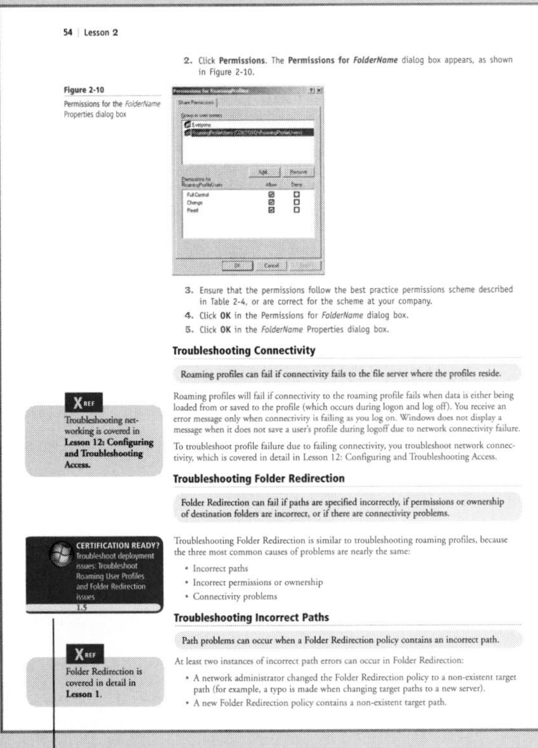

54 | Lesson 2

2. Click **Permissions**. The **Permissions for *FolderName*** dialog box appears, as shown in Figure 2-10.

Figure 2-10
Permissions for the *FolderName* Properties dialog box

3. Ensure that the permissions follow the best practice permissions scheme described in Table 2-4, or are correct for the scheme at your company.
4. Click **OK** in the Permissions for *FolderName* dialog box.
5. Click **OK** in the *FolderName* Properties dialog box.

Troubleshooting Connectivity

Roaming profiles can fail if connectivity fails to the file server where the profiles reside.

X REF Troubleshooting networking is covered in **Lesson 12: Configuring and Troubleshooting Access.**

Roaming profiles will fail if connectivity to the roaming profile fails when data is either being loaded from or saved to the profile (which occurs during logon and log off). You receive an error message only when connectivity is failing as you log on. Windows does not display a message when it does not save a user's profile during logoff due to network connectivity failure.

To troubleshoot profile failure due to failing connectivity, you troubleshoot network connectivity, which is covered in detail in Lesson 12: Configuring and Troubleshooting Access.

Troubleshooting Folder Redirection

Folder Redirection can fail if paths are specified incorrectly, if permissions or ownership of destination folders are incorrect, or if there are connectivity problems.

CERTIFICATION READY? Troubleshoot deployment issues: Troubleshoot Roaming User Profiles and Folder Redirection issues 1.5

Troubleshooting Folder Redirection is similar to troubleshooting roaming profiles, because the three most common causes of problems are nearly the same:

- Incorrect paths
- Incorrect permissions or ownership
- Connectivity problems

Troubleshooting Incorrect Paths

Path problems can occur when a Folder Redirection policy contains an incorrect path.

X REF Folder Redirection is covered in detail in **Lesson 1.**

At least two instances of incorrect path errors can occur in Folder Redirection:

- A network administrator changed the Folder Redirection policy to a non-existent target path (for example, a typo is made when changing target paths to a new server).
- A new Folder Redirection policy contains a non-existent target path.

MCTS Certification Objective Alert

Case Scenarios

Windows Vista Deploying Windows Vista | 63

c. Create a separate WIM image for desktops and laptops and then combine the images using ImageX /combine.
d. You have to create a separate WIM image for the desktops and laptops because they have different HALs.

Review Questions

1. Describe the roll of Windows PE and WIM images in the following deployment schemes:
   - Installing a single copy of Windows Vista Ultimate on a personal, home computer using the Windows Vista Ultimate DVD
   - Applying an image from a network share
   - Using BDD 2007 for a large-scale deployment
2. For the parent folder in a roaming profile scheme (see Table 2-4), explain in qualitative terms the recommended NTFS permissions for administrators and the security group of roaming profile users. Provide your own reasoning about why the settings are what they are.

■ **Case Scenarios**

Scenario 1: Event 502

The IT department has redirected the Pictures folders for the art department this morning. A user logs on, puts some art files in his Pictures folder, and then goes to a colleague's office and logs on, expecting to be able to show his colleague the pictures. But they are not there. In diagnosing the problem, you discover that Event 502 is occurring each time he logs on. You check the redirection paths, and they are correct. What is likely the problem, and how can you fix it?

Scenario 2: Event 1525

A user says some items on his desktop have "disappeared." No matter which workstation he logs onto, you find that event 1525 is logged during the time when he is logging on. What is the likely cause of this issue and what steps can you take to address it?

Sumnmary Skill Matrix

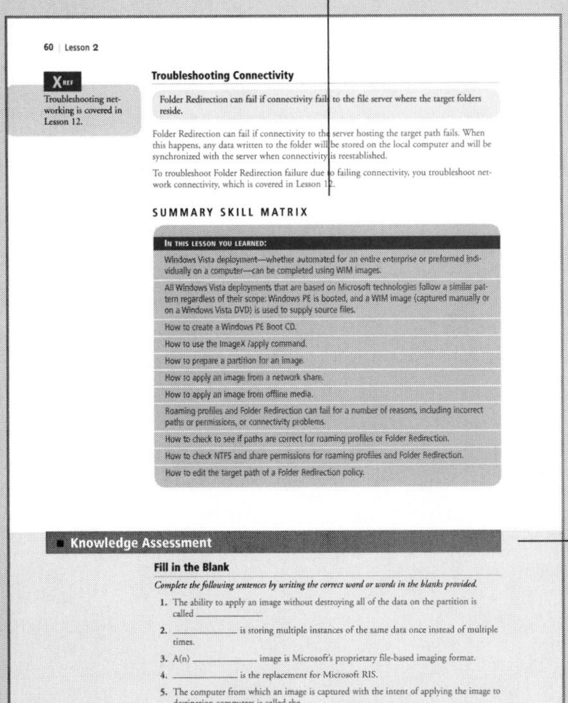

60 | Lesson 2

X REF Troubleshooting networking is covered in Lesson 12.

Troubleshooting Connectivity

Folder Redirection can fail if connectivity fails to the file server where the target folders reside.

Folder Redirection can fail if connectivity to the server hosting the target path fails. When this happens, any data written to the folder will be stored on the local computer and will be synchronized with the server when connectivity is reestablished.

To troubleshoot Folder Redirection failure due to failing connectivity, you troubleshoot network connectivity, which is covered in Lesson 12.

SUMMARY SKILL MATRIX

IN THIS LESSON YOU LEARNED:
Windows Vista deployment—whether automated for an entire enterprise or preformed individually on a computer—can be completed using WIM images.
All Windows Vista deployments that are based on Microsoft technologies follow a similar pattern regardless of their scope: Windows PE is booted, and a WIM image (captured manually or on a Windows Vista DVD) is used to supply source files.
How to create a Windows PE Boot CD.
How to use the ImageX /apply command.
How to prepare a partition for an image.
How to apply an image from a network share.
How to apply an image from offline media.
Roaming profiles and Folder Redirection can fail for a number of reasons, including incorrect paths or permissions, or connectivity problems.
How to check to see if paths are correct for roaming profiles or Folder Redirection.
How to check NTFS and share permissions for roaming profiles and Folder Redirection.
How to edit the target path of a Folder Redirection policy.

■ **Knowledge Assessment**

Fill in the Blank

Complete the following sentences by writing the correct word or words in the blanks provided.

1. The ability to apply an image without destroying all of the data on the partition is called ________.
2. ________ is storing multiple instances of the same data once instead of multiple times.
3. A(n) ________ image is Microsoft's proprietary file-based imaging format.
4. ________ is the replacement for Microsoft RIS.
5. The computer from which an image is captured with the intent of applying the image to destination computers is called the ________.

Knowledge Assessment Questions

Conventions and Features Used in This Book

This book uses particular fonts, symbols, and heading conventions to highlight important information or to call your attention to special steps. For more information about the features in each lesson, refer to the Illustrated Book Tour section.

CONVENTION	MEANING
NEW FEATURE	This icon indicates a new or greatly improved Windows feature in this version of the software.
THE BOTTOM LINE	This feature provides a brief summary of the material to be covered in the section that follows.
CLOSE	Words in all capital letters and in a different font color than the rest of the text indicate instructions for opening, saving, or closing files or programs. They also point out items you should check or actions you should take.
CERTIFICATION READY?	This feature signals the point in the text where a specific certification objective is covered. It provides you with a chance to check your understanding of that particular MCTS objective and, if necessary, review the section of the lesson where it is covered.
TAKE NOTE	Reader aids appear in shaded boxes found in your text. *Take Note* provides helpful hints related to particular tasks or topics.
ANOTHER WAY	*Another Way* provides an alternative procedure for accomplishing a particular task.
DOWNLOAD	*Downloads* provides information on where to download useful software.
X REF	These notes provide pointers to information discussed elsewhere in the textbook or describe interesting features of Windows Vista that are not directly addressed in the current topic or exercise.
Alt + Tab	A plus sign (+) between two key names means that you must press both keys at the same time. Keys that you are instructed to press in an exercise will appear in the font shown here.
A ***shared printer*** can be used by many individuals on a network.	Key terms appear in bold italic.
Key **My Name is.**	Any text you are asked to key appears in color.
Click **OK**.	Any button on the screen you are supposed to click on or select will also appear in color.

www.wiley.com/college/microsoft ***or***
call the MOAC Toll-Free Number: 1+(888) 764-7001 (U.S. & Canada only)

Instructor Support Program

The *Microsoft Official Academic Course* programs are accompanied by a rich array of resources that incorporate the extensive textbook visuals to form a pedagogically cohesive package. These resources provide all the materials instructors need to deploy and deliver their courses. Resources available online for download include:

- The **MSDN Academic Alliance** is designed to provide the easiest and most inexpensive developer tools, products, and technologies available to faculty and students in labs, classrooms, and on student PCs. A free 1-year membership is available to qualified MOAC adopters.

  Note: Microsoft Windows Vista Enterprise Edition can be downloaded from MSDNAA for use by students in this course

- **Windows Server 2003 Trial Software.** A 180-day trial version of the Windows Server 2003 software can be downloaded for use with this course from the Microsoft TechNet site (http://technet.microsoft.com/). A CD containing a trial version of this software is also bundled within this text.
- The **Instructor's Guide** contains Solutions to all the textbook exercises and Syllabi for various term lengths. The Instructor's Guide also includes chapter summaries and lecture notes. The Instructor's Guide is available from the Book Companion site (http://www.wiley.com/college/microsoft) and from Wiley*PLUS*.
- The **Test Bank** contains hundreds of multiple-choice, true-false, and short answer questions and is available to download from the Instructor's Book Companion site (http://www.wiley.com/college/microsoft) and from Wiley*PLUS*. A complete answer key is provided. It is available as a computerized test bank and in Microsoft Word format. The easy-to-use test-generation program fully supports graphics, print tests, student answer sheets, and answer keys. The software's advanced features allow you to create an exam to meet your exact specifications. The computerized test bank provides:
  - Varied question types to test a variety of comprehension levels—multiple-choice, true-false, and short answer.
  - Allows instructors to edit, randomize, and create questions freely.
  - Allows instructors to create and print different versions of a quiz or exam.
- **PowerPoint Presentations and Images.** A complete set of PowerPoint presentations is available on the Instructor's Book Companion site (http://www.wiley.com/college/microsoft) and in Wiley*PLUS* to enhance classroom presentations. Approximately 50 PowerPoint slides are provided for each lesson. Tailored to the text's topical coverage and Skills Matrix, these presentations are designed to convey key Windows Vista concepts addressed in the text.

  All figures from the text are on the Instructor's Book Companion site (http://www.wiley.com/college/microsoft) and in Wiley*PLUS*. You can incorporate them into your PowerPoint presentations, or create your own overhead transparencies and handouts.

  By using these visuals in class discussions, you can help focus students' attention on key elements of Windows Vista and help them understand how to use it effectively in the workplace.

- **The Wiley Faculty Network** lets you tap into a large community of your peers effortlessly. Wiley Faculty Network mentors are faculty like you, from educational institutions around the country, who are passionate about enhancing instructional efficiency and effectiveness through best practices. Faculty Network activities include technology training and tutorials, virtual seminars, peer-to-peer exchanges of experience and ideas, personal consulting, and sharing of resources. To register for a seminar, go to www.wherefacultyconnect.com or phone 1-866-4FACULTY (U.S. and Canada only).

Wiley*PLUS*

Broad developments in education over the past decade have influenced the instructional approach taken in the Microsoft Official Academic Course programs. The way that students learn, especially about new technologies, has changed dramatically in the Internet era. Electronic learning materials and Internet-based instruction is now as much a part of classroom instruction as printed textbooks. Wiley*PLUS* provides the technology to create an environment where students reach their full potential and experience academic success that will last them a lifetime!

Wiley*PLUS* is a powerful and highly-integrated suite of teaching and learning resources designed to bridge the gap between what happens in the classroom and what happens at home and on the job. Wiley*PLUS* provides instructors with the resources to teach their students new technologies and guide them to reach their goals of getting ahead in the job market by having the skills to become certified and advance in the workforce. For students, Wiley*PLUS* provides the tools for study and practice that are available to them 24/7, wherever and whenever they want to study. Wiley*PLUS* includes a complete online version of the student textbook, PowerPoint presentations, homework and practice assignments and quizzes, image galleries, test bank questions, gradebook, and all the instructor resources in one easy-to-use website.

Organized around the everyday activities you and your students perform in the class, Wiley*PLUS* helps you:

- **Prepare & Present** outstanding class presentations using relevant PowerPoint slides and other Wiley*PLUS* materials—and you can easily upload and add your own.
- **Create Assignments** by choosing from questions organized by lesson, level of difficulty, and source—and add your own questions. Students' homework and quizzes are automatically graded, and the results are recorded in your gradebook.
- **Offer context-sensitive help to students, 24/7.** When you assign homework or quizzes, you decide if and when students get access to hints, solutions, or answers where appropriate—or they can be linked to relevant sections of their complete, online text for additional help whenever—and wherever they need it most.
- **Track Student Progress:** Analyze students' results and assess their level of understanding on an individual and class level using the Wiley*PLUS* gradebook, or export data to your own personal gradebook.
- **Administer Your Course:** Wiley*PLUS* can easily be integrated with another course management system, gradebook, or other resources you are using in your class, providing you with the flexibility to build your course, your way.
- **Seamlessly integrate all of the rich Wiley*PLUS* content and resources with WebCT and Blackboard**—with a single sign-on.

Please view our online demo at **www.wiley.com/college/wileyplus.** Here you will find additional information about the features and benefits of Wiley*PLUS*, how to request a "test drive" of Wiley*PLUS* for this title, and how to adopt it for class use.

MSDN ACADEMIC ALLIANCE—FREE 1-YEAR MEMBERSHIP AVAILABLE TO QUALIFIED ADOPTERS!

MSDN Academic Alliance (MSDN AA) is designed to provide the easiest and most inexpensive way for universities to make the latest Microsoft developer tools, products, and technologies available in labs, classrooms, and on student PCs. MSDN AA is an annual membership program for departments teaching Science, Technology, Engineering, and Mathematics (STEM) courses. The membership provides a complete solution to keep academic labs, faculty, and students on the leading edge of technology.

Software available in the MSDN AA program is provided at no charge to adopting departments through the Wiley and Microsoft publishing partnership.

As a bonus to this free offer, faculty will be introduced to Microsoft's Faculty Connection and Academic Resource Center. It takes time and preparation to keep students engaged while giving them a fundamental understanding of theory, and the Microsoft Faculty Connection is designed to help STEM professors with this preparation by providing articles, curriculum, and tools that professors can use to engage and inspire today's technology students.

* Contact your Wiley rep for details.

For more information about the MSDN Academic Alliance program, go to:

http://msdn.microsoft.com/academic/

Note: Microsoft Windows Vista Enterprise Edition can be downloaded from MSDNAA for use by students in this course.

Important Web Addresses and Phone Numbers

To locate the Wiley Higher Education Rep in your area, go to the following Web address and click on the "*Who's My Rep?*" link at the top of the page.

http://www.wiley.com/college

Or Call the MOAC Toll Free Number: 1 + (888) 764-7001 (U.S. & Canada only).

To learn more about becoming a Microsoft Certified IT Professional (MCITP) and exam availability, visit www.microsoft.com/learning/mcp/mcitp/.

www.wiley.com/college/microsoft ***or***
call the MOAC Toll-Free Number: 1+(888) 764-7001 (U.S. & Canada only)

Student Support Program

Book Companion Website (www.wiley.com/college/microsoft)

The book companion site for the MOAC series includes the Instructor Resources, the student CD files, and Web links to important information for students and instructors.

Wiley*PLUS*

Wiley*PLUS* is a powerful and highly-integrated suite of teaching and learning resources designed to bridge the gap between what happens in the classroom and what happens at home and on the job. For students, Wiley*PLUS* provides the tools for study and practice that are available 24/7, wherever and whenever they want to study. Wiley*PLUS* includes a complete online version of the student textbook, PowerPoint presentations, homework and practice assignments and quizzes, image galleries, test bank questions, gradebook, and all the instructor resources in one easy-to-use website.

Wiley*PLUS* provides immediate feedback on student assignments and a wealth of support materials. This powerful study tool will help your students develop their conceptual understanding of the class material and increase their ability to answer questions.

- A **Study and Practice** area links directly to text content, allowing students to review the text while they study and answer. Access to Microsoft's Pre-Test, Learning Plan, and a code for taking the MCAS certification exam is available in Study and Practice. Additional Practice Questions tied to the MCAS certification that can be re-taken as many times as necessary, are also available.
- An **Assignment** area keeps all the work you want your students to complete in one location, making it easy for them to stay on task. Students have access to a variety of interactive self-assessment tools, as well as other resources for building their confidence and understanding. In addition, all of the assignments and quizzes contain a link to the relevant section of the multimedia book, providing students with context-sensitive help that allows them to conquer obstacles as they arise.
- A **Personal Gradebook** for each student allows students to view their results from past assignments at any time.

Please view our online demo at www.wiley.com/college/wileyplus. Here you will find additional information about the features and benefits of Wiley*PLUS*, how to request a "test drive" of Wiley*PLUS* for this title, and how to adopt it for class use.

You can use the Search function in the Open dialog box to quickly find the specific file for which you are looking.

Wiley Desktop Editions

Wiley MOAC Desktop Editions are innovative, electronic versions of printed textbooks. Students buy the desktop version for 50% off the U.S. price of the printed text, and get the added value of permanence and portability. Wiley Desktop Editions provide students with numerous additional benefits that are not available with other e-text solutions.

Wiley Desktop Editions are NOT subscriptions; students download the Wiley Desktop Edition to their computer desktops. Students own the content they buy to keep for as long as they want. Once a Wiley Desktop Edition is downloaded to the computer desktop, students have instant access to all of the content without being online. Students can also print out the sections they prefer to read in hard copy. Students also have access to fully integrated resources within their Wiley Desktop Edition. From highlighting their e-text to taking and sharing notes, students can easily personalize their Wiley Desktop Edition as they are reading or following along in class.

Preparing to Take the Microsoft Certified Information Technology Professional (MCITP) Exam

The Microsoft IT Professional credential and associated exams help to validate specific job-role skills outside of the core technology, such as operational processes, operational procedures, and analyzing business problems.

For organizations, the new certification program provides better skills verification tools that help with assessing not only in-demand skills on Windows Vista and other Microsoft technologies, but also the ability to quickly complete on-the-job tasks. Individuals will find it easier to identify and work towards the certification credential that meets their personal and professional goals.

To learn more about becoming a Microsoft Certified Information Technology Professional and exam availability, visit www.microsoft.com/learning/mcp/mcitp.

Microsoft Certified Information Technology Professional (MCITP) Program

Microsoft Certifications for IT Professionals

The new Microsoft Certified Technology Specialist (MCTS) and Microsoft Certified IT Professional (MCITP) credentials provide IT professionals with a simpler and more targeted framework to showcase their technical skills in addition to the skills that are required for specific developer job roles.

The Microsoft Certified Database Administrator (MCDBA), Microsoft Certified Desktop Support Technician (MCDST), Microsoft Certified System Administrator (MCSA), and Microsoft Certified Systems Engineer (MCSE) credentials continue to provide IT professionals who use Microsoft SQL Server 2000, Windows XP, and Windows Server 2003 with industry recognition and validation of their IT skills and experience.

Microsoft Certified IT Professional

The new Microsoft Certified IT Professional (MCITP) credential lets you highlight your specific area of expertise. Now, you can easily distinguish yourself as an expert in database administration, database development, business intelligence, or support.

By becoming certified, you demonstrate to employers that you have achieved a predictable level of skill not only in the use of the Windows Vista operating system, but with a comprehensive set of Microsoft technologies. Employers often require certification either as a condition of employment or as a condition of advancement within the company or other organization.

The certification examinations are sponsored by Microsoft but administered through exam delivery partners like Thomson Prometric.

Preparing to Take an Exam

Unless you are a very experienced user, you will need to use a test preparation course to prepare to complete the test correctly and within the time allowed. The *Microsoft Official Academic Course* series is designed to prepare you with a strong knowledge of all exam topics, and with some additional review and practice on your own. You should feel confident in your ability to pass the appropriate exam.

After you decide which exam to take, review the list of objectives for the exam. You can easily identify tasks that are included in the objective list by locating the Objective Domain Matrix at the start of each lesson and the Certification Ready sidebars in the margin of the lessons in this book.

To take the MCITP test, visit *www.microsoft.com/learning/mcp/mcitp* to locate your nearest testing center. Then call the testing center directly to schedule your test. The amount of advance notice you should provide will vary for different testing centers, and it typically depends on the number of computers available at the testing center, the number of other testers who have already been scheduled for the day on which you want to take the test, and the number of times per week that the testing center offers MCITP testing. In general, you should call to schedule your test at least two weeks prior to the date on which you want to take the test.

When you arrive at the testing center, you might be asked for proof of identity. A driver's license or passport is an acceptable form of identification. If you do not have either of these items of documentation, call your testing center and ask what alternative forms of identification will be accepted. If you are retaking a test, bring your MCITP identification number, which will have been given to you when you previously took the test. If you have not prepaid or if your organization has not already arranged to make payment for you, you will need to pay the test-taking fee when you arrive.

www.wiley.com/college/microsoft *or*
call the MOAC Toll-Free Number: 1+(888) 764-7001 (U.S. & Canada only)

Acknowledgments

MOAC Instructor Advisory Board

We would like thank to our Instructor Advisory Board, an elite group of educators who has assisted us every step of the way in building these products. Advisory Board members have acted as our sounding board on key pedagogical and design decisions leading to the development of these compelling and innovative textbooks for future Information Workers. Their dedication to technology education is truly appreciated.

Catherine Binder, Strayer University & Katharine Gibbs School–Philadelphia

Catherine currently works at both Katharine Gibbs School in Norristown, PA and Strayer University in King of Prussia, PA. Catherine has been at Katharine Gibbs School for 4 years. Catherine is currently the Department Chair/Lead instructor for PC Networking at Gibbs and the founder/advisor of the TEK Masters Society. Since joining Strayer University a year and a half ago she has risen in the ranks from adjunct to DIT/Assistant Campus Dean.

Catherine has brought her 10+ year's industry experience as Network Administrator, Network Supervisor, Professor, Bench Tech, Manager and CTO from such places as Foster Wheeler Corp, KidsPeace Inc., Victoria Vogue, TESST College, AMC Theatres, Blue Mountain Publishing and many more to her teaching venue.

Catherine began as an adjunct in the PC Networking department and quickly became a full-time instructor. At both schools she is in charge of scheduling, curricula and departmental duties. She happily advises about 80+ students and is committed to Gibbs/Strayer life, her students, and continuing technology education every day.

Penny Gudgeon, CDI College

Penny is the Program Manager for IT curriculum at Corinthian Colleges, Inc. Until January 2006, Penny was responsible for all Canadian programming and web curriculum for five years. During that time, Corinthian Colleges, Inc. acquired CDI College of Business and Technology in 2004. Before 2000 she spent four years as IT instructor at one of the campuses. Penny joined CDI College in 1997 after her working for 10 years first in programming and later in software productivity education. Penny previously has worked in the fields of advertising, sales, engineering technology and programming. When not working from her home office or indulging her passion for life long learning, and the possibilities of what might be, Penny likes to read mysteries, garden and relax at home in Hamilton, Ontario, with her Shih-Tzu, Gracie, and husband, Al.

Jana Hambruch, School District of Lee County

Ms. Hambruch currently serves as Director for the Information Technology Magnet Programs at The School District of Lee County in Ft Myers, Florida. She is responsible for the implementation and direction of three schools that fall under this grant program. This program has been recognized as one of the top 15 most innovative technology programs in the nation. She is also co-author of the grant proposal for the IT Magnet Grant prior to taking on the role of Director.

Ms. Hambruch has over ten years experience directing the technical certification training programs at many Colleges and Universities, including Barry University, the University of South Florida, Broward Community College, and at Florida Gulf Coast University, where she served as the Director for the Center for Technology Education. She excels at developing alternative training models that focus on the tie between the education provider and the community in which it serves.

Ms. Hambruch is a past board member and treasurer of the Human Resources Management Association of SW Florida, graduate of Leadership Lee County Class of 2002, Steering Committee Member for Leadership Lee County Class of 2004 and a former board member of the Career Coalition of Southwest Florida. She has frequently lectured for organizations such as Microsoft, American Society of Training and Development, Florida Gulf Coast University, Florida State University, University of Nevada at Las Vegas, University of Wisconsin at Milwaukee, Canada's McGill University, and Florida's State Workforce Summit.

Dee Hobson, **Richland College**

Dee Hobson is currently a faculty member of the Business Office Systems and Support Division at Richland College. Richland is one of seven colleges in the Dallas County Community College District and has the distinction of being the first community college to receive the Malcolm Baldrige National Quality Award in 2005. Richland also received the Texas Award for Performance Excellence in 2005.

The Business Office Systems and Support Division at Richland is also a Certiport Authorized Microsoft Office testing center. All students enrolling in one of Microsoft's application software courses (Word, Excel, PowerPoint, and Access) are required to take the respective Microsoft certification exam at the end of the semester.

Dee has taught computer and business courses in K-12 public schools and at a proprietary career college in Dallas. She has also been involved with several corporate training companies and with adult education programs in the Dallas area. She began her computer career as an employee of IBM Corporation in St. Louis, Missouri. During her ten-year IBM employment, she moved to Memphis, Tennessee, to accept a managerial position and to Dallas, Texas, to work in a national sales and marketing technical support center.

Keith Hoell, **Katharine Gibbs School–New York**

Keith has worked in both non-profit and proprietary education for over 10 years, initially at St. John's University in New York, and then as full-time faculty, Chairperson and currently Dean of Information Systems at the Katharine Gibbs School in New York City. He also worked for General Electric in the late 80's and early 90's as the Sysop of a popular bulletin board dedicated to ASCII-Art on GE's pioneering GEnie on-line service before the advent of the World Wide Web. He has taught courses and workshops dealing with many mainstream IT issues and varied technology, especially those related to computer hardware and operating system software, networking, software applications, IT project management and ethics, and relational database technology. An avid runner and a member of The New York Road Runners, he won the Footlocker Five Borough Challenge representing Queens at the 2005 ING New York City Marathon while competing against the 4 other borough reps. He currently resides in Queens, New York.

Michael Taylor, **Seattle Central Community College**

Michael worked in education and training for the last 20 years in both the public and private sector. He currently teaches and coordinates the applications support program at Seattle Central Community College and also administers the Microsoft IT Academy. His experience outside the educational world is in Travel and Tourism with wholesale tour operations and cruise lines.

Interests outside of work include greyhound rescue. (He adopted 3 ex-racers who bring him great joy.) He also enjoys the arts and is fortunate to live in downtown Seattle where there is much to see and do.

MOAC Windows Vista Reviewers

We also thank the many reviewers who pored over the manuscript, providing invaluable feedback in the service of quality instructional materials.

Microsoft® Windows Vista™ Configuring Microsoft® Certified Technology Specialist Exam 70-620

Sue Bailey, Ouachita Technical College
David Courtaway, DeVry University—Pomona
Jason Eckert, TriOS College
Rob Hillard, National Park Community College
Katherine James, Seneca College
Steven Singer, Kapi'olani Community College
Steve Strom, Butler Community College
Joyce Thompson, Lehigh Carbon Community College
Dennis Yeadon, CDI College—Brampton

Microsoft® Supporting and Troubleshooting Applications on a Windows Vista™ Client for Enterprise Support Technicians

Microsoft® Certified Information Technology Professional Exam 70-622

Mohan Bala, CDI College—Toronto
Brian Bordelon, Lantec Computer Training Center
Wendy Corbin, Baker College
Nanci Ford, Fanshawe College
Vijay Navghare, CDI College—Scarborough
Richard Tamme, Elgin Community College
Sam Valcaniant, Chattanooga State Technical Community College

Focus Group and Survey Participants

Finally, we thank the hundreds of instructors who participated in our focus groups and surveys to ensure that the Microsoft Official Academic Courses best met the needs of our customers.

Jean Aguilar, Mt. Hood Community College
Konrad Akens, Zane State College
Michael Albers, University of Memphis
Diana Anderson, Big Sandy Community & Technical College
Phyllis Anderson, Delaware County Community College
Judith Andrews, Feather River College
Damon Antos, American River College
Bridget Archer, Oakton Community College
Linda Arnold, Harrisburg Area Community College–Lebanon Campus
Neha Arya, Fullerton College
Mohammad Bajwa, Katharine Gibbs School–New York
Virginia Baker, University of Alaska Fairbanks
Carla Bannick, Pima Community College
Rita Barkley, Northeast Alabama Community College
Elsa Barr, Central Community College–Hastings
Ronald W. Barry, Ventura County Community College District
Elizabeth Bastedo, Central Carolina Technical College
Karen Baston, Waubonsee Community College
Karen Bean, Blinn College
Scott Beckstrand, Community College of Southern Nevada
Paulette Bell, Santa Rosa Junior College
Liz Bennett, Southeast Technical Institute
Nancy Bermea, Olympic College
Lucy Betz, Milwaukee Area Technical College
Meral Binbasioglu, Hofstra University
Catherine Binder, Strayer University & Katharine Gibbs School–Philadelphia

Terrel Blair, El Centro College
Ruth Blalock, Alamance Community College
Beverly Bohner, Reading Area Community College
Henry Bojack, Farmingdale State University
Matthew Bowie, Luna Community College
Julie Boyles, Portland Community College
Karen Brandt, College of the Albemarle
Stephen Brown, College of San Mateo
Jared Bruckner, Southern Adventist University
Pam Brune, Chattanooga State Technical Community College
Sue Buchholz, Georgia Perimeter College
Roberta Buczyna, Edison College
Angela Butler, Mississippi Gulf Coast Community College
Rebecca Byrd, Augusta Technical College
Kristen Callahan, Mercer County Community College
Judy Cameron, Spokane Community College
Dianne Campbell, Athens Technical College
Gena Casas, Florida Community College at Jacksonville
Jesus Castrejon, Latin Technologies
Gail Chambers, Southwest Tennessee Community College
Jacques Chansavang, Indiana University–Purdue University Fort Wayne
Nancy Chapko, Milwaukee Area Technical College
Rebecca Chavez, Yavapai College
Sanjiv Chopra, Thomas Nelson Community College
Greg Clements, Midland Lutheran College
Dayna Coker, Southwestern Oklahoma State University–Sayre Campus
Tamra Collins, Otero Junior College
Janet Conrey, Gavilan Community College
Carol Cornforth, West Virginia Northern Community College
Gary Cotton, American River College
Edie Cox, Chattahoochee Technical College
Rollie Cox, Madison Area Technical College
David Crawford, Northwestern Michigan College
J.K. Crowley, Victor Valley College
Rosalyn Culver, Washtenaw Community College
Sharon Custer, Huntington University
Sandra Daniels, New River Community College
Anila Das, Cedar Valley College
Brad Davis, Santa Rosa Junior College
Susan Davis, Green River Community College
Mark Dawdy, Lincoln Land Community College
Jennifer Day, Sinclair Community College
Carol Deane, Eastern Idaho Technical College
Julie DeBuhr, Lewis-Clark State College
Janis DeHaven, Central Community College
Drew Dekreon, University of Alaska–Anchorage
Joy DePover, Central Lakes College
Salli DiBartolo, Brevard Community College
Melissa Diegnau, Riverland Community College
Al Dillard, Lansdale School of Business
Marjorie Duffy, Cosumnes River College
Sarah Dunn, Southwest Tennessee Community College
Shahla Durany, Tarrant County College–South Campus
Kay Durden, University of Tennessee at Martin
Dineen Ebert, St. Louis Community College–Meramec
Donna Ehrhart, State University of New York–Brockport
Larry Elias, Montgomery County Community College
Glenda Elser, New Mexico State University at Alamogordo
Angela Evangelinos, Monroe County Community College
Angie Evans, Ivy Tech Community College of Indiana
Linda Farrington, Indian Hills Community College
Dana Fladhammer, Phoenix College
Richard Flores, Citrus College
Connie Fox, Community and Technical College at Institute of Technology West Virginia University
Wanda Freeman, Okefenokee Technical College
Brenda Freeman, Augusta Technical College
Susan Fry, Boise State University
Roger Fulk, Wright State University–Lake Campus
Sue Furnas, Collin County Community College District
Sandy Gabel, Vernon College
Laura Galvan, Fayetteville Technical Community College
Candace Garrod, Red Rocks Community College
Sherrie Geitgey, Northwest State Community College
Chris Gerig, Chattahoochee Technical College
Barb Gillespie, Cuyamaca College
Jessica Gilmore, Highline Community College
Pamela Gilmore, Reedley College
Debbie Glinert, Queensborough Community College
Steven Goldman, Polk Community College
Bettie Goodman, C.S. Mott Community College
Mike Grabill, Katharine Gibbs School–Philadelphia
Francis Green, Penn State University
Walter Griffin, Blinn College
Fillmore Guinn, Odessa College
Helen Haasch, Milwaukee Area Technical College
John Habal, Ventura College
Joy Haerens, Chaffey College
Norman Hahn, Thomas Nelson Community College
Kathy Hall, Alamance Community College
Teri Harbacheck, Boise State University
Linda Harper, Richland Community College
Maureen Harper, Indian Hills Community College
Steve Harris, Katharine Gibbs School–New York
Robyn Hart, Fresno City College
Darien Hartman, Boise State University
Gina Hatcher, Tacoma Community College
Winona T. Hatcher, Aiken Technical College
BJ Hathaway, Northeast Wisconsin Tech College
Cynthia Hauki, West Hills College – Coalinga
Mary L. Haynes, Wayne County Community College
Marcie Hawkins, Zane State College
Steve Hebrock, Ohio State University Agricultural Technical Institute

Sue Heistand, Iowa Central Community College
Heith Hennel, Valencia Community College
Donna Hendricks, South Arkansas Community College
Judy Hendrix, Dyersburg State Community College
Gloria Hensel, Matanuska-Susitna College University of Alaska Anchorage
Gwendolyn Hester, Richland College
Tammarra Holmes, Laramie County Community College
Dee Hobson, Richland College
Keith Hoell, Katharine Gibbs School–New York
Pashia Hogan, Northeast State Technical Community College
Susan Hoggard, Tulsa Community College
Kathleen Holliman, Wallace Community College Selma
Chastity Honchul, Brown Mackie College/Wright State University
Christie Hovey, Lincoln Land Community College
Peggy Hughes, Allegany College of Maryland
Sandra Hume, Chippewa Valley Technical College
John Hutson, Aims Community College
Celia Ing, Sacramento City College
Joan Ivey, Lanier Technical College
Barbara Jaffari, College of the Redwoods
Penny Jakes, University of Montana College of Technology
Eduardo Jaramillo, Peninsula College
Barbara Jauken, Southeast Community College
Susan Jennings, Stephen F. Austin State University
Leslie Jernberg, Eastern Idaho Technical College
Linda Johns, Georgia Perimeter College
Brent Johnson, Okefenokee Technical College
Mary Johnson, Mt. San Antonio College
Shirley Johnson, Trinidad State Junior College–Valley Campus
Sandra M. Jolley, Tarrant County College
Teresa Jolly, South Georgia Technical College
Dr. Deborah Jones, South Georgia Technical College
Margie Jones, Central Virginia Community College
Randall Jones, Marshall Community and Technical College
Diane Karlsbraaten, Lake Region State College
Teresa Keller, Ivy Tech Community College of Indiana
Charles Kemnitz, Pennsylvania College of Technology
Sandra Kinghorn, Ventura College
Bill Klein, Katharine Gibbs School–Philadelphia
Bea Knaapen, Fresno City College
Kit Kofoed, Western Wyoming Community College
Maria Kolatis, County College of Morris
Barry Kolb, Ocean County College
Karen Kuralt, University of Arkansas at Little Rock
Belva-Carole Lamb, Rogue Community College
Betty Lambert, Des Moines Area Community College
Anita Lande, Cabrillo College
Junnae Landry, Pratt Community College
Karen Lankisch, UC Clermont
David Lanzilla, Central Florida Community College
Nora Laredo, Cerritos Community College
Jennifer Larrabee, Chippewa Valley Technical College
Debra Larson, Idaho State University
Barb Lave, Portland Community College
Audrey Lawrence, Tidewater Community College
Deborah Layton, Eastern Oklahoma State College
Larry LeBlanc, Owen Graduate School–Vanderbilt University
Philip Lee, Nashville State Community College
Michael Lehrfeld, Brevard Community College
Vasant Limaye, Southwest Collegiate Institute for the Deaf – Howard College
Anne C. Lewis, Edgecombe Community College
Stephen Linkin, Houston Community College
Peggy Linston, Athens Technical College
Hugh Lofton, Moultrie Technical College
Donna Lohn, Lakeland Community College
Jackie Lou, Lake Tahoe Community College
Donna Love, Gaston College
Curt Lynch, Ozarks Technical Community College
Sheilah Lynn, Florida Community College–Jacksonville
Pat R. Lyon, Tomball College
Bill Madden, Bergen Community College
Heather Madden, Delaware Technical & Community College
Donna Madsen, Kirkwood Community College
Jane Maringer-Cantu, Gavilan College
Suzanne Marks, Bellevue Community College
Carol Martin, Louisiana State University–Alexandria
Cheryl Martucci, Diablo Valley College
Roberta Marvel, Eastern Wyoming College
Tom Mason, Brookdale Community College
Mindy Mass, Santa Barbara City College
Dixie Massaro, Irvine Valley College
Rebekah May, Ashland Community & Technical College
Emma Mays-Reynolds, Dyersburg State Community College
Timothy Mayes, Metropolitan State College of Denver
Reggie McCarthy, Central Lakes College
Matt McCaskill, Brevard Community College
Kevin McFarlane, Front Range Community College
Donna McGill, Yuba Community College
Terri McKeever, Ozarks Technical Community College
Patricia McMahon, South Suburban College
Sally McMillin, Katharine Gibbs School–Philadelphia
Charles McNerney, Bergen Community College
Lisa Mears, Palm Beach Community College
Imran Mehmood, ITT Technical Institute–King of Prussia Campus
Virginia Melvin, Southwest Tennessee Community College
Jeanne Mercer, Texas State Technical College

Denise Merrell, Jefferson Community & Technical College
Catherine Merrikin, Pearl River Community College
Diane D. Mickey, Northern Virginia Community College
Darrelyn Miller, Grays Harbor College
Sue Mitchell, Calhoun Community College
Jacquie Moldenhauer, Front Range Community College
Linda Motonaga, Los Angeles City College
Sam Mryyan, Allen County Community College
Cindy Murphy, Southeastern Community College
Ryan Murphy, Sinclair Community College
Sharon E. Nastav, Johnson County Community College
Christine Naylor, Kent State University Ashtabula
Haji Nazarian, Seattle Central Community College
Nancy Noe, Linn-Benton Community College
Jennie Noriega, San Joaquin Delta College
Linda Nutter, Peninsula College
Thomas Omerza, Middle Bucks Institute of Technology
Edith Orozco, St. Philip's College
Dona Orr, Boise State University
Joanne Osgood, Chaffey College
Janice Owens, Kishwaukee College
Tatyana Pashnyak, Bainbridge College
John Partacz, College of DuPage
Tim Paul, Montana State University–Great Falls
Joseph Perez, South Texas College
Mike Peterson, Chemeketa Community College
Dr. Karen R. Petitto, West Virginia Wesleyan College
Terry Pierce, Onandaga Community College
Ashlee Pieris, Raritan Valley Community College
Jamie Pinchot, Thiel College
Michelle Poertner, Northwestern Michigan College
Betty Posta, University of Toledo
Deborah Powell, West Central Technical College
Mark Pranger, Rogers State University
Carolyn Rainey, Southeast Missouri State University
Linda Raskovich, Hibbing Community College
Leslie Ratliff, Griffin Technical College
Mar-Sue Ratzke, Rio Hondo Community College
Roxy Reissen, Southeastern Community College
Silvio Reyes, Technical Career Institutes
Patricia Rishavy, Anoka Technical College
Jean Robbins, Southeast Technical Institute
Carol Roberts, Eastern Maine Community College and University of Maine
Teresa Roberts, Wilson Technical Community College
Vicki Robertson, Southwest Tennessee Community College
Betty Rogge, Ohio State Agricultural Technical Institute
Lynne Rusley, Missouri Southern State University
Claude Russo, Brevard Community College
Ginger Sabine, Northwestern Technical College
Steven Sachs, Los Angeles Valley College
Joanne Salas, Olympic College
Lloyd Sandmann, Pima Community College–Desert Vista Campus
Beverly Santillo, Georgia Perimeter College
Theresa Savarese, San Diego City College
Sharolyn Sayers, Milwaukee Area Technical College
Judith Scheeren, Westmoreland County Community College
Adolph Scheiwe, Joliet Junior College
Marilyn Schmid, Asheville-Buncombe Technical Community College
Janet Sebesy, Cuyahoga Community College
Phyllis T. Shafer, Brookdale Community College
Ralph Shafer, Truckee Meadows Community College
Anne Marie Shanley, County College of Morris
Shelia Shelton, Surry Community College
Merilyn Shepherd, Danville Area Community College
Susan Sinele, Aims Community College
Beth Sindt, Hawkeye Community College
Andrew Smith, Marian College
Brenda Smith, Southwest Tennessee Community College
Lynne Smith, State University of New York–Delhi
Rob Smith, Katharine Gibbs School–Philadelphia
Tonya Smith, Arkansas State University–Mountain Home
Del Spencer – Trinity Valley Community College
Jeri Spinner, Idaho State University
Eric Stadnik, Santa Rosa Junior College
Karen Stanton, Los Medanos College
Meg Stoner, Santa Rosa Junior College
Beverly Stowers, Ivy Tech Community College of Indiana
Marcia Stranix, Yuba College
Kim Styles, Tri-County Technical College
Sylvia Summers, Tacoma Community College
Beverly Swann, Delaware Technical & Community College
Ann Taff, Tulsa Community College
Mike Theiss, University of Wisconsin–Marathon Campus
Romy Thiele, Cañada College
Sharron Thompson, Portland Community College
Ingrid Thompson-Sellers, Georgia Perimeter College
Barbara Tietsort, University of Cincinnati–Raymond Walters College
Janine Tiffany, Reading Area Community College
Denise Tillery, University of Nevada Las Vegas
Susan Trebelhorn, Normandale Community College
Noel Trout, Santiago Canyon College
Cheryl Turgeon, Asnuntuck Community College
Steve Turner, Ventura College
Sylvia Unwin, Bellevue Community College
Lilly Vigil, Colorado Mountain College
Sabrina Vincent, College of the Mainland
Mary Vitrano, Palm Beach Community College
Brad Vogt, Northeast Community College
Cozell Wagner, Southeastern Community College
Carolyn Walker, Tri-County Technical College
Sherry Walker, Tulsa Community College

Qi Wang, Tacoma Community College
Betty Wanielista, Valencia Community College
Marge Warber, Lanier Technical College–Forsyth Campus
Marjorie Webster, Bergen Community College
Linda Wenn, Central Community College
Mark Westlund, Olympic College
Carolyn Whited, Roane State Community College
Winona Whited, Richland College
Jerry Wilkerson, Scott Community College
Joel Willenbring, Fullerton College
Barbara Williams, WITC Superior
Charlotte Williams, Jones County Junior College
Bonnie Willy, Ivy Tech Community College of Indiana
Diane Wilson, J. Sargeant Reynolds Community College
James Wolfe, Metropolitan Community College
Marjory Wooten, Lanier Technical College
Mark Yanko, Hocking College
Alexis Yusov, Pace University
Naeem Zaman, San Joaquin Delta College
Kathleen Zimmerman, Des Moines Area Community College

We would also like to thank Lutz Ziob, Sanjay Advani, Jim DiIanni, Merrick Van Dongen, Jim LeValley, Bruce Curling, Joe Wilson, and Naman Kahn at Microsoft for their encouragement and support in making the Microsoft Official Academic Course programs the finest instructional materials for mastering the newest Microsoft technologies for both students and instructors.

www.wiley.com/college/microsoft ***or***
call the MOAC Toll-Free Number: 1+(888) 764-7001 (U.S. & Canada only)

Brief Contents

www.wiley.com/college/microsoft ***or***
call the MOAC Toll-Free Number: 1+(888) 764-7001 (U.S. & Canada only)

Contents

Lesson 11: Understanding, Configuring, and Securing TCP/IP Networks 312

Lesson 12: Configuring and Troubleshooting Access 343

Lesson 13: Supporting and Maintaining Desktop Applications 388

www.wiley.com/college/microsoft *or*
call the MOAC Toll-Free Number: 1+(888) 764-7001 (U.S. & Canada only)

FOR INSTRUCTORS

Wiley*PLUS* is built around the activities you perform in your class each day. With Wiley*PLUS* you can:

Prepare & Present

Create outstanding class presentations using a wealth of resources such as PowerPoint™ slides, image galleries, interactive simulations, and more. You can even add materials you have created yourself.

Create Assignments

Automate the assigning and grading of homework or quizzes by using the provided question banks, or by writing your own.

Track Student Progress

Keep track of your students' progress and analyze individual and overall class results.

Now Available with WebCT

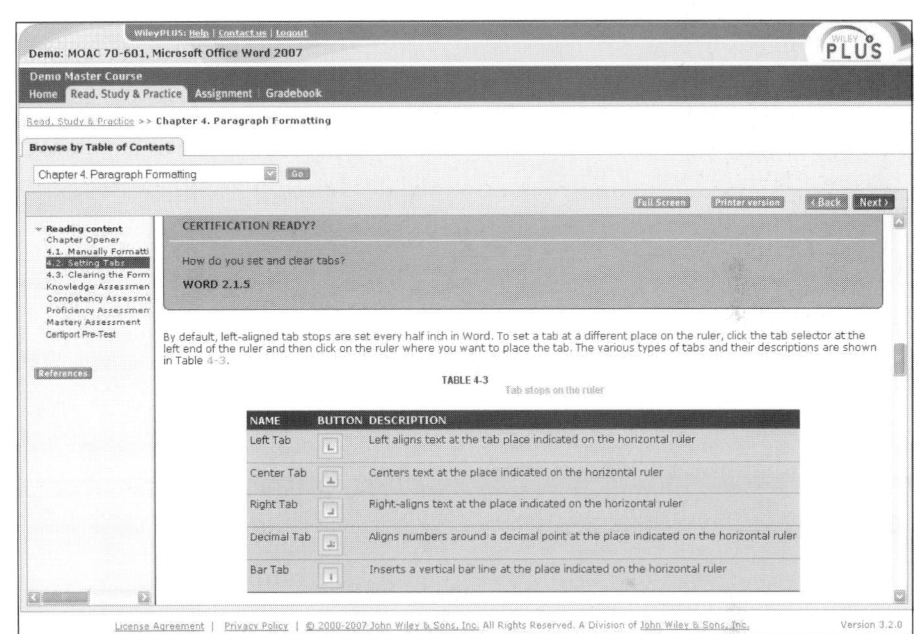

"It has been a great help, and I believe it has helped me to achieve a better grade."

Michael Morris,
Columbia Basin College

FOR STUDENTS

You have the potential to make a difference!

Wiley*PLUS* is a powerful online system packed with features to help you make the most of your potential and get the best grade you can!

With Wiley*PLUS* you get:

A complete online version of your text and other study resources.

•

Problem-solving help, instant grading, and feedback on your homework and quizzes.

•

The ability to track your progress and grades throughout the term.

For more information on what Wiley*PLUS* can do to help you and your students reach their potential, please visit www.wiley.com/college/*wileyplus*.

76% of students surveyed said it made them better prepared for tests.*

*Based on a survey of 972 student users of Wiley*PLUS*

www.wiley.com/college/microsoft *or*
call the MOAC Toll-Free Number: 1+(888) 764-7001 (U.S. & Canada only)

Microsoft® Official Academic Course

Supporting and Troubleshooting Applications on a Windows Vista® Client for Enterprise Support Technicians

Microsoft® Certified IT Professional Exam 70-622

Owen Fowler

www.wiley.com/college/microsoft ***or***
call the MOAC Toll-Free Number: 1+(888) 764-7001 (U.S. & Canada only)

Preparing to Deploy Windows Vista

LESSON 1

OBJECTIVE DOMAIN MATRIX

Technology Skill	Objective Domain	Objective Domain Number
Choosing a Deployment Method	Analyze the business environment and select an appropriate deployment method • Network • Offline Media • USB • DVD	1.1
Preparing for Deployment	Prepare a system for clean installation or upgrade	1.2
Understanding System Requirements	Prepare a system for clean installation or upgrade • Verify Windows Vista installation requirements	1.2
Analyzing Application and Device Compatibility	Troubleshoot deployment issues • Resolve application compatibility issues • Resolve device driver issues	1.5
Analyzing User Profile and Data Storage Requirements	Prepare a system for clean installation or upgrade • Analyze user profile and data requirements • Roaming User Profiles/Folder Redirection	1.2
Migrating User Profiles by Using USMT	Prepare a system for clean installation or upgrade • Perform user state backup with USMT Perform post-installation tasks • Restore user state with USMT	1.2 1.4
Understanding USMT	Prepare a system for clean installation or upgrade • Perform user state backup with USMT Perform post-installation tasks • Restore user state with USMT	1.2 1.4
Understanding What USMT Migrates	Prepare a system for clean installation or upgrade • Perform user state backup with USMT Perform post-installation tasks • Restore user state with USMT	1.2 1.4
Using USMT	Prepare a system for clean installation or upgrade • Perform user state backup with USMT Perform post-installation tasks • Restore user state with USMT	1.2 1.4

(continued)

OBJECTIVE DOMAIN MATRIX (*continued*)

Technology Skill	Objective Domain	Objective Number
Understanding ScanState	Prepare a system for clean installation or upgrade • Perform user state backup with USMT	1.2
Understanding LoadState	Perform post-installation tasks • Restore user state with USMT	1.4
Understanding the .xml Control Files	Prepare a system for clean installation or upgrade • Perform user state backup with USMT Perform post-installation tasks • Restore user state with USMT	1.2 1.4
Understanding Manifests	Prepare a system for clean installation or upgrade • Perform user state backup with USMT Perform post-installation tasks • Restore user state with USMT	1.2 1.4
Completing a Simple Profile Migration by Using USMT	Prepare a system for clean installation or upgrade • Perform user state backup with USMT Perform post-installation tasks • Restore user state with USMT	1.2 1.4

KEY TERMS

image
Windows Imaging Format (WIM) image
Windows Vista Capable PC
Windows Vista Premium Ready PC
Windows Vista Hardware Assessment tool
Application Compatibility Toolkit 5.0 (ACT)
distributed compatibility evaluators
Inventory Collector
User Account Control Compatibility Evaluator (UACCE)
Update Compatibility Evaluator (UCE)
Internet Explorer Compatibility Evaluator (IECE)
Vista Compatibility Evaluator (VCE)
Windows Vista Upgrade Advisor
user profile
roaming profiles
All Users profile
Public profile
Folder Redirection
local UserProfile location
Microsoft Windows User State Migration Tool (USMT)
ScanState
LoadState
.xml control files
Component Manifests
Downlevel Manifests
MigSys.xml
MigApp.xml
MigUser.xml
Config.xml

Contoso Incorporated, where you are a senior desktop support technician, is going to do a pilot deployment of Windows Vista in the accounting department. You have been assigned to a committee whose purpose is to plan and execute the deployment. Your role on the committee is to coordinate the pre-deployment tasks and make recommendations as to what deployment method to use. If the pilot goes well, you will deploy Windows Vista to the entire enterprise over the next two quarters.

Choosing a Deployment Method

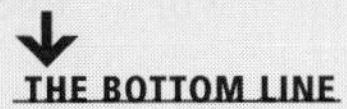

THE BOTTOM LINE

Deciding what deployment method to use depends primarily on how many workstations you want to deploy Windows Vista to and how hands-off you want the deployment process to be.

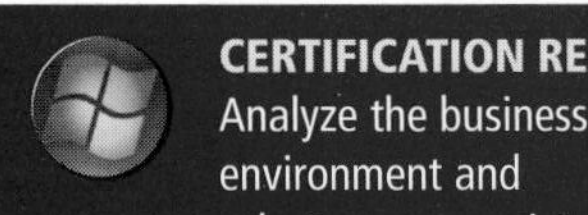

CERTIFICATION READY?
Analyze the business environment and select an appropriate deployment method
- Network
- Offline media
- USB
- DVD

1.1

For large Windows Vista deployments to networked workstations, Microsoft recommends that you deploy from a ***Windows Imaging Format (WIM)*** image over the network. An ***image*** is a file that contains the contents and structure of a data medium, such as a hard disk. A WIM image (herein shortened to *image*) is Microsoft's proprietary image file format for storing images of Windows operating systems. Deploying by using an image over the network enables you to deploy the operating system to many workstations simultaneously without being present at the workstations.

XREF

You can find more information on the WIM file format in Lesson 2: Deploying Windows Vista.

Another way to deploy Windows Vista is by using offline media, such as a DVD disc or a Universal Serial Bus (USB) storage device that contains a Windows Vista image. The primary reason that you would choose to deploy using offline media is if you are deploying to a small number of workstations. For example, you might decide the best way to deal with a troubleshooting problem on an individual workstation is to reinstall the operating system by using a portable USB device containing the appropriate image. Or, you might be setting up an isolated lab of three workstations in a workgroup and decide that the most convenient way to install Windows Vista on each workstation is by using a DVD disc containing an image.

TAKE NOTE*

When you install Windows Vista by using an original Windows Vista DVD disc, you are still installing from a WIM image. Though there are other support files on the DVD disc, the actual installation files are stored in a WIM image.

Preparing for Deployment

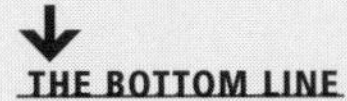

THE BOTTOM LINE

Preparing for deployment includes understanding system requirements, analyzing device and application compatibility issues, and analyzing and planning for user data migration and data storage.

CERTIFICATION READY?
Prepare a system for clean installation or upgrade: Verify Windows Vista installation requirements

1.2

Understanding System Requirements

Microsoft specifies three sets of system requirements: minimum system requirements, Windows Vista Capable PC requirements, and Windows Vista Premium Ready PC requirements.

The minimum system requirements to run the core features of Windows Vista according to Microsoft are:

- 800MHz 32-bit (x86) or 64-bit (x64) processor
- 512MB system memory
- SVGA (800×600) graphics processing unit (GPU)
- 20GB hard disk drive (HDD) with 15GB free space
- CD-ROM optical drive

In addition to these minimum requirements, Microsoft has created two logos that indicate if a new computer is capable of running Windows Vista: the Windows Vista Capable PC logo (Figure 1-1) and the Windows Vista Premium Ready PC logo (Figure 1-2). When you purchase a computer that has one of these logos, you can rest assured that it will be able to run Windows Vista.

Figure 1-1

Windows Vista Capable PC logo

Figure 1-2

Windows Vista Premium Ready PC logo

Microsoft describes a ***Windows Vista Capable PC*** as follows: "A new PC running Windows XP that carries the Windows Vista Capable PC logo can run Windows Vista. All editions of Windows Vista will deliver core experiences such as innovations in organizing and finding information, security, and reliability. All Windows Vista Capable PCs will run these core experiences at a minimum. Some features available in the premium editions of Windows Vista—like the new Windows Aero user experience—may require advanced or additional hardware."

The minimum system requirements for a Windows Vista Capable PC are:

- A modern processor (at least 800MHz)
- 512MB system memory
- DirectX 9 capable GPU

Microsoft describes a ***Windows Vista Premium Ready PC*** as follows: "To get an even better Windows Vista experience, including the Windows Aero user experience, ask for a Windows Vista Capable PC that is designated Premium Ready, or choose a PC that meets or exceeds the Premium Ready requirements described below. Features available in specific premium editions of Windows Vista, such as the ability to watch and record live TV, may require additional hardware."

The minimum system requirements for a Windows Vista Premium Ready PC are:

- 1GHz 32-bit (x86) or 64-bit (x64) processor
- 1GB system memory
- GPU that supports DirectX 9 graphics with a Microsoft Windows Vista Display Driver Model (WDDM) driver, 128MB of graphics memory (minimum), Pixel Shader 2.0 and 32 bits per pixel
- 40GB HDD with 15GB free space
- DVD-ROM drive
- Audio output capability
- Internet access capability

MORE INFORMATION

You can find more information on system requirements in an enterprise environment here: *technet.microsoft.com/en-us/windowsvista/aa905075.aspx*

Analyzing Application and Device Compatibility

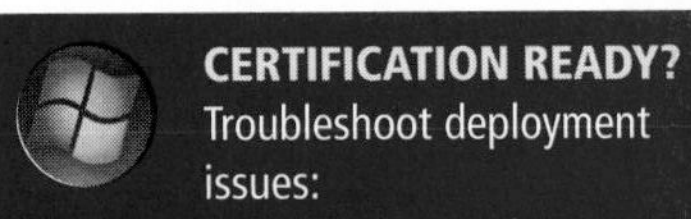

CERTIFICATION READY?
Troubleshoot deployment issues:
- Resolve application compatibility issues
- Resolve device driver issues

1.5

Microsoft provides two tools for analyzing application and device compatibility with Windows Vista for many computers simultaneously in an enterprise: the Windows Vista Hardware Assessment tool and the Application Compatibility Toolkit 5.0. In addition, you can use the Windows Vista Upgrade Advisor to analyze both software and hardware compatibility on stand-alone computers.

Microsoft provides two tools for analyzing application and device compatibility with Windows Vista in an enterprise: the ***Windows Vista Hardware Assessment tool*** and the ***Application Compatibility Toolkit 5.0 (ACT)***. You use the first to analyze device compatibility, and the second to analyze application compatibility. In addition, for stand-alone computers both at home and in a business environment, you can use the Windows Vista Upgrade Advisor to analyze both application and device compatibility.

TAKE NOTE* The word *device* in this context includes both devices that you attach to your computer, such as USB drives or digital music players, as well as hardware components of the computer, such as CPUs and hard disks.

X REF Troubleshooting application and device compatibility issues are covered in Lesson 3: Configuring Devices and Applications.

The following are five ways that you can check to see if an application is compatible with Windows Vista:

- Check the packaging of the software (or the website from which it is downloaded) for the Microsoft Vista Compatible logo.
- Check the Windows Marketplace.
- Use the Windows Vista Upgrade Advisor (for stand-alone computers).
- Use the Application Compatibility Toolkit 5.0 (for large numbers of networked computers in an enterprise).
- Install the application.

The Microsoft Vista Compatible logo ensures that the application is compatible with Windows Vista. If a product lacks the logo, it still may be compatible.

The ***Windows Marketplace*** is a portal for selling computer related products. If you can find the software in the Windows Marketplace, you will be presented with compatibility information. The Windows Marketplace URL is *www.windowsmarketplace.com*.

The following is a list of steps you can take to determine if a device is compatible with Windows Vista:

- See if the device is listed in the ***Windows VistaHardware Compatibility List (HCL)***: *winqual.microsoft.com/hcl/*.
- Check the packaging and manual for an indication of Windows Vista compatibility.
- For enterprise computers, run the Windows Vista Hardware Assessment tool.
- For stand-alone computers, run the Windows Vista Upgrade Advisor tool.

Getting Started with the Windows Vista Hardware Assessment Tool

The Windows Vista Hardware Assessment tool can analyze and report on device compatibility across many computers on a large network.

The Windows Vista Hardware Assessment tool aggregates and organizes system resource and device data across your network onto a single computer. It does not require you to install agents on target computers, as many assessment tools do. The Windows Vista Hardware Assessment tool encrypts what it sends between the target computers and the computer that aggregates the data.

The Windows Vista Hardware Assessment tool can only scan computers that support Windows Management Instrumentation (WMI). This includes computers running the following operating systems:

- Windows Vista
- Windows XP Professional (SP2)
- Windows Server 2003 (R1 and R2)
- Windows 2000 Professional
- Windows 2000 Server

The Windows Vista Hardware Assessment tool does the following in its analysis:

- Identifies which computers are ready for migration to Windows Vista as is
- Identifies which computers need upgrades to become ready for migration to Windows Vista
- Recommends reasonable hardware upgrades (does not recommend costly hardware upgrades, for example, CPU upgrades)
- Determines which hardware devices have device drivers available on the Windows Vista installation DVD
- Determines which hardware drivers can be downloaded from Windows Update
- Determines which devices require manufacturer device drivers

Following its analysis, the Windows Vista Hardware Assessment tool creates the following reports:

- A Microsoft Office Excel workbook comprehensively covering the device inventory and assessment. The information in this report provides all the details required for you to address device issues prior to migration to Windows Vista.
- A Microsoft Office Word document summarizing the device inventory and assessment. This report is targeted at business decision makers and is intended to aide strategic decisions. It is not helpful in addressing specific device issues.

MORE INFORMATION

You can get more information and download the Windows Vista Hardware Assessment tool here: *www.microsoft.com/technet/solutionaccelerators/.*

Getting Started with the Application Compatibility Toolkit 5.0

The Application Compatibility Toolkit 5.0 (ACT 5.0) can analyze and report on application compatibility across many computers on a large network.

ACT uses ***distributed compatibility evaluators***, which are small programs installed on each computer being evaluated, to gather and send application compatibility data to a single, centralized store where it is organized and can be viewed.

TAKE NOTE*

Distributed compatibility evaluators is Microsoft's fancy term for agents.

ACT uses the following distributed compatibility evaluators:

- ***Inventory Collector*** Identifies installed applications and gathers system information
- ***User Account Control Compatibility Evaluator (UACCE)*** Identifies potential compatibility issues due to permissions restrictions enforced by User Account Control (UAC)
- ***Update Compatibility Evaluator (UCE)*** Gathers information on application dependencies and can identify potential effects of Windows operating system security updates on applications
- ***Internet Explorer Compatibility Evaluator (IECE)*** Identifies potential Web application and Web site issues that occur due to the release of a new operating system
- ***Vista Compatibility Evaluator (VCE)*** Identifies other issues related to compatibility with Windows Vista, such as potential Graphical Identification and Authentication (GINA) dynamic-link library (DLL) issues, services running in Session 0 in a production environment, and deprecation issues

X REF

UAC is covered in Lesson 8: Troubleshoot Access, Authentication, and User Account Control Issues.

ACT, in addition to gathering data, provides recommendations on how to resolve some of the compatibility issues that it identifies.

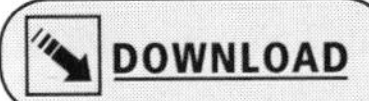

DOWNLOAD You can download and find links to more information on ACT 5.0 by searching here: *www.microsoft.com/downloads/.*

Using the Windows Vista Upgrade Advisor

You can use the Windows Vista Upgrade Advisor on stand-alone computers to analyze both hardware and application compatibility issues before upgrading to Windows Vista.

The ***Windows Vista Upgrade Advisor*** can catch compatibility issues before you upgrade a stand-alone computer to Windows Vista.

DOWNLOAD You can download the Windows Vista Upgrade Advisor here: *www.microsoft.com/windows/products/windowsvista/buyorupgrade/.*

RUN THE WINDOWS VISTA UPGRADE ADVISOR

To run the Windows Vista Upgrade Advisor, the target computer must be running Windows XP or newer. The Windows Vista Upgrade Advisor gives information on system, device, and application compatibility.

DOWNLOAD and install the Windows Vista Upgrade Advisor. Launch it from the Start menu.

1. In the Windows Vista Upgrade Adviser window, click **Start Scan**. The Scanning system page appears while the scan takes place, as shown in Figure 1-3. When the scan is complete, the Scan complete page appears.
2. Click **See Details**. A summary page appears.

Figure 1-3

The Scanning System page of the Windows Vista Upgrade Adviser setup wizard

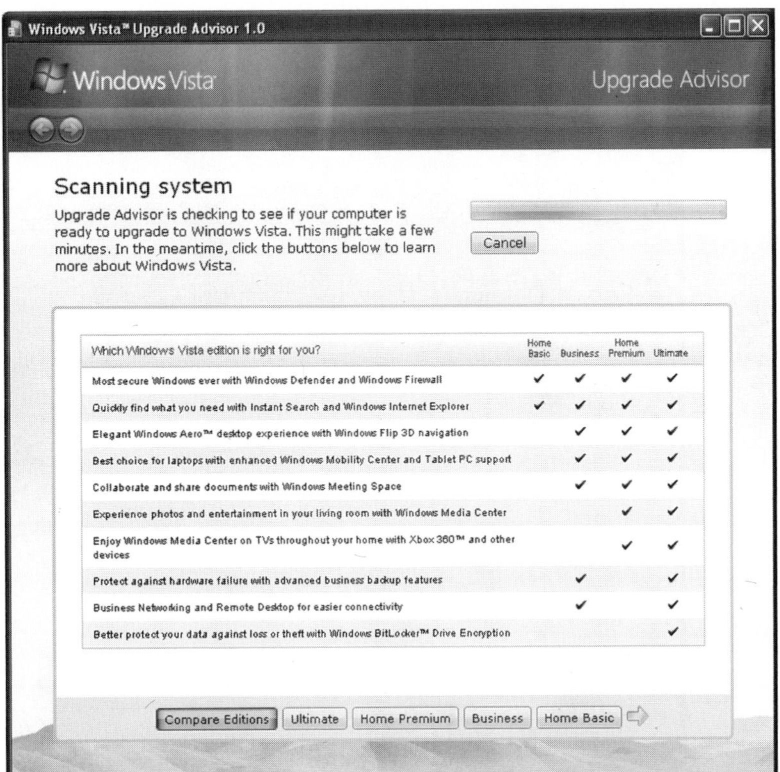

The summary page contains four sections of interest, as shown in the example in Figure 1-4:

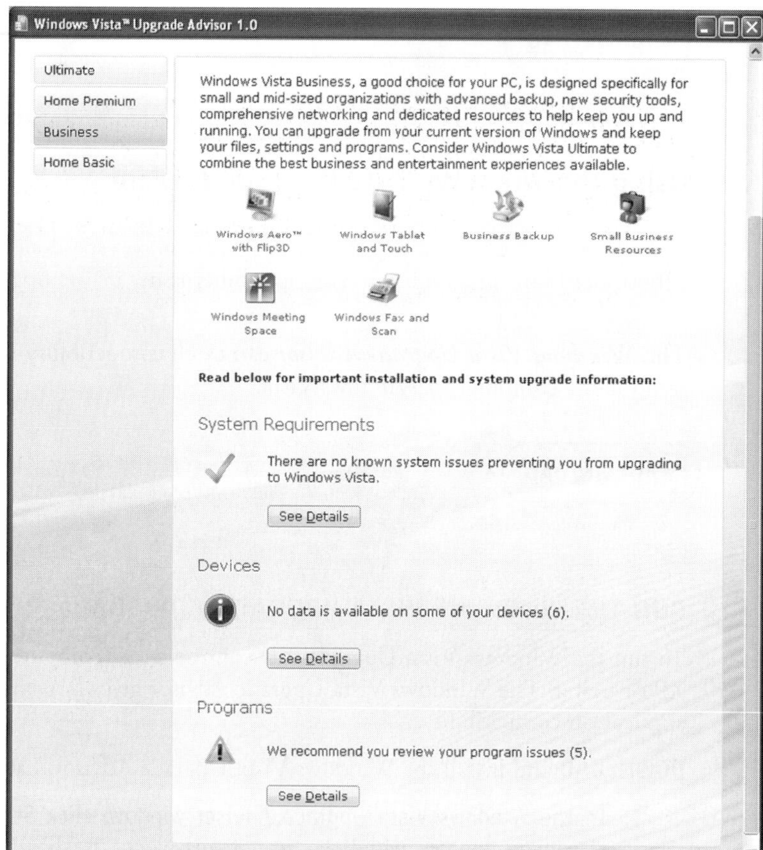

Figure 1-4

Summary for Windows Vista Upgrade Advisor

Each of these sections contains a See Details button, which when clicked will open the same page but with a different tab open. The four tabs are:

- **System** Contains information on any required system upgrades prior to upgrading. An example of the System tab is shown in Figure 1-5.

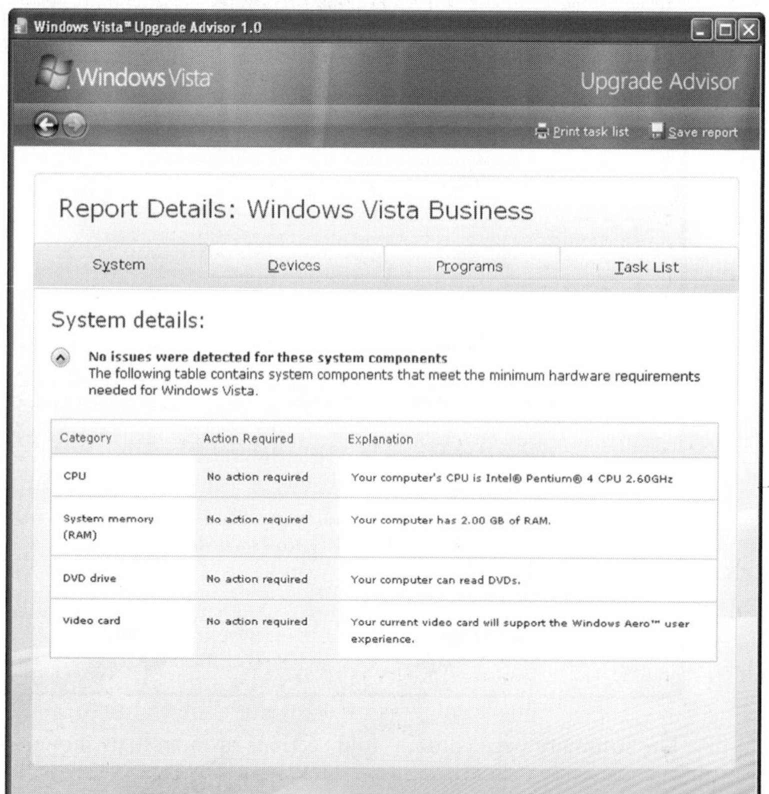

Figure 1-5

System tab of the Windows Vista Upgrade Advisor

- **Devices** Lists any incompatibilities with attached devices. An example of the Devices tab is shown in Figure 1-6.

Figure 1-6

Devices tab of the Windows Vista Upgrade Advisor

- **Programs** Details any application compatibility issues. An example of the Programs tab is shown in Figure 1-7.

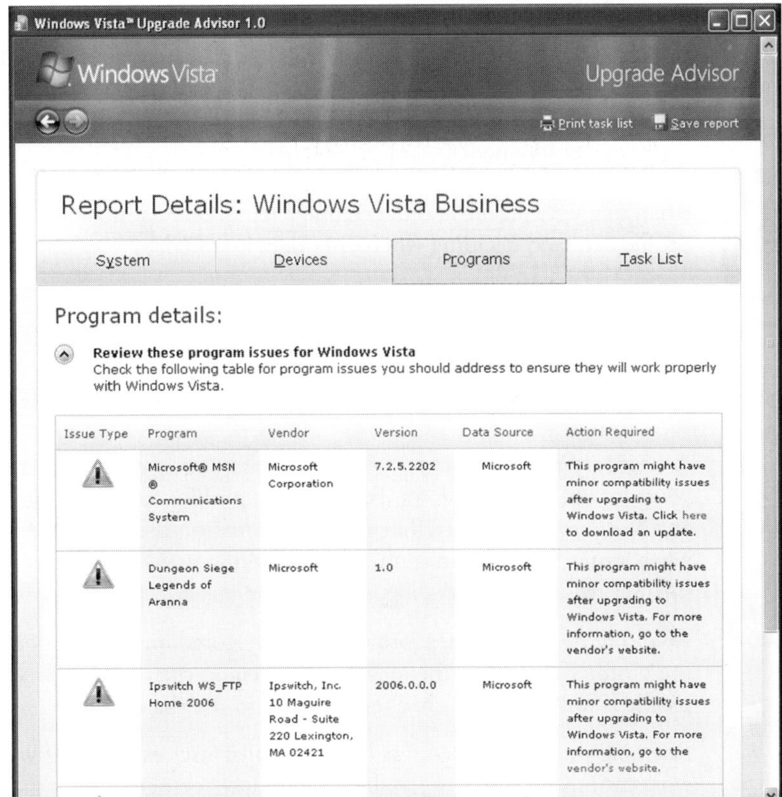

Figure 1-7

Programs tab of the Windows Vista Upgrade Advisor

- **Task List** Summarizes tasks from the other three tabs that you need to address before upgrading. An example of the Task List tab is shown in Figure 1-8.

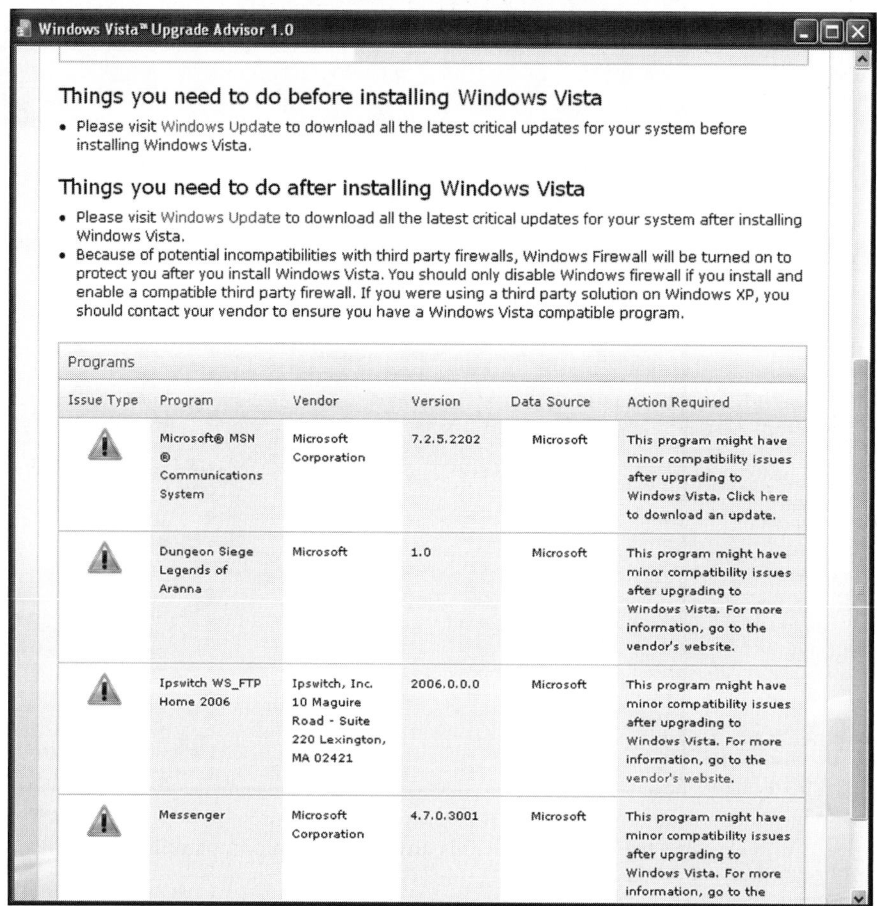

Figure 1-8

Task List tab of the Windows Vista Upgrade Advisor

Analyzing User Profile and Data Storage Requirements

Before deploying Windows Vista, you need to plan and prepare for user profile and data storage requirements.

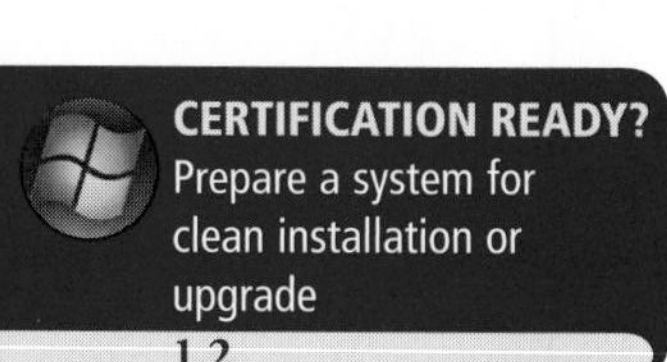

CERTIFICATION READY?
Prepare a system for clean installation or upgrade
1.2

Analyzing user profile and data storage requirements includes deciding how to organize user profile data and deciding where user data is stored.

Understanding User Profiles

A user profile is a collection of user data.

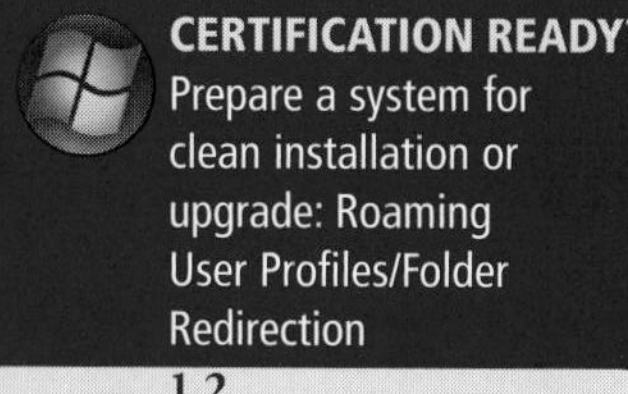

CERTIFICATION READY?
Prepare a system for clean installation or upgrade: Roaming User Profiles/Folder Redirection
1.2

A ***user profile*** is a collection of user data that partly dictates user settings and user experience when logged onto Windows. For example, profiles contain information on desktop appearance and Start menu structure. The profile is stored on the local hard drive, is loaded into memory when a user logs on, and is unloaded when the user logs off. Any changes to the profile that the user makes during the logon session are saved to the profile when the user logs off.

Roaming profiles are user profiles that are stored on a network share. When a user logs on, the profile is copied to the local hard drive and then is loaded. When the user logs off, the profile is unloaded and changes are saved to the share.

Roaming profiles enable users to have similar user experiences when logging onto different workstations on the network, because the user profile follows the user.

X REF

Migrating profile data is covered in the Migrating User Profiles by Using USMT section later in this lesson.

Before deploying Windows Vista, you should determine if affected users are configured to use roaming or local profiles. In either case, if you want to preserve their current profile data through the migration (which is highly likely), you will need to migrate the profile data.

One disadvantage of roaming profiles is that they can get rather large, and therefore can take a lot of time to load when a user logs on. This was especially true in previous versions of Windows. Windows Vista mitigates this problem by better separating application data that needs to roam with a user from application data that can remain on the local machine. This separation enables Windows Vista to reduce the amount of application data stored in a roaming profile.

A user profile (roaming or otherwise) is made up of a folder structure and user data (including registry settings). Windows Vista profiles use a different folder structure for profiles than do Windows XP profiles.

TAKE NOTE*

You can view the folder structure of your own profile. Navigate to the Users folder and then open the folder that corresponds to your user name. The folder structure within is the folder structure stored in your user profile. Some folders are hidden by default.

Table 1-1 shows the folder locations in XP and Windows Vista for the most important folders in a profile. Understanding this structure is key to understanding how folder direction works in Windows XP versus Windows Vista, and it can help in troubleshooting Folder Redirection.

Table 1-1

Folder locations in XP and Windows Vista for important profile folders

WINDOWS VISTA FOLDER LOCATION: \USERS\USERNAME\	XP FOLDER LOCATION: \DOCUMENTS AND SETTINGS\USERNAME\	FOLDER PURPOSE
Contacts	Does not exist in XP	Default location for user's contacts
Desktop	Desktop	Contains items stored on the desktop
Documents	My Documents	Default location for user created documents
Downloads	Does not exist in XP	Default location for user downloaded files
Favorites	Favorites	Contains Internet Explorer favorite links
Music	My Documents\My Music	Default location for user's music
Videos	My Documents\My Videos	Default location for user's videos
Pictures	My Documents\My Pictures	Default location for user's pictures
Searches	Does not exist in XP	Default location for saved searches
Links	Documents And Settings*UserName*\ Favorites\ Links\	Contains Windows Explorers favorite links
Saved Games	Does not exist in XP	Contains files for saved games
AppData\Roaming	Application Data	Contains data for applications that are machine independent, such as custom dictionaries

(continued)

Table 1-1 ***(continued)***

Windows Vista folder location: \Users\username\	XP folder location: \Documents and Settings\username\	Folder purpose
AppData\Local	Local Settings\Application Data	Contains data for applications and does not roam with the user because the data file is too large to roam, or is machine specific
AppData\LocalLow	Does not exist in XP	Contains low integrity-level data for applications and does not roam with the user
AppData\Local\Microsoft\Windows\History	Local Settings\History	Contains browsing history data for Internet Explorer
AppData\Local\Temp	Local Settings\Temp	Contains temporary data
AppData\Local\Microsoft\Windows\Temporary Internet Files	Local Settings\Temporary Internet Files	Contains temporary Internet files
AppData\Roaming\Microsoft\Windows\Cookies	Cookies	Contains Internet Explorer cookies
AppData\Roaming\Microsoft\Windows\	Nethood	Contains shortcuts to network resources Network Shortcuts
AppData\Roaming\Microsoft\Windows\Printer Shortcuts	PrintHood	Contains shortcuts to printers
AppData\Roaming\Microsoft\Windows\Recent	Recent	Contains shortcuts to recently used documents
AppData\Roaming\Microsoft\Windows\Send To	SendTo	Contains shortcuts to SendTo locations
AppData\Roaming\Microsoft\Windows\Start Menu	Start Menu	Contains Start menu entries
AppData\Roaming\Microsoft\Windows\Templates	Templates	Contains templates

Profiles created for earlier versions of Windows will not work in Windows Vista, nor will Windows Vista profiles work in earlier versions of Windows. Windows Vista appends roaming profile folders with a V2 to distinguish them from profiles from earlier versions of Windows.

Previous versions of Windows, in addition to normal user profiles, have an All Users profile. The ***All Users profile*** contains data that it applies to all users who log onto the workstation. The All Users profile folder structure and items are merged with those of the user profile when a user logs on. For example, adding a shortcut to the Desktop folder of the All Users profile on a workstation will cause all users who log onto that workstation to have same shortcut appear on their desktops.

The ***Public profile*** is the Windows Vista version of the All Users profile, and it works the same way. The default location of the Public profile is in the Users folder.

The Recycle Bin in Windows Vista is stored in the root of a user's profile. In previous versions of Windows, the system stored the folder publicly in the root of the local computer on which the user deleted the files.

TAKE NOTE*

You can encrypt user profiles using Encrypting File System (EFS) except for the ntuser.dat file and the \AppData\Roaming\Microsoft\Credentials folder.

Configuring Roaming Profiles

Roaming profiles are configured in the Active Directory Users and Computers Properties dialog box for the user.

CONFIGURE A ROAMING PROFILE FOR A USER

TAKE NOTE*

This procedure was written and tested using Windows Server 2003.

You can configure a roaming profile for a user by using the Active Directory Users and Computers console.

1. Log on to a Windows server with a domain administrator account.
2. Click **Start**, point to **Administrative Tools**, and then click **Active Directory Users and Computers**. The Active Directory Users and Computers console appears.
3. In the Active Directory Users and Computers console, in the console tree, expand ***ServerName*** and then select **Users**, as shown in the example in Figure 1-9:

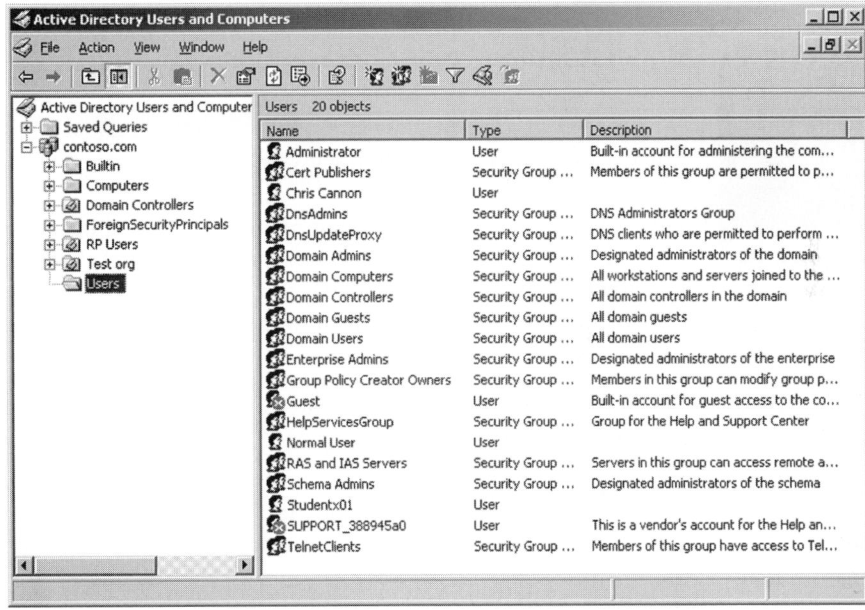

Figure 1-9

Active Directory Users and Computers console with Users selected

4. In the details pane, right-click the user for which you want to configure a roaming profile and then click **Properties**. The *UserName* Properties dialog box appears.
5. Click the **Profile** tab.
6. In the User Profile section, key the path where the roaming profile will reside, as shown in the example in Figure 1-10.

Figure 1-10

The Profile tab of the Properties dialog box for an example user

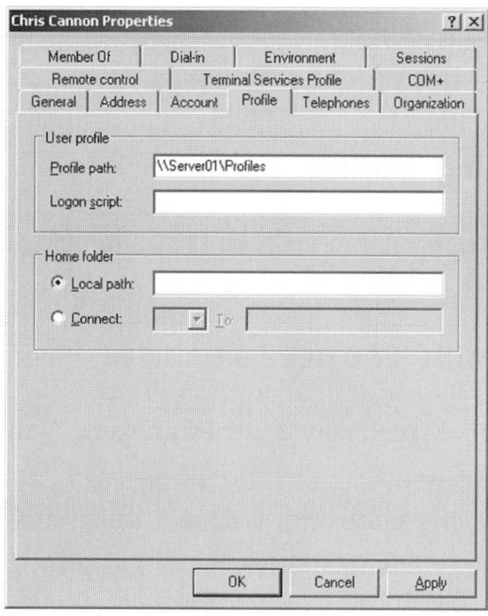

7. Click **OK**.

Understanding Folder Redirection

Folder Redirection enables you to redirect the saving and loading of data from a profile folder to another folder (almost always a network share).

Folder Redirection is the process of redirecting the saving and loading of data from a profile folder to another folder (almost always a network share). For example, if you redirect the Desktop folder for a group of users, then when they save items to their desktops, Windows saves the data to a share rather than to the Desktop folders in their profiles.

TAKE NOTE*

Folder Redirection enables you to direct data out of users' profiles into a share, which shrinks the size of the profiles, thus decreasing log-on time with roaming profiles.

When Vista redirects a profile folder, it is referred to as a redirected folder. The folder to which it is redirected is referred to as a target folder.

When you migrate to Windows Vista, you want to try to create as seamless a transition for your users as possible. If you are using Folder Redirection, you will want to be sure that the new Windows Vista installations access the redirected folders correctly. Also, if you are not using Folder Redirection, you might consider redirecting at least some user folders before migrating so that you don't need to migrate as much profile data.

Windows XP gives you the ability to redirect five profile folders:

- Application Data
- Desktop
- My Documents
- My Pictures
- Start Menu

Windows Vista gives you the ability to redirect 13 profile folders:

- AppData\Roaming
- Desktop
- AppData\Roaming\Start Menu

- Documents
- Pictures
- Music
- Videos
- Favorites
- Contacts
- Downloads
- Links
- Searches
- Saved Games

If you set up Folder Redirection for folders in Windows XP or earlier, those redirections will work correctly when a user logs onto a Windows Vista workstation. Table 1-2 shows how Folder Redirection on an XP client compares to Folder Redirection on a Windows Vista client:

Table 1-2

How Folder Redirection on an XP client compares to Folder Redirection on a Windows Vista client

XP REDIRECTED FOLDER	WINDOWS VISTA REDIRECTED FOLDER
Application Data	AppData\Roaming
Desktop	Desktop
Start Menu	Start Menu
My Documents	Documents

Configuring Folder Redirection

Folder Redirection in an enterprise environment is configured through Group Policy objects.

X REF

Group Policy is covered in Lesson 4: Using Group Policy.

In an enterprise, Folder Redirection should be configured through a Group Policy object (GPO) linked to the site, domain, or organizational unit containing the users for which you want to configure Folder Redirection. A ***Group Policy object*** is a set of policies that is applied to users or computers in an Active Directory directory service domain.

Before configuring Folder Redirection, you need to create a share or shares to contain the target folders. The following permissions will allow only the user and domain administrators to open the target folder for a redirected folder.

1. Create a folder on the file server.
2. Set the Share Permissions for the Everyone group to Full Control.
3. Set the NTFS permissions according to Table 1-3.

Table 1-3

NTFS permissions for a shared folder containing target folders for Folder Redirection.

GROUP OR USER NAME	NTFS PERMISSION	APPLY ONTO
CREATOR OWNER	Full Control	Subfolders and Files Only
SYSTEM	Full Control	This Folder, Subfolder, and Files
Domain Admins	Full Control	This Folder, Subfolder, and Files
Everyone	Create Folders/Append Data List Folder/Read Data Read Attributes Traverse Folder/Execute File	This Folder Only

REDIRECT A FOLDER TO SEPARATE TARGET FOLDERS IN THE SAME ROOT PATH FOR EACH USER

Redirecting a folder to separate target folders is the most common Folder Redirection configuration.

1. Click **Start**.
2. In the Start Search box, key **gpmc.msc** and then press **Ctrl** + **Shift** + **Enter.** A User Account Control dialog box appears.
3. Provide administrator credentials and then click **OK**. The Group Policy Management Console appears.
4. In the console tree, expand **Forest:** ***ForestName*.Domains>*DomainName*>Group Policy Objects** to expose the GPO that you want to configure, as shown in the example in Figure 1-11.

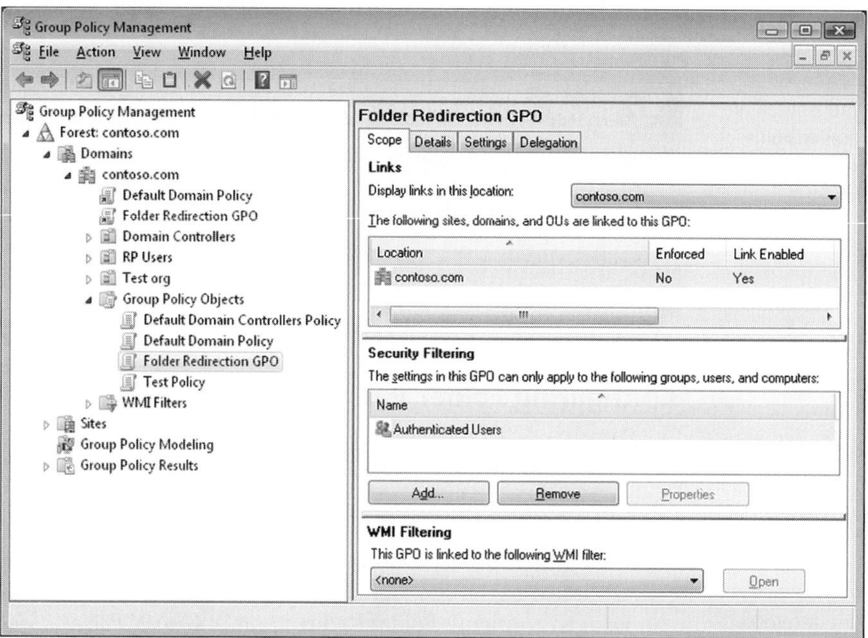

Figure 1-11

Group Policy Management console with the Folder Redirection GPO selected

5. Right-click the GPO you want to edit and then click **Edit**. The Group Policy Object Editor appears with the selected GPO loaded, as shown in the example in Figure 1-12.

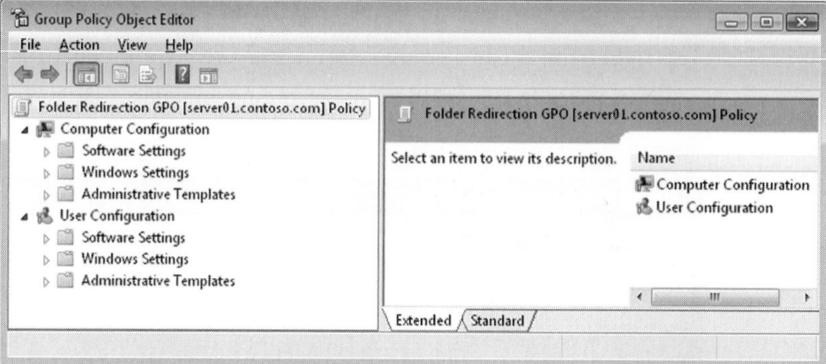

Figure 1-12

Group Policy Object Editor with an example GPO loaded

6. In the console tree, expand **User Configuration>Windows Settings>Folder Redirection**, as shown in Figure 1-13.

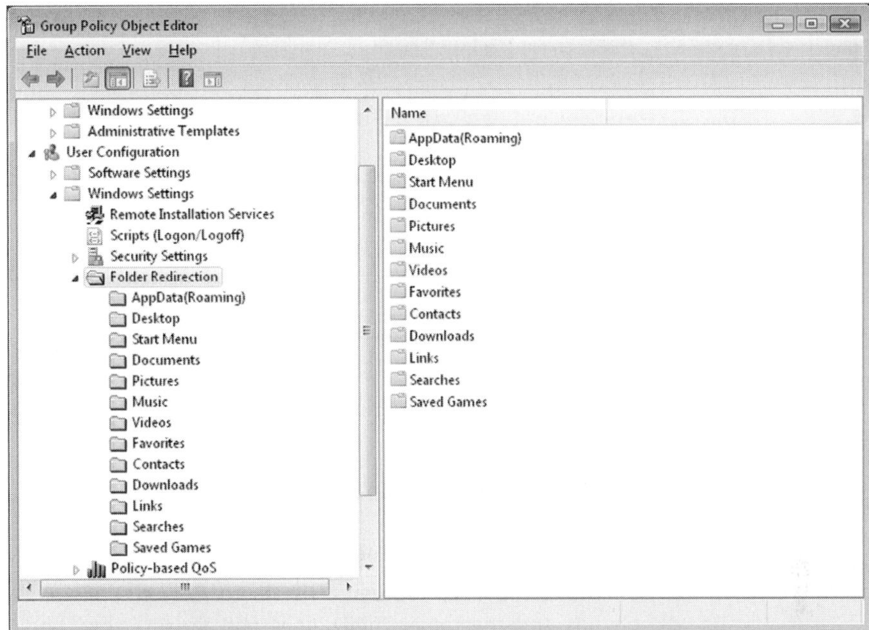

Figure 1-13

Group Policy Object Editor with Folder Redirection selected.

7. In the details pane, right-click the fzolder that you want to redirect and then click **Properties.** The *RedirectedFolderName* Properties dialog box appears.
8. In the Setting drop-down list, ensure that **Basic – Redirect everyone's folder the same location** is selected.
9. In the Target folder location section, in the drop-down list, select **Create a folder for each user under the root path.**
10. Enter the share location for Folder Redirection in the **Root Path** text box, as shown in the example in Figure 1-14. The root path is where a separate folder is created for each user, under which are created the target folders. For example, if you are redirecting the Pictures folder for a user with username ChrisC to a share named RedirectStore1 on a computer named server01, the root path you key will be **\\server01\RedirectStore1** and the target folder created will be \\server01\RedirectStore1\ChrisC\Pictures. Group Policy will redirect the data Chris places in the Pictures folder on any workstation to this folder.

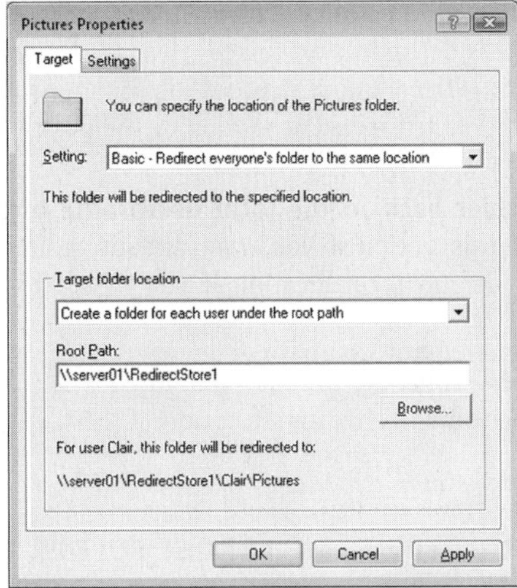

Figure 1-14

Target tab of the *RedirectedFolderName* Properties dialog box

11. Click the **Settings** tab. Example settings are shown in Figure 1-15.

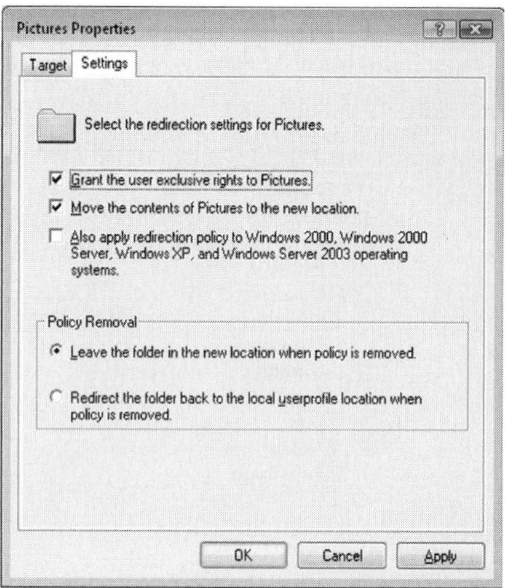

Figure 1-15

Settings tab of the *RedirectedFolderName* Properties dialog box.

12. Configure the following check boxes:

    Grant the user exclusive rights to *RedirectedFolderName* If you select this check box and the target folder does not already exist, the target folder will be created with permissions set to allow Full Control for the SYSTEM account and for the user. If the target folder does exist, and another user owns the folder, Folder Redirection will fail. Finally, if you clear this check box, the ownership of the folder will not be checked and therefore access will not be exclusive to the user.

    Move the contents of *RedirectedFolderName* to the new location Select this check box to move the contents of *RedirectedFolder* to *TargetFolder* at next user logon.

    Also apply redirection to Windows 2000, Windows 2000 Server, Windows XP, and Windows Server 2003 operating systems Select this check box if you want Folder Redirection to apply to the listed operating systems as well as to Windows Vista.

13. Select one of the following:

    Leave the folder in the new location when policy is removed Select this option if you want already redirected user folders to remain where they are if you delete or un-link the GPO.

TAKE NOTE* Users who did not log on after the policy was in effect were never subject to the policy. Therefore, after the GPO is deleted or un-linked, their folders will remain as they were before the policy went into effect. Those that did log on after the policy was in effect will continue to have their folders redirected according to the policy.

Redirect the folder back to the local userprofile location when policy is removed Select this option if you want already redirected user folders to be returned to the default local location if you delete or un-link the GPO.

TAKE NOTE* Changing the policy in the Target tab to Not Configured will not have any effect on already redirected folders. The option will have an effect only if the GPO is deleted or unlinked.

REDIRECT A FOLDER TO THE SAME TARGET FOLDER FOR ALL USERS

Use this procedure to redirect all users' folders to the same target folder. This is useful if all users need access to the same folder for collaboration purposes. For example, an art department might want the Pictures folder for all users to redirect to the same location where stock images are stored.

OPEN the GPO you want to edit in the Group Policy Object Editor.

1. In the Group Policy Object Editor, in the console tree, expand **User Configuration > Windows Settings > Folder Redirection.**
2. In the details pane, right-click the folder that you want to redirect and then click **Properties.** The *RedirectedFolderName* Properties dialog box appears.
3. Ensure that **Basic - Redirect everyone's folder to the same location** is selected in the Setting drop-down list.
4. In the Target folder location section, in the drop-down list, select **Redirect to the following location.**
5. In the **Root Path** text box, browse to or key *ServerName**ShareName**TargetFolderName,* as shown in the example in Figure 1-16.

   If *TargetFolderName* does not exist, it will be created with correct permissions assuming that the permissions are correct for ShareName.

   If *TargetFolderName* does exist, you need to configure the permissions so that all users to which the GPO applies and the SYSTEM account have the Full Control permission.

   After the policy is applied, data deposited in the redirected folder will be redirected to the target folder called *TargetFolderName.*

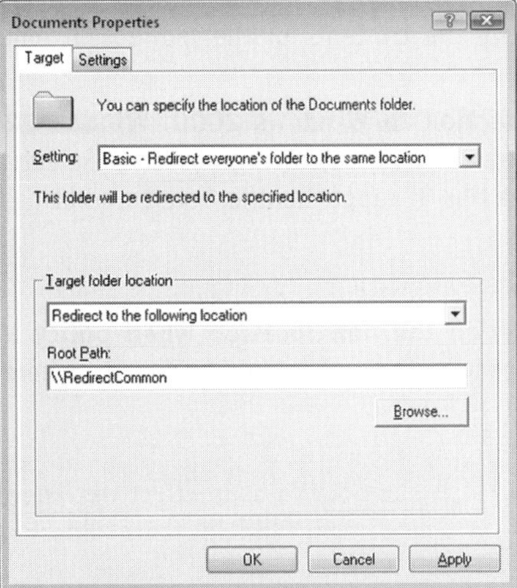

Figure 1-16

Target tab of an example Properties dialog box for a redirected folder

TAKE NOTE*

The term *root path* used in the interface is a misnomer, because you are not specifying a root path as in the previous procedure, but a folder location.

TAKE NOTE*

During testing of Folder Redirection using the Redirect to the following location option, you may observe some inconsistencies in the display name of the redirected folder on Windows Vista desktops. Immediately after the application of the policy, the first user to log on might see the name of the target folder instead of the name of the folder being redirected (the latter naming is correct). This issue will go away after subsequent logons.

6. Click the **Settings** tab. Example settings are shown in Figure 1-17.

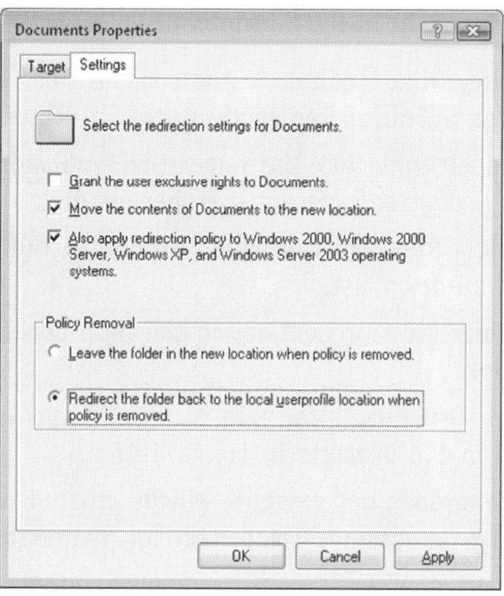

Figure 1-17

Settings tab of an example Properties dialog box for a redirected folder

WARNING The Grant the user exclusive rights to the RedirectedFolderName check box is selected by default, which will cause Folder Redirection to fail in this instance. If you select this check box (or leave it selected), the first user to which the policy is applied will assume exclusive permissions to the target folder. Therefore, when other users log on subsequently, they will not be able to access the target folder.

7. Configure the following check boxes:

   Grant the user exclusive rights to *RedirectedFolderName* Always clear this check box when you select the *Redirect to the following location* option.

   Move the contents of *RedirectedFolderName* to the new location Select this check box to move the contents of the redirected folder to the target folder at next user logon.

   Also apply redirection to Windows 2000, Windows 2000 Server, Windows XP, and Windows Server 2003 operating systems Select this check box if you want the Folder Redirection to apply to the listed operating systems as well as to Windows Vista.

8. Select one of the following:

   Leave the folder in the new location when policy is removed Select this option if you want already redirected folders to remain where they are if you delete or un-link the GPO.

TAKE NOTE* Users who did not log on after the policy was in effect were never subject to the policy. Therefore, after the GPO is deleted or un-linked, their folders will remain as they were before the policy was in effect. Those that did log on after the policy was in effect will continue to have their folders redirected according to the policy.

   Redirect the folder back to the local userprofile location when policy is removed Select this option if you want redirected folders to be restored to the default local location if you delete or un-link the GPO.

TAKE NOTE* Changing the policy in the Target tab to Not Configured will not have any effect on already redirected folders. The option will only have an effect if the GPO is deleted or unlinked.

REDIRECT A FOLDER TO THE LOCAL USERPROFILE LOCATION

By default, folders are directed to the ***local userprofile location***. For example, the Downloads folder is directed to %SYSTEMROOT%\Users\Username\Downloads.

There are at least two reasons that you might want to configure Group Policy to redirect a folder to the local userprofile location:

- To restore folder direction to the local userprofile location if a Folder Redirection policy is persisting after the responsible Group Policy object is deleted or unlinked

- To restore folder direction to the local userprofile location without deleting or unlinking the responsible GPO

OPEN the GPO you want to edit in the Group Policy Object Editor.

1. In the Group Policy Object Editor, in the console tree, expand **User Configuration > Windows Settings > Folder Redirection.**
2. In the details pane, right-click the folder that you want to redirect and then click **Properties.** The *RedirectedFolderName* Properties dialog box appears.
3. Ensure that **Basic – Redirect everyone's folder to the same location** is selected in the Setting drop-down list.
4. In the Target folder location section, in the drop-down list, select **Redirect to the local userprofile location**, as shown in the example in Figure 1-18.

Figure 1-18

Target tab of an example Properties dialog box for a redirected folder

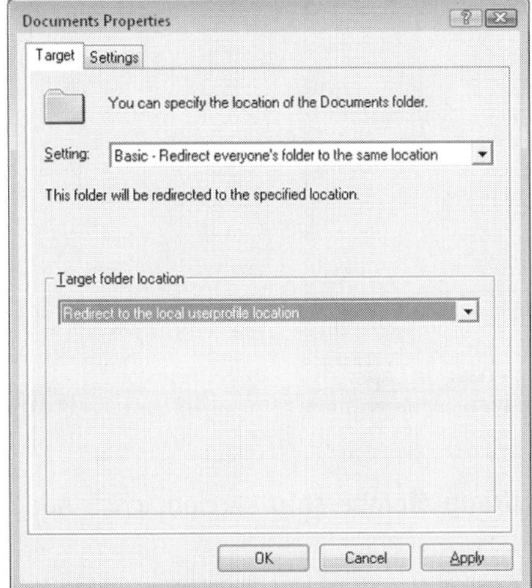

5. Click the **Settings** tab.
6. Configure the following check boxes:

   Grant the user exclusive rights to *RedirectedFolderName* In most circumstances it makes sense to select this check box because the redirected folder is local and only the user needs access to it.

   Move the contents of *RedirectedFolderName* to the new location Select this check box to move the contents of the redirected folder to the target folder at next user logon.

   Also apply redirection to Windows 2000, Windows 2000 Server, Windows XP, and Windows Server 2003 operating systems Select this check box if you want the Folder Redirection to apply to the listed operating systems as well as to Windows Vista.
7. Select one of the following (because the new location is the local userprofile location, the options result in the same behavior):

   Leave the folder in the new location when policy is removed.

   Redirect the folder back to the local userprofile location when policy is removed.

REDIRECT A FOLDER ACCORDING TO GROUP MEMBERSHIP

You may not want all users to have their folders directed to the same location. For example, you could redirect pictures for all members of a graphics design department to the same folder, and pictures for all members of the product development team to individual folders for each user.

OPEN the GPO you want to edit in the Group Policy Object Editor.

1. In the Group Policy Object Editor, in the console tree, expand **User Configuration>Windows Settings>Folder Redirection.**
2. In the details pane, right-click the folder that you want to redirect and then click **Properties.** The *RedirectedFolderName* Properties dialog box appears.
3. In the Setting drop-down list, select **Advanced - Specify locations for various user groups**, as shown in the example in Figure 1-19.

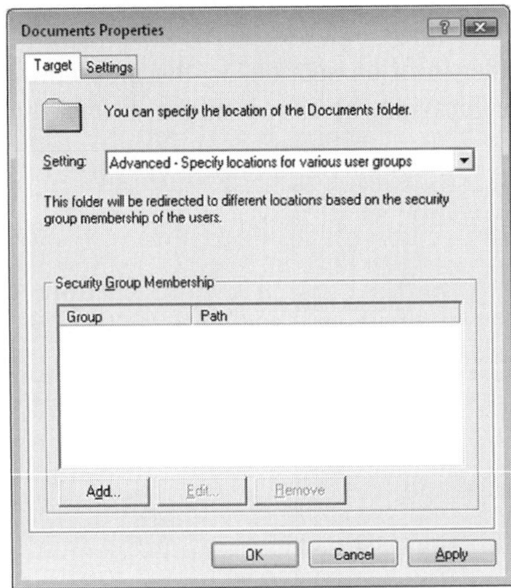

Figure 1-19

Target tab of an example Properties dialog box for a redirected folder

4. In the **Security Group Membership** section, click **Add**. The **Specify Group and Location** dialog box appears.
5. In the **Security Group Membership** text box, enter the security group for which you want to configure Folder Redirection.
6. In the **Target Folder Location** section, in the drop-down list, select one of the following:

   Create a folder for each user under the root path Select this option if you want users within the specified security groups to have the folder redirected to individual target folders. If you select this option, enter a root path in the Root Path text box.

   Redirect to the following location Select this option if you want users within the specified security groups to have the folder redirected to the same target folder. If you select this option, enter the target folder location in the Root Path text box.

   Redirect to the local userprofile location Select this option if you want users within the specified security groups to have the folder redirected to the local user-profile location, which is the default location.
7. Click the **Settings** tab and configure the settings as needed, as shown in the example in Figure 1-20. Note that the settings apply to all security groups (to define different settings for different security groups, you would need to configure multiple GPOs).

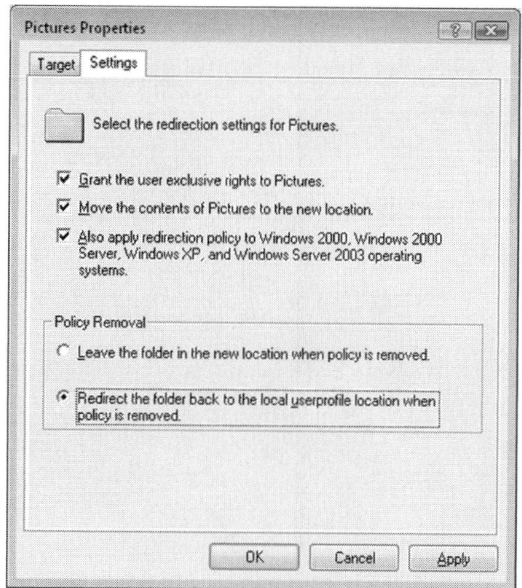

Figure 1-20

Settings tab of an example Properties dialog box for a redirected folder

CONFIGURE THE PICTURES, MUSIC, OR VIDEO FOLDERS TO FOLLOW THE DOCUMENTS FOLDER

When you redirect the Pictures, Music, or Video folders to follow the Documents folder, they are redirected to a target folder in the Documents folder. This redirection follows the Documents folder whenever it is redirected.

In Windows XP, the My Picture, My Music, and My Videos folders are contained within the My Documents folder. This means that when the My Documents folder is redirected in Windows XP, the other folders are also redirected.

In Windows Vista, the Pictures, Music, and Videos folders are not contained within the Documents folder. Therefore, when the Documents folder is redirected, the other folders are not automatically redirected. By configuring these folders to follow the Documents folder, Windows Vista's redirection of the Documents folder mimics the behavior of Windows XP when the My Documents folder is redirected.

One common reason to implement this configuration is when migrating from Windows XP to Windows Vista where the Windows XP users have their My Documents folders redirected. When migrating to Windows Vista, you will need to configure the Pictures, Music, and Videos folders to follow the Documents folder in order to achieve a seamless transition.

OPEN the GPO you want to edit in the Group Policy Object Editor.

1. In the Group Policy Object Editor, in the console tree, expand **User Configuration > Windows Settings > Folder Redirection**, as shown in Figure 1-7.
2. In the details pane, select one of the following:
   - **Pictures**
   - **Music**
   - **Videos**
3. Click **Properties** in the Action menu. The *RedirectedFolderName* Properties dialog box appears.
4. In the Setting drop-down list, select **Follow the Documents Folder**, as shown in the example in Figure 1-21.

...e target ...d folder using the targ... of the Properties dialog box for the redirected folder.

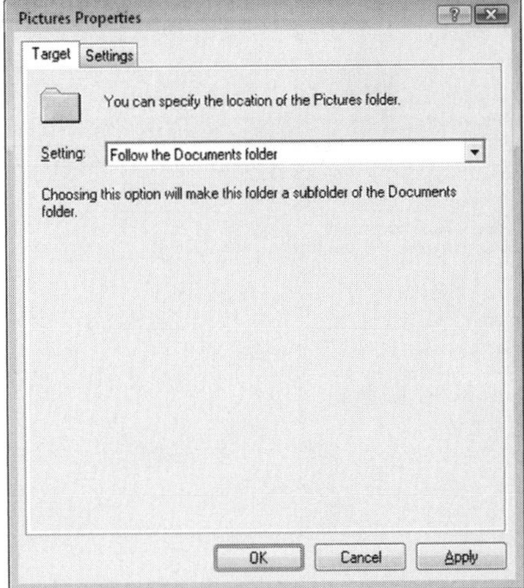

Migrating User Profiles by Using USMT

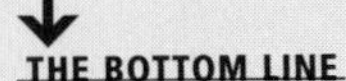

THE BOTTOM LINE You can use USMT 3.0 to migrate profile settings and data in an enterprise environment.

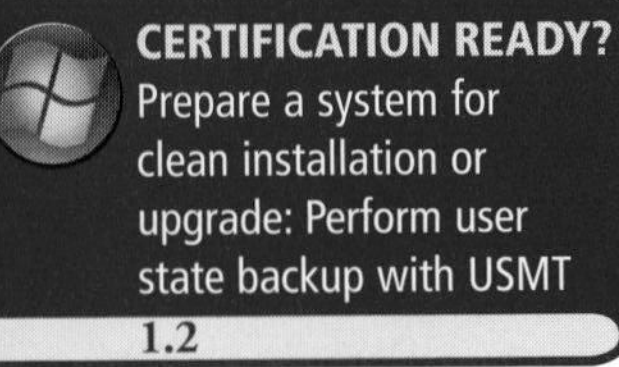

CERTIFICATION READY? Prepare a system for clean installation or upgrade: Perform user state backup with USMT 1.2

Because Windows Vista profiles are different from previous versions, whether upgrading a single system or an entire enterprise, profiles need to be migrated if you want to keep profile settings and data.

If you are upgrading a single home system, you probably just want to use the Windows Easy Transfer tool provided on the Windows Vista installation disk. The Windows XP tool can read settings from almost any version of Windows, but it cannot transfer settings to Windows Vista. The Windows Vista tool can read settings from Windows 2000, XP, and Windows Vista only, and can transfer settings to Windows Vista. However, when you are migrating large numbers of profiles on numerous workstations, the tool of choice is the User State Migration Tool version 3.0 (USMT 3.0).

Understanding USMT

USMT 3.0 is a tool for migrating profile settings and data that consists of two command-line executables (ScanState and LoadState) as well as other components.

USMT 3.0 is a tool for migrating profile data and settings from source workstations to destination workstations during large deployments of Windows XP and Windows Vista. The data is stored in a share after it is collected from the source workstations, and then it is loaded onto the destination workstations.

USMT is composed of five major components:

- **ScanState** A command-line executable that collects files, profile data, and settings from a source workstation. ScanState compresses and then stores the files as an image file named USMT3.mig.
- **LoadState** A command-line executable that migrates data and settings to a destination workstation.
- **.xml control files** Files that control ScanState and LoadState.

- **Component Manifests** Files that contain Windows Vista data and settings that determine which operating system and browser settings are migrated and how they are migrated.
- **Downlevel Manifests** Files that list settings and data for Windows XP and Windows 2000 that determine which operating system and browser settings are migrated and how they are migrated.

This lesson covers only parts of USMT:

- What USMT migrates
- Using USMT
- Understanding ScanState
- Understanding LoadState
- Understanding control files
- Understanding manifests
- Completing a simple migration using USMT

Using USMT in an enterprise environment requires modifying existing XML control files, creating custom XML control files, and automating the running of ScanState and LoadState on large numbers of workstations through scripting or other means. These tasks are not covered here.

MORE INFORMATION

One of the best resources for information on using USMT in a large deployment is the **User State Migration Feature Team Guide**, which is part of the documentation set that comes with the **Microsoft Solution Accelerator for Business Desktop Deployment 2007**: *technet.microsoft.com/enus/library/bb490308.aspx*. The **Microsoft Solution Accelerator for Business Desktop Deployment 2007** also contains many tools including scripts to automate the use of USMT and other deployment tools. Additionally, you can find a reference for the XML elements used in USMT.xml control files here: *go.microsoft.com/fwlink/?LinkId=64519*. Finally, the USMT 3.0 help file contains a lot of information on using USMT.

Installing USMT 3.0 is very simple. You simply launch the install program and follow the instructions of the install wizard.

You can download USMT 3.0 install program by searching for it here: *www.microsoft.com/downloads/*. Versions are available for Windows XP and Windows Vista, for both 32-bit and 64-bit systems.

Understanding What USMT Migrates

The .xml control files determine what USMT migrates.

You can customize what profile data and settings are migrated by USMT by customizing the .xml control files. The following are migrated using the default control files:

- User data
- Operating system settings
- Supported application data and settings

Table 1-4 shows the user data that is migrated.

Table 1-4

What profile data USMT migrates

From User Profile folders	From All Users Profile folders	From Fixed disks
My Documents	Shared Documents	Files with the following extensions: .qdf,.qsd,.qel,.qph,.doc,.dot,.rtf,.mcw, .wps,.scd,.wri,.wpd,.xl*,.csv,.iqy,.dqy,.oqy, .rqy,.wk*,.wq1,.slk,.dif,.ppt*,.pps*,.pot*, .sh3,.ch3,.pre,.ppa,.txt,.pst,.one*,.mpp, .vsd,.vl*,.or6,.accdb,.mdb,.pub
My Video	Shared Video	
My Music	Shared Music	
My Pictures	Shared Desktop files	
Desktop files	Shared Pictures	
Start Menu	Shared Start Menu	
Quick launch settings	Shared Favorites	
Favorites		

USMT also migrates access control lists (ACLs) for files and folders from both Windows XP and Windows Vista. This means that file permissions are migrated for files that are migrated. For example, if a text file has Read Only permissions for a user on the source computer, that permission will be preserved on the destination computer.

The following is a list of operating system settings that USMT migrates:

- Accessibility settings
- Classic desktop
- Command prompt settings
- Dial-up connections
- Favorites
- Folder options
- Fonts
- Group membership
- Taskbar settings
- Microsoft Internet Explorer settings (all versions through version 6.0)
- Microsoft Open Database Connectivity settings
- Microsoft Outlook Express mail (.dbx) files
- Mouse and keyboard settings
- Multimedia settings
- Phone and modem options
- RAS connection phonebook (.pbk) files
- Regional options
- Remote Access
- Screen saver selection
- Wallpaper settings

WARNING USMT may not migrate application settings that have not been set or modified by the user.

With the Exception of Microsoft Office applications, when migrating application settings by using USMT, the versions of the applications on the source and destination workstations must match. USMT does not support migrating settings of an older version of an application to that of a newer.

Using USMT

Using USMT requires planning, using ScanState to collect profile data and settings, and using LoadState to restore profile data and settings.

Using USMT in an enterprise environment to migrate data and settings can be divided into three broad stages:

1. Planning the migration
2. Collecting files and settings from the source workstation
3. Migrating files and settings to the destination workstation

The following sections outline broad steps for each of the preceding three stages. Actual procedures for using USMT to migrate profile data is covered after that.

Stage 1: Planning the Migration

Planning user profile migration includes deciding what to migrate and how to migrate it.

The following steps can be used to plan a migration of user profile data.

1. Choose what to migrate within the following categories:

   Users
   - Application settings
   - Operating system settings
   - Files and folders
   - Registry keys
2. Determine where to store the migration data:
   - On the source workstation
   - On a network share
   - On the destination workstation
3. Modify the migration .xml files and create Custom.xml files if necessary:
   - To configure user data migration, modify the MigUser.xml file.
   - To configure application data migration, modify the MigApp.xml file.
   - To exclude anything from the migration, create a custom Config.xml file.
   - To customize the migration for your organization's unique needs, create a Custom.xml file.

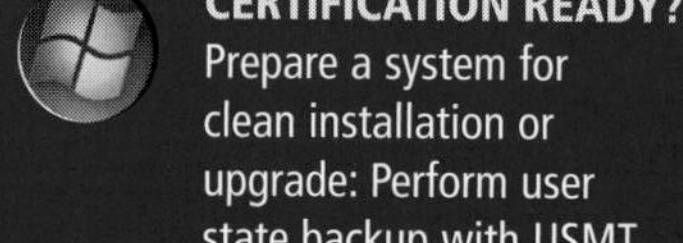

CERTIFICATION READY?
Prepare a system for clean installation or upgrade: Perform user state backup with USMT
1.2

Stage 2: Collecting Profile Data and Settings from the Source Workstation

You collect profile data and settings from the source workstation by using ScanState.

The following steps can be used to collect profile data and settings from a source workstation.

1. Back up the source workstation.
2. Close all applications. If any applications are running, they might prevent USMT from being able to capture files.

TAKE NOTE* ScanState by default will fail (stop running) if it cannot migrate a file that it is supposed to. You can change this behavior using the */c* option. ScanState options are covered later in the **Understanding ScanState** section.

3. Run ScanState on the source workstation to collect the profile data and settings as specified in the.xml control files.

Running ScanState is covered later in the **Understanding ScanState** section.

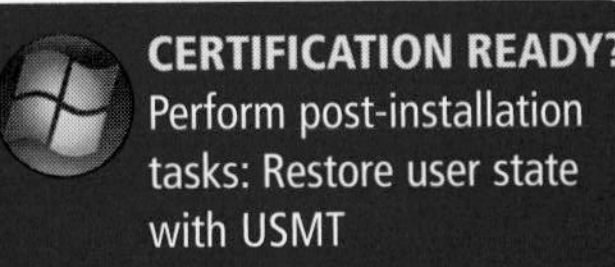

CERTIFICATION READY? Perform post-installation tasks: Restore user state with USMT

1.4

Stage 3: Restore Profile Data and Settings to the Destination workstation

You restore profile data and settings to the destination computer using LoadState.

The following steps can be used to restore profile data and settings to a destination workstation.

1. Deploy the operating system to the destination workstation.
2. Install all of the applications that were on the source workstation that will be on the destination workstation. Be sure that the application versions are the same (except in the case of Microsoft Office, which is designed to be able to be upgraded and still preserve migrated data and settings from older versions).

TAKE NOTE* You are not required to install all of the applications that were on the source workstation that are going to be on the destination workstation at this time, but is recommended. If you run LoadState first, application settings and data can be lost in some cases when the applications are installed. This problem is known to occur with the following applications: Lotus SmartSuite, RealPlayer Basic, and Quicken 2004 Home and Business.

3. Close all applications. If any applications are running, LoadState might not be able to restore all data and settings.

TAKE NOTE* LoadState by default will fail (stop running) if it cannot restore a file that it is supposed to. You can change this behavior using the */c* option. LoadState options are covered later in the **Understanding LoadState** section.

4. Run LoadState on the destination workstation to restore the files and settings as specified in the .xml control files.

X REF Running LoadState is covered later in the **Understanding LoadState** section.

5. Log off after running LoadState so that settings are fully refreshed during the next logon.

Understanding ScanState

ScanState is a command-line executable that collects profile data an source workstation. It is a key component of USMT 3.0.

CERTIFICATION READY? Prepare a system for clean installation or upgrade: Perform user state backup with USMT 1.2

ScanState collects profile data and settings on a source workstation and save called USMT3.mig in the specified data store. ScanState can use the followi ...ol files:

- MigSys.xml
- MigApp.xml
- MigUser.xml
- Config.xml
- Custom.xml

X REF The .xml control files are covered in **Understanding the .xml Control Files** later in this lesson.

ScanState is a command-line executable, meaning that you run it from a command prompt. This means that options are configured using text. The set of rules that dictates how you run the tool and specify the options is called the ***syntax***.

The ScanState syntax specification is as follows:

```
scanstate [StorePath] [/i:[Path\]FileName] [/o]
[/v:VerbosityLevel] [/nocompress] [/localonly]
[/encrypt /key:KeyString|/keyfile:[Path\]FileName]
[/l:[Path\]FileName] [/progress:[Path\]FileName]
[/r:TimesToRetry] [/w:SecondsBeforeRetry] [/c] [/p]
[/all] [/ui:[DomainName\]UserName]|LocalUserName]
[/ue:[DomainName\]UserName]|LocalUserName]
[/uel:NumberOfDays|YYYY/MM/DD|0]
[/efs:abort|skip|decryptcopy|copyraw]
[/genconfig:[Path\]FileName] [/targetxp]
[/config:[Path\]FileName] [/?|help]
```

ScanState requires elevated privileges. If you are running ScanState under Windows Vista, you should start the command prompt in administrator mode. If you are running ScanState under Windows XP, you need to log on with an administrator account.

You can run ScanState, like most command-line executables, with the /? option to see a list of options and their descriptions, along with other helpful information. The following text and Table 1-5 is what is output (with formatting added for readability) to the Command Prompt window when you run `ScanState /?`:

```
You can use ScanState to collect files and settings from the source
computer.
See Usmt.chm for more information about these options.
Syntax: scanstate <StorePath> [Options]
```

Table 1-5

Output from ScanState /? in table format

OPTION	DESCRIPTION
StorePath	Indicates where to save the files and settings.
/targetxp	Optimizes ScanState when the destination computer is running Windows XP; you should use this option with /genconfig and when you create a store.
/genconfig:FileName	Generates a Config.xml file. You cannot specify <StorePath>. The only other options that you can specify are /i, /v, /l, and /targetxp.
/o	Overwrites any existing data in the store.

(continued)

(continued)

Option	Description
/p	Generates a space-estimate file called USMTSIZE.TXT that is saved in the store. This option does not collect the user state. You must also specify /nocompress.
/localonly	Specifies that only files that are stored on the local computer will be migrated.
/efs:abort|skip|decryptcopy |copyraw	abort: Fails if Encrypting File System (EFS) files are found. skip: Ignores all EFS files. decryptcopy: Decrypts and copies files if possible. Fails if the files cannot be decrypted. copyraw: Copies encrypted EFS files.
/encrypt	Encrypts the store.
	You must also specify /key or /keyfile.
/key:KeyString	Specifies the key.
/keyfile:FileName	Specifies the location and name of a.txt file that contains the key.
/nocompress	Specifies that the store is not compressed.
/l:FileName	Specifies the location and name of the log.
/v:Level	Enables verbose output in the log. You can specify 0, 1, 4, 5, 8, 9, 12, or 13. Default is 0.
/progress:FileName	Specifies the location and name of the optional progress log.
/c	When specified, the command continues to run even if there are nonfatal errors.
/r:TimesToRetry	Specifies the number of times to retry when an error occurs (default is 3).
/w:SecondsToWait	Specifies the time to wait before retrying a failed attempt (default is 1 second).
/all	Migrates all the users.
/ui:[Domain\]UserName	Migrates the specified user(s). To migrate a local user, specify UserName only. Domain and UserName can contain wildcard characters (* or ?).
/ue:[Domain\]UserName	Excludes the specified user(s) from the migration. To exclude a local user, specify UserName only. Domain and UserName can contain wildcard characters (* or ?).
/uel:NumberOfDays |YYYY/MM/DD	Specifies that the migration should exclude users that have not logged on within the specified time. NumberOfDays can be 0 to exclude all users who are not currently logged on.
/i:FileName	Specifies the location and name of a.xml file that contains rules that define what state to migrate.
/help or /?	Displays Help at the command line.
/config:FileName	Specifies the Config.xml file that USMT should use.

```
Notes:
* For more information about these options, see Us
* You cannot specify /all with the /ui, /ue or /uel
* You can specify /i, /ui, /ue and /uel more than on
* You cannot specify /key and /keyfile together.
* You cannot specify /encrypt and /nocompress together.
```

MORE INFORMATION

You can find detailed descriptions of each option in the USMT 3.0 help file named USMT.chm.

Understanding LoadState

LoadState is a command-line executable that restores profile data and settings to a destination workstation. It is a key component of USMT 3.0.

CERTIFICATION READY?
Perform post-installation tasks: Restore user state with USMT
1.4

LoadState restores profile data and settings to a destination workstation from the specified data store. LoadState can use the following.xml control files:

- MigSys.xml
- MigApp.xml
- MigUser.xml
- Config.xml
- Custom.xml

X REF The .xml control files are covered in **Understanding the .xml Control Files** later in this lesson.

TAKE NOTE* LoadState requires connectivity to a domain controller to solicit the security identifier (SID) of profiles that it is migrating.

LoadState is a command-line executable, meaning that you run it from a command prompt. This means that options are configured using text. The LoadState syntax specification is as follows:

```
loadstate [StorePath] [/i:[Path\]FileName] [/o]
[/v:VerbosityLevel] [/nocompress] [/decrypt
/key:KeyString|/keyfile:[Path\]FileName]
[/l:[Path\]FileName] [/progress:[Path\]FileName]
[/r:TimesToRetry] [/w:SecondsToWait] [/c] [/all]
[/ui:[[DomainName\]UserName]|LocalUserName]
[/ue:[[DomainName\]UserName]|LocalUserName]
[/uel:NumberOfDays|YYYY/MM/DD|0]
[/md:OldDomain:NewDomain]
[/mu:OldDomain\OldUserName:[NewDomain\]NewUserName]
[/lac:[Password]] [/lae] [/q]
[/config:[Path\]FileName] [/?|help]
```

MORE INFORMATION

You can find examples of LoadState being used in the USMT 3.0 help file. You can also find a simple example in **Completing a Simple Profile Migration Using USMT** later in this lesson.

LoadState requires elevated privileges. If you are running LoadState under Windows Vista, you should start the Command Prompt window by using the Run as administrator option. If you are running LoadState under Windows XP, you need to log on with an administrator account.

Running a command prompt in administrator mode is covered in the **Understanding ScanState** section earlier in this lesson.

You can run LoadState, like most command-line executables, with the /? option to see a list of options and their descriptions, along with other helpful information. The following text and Table 1-6 is what is output (with formatting added for readability) to the Command Prompt window when you run LoadState /?:

```
You can use LoadState to restore the user state onto the destination
computer.
See Usmt.chm for more information about these options.
Syntax: loadstate <StorePath> [options]
```

Table 1-6

Output from LoadState /? in table format

OPTION	DESCRIPTION
StorePath	Indicates where the settings are stored.
/lac[:Password]	Creates disabled local accounts if they do not already exist on the destination computer. Password is the password for the created accounts. An empty password is used by default.
/lae	Enables local accounts created by /lac. You must also specify /lac.
/q	Allows LoadState to run without administrative credentials.
/mu:[OldDomain\]OldUserName:[NewDomain\]NewUserName	Specifies a new user name. For local users, specify OldUserName and NewUserName. Wildcard characters are not allowed.
/md:OldDomain:NewDomain	Specifies a new domain for the user(s). OldDomain can contain wildcard characters (* or ?).
/decrypt	Specifies that the store is encrypted and needs to be decrypted. You must also specify /key or /keyfile.
/key:KeyString	Specifies the key.
/keyfile:FileName	Specifies the location and name of a. txt file that contains the key.
/nocompress	Specifies that the store is not compressed.
/l:FileName	Specifies the location and name of the log.
/v:Level	Enables verbose output in the log. You can specify 0, 1, 4, 5, 8, 9, 12, or 13. Default is 0.
/progress:FileName	Specifies the location and name of the optional progress log.
/c	When specified, the command continues to run even if there are nonfatal errors.

(*continued*)

Table 1-6 (*continued*)

Option	Description
/r:TimesToRetry	Specifies the number of times to retry when an error occurs (defaul
/w:SecondsToWait	Specifies the time to wait before retrying a failed attempt (default is 1 second).
/all	Migrates all the users.
/ui:[Domain\]UserName	Migrates the specified user(s). To migrate a local user, specify UserName only. Domain and UserName can contain wildcard characters (* or ?).
/ue:[Domain\]UserName	Excludes the specified user(s) from the migration. To exclude a local user, specify UserName only. Domain and UserName can contain wildcard characters (* or ?).
/uel:NumberOfDays|YYYY/MM/DD	Specifies that the migration should exclude users that have not logged on within the specified time. NumberOfDays can be 0 to exclude all users who are contains rules that define what state to migrate.
/i:FileName	Specifies the location and name of a .xml file that contains rules that define what state to migrate.
/help or /?	Displays Help at the command line.
/config:FileName	Specifies the Config.xml file that USMT should use.

```
Notes:
*For more information about these options, see Usmt.chm.
*You cannot specify /all with the /ui, /ue or /uel options.
*You can specify /i, /ui, /ue and /uel more than once if necessary.
*You cannot specify /key and /keyfile together.
*You cannot specify /decrypt and /nocompress together.
*You can specify /md and /mu more than once if necessary.
```

MORE INFORMATION

You can find detailed descriptions of each option in the USMT 3.0 help file.

Understanding the.xml Control Files

The .xml control files control ScanState and LoadState.

The.xml control files control ScanState and LoadState and can be customized to the needs of the profile migration. The following are the.xml control files that ScanState and LoadState use:

- **MigSys.xml** Controls which operating system and browser settings to migrate when the source workstation is running Windows XP.
- **MigApp.xml** Controls which application settings are migrated from the source workstation.
- **MigUser.xml** Controls which profile folders, files, and file types to migrate from the source workstation.
- **Config.xml** Contains all settings defined by Component Manifests or by Downlevel Manifests. You create this file by using the ScanState **/genconfig** option.
- **Custom.xml** Defines custom migration rules. Can be used for such tasks as migrating the settings for a custom business application. You can define multiple custom control files. To call custom control files, you modify CustomSettings.ini.

X REF

The Component Manifests and Downlevel Manifests are covered in the **Understanding Manifests** section later in this lesson.

Understanding Manifests

Manifests are files that contain lists of operating system and browser settings. They cannot be modified.

There are two types of manifests: Component Manifests and Downlevel Manifests.

Component Manifests are used only when the source or destination workstation is running Windows Vista. The Component Manifests are files that control which operating system and browser settings are migrated and how. Component Manifests are located on Windows Vista installations, and you cannot modify them. Therefore, to exclude certain operating system settings when the source workstation is running Windows Vista, you need to create and customize a Config.xml file.

Component Manifests are not used when the destination workstation is running Windows XP. Windows XP uses the MigSys.xml control file instead.

The other type of manifests are Downlevel Manifests. Downlevel Manifests are used only when the source workstation is running Windows 2000 or Windows XP. These manifests are files that control how ScanState collects operating system and browser settings (LoadState does not use Downlevel Manifests).

The Downlevel Manifests are located in the USMT\dlmanifests folder. You cannot modify these files. Therefore, to exclude certain operating system settings when the destination workstation is running Windows Vista, you need to create and customize a Config.xml file.

Downlevel Manifests are not used when the destination workstation is running Windows XP. Windows XP uses the MigSys.xml control file instead.

Completing a Simple Profile Migration by Using USMT

Using USMT to migrate profile data and settings means using the ScanState and LoadState command-line executables.

COLLECT PROFILE DATA AND SETTINGS USING SCANSTATE

GET READY. Before you begin these steps, create a folder to contain the user account and settings data. The folder can be remote or local. The account that you log on with in step 1 must have full access to the folder.

TAKE NOTE* This procedure assumes that the source workstation is running Windows XP.

1. Log onto the source workstation with a domain administrator account.
2. Click **Start**, point to **All Programs**, point to **Accessories**, and then click **Command Prompt**. The Command Prompt window appears.
3. At the command prompt, key **cd c:\program files\USMT30** and then press **Enter**. This changes the current directory to where ScanState resides, as shown in the example in Figure 1-22. The path may vary depending on the installation of USMT.

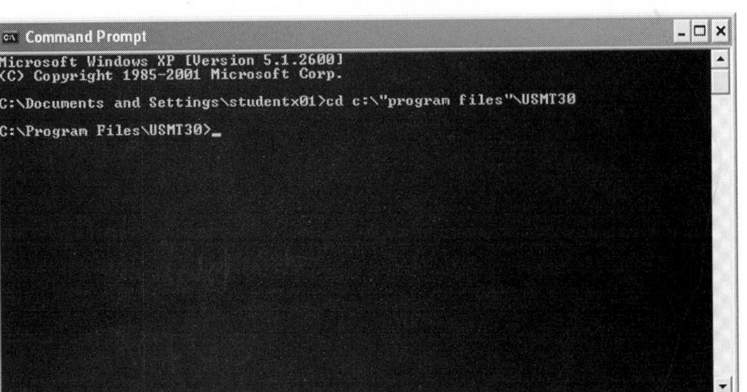

Figure 1-22

Command Prompt window with the path set to the USTM30 directory

TAKE NOTE*

Note that in step 4, the migsys.xml file was not specified. The migsys.xml file is not used for migrations to Windows Vista.

4. Key **scanstate \\ServerName\path /i:miguser.xml /i:migapp.xml /o** and then press **Enter.** *ServerName* is the server on which the folder that will contain the USMT data will reside, and *path* is the network path to that folder. ScanState will begin its scan, which can take significant time depending on the size of the profiles that are being migrated. Text similar to the following is output to the Command Prompt window as the scan takes place:

```
Log messages are being sent to 'C:\Program Files\USMT30\ScanState.log'
Scanning the computer for files and settings...
Collecting files and settings for:
     This Computer
     'XP1\Owen' (user 1 of 3)
     'CONTOSO\RPUser1' (user 2 of 3)
     'CONTOSO\studentx01' (user 3 of 3)
Saving files and settings - 2 minute(s) remaining...
ScanState has successfully collected the files and settings.
```

RESTORE PROFILE DATA AND SETTINGS USING LOADSTATE

TAKE NOTE*

This procedure assumes that the destination workstation is running Windows Vista.

1. Log onto the destination workstation with a normal user account.
2. Click **Start**. In the **Start Search** text box, key **cmd** and then press **Ctrl** + **Shift** + **Enter**. A User Account Control dialog box appears.
3. Provide administrator credentials and then click **OK**. A Command Prompt window appears.
4. At the command prompt, key **cd c:\program files\USMT30** and then press **Enter**. This changes the current directory to where LoadState resides, as shown in Figure 1-16. The path may vary depending on the installation of USMT.
5. Key **loadstate \\ServerName\path /i:miguser.xml /i:migapp.xml /lac /lae** and then press **Enter.** ***Migrating Profile Data Using USMT*** is the server on which the folder that contains the USMT data resides, and *path* is the network path to that folder. LoadState will restore the profile data and settings, which can take significant time depending on the size of the profiles that are being migrated. Text similar to the following is output to the Command Prompt window as the restoration takes place:

TAKE NOTE*

The /lac and /lae switches migrate the local accounts and enable the local accounts respectively. If there are no local accounts in the source folder, then you do not need these switches. You can also leave off /lae, in which case a local administrator will need to enable the accounts before they are usable.

```
Log messages are being sent to 'c:\Program Files\USMT30\LoadState.log'

Scanning the computer for files and settings...

Applying files and settings - 1 minute(s) remaining... -

C:\ProgramData\Microsoft\Windows NT\MSFax\Inbox.rename dir Unassigned$dir

The system cannot find the file specified.

LoadState has successfully restored the files and settings.
```

SUMMARY SKILL MATRIX

IN THIS LESSON YOU LEARNED:
How to choose a deployment method.
How to judge system requirements based on Windows Vista Capable PC minimum requirements and Windows Vista Premium Ready PC minimum requirements.
The Windows Vista Hardware Assessment tool analyzes and reports on device compatibility across an enterprise.
The Application Compatibility Toolkit 5.0 analyzes and reports on application compatibility across an enterprise.
You can use the Windows Vista Upgrade Advisor on stand-alone computers to analyze both hardware and application compatibility issues before upgrading to Windows Vista.
Before deploying Windows Vista, you need to plan and prepare for user profile and data storage requirements.
Roaming profiles are configured in the Active Directory Users and Computers Properties dialog box for the user.
Folder Redirection enables you to redirect the saving and loading of data from a profile folder to another folder (almost always a network share).
How to redirect folders.
How to configure the Pictures, Music, or Video folder to follow the Documents folder for Folder Redirection.
USMT 3.0 is a tool for migrating profile settings and data that consists of two command-line executables (ScanState and LoadState) as well as other components.
The.xml control files determine what USMT migrates.
How to collect and restore profile data and settings using ScanState and LoadState.

■ Knowledge Assessment

Fill in the Blank

Complete the following sentences by writing the correct word or words in the blanks provided.

1. The _______________ file controls USMT migration of User settings.
2. The behavior of USMT is dictated by the _______________.
3. _______________ contain user settings and data and are loaded from a share when a user logs on.
4. The _______________ is an excellent tool for large profile migrations.
5. The _______________ file controls USMT migration of application settings.
6. To decrease the size of profiles, you can offload user data from the profiles by using _______________.
7. In Windows Vista, user profiles of all users on a computer are merged with the _______________ when the users log on.
8. _______________ is a command-line executable that restores profile data and settings during a USMT profile migration.
9. The _______________ are used only when the source workstation is running Windows 2000 or Windows XP.
10. The _______________ collects data from target computers using distributed compatibility evaluators.

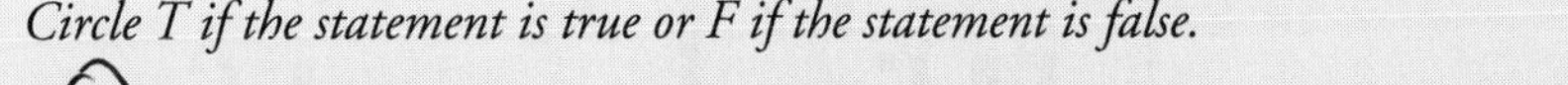

True / False

Circle T if the statement is true or F if the statement is false.

T F 1. The MigSys.xml is always used by ScanState when migrating profile settings and data to Windows Vista Workstations.

T F 2. The WIM image format is sector based imaging format for creating images of Windows operating systems.

T F 3. The All Users profile is the Windows XP equivalent of the Windows Vista Public profile.

T F 4. Component Manifests are not used when the destination workstation is running Windows XP.

T F 5. User profiles in Windows Vista are by default stored locally in the Documents and Settings folder.

T F 6. Windows Vista Premium Ready PCs have a 60GB HDD as a minimum requirement.

T F 7. Windows Vista Capable PCs require at least 512MB of system memory.

T F 8. The local userprofile location for the Documents folder in Windows Vista is in the Users*UserName* folder.

T F 9. ScanState is used to scan the registry to collect system state data.

T F 10. The config.xml control file is created using the ScanState command-line executable with the /genconfig option.

Review Questions

1. What are the two official Windows Vista system requirements specifications called? What is the CPU speed cutoff for the higher-performance requirements specification?
2. What are the three tools you can use to analyze device (hardware) and application compatibility, and in what environments should you use each?

■ Case Scenarios

Scenario 1: Folder Redirection

Contoso's Graphic Design Department has a need for a central repository of images that all of the employees can access. It should contain all of the images currently in the employees' Pictures folders. Outline a scheme where:

1. The Pictures folder for each user is redirected to a single, shared folder that each member of the department has access to. In your answer, specify the location in the GPO where you need to configure settings, and specify the value for each setting.
2. All the files currently in each user's Pictures folder are transferred to the share when the policy is instituted.
3. The Pictures folder for each user will revert to being local if the Folder Redirection policy is ever removed.

Scenario 2: Making a Shortcut Available to All Users

A kiosk computer in the IT department lobby is available to users so that they can reset their smartcard PIN numbers. To do this, they log onto the kiosk computer and then access a PIN reset application. Regardless of the user, you want a shortcut to appear on the desktop for the PIN Reset application. How can you accomplish this? The solution needs to work for users both with and without roaming profiles.

Deploying Windows Vista

OBJECTIVE DOMAIN MATRIX

Technology Skill	Objective Domain	Objective Domain Number
Understanding Windows Vista Deployment	Deploy Windows Vista from a custom image	1.3
Deploying Windows Vista from an Image	Deploy Windows Vista from a custom image	1.3
Creating a Windows PE Boot CD	Deploy Windows Vista from a custom image	1.3
Applying a WIM Image	Deploy Windows Vista from a custom image • Apply an image over the network • Apply an image from offline media	1.3
Troubleshooting Roaming Profiles	Troubleshoot deployment issues • Troubleshoot Roaming User Profiles and Folder Redirection issues	1.5
Troubleshooting Folder Redirection	Troubleshoot deployment issues • Troubleshoot Roaming User Profiles and Folder Redirection issues	1.5

KEY TERMS

modularization
Windows Imaging Format (WIM) image
master computer
single instancing
non-destructive imaging
ImageX
Windows Automated Installation Kit (WAIK)
Windows Preinstallation Environment (Windows PE)
Windows Deployment Services (Windows DS)

In preparation for a full-scale deployment, you are going to test a Windows Imaging Format image (WIM image) by deploying it to a test computer. To do this, you will use the Windows Preinstallation Environment (Windows PE) and ImageX. Once the installation is complete, you will restore roaming profile data by using the User State Migration Tool. Finally, you will troubleshoot any issues with roaming profiles or Folder Redirection. This test will be used to help inform a full-scale deployment plan.

Understanding Windows Vista Deployment

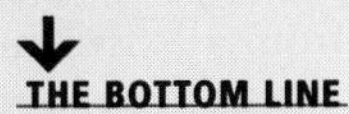

Windows Vista deployment, whether automated for an entire enterprise or preformed individually on a computer, can be completed using WIM images.

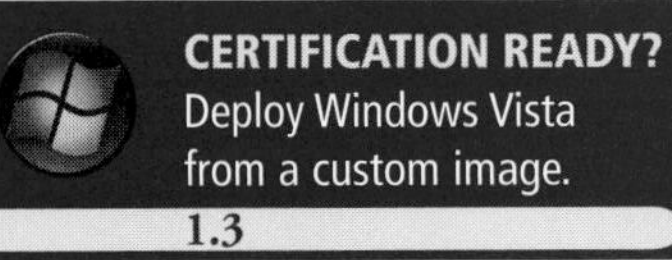

CERTIFICATION READY?
Deploy Windows Vista from a custom image.
1.3

Many new innovations make deploying Windows Vista in an enterprise easier than it was for previous versions of Windows. Two of the biggest innovations are greater modularization and the introduction of WIM images.

Windows Vista is divided into modules that communicate with each other to form the operating system as a whole. This is called modularization. The modules can be mixed and matched to customize deployments. For example, you used to have to install different versions of Windows for different languages. Updates had to come in different versions to match these different versions. In Windows Vista, the language components have been modularized so that they are separate from the underlying operating system. This means that different language versions of Windows Vista can be achieved by adding a language module on top of the same base operating system module. It also means that operating system updates only need to come in a single version.

A ***WIM image*** is Microsoft's proprietary file-based (as opposed to sector-based) image format for storing images of Windows operating systems. An ***image*** is a file that contains the contents and sometimes the structure of a data medium, such as a hard disk. You can capture an image from an existing computer's hard drive that contains a Windows installation and applications and apply it onto another computer's hard drive. This bypasses the laborious task of manual installation and can be completed more quickly than even automated installation. On a fast computer, Windows Vista can be installed by applying a WIM image in less than ten minutes.

The computer from which you capture the customized image is called the ***master computer***, and the computer to which the image is applied is called the ***destination computer***.

Some of the highlights of WIM images over traditional sector-based images are:

- Smaller image size because of single instancing. ***Single instancing*** is the storing of one instance of identical files in the WIM image instead of the previous sector-based approach of storing multiple copies of the same file in different locations in a CAB file. This new approach is possible with Windows Vista because the path data is stored separately from the file data, and the path data can indicate that a file exists in more than one location.
- Storage of more than one volume image in a single WIM image.
- Non-destructive imaging. ***Non-destructive imaging*** allows you to partially apply an image without overwriting the target drive. This means that you can selectively install part of an image to an existing installation.
- Interoperability with any platform that supports Windows.
- Internet Explorer access to the image. You can perform normal file operations, such as copy and paste, directly to the image using Windows Explorer or other file management tools (you must first mount the image to a folder).
- Ability to modify drivers, configure operating system components, and install updates directly to the image.
- Hardware abstraction layer (HAL) independence. You can apply the same image to computers with different hardware.
- Three compression options: fast, maximum, and none. Fast compression is the default compression type. Compression can be configured per WIM image only; separate volume images within a WIM all must have the same compression setting.
- The destination computer does not have to boot from the same type of mass-storage controller as the master computer.

- The image does not have to be applied to the same partition type as that of the master, and it does not have to be as large as that of the master computer.

Whether you deploy Windows Vista from a Windows Vista DVD, Universal Serial Bus (USB) storage device, or a network share, the source files will come from a WIM image (unless, of course, you use a third-party imaging technology).

TAKE NOTE* Your Windows Vista installation DVD contains a WIM image file, which actually contains seven images for different versions of Windows Vista. Single instancing enables these seven images to be stored in much less space than they would be otherwise.

Understanding the Deployment Process

All Windows Vista deployments that are based on Microsoft technologies follow a similar pattern regardless of their scope: Windows PE is booted and a WIM image (captured manually or on a Windows Vista DVD) is used to supply source files.

The two primary tools used in capturing and deploying Windows Vista images are `ImageX` and Windows PE.

ImageX is a command-line tool that enables you to capture, apply, and manage WIM images. ***Windows PE*** is a minimal operating system that you can boot from CD or other media so that you can run ImageX and other tools.

TAKE NOTE* When you install from the Windows Vista installation DVD, it boots Windows PE, from which it then installs using a WIM image.

The first step you take in a deployment using WIMs is to create a master computer that contains the installation of Windows Vista (including applications) that you want to deploy. You then use the Windows System Preparation tool to prepare the operating system to be an image. You boot the master computer from bootable medium containing Windows PE (this could be a USB memory stick, USB drive, CD, or Preboot Execution Environment (PXE) network location) and then use `ImageX` to capture the image. You can capture the image to a network share, offline media, or to the local computer. In an enterprise, you would most likely store the image on a network share so that it is available anywhere on the network. Doing so enables you to remotely complete Windows Vista deployment.

MORE INFORMATION

You can find more information on the System Preparation tool in the Windows Automated Installation Kit User's Guide.

The next step is to boot Windows PE on the destination systems. Again, you can do this from any bootable medium, including over the network. After that, you prepare the hard disks by partitioning and formatting them. Next, you use ImageX to apply the image to the destination computers. Finally, you perform any post-installation tasks.

Figure 2-1 shows a high-level overview of the deployment process.

Figure 2-1
WIM Image deployment overview

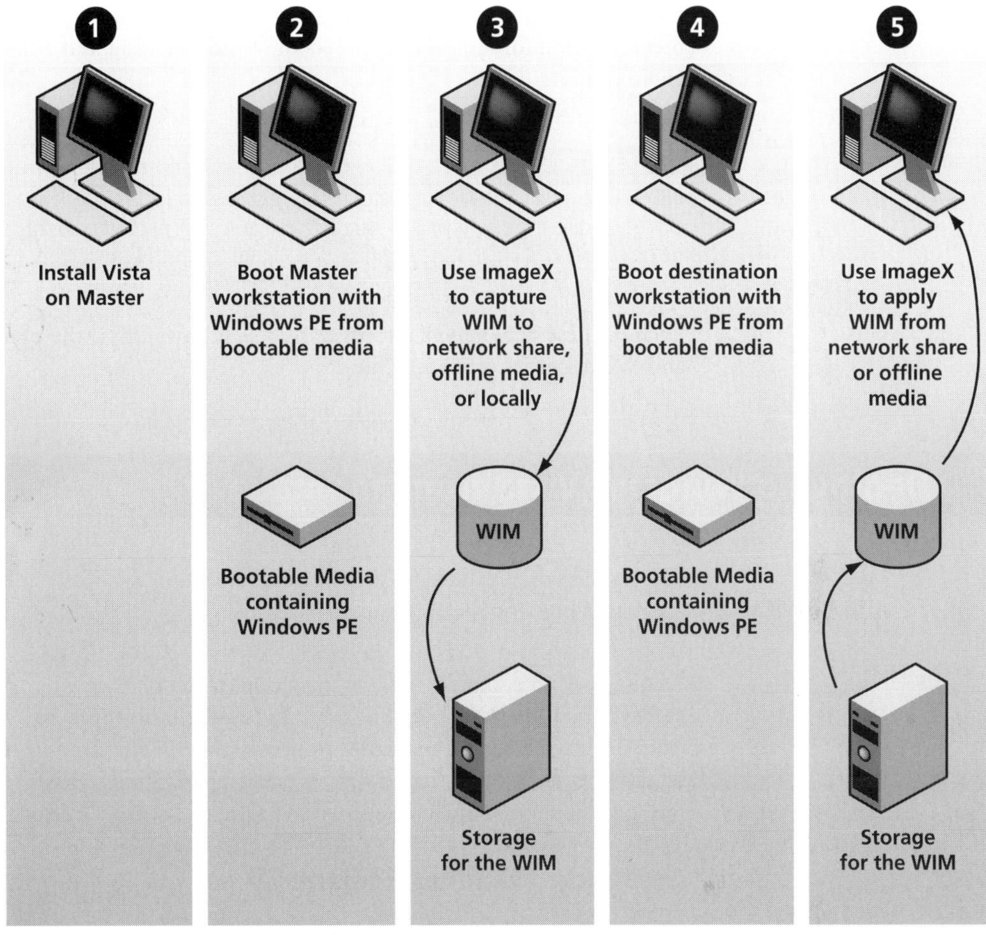

Of course, in a large deployment, you would want to automate some of the preceding tasks by using scripting or a deployment management tool. Microsoft provides some tools to help you do this.

Windows Deployment Services (Windows DS) enables you to deploy Windows Vista remotely using Windows PE and Windows DS Server. Deployments using Windows DS are customizable, scalable, and can be fully unattended. Windows DS comes as part of the ***Windows Automated Installation Kit (WAIK)***.

TAKE NOTE* Windows DS is a server update for the Windows Server 2003 operating systems. It replaces Remote Operating System Installation (RIS).

The WAIK can be used to automate Windows Vista deployment through deployment life cycle, including planning; preparing the deployment environment; creating and customizing an image; capturing, modifying, and testing the image; and deploying, maintaining, and servicing the image. The WAIK also includes the ***Windows System Image Manager (Windows SIM)***, which manages WIM files and can be used to create an autounnatend.xml file for use in unattended installations.

DOWNLOAD You can download WAIK by searching for it here: *www.microsoft.com/downloads/*. It is a large IMG file (992.2MB). To install it, you need to either burn it to a DVD or mount it using a virtual CD/DVD ROM drive.

The Systems Management Server (SMS) Operating System Deployment Feature Pack enables you to deploy Windows Vista in a customizable, centralized, and scalable way.

Finally, the Business Desktop Deployment (BBD) 2007 is a complete and automated deployment solution for large deployments of Windows Vista and Microsoft Office in an enterprise environment.

MORE INFORMATION

BBD 2007 is a complete and automated deployment solution for large deployments of Windows Vista and Microsoft Office in an enterprise environment. You can find it at *technet.microsoft.com/en-us/library/bb490308.aspx*.

Each of these deployment processes uses Windows PE as the preinstallation operating system and WIM images for source files.

■ Deploying Windows Vista from an Image

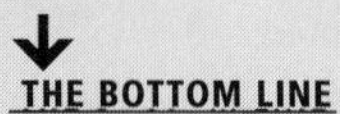

You can deploy Windows Vista by booting Windows PE on the destination computer and then applying an image by using ImageX.

As discussed in earlier, Windows Vista deployment in an enterprise will ordinarily be automated. The Objective Domains for exam 70-622, however, cover applying an image both from offline media and manually from a network. This section covers those objective domains by taking you through the process of creating a Windows PE boot CD, booting Windows PE, and then applying an image either from a network share or from offline media.

Creating a Windows PE Boot CD

Creating a Windows PE Boot CD will enable you to boot the Windows PE operating system on the destination computer so that you can apply a WIM image to it.

CREATE A WINDOWS PE BOOT CD

Whether you are installing from a DVD directly, using an automated solution such as BDD 2007, or manually applying an image (as in the example in this lesson), you boot the destination computer by using Windows PE. The following procedure explains how to create a Windows PE ISO image (along with a copy of ImageX), which you can burn to a CD-ROM. You can then boot a destination computer from the CD so that you can apply an image to it using ImageX.

GET READY. Before you begin this procedure, download and install WAIK to the default location. The installation wizard will guide you through the simple installation process.

1. Click **Start.** In the Start Search box, type **cmd** and then press **Ctrl** + **Shift** + **Enter.** A User Account Control dialog box appears.
2. Provide administrator credentials and then click **OK.** A command prompt window appears.
3. At the command prompt, type **cd c:\program files\windows aik\tools\petools** and then press **Enter.** The current directory changes to C:\Program Files\Windows AIK\Tools\PETools.
4. Type **copype *ArchitectureDesignation DestinationPath*** (for example, **copype x86 c:\winpe**) and then press **Enter.**
   - *ArchitectureDesignation* is the architecture designation for the processor (x86, amd64, or ia64).
   - *DestinationPath* is a path to a local directory (if the directory does not exist, it will be created).

Text similar to the following will be output to the command prompt window:

```
===============================================================
Creating Windows PE customization working directory
c:\winpe
===============================================================
        1 file(s) copied.
        1 file(s) copied.

C:\Program Files\Windows
   AIK\Tools\PETools\x86\boot\bcd
C:\Program Files\Windows
   AIK\Tools\PETools\x86\boot\boot.sdi
C:\Program Files\Windows
   AIK\Tools\PETools\x86\boot\bootfix.bin
C:\Program Files\Windows
   AIK\Tools\PETools\x86\boot\etfsboot.com
C:\Program Files\Windows
   AIK\Tools\PETools\x86\boot\fonts\chs_boot.ttf
C:\Program Files\Windows
   AIK\Tools\PETools\x86\boot\fonts\cht_boot.ttf
C:\Program Files\Windows
   AIK\Tools\PETools\x86\boot\fonts\jpn_boot.ttf
C:\Program Files\Windows
   AIK\Tools\PETools\x86\boot\fonts\kor_boot.ttf
C:\Program Files\Windows
   AIK\Tools\PETools\x86\boot\fonts\wgl4_boot.ttf
9 File(s) copied
C:\Program Files\Windows
   AIK\Tools\PETools\x86\EFI\microsoft\boot\bcd
C:\Program Files\Windows
   AIK\Tools\PETools\x86\EFI\microsoft\boot\fonts\chs_boot.ttf
C:\Program Files\Windows
   AIK\Tools\PETools\x86\EFI\microsoft\boot\fonts\cht_boot.ttf
C:\Program Files\Windows
   AIK\Tools\PETools\x86\EFI\microsoft\boot\fonts\jpn_boot.ttf
C:\Program Files\Windows
   AIK\Tools\PETools\x86\EFI\microsoft\boot\fonts\kor_boot.ttf
C:\Program Files\Windows
   AIK\Tools\PETools\x86\EFI\microsoft\boot\fonts\wgl4_boot.ttf
6 File(s) copied
   1 file(s) copied.
   1 file(s) copied.

Success

Updating path to include peimg, oscdimg, imagex

  C:\Program Files\Windows AIK\Tools\PETools\
  C:\Program Files\Windows AIK\Tools\PETools\..\x86
```

ANOTHER WAY

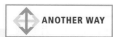

You can use Windows Explorer to copy the file Imagex.exe from the x86 folder to the Winpe\ISO folder.

5. Type **copy "c:\program files\windows aik\tools\x86\imagex.exe" c:\winpe\iso** and then press **Enter**. ImageX is copied to the ISO directory in the winpe directory. Files in the ISO directory will be part of an ISO image created later in this procedure.
6. Type **cd c:\program files\windows aik\tools\petools** and then press **Enter**. The current directory changes to C:\Program Files\Windows AIK\Tools\PETools.
7. Type **oscdimg -n -bc:\winpe\etfsboot.com c:\winpe\ISO c:\winpe\winpe.iso**. This creates a bootable ISO image file from the contents of the C:\winpe\ISO directory.

   The -n allows long file names.

   The -b option creates a bootable ISO using etfsboot.com as the bootable program.

   c:\winpe\ISO is the location of the files with which to create the ISO image.

   c:\winpe\winpe.iso is the destination file for the ISO image.

Text similar to the following is output to the command prompt window:

```
OSCDIMG 2.45 CD-ROM and DVD-ROM Premastering Utility

Copyright (C) Microsoft, 1993-2000. All rights reserved.

For Microsoft internal use only.

Scanning source tree complete (18 files in 8 directories)

Computing directory information complete

Image file is 192542720 bytes

Writing 18 files in 8 directories to c:\winpe\winpe_x86.iso

100% complete

Final image file is 192542720 bytes

Done.
```

8. Use third-party CD burning software to burn the winpe.iso ISO image to a writable CD.

Applying a WIM Image

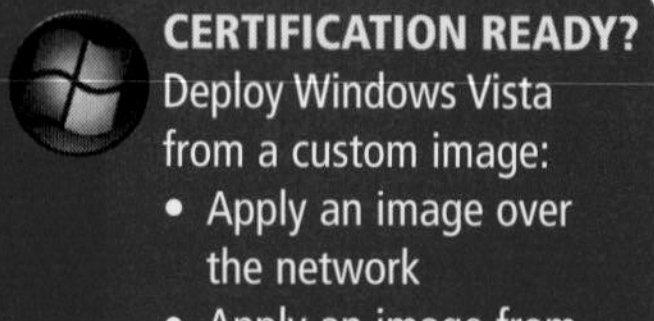

CERTIFICATION READY?
Deploy Windows Vista from a custom image:
- Apply an image over the network
- Apply an image from offline media

1.3

You can apply a WIM image to a destination computer using the ImageX /apply command.

As stated earlier, WIM images are both captured and applied using the ImageX command-line tool.

Table 2-1 summarizes the actions `ImageX` completes when it captures an image from an existing deployment of Windows Vista.

Table 2-1

Actions ImageX completes when it captures an image

ACTION	DESCRIPTION
Captures volume metadata	ImageX gathers data about file names, NTFS ACLs, and other file system attributes across the volume. (You can opt to exclude certain files with a script file.)
Captures file data	Each file is captured and along with its metadata.
Generates a hash for each file captured	For each file captured, a cryptographic hash is generated. This identifies the file and is used, for example, in single instancing.
Checks for and removes duplicate files	Removing duplicate files is possible because of single instancing.
Compresses on a file-by-file basis	Each file is compressed individually (if compression is specified), which, among other advantages, makes it easier to implement technologies that can browse WIM images.
Compresses volume metadata	After all the files are stored, a metadata entry that lists each file added to the volume image is created, compressed, and stored.
Generates and stores Image XML data	The XML image data provides information for each volume image in the WIM image. You can run imagex /info to see this data.
Stores cached WIM Data Index	The master data index (along wit the cached data) is stored. This is the master index for the WIM image and contains only one entry per hash (and therefore one entry per unique file).

Table 2-2 summarizes the actions `ImageX` completes when it applies an image to a destination computer.

Table 2-2

Actions ImageX completes when it applies an image

ACTION	DESCRIPTION
Retrieves and loads image metadata	The metadata for each volume image is retrieved and loaded.
Creates directory structure	The directory tree for the volume image is created on the destination computer in the specified path.
Extracts file data	Each file is extracted from the image in the same order in which the file was stored.
Applies files	The extracted files are loaded, decompressed if necessary, and copied into their place on the destination computer. The metadata for each file is applied.
Applies directory metadata	This step is completed last so that permissions on directories don't interfere with applying files.

The usage of `imagex /apply` is as follows:

`imagex /apply ImageFile ImageNumber | IamgeName ImagePath`

- *`ImageFile`* is the path and image file that `ImageX` will apply
- *`ImageNumber`* is the number of the volume image in the WIM image that `ImageX` will apply
- *`IamgeName`* is the name of the image (this is optional)
- *`ImagePath`* is the path that `ImageX` will apply the image to

For example, to apply the first volume image in a WIM image located on a network drive y named workstation1.wim to the root of the C drive, type `imagex /apply y:\workstation1.wim 1 c:.`

Several options can be appended to `ImageX /apply`, which are summarized in Table 2-3.

Table 2-3

Command-line options for `ImageX /apply`

OPTION	DESCRIPTION
/check	Verifies the integrity of data in the WIM image before it is applied.
/ref *splitwim.swm*	Enables the reference of split.wim files (SWMs). WIM files can be split so that they can span across media. *splitwim.swm* is the name and location of additional split files. Wildcards are accepted.
/scroll	Scrolls output for redirection.
/verify	Enables file resource verification by checking for errors and file duplication.

PREPARE A PARTITION FOR AN IMAGE

Because WIM Images are file-based rather than sector-based, you need to prepare a partition on which to apply a WIM image. To do this, you use diskpart, a Windows PE tool. The following procedure creates a primary partition on which to apply an image by using ImageX.

GET READY. Configure the BIOS of the destination computer so that you can boot from the CD-ROM drive.

1. Boot using a bootable Windows PE CD. The Windows PE operating system loads and a command prompt window appears, as shown in Figure 2-2.

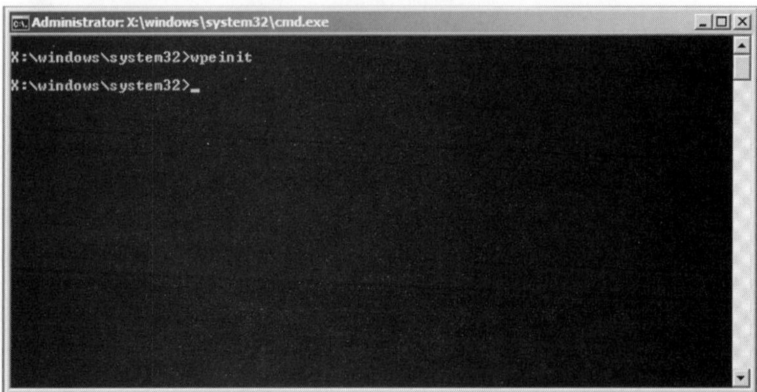

Figure 2-2

The Windows PE Operating System runs in a command prompt and does not have a graphical user interface.

2. In the Windows PE command prompt window, type **diskpart** and then press **Enter**. DiskPart starts, which enables you to configure and format disk partitions.
3. Type **select disk 0** and then press **Enter**. Disk 0 is selected for configuration.
4. Type **clean** and then press **Enter**. All information is cleaned from Disk 0.
5. Type **create partition primary** and press **Enter**. A partition is created equal to the size of the space remaining on the disk. You can optionally specify a size by appending size=*NumberOfMegaBytes*.
6. Type **select partition 1** and then press **Enter**. Partition 1 is selected for configuration.
7. Type **active**. Partition 1 is set as the active partition, which is the partition that will boot on start-up.
8. Type **format**. Partition 1 is formatted in NTFS.
9. Type **exit** and then press **Enter**. The DiskPart tool is exited. The following is an example of this procedure being implemented:

```
X:\Windows\System32>diskpart

Microsoft DiskPart version 6.0.6000

Copyright (c) 1999-2007 Microsoft Corporation

On Compter: MININT-R9AD2IL

DISKPART> clean

DiskPart succeded in cleaning the disk

DISKPART> select partition 1

Parition 1 is now the selected partition

DISKPART> active

DiskPart marked the current partition as active.

DISPART> format

100 percent complete

DiskPart successfully formatted the volume.

DISKPART> exit

Leaving DiskPart...
```

APPLY AN IMAGE FROM A NETWORK SHARE

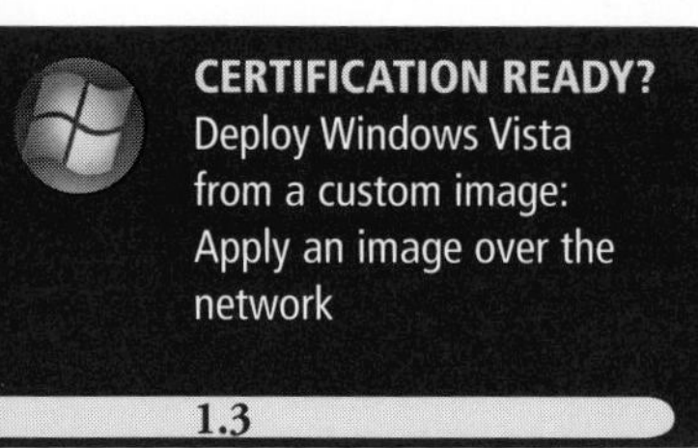

CERTIFICATION READY?
Deploy Windows Vista from a custom image: Apply an image over the network
1.3

The most common option in an enterprise environment is to apply an image located on a network share. For mass deployments, this will typically be automated. However, in some circumstances a one-off is appropriate, for example, when you are repairing a broken system and find the easiest fix is to apply a new image.

CONTINUE from the previous procedure.

1. In the Windows PE command prompt window, type **net use Y: *ServerName**ShareName*** and then press **Enter**.

TAKE NOTE

Ensure that after *Y:* there is a space before *//...*

Net use is a command-line tool that lets you configure network settings. In this case, you are using it to map a network share to the drive letter Y, which will enable you to refer to the network share by referring to drive Y.

Server Name is the name of the file server on which the share containing the image resides.

Share Name is the name of the shared folder where the image resides.

2. When prompted, provide credentials for a user who has read privileges to the shared folder. Provide the user name in the form *DomainName\UserName*.
3. Type **D:\imagex /apply y:*ImageFile ImageNumber ImagePath*** (for example, *D:\imagex /apply y:\workstation1.wim 1 C:*) and then press **Enter**. In the example:

   D is the drive letter where the Windows PE CD is. Substitute the correct drive letter if D is not the drive letter for your optical drive.

   workstation1.wim is the name of an example WIM image that ImageX is applying.

   1 identifies which volume image within the WIM image that ImageX will apply.

   C: is the path where ImageX will apply the image.

+ MORE INFORMATION

You can find more information on ImageX here: *technet2.microsoft.com/WindowsVista/en/library/2154c2e3-90a1-46c2-80e8-57bea12542491033.mspx?mfr=true.*

The application of the image can take considerable time. Information about the installation will be output to the command prompt window during installation. After the preliminary stages, progress will be represented by a percentage complete and an estimate of time remaining. An example image application in progress is shown in Figure 2-3.

Figure 2-3

ImageX applying a WIM image

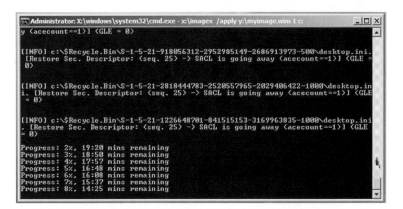

```
Administrator: X:\windows\system32\cmd.exe - x:\imagex /apply y:\myimage.wim 1 c:
y (acecount==1)] (GLE = 0)

[INFO] c:\$Recycle.Bin\S-1-5-21-918056312-2952985149-2686913973-500\desktop.ini.
 [Restore Sec. Descriptor: (seq. 25) -> SACL is going away (acecount==1)] (GLE =
 0)

[INFO] c:\$Recycle.Bin\S-1-5-21-2818444783-2520557965-2029406422-1000\desktop.in
i. [Restore Sec. Descriptor: (seq. 25) -> SACL is going away (acecount==1)] (GLE
 = 0)

[INFO] c:\$Recycle.Bin\S-1-5-21-1226648701-841515153-3169963835-1000\desktop.ini
. [Restore Sec. Descriptor: (seq. 25) -> SACL is going away (acecount==1)] (GLE
= 0)

Progress: 2%, 19:20 mins remaining
Progress: 3%, 18:50 mins remaining
Progress: 4%, 17:57 mins remaining
Progress: 5%, 16:48 mins remaining
Progress: 6%, 16:08 mins remaining
Progress: 7%, 15:37 mins remaining
Progress: 8%, 14:25 mins remaining
```

APPLY AN IMAGE FROM OFFLINE MEDIA

Applying an image from offline media is not a mass deployment option, but it can be useful to deploy Windows Vista in a one-off scenario. For example, a computer becomes corrupted, and the most efficient way to address the problem is to replace the operating system.

CONTINUE from the "Prepare a Partition for an Image" procedure earlier in this lesson.

1. In the Windows PE command prompt window, type **copy d:\imagex.exe x:** and then press **Enter**. Doing so copies the ImageX program to the RAM drive so that it will be accessible without the Windows PE CD in the drive.
2. If necessary, insert the DVD containing the WIM image (the image could also be on a USB drive or other offline media).

3. Type **X:\imagex /apply y:*ImageFile ImageNumber ImagePath*** (for example, `X:\imagex /apply y:\workstation2.wim 1 C:`) and then press **Enter**. In the example:

   D is the drive letter where the Windows PE CD is. Substitute the correct drive letter if D is not the drive letter for your optical drive.

   Workstation2.wim is the name of an example WIM image that ImageX is applying.

   1 identifies which volume image within the WIM image ImageX will apply.

   C: is the path where ImageX will apply the image.

The application of the image can take considerable time. Information about the installation will be output to the command prompt window during installation. After the preliminary stages, progress will be represented by a percentage complete and an estimate of time remaining (see Figure 2-2).

■ Post-Deployment Tasks

In a successful deployment, any issues concerning roaming profiles and Folder Redirection should have been worked out in a test deployment before the main roll-out. If not, you may have to troubleshoot those issues. Also, if you are migrating settings by using the User State Migration Tool (USMT), you do so after installation.

Post-installation tasks covered in this lesson include:

- Restoring the profile data and settings (also called user state) by using USMT 3.0
- Troubleshooting roaming profiles
- Troubleshooting Folder Redirection

More post-deployment tasks are covered in **Lesson 3: Configuring Devices and Applications.**

Restoring Profile Data and Settings by Using USMT 3.0

The User State Migration Tool can be used to migrate user settings to new Windows Vista installations.

When you are migrating to Windows Vista, you may want to capture profile data from the destination computers before you deploy Windows Vista and then restore the profile data after. You can do this using LoadState, a command-line tool that is part of USMT 3.0.

Using USMT, including LoadState, is covered in Lesson 1: Preparing to Deploy Windows Vista.

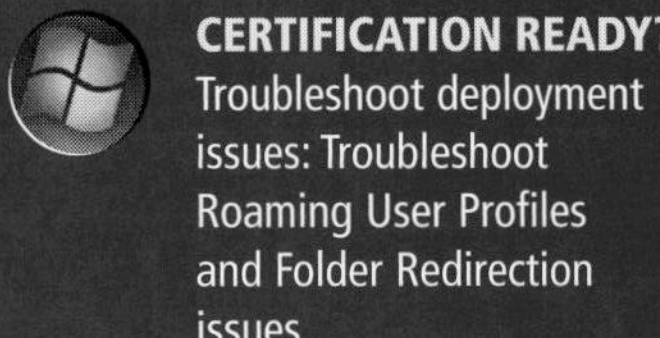

CERTIFICATION READY?
Troubleshoot deployment issues: Troubleshoot Roaming User Profiles and Folder Redirection issues
1.5

Troubleshooting Roaming Profiles

Roaming profiles can fail for a number of reasons, including incorrect paths or permissions, or connectivity problems.

Roaming profiles are covered in detail in **Lesson 1.**

Roaming profile problems are most commonly caused by the following:

- Incorrect paths
- Incorrect permissions
- Connectivity problems

Troubleshooting Incorrect Paths

Path problems can occur when the path specified for a roaming profile is incorrect.

Path problems occur when the roaming profile path indicated in the user's properties does not point to the path where the roaming profile resides. In such cases, the roaming profile will not load, and you will be presented with the message shown in Figure 2-4.

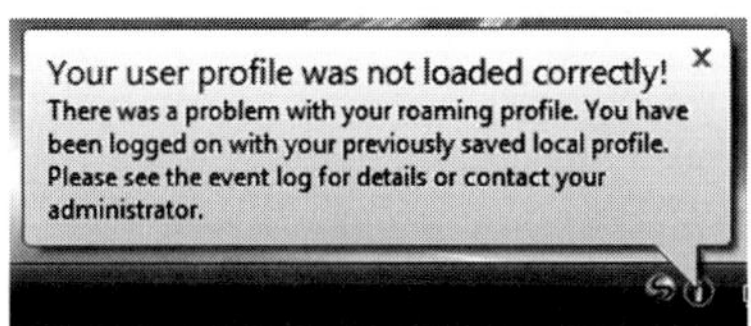

Figure 2-4

Message that the roaming profile did not load

If the path is wrong, you will see the following error in Event Viewer:

```
Event 1525: User Profile Service
```

```
Windows cannot locate the server copy of your roaming profile and is attempting to log you on with your local profile. Changes to the profile will not be copied to the server when you log off. This error may be caused by network problems or insufficient security rights.
```

```
DETAIL - The network path was not found.
```

Event Viewer is covered in detail in **Lesson 6: Troubleshooting Security Issues.**

CHECK TO SEE IF THE PROFILE PATH IS CORRECT

1. Log onto a domain controller.
2. Click **Start**, point to **Administrative Tools**, and then click **Active Directory Users and Computers.** The Active Directory Users and Computers console appears, as shown in Figure 2-5.

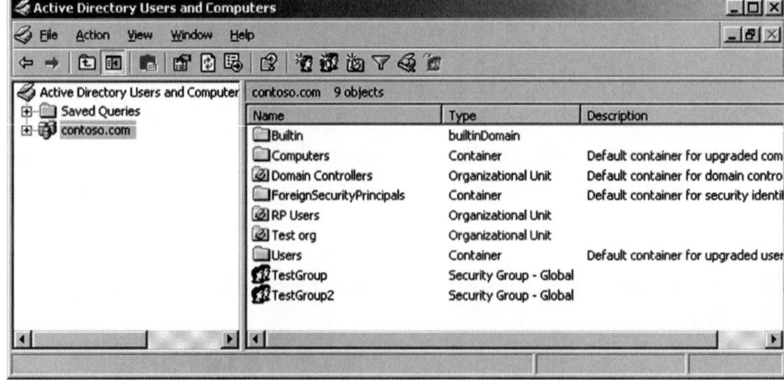

Figure 2-5

The Active Directory Users and Computers console

3. Expand as necessary to select the container that holds the user for which there is a roaming profile problem. For example, expand **contoso.com** and then select **Users.**
4. In the details pane, right-click the user and then click **Properties.** The *UserName* Properties dialog box appears.
5. Click the **Profile** tab.

6. Ensure that the entry in the Profile Path text box matches he intended profile path. You can also see if the path is accessible from the user's workstation. An example path is shown in Figure 2-6.

Figure 2-6

The profile path is shown in the the Profile tab of the *UserName* Properties dialog box

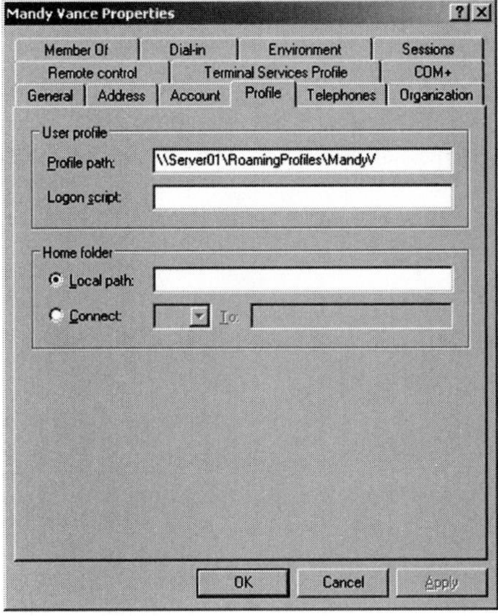

7. Click **OK**.

Troubleshooting Incorrect Permissions

Roaming profiles can fail if the permissions where the profiles are stored are incorrect.

If the profile path is correct, but permissions on the path are not sufficient to allow the user access, the roaming profile can fail. And then the user may receive a message the same as or similar to that in Figure 2-4. One of the most common causes of this error is incorrect permissions on the profile share.

If the permissions are not sufficient, you will see the following error in Event Viewer:

```
Event 1521- User Profile Service
```

```
Windows cannot locate the server copy of your roaming profile and is
attempting to log you on with your local profile. Changes to the pro-
file will not be copied to the server when you log off. This error
may be caused by network problems or insufficient security rights.
```

```
DETAIL - Access is denied.
```

X REF

Event Viewer is covered in detail in **Lesson 6: Troubleshooting Security Issues.**

If a profile won't load correctly, check permissions related to reading data within the profile folder. Likewise, if a profile cannot save correctly, check permissions related to writing data to the profile folder.

Table 2-4 summarizes the permissions Microsoft recommends for user profile folders.

Table 2-4

Recommended permissions for user profile folders

Folder	User account or group	Permissions type	Permissions	Apply to
Parent folder	CREATER OWNER	NTFS	Full Control	Subfolders and files only
Parent folder	Administrator(s)	NTFS	None	N/A
Parent folder	Security group of users with roaming profiles	NTFS	• List Folder/Read Data • Create Folders/ Append Data	This folder only
Parent folder	Everyone	NTFS	None	N/A
Parent folder	SYSTEM	NTFS	Full Control	This folder, subfolders, and files
Parent folder	Security group of users with roaming profiles	Share-level permissions	Read	N/A
User profile folder (within parent folder, for example, a folder named ChrisC.V2)	*UserName*	NTFS	• Full Control • Owner	This folder, subfolders, and files

CHECK NTFS PERMISSIONS

1. Log onto the file server where the roaming profile share is located.
2. Locate the shared folder, right-click it, and then click **Properties**. The *FolderName* Properties dialog box appears.
3. Click the **Security** tab, shown in Figure 2-7.

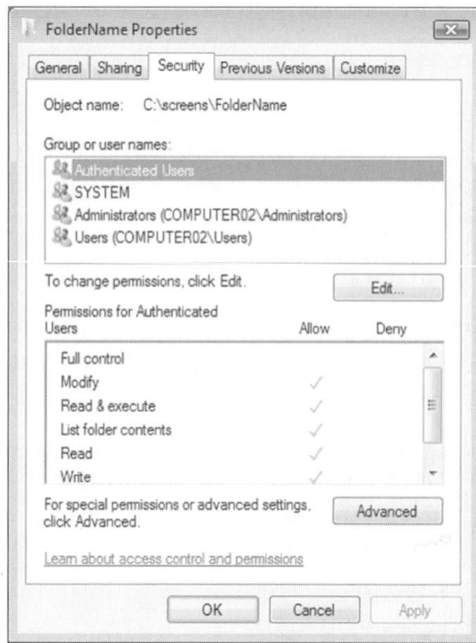

Figure 2-7

The Security tab of the *FolderName* Properties dialog box

4. Click **Advanced.** The Advanced Security Settings for *FolderName* dialog box appears, as shown in Figure 2-8.

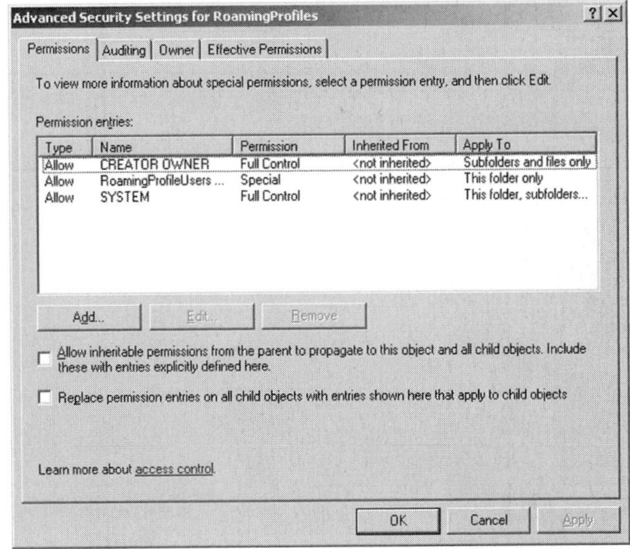

Figure 2-8

The Advanced Security Settings for *FolderName* dialog box

5. In the Permissions entries list box, select the user or group for which you want to check permissions and then click **Edit.** The Permission Entry for *FolderName* dialog box appears. The group or user to whom the permissions apply is listed in the Name box.
6. Ensure that the permissions follow the best practice permissions scheme described in Table 2-4, or are correct for the scheme at your company.
7. Click **OK** in the Permission Entry for *FolderName* dialog box.
8. Click **OK** in the Advanced Security Settings for *FolderName* dialog box.

CHECK SHARE-LEVEL PERMISSIONS

OPEN the properties dialog box for the roaming profile share folder (see the previous procedure).

1. In the *FolderName* Properties dialog box, click the **Sharing** tab, which is shown in Figure 2-9.

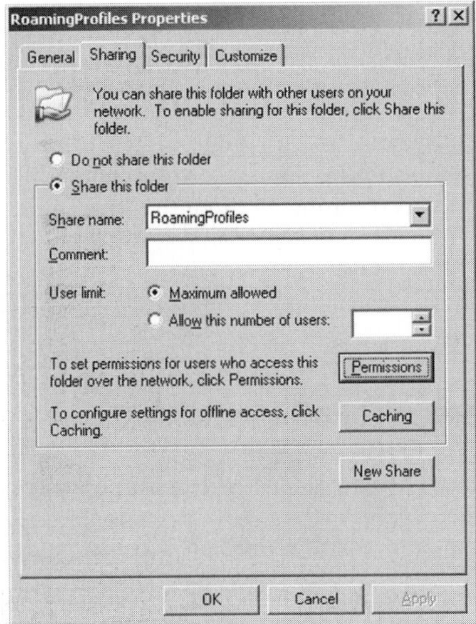

Figure 2-9

Sharing tab of the *FolderName* Properties dialog box

2. Click **Permissions**. The **Permissions for *FolderName*** dialog box appears, as shown in Figure 2-10.

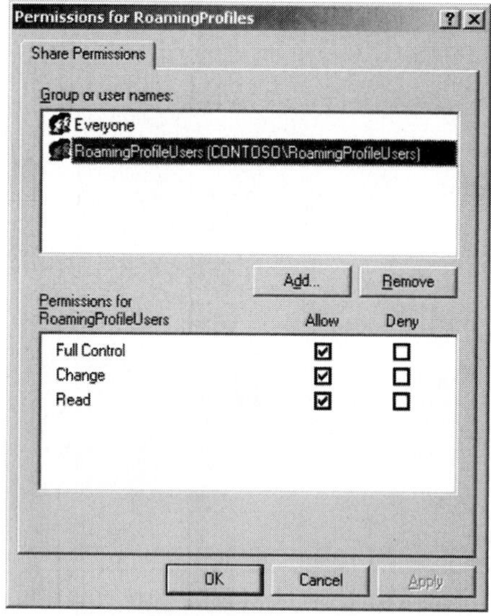

Figure 2-10

Permissions for the *FolderName* Properties dialog box

3. Ensure that the permissions follow the best practice permissions scheme described in Table 2-4, or are correct for the scheme at your company.
4. Click **OK** in the Permissions for *FolderName* dialog box.
5. Click **OK** in the *FolderName* Properties dialog box.

Troubleshooting Connectivity

Roaming profiles can fail if connectivity fails to the file server where the profiles reside.

Troubleshooting networking is covered in **Lesson 12: Configuring and Troubleshooting Access.**

Roaming profiles will fail if connectivity to the roaming profile fails when data is either being loaded from or saved to the profile (which occurs during logon and log off). You receive an error message only when connectivity is failing as you log on. Windows does not display a message when it does not save a user's profile during logoff due to network connectivity failure.

To troubleshoot profile failure due to failing connectivity, you troubleshoot network connectivity, which is covered in detail in Lesson 12: Configuring and Troubleshooting Access.

Troubleshooting Folder Redirection

Folder Redirection can fail if paths are specified incorrectly, if permissions or ownership of destination folders are incorrect, or if there are connectivity problems.

CERTIFICATION READY?
Troubleshoot deployment issues: Troubleshoot Roaming User Profiles and Folder Redirection issues
1.5

Troubleshooting Folder Redirection is similar to troubleshooting roaming profiles, because the three most common causes of problems are nearly the same:

- Incorrect paths
- Incorrect permissions or ownership
- Connectivity problems

Troubleshooting Incorrect Paths

Path problems can occur when a Folder Redirection policy contains an incorrect path.

Folder Redirection is covered in detail in **Lesson 1.**

At least two instances of incorrect path errors can occur in Folder Redirection:

- A network administrator changed the Folder Redirection policy to a non-existent target path (for example, a typo is made when changing target paths to a new server).
- A new Folder Redirection policy contains a non-existent target path.

In the first instance—in which a Folder Redirection policy was changed from having a correct to a non-existent target path—the new policy will not take effect, and the previous one will remain in effect. Event Viewer will show errors similar to the following:

```
Event 502 - Folder Redirection

Failed to apply policy and redirect folder "RedirectedFolderName" to
"\\ServerName\ShareName\UsernName\RedirectedFolderName".

Redirection options=1231.

The following error occurred: "Can not create folder "\\ServerName\
ShareName\UsernName\RedirectedFolderName".

Error details: "The network path was not found."
```

In the second instance—a new Folder Redirection policy contains a non-existent target path—Windows will not apply the new policy. Event Viewer may not show an error. However, the Resultant Set of Policy console will show the following error:

```
Failed to apply policy and redirect folder "RedirectedFolderName" to
"\\ServerName\ShareName\UserName\RedirectedFolderName".

Redirection options=1211.

The following error occurred: "Can not create folder "\\ServerName\
ShareName\UserName\RedirectedFolderName".

Error details: "The network path was not found."
```

EDIT THE TARGET PATH OF A FOLDER REDIRECTION POLICY

1. Click **Start.** In the **Start Search** text box, type **gpmc.msc** and then press **Ctrl** + **Shift** + **Enter**. A User Account Control dialog box appears.
2. Provide administrator credentials and then click **OK**. The Group Policy Management console appears.
3. In the console tree, expand **Forest:** ***ForestName*>Domains>*Domain Name*>Group Policy Objects** and then select the GPO where the Folder Redirection policy resides, as the example in Figure 2-11 shows.

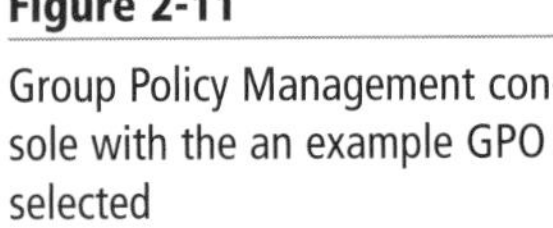

Figure 2-11

Group Policy Management console with the an example GPO selected

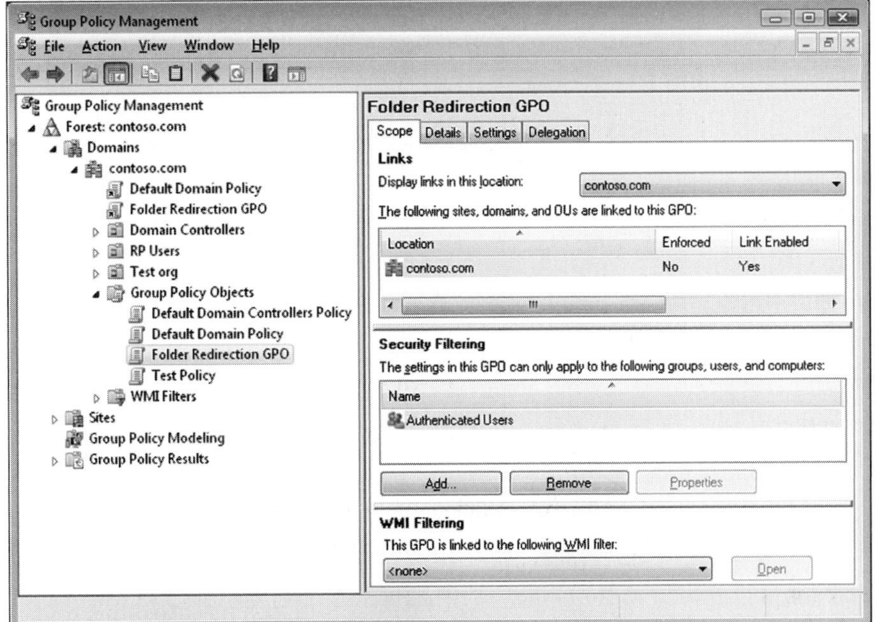

4. Right-click the Group Policy object and then click **Edit.** The Group Policy Object Editor console appears with the selected Group Policy object loaded.
5. In the console tree, expand **User Configuration>Windows Settings>Folder Redirection**, as shown in Figure 2-12.

Figure 2-12

Group Policy Object Editor console with the Folder Redirection node selected

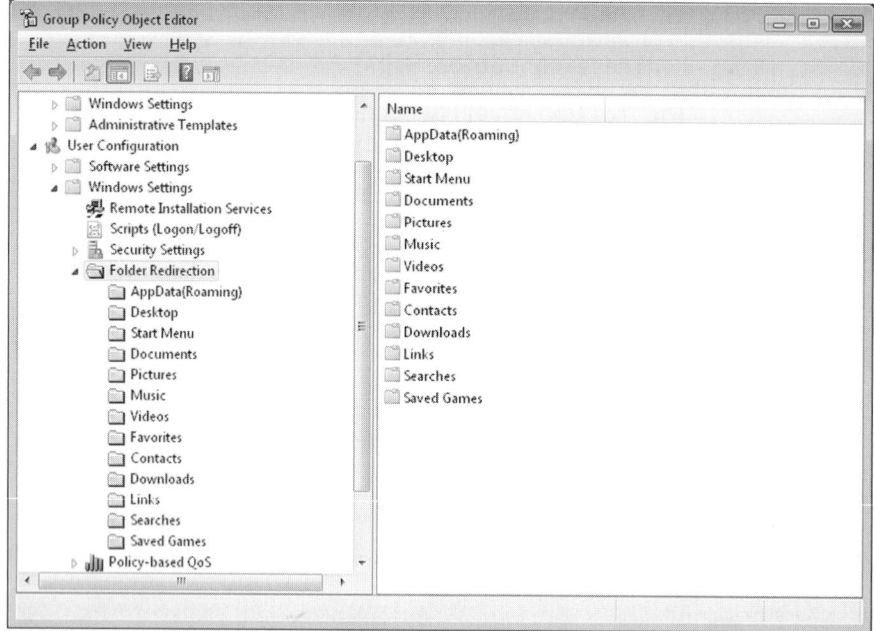

6. In the details pane, right-click the folder for which you want to edit the target path and then click **Properties.** The *RedirectedFolderName* Properties dialog box appears, as the example in Figure 2-13 shows.

Figure 2-13

The *RedirectedFolderName* Properties dialog box

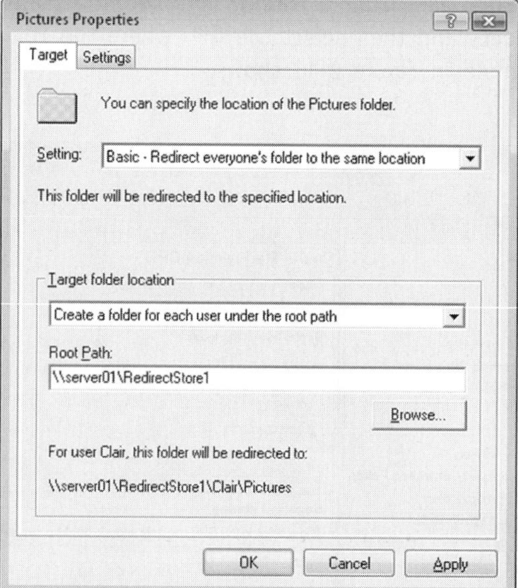

TAKE NOTE*

If you browse to the path rather than typing it, you cannot commit a typographical error.

7. Edit the target path in the **Root Path** text box as needed.
8. Click **OK** in the *RedirectedFolderName* Properties dialog box.

Troubleshooting Incorrect Permissions and Ownership

Incorrect NTFS permissions and ownership can cause Folder Redirection to fail.

If you create a new Folder Redirection policy, and the permissions on the target path are not sufficient to allow a user access, the policy will not be applied.

If the permissions are wrong, you may see the following error in Event Viewer:

```
Event 502 - Folder Redirection

Failed to apply policy and redirect folder "RedirectedFolderName" to
"\\ServerName\ShareName\UserName\RedirectedFolderName".

Redirection options=1211.

The following error occurred: "Can not create folder "\\ServerName\
ShareName\UserName\RedirectedFolderName".

Error details: "Access is denied."
```

Table 2-5 contains permissions Microsoft recommends for Folder Redirection.

Table 2-5

Recommended permissions for Folder Redirection shares

GROUP OR USER NAME	NTFS PERMISSION	APPLY TO
CREATOR OWNER	Full Control	Subfolders and files only
SYSTEM	Full Control	This folder, subfolder, and files
Domain Admins	Full Control	This folder, subfolder, and files
Everyone	Create Folders/Append Data List Folder/Read Data Read Attributes Traverse Folder/Execute File	This folder only

If the user does not own the folder named for him inside the redirection path, then Folder Redirection will fail. This can happen if an administrator takes ownership of the folder for administrative purposes and fails to give it back to the user. If the ownership is incorrect, Event Viewer will show the following error:

```
Event 502 - Folder Redirection

Failed to apply policy and redirect folder "RedirectedFolderName" to
"\\ServerName\ShareName\UserName\RedirectedFolderName".

Redirection options=9220.

The following error occurred: "Can not create folder "\\ServerName\
ShareName\UserName\RedirectedFolderName".

Error details: "This security ID may not be assigned as the owner of
this object."
```

CHECK PERMISSIONS

1. Log onto the file server where the redirected folder share is located.
2. Locate the shared folder, right-click it, and then click **Properties**. The *FolderName* Properties dialog box appears.
3. Click the **Security** tab. Figure 2-14 shows the Security tab.

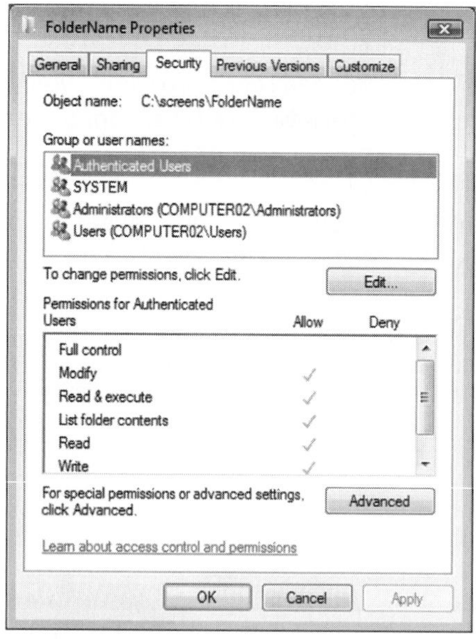

Figure 2-14

The Security tab of the *FolderName* Properties dialog box

4. Click **Advanced**. The Advanced Security Settings for *FolderName* dialog box appears, as shown in Figure 2-15.

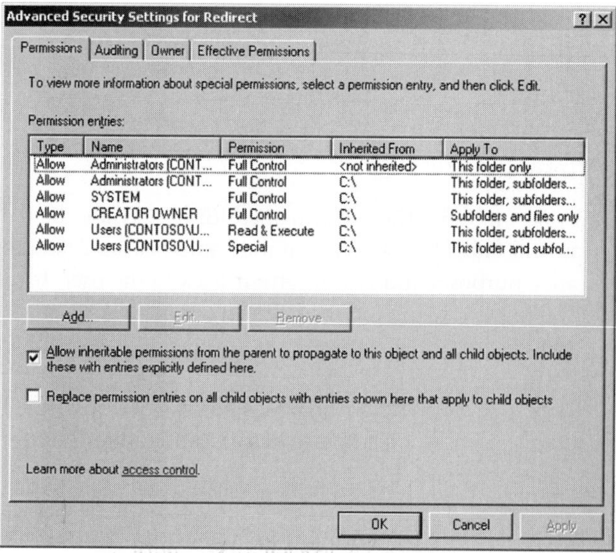

Figure 2-15

The Advanced Security Settings dialog box for an example folder

5. In the Permissions entries list box, select the user or group for which you want to check permissions and then click **Edit**. The Permission Entry for *FolderName* dialog box appears, as shown in Figure 2-16. The group or user to whom the permissions apply is listed in the Name box.

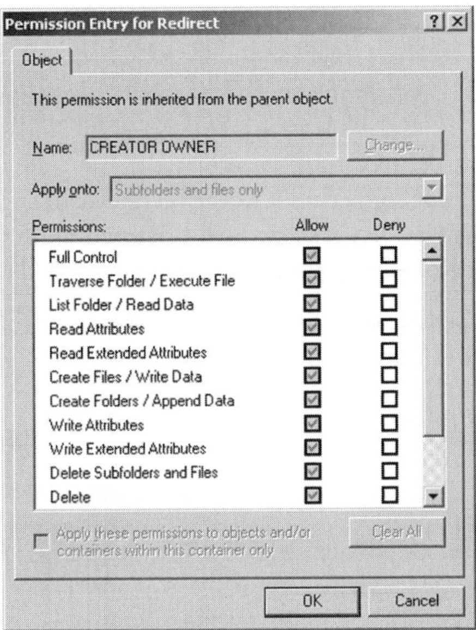

Figure 2-16

The Permissions Entry dialog box for an example folder

6. Ensure that the permissions follow the best practice permissions scheme described in Table 2-5, or are correct for the scheme at your company.
7. Click **OK** in the Permission Entry for *FolderName* dialog box.

CHECK OWNERSHIP

OPEN the Advanced Security Settings dialog box for the folder for which you want to check ownership (see the previous procedure).

1. In the Advanced Security Settings dialog box, click the **Owner** tab. The **Owner** tab is shown in Figure 2-17.

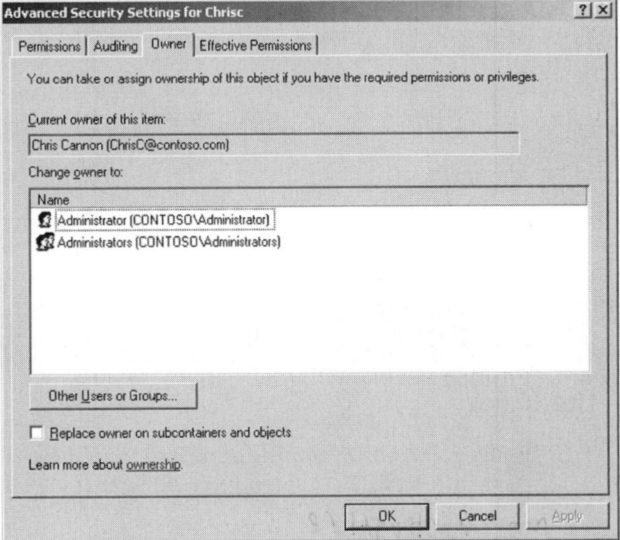

Figure 2-17

The Owner tab of the Advanced Security Settings dialog box for an example folder

2. The owner of the item is listed in the Current owner of this item box. The owner of the target folder should be the user. If the user is not the owner, click **Other users or groups** to add the user to the list of possible owners, select the user in the list, and then click **Apply**.
3. When you are finished, click **OK** in the Advanced Security Settings for *FolderName* dialog box.
4. Click **OK** in the *FolderName* Properties dialog box.

Troubleshooting networking is covered in Lesson 12.

Troubleshooting Connectivity

Folder Redirection can fail if connectivity fails to the file server where the target folders reside.

Folder Redirection can fail if connectivity to the server hosting the target path fails. When this happens, any data written to the folder will be stored on the local computer and will be synchronized with the server when connectivity is reestablished.

To troubleshoot Folder Redirection failure due to failing connectivity, you troubleshoot network connectivity, which is covered in Lesson 12.

SUMMARY SKILL MATRIX

IN THIS LESSON YOU LEARNED:
Windows Vista deployment—whether automated for an entire enterprise or preformed individually on a computer—can be completed using WIM images.
All Windows Vista deployments that are based on Microsoft technologies follow a similar pattern regardless of their scope: Windows PE is booted, and a WIM image (captured manually or on a Windows Vista DVD) is used to supply source files.
How to create a Windows PE Boot CD.
How to use the ImageX /apply command.
How to prepare a partition for an image.
How to apply an image from a network share.
How to apply an image from offline media.
Roaming profiles and Folder Redirection can fail for a number of reasons, including incorrect paths or permissions, or connectivity problems.
How to check to see if paths are correct for roaming profiles or Folder Redirection.
How to check NTFS and share permissions for roaming profiles and Folder Redirection.
How to edit the target path of a Folder Redirection policy.

■ Knowledge Assessment

Fill in the Blank

Complete the following sentences by writing the correct word or words in the blanks provided.

1. The ability to apply an image without destroying all of the data on the partition is called ____________.
2. ____________ is storing multiple instances of the same data once instead of multiple times.
3. A(n) ____________ image is Microsoft's proprietary file-based imaging format.
4. ____________ is the replacement for Microsoft RIS.
5. The computer from which an image is captured with the intent of applying the image to destination computers is called the ____________.

6. To apply an image, the ______________ command-line tool is used with the /apply option.
7. LoadState is a part of the ______________ and can be used to restore user profile settings.
8. ______________ is a simplified operating system that is booted when you install Windows Vista from a Windows Vista DVD.
9. A(n) ______________ is used in a WIM image to uniquely identify every file.
10. WIM images are ______________ independent, meaning that they can be used to install on computers with varying hardware.

Multiple Choice

Select the best response for the following questions.

1. The tool that you use to capture a WIM image from a Windows Vista installation is:
   a. ImageX.
   b. Windows Image.
   c. Windows DS.
   d. Windows PE.
2. When you install Windows Vista from the installation DVD, the following operating system is booted, and the installation is launched from it:
   a. ImageX
   b. Windows Vista
   c. Windows DS
   d. Windows PE
3. Which of the following is not a commonly occurring reason for Folder Redirection to fail?
   a. Network connectivity problems
   b. Incorrect profile path specified in the user's properties
   c. Incorrect permissions
   d. Incorrect specification of the target path
4. In the command d:\imagex /apply y:\AccountingImage.wim 3 c:, the 3 specifies:
   a. Use verbosity level three
   b. Apply the fourth image within the WIM image, the root image being image 0
   c. Apply the third image within the WIM image
   d. None of the above
5. The command-line Windows PE program used to prepare a partition before deploying Windows Vista is:
   a. Format.
   b. Fdisk.
   c. PartDsk.
   d. Diskpart.
6. To verify the integrity of the data within a WIM image before applying the image, you can do the following:
   a. Use the Windows System Image Manager (windows SIM) and select Verify integrity now from the Actions menu
   b. Run ImageX /apply with the /check option
   c. Run Imagex /apply with the /verify option
   d. Mount the WIM image and inspect it manually

7. The following about WIM Image compression is true:
   a. Each volume image within the WIM image must have the same compression settings and compression is applied to each file.
   b. Each volume image within the WIM Image can have an independent compression level and compression is applied to volume images as a whole.
   c. Each volume image within the WIM image can have an independent compression level and compression is applied to each file individually.
   d. Each volume image within the WIM image must have the same compression settings because compression is applied at the WIM image level.

8. Examine the permissions in Figure 2-18. If this is a parent folder for roaming user profiles, which of the following is true about the permissions and settings?
   a. The CREATOR OWNER should not have full permissions assigned on this folder, but on the individual folders for each user that has a roaming profile.
   b. The permissions and settings are correct.
   c. The permissions are correct, but the Apply onto setting is incorrect.
   d. The permissions are not correct; on the parent folder, the CREATOR OWNER only needs to be able to read and write data.

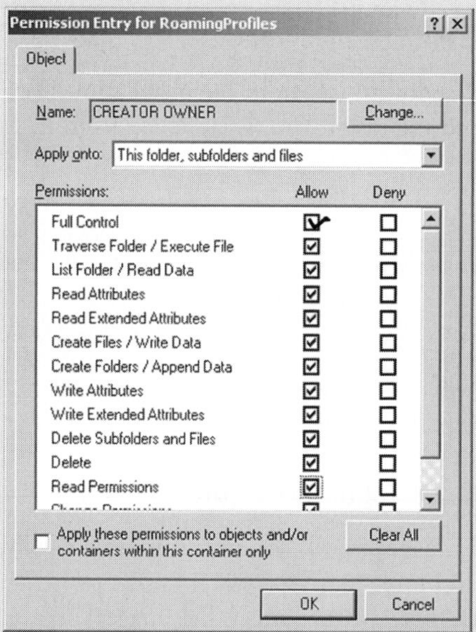

Figure 2-18

Example permissions for a roaming profile parent folder.

9. As part of designing a full-scale Windows Vista deployment scheme, you want a deployment option where you can deploy Windows Vista onto non-domain kiosk computers using a DVD. You want to be able to start the install process and then walk away, and have the install finish unattended. You should:
   a. Use setupmgr.exe to create a winnt.sif file to automate installation configuration options.
   b. Use Windows SIM to create an autounattend.xml file to automate installation configuration options.
   c. Use setupmgr.exe to create an autounattend.xml file to automate installation configuration options.
   d. Use Powershell to write a script to configure installation options.

10. You are creating a WIM image or images that will be used for deployment across the domain. The volume image for desktops and laptops is to be different. The most efficient way to organize the images is to:
    a. Create a WIM image for either the desktop or laptop and then append the other volume image to create a single WIM image with two volume images.
    b. You only need to create a single image because WIM images implement single-instancing.

c. Create a separate WIM image for desktops and laptops and then combine the images using ImageX /combine.
d. You have to create a separate WIM image for the desktops and laptops because they have different HALs.

Review Questions

1. Describe the roll of Windows PE and WIM images in the following deployment schemes:
   - Installing a single copy of Windows Vista Ultimate on a personal, home computer using the Windows Vista Ultimate DVD
   - Applying an image from a network share
   - Using BDD 2007 for a large-scale deployment
2. For the parent folder in a roaming profile scheme (see Table 2-4), explain in qualitative terms the recommended NTFS permissions for administrators and the security group of roaming profile users. Provide your own reasoning about why the settings are what they are.

■ Case Scenarios

Scenario 1: Event 502

The IT department has redirected the Pictures folders for the art department this morning. A user logs on, puts some art files in his Pictures folder, and then goes to a colleague's office and logs on, expecting to be able to show his colleague the pictures. But they are not there. In diagnosing the problem, you discover that Event 502 is occurring each time he logs on. You check the redirection paths, and they are correct. What is likely the problem, and how can you fix it?

Scenario 2: Event 1525

A user says some items on his desktop have "disappeared." No matter which workstation he logs onto, you find that event 1525 is logged during the time when he is logging on. What is the likely cause of this issue and what steps can you take to address it?

Configuring Devices and Applications

OBJECTIVE DOMAIN MATRIX

Technology Skill	Objective Domain	Objective Domain Number
Installing and Configuring Devices and Device Drivers	Perform post-installation tasks • Install and configure devices and drivers	1.4
Understanding Devices and Device Drivers	Perform post-installation tasks • Install and configure devices and drivers	1.4
	Troubleshoot deployment issues • Resolve device driver issues	1.5
Checking Device Compatibility	Troubleshoot deployment issues • Resolve device driver issues	1.5
Installing Devices	Perform post-installation tasks • Install and configure devices and drivers	1.4
Configuring Display Devices	Perform post-installation tasks • Configure display devices	1.4
Troubleshooting Devices and Device Drivers	Troubleshoot deployment issues • Resolve device driver issues	1.5
Using Device Manager	Troubleshoot deployment issues • Resolve device driver issues	1.5
Understanding and Configuring Device Installation Restrictions	Troubleshoot deployment issues • Group policy vs. local policy for user devices	1.5
Configuring Device Installation Restrictions through Group Policy	Troubleshoot deployment issues • Group policy vs. local policy for user devices	1.5
Configuring Application Compatibility	Troubleshoot deployment issues • Resolve application compatibility issues	1.5
Troubleshooting Application Compatibility	Troubleshoot deployment issues • Resolve application compatibility issues	1.5

KEY TERMS

device
device driver
Plug and Play (PnP)
signed drivers
screen resolution
pixels
color depth
maximum resolution
liquid crystal display (LCD) monitor
cathode-ray tube (CRT) monitor
native resolution
refresh rate
Device Manager
device installation restrictions
hardware IDs
device class GUIDs (Globally Unique Identifiers)
file and registry virtualization
compatibility layers

You are a support technician at Contoso, Incorporated. Contoso has recently deployed Windows Vista to 30 percent of its workstations on its main campus. Although you and your team were diligent in preparing for the deployment, you are likely to face some issues concerning devices and applications.

Installing and Configuring Devices and Device Drivers

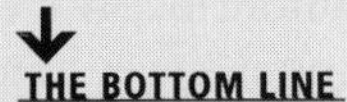

THE BOTTOM LINE

There is a broad range of tasks device–related tasks, from installing legacy devices to configuring and troubleshooting device installation restriction policies.

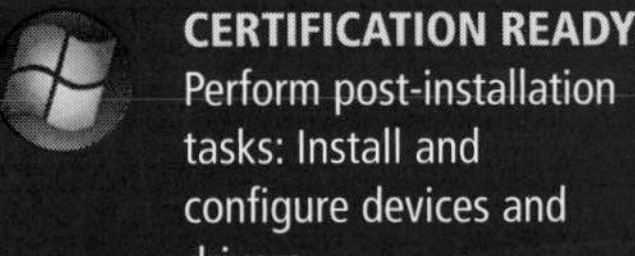

CERTIFICATION READY?
Perform post-installation tasks: Install and configure devices and drivers
1.4

Understanding Devices and Device Drivers

Device drivers enable computers to interact with devices, from hard drives to digital music players.

Devices are the various hardware items that your computer interacts with, from disk drives and modems, to graphics tablets and digital cameras.

A ***device driver***, often shortened to ***driver***, is a hardware-dependent, operating specific program that enables a computer to interact with a device.

Most devices today are Plug and Play. ***Plug and Play (PnP)*** devices automatically communicate information about themselves either during start-up or when you plug them in while the computer is running (called hot plugging), as in the case of Universal Serial Bus (USB) and some other devices. According to what the device communicates to the computer, the computer allocates system resources to the device, such as memory and communications channels, and installs a device driver if necessary.

All USB and IEEE 1394 Port (firewire) devices are PnP. Almost all interface cards that connect to Peripheral Component Interconnect (PCI), PCI Express, or Accelerated Graphics Port (AGP) slots are PnP. Devices that connect to serial, parallel, or PS/2 ports may or may not be PnP (most modern ones are). Devices that plug into Industry Standard Architecture (ISA) slots are not PnP.

Installing devices in Windows Vista is very similar to installing devices in Windows XP. In fact, many XP drivers will work in Windows Vista, although it is always recommended to use a Windows Vista driver when possible.

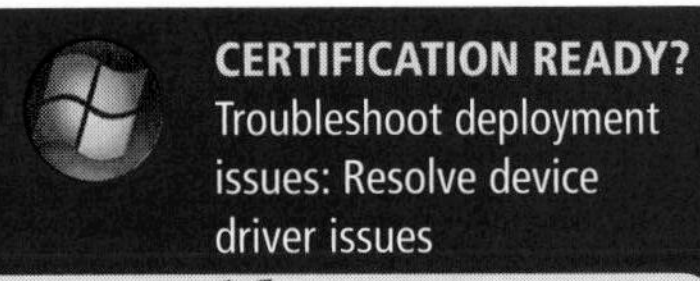

CERTIFICATION READY?
Troubleshoot deployment issues: Resolve device driver issues
1.5

Some devices, especially older ones, are not compatible with Windows Vista. Microsoft maintains a list of compatible devices called the hardware compatibility list (HCL). These devices have been submitted to and passed the quality tests of the Windows Quality Online Services team. Although the HCL contains many devices, it is by no means a complete listing of compatible devices. You can find the HCL for Windows Vista here: *winqual.microsoft.com/hcl/*.

Signed drivers are drivers that have met the Designed for Windows Vista requirements and have been given a digital signature. If you are using one of the install wizards and attempt to install an unsigned driver, you will be presented with the dialog box in Figure 3-1.

Figure 3-1

Windows Vista will ask if you want to install an unsigned driver.

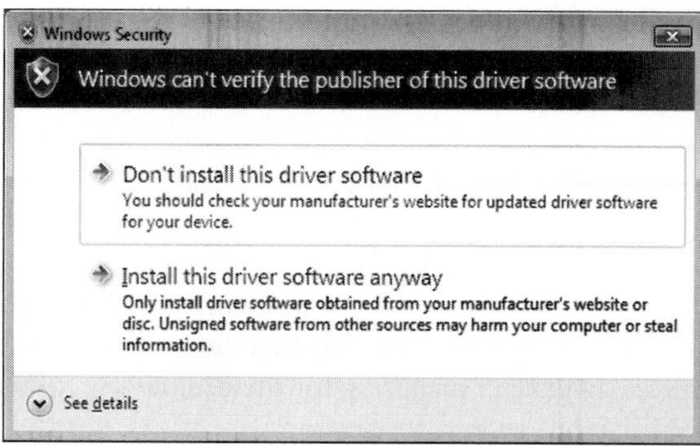

Installing an unsigned driver is more likely to cause system instability than installing a signed driver. In addition, some unsigned drivers are malware that steal information and send it to third parties. Always be wary of installing an unsigned driver that is not from the manufacturer of the device.

Windows Vista recognizes the risky nature of unsigned drivers and automatically creates a restore point whenever you install one so that if things do become unstable, you can return the system to the way it was before.

Checking Device Compatibility

Most new devices are compatible with Windows Vista.

CERTIFICATION READY?
Troubleshoot deployment issues: Resolve device driver issues
1.5

The following is a list of steps you can take to determine if a device is compatible with Windows Vista:

1. See if the device is listed in the HCL, at winqual.microsoft.com/hcl/.
2. Check the packaging and manual for an indication of Windows Vista compatibility.
3. Run the Windows Vista Upgrade Advisor Tool.
4. Check the manufacturer website for a Windows Vista driver for the device.
5. If the manufacturer does not have a Windows Vista driver for the device, check the manufacturer's website for a Windows XP driver for the device (this may get you the information you are looking for, or it may not).
6. Use a Windows Vista generic driver (a generic driver is a driver published by Microsoft rather than the device manufacturer).
7. See if it works to install the device by using the latest drivers from the manufacturer.
8. Check Windows Update to see if a driver is available for the device.

X REF

Installing a generic driver is covered later in this lesson in the **Installing Devices** section.

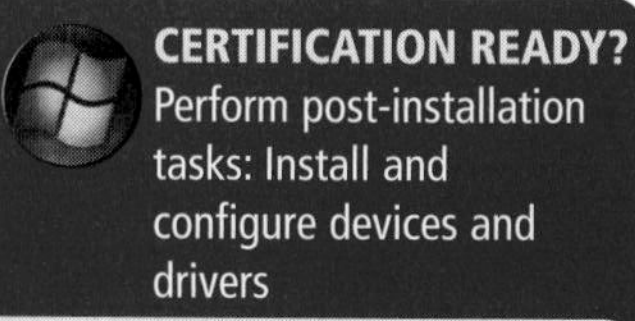

CERTIFICATION READY?
Perform post-installation tasks: Install and configure devices and drivers
1.4

Installing Devices

Windows Vista installs most new devices with little or no user interaction. You can install legacy devices manually.

INSTALL WINDOWS VISTA COMPATIBLE PnP DEVICES

Installing devices that are PnP and Windows Vista compatible is typically very straightforward. Most often you simply follow the manufacturer's instructions. The following are generic steps you can follow to install devices if you don't have instructions from the manufacturer:

1. Turn off the computer and physically install the device (or hot plug the device if applicable).
2. Start the computer and log on if needed. Windows Vista will detect the device, and if Windows Vista does not find a driver, the Found New Hardware wizard will appear, as shown in Figure 3-2.

Figure 3-2

The Found New Hardware wizard

3. Click **Locate and install driver software (recommended)**. This option will search Windows Update for a driver. A User Account Control dialog box appears.
4. Provide administrator credentials and then click **OK**. If Windows Vista finds a driver, complete the installation by following the prompts. If not, the Found New Hardware wizard will report that it cannot find a driver.
5. Select one of the following:

   Check for a solution. Select this option if you think something is preventing correct installation of the driver. Windows Vista will check for a known solution. If there is one, follow the prompts to complete the solution.

   Browse my computer for driver software (advanced). Select this option to select a driver from a known location. Continue to step 6.
6. The Browse for driver software on your computer page appears. In the **Search for driver software in this location** text box, enter a folder to search.
7. Select the **Include subfolders** check box to search subfolders. Click **Next**. Follow the onscreen prompts to complete the installation.

INSTALL A LEGACY MODEM

The following procedure is for installing a legacy modem (an older modem) by using a generic driver (one provided by Microsoft that is not from the manufacturer and may work for more than one device), or a driver in a location that you specify. You can use this procedure to install non-legacy modems, but to install any device, you should follow the manufacturer's instructions.

1. Click **Start** and then click **Control Panel**. The Control Panel window appears, as shown in Figure 3-3.

Figure 3-3

The Control Panel

2. In the Control Panel window, click **Hardware and Sound**. The Hardware and Sound control panel appears.
3. Click **Phone and Modem Options**. The Location Information dialog box appears.
4. In the **What country/region are you in now** drop-down list, select the appropriate country/region.
5. In the **What area code (or city code) are you in now** text box, key your area code.
6. In the **If you need to specify a carrier code, what is it** text box, key a carrier code if necessary.
7. In the **If you dial a number to access an outside line, what is it** text box, key a number used to access an outside line, if necessary.
8. For the *The phone system at this location uses* option, select either Tone dialing or Pulse dialing as appropriate.
9. Click **OK**. The Phone and Modem Options dialog box appears.
10. Click the **Modems** tab, as shown in Figure 3-4.

Figure 3-4

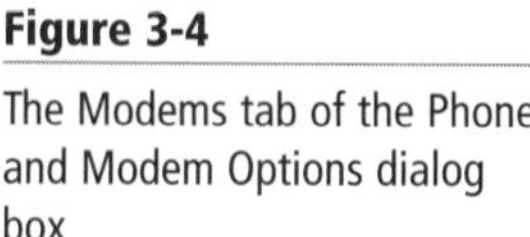

The Modems tab of the Phone and Modem Options dialog box

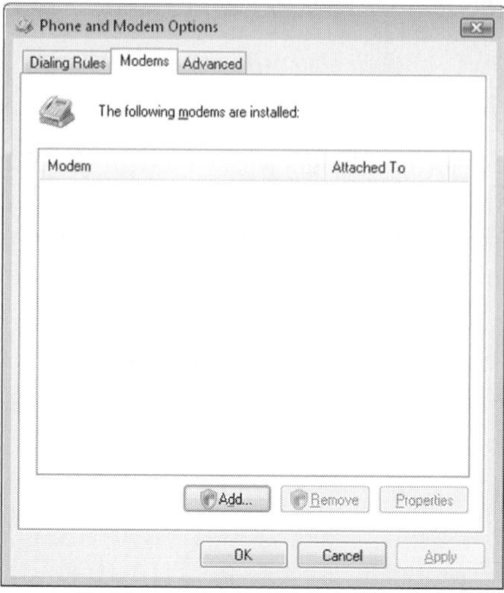

11. Click **Add**. A User Account Control dialog box appears.
12. Provide administrator credentials and then click **OK**. The Add Hardware Wizard opens to the *Install New Modem, Do you want Windows to detect your modem?* page, as shown in Figure 3-5.

Figure 3-5

The Install New Modem page of the Add Hardware Wizard

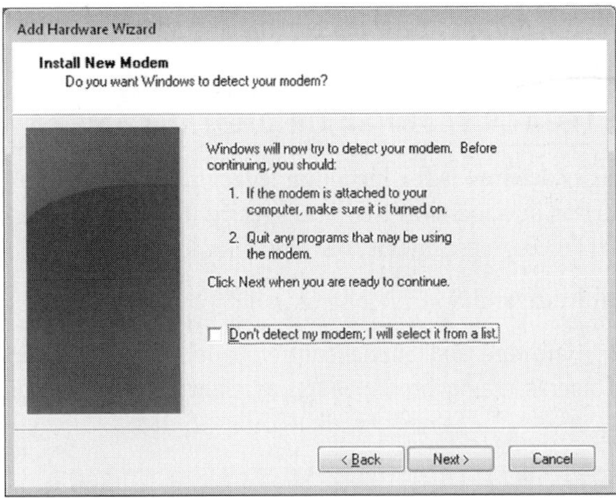

13. Select the **Don't detect my modem; I will select it from a list** check box.
14. On the next Install New Modem page, select a manufacturer and model to select a generic driver, or click **Have Disk** if you want to provide a driver from another location.
15. Click **Next**.
16. On the *Select the port(s) you want to install the modem on* page, select one of the following:

    All ports. Select this option to duplicate the modem installation to all the ports listed in the Selected ports standard list box.

    Selected ports. Select this option to select the specific port on which to install the modem. If you select this option, then select a port in the corresponding list box.
17. Click **Next**.
18. The *Windows is installing the modem(s)* page appears. After a few moments, the *Modem installation is finished!* page appears. Click **Finish**.

INSTALL A LEGACY PRINTER

The following procedure is for installing a legacy printer by using a generic driver, or a driver in a location that you specify. This procedure *can* be used to install non-legacy printers, but it's best to follow the manufacturer's instructions instead.

OPEN the Hardware and Sound control panel.

1. In the Hardware and Sound control panel, under Printers, click **Add a Printer**. The Add Printer Wizard appears.
2. Select **Add a local printer**. The Choose a printer port page appears.
3. Select one of the following:

    Use an existing port. If you select Use an existing port, select a port in the drop-down list and then click **Next**. Continue to step 4.

    Create a new port. If you select Create a new port, after you have created the new port, continue to step 4.

4. The *Install the printer driver* page appears. Select a manufacturer and model to select a generic driver, or click Have Disk if you want to provide a driver from another location. You can also click Windows Update to see if a newer driver is available through Windows Update.
5. Click **Next.**
6. Follow the prompts to complete the installation.

INSTALL A LEGACY SCANNER OR DIGITAL CAMERA

The following procedure is for installing legacy scanners or digital cameras by using a generic driver, or a driver in a location that you specify. This procedure can be used to install non-legacy scanners or digital cameras, but you should follow the manufacturer's instructions.

OPEN the Hardware and Sound control panel.

1. In the Hardware and Sound control panel, click **Scanners and Cameras.** The Scanners and Cameras dialog box appears, as shown in Figure 3-6.

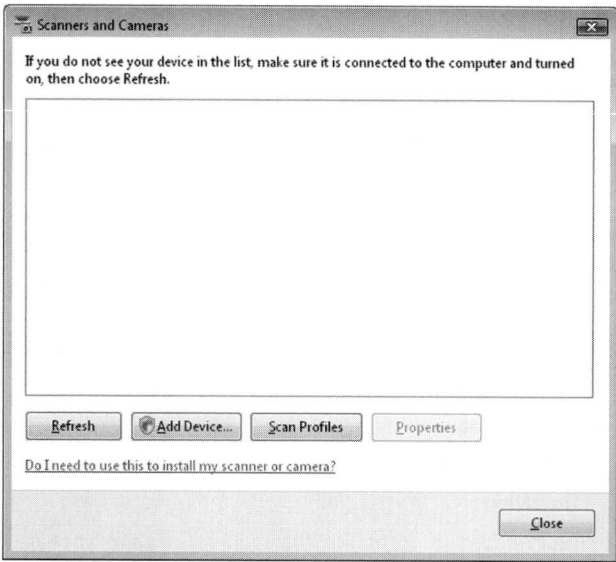

Figure 3-6

The Scanners and Cameras dialog box

2. Click **Add Device.** A User Account Control dialog box appears. Provide administrator credentials and then click **OK.** The Scanner and Camera Installation Wizard appears.
3. Click **Next**. The *Which scanner or camera do you want to install?* page appears.
4. To select a generic driver, select a manufacturer and model, or click **Have Disk** if you want to provide a driver from another location.
5. Click **Next**. Follow the prompts to complete the installation.

INSTALL LEGACY DEVICES

The following procedure is for installing legacy devices of all sorts by using a generic driver, or a driver in a location that you specify. This procedure can be used to install non-legacy devices, but you should follow the manufacturer's instructions.

OPEN the Hardware and Sound control panel.

1. In the Hardware and Sound control panel, click **View hardware and devices** under Device Manager. A User Account Control dialog box appears.
2. Provide administrator credentials and then click **OK.** The Device Manager console appears.

3. Select any device in the console tree. On the **Action** menu, click **Add legacy hardware**. The Add Hardware Wizard appears. Click **Next**.
4. Select one of the following:

   Search for and install the hardware automatically (Recommended). If you select this option, click **Next**. If the hardware is found, follow the prompts and complete installation. If it is not, click **Next** and continue to step 5.

   Install the hardware that I manually select from a list (Advanced). If you select this option, click **Next** and continue to step 5.
5. The *From the list below, select the type of hardware you are installing* page appears. In the standard list box, select the type of hardware you are installing. Depending on what you choose, different install wizards may start. Follow the onscreen prompts to complete the installation.

Configuring Display Devices

Correctly configuring display devices improves users' work experience.

CERTIFICATION READY?
Perform post-installation tasks: configure display devices
1.4

Before jumping into configuring display devices, you should be familiar with the following terms:

Screen resolution is how many pixels horizontally by how many pixels vertically your screen displays. It is expressed *HorizontalResolution* × *VerticalResolution* (for example, 1024×768).

Pixels are single points in graphics images. Everything you see on the screen is a combination of pixels.

Color depth is the number of colors each pixel can be. This is often measured in the number of bits that is used to specify the color of a single pixel. For example, if the color depth is 8 bits, then the number of colors that each pixel can be is 2^8 (or 2×2×2×2×2×2×2×2 = 256 colors).

Maximum resolution is the highest screen resolution that your monitor and video card combination is able to display.

Liquid crystal display (LCD) monitors use liquid crystal technology to display pixels. They are very flat in physical dimension compared to traditional (CRT) monitors.

Cathode-ray tube (CRT) monitors use a CRT to project the image on the screen, and they are similar in design to traditional television sets.

Native resolution is the highest resolution that an LCD monitor is able to display without cheating (i.e., removing pixels from images to mimic higher resolutions). Unlike CRT monitors, LCD monitors only look their best when they run at their native resolution, or half in each direction of their native resolution (and half of that again and so on). For example, an LCD monitor with a native resolution of 1600×1200 would also look good at 800×600. CRT monitors do not have a native resolution.

The ***Refresh rate*** is how fast in hertz (Hz; number of times per second) the screen is redrawn. For example, if your refresh rate is 70 Hz, the screen redraws from top to bottom 70 times per second.

Both screen resolution and color depth require access to video RAM. Therefore, if you have a lot of one, you may be restricted to having little of the other, depending on how much video RAM your video card has.

Low refresh rates can cause flickering (which can be compounded when under fluorescent lights, which also cause flicker), whereas high refresh rates can cause blurriness. Refresh rates are more of an issue with CRT monitors than with LCD monitors. Most people find that a refresh rate of 70 Hz or above limits flickering adequately on a CRT. LCDs are comfortable to look at with a refresh rate of 60 Hz. Specifying a high screen resolution can limit the refresh rates available (and vice-versa), as can limitations of the monitor and video card. Setting a refresh rate higher than the monitor is capable of can permanently damage the monitor.

CONFIGURE DISPLAY SETTINGS

1. Right-click the **desktop** and then click **Personalize**. The Personalization control panel appears, as shown in Figure 3-7.

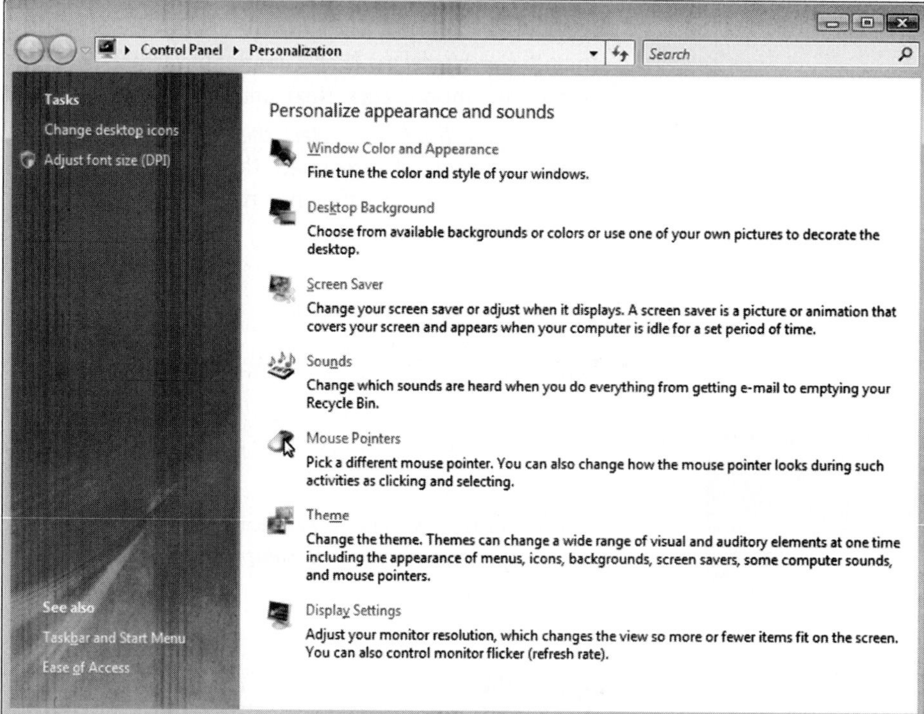

Figure 3-7
The Personalization control panel

2. Click **Display Settings**. The Display Settings dialog box appears, as shown in Figure 3-8.

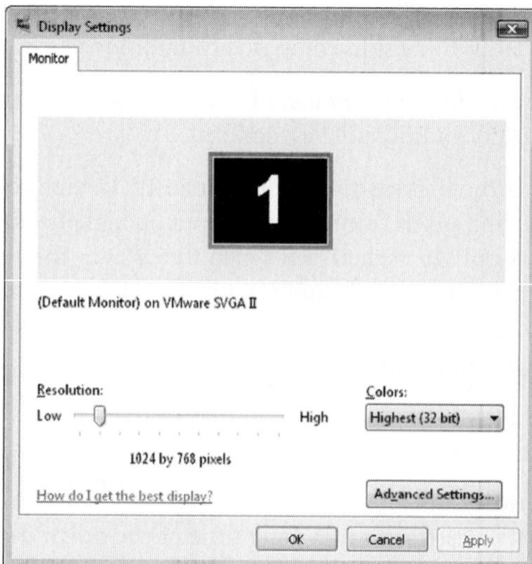

Figure 3-8
The Display Settings dialog box

3. To change the screen resolution, use the Resolution slider.
4. To change the color depth, use the Colors drop-down list.
5. To change the refresh rate, click **Advanced Settings**. The *MonitorName* and *VideoCardName* dialog box appears.

6. Click the **Monitor** tab, as shown in Figure 3-9.

Figure 3-9

The Monitor tab

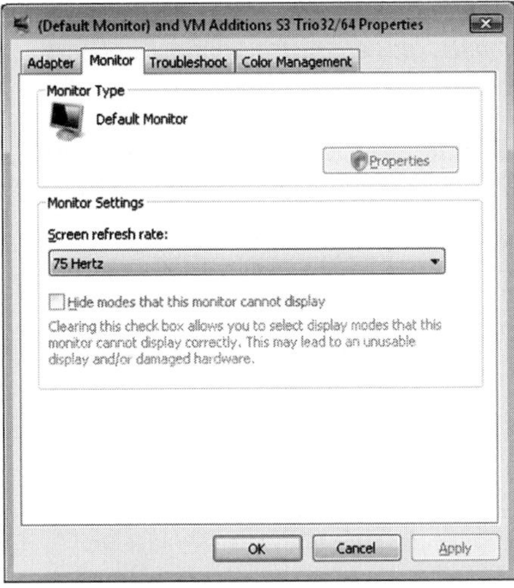

7. Select a refresh rate in the Screen refresh rate drop-down list.

CONFIGURE APPEARANCE SETTINGS

In addition to configuring display settings, you can configure colors and appearance. This includes applying or creating themes (which are collections of colors and settings).

OPEN the Personalization control panel.

1. Click **Window Color and Appearance**. The Appearance Settings dialog box appears, as shown in Figure 3-10.

Figure 3-10

The Appearance Settings dialog box

2. To select an existing color scheme, select one in the Color scheme standard list box.
3. To define your own color scheme, click **Advanced** in the Appearance Settings dialog box.
4. To change the effects settings, click **Effects** in the Appearance Settings dialog box. The Effects dialog box appears. Configure the effects as desired.

RECEIVE RECOMMENDATIONS ON EASE OF ACCESS SETTINGS

If you have a user who is visually impaired, you can adjust the appearance to attempt to make the display easier to see. To make this easier, Windows Vista provides a wizard that will make recommendations for settings once you give it answers to questions about ease of access. The questions and recommendations help to mitigate visual and other types of impairments.

OPEN Control Panel.

1. Click **Let Windows suggest settings** under Ease of Access. The *Get recommendations to make your computer easier to use* window appears, as shown in Figure 3-11.

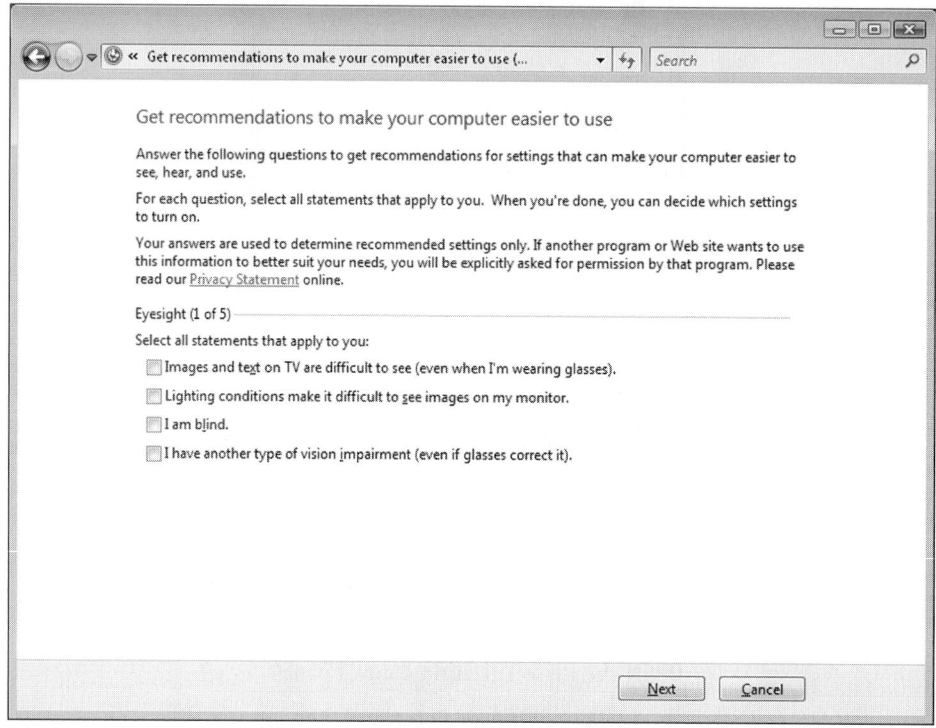

Figure 3-11

Windows Vista will provide ease of access recommendations based on your answers to questions.

2. Answer the questions and follow the onscreen prompts to receive a recommendation. Figure 3-12 shows sample recommendations.

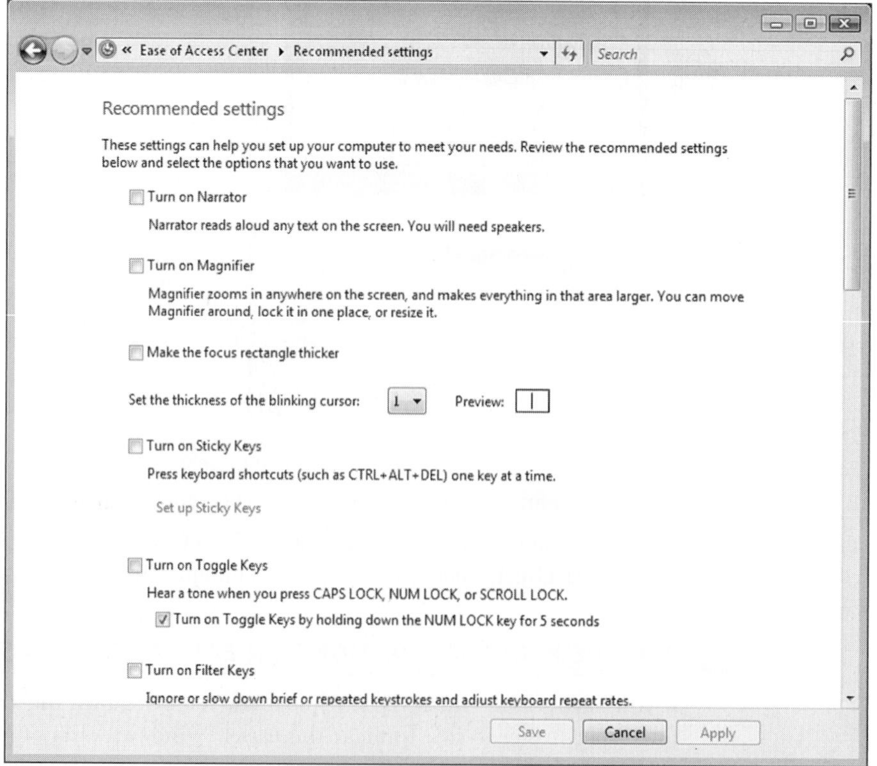

Figure 3-12

Sample ease of access recommendations

Using Group Policy to Configure Display Devices

You can use Group Policy to manage settings for display devices centrally.

You can use Group Policy to manage settings for display devices centrally. Table 3-1 describes Group Policy settings for display settings, which are located in the User Configuration> Administrative Templates>Control Panel>Display folder of Group Policy Objects (GPOs).

You can find more information on Group Policy Objects and configuring Group Policy in **Lesson 4: Using Group Policy.**

Table 3-1

Display settings in Group Policy

Setting	Description
Remove Display in Control Panel Properties	Prevents users from accessing all display-related Control Panel settings. The remaining policy settings in this table apply to narrower sets of Control Panel display settings (e.g., access to themes settings). • **Enabled**: Prevents users from accessing all display-related Control Panel settings. • **Disabled**: No effect. • **Not Configured**: Same as Disabled.
Hide Appearance and Themes tab	Prevents users from accessing Control Panel display settings related to themes and color schemes. • **Enabled**: Prevents users from accessing Control Panel display settings related to themes and color schemes. • **Disabled**: No effect. • **Not Configured**: Same as Disabled.
Hide Desktop tab	Prevents users from accessing Control Panel desktop background and desktop icons settings. • **Enabled**: Prevents users from accessing Control Panel desktop background and desktop icons settings. • **Disabled**: No effect. • **Not configured**: Same as Disabled.
Hide Screen Saver tab	Prevents users from accessing Control Panel screen saver settings. • **Enabled**: Prevents users from accessing Control Panel screen saver settings. • **Disabled**: No effect. • **Not configured**: Same as Disabled.
Hide Settings tab	Prevents users from accessing Control Panel display configuration settings (screen resolution, refresh rate, and so on). • **Enabled**: Prevents users from accessing Control Panel display configuration settings. • **Disabled**: No effect. • **Not Configured**: Same as disabled.

(continued)

Table 3-1 (*continued*)

Setting	Description
Screen Saver	Enables desktop screen savers. • **Enabled**: No effect (screen saves can run, which is the default behavior). • **Disabled**: Prevents screen savers from running. • **Not configured**: Same as Enabled.
Screen Saver executable name	Enables you to specify the screen saver for the user's desktop. Also prevents users from using Control Panel to change the screen saver. If the Screen Saver setting is disabled (see previous row in this table), Group Policy ignores this setting and prevents screen savers from running. • **Enabled**: Enables you to specify the screen saver for the user's desktop. Also prevents users from using Control Panel to change the screen saver. If you enable this setting, key the name of the screen saver file in the *Screen Saver executable name* text box. If the screen saver file is not in the *Systemroot*\System32 directory, type the fully qualified path to the screen saver file. If the specified file is not found, the policy setting is treated as Not Configured. • **Disabled**: No effect. • **Not Configured**: Same as Disabled.
Password protect the screen saver	Determines whether screen savers used on the computer are password protected. Password protected screen savers require the user or an administrator to provide credentials to return to the desktop from a screen saver. • **Enabled**: All screen savers are password protected. • **Disabled**: Password protection cannot be set on any screen saver. • **Not Configured**: Users can choose whether to password protect each screen saver individually. If you select Enabled or Disabled, the Password protected check box is disabled, preventing users from changing the password protection setting. Password protection will not be used if the user's computer never runs a screen saver. Therefore, to ensure that password protection is used, you can enable the *Screen Saver* and *Screen Saver executable name* policy settings to enforce screen saver use.
Screen Saver timeout	Enables you to specify how much user idle time must elapse before the user's computer launches a screen saver. • **Enabled**: You can set idle time from 1 second to 86,400 seconds (24 hours). If you set the idle time to zero, the screen saver will not start. • **Disabled**: The user can set the idle time, which defaults to 15 minutes. • **Not Configured**: Same as Disabled.
Prevent changing wallpaper	Prevents users from adding a desktop background or from using Control Panel to change the existing desktop background. • **Enabled**: Prevents users from adding a desktop background or from using Control Panel to change the existing desktop background. • **Disabled**: No effect. • **Not Configured**: Same as Disabled.

Group Policy also provides policy settings for controlling user interaction with themes. These policy settings are contained in the User Configuration>Administrative Templates> Control Panel>Display>Desktop Themes folder of GPOs. Table 3-2 lists each setting and its description.

Table 3-2

Group policy desktop theme settings

Policy setting	Description
Prohibit Theme color selection	Sets the color scheme to that of the current desktop theme and prevents users from using Control Panel to change the color scheme. • **Enabled**: Sets the color scheme to that of the current desktop theme, and prevents users from changing the color scheme. • **Disabled**: No effect. • **Not Configured**: Same as Disabled.
Remove Theme option	Prevents users from accessing Control Panel desktop theme settings. • **Enabled**: Prevents users from accessing Control Panel desktop theme settings. If you enable this setting, you can specify a theme. If you do not specify a theme, the computer will use the last theme selected. • **Disabled**: No effect. • **Not Configured**: Same as Disabled.
Prevent selection of windows and buttons styles	Prevents users from accessing Control Panel buttons and fonts settings. • **Enabled**: Prevents users from accessing Control Panel buttons and fonts settings. • **Disabled**: No effect. • **Not Configured**: Same as Disabled.
Load a specific visual style file or force Windows Classic	Enables you to specify a visual style for the user's computer. Also prevents the user from using Control Panel to change the visual style. • **Enabled**: Enables you to specify a visual style for the user's computer. Also prevents the user from using Control Panel to change the visual style. If you enable this option, you can specify the visual style file for the user's computer by specifying a visual style file (paths to shares are acceptable). If you do not specify a style file and the client computer is running Windows XP or newer, the Windows classic style is used. • **Disabled**: No effect. • **Not Configured**: Same as Disabled.
Prohibit selection of font size	Prevents users from changing the size of the font used in windows and buttons. • **Enabled**: Prevents users from changing the size of the font used in windows and buttons. • **Disabled**: No effect. • **Not Configured**: Same as Disabled.

■ Troubleshooting Devices and Device Drivers

Most large-scale deployments of Windows Vista will be followed by at least some device issues.

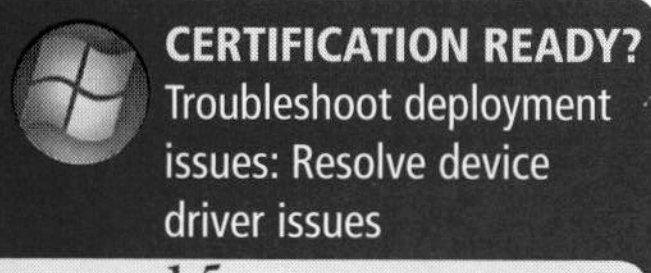

CERTIFICATION READY? Troubleshoot deployment issues: Resolve device driver issues 1.5

Ideally, you'll have worked out most of your device issues by using Windows Vista Hardware Assessment before you deploy Windows Vista on a large scale. However, post-deployment service calls for device issues are common in an enterprise, and they will continue to be so with Windows Vista.

In addition to doing so before deployment, you may want to run the Windows Vista Hardware Assessment tool after deployment of Windows Vista to detect any compatibility issues that were not resolved before deployment.

You can find more information on addressing hardware compatibility issues before deploying Windows Vista in **Lesson 1: Preparing to Deploy Windows Vista.**

Troubleshooting devices and device drivers falls into two broad categories:

- Troubleshoot devices that are not working properly
- Troubleshoot devices that are causing system instability

Because device drivers interact with the operating system on a basic level, they can cause system instability. If you have recently installed drivers, be sure to check the system for stability problems. If any are present, roll back the driver to the previous version or uninstall the device and look for a better driver.

Table 3-3 shows actions to take regarding devices and device driver issues.

Table 3-3

Common device driver–related actions and reasons for performing them

ACTION	REASON
Reinstall the driver	This may be necessary if a driver is malfunctioning because one or more of its files has been corrupted. You should also check the disk for errors if this is the case.
Upgrade to a signed driver	Signed drivers are much less likely to cause problems because they have been certified by Microsoft.
Install the latest driver from the manufacturer	The manufacturer may have fixed a driver that is faulty. Download and install the latest driver from the manufacturer's web page.
Use Windows Update	Windows Update offers drivers for many different products on a regular basis.
Roll back a driver	If a new driver is causing troubles and the previous driver worked, you can roll back the driver.
Use a system restore point	When an unsigned driver is installed, Windows Vista automatically creates a system restore point. If a new, unsigned driver is giving you trouble, restore the system to the last restore point before the driver was installed.
Configure device resource allocation	For legacy devices, you may need to configure resource allocation to ensure that there are no resource conflicts.

Using Device Manager

You can manage devices and device drivers by using Device Manager.

The place you will usually begin device troubleshooting is Device Manager. ***Device Manager*** is a tool for managing devices and device drivers.

START DEVICE MANAGER

1. Click **Start**, right-click **Computer**, and then click **Manage.** A User Account Control dialog box appears.
2. Provide administrator credentials and then click **OK.** The Computer Management console appears.
3. In the console tree, expand **System Tools** and then select **Device Manager**, as shown in Figure 3-13.

Figure 3-13

Device Manager in the Computer Management console

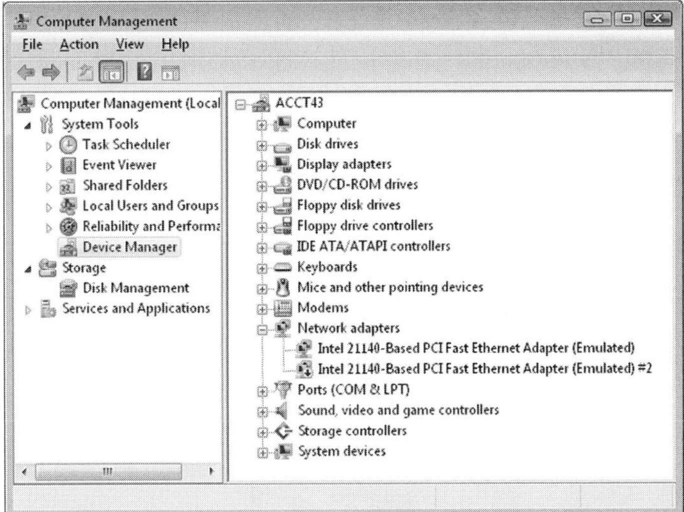

The device tree in Device Manager is by default organized according to hardware type, but several other views are available in the **View** menu:

- **Devices by Connection** Device Manager displays devices according to what they are connected to on your computer. This view is useful if, for example, you want to know what devices are attached to the PCI bus.
- **Resources by Type** Devices are displayed according to resource allocation. The types of resources are direct memory access (DMA) channels, input/output ports (I/O ports), interrupt request (IRQ), and memory addresses.
- **Resources by Connection** Allocated resources are displayed according to how they are connected within the computer.
- **Show Hidden Devices** Displays non–Plug and Play devices that aren't normally displayed, as well as devices that are installed but are not currently attached to the computer.

Device Manager will mark devices with one of four icons if there is an issue with the device:

- **Black exclamation mark** Indicates that there is a problem with the device.
- **Black Down Arrow** Indicates that the device is disabled.
- **Red X** Indicates that the device is missing.
- **Blue I** Indicates that at least one of the device's resources was allocated manually. This does not in and of itself mean that there is a problem. However, if you have a device that is not working properly and this icon is present, there is a good chance that the problem is with resource allocation.

Device Manager gives you access to the Property dialog boxes for any device on your system. From the *DeviceName* Properties dialog box, you can complete the following common device troubleshooting tasks:

- Update the driver
- Roll back the driver
- Disable the device
- Uninstall the device
- Configure the device resources

UPDATE A DEVICE DRIVER

1. Click Start. Right-click Computer and then click Manage. A User Account Control dialog box appears.
2. Provide administrator credentials and then click **OK**. The Computer Management console appears.
3. In the console tree, expand System Tools and then select Device Manager.
4. In the Details pane, right-click the device you want to update the driver for and click **Properties**. The *DeviceName* Properties dialog box appears, as shown in Figure 3-14.

Figure 3-14

Properties dialog box

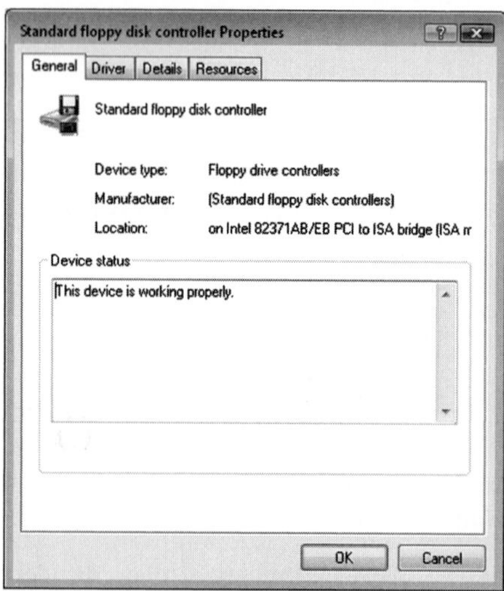

5. In the *DeviceName* Properties dialog box, click the **Driver** tab, as shown in Figure 3-15.

Figure 3-15

Driver tab of a properties dialog box

6. Click **Update Driver.** The Update Driver Software-*DeviceName* Wizard appears. Follow the onscreen prompts to update the driver.

CONFIGURE DEVICE RESOURCE ALLOCATION

OPEN the properties dialog box for the device for which you want to configure resource allocation.

1. In the *DeviceName* Properties dialog box, click the **Resources** tab.
2. Clear the **Use automatic settings** check box if it is present (not all devices have this check box).
3. In the **Resource settings** list box, select the resource you want to configure and then click **Change Setting.** The *ResourceName* dialog box appears.
4. Configure the resource as desired.

DISABLE A DEVICE

OPEN the properties dialog box for the device you want to disable.

1. In the *DeviceName* Properties dialog box, click the **Driver** tab.
2. Click **Disable.** The *DeviceName* warning box appears. Click **Yes.**

UNINSTALL A DEVICE

OPEN the properties dialog box for the device you want to uninstall.

1. In the *DeviceName* Properties dialog box for the device, click the **Driver** tab.
2. Click **Uninstall.** The Confirm Device Uninstall warning box appears. Click **OK.**

Understanding and Configuring Device Installation Restrictions

THE BOTTOM LINE Device installation restrictions enable you to restrict what devices users are allowed to install.

CERTIFICATION READY?
Troubleshoot deployment issues: Group policy vs. local policy for user devices
1.5

New in Windows Vista is the ability through Group Policy to restrict the installation of devices. These restrictions are collectively called ***device installation restrictions***. You can configure Group Policy to prevent users from installing devices except those explicitly allowed (a whitelist), or to allow users to install all devices except those explicitly disallowed (a blacklist). Some additional options are covered in Table 3-4.

Restricting device installation will prevent users from installing devices; it will not prevent users from using already installed devices. Therefore, if you want to control device use through device installation restrictions, you should do so before you roll out Windows Vista to client computers so that users don't have a chance to install unwanted devices.

TAKE NOTE*

In addition to preventing users from installing new device drivers, device installation restrictions also prevent users from upgrading already installed device drivers.

One of the primary reasons that you might want to block device installation is to strengthen security. For example, it is very easy for a user to copy sensitive data to a USB drive and leave the premises with it undetected. To prevent this, you can use device installation restrictions to prevent computers from installing device drivers for USB drives.

Another reason to use device installation restrictions is to limit installation of devices that are not work related. For example, you could prevent users from installing video game controllers.

When you specify devices in either a blacklist or whitelist, you can specify specific devices or classes of devices. This enables you, for example, to restrict installation of all USB drives or a specific model of USB drives.

You specify devices in blacklists or whitelists in device installation restrictions by using two types of identification. The first is the ***hardware ID***, which identifies specific devices. Devices often have more than one hardware ID: the first listed is the most specific, and the rest are increasingly more general.

The second type of identification you can use to identify devices in device installation restriction policies is the device class GUID (Globally Unique Identifier). ***Device class GUIDs*** specify entire classes of devices (e.g., all optical drives).

Before you can configure device installation restriction polices, you need to know the hardware IDs and device class GUIDs that you want to blacklist or whitelist. The easiest way to do this is to install the device in question on a test computer and then follow the next procedure.

USE DEVICE MANAGER TO OBTAIN HARDWARE IDS AND DEVICE CLASS GUIDS FOR DEVICES

OPEN Device Manager.

1. In the device tree in the Details pane, right-click the device for which you want to obtain identification and then click **Properties.** The *DeviceName* Properties dialog box appears.
2. Click the **Details** tab.
3. In the Property drop-down list, select **Hardware Ids**, as shown in Figure 3-16.

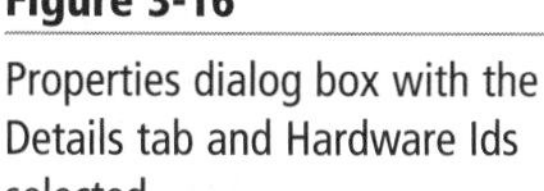

Figure 3-16

Properties dialog box with the Details tab and Hardware Ids selected

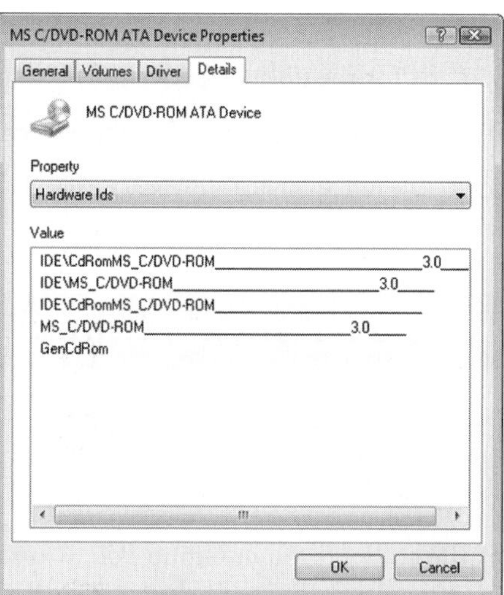

4. The hardware IDs are listed in order of specificity in the Value list box. You can right-click any of them and then click **copy** to copy the ID to the clipboard.
5. In the Property drop-down list, select **Device class guid**. The device class GUID is displayed in the Value list box. Right-click the GUID and then click copy to copy the GUID to the clipboard.

Configuring Device Installation Restrictions through Group Policy

You can use Group Policy to configure device installation restrictions for multiple computers.

Although it is users who are restricted by device installation restrictions, Group Policy restricts device installation according to computer policy, not user policy. You therefore cannot restrict device installation for specific users or groups of users, only for specific computers or groups

You can find more information on Group Policy Objects and configuring Group Policy in **Lesson 4**.

of computers (the users that use those computers face the actual restrictions). The exception to this is that you can use Group Policy to enable administrators to install restricted devices (see Table 3-4).

Device installation restriction Group Policy settings reside in the Computer Configuration> Administrative Templates>System>Device Installation>Device Installation Restrictions folder of GPOs. Table 3-4 describes each policy setting.

Table 3-4

Group policy display settings

POLICY SETTING	DESCRIPTION
Allow administrators to override Device Installation Restriction policies	Enables administrators to install or update device drivers regardless of any device installation restrictions in other policy settings. • **Enabled**: Enables administrators to install or update device drivers regardless of device installation restrictions. • **Disabled**: Administrators are subject to device installation restrictions. • **Not Configured**: Same as Disabled.
Allow installation of devices using drivers that match these device setup classes	Enables users to install devices that are part of any device class GUID in a list of device class GUIDs that you provide. Use this policy setting in conjunction with the Prevent installation of devices not described by other policy settings policy setting described later in this table. When you enable that policy setting, you use this policy setting to create a whitelist of allowed device classes. Any policy setting that prevents users from installing devices takes precedence over this policy setting. • **Enabled**: Enables users to install devices that are part of any device class GUID in a list of device lass GUIDs that you provide. If you enable this policy setting, specify the device class GUIDs of the device classes you want to enable users to install. • **Disabled**: Policy setting has no effect. • **Not Configured**: Same as disabled.
Prevent installation of devices using drivers that match these device setup classes	Prevents users from installing devices that are part of a device class GUID if that device class GUID is in a list that you provide. This policy setting takes precedence over any device restriction policy settings that enable users to install devices. • **Enabled**: Prevents users from installing devices that are part of a device class GUID if that device class GUID is in a list that you provide. If you enable this setting, specify the list of device class GUIDs that you want to blacklist. • **Disabled**: Policy setting has no effect. • **Not Configured**: Same as Disabled.
Display a custom message when installation is prevented by policy (balloon text)	Enables you to specify a message that the computer displays when a device installation restriction policy prevents the user from installing a device. • **Enabled**: Enables you to specify a message that the computer displays when a device installation restriction policy prevents the user from installing a device. If you enable this policy setting, key the message you want users to see in the *Detail text* text box (maximum length of 128 characters). • **Disabled**: The computer displays a default message when a device installation restriction policy prevents the user from installing a device. • **Not Configured**: Same as Disabled.

(continued)

Table 3-4 (*continued*)

Policy Setting	Description
Display a custom message when installation is prevented by policy (balloon title)	Enables you to provide a title for the message described in the previous policy setting. • **Enabled**: Enables you to provide a title for the message described in the previous policy setting. If you enable this policy setting, key the title you want for the message in the *Main text* text box. • **Disabled**: A default title is used. • **Not Configured**: Same as Disabled.
Allow installation of devices that match any of these device IDs	Enables users to install devices whose hardware ID is in a list you provide. Use this policy setting in conjunction with the Prevent installation of devices not described by other policy settings policy setting described later in this table. When you enable that policy setting, you use this policy setting to create a whitelist of allowed devices. Any policy setting that prevents users from installing devices takes precedence over this policy setting. • **Enabled**: Enables users to install devices whose hardware ID is in a list you specify. If you enable this policy setting, specify the GUIDs of the devices that you want to enable users to install. • **Disabled**: No effect. • **Not Configured**: Same as Disabled.
Prevent installation of devices that match any of these device IDs	Prevents users from installing devices whose hardware IDs are in a list you provide. You use this setting to create a blacklist of restricted devices. This policy setting takes precedence over any device restriction policy settings that enable users to install devices. • **Enabled**: Prevents users from installing devices whose hardware IDs are in a list you provide. If you enable this setting, specify the list of hardware IDs that you want to blacklist. • **Disabled**: No effect. • **Not Configured**: Same as Disabled. This policy setting takes precedence over any other policy settings that enable users to install devices.
Prevent installation of removable devices	Prevents users from installing removable devices. This policy setting takes precedence over any device restriction policy settings that enable users to install devices. • **Enabled**: Prevents users from installing removable devices. • **Disabled**: No effect. • **Not Configured**: Same as Disabled.
Prevent installation of devices not described by other policy settings	Prevents users from installing all devices that other policy settings do not explicitly allow. Use this policy setting in conjunction with the Allow installation of devices using drivers that match these device setup classes and Allow installation of devices that match any of these device IDs policy settings. • **Enabled**: Prevents users from installing all devices that other policy settings do not explicitly allow. • **Disabled**: No effect. • **Not Configured**: Same as Disabled

USE BLACKLISTS TO RESTRICT DEVICE INSTALLATION

You can restrict device installation using blacklists, which enable users to install all devices except those listed in the blacklists.

1. Click **Start**. In the **Start Search** text box, key **gpmc.msc** and then press **Ctrl + Shift + Enter**. A User Account Control dialog box appears.
2. Provide administrator credentials and then click **OK**. The Group Policy Management Console appears.
3. In the console tree, expand **Forest: *ForestName*>Domains>*DomainName*> Group Policy Objects**.
4. Right-click the Group Policy object for which you want to configure device installation restrictions and then click **Edit**. The Group Policy Object Editor opens with the selected GPO loaded.
5. In the console tree, expand **Computer Configuration>Administrative Templates> System>Device Installation>Device Installation Restrictions**.
6. In the details pane, right-click **Prevent installation of devices using drivers that match these device setup classes** and then click **Properties**. The *Prevent installation of devices using drivers that match these device setup classes Properties* dialog box appears, as shown in Figure 3-17.

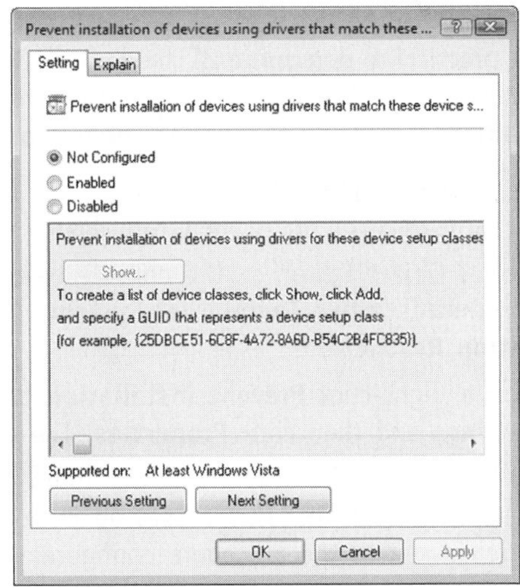

Figure 3-17

The *Prevent installation of devices using drivers that match these device setup classes Properties* dialog box enables you to specify classes of devices that users are prevented from installing.

TAKE NOTE*

The easiest way to complete step 11 is to copy the GUID to the clipboard from Device Manager.

7. Click **Enabled**.
8. Click **Show**. The Show Contents dialog box appears.
9. Click **Add**. The Add Item dialog box appears.
10. Key or paste the device class GUID in the **Enter the item to be added** text box for the device class that you want to blacklist.
11. Click **OK**. The device class GUID is added to the list box in the Show Contents dialog box, as shown in Figure 3-18.

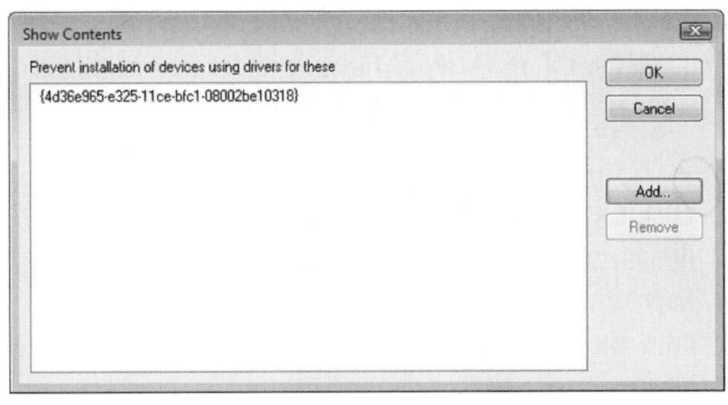

Figure 3-18

The Show Contents dialog box with a device class GUID added

12. Repeat steps 10–11 for each device class that you want to add to the blacklist.
13. Click **OK** in the Show Contents dialog box. Click **OK** in the *Prevent installation of devices using drivers that match these device setup classes Properties* dialog box.
14. In the Group Policy Object Editor, in the Details pane, right-click **Prevent installation of devices that match any of the device IDs** and then click **Properties**. The *Prevent installation of devices that match any of the device IDs Properties* dialog box appears.
15. Click **Enabled.**
16. Click **Show**. The Show Contents dialog box appears.
17. Click **Add**. The Add Item dialog box appears.
18. In the **Enter the item to be added** text box, key or paste the hardware ID of the device you want to blacklist.
19. Repeat steps 17 and 18 for all the devices that you want to blacklist.
20. Click **OK** in the Show Contents dialog box. Click **OK** in the *Prevent installation of devices that match any of the device IDs* dialog box.

USE WHITELISTS TO RESTRICT DEVICE INSTALLATION

You can use whitelists to restrict device installation, which allow users to install only devices specified in those whitelists. Restricting devices this way can be burdensome for technical support because it is not practical to determine all the devices that an enterprise is going to need to install. You should therefore restrict use of blacklists most of the time, and only use whitelists in small environments that you need to lock down, for example, kiosk computers or computers accessible by many users in a reception area.

OPEN the GPO that you want to configure in the Group Policy Object Editor.

1. In the Group Policy Object Editor, in the console tree, expand **Computer Configuration>Administrative Templates>System>Device Installation>Device Installation Restrictions**.
2. In the Details pane, right-click **Prevent installation of devices not described by other policy settings** and then click **Properties**. The *Prevent installation of devices not described by other policy settings Properties* dialog box appears.
3. Click **Enabled** and then click **OK**. This causes all device installation to be blocked by default; the remainder of the procedure configures exceptions to this behavior.
4. In the Details pane of the Group Policy Object Editor, right-click **Allow installation of devices using drivers for these device classes** and then click **Properties**. The *Allow installation of devices using drivers for these device classes Properties* dialog box appears.
5. Click **Show**. The Show Contents dialog box appears.
6. Click **Add**. The Add Item dialog box appears.
7. Key or paste the device class GUID in the **Enter the item to be added** text box for the device class that you want to whitelist.

TAKE NOTE*

The easiest way to complete step 7 is to copy the GUID to the clipboard from Device Manager. See the **Using Device Manager to Obtain Hardware IDs and Device Class GUIDS for Devices** procedure earlier in this lesson.

8. Click **OK**. The device class GUID is added to the list box in the Show Contents dialog box.
9. Repeat steps 6–8 for each device class that you want to whitelist.
10. Click **OK** in the Show Contents dialog box. Click **OK** in the *Allow installation of devices using drivers for these device classes Properties* dialog box.

11. In the Group Policy Object Editor, in the Details pane, right-click **Prevent installation of devices that match any of the device IDs** and then click **Properties.** The *Allow installation of devices that match any of the device IDs Properties* dialog box appears.
12. Click **Enabled.**
13. Click **Show.** The Show Contents dialog box appears.
14. Click **Add.** The Add Item dialog box appears.
15. In the **Enter the item to be added** text box, key or paste the hardware ID of the device you want to whitelist.
16. Repeat steps 14 and 15 for all the devices that you want to whitelist.
17. Click **OK** in the Show Contents dialog box. Click **OK** in the *Allow installation of devices that match any of these device IDs* dialog box.

Configuring Application Compatibility

THE BOTTOM LINE Some new features of Windows Vista may cause application compatibility issues, which you may be able to resolve using the Compatibility tab.

CERTIFICATION READY? Troubleshoot deployment issues: Resolve application compatibility issues 1.5

X REF You can find more information on addressing application compatibility issues before deploying Windows Vista in **Lesson 1.**

As with hardware compatibility issues, it is best to deal with application compatibility issues before you complete a large deployment of Windows Vista. However, you may face some compatibility problems despite your best efforts.

Windows Vista is built on the Windows NT code base, and as such, most applications that work on Windows NT, Windows 2000, and Windows XP will work on Windows Vista. Windows Vista does offer greater security than these operating systems, and that security, along with other changes, will affect some applications adversely.

One new technology that Windows Vista uses to increase compatibility while maintaining security is file and registry virtualization. ***File and registry virtualization*** is the redirecting of attempts by an application to write data to secure areas of the file system or registry. Instead, the data will write to non–security sensitive areas of a user's profile or the registry, as appropriate. For example, when an application attempts to write data to the Program Files folder, File and registry virtualization redirects the writing to a location in the user's profile. When the application attempts to read data from the Program Files folder, it is redirected to the alternate user profile location and only resorts to reading from Program Files if that fails. A similar scheme is used for registry writes and reads.

File and registry virtualization enables some programs that otherwise might need to run with administrator credentials to run with standard user credentials, which heightens security.

X REF File and registry virtualization is part of User Account Control and is covered in **Lesson 8: Troubleshoot Access, Authentication, and User Account Control Issues.**

Another compatibility feature of Windows Vista is compatibility layers. ***Compatibility layers*** (also sometimes called compatibility modes) are settings you can configure for individual applications on the Compatibility tab of the Properties dialog box for the application. Among other things, you can choose to emulate an older Windows operating system, as well as adjust display settings to match those of a legacy application.

As discussed in Lesson 1, you should resolve application compatibility issues as best you can before you complete a large-scale deployment of Windows Vista. It is still possible, however, that you will run into some compatibility issues after a large-scale deployment regardless of your actions before the deployment.

Troubleshooting Application Compatibility

You can use the Compatibility tab in a program file's Properties dialog box to configure compatibility settings.

The best first step in dealing with application compatibility problems is to do some research on the Internet. Check the software manufacturer's website and check for any upgrades that might help with compatibility. Also check with user groups for the application and see if others have found solutions to your problem.

For applications designed for older versions of Windows, you can use the Compatibility tab in the Properties dialog box of the application, as shown in Figure 3-19.

Figure 3-19

The Compatibility tab in an application's Properties dialog box

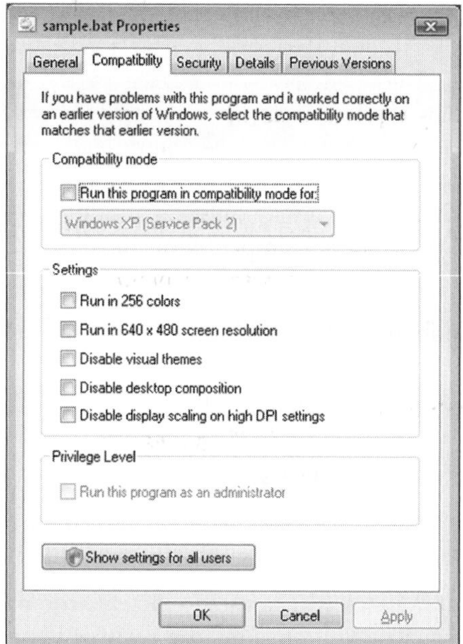

The Compatibility tab has three sections:

- Compatibility mode
- Settings
- Privilege Level

The compatibility mode section enables you to run the program under an emulation of a previous Windows operating system. You can specify the following operating system emulations:

- Microsoft Windows 95
- Microsoft Windows 98/Windows Me
- Microsoft Windows NT 4.0 (Service Pack 5)
- Microsoft Windows 2000
- Microsoft Windows XP (Service Pack 2)
- Windows Server 2003 (Service Pack 1)

If a program will not run correctly under Windows Vista, you can select to emulate whichever operating system the program was originally designed to run on, or an operating system that it was known to run on correctly.

The second section contains settings having to do with graphics compatibility:

- 256 colors
- 640×480 screen resolutions

- Disable visual themes
- Disable desktop composition
- Disable display scaling on high DPI settings

TAKE NOTE* The last two compatibility settings, Disable desktop composition and Disable display scaling on high DPI settings are new to Windows Vista.

Again, select these options to best match the environment for which the application was created.

The only option in the Does the program require administrator privileges? page is the Run this program as administrator check box. If you select the Run this program as administrator check box when you run the program, you will be prompted by a User Account Control dialog box because the program's privileges have been elevated. Additionally, if you do not log on as an administrator, you will be asked for credentials. Before selecting the Run this program as administrator check box, make sure that it is necessary by logging on as an administrator and running the program, or by right-clicking the program and selecting Run as administrator. If neither of these actions help, then there is no reason to select this option.

X REF

User Account Control is covered in detail in **Lesson 8.**

CONFIGURE THE COMPATIBILITY TAB FOR AN APPLICATION

1. Locate the program or a shortcut to the program.
2. Right-click the program (or shortcut) and then click **Properties.** The *ApplicationName* Properties dialog box appears.
3. Click the **Compatibility** tab.
4. Configure the settings as needed. If you want the settings to apply for all users, click **Show settings for all users.**

SUMMARY SKILL MATRIX

IN THIS LESSON YOU LEARNED:
There is a broad range of device-related tasks, from installing legacy devices to troubleshooting device installation restriction policies.
Device drivers enable computers to interact with devices, from hard drives to digital music players.
Windows Vista installs most new devices with little or no user interaction. You can install legacy devices manually.
How to install a legacy modem, printer, and scanner or digital camera.
How to configure display devices correctly to improve user satisfaction and productivity.
How to solicit recommendations on ease of access settings.
How to use Group Policy to centrally manage settings for display devices.
How to use Device Manager to manage devices and device drivers.
How to update and configure device drivers.
How to use device installation restrictions to restrict what devices users can install.
How to troubleshoot application compatibility by using the Compatibly tab.

■ Knowledge Assessment

Fill in the Blank

Complete the following sentences by writing the correct word or words in the blanks provided.

1. ________________ is measured in bits and defines how many colors a display device can display.
2. ________________ is the part of UAC that redirects the writing and reading of data from sensitive areas of the operating system to non-sensitive areas.
3. The software that enables your computer to communicate with, for example, your keyboard, is called a(n) ________________.
4. ________________ can be used to specify specific devices in a device installation restriction blacklist.
5. The compatibility options that you can set on the Compatibility tab are collectively referred to as ________________.
6. Traditional monitors that look like televisions sets are called ________________.
7. The frequency at which a screen is updated per second is called the ________________.
8. A(n) ________________ is an identification string that can be used in device installation restrictions to whitelist classes of devices.
9. LCD monitors look best when run in their ________________, or half of it (or half of that).
10. Using ________________, you can centrally manage display settings for large groups of users.

Multiple Choice

Select all answers that apply for the following questions.

1. Select the following statements that are true about PnP devices:
   a. All USB and IEEE 1394 Port (firewire) devices are PnP.
   b. Chances are that if you have an AGP display adapter, it is not PnP.
   c. Legacy ISA cards are usually not PnP.
   d. Serial devices are never PnP because serial ports do not support PnP.
2. A color depth of 16 bits provides access to how many colors?
   a. 16^2 colors.
   b. 2^{16} colors.
   c. 16 colors.
   d. 16,000 colors.
3. An increase in the color depth can result in a decrease in your choices for:
   a. Font size.
   b. Native resolution.
   c. Refresh rate.
   d. Screen Resolution.
4. You can prevent users from changing display settings by using Group Policy. These policies are:
   a. Applied to users only. You cannot configure these restrictions by using Group Policy on specific computers or groups of computers.
   b. Applied to computers. Users face the restrictions according to what computer they log onto.
   c. Applied to users or computers. The policy settings appear in both the User Configuration and Computer Configuration folders of GPOs.
   d. Applied according to membership in organizational units, regardless if the member is a computer or a user.

5. You want to configure Group Policy so that if users leave their desks for more than a specified amount of time, another person cannot sit down at their workstations and have access to their data. To do this through Group Policy, you should enable the following policy setting(s):
   a. The Password protect the screen saver setting.
   b. There is no way to do this through Group Policy.
   c. Password protect standby mode and Activate standby mode after settings.
   d. Password protect the screen saver, Screen Saver, and Screen Saver executable name settings.
6. Device installation restrictions use the following to prevent installation of specific devices:
   a. Device class GUIDs
   b. Hardware GUIDs
   c. Hardware IDs
   d. Device GUIDs
7. Device installation restrictions use the following to allow installation of classes of devices:
   a. Device class GUIDs
   b. Hardware GUIDs
   c. Device class IDs
   d. Class GUIDs
8. Contoso has several hundred kiosk computers on its main campus that restrict device installation by using whitelists. You are an administrator and need to be able to install smart card readers on some of the kiosk computers. Select all of the following that are solutions:
   a. Blacklist the smart card device to counteract the whitelist and install the smart card devices.
   b. Determine the hardware ID for the smartcard devices and whitelist it.
   c. Determine the Device GUID for the smartcard readers and whitelist it.
   d. Enable the Allow administrators to override Device Installation Restriction policies.
9. File and registry virtualization:
   a. Creates a virtual file system and registry for each user so that the real file system and registry are immune to attacks from viruses and other malware.
   b. Enables some programs to run without elevated privileges by removing security restrictions to the areas of the file system and registry so that reads and writes to those areas do not fail.
   c. Restricts devices with unsigned drivers from using sensitive areas of the file system and registry to lessen the probability that they will cause system instability.
   d. Enables some programs to run without elevated privileges by redirecting reads and writes from areas that only administrators are allowed to write and read from, to areas within the users profile.
10. A user complains that ever since his computer was upgraded to Windows Vista, his monitor screen is flickering. You should:
    a. Adjust the color depth to a lower level because color saturation can cause flicker.
    b. Adjust the refresh rate to a lower refresh rate if one is available.
    c. Adjust the refresh rate to a higher refresh rate if one is available.
    d. Increase the screen resolution.

Review Questions

1. Describe the four icons that Vista can tag to devices in Device Manager and what each of them indicates.
2. Explain the difference between a whitelist and a blacklist in device installation restrictions, and list the essential Group Policy settings you use to implement each.

Case Scenarios

Scenario 1: Unstable driver and software

The engineering department at Contoso uses a legacy serial port device that can simultaneously measure the temperatures of many electrical components. The device sends the data to the computer, and the temperatures are graphed real-time in a Windows 95 application. When you upgrade to Windows Vista and install the device on the laboratory computer, you use the unsigned driver that came with the hardware. The system becomes unstable when the graphing application is active. Discuss steps you could take regarding both the graphing application and the device driver to attempt to restore system stability.

Scenario 2: Using Device Installation Restrictions

Outline the broad procedure for configuring a GPO with the following device installation restriction policies:

- Users cannot install any Removable storage devices.
- Users cannot install any game controller devices.
- Administrators can install any device.

Using Group Policy

LESSON 4

OBJECTIVE DOMAIN MATRIX

Technology Skill	Objective Domain	Objective Domain Number
Understanding Group Policy	Troubleshoot policy settings	3.1
Understanding Group Policy Objects	Troubleshoot policy settings • Local vs. group	3.1
What's New in Group Policy for Windows Vista	Troubleshoot policy settings • New settings in Windows Vista	3.1
Configuring Group Policy	Troubleshoot policy settings	3.1
Creating and Understanding Group Policy Modeling and Group Policy Results Reports	Troubleshoot security configuration issues Troubleshoot policy settings	2.2 3.1
Using the Group Policy Modeling Wizard	Troubleshoot policy settings	3.1
Understanding Group Policy Modeling Reports	Troubleshoot policy settings	3.1
Using the Group Policy Results Wizard	Troubleshoot security configuration issues • Run the RSoP tool Troubleshoot policy settings	2.2 3.1
Understanding Group Policy Results Reports	Troubleshoot security configuration issues • Run the RSoP tool Troubleshoot policy settings	2.2 3.1

KEY TERMS

Active Directory
Group Policy
Group Policy objects (GPO)
Local Group Policy objects (LGPO)
organizational unit (OU)
scope
Administrators LGPO
Non-Administrators LGPO
user-specific LGPOs
last writer wins
GPO link order
Group Policy Modeling Wizard
Group Policy Modeling
Group Policy Results Wizard
Resultant Set of Policy (RSoP)

Like any enterprise environment that uses Active Directory directory service, Contoso uses Group Policy to enforce policy settings for users, computers, printers, and other Active Directory directory service objects. As a support technician, it is your job to be able to edit these Group Policy objects (GPOs) to change settings and to create new GPOs when necessary.

Currently, Contoso is doing an audit of Group Policy in preparation for rolling out some new GPOs. Your task is to use the Group Policy Results Wizard to analyze Group Policy and then use the Group Policy Modeling Wizard to test new GPOs before they are deployed to a pilot group of users and computers.

■ Understanding Group Policy

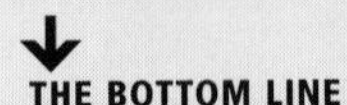

Group Policy can be used to configure settings for groups of users and computers and other Active Directory objects.

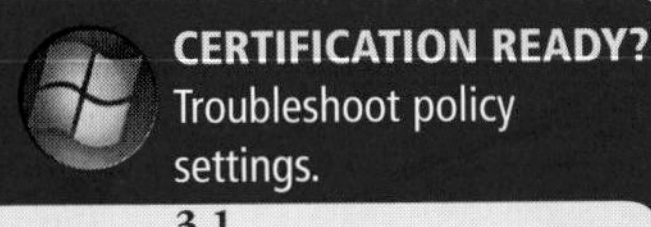

Active Directory is a database that contains a directory of the objects in your network, combined with a service that interfaces with applications to enable you to manage the objects in the network. The database contains information on the network, and the computers, printers, users, and so on, in the domain. The service makes this information available to applications (such as operating systems).

Group Policy is the collective set of policy settings for users, computers, and other entities within Active Directory as applied through Group Policy objects (Group Policy can also include policy settings local to a specific computer). ***Group Policy objects (GPO)*** are collections of settings that are applied through Active Directory. As you will see in subsequent lessons, there are Group Policy settings for a wide variety of security and user experience components of Windows Vista.

Group Policy for a particular computer being used by a particular user is determined according to Group Policy (applied through Active Directory) and local Group Policy (applied through the local computer).

Understanding Group Policy Objects

Group Policy objects are collections of Group Policy settings and are the mechanism by which administrators configure Group Policy.

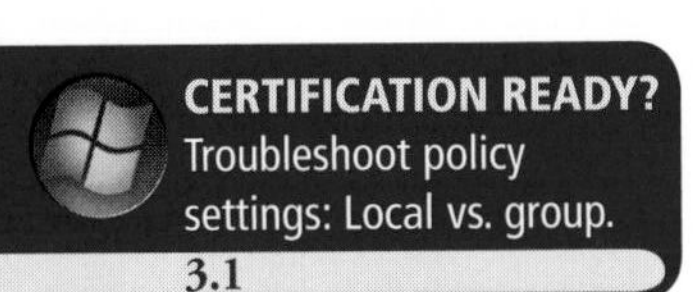

CERTIFICATION READY?
Troubleshoot policy settings: Local vs. group.
3.1

The actual policy settings that determine Group Policy are contained in GPOs. GPOs can be stored either in Active Directory or locally. Group Policy objects stored on the local computer are called ***Local Group Policy objects (LGPOs)***. Local Group Policy affects only the local machine. Group Policy for domain-attached computers is determined by a combination of Active Directory GPOs and LGPOs (unless you disable local Group Policy, which is discussed later).

The scope of a GPO (the ***scope*** is the set of objects to which the policies in the GPO apply) is determined by what the GPO is linked to in Active Directory. GPOs can link to sites, domains, and organizational units (OUs). ***Organizational units (OUs)*** are containers in Active Directory that can contain other OUs and objects such as users and computers (an enterprise, for example, might have an Accountants OU and a Marketing OU, among others). A single GPO can link to more than one object in Active Directory (e.g., it could link two different OUs).

The scope of an LGPO is determined by what type of LGPO it is. In previous versions of Windows, there is only one LGPO. Windows Vista has three types of LGPOs:

- **Administrators LGPO** Each Windows Vista installation has only one of these LGPOs. The settings in this LGPO are applied when an administrator logs on.
- **The Non-Administrators LGPO** Each Windows Vista installation has only one of these LGPOs. The settings in this LGPO are applied when a non-administrator logs on.
- **User-specific LGPOs** Each Windows Vista installation can have as many of these as there are local users. The settings in these LGPOs are applied if the user is within the scope of the particular LGPO.

X REF

In an enterprise environment, it is common to turn off local Group Policy for domain connected computers. This way, computer and user Group Policy settings can be centralized in Active Directory–stored GPOs. Turning off local Group Policy is covered in the **Turn Off Local Group Policy** procedure later in this lesson.

Group Policy settings in GPOs are applied cumulatively, so that overall group policy is a combination of all GPOs within scope. When a policy setting is defined in two or more GPOs, the policy setting of the last GPO applied is used. This method of determining which setting is applied is called ***last writer wins***. The order in which GPOs are applied is critical in understanding what policies are applied and in troubleshooting policy settings. The following is the order in which Group Policies objects are applied:

1. Local GPOs in the following order:
   a. The Administrators LGPO
   b. The Non-Administrators LGPO
   c. User-specific LGPOs
2. Active Directory GPOs in the following order:
   a. GPOs linked to sites
   b. GPOs linked to domains
   c. GPOs linked to organizational units; in the case of nested organizational units, GPOs associated with parent organizational units are applied before GPOs associated with child organizational units

A site, domain, or OU can also have multiple GPOs linked to it. Such GPOs are applied according to the ***GPO link order***, which you can adjust.

GPO application order and the scope can also be affected by the following:

- **Filtering using security groups** You can filter GPO settings by security group.
- **Windows Management Instrumentation filters (WMI filters)** WMI filters can filter the application of GPOs according to queries written in WMI Query Language (WQL), a SQL-like language. WMI filters are linked to GPOs in a similar fashion to how GPOs are linked to sites, domains, or OUs.
- **Blocking Group Policy inheritance** You can block policy inheritance for a domain or OU. Using block inheritance prevents GPOs linked to higher sites, domains, or OUs from being automatically inherited by child domains or OUs. By default, children inherit all GPOs from the parent.
- **Enforcing a GPO link** You can specify that the settings in a GPO link should take precedence over the settings of any child object by setting that link to Enforced. In tools prior to Group Policy Management console, *enforced* is known as *No override*.
- **Disabling a GPO link** By default, processing is enabled for all GPO links. You can completely block the application of a GPO for a given site, domain, or OU by disabling the link for the GPO to that domain, site, or OU.

Given the somewhat complex rules for GPO application and scope, and the fact that many environments will have numerous GPOs, determining what Group Policy will be for a particular user and computer (or other combination of Active Directory objects) can be difficult. Windows Vista, however, provides two tools within the Group Policy Management console to help: Group Policy Modeling and Group Policy Results. For more information, see the **Creating and Understanding Group Policy Modeling and Group Policy Results Reports** section later in this lesson.

MORE INFORMATION

For more information on limiting the scope of GPOs, search for it here: *technet2.microsoft.com/WindowsServer/en/library/*.

What's New in Group Policy for Windows Vista

Group Policy in Windows Vista includes more than 700 new settings, as well as an expansion of some existing settings.

CERTIFICATION READY? Troubleshoot policy settings: New settings in Windows Vista. 3.1

In previous versions of Windows, there is only one LGPO per Windows installation. This makes it difficult to administer non–domain attached computers, such as kiosk computers, because locking down Group Policy for one user meant locking down Group Policy for all users, including administrators.

With multiple LGPOs (MLGPOs), you can configure Group Policy for administrators, non-administrators, and individual users, as well as for the computer—all separately. This enables you to lock down security for non-administrators while allowing less stringent security for administrators.

Windows Vista also introduces 700-plus new Group Policy settings and has expanded other settings. These new additions and expansions are summarized in Table 4-1 (note that some Group Policy categories, listed in the first column, are represented by Group Policy settings in multiple locations in a GPOs, which are listed in the third column).

Table 4-1

Windows Vista has more than 700 new Group Policy settings, in addition to some expanded legacy Group Policy settings.

Group Policy category	Description	Location of Group Policy settings
Antivirus	Manages behavior for evaluating high-risk attachments.	User Configuration\Administrative Templates\Windows Components\Attachment Manager
Background Intelligent Transfer Service (BITS)	Configures the new BITS Neighbor Casting feature to facilitate peer-to-peer file transfer within a domain. This feature is supported in Windows Vista and Windows Server 2008.	Computer Configuration\Administrative Templates\Network\Background Intelligent Transfer Service
Client Help	Determines where users access Help systems that may include untrusted content. You can direct users to Help or to local offline Help.	• Computer Configuration\Administrative Templates\Online Assistance • User Configuration\Administrative Templates\Online Assistance

(continued)

Table 4-1 (*continued*)

Group Policy category	Description	Location of Group Policy settings
Deployed Printer Connections	Deploys a printer connection to a computer. This is useful when the computer is shared in a locked-down environment, such as a school, or when a user roams to a different location and needs to have a printer connected automatically.	• Computer Configuration\Windows Settings\Deployed Printers • User Configuration\Windows Settings\Deployed Printers • Computer Configuration\Administrative Templates\System\Device Installation
Device Installation	Allows or denies a device installation, based on the device class or ID.	Computer Configuration\Administrative Templates\System\Device Installation
Disk Failure Diagnostic	Controls the level of information displayed by the disk failure diagnostics.	• Computer Configuration\Administrative Templates\System\Troubleshooting • Computer Configuration\Administrative Templates\System\Diagnostics\Disk Diagnostic
DVD Video Burning	Configures DVD video burning.	• Computer Configuration\Administrative Templates\Windows Components\Import Video • User Configuration\Administrative Templates\Windows Components\Import Video
Enterprise Quality of Service (QoS)	Alleviates network congestion issues by enabling central management of Windows Vista network traffic. Without requiring changes to applications, you can define flexible policies to prioritize the Differentiated Services Code Point (DSCP) marking and throttle rate.	Computer Configuration\Windows Settings\Policy-based QoS
Hybrid Hard Disk	Configures the hybrid hard disk (with non-volatile cache) properties, enabling you to manage: • Use of non-volatile cache. • Startup and resume optimizations. • Solid state mode. • Power savings mode.	Computer Configuration\Administrative Templates\System\Disk NV Cache
Internet Explorer 7	Replaces and expands the current settings in the Internet Explorer Maintenance extension to enable administrators to read the current settings without affecting values.	• Computer Configuration\Administrative Templates\Windows Components\Internet Explorer • User Configuration\Administrative Templates\Windows Components\Internet Explorer
Networking: Quarantine	Manages three components: • Health Registration Authority (HRA) • Internet Authentication Service (IAS) • Network Access Protection (NAP)	Computer Configuration\Windows Settings\Security Settings\Network Access Protection

(*continued*)

Table 4-1 ***(continued)***

Group Policy category	Description	Location of Group Policy settings
Networking: Wired Wireless	Applies a generic architecture for centrally managing existing and future media types.	• Computer Configuration\Windows Settings\Security Settings\Wired Network (IEEE 802.11) Policies • Computer Configuration\Windows Settings\Security Settings\Wireless Network (IEEE 802.11) Policies
Power Management	Configures power management options in Control Panel.	• Computer Configuration\Administrative Templates\System\Power Management
Removable Storage	Enables administrators to protect corporate data by limiting the data that can be read from and written to removable storage devices. Administrators can enforce restrictions on specific computers or users without relying on third-party products or disabling the buses.	• Computer Configuration\Software\Policies\Microsoft\Windows\RemovableStorageDevices • User Configuration\Software\Policies\Microsoft\Windows\RemovableStorageDevices
Security Protection	Combines the management of both the Windows Firewall and IIPsec technologies to reduce the possibility of creating conflicting rules. Administrators can specify which applications or ports to open and whether connections to those resources must be secure.	Computer Configuration\Windows Settings\Security Settings\Windows Firewall with Advance Security
Shell Application Management	Manages access to the toolbar, taskbar, Start menu, and icon displays.	User Configuration\Administrative Templates\Start Menu and Taskbar
Shell First Experience, Logon, and Privileges	Configures the logon experience to include expanded Group Policy settings in: • Roaming User Profiles. • Redirected folders. • Logon dialog screens.	User Configuration\Administrative Templates\Windows Components\
Shell Sharing, Sync, and Roaming	Configures: • Autorun for different devices and media. • Creation and removal of partner-ships. • Synchronization schedule and behavior. • Creation and access to work-spaces.	User Configuration\Administrative Templates\Windows Components\
Shell Visuals	Configures the desktop display to include: • AERO Glass display. • New screen saver behavior. • Search and views.	User Configuration\Administrative Templates\Windows Components\

(continued)

Table 4-1 ***(continued)***

GROUP POLICY CATEGORY	DESCRIPTION	LOCATION OF GROUP POLICY SETTINGS
Tablet PC	Configures Tablet PC to include: • Tablet Ink Watson and Personalization features. • Tablet PC desktop features. • Input Panel features. • Tablet PC touch input.	• Computer Configuration\Administrative Templates\Windows Components\Input Personalization • Computer Configuration\Administrative Templates\Windows Components\Pen Training • Computer Configuration\Administrative Templates\Windows Components\TabletPC\Tablet PC Input Panel • Computer Configuration\Administrative Templates\Windows Components\TabletPC\Touch Input • User Configuration\Administrative Templates\Windows Components\Input Personalization • User Configuration\Administrative Templates\Windows Components\Pen Training • User Configuration\Administrative Templates\Windows Components\TabletPC\Tablet PC Input Panel • User Configuration\Administrative Templates\Windows Components\TabletPC\Touch Input
Terminal Services	Configures the following features to enhance the security, ease-of-use, and manageability of Terminal Services remote connections: • Allow or prevent redirection of additional supported devices to the remote computer in a Terminal Services session. • Require the use of Transport Layer Security (TLS) 1.0 or native Remote Desktop Protocol (RDP) encryption, or negotiate a security method. • Require the use of a specific encryption level (FIPS Compliant, High, Client Compatible, or Low).	• Computer Configuration\Administrative Templates\Windows Components\Terminal Services • User Configuration\Administrative Templates\Windows Components\Terminal Services
Troubleshooting and Diagnostics	Controls the diagnostic level from automatically detecting and fixing problems to indicating to the user that assisted resolution is available for: • Application issues. • Leak detection. • Resource allocation.	Computer Configuration\Administrative Templates\System\Troubleshooting and Diagnostics

(continued)

Table 4-1 (*continued*)

Group Policy Category	Description	Location of Group Policy Settings
User Account Protection	Configures the properties of user accounts to: • Determine behavior for the elevation prompt. • Elevate the user account during application installs. • Identify the least-privileged user accounts. • Virtualize file and registry write failures to per-user locations.	Computer Configuration\Windows Settings\Security Settings\Local Policies\Security Options
Windows Error Reporting	Disables Windows Feedback only for Windows or for all components. By default, Windows Feedback is turned on for all Windows components.	• Computer Configuration\Administrative Templates\Windows Components\Windows Error Reporting • User Configuration\Windows Components\Administrative Templates\Windows Error Reporting

Configuring Group Policy

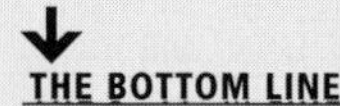

THE BOTTOM LINE

You configure Group Policy by using the Group Policy Object Editor to edit GPOs and by using the Group Policy Management console to arrange the GPOs within Active Directory.

EDIT A GPO

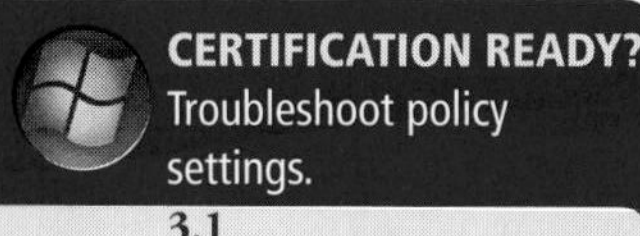

CERTIFICATION READY? Troubleshoot policy settings. 3.1

You can use the Group Policy Object Editor to edit the policy settings in a GPO.

1. In the **Start Search** text box, type **gpmc.msc** and then press **Ctrl** + **Shift** + **Enter**. A User Account Control dialog box appears.
2. Provide administrator credentials and then click **OK**. The Group Policy Management console appears.
3. In the console tree, expand **Forest:** ***Forest Name*>Domains>*Domain Name*> Group Policy Objects.**
4. Right-click the Group Policy object that you want to edit and then click **Edit.** The Group Policy Object Editor appears with the selected GPO loaded.

CREATE A GPO

OPEN the Group Policy Management console.

1. In the Group Policy Management console, in the console tree, expand **Forest:** ***ForestName*>Domains>*DomainName*.**
2. Right-click Group Policy Objects and then click **New**. The New GPO dialog box appears.

3. In the Name text box, type a name for the GPO and then click **OK**. The new GPO will appear in the console tree under the Group Policy Objects node.

LINK A GPO

GPOs can link to sites, domains, and organizational units (OUs). Linking to an Active Directory object applies the settings in the GPO to that object and its children.

OPEN the Group Policy Management console.

1. In the Group Policy Management console, in the console tree, right-click the site, domain, or OU to which you want to link a GPO and then click **Link an Existing GPO**. The Select GPO dialog box appears.
2. In the Group Policy objects list box, select the GPO that you want to link and then click **OK**. The linked GPO will appear in the console tree under the object you linked it to.

CHANGE GPO LINK ORDER

GPOs are applied according to the link order. The highest numbered link is applied last (and appears at the top of the link list), meaning that it takes precedence over lower-numbered links.

OPEN the Group Policy Management console.

1. In the Group Policy Management console, in the console tree, select the site, domain, or OU for which you want to change the GPO link order.
2. In the details pane (an example is shown in Figure 4-1), select the link that you want to move in the list and use the arrow buttons on the left to move the link up or down. In order from top to bottom, the four arrow buttons:
   1. Move a link to the top.
   2. Move a link up one position.
   3. Move a link down one position.
   4. Move a link to the bottom.

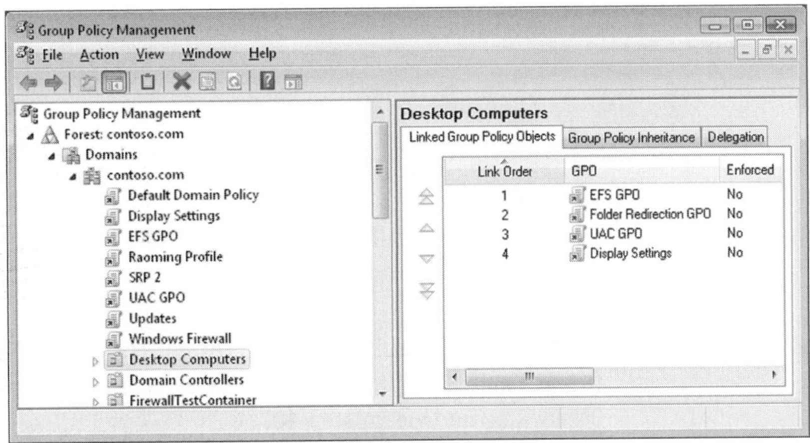

Figure 4-1

The details pane of an example OU (Desktop Computers) in the Group Policy Management console. You can change the link order of the GPOs by using the arrows on the left of the details pane.

TURN OFF LOCAL GROUP POLICY

You can turn off local Group Policy through a setting in an Active Directory GPO. You may want to do this for domain attached computers so that local policy doesn't conflict with the Group Policy settings you are configuring in Active Directory.

OPEN the GPO for which you want to turn off local Group Policy.

1. In the Group Policy Object Editor, expand **Computer Configuration>Administrative Templates>System>Group Policy**.
2. In the details pane, right-click **Turn off Local Group Policy objects processing** and then click **Properties.** The *Turn off Local Group Policy objects processing Properties* dialog box appears.
3. Select **Enabled** and then click **OK.**

EDIT LGPOs

LOG ON to the computer for which you want to edit an LGPO.

1. Click **Start.** In the Start Search text box, type **mmc** and then press **Ctrl + Shift + Enter.** A User Account Control dialog box appears.
2. Provide local administrator credentials and then click **OK.** If you do not provide local administrator credentials, you will not be able to edit all LGPOs. The Microsoft Management Console appears.
3. In the File menu, click **Add/Remove Snap-in.** The Add or Remove Snap-ins dialog box appears.
4. In the Available snap-ins list box, select **Group Policy Object Editor** and then click **Add.** The Select Group Policy Object Wizard appears.
5. Click **Browse.** The Browse for a Group Policy Object dialog box appears.
6. To select the LGPO for the computer, click the **Computers** tab, ensure that **This computer** is selected, click **OK,** and then continue to step 8. To select an LGPO for a user or group, click the **Users** tab and continue to step 7.
7. In the Local Users and Groups compatible with Local Group Policy list box, select the LGPO that you want to edit and then click **OK.** An example of selecting the Non-Administrators LGPO is shown in Figure 4-2.

Figure 4-2

Selecting the Non-Administrators LGPO in the *Browse for s Group Policy Object* dialog box

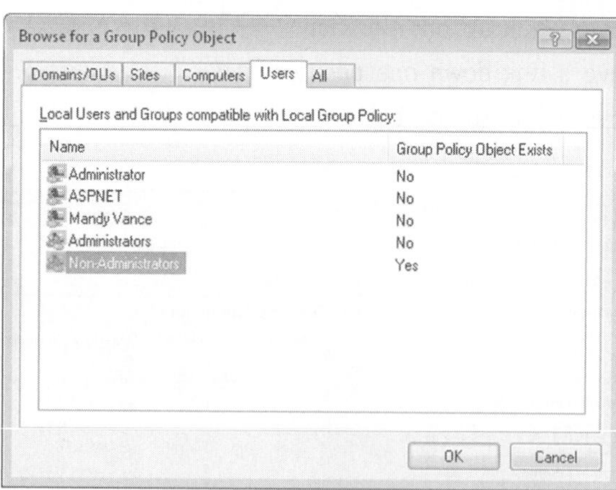

8. In the Select Group Policy Object Wizard, click **Finish.**
9. If you want to add other LGPOs to the console for editing, repeat steps 4–8. Otherwise, continue to step 10.
10. In the Add or Remove Snap-ins dialog box, click **OK.**
11. To save the console for later use, click **File** and then click **Save as.**

Gpupdate is a command-line tool used to update Group Policy settings on Active Directory objects (such as users and computers) before the normal update process takes place. This can be useful if you want to immediately apply Group Policy changes to a computer or user for testing or other purposes.

The syntax for `gpupdate` is as follows:

```
gpupdate [/target:{computer|user}] [/force]
[/wait:value] [/logoff] [/boot]
```

Table 4-2 describes the gpupdate parameters.

Table 4-2

Gpupdate parameters

PARAMETER	DESCRIPTION
/target:{*computer*|*user*}	Processes only the *computer* settings or the current *user* settings. By default, both the computer settings and the user settings are processed.
/force	Ignores all processing optimizations and reapplies all settings.
/wait:*value*	Number of seconds that policy processing waits to finish. The default is 600 seconds. **0** means no wait and **−1** means wait indefinitely.
/logoff	Logs off after the refresh has completed. This is required for those Group Policy client-side extensions that do not process on a background refresh cycle but that do process when the user logs on, such as user Software Installation and Folder Redirection. This option has no effect if no extensions are called that require the user to log off.
/boot	Restarts the computer after the refresh has completed. This is required for those Group Policy client-side extensions that do not process on a background refresh cycle but that do process when the computer starts up, such as computer Software Installation. This option has no effect if no extensions are called that require the computer to be restarted.
/?	Displays help at the command prompt.

USE GPUPDATE TO REAPPLY ALL SETTINGS

You can force a Group Policy update earlier than it would normally occur by using gpupdate.

1. Click **Start.** In the Start Search text box, type **cmd** and then press **Enter.** A command prompt window appears.
2. At the command prompt, type **gpupdate /force** and then press **Enter.** Group Policy will update, and if the update is successful, the following text will be output to the command prompt window:

```
C:\Users\garretv>gpupdate /force

Updating Policy...

User Policy update has completed successfully.

Computer Policy update has completed successfully.
```

■ Creating and Understanding Group Policy Modeling and Group Policy Results Reports

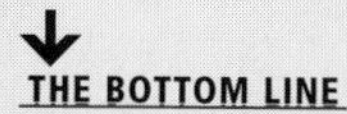

THE BOTTOM LINE

Group Policy Modeling and Group Policy Results reports enable you to model Group Policy through simulation and determine actual Group Policy. These are essential tools in both testing Group Policy settings before rolling them out and in troubleshooting Group Policy issues.

CERTIFICATION READY?
Troubleshoot policy settings.
Troubleshoot security configuration issues.
3.1, 2.2

Because of the flexibility and scope of Group Policy, assigning policy settings to users and groups can become very complex. The result is that it can be very difficult to manually investigate the relevant GPOs to determine what policies apply to a particular user or group.

Microsoft provides two tools within the Group Policy Management console to solve this problem: Group Policy Modeling and Group Policy Results.

Using the Group Policy Modeling Wizard

The Group Policy Modeling Wizard enables you to model Group Policy before rolling it out to either a production environment or a test environment.

Group Policy Modeling simulates and reports on what Group Policy will be for selected configurations of users, computers, containers, security groups, and Windows Management Instrumentation (WMI) filters. When making a change to Group Policy that is even a little bit complex or critical, it is a good idea to use Group Policy Modeling to make sure that the policy settings will be implemented correctly. Another reason to use Group Policy Modeling is to inspect what a particular user's or computer's policy settings will be if you move that user or computer into a different security group or container.

The settings you configure when modeling a Group Policy are collectively called a query.

USE THE GROUP POLICY MODELING WIZARD

1. Click **Start**.
2. In the **Start Search** text box, type **gpmc.msc** and then press **Ctrl + Shift + Enter** to run the Group Policy Management console as an administrator. A User Account Control dialog box appears.
3. Provide administrator credentials and then click **OK**. The Group Policy Management console appears.
4. In the console tree, expand **Forest: *ForestName***.
5. Right-click **Group Policy Modeling** and then click **Group Policy Modeling Wizard**. The Group Policy Modeling Wizard appears.
6. Click **Next**. The Domain Controller Selection page appears.
7. Select the domain for which you want to model Group Policy in the **Show domain controllers in this domain** drop-down list.
8. Select one of the following:

   Any available domain controller running Windows Server 2003 or later. Select this option if you do not know which domain controller within the domain will be used to model Group Policy.

   This domain controller. Select this option if you want to specify the domain controller that will be used to model Group Policy. If you select this option, select the domain controller that you want to use, as Figure 4-3 shows.

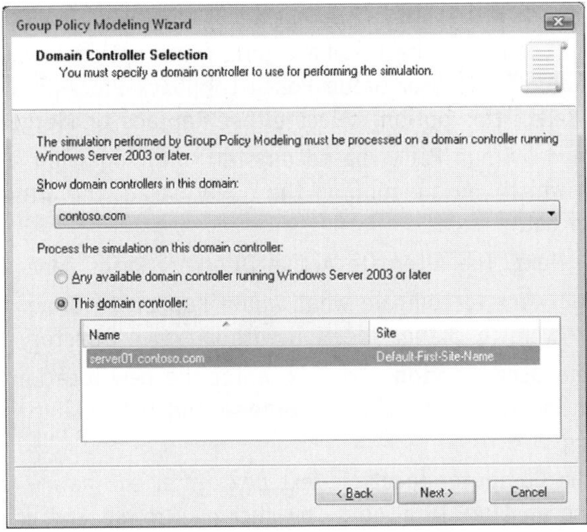

Figure 4-3

Selecting a domain controller in the Group Policy Modeling Wizard

9. Click **Next.** The User and Computer Selection page appears.
10. In the User information section, select one of the following:

    Container. Select this option of you want to model policy for all users contained within a container. Either type the name of the container manually using Light Directory Access Protocol (LDAP) syntax or click **Browse** to select a container in the Choose Container dialog box, as Figure 4-4 shows.

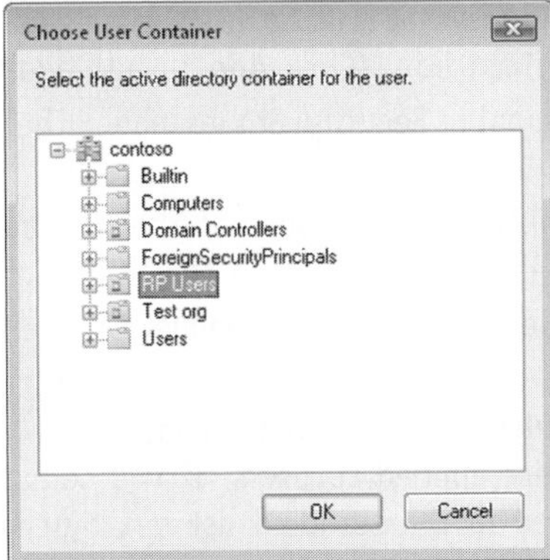

Figure 4-4

Selecting a container in the Choose User Container dialog box

    User. Select this option if you want to model policy for a particular user. Either type the name of the container manually using LDAP syntax or click **Browse** to select the user by using the Select User dialog box.

11. In the Computer information section, select one of the following:

    Container. Select this option if you want to model policy for all computers contained within a container. Either type the container manually using LDAP syntax or click **Browse** to select the container in Choose Computer Container dialog box.

    User. Select this option if you want to model policy for a particular user. Either type the container manually using LDAP syntax or click **Browse** to select the computer by using the Select User dialog box.

12. Click **Next.** The Advanced Simulation Options page appears.
13. Under Simulate policy implementation for the following, configure the following:

    Slow network connection (for example, a dial-up connection). Select this check box if you want to simulate a slow Internet connection. You might do this, for example, if the computer in question is a laptop that often accesses the domain from slow Internet connections when its user is traveling. Slow connections can limit the application of policies.

Loopback processing. This option is only available if you are modeling a user and a computer. The Loopback processing option lets you simulate the effect of configuring the User Group Policy Loopback Processing Mode policy for a GPO. If you select this option, select either **Replace** or **Merge.**

14. To model Group Policy based on startup or logon on a subnet other than the one from which you are running the query, select the alternate site in the **Site** drop-down list.
15. Click **Next.** The Alternate Active Directory Paths page appears.
16. If you want to compare what would happen to Group Policy if the user or computer were to change location within Active Directory, then do the following:

    In the **User location** text box, enter the new location for the user by typing the LDAP location or by clicking **Browse** and then using the Choose User Container dialog box.

    In the **Computer location** text box, enter the new location for the computer by typing an LDAP location or by clicking **Browse** and using the Choose Computer Container dialog box.
17. Click **Next.** The User Security Groups page appears.
18. The security groups to which the user belongs (or if you selected a container, the security groups that will be used for modeling purposes) are displayed in the Security groups list box. (Click **Add** to add additional security groups.)
19. Click **Next** on the User Security Groups page. The Computer Security Groups page appears.
20. The security groups to which the computer belongs (or, if you selected a container, the security groups that will be used for modeling purposes) are displayed in the Security groups list box. (Click **Add** to add additional security groups.)
21. Click **Next** on the Computer Security Groups page. The WMI Filters for Users page appears.
22. WMI filters can be linked to a GPO so that the GPO applies only to users or computers that meet the criteria specified in the filter. Select one of the following:

    All linked filters. Select this option to model Group Policy with all linked WMI filters applied to users.

    Only these filters. Select this option to model Group Policy with only the linked WMI filters that you list applied to users. If you select this option, select the filters you want applied in the standard list box by clicking **List Filters.**
23. Click **Next.** The WMI Filters for Computers page appears.
24. To configure this page, follow the instructions in step 22, but replace computers for users.
25. Click **Next.** The Summary of Selections page appears and summarizes your selections, as Figure 4-5 shows.

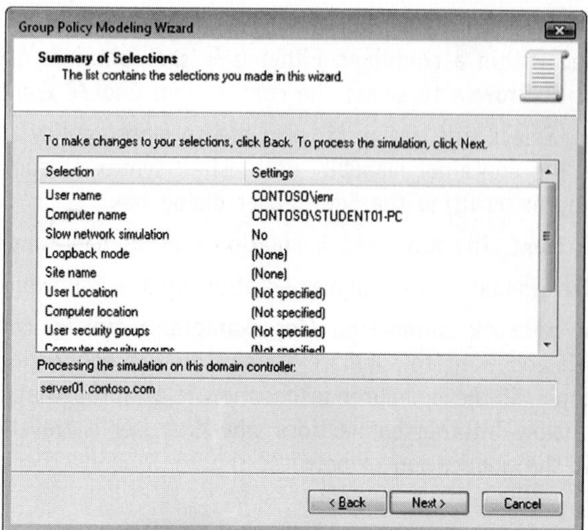

Figure 4-5

The Summary of Selections page of the Group Policy Modeling Wizard

26. Ensure that the selections are correct and then click **Next.** After that, the Completing the Group Policy Modeling Wizard page appears.
27. Click **Finish.**

Group Policy is modeled according to the selections you made. When the modeling completes, a node representing the query appears in the console tree under Group Policy Modeling. The report, which is discussed in the next section, is given in the details pane when you select the query in the console tree. The query is saved automatically and will be present the next time you open the Group Policy Management console.

Understanding Group Policy Modeling Reports

Group Policy Modeling reports contain all the information you need to understand how a particular Group Policy scheme will work.

A Group Policy Modeling report contains three tabs and can be saved as an HTML file. To save the report as an HTML file, right-click the report node in the console tree and then click Save Report.

Each tab in the report is divided into sections that you can expand or collapse using the show/hide toggles to the right of the section titles. Sections can also contain subsections. To expand or collapse all sections and subsections in a tab, use the show all/hide all toggle in the upper right corner.

The Summary Tab This tab summarizes the information gathered during the modeling process. For a query based on a user and a computer, the summary will contain two main sections: Computer Configuration Summary and User Configuration Summary. These sections will change if the modeling uses containers instead of users or computers. Figure 4-6 shows the Summary tab.

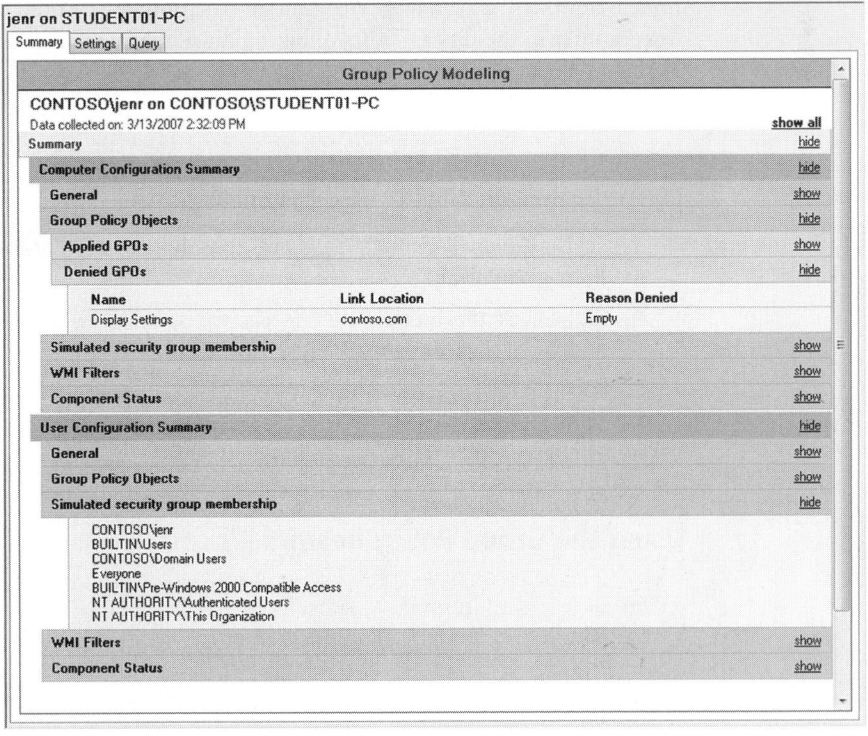

Figure 4-6

The Summary tab of a Group Policy Modeling report, with the Denied GPOs and Simulated security group membership sections expanded

The Settings Tab This tab contains the most pertinent information. It reports on individual policies (in the Policy column), displays their setting (in the Setting column), and displays from which GPO they take their settings (in the Winning GPO column). If you want to know in the given model what the setting is for a particular policy and which GPO is responsible for that setting, this is the place. Figure 4-7 shows the Settings tab.

Figure 4-7

The Settings tab of a Group Policy Modeling report, with all of the sections expanded

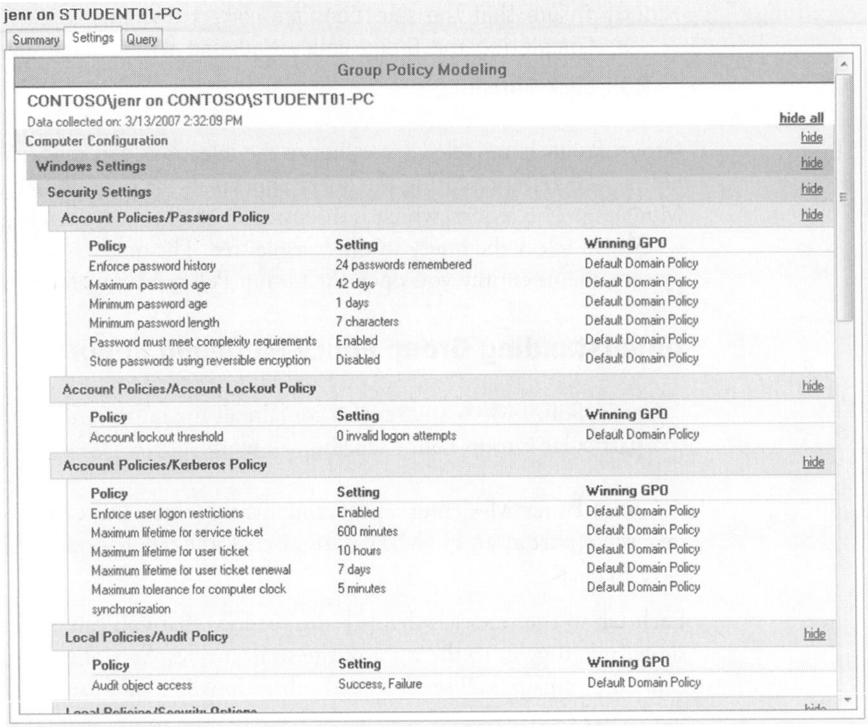

The Query Tab This tab is a list of the settings on which Group Policy was modeled. It repeats the information that is on the Summary of Selections page of the Group Policy Modeling Wizard.

The information presented in the report is well organized and easy to navigate. However, there is another useful way to view the information: as it would appear for an actual user or computer in the Group Policy Object Editor Snap-in. That view is achieved using the Resultant Set of Policy (RSoP) Snap-in.

VIEW GROUP POLICY MODELING DATA IN THE RSoP SNAP-IN

CONTINUE from or complete steps 1–4 of the previous procedure.

1. In the Group Policy Management console, expand **Forest: *ForestName*>Group Policy Modeling.**
2. Right-click the Group Policy Modeling query for which you want to view RSoP data and then click **Advanced View.** The Resultant Set of Policy Snap-in appears.

   You can browse the console tree just like you would a GPO in the Group Policy Object Editor.
3. **CLOSE** the Resultant Set of Policy console when you have finished.

Using the Group Policy Results Wizard

You can use the Group Policy Results Wizard to analyze existing Group Policy as it applies to a specific computer and user (from which you can extrapolate to other users and computers).

CERTIFICATION READY?
Troubleshoot security configuration issues: Run the RSoP tool.
2.2

Though Group Policy Modeling simulates and reports on what Group Policy will be for different configurations of users, computers, containers, security groups, and WMI filters, the ***Group Policy Results Wizard*** accesses the actual client computer to calculate what Group Policy is for a specific user on a specific computer as Group Policy is currently configured.

The settings you configure in the Group Results Wizard are collectively called a query.

USE THE GROUP POLICY RESULTS WIZARD

CONTINUE from or complete steps 1–4 of the **Use the Group Policy Modeling Wizard** procedure earlier in this lesson.

1. In the Group Policy Management console, right-click **Group Policy Results** and then click **Group Policy Results Wizard.** The Group Policy Results Wizard appears.
2. Click **Next.** The Computer Selection page appears.
3. Select one of the following:

   This computer. Select this option to use the local computer to generate Group Policy Results data.

   Another computer. Select this option to use another computer to generate the Group Policy Results data. If you select this option, enter the other computer in the **Another computer** text box.
4. Select the Do not display policy settings for the selected computer in the results (display user policy settings only) check box if you want to limit the results to user settings only.
5. Click Next. The User Selection page appears.
6. Select one of the following:

   Current User. Select this option to use the current user (which is the administrator account you used to run the Group Policy Management console) to generate Group Policy Results data.

   Select a specific user. Select this option to select a specific user (which can be the current user or a different user) to generate the Group Policy Results data. If you select this option, select the user in the Select a specific user list box.

   Do not display user policy settings in the results (display computer policy settings only). Select this option if you want to limit the results to computer settings only.
7. Click **Next.** The Summary of Selections page appears and summarizes your selections, as Figure 4-8 shows.

Figure 4-8

The Summary of Selections page for the Group Policy Results Wizard

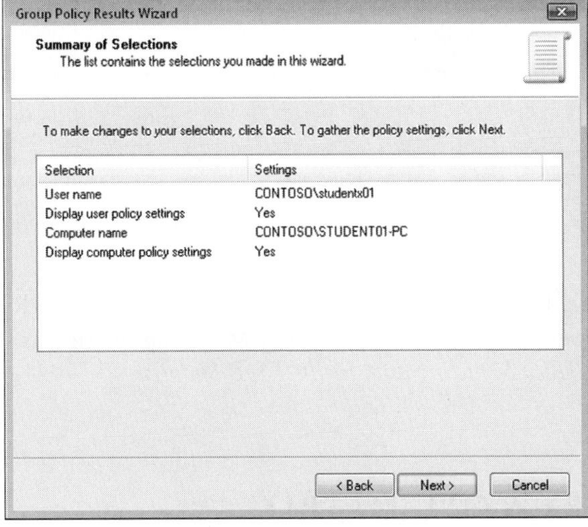

8. Ensure that the selections are correct and then click **Next.** The Completing the Group Policy Results Wizard page appears.
9. Click **Finish.**

   Group Policy Results are ascertained according to the selections you made. A node representing the query appears in the console tree under Group Policy Results. The report is given in the details pane when the query is selected in the console tree. The query is saved automatically and will be present the next time you open the Group Policy Management console.
10. **CLOSE** the Group Policy Management console when you are finished.

Understanding Group Policy Results Reports

Group Policy Results reports contain all the information you need to understand the Group Policy settings that are applied to a particular user on a particular computer.

A Group Policy Results report is similar to the Group Policy Modeling report described earlier in this lesson. It can be saved and navigated in the same way. The difference is in the third tab, which is replaced in the Group Policy Results report with the Policy Events tab.

The Policy Events tab contains all of the policy events on the computer used in the query. These events can be useful in troubleshooting policy application issues. Each event can be double-clicked to open an Event Properties dialog box for the event. Figure 4-9 shows The Policy Events tab and an Event Properties dialog box.

Figure 4-9

The Policy Events tab of a Group Policy Results report. The Properties dialog box for the highlighted event has been opened.

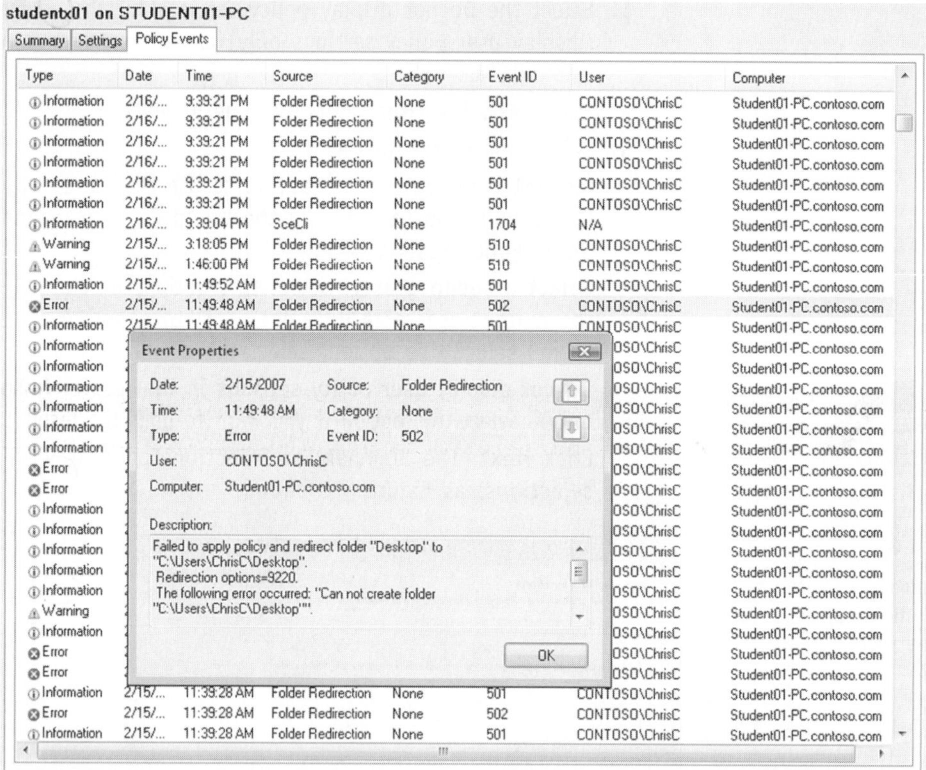

Understanding Group Policy Results reports is similar to understanding Group Policy Modeling reports, which is covered in the **Understanding Group Policy Modeling Reports** section earlier in this lesson.

You can view the Group Policy Results data for a query in the Resultant Set of Policy Snap-in in the same way you can for Group Policy Modeling queries, as we discussed in the procedure *View Group Policy Modeling data in the RSoP Snap-in.*

SUMMARY SKILL MATRIX

In this lesson you learned:
Group Policy can be used to configure settings for groups of users and computers and other Active Directory objects.
Group Policy objects are collections of Group Policy settings and are the mechanism by which administrators configure Group Policy.
Group Policy in Windows Vista includes more than 700 new settings, as well as an expansion of some existing settings.

(continued)

SUMMARY SKILL MATRIX (*continued*)

IN THIS LESSON YOU LEARNED:
You configure Group Policy by using the Group Policy Object Editor to edit GPOs and by using the Group Policy Management console to arrange the GPOs within Active Directory.
How to create, edit, and link GPOs.
How to change GPO link order.
How to turn off local Group Policy.
How to edit LGPOs.
How to use gpupdate to reapply all Group Policy settings.
Group Policy Modeling and Group Policy Results reports enable you to model Group Policy through simulation and determine actual Group Policy. These are essential tools in both testing Group Policy settings before rolling them out and in troubleshooting Group Policy issues.
The Group Policy Modeling Wizard enables you to model Group Policy before rolling it out to either a production environment or a test environment.
How to use the Group Policy Modeling Wizard.
How to view Group Policy Modeling data in the RSoP Snap-in.
How to use the Group Policy Results Wizard.

■ Knowledge Assessment

Fill in the Blank

Complete the following sentences by writing the correct word or words in the blanks provided.

1. The ________ is the object that stores local Group Policy settings for administrator users.
2. The ________ Wizard is a tool in the Group Policy Management console that enables you to determine the current setting from Group Policy applied to a specific user on a specific computer.
3. ________ combines a service with a directory of objects in your network to enable management of the objects in the network.
4. Policy Settings are grouped into ________ that can be applied by linking them to OUs, sites, and domains in Active Directory.
5. ________ is the collective set of policies applied through GPOs to administer objects such as users and computers.
6. Both Group Policy Modeling data and Group Policy Results data can be viewed as if it were a GPO being viewed in the Group Policy Object Editor by using the ________ Snap-in.
7. The ________ determines the order of application of GPOs linked to the same OU in Active Directory.
8. ________ is the name of the method which Active Directory uses to determine which of conflicting settings in different GPOs is applied.
9. A(n) ________ is the type of LGPO that enables you to create policy settings for a specific local user.
10. The ________ is a tool within the Group Policy Management console that enables you to test Group Policy schemes before they are deployed.

Multiple Choice

Select all answers that apply for the following questions.

1. Active Directory:
   a. Is partly a directory of the objects in your network.
   b. Is a service that applications can interact with to get and modify information on your network.
   c. Enables management of items in your network.
   d. All of the above.
2. Which of the following is true about the relationship between GPOs and LGPOs (select all that apply)?
   a. LGPOs take precedence over GPOs because they determine settings on the local computer.
   b. GPOs take precedence over LGPOs because application of GPOs uses the last writer wins method.
   c. Each GPO has an equivalent LGPO to determine what the local policies are.
   d. GPOs and LGPOs are both applied through Active Directory.
3. The Contoso domain has an OU called Laptop Computers. A GPO called Domain Security Policies is linked to the Contoso domain, and a GPO called Laptop Security Policies is linked to the Laptop Computers OU. Furthermore, a computer that is in the Laptop Computers OU has an Administrators LGPO. A policy setting in each of these three GPOs is defined with a different setting. Which GPO wins?
   a. The Administrators LGPO wins because LGPOs are not subject to last writer wins.
   b. The Domain Security Policies GPO wins because domain GPOs are written after OU GPOs and LGPOs.
   c. The Domain Security Policies GPO wins because it applies to the broadest set of objects.
   d. The Laptop Computers GPO wins because it is written after the other two GPOs.
4. The following tool within the Group Policy Management console simulates which group policy would be given a Group Policy query:
   a. Group Policy Modeling
   b. Group Policy Results
   c. Resultant Set of Policy
   d. Security Configuration and Analysis
5. Policy inheritance in the Contoso domain is blocked for an OU called Desktop Computers. Which of the following are true (select all that apply)?
   a. GPOs attached to OUs that are children of Desktop Computers will not be applied.
   b. LGPOs will not inherit policies from the Desktop Computer OU.
   c. GPOs attached to higher sites or OUs will not be applied to Desktop Computers and child OUs.
   d. You will not be able to link GPOs to the Desktop Computer OU.
6. Select all statements about Windows Vista Group Policy that are true:
   a. There are more than 700 new Group Policy settings in Windows Vista.
   b. The number of Group Policy settings in Windows Vista has been reduced to make setting policies easier.
   c. The Power Users LGPO has been deprecated.
   d. Windows Vista introduces multiple LGPOs.
7. To turn off Local Group policy:
   a. Delete the LGPOs in Active Directory.
   b. Enable the *Turn off Local Group Policy objects processing* policy setting in Computer Configuration>Administrative Templates>System>Group Policy.
   c. Disable the links for all LGPOs in Active Directory.
   d. Disable the *Apply local Group Policy objects at startup* policy setting in Computer Configuration>Administrative Templates>System>Group Policy.

8. The command `gpupate /target:computer /logoff:`
   a. Will update Group Policy for computer settings and will log off the user regardless of whether it is necessary to complete policy updates.
   b. Will not work because a parameter is missing: after `computer`, a computer name needs to be specified.
   c. Will update Group Policy settings for the computer settings and user settings, and will log the user off whether or not it is necessary.
   d. Will update Group Policy for computer settings and will log the user off only if it is necessary to complete policy updates.

9. Before you move a user from one container to another, you can use which tool to determine how Group Policy settings will be affected for the user?
   a. Group Policy Results Wizard
   b. Security Configuration and Analysis Snap-in
   c. Group Policy Modeling Wizard
   d. Security Template Export Wizard

10. After the user is moved in question nine, you can use which tool to determine the actual Group Policy settings for the user on a specific computer in the domain?
    a. Group Policy Results Wizard
    b. Security Configuration and Analysis Snap-in
    c. Group Policy Modeling Wizard
    d. Security Template Export Wizard

Review Questions

1. Explain the overall scheme for GPO setting precedence for conflicting settings. Include discussion on the principle of last writer wins and link order.

2. Windows Vista introduces 700-plus new Group Policy settings. Describe any three areas of new Group Policy settings.

■ Case Scenarios

Scenario 1: Updating LGPO Settings on a Kiosk Computer Upgraded from Windows XP Professional

A kiosk computer not attached to the domain has recently been upgraded from Windows XP Professional to Windows Vista. The local computer LGPO settings have been maintained from XP. The computer is difficult to administer because of restrictive local Group Policy settings. How can you configure local Group Policy so that the computer is secure but easier for administrators to administer?

Scenario 2: Creating and Linking GPOs

Contoso has decided to implement software restriction policies by using Group Policy. Create a GPO called SRPs and link it to the domain. Without defining any of the settings in the GPO, run the Group Policy Modeling Wizard by using your computer and your standard user account as parameters. Is the GPO applied or denied, and why? When you are done, delete the GPO.

Configuring Windows Internet Explorer 7 Security

OBJECTIVE DOMAIN MATRIX

Technology Skill	Objective Domain	Objective Domain Number
Understanding Internet Explorer Security	Configure and troubleshoot security for Windows Internet Explorer 7+ • Troubleshoot policy-setting issues	2.1
Understanding Security Zones	Configure and troubleshoot security for Windows Internet Explorer 7+ • Troubleshoot policy-setting issues	2.1
Understanding Internet Explorer Protected Mode	Configure and troubleshoot security for Windows Internet Explorer 7+ • Troubleshoot Protected Mode issues	2.1
Understanding ActiveX Opt-In and ActiveX Installer Services	Configure and troubleshoot security for Windows Internet Explorer 7+ • ActiveX Opt-In and ActiveX Installer Service	2.1
Understanding ActiveX Opt-In	Configure and troubleshoot security for Windows Internet Explorer 7+ • ActiveX Opt-In and ActiveX Installer Service	2.1
Understanding and Configuring the ActiveX Installer Service	Configure and troubleshoot security for Windows Internet Explorer 7+ • ActiveX Opt-In and ActiveX Installer Service	2.1
Understanding and Managing Add-Ons	Configure and troubleshoot security for Windows Internet Explorer 7+	2.1
Understanding Certificates	Configure and troubleshoot security for Windows Internet Explorer 7+ • Troubleshoot certificate issues	2.1
Understanding and Configuring the Phishing Filter	Configure and troubleshoot security for Windows Internet Explorer 7+	2.1
Resetting Internet Explorer Settings	Configure and troubleshoot security for Windows Internet Explorer 7+ • Troubleshoot policy-setting issues	2.1

(continued)

OBJECTIVE DOMAIN MATRIX (*continued*)

TECHNOLOGY SKILL	OBJECTIVE DOMAIN	OBJECTIVE DOMAIN NUMBER
Configuring Additional Group Policy Security Settings	Configure and troubleshoot security for Windows Internet Explorer 7+ • Troubleshoot policy-setting issues	2.1

KEY TERMS

security zones
Internet Explorer Protected Mode
ActiveX
ActiveX Opt-In
ActiveX controls
ActiveX Installer Service (AxIS)
approved installation site for ActiveX controls
Internet Explorer 7 (IE7)
Internet Explorer add-ons
certificates
certificate authority (CA)
Phishing Filter
Reset Internet Explorer Settings (RIES)

The Internet is a commonly used attack route for hackers, and is therefore a serious security vulnerability. With the introduction of Windows Vista and Internet Explorer 7, Contoso is reviewing all of its Internet security practices. You need to understand and make good use of the new security features, such as Internet Explorer Protected Mode and Active X Opt-in.

Understanding Internet Explorer Security

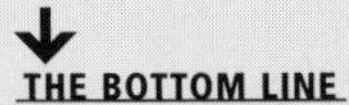

THE BOTTOM LINE

Internet Explorer 7 security has several new options, including Internet Explorer Protected Mode (available only in Windows Vista) and ActiveX Opt-in.

CERTIFICATION READY? Configure and troubleshoot security for Windows Internet Explorer 7+
2.1

Windows Internet Explorer 7 (IE7) includes new technology to help prevent the installation of unwanted software and the unauthorized transmission of data. New technology covered in this lesson includes:

- Explorer Protected Mode
- ActiveX Opt-in and ActiveX Installer Services
- The Phishing Filter
- Reset Internet Explorer Settings (RIES)

We'll also discuss the following legacy Internet Explorer security topics:

- Security Zones
- Group Policy security settings
- Certificates

MORE INFORMATION

You can also manage Internet Explorer 7 by using the Internet Explorer Administration Kit (IEAK) 7, which enables you to easily deploy Internet Explorer 7 and manage custom browser software packages. You can find more information and a download link here: *technet.microsoft.com/en-us/ie/*.

Many IE7 security settings can be configured both locally inside Internet Explorer (using the Internet Options dialog box) and through Group Policy. Settings configured in Group Policy override settings that are configured locally in Internet Explorer.

CONFIGURE INTERNET EXPLORER SECURITY SETTINGS THROUGH GROUP POLICY

CERTIFICATION READY?
Configure and troubleshoot security for Windows Internet Explorer 7+: Troubleshoot policy-setting issues
2.1

Most of the security settings covered in this lesson can be performed locally using the Internet Explorer 7 interface, and through Group Policy using a Group Policy Object (GPO). When a procedure for configuring IE7 security settings locally has a Group Policy equivalent, the Group Policy equivalent procedure follows the local procedure. This procedure explains how to access the IE7 Group Policy security settings, which is necessary before you can follow any of the procedures on configuring specific IE7 Group Policy security settings.

1. Click **Start**. In the Start Search box, key **gpmc.msc** and then press **Ctrl** + **Shift** + **Enter**. A User Account Control dialog box appears.
2. Provide administrator credentials and then click **OK**. The Group Policy Management console appears, as shown in Figure 5-1.

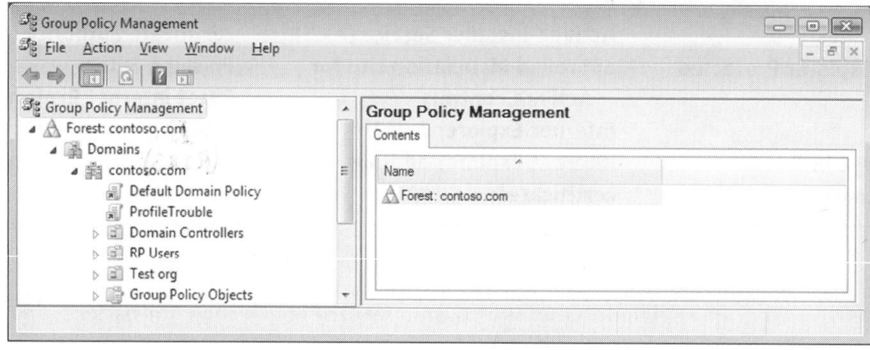
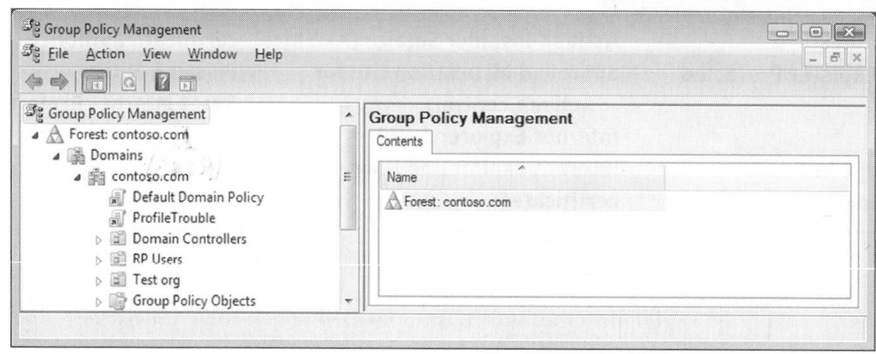

Figure 5-1
The Group Policy Management console

3. In the console tree, expand **Forest:** ***ForestName*****>Domains>*****DomainName*****>Group Policy Objects.**
4. Right-click the Group Policy object for which you want to configure Internet Explorer security settings and then click **Edit**. The Group Policy Object Editor opens with the GPO you selected loaded.
5. In the console tree, expand **Computer Configuration>Administrative Templates> Windows Components>Internet Explorer,** as shown in Figure 5-2.

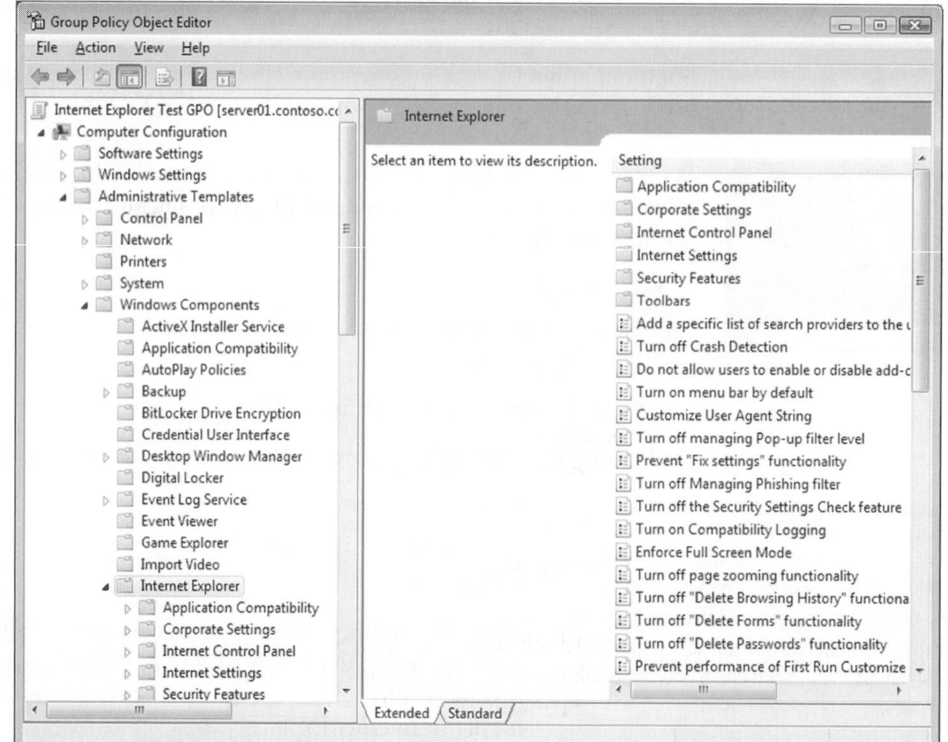

Figure 5-2
The Group Policy Object Editor console

■ Understanding Security Zones

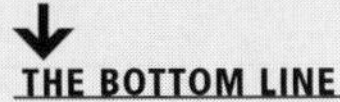
THE BOTTOM LINE

Security zones divide URL namespaces and enable you to vary security according to where the content is coming from.

CERTIFICATION READY?
Configure and troubleshoot security for Windows Internet Explorer 7+: Troubleshoot policy-setting issues
2.1

Internet Explorer divides URL namespaces into five ***security zones*** according to level of trust. URL actions are restricted according to which zone the current URL is a part. URL actions are actions that Internet Explorer can take that have been judged risky enough that they need to be able to be restricted from occurring.

The five security zones in Internet Explorer are:

- Internet
- Local Intranet
- Trusted Sites
- Restricted Sites
- Local machine

TAKE NOTE*

The Local Machine zone contains URLs that reside on the local machine. Local Machine zone security settings are not configurable through Internet Explorer, but are configurable through Group Policy. URLs within the Local Machine zone are by default treated with a high level of trust.

Zones can be configured to restrict various URL actions. You can adjust each security setting individually using the Custom level button located on the Security tab of the Internet Options dialog box, or you can apply one of five templates:

1. Low
   - Default template for the Local Machine zone
   - Minimal safeguards and warning prompts provided
   - Most content is downloaded and run without prompts
   - All active content can run
   - Appropriate for sites that you absolutely trust
2. Medium-Low
   - Default template for the Local Intranet zone
   - Appropriate for websites on your local network (intranet)
   - Most content will be run without prompts
   - Unsigned ActiveX controls will not be downloaded
   - Same as Medium level without prompts
3. Medium
   - Default template for the Trusted sites zone
   - Prompts before downloading potentially unsafe content
   - Unsigned ActiveX controls will not be downloaded
4. Medium-high
   - Default template for the Internet zone
   - Appropriate for most websites
   - Prompts before downloading potentially unsafe content
   - Unsigned ActiveX controls will not be downloaded
5. High
   - Default template for the Restricted Sites zone
   - Appropriate for websites that might contain harmful content
   - Maximum safeguards
   - Less secure features are disabled

It is not uncommon for a user to experience browser problems when the user tries to perform an action that is disallowed by the settings for the security zone.

CONFIGURE ZONE SECURITY SETTINGS LOCALLY

1. In Internet Explorer, in the **Tools** menu, click **Internet Options**. The Internet Options dialog box appears, as shown in Figure 5-3.

Figure 5-3

The Internet Options dialog box

2. Click the **Security** tab, as shown in Figure 5-4.

Figure 5-4

The Security tab of the Internet Options dialog box

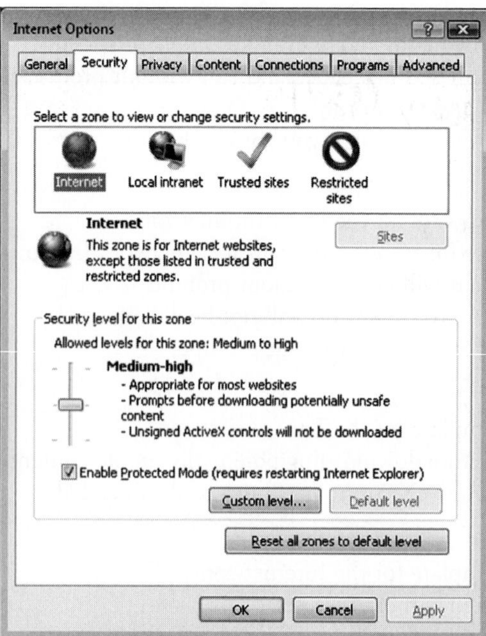

3. In the *Select a zone to view or change security settings* section, select the zone for which you want to configure security settings.
4. To change the template that Windows assigns to the zone, use the slide in the *Security level for this zone* section.

5. To customize security for the selected zone, click **Custom level**. The Settings – *ZoneName* Zone dialog box appears, as shown in Figure 5
   Do one of the following:
   - To configure custom settings, select the options as desired for each of the security settings in the Settings standard list box.
   - To restore all settings to their original configuration, click **Reset**.

Figure 5-5

The Security Settings – Restricted Sites Zone dialog box

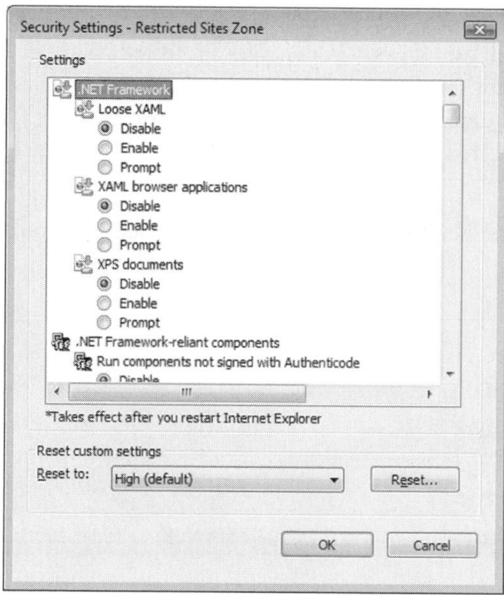

When you are finished configuring settings, click **OK** to close the Security Settings – *ZoneName* Zone dialog box.

Understanding Internet Explorer Protected Mode

THE BOTTOM LINE

Internet Explorer Protected Mode is a feature of Internet Explorer 7 available on Windows Vista. Protected Mode protects against unsolicited installation of software and modification of data.

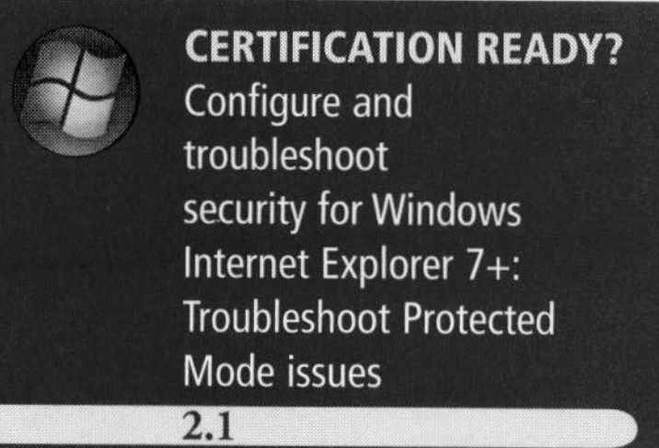

CERTIFICATION READY?
Configure and troubleshoot security for Windows Internet Explorer 7+: Troubleshoot Protected Mode issues
2.1

Internet Explorer Protected Mode heightens security by taking advantage of features new to Windows Vista, primarily User Account Control (UAC), and it is therefore not available in Windows XP or earlier. ***Internet Explorer Protected Mode*** gives Internet Explorer the privileges it needs to browse the Internet while withholding privileges needed to silently install programs or modify sensitive system data. These limited user privileges reduce the chance of malicious software being installed and then run, thus restricting malicious code from carrying out damaging actions.

Internet Explorer Protected Mode will prompt you both when web pages try to install software, and when they try to run software. You are also prompted when a program attempts to run outside of Internet Explorer or outside of Protected Mode, because your system faces increased exposure in those cases.

The status bar indicates when Internet Explorer is running in Protected Mode, as shown in Figure 5-6.

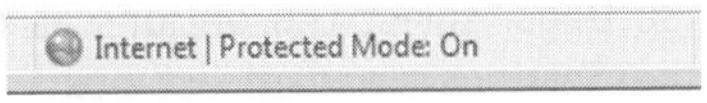

Figure 5-6

The status bar in Internet Explorer will tell you when Protected Mode is on

Internet | Protected Mode: On

Although by default Windows Vista enables Protected Mode in Internet Explorer 7 in all security zones except the Trusted Sites and Local Machine zones, users can disable Protected Mode in any zone unless the administrator configures it using Group Policy. It is a best practice to enable Protected Mode in Group Policy for all zones except the Trusted Site and Local Machine zones.

Protected Mode can be enabled separately for the following four security zones in Internet Explorer:

- Internet
- Local Intranet
- Trusted Sites
- Restricted Sites

MORE INFORMATION

You can find more detailed information about how Protected Mode works here:*msdn2.microsoft.com/en-us/library/Bb250462.aspx.*

If the administrator has not configured a Group Policy setting for a particular zone for Protected Mode, users can disable or enable Protected Mode for that zone. If a Group Policy setting is defined, users no longer have any control over the defined setting.

ENABLE OR DISABLE PROTECTED MODE LOCALLY

1. In Internet Explorer, in the **Tools** menu, click **Internet Options**. The Internet Options dialog box appears, as shown in Figure 5-3.
2. Click the **Security** tab, as shown in Figure 5-4.
3. In the *Select a zone to view or change security settings* section, select the zone for which you want to enable or disable Protected Mode.

   a. Do one of the following:
   - Clear the *Enable Protected Mode (requires restarting Internet Explorer)* check box to disable Protected Mode for the selected zone.
   - Select the *Enable Protected Mode (requires restarting Internet Explorer)* check box to enable Protected Mode for the selected zone.

   b. When you are finished, click **OK** to close the Internet Options dialog box.

CONFIGURE INTERNET EXPLORER PROTECTED MODE THROUGH GROUP POLICY

OPEN the GPO you want to edit in the Group Policy Object Editor.

1. In the Group Policy Object Editor console tree, expand **Computer Configuration>Administrative Templates>Windows Components>Internet Explorer>Internet Control Panel>Security Page**.
2. Select ***ZoneName,*** where *ZoneName* is the zone for which you want to configure Windows Protected Mode policy. For example, Figure 5-7 shows Intranet Zone selected.

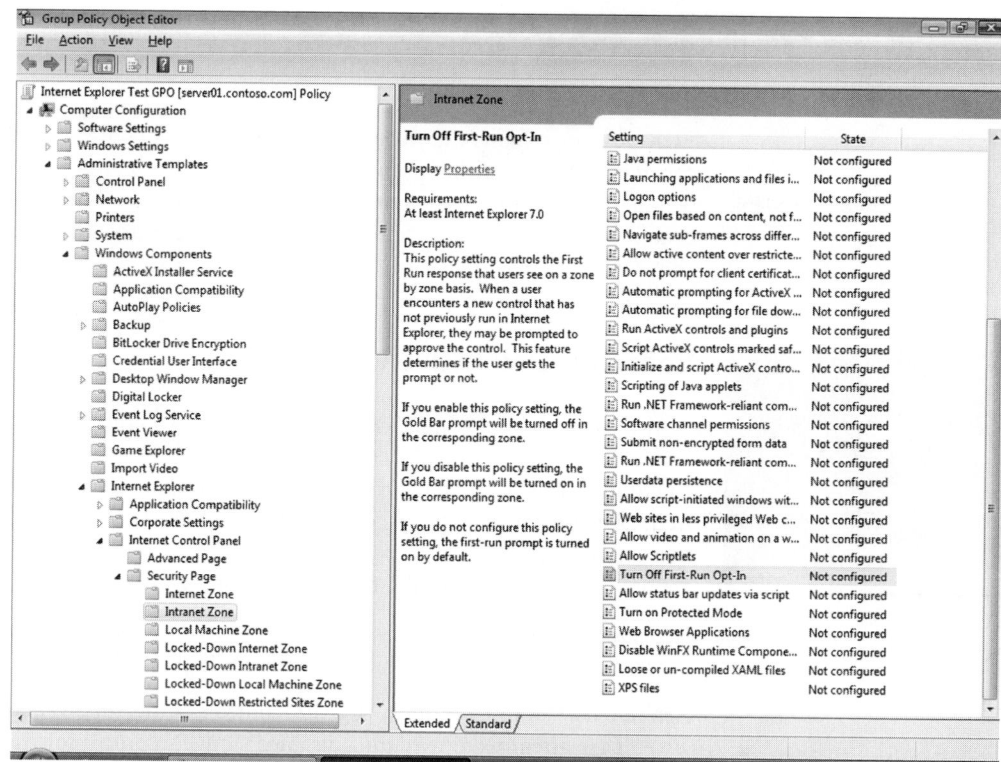

Figure 5-7

Intranet Zone selected in the Group Policy Object Editor console

3. In the details pane, right-click **Turn on Protected Mode** and then click **Properties**. The Turn on Protected Mode Properties dialog box appears, as shown in Figure 5-8.

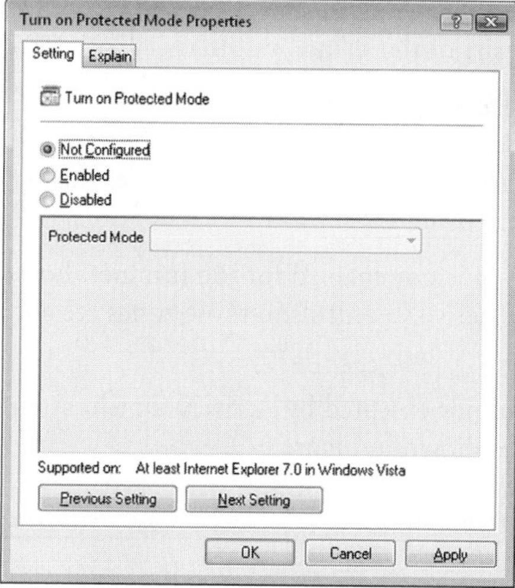

Figure 5-8

Turn on Protected Mode Properties dialog box

4. Select one of the following:

   Not Configured Select this option to enable users to turn Windows Protected Mode on or off for this zone. This is the default option in Group Policy Object Editor.

   Enabled Select this option to turn on Protected Mode for this zone and to disallow users the ability to turn it off.

   Disabled Select this option to turn off Protected Mode for this zone and to disallow users the ability to turn it on.

Understanding ActiveX Opt-In and ActiveX Installer Services

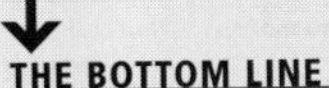

THE BOTTOM LINE

ActiveX Opt-in limits exposure to malicious ActiveX controls by disabling most ActiveX controls and by requiring permission from a user with administrator credentials before installing any of the remaining ActiveX controls. The ActiveX Installer Services enable administrators to specify a list of ActiveX controls that users can install without administrator credentials.

Understanding ActiveX Opt-In

CERTIFICATION READY? Configure and troubleshoot security for Windows Internet Explorer 7+: ActiveX Opt-In and ActiveX Installer Service
2.1

By default, ActiveX Opt-in disables most ActiveX controls.

Microsoft has used the term *ActiveX* to brand a number of technologies. For our purposes, ***ActiveX*** is the set of ActiveX controls that are linked to a web page and can be downloaded and executed by an ActiveX compliant browser, such as Internet Explorer. ***ActiveX controls*** are programs that expand the functionality of web pages.

ActiveX controls are a security vulnerability because they can interact with data on your computer. To mitigate this vulnerability, Internet Explorer 7 introduces ActiveX Opt-in.

ActiveX Opt-in disables most ActiveX controls by default. When a user is browsing and a web page attempts to execute a disabled ActiveX control for the first time, the user is prompted to either allow the control to run or not. If the user allows the control to run, then the control runs without requesting permission the next time it is encountered.

By default, ActiveX Opt-in will not disable the following ActiveX controls (meaning that they are allowed to run without user permission):

- Commonly used controls whose security Microsoft has already deemed acceptable. These controls are part of the Windows Internet Explorer 7 pre-approved list.
- Controls used in a previous version of Internet Explorer before the user upgraded to Internet Explorer 7.
- Controls that ActiveX Opt-in automatically enables during the install process when the user downloads them using IE7.

By default, ActiveX Opt-in is not enabled for the Intranet, Local Machine, and Trusted Site zones, which means that ActiveX controls in those zones are allowed to run the first time without user permission.

When an ActiveX control not excepted by ActiveX Opt-in attempts to run, you are notified in the information bar, as shown in Figure 5-9.

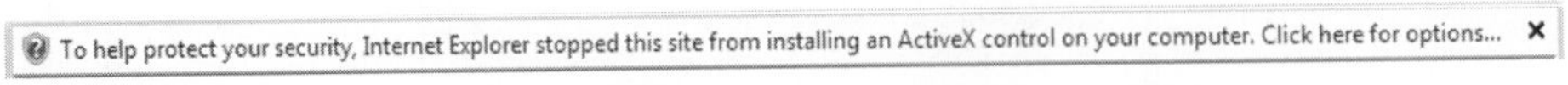

To help protect your security, Internet Explorer stopped this site from installing an ActiveX control on your computer. Click here for options... ×

Figure 5-9

ActiveX Opt-in first notifies the user in the information bar

If you click the information bar as prompted, you will be presented with a context menu, as shown in Figure 5-10.

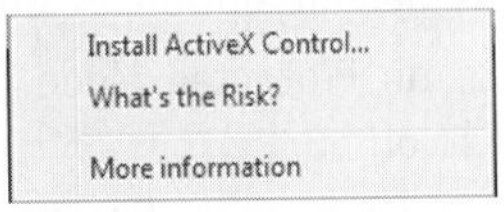

Install ActiveX Control...
What's the Risk?
More information

Figure 5-10

Context menu for ActiveX installation

If you select Install ActiveX Control, a User Account Control dialog box will open, and you can then provide administrator credentials to install the ActiveX Control. If Internet Explorer cannot verify the publisher of the ActiveX Control, an Internet Explorer Add-on Installer - Security Warning dialog box similar to that in Figure 5-11 will open.

Figure 5-11

Internet Explorer Add-on Installer - Security Warning dialog box

To install the ActiveX Control, click Install and follow any additional prompts. Once you install the ActiveX control, it has been excepted and is no longer subject to ActiveX Opt-in.

ENABLE OR DISABLE ACTIVEX OPT-IN LOCALLY

OPEN the Security Settings – *ZoneName* Zone dialog box for the zone in which you want to enable or disable ActiveX Opt-in.

1. In the Security Settings – *ZoneName* Zone dialog box, scroll the list box until you find the *ActiveX controls and plug-ins* section.
2. Under *Allow previously unused ActiveX controls to run without prompt*, select one of the following:
    - **Disable** Select this option to Enable ActiveX Opt-in (this is correct: you disable this setting to enable ActiveX Opt-in).
    - **Enable** Select this option to disable ActiveX Opt-in (this is correct: you enable this setting to disable ActiveX Opt-in).

CONFIGURE ACTIVEX OPT-IN THROUGH GROUP POLICY

OPEN the GPO you want to edit in the Group Policy Object Editor.

1. In the Group Policy Object Editor console tree, expand **Computer Configuration> Administrative Templates>Windows Components>Internet Explorer>Internet Control Panel>Security Page.**
2. Select the ***ZoneName*** node, where *ZoneName* is the zone for which you want to configure First-Run Opt-In policy. For example, Figure 5-7 shows the Intranet Zone node selected.
3. In the details pane, right-click **Turn Off First-Run Opt-In** and then click **Properties.** The Turn Off First-Run Opt-In Properties dialog box appears (as shown in Figure 5-12).

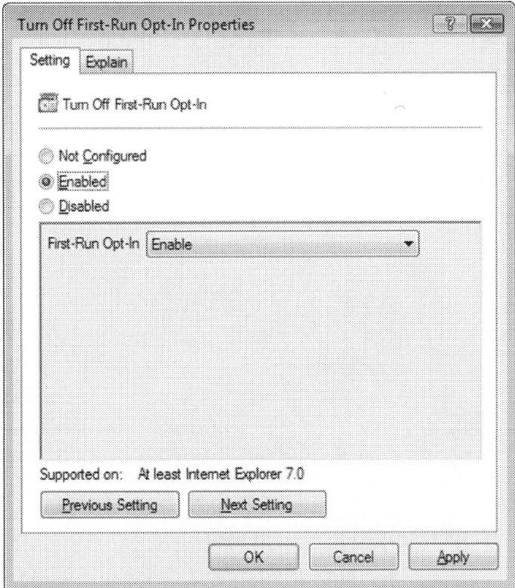

Figure 5-12

The Turn Off First-Run Opt-In Properties dialog box with Enabled selected

4. Select one of the following:
   - **Not Configured** Select this option to enable users to enable or disable ActiveX Opt-in for this zone. This is the default option in Group Policy Object Editor.
   - **Enabled** Select this option to disable ActiveX Opt-in for this zone and to disallow users the ability to enable it.
   - **Disabled** Select this option to enable ActiveX Opt-in for this zone and to disallow users the ability to disable it.

Understanding and Configuring the ActiveX Installer Service

The ActiveX Installer Service enables administrators to specify ActiveX controls that users are allowed to install without administrator credentials.

Unless you have administrator credentials, you cannot install an ActiveX control. This means that standard users are unable to install ActiveX controls, which can be a serious problem if your enterprise uses ActiveX controls in critical web applications. For example, your intranet may use ActiveX controls to host a suite of collaboration tools. Standard users will not be able to install the ActiveX controls without administrator credentials. This can be particularly annoying if your organization releases new ActiveX controls frequently.

The ***ActiveX Installer Service (AxIS)*** enables administrators to allow standard users to install ActiveX controls that reside in a specified URL called an ***approved installation site for ActiveX controls***. The URL can be any URL; it does not need to be internal. ActiveX Installer Services is available in Windows Vista Ultimate, Enterprise, and Business. The ActiveX Installer Service is an optional component that Windows enables only on the client computers where you install it.

When a user requests an Active X control to be installed or updated, the IE7 asks AxIS to carry out the installation. Before AxIS proceeds, it checks to see if the ActiveX control is listed in an approved installation site for ActiveX controls. If it is, AXiS proceeds with the installation or upgrade. If not, the user is prompted for administrator credentials.

Using the ActiveX Installer Service requires four components:

- Internet Explorer 7+
- ActiveX Installer Service
- Group Policy configuration
- Approved installation sites for ActiveX controls

LOCALLY TURN ON THE ACTIVEX INSTALLER SERVICE

1. Click **Start** and then click **Control Panel**. The Control Panel appears, as shown in Figure 5-13.

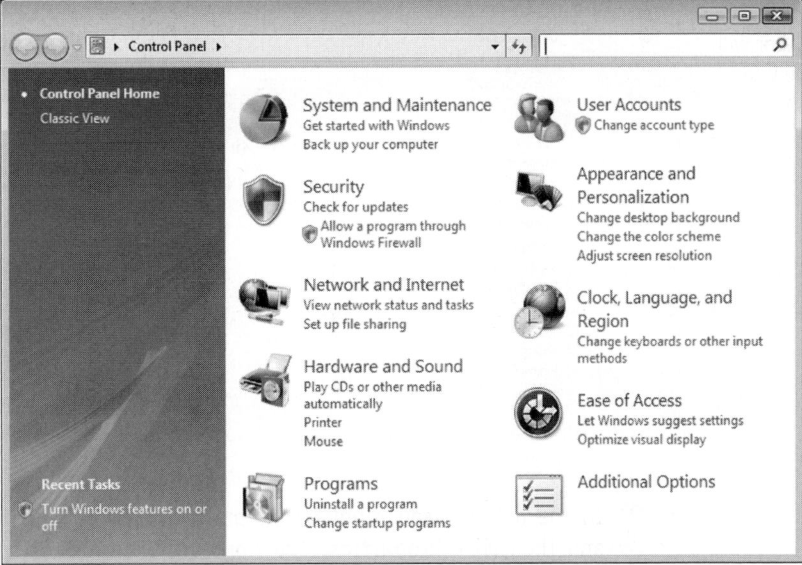

Figure 5-13

The Control Panel

2. Click **Programs**. The Programs window appears.
3. Under Programs and Features, click **Turn Windows features on or off**. A User Account Control dialog box appears.
4. Provide administrator credentials and then click **OK**. The Windows Features dialog box appears, as shown in Figure 5-14.

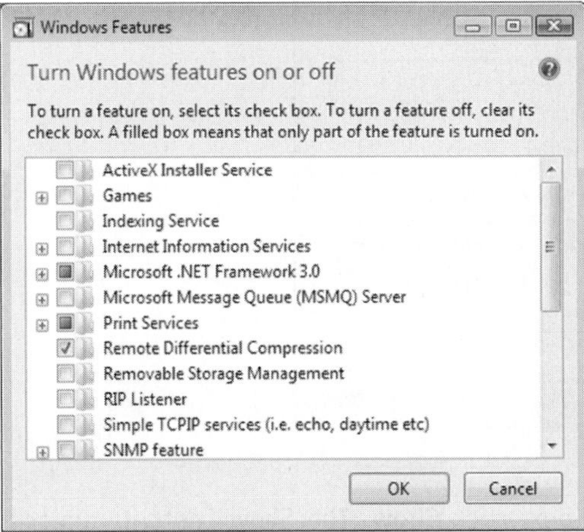

Figure 5-14

The Windows Features dialog box

5. Select the **ActiveX Installer Service** check box and then click **OK**.

CONFIGURE ACTIVEX INSTALLER SERVICE THROUGH GROUP POLICY

OPEN the GPO you want to edit in the Group Policy Object Editor.

1. In the Group Policy Object Editor console tree, expand **Computer Configuration>Administrative Templates>Windows Components>ActiveX Installer Service**, as shown in Figure 5-15.

Figure 5-15

Group Policy Object Editor with the ActiveX Installer Service node selected

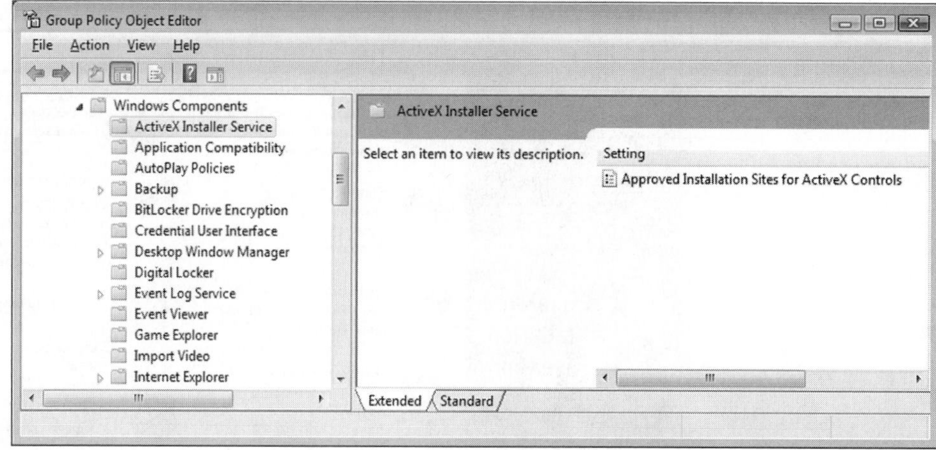

2. In the details pane, right-click **Approved Installation Sites for ActiveX controls** and then click **Properties**. The Approved Installation Sites for ActiveX controls Properties dialog box appears.
3. Select **Enabled**, as shown in Figure 5-16.

Figure 5-16

The Approved Installation Sites for ActiveX controls Properties dialog box with Enabled selected

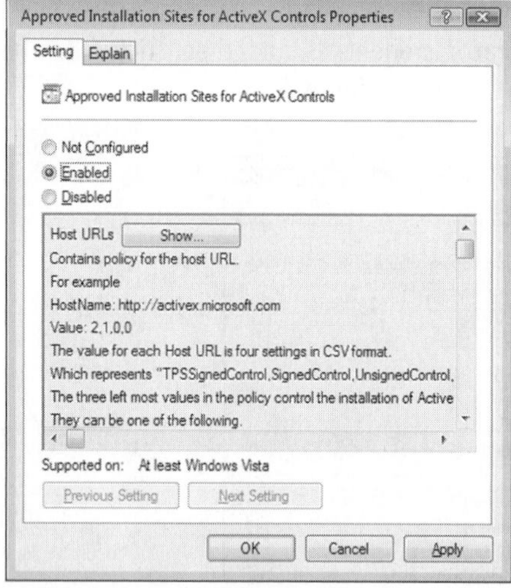

4. In the list box, click **Show**. The Show Contents dialog box appears, as shown in Figure 5-17.

Figure 5-17

Use the Show Contents dialog box for adding or removing approved ActiveX control installation sites

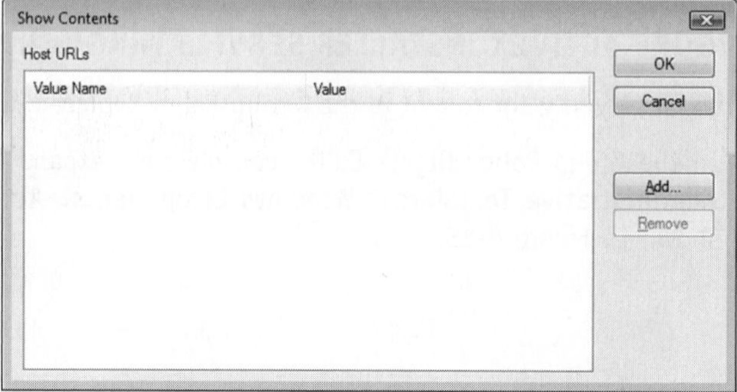

5. Click **Add.** The Add Item dialog box appears, as shown in Figure 5-18.

Figure 5-18

The Add Item dialog box for adding ActiveX controls to an approved installation site

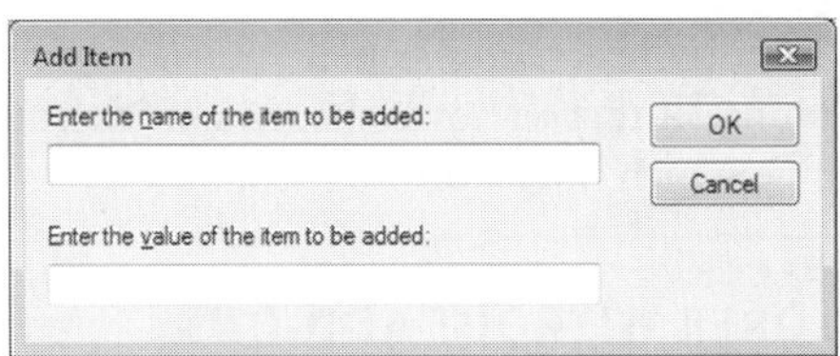

6. In the *Enter the name of the item to be added* text box, key the approved installation site for the ActiveX controls URL. For example, http://contoso.com/ActiveXAprroved.
7. In the *Enter the value of the item to be added* text box, key comma-separated values in the form *TPSSignedControl,SignedControl,UnsignedControl,ServerCertificatePolicy*, according to the chart in Table 5-1.

Table 5-1

Variable names are listed horizontally and possible values vertically.

	TPSSignedControl	SignedControl	UnsignedControl	ServerCertificatePolicy
0	ActiveX control will not be installed	ActiveX control will not be installed	ActiveX control will not be installed	Must pass all security checks
1	Prompt the user to install ActiveX control	Prompt the user to install ActiveX control	Prompt the user to install ActiveX control	NA
2	ActiveX control will be silently installed	ActiveX control will be silently installed	ActiveX control will be silently installed	NA
0x00000100	NA	NA	NA	Ignore unknown CA
0x00001000	NA	NA	NA	Ignore invalid CN
0x00002000	NA	NA	NA	Ignore invalid certificate date
0x00000200	NA	NA	NA	Ignore wrong certificate usage

For example, to install all signed ActiveX controls silently (*TPSSignedContro*=2 *and SignedControl*=2), to require user permission to install unsigned ActiveX controls (*UnsignedControl*=1), and to ignore invalid certificate dates for ActiveX controls (*ServerCertificatePolicy*=0×00002000), key 2,2,1,0×00002000.

8. Click **OK.**

■ Understanding and Managing Add-Ons

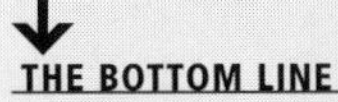

You can manage add-ons by using the Manage Add-ons dialog box. Add-ons extend the functionality of Internet Explorer, but they can also be malicious or cause instability or poor performance.

Internet Explorer add-ons are software components that extend the functionality of Internet Explorer (ActiveX controls are a type of add-on). Most add-ons come from the Internet and require your permission to download and install. However, add-ons can be added as parts of

CERTIFICATION READY?
Configure and troubleshoot security for Windows Internet Explorer 7+
2.1

other programs and therefore can be installed without your knowledge. Furthermore, some add-ons are pre-installed before you ever start Internet Explorer.

If Internet Explorer has recently become unstable, you can try running Internet Explorer without any add-ons running. If that removes the instability, you can systematically disable add-ons to try to determine which one is causing trouble.

RUN INTERNET EXPLORER WITHOUT ADD-ONS

1. Click **Start**, click **All Programs**, click **Accessories**, click **System Tools**, and then click **Internet Explorer (No Add-ons)**. Internet Explorer opens to an intercept page, shown in Figure 5-19.

Figure 5-19

An intercept page indicates that Internet Explorer is running without add-ons

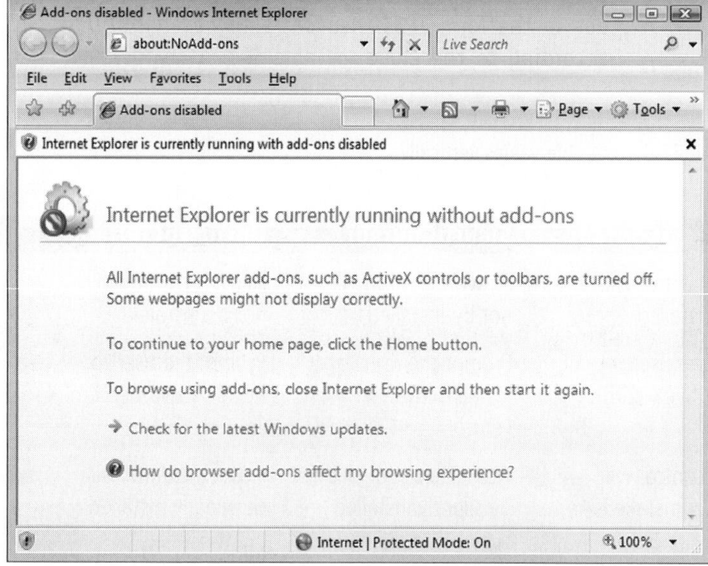

2. You can now browse as you like. If you are troubleshooting, you can visit the web pages that are causing problems and see if they perform correctly when add-ons are disabled.

MANAGE INTERNET EXPLORER ADD-ONS

1. In Internet Explorer, in the **Tools** menu, click **Internet Options**. The Internet Options dialog box appears, as shown in Figure 5-3.
2. Click the **Programs** tab, as shown in Figure 5-20.

Figure 5-20

The Programs tab of the Internet Options dialog box

3. Click **Manage add-ons**. The Manage Add-ons dialog box appears.
4. In the **Show** drop-down list, select one of the following:
   - **Add-ons that have been used by Internet Explorer** Select this option to display a complete list of the add-ons that reside on your computer.
   - **Add-ons currently loaded in Internet Explorer** Select this option to display only those add-ons that were needed for the current web page or a recently viewed web page. This can be useful if Internet Explorer is not performing correctly and you suspect it is because of a loaded add-on.
   - **Add-ons that run without requiring permission** Select this option to display add-ons that are pre-approved by Microsoft, your computer manufacturer, or a service provider. These add-ons are less likely to be the cause of problems.
   - **Downloaded ActiveX controls (32-bit)** Select this option to display only 32-bit ActiveX controls.
5. To enable or disable an add-on, select the add-on in the standard list box and then select **Enable** or **Disable** in the Settings section.
6. To delete an ActiveX control, select the control in the standard list box and then click **Delete** in the Delete ActiveX section.

■ Understanding Certificates

THE BOTTOM LINE

Certificates identify the owner of Internet entities, such as websites. They also enable you to communicate with other users through public key encryption.

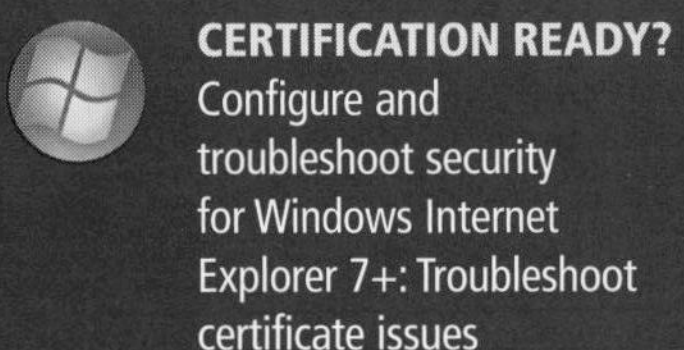

CERTIFICATION READY?
Configure and troubleshoot security for Windows Internet Explorer 7+: Troubleshoot certificate issues
2.1

Certificates, as they relate to the Internet, serve two purposes. The first is to identify the owner of Internet entities, such as websites or electronic messages. The second is to enable users to respond to those entities securely, through public key encryption.

The first purpose, to identify the owner of an Internet entity, is accomplished by a certificate being issued to the entity by a trusted third party, called a ***certificate authority (CA)***. If you trust the third party, then it is a small step to trust the identity of the certificate owner. The certificate authority can be outside of the organization that owns the certificate, or it can be internal if the certificate is self-issued (useful for secure internal communications). Deciding whether you trust a particular certificate authority is a judgment call. There are many reputable certificate authorities such as VeriSign and GoDaddy.

The second purpose, to enable users to respond to the certificate owner securely, is accomplished by a public key being attached to the certificate. Anyone possessing the public key can send encrypted information to the certificate owner. Note that if the certificate is self-issued by the certificate owner—for example, Contoso, Inc.—a fraudulent party could issue themselves a certificate claiming that they are Contoso, Inc., and receive transmissions intended for Contoso. This is why third-party certificate authorities are critical.

If you browse to a website, and it offers a certificate that is not from a trusted certificate authority, Internet Explorer will present you with an intercept page, as shown in Figure 5-21.

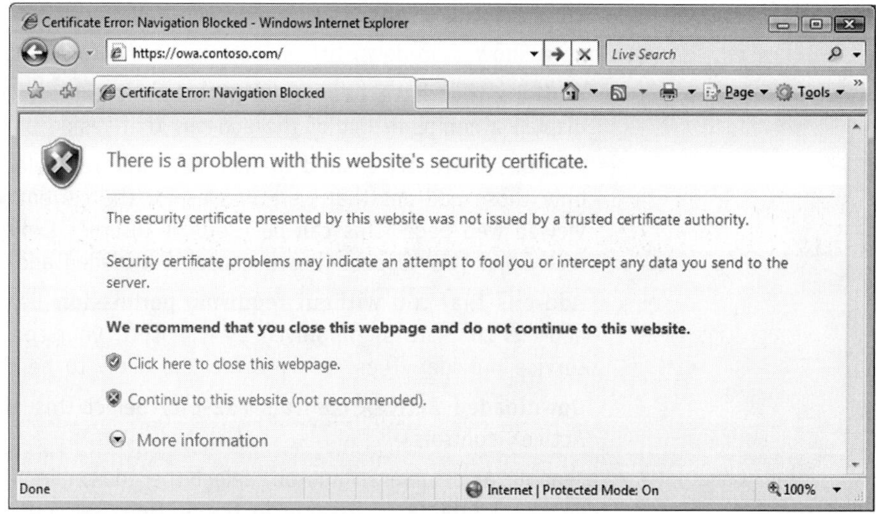

Figure 5-21

The Internet Explorer 7 Certificate Error intercept page

If you click *Continue to this website (not recommended)*, then Internet Explorer will remember that you accepted the certificate until you restart Internet Explorer.

If you continue to the website, the address bar will be highlighted red, and a Certificate Error warning will be displayed to the right of the address, as shown in Figure 5-22.

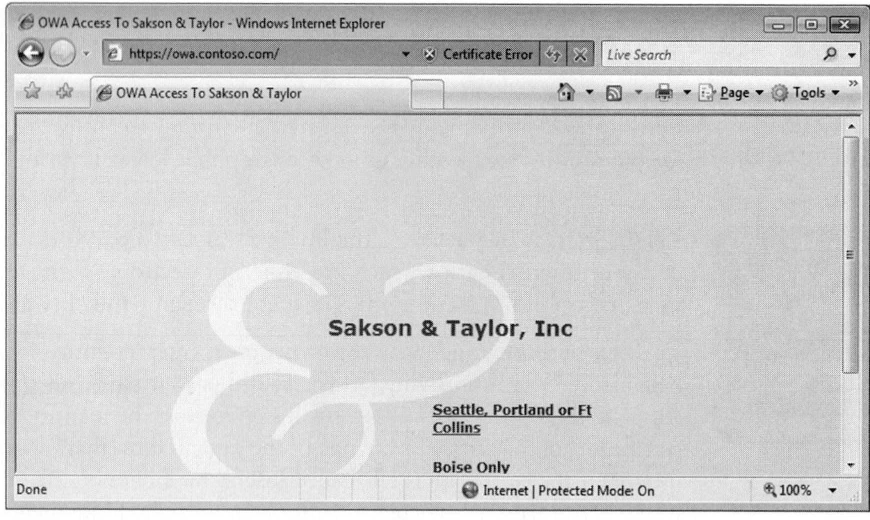

Figure 5-22

The Explorer bar turns red, and a Certificate Error warning is displayed when a there is an error with a certificate

If you click Certificate Error, the Untrusted Certificate warning box will open, as shown in Figure 5-23. You can click View certificates to see detailed information on the certificate, including who issued it.

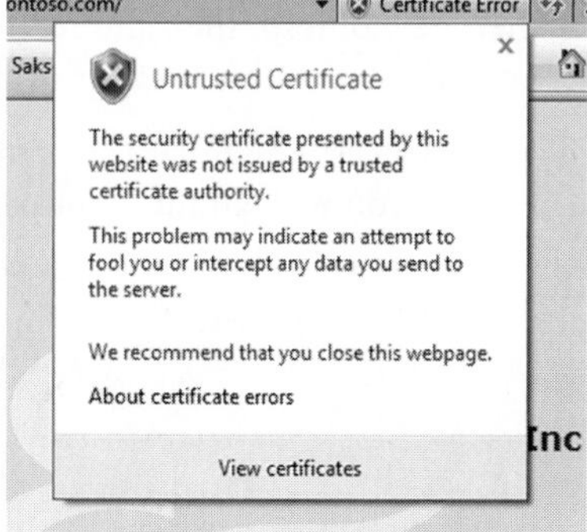

Figure 5-23

The Untrusted Certificate warning box

Internet Explorer 7 also introduces support for highly secure certificates (also called extended validation certificates), which have more stringent requirements than ordinary certificates. The address bar is highlighted green when such certificates are encountered.

Understanding and Configuring the Phishing Filter

THE BOTTOM LINE The Phishing Filter monitors websites and alerts you when it suspects that you have encountered a phishing website.

CERTIFICATION READY? Configure and troubleshoot security for Windows Internet Explorer 7+
2.1

Phishing is when attackers attempt identity theft by using fraudulent emails to trick users into giving personal or financial information. Typically, the attackers masquerade as a legitimate business or organization to attempt to solicit sensitive information by urging the recipient to click an email's hyperlink and then to supply the requested information at the destination website.

The ***Phishing Filter*** in Internet Explorer 7 is a monitor that alerts users about suspicious or known phishing websites.

The Phishing Filter helps protect users from phishing in the following three ways:

- It compares the addresses of sites a user attempts to visit with a list of reported legitimate sites stored on the user's computer.
- It analyzes websites that users attempt to visit for characteristics common to phishing sites that are uncommon to other sites. For example, sites that solicit personal or financial information but do not use Secure Socket Layer (SSL) for encryption. SSL is a form of encryption sometimes used to secure communication across the Internet.
- It submits website URLs that a user attempts to visit to an online Microsoft service that checks the URLs against known phishing sites.

LOCALLY ENABLE OR DISABLE THE PHISHING FILTER

OPEN Internet Explorer and then the Security Settings – *ZoneName* Zone dialog box for the zone in which you want to enable or disable the Phishing Filter.

1. In the Security Settings – *ZoneName* Zone dialog box, scroll the list box until you find the Miscellaneous section.
2. Continue scrolling down to the Use Phishing Filter setting and then select one of the following:

   Disable Select this option to disable the Phishing Filter.

   Enable Select this option to enable the Phishing Filter.

CONFIGURE THE PHISHING FILTER THROUGH GROUP POLICY

Unlike many other security settings for Internet Explorer, this setting is configured in only one place for all security zones.

OPEN the GPO you want to edit in the Group Policy Object Editor.

1. In the Group Policy Object Editor console tree, expand **Computer Configuration**> **Administrative Templates**>**Windows Components**>**Internet Explorer.**
2. In the details pane, right-click **Turn Off Managing Phishing filter** and then click **Properties.** The Turn off Managing Phishing filter Properties dialog box appears (as shown in Figure 5-24).

Figure 5-24

The Turn off Managing Phishing filter Properties dialog box

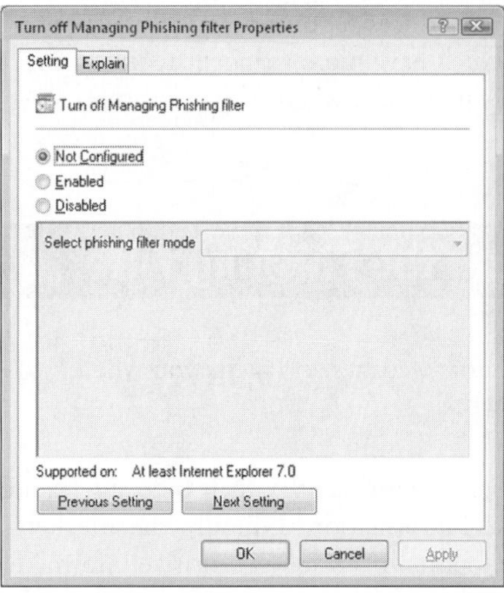

3. Select one of the following:

   Not Configured Select this option to prompt users to choose the mode of operation for the Phishing Filter. This option results in the same behavior as the Disabled option.

   Enabled Select this option to enable the Phishing Filter without prompting the user. If you select this option, select one of the following modes from the *Select phishing filter mode list* box: Automatic, Manual, or Off. If you select Manual, the Phishing Filter performs local analysis, and users are prompted before any data is sent to Microsoft for analysis. If you select Automatic, then data is automatically sent to Microsoft.

   Disabled Select this option to prompt users to choose the mode of operation for the Phishing Filter. This option results in the same behavior as the Not Configured option.

■ Resetting Internet Explorer Settings

THE BOTTOM LINE

You can reset many Internet Explorer settings simultaneously to restore the browser to a more uncorrupted state in an attempt to remedy instability.

Internet browsing is an inherently dangerous activity from a security point of view because the browsing computer is exposed to literally millions of other computers. In addition, poorly written add-ons, even if not malicious, can degrade the browsing experience.

Reset Internet Explorer Settings (REIS) in Internet Explorer 7 enables you to reset many Internet Explorer settings to the default state. If the browser becomes unstable, this can be a quick way to restore the browser closer to the state it was in before it was used.

REIS resets the following:

- **Browser settings** Resets all user-defined browser settings (configured by using the Internet Options dialog box) to Internet Explorer 7 defaults. This includes security settings, privacy settings, and zone settings.
- **Extensibility** Any extensions that you have added, such as toolbars, are prevented from running automatically. Also, ActiveX Opt-in is reset so that any ActiveX controls that have been allowed to run by the user will require user permission to run again.
- **Browsing history and temporary files** are restored. This includes temporary Internet files, cookies, browsing history, form data, passwords, and auto-complete data.
- **Manufacturer settings** for Internet Explorer as set by the computer manufacturer are restored.

TAKE NOTE *

REIS does not affect Group Policy settings.

USE REIS TO RESET INTERNET EXPLORER SETTINGS

1. In Internet Explorer, in the **Tools** menu, click **Internet Options**. The Internet Options dialog box appears, as shown in Figure 5-3.
2. Click the **Advanced** tab, as shown in Figure 5-25.

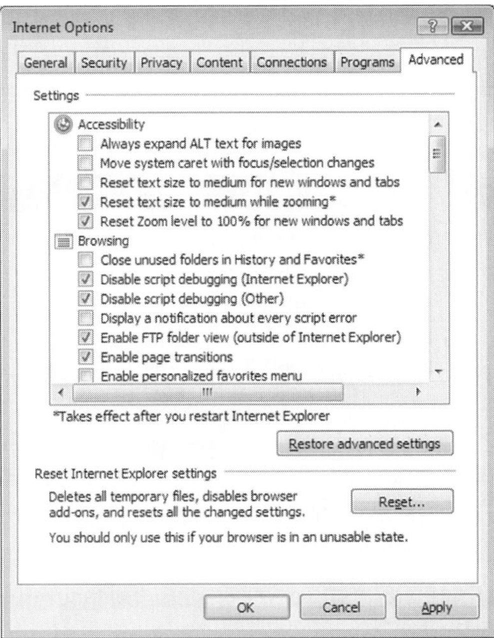

Figure 5-25

Advanced tab of the Internet Options dialog box

3. Click **Reset**. The Reset Internet Explorer Settings warning box appears, as shown in Figure 5-26.

Figure 5-26

Reset Internet Explorer Settings warning box

4. Click **Reset**. The Reset Internet Explorer Settings indicator box appears.
5. Click **Close**. An Internet Explorer information box appears to inform you that you need to restart Internet Explorer.
6. Click **OK**.
7. Restart Internet Explorer.

■ Configuring Additional Group Policy Security Settings

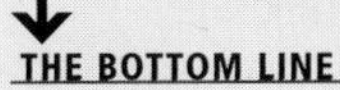

THE BOTTOM LINE You can centrally manage Internet Explorer 7 security settings by using Group Policy.

CERTIFICATION READY?
Configure and troubleshoot security for Windows Internet Explorer 7+: Troubleshoot policy-setting issues
2.1

Many Internet Explorer security settings can be configured through Group Policy. Table 5-2 highlights some of the more important settings. For a more complete explanation of a Group Policy setting, access the Explain tab for that setting in the Group Policy Object Editor.

Table 5-2

Summary of IE7 Group Policy security settings

Security Area	Group Policy Setting	Location	Description
Protected Mode	Turn on Protected Mode	Computer Configuration> Administrative Templates>Windows Components>Internet Explorer> Internet Control Panel>Security Page>*ZoneName*	Turn on or off Protected Mode while disallowing user control, or enable the user to decide.
ActiveX Opt-in	Turn Off First-Run Opt-In	Computer Configuration> Administrative Templates>Windows Components>Internet Explorer> Internet Control Panel>Security Page>*ZoneName*	Configure first time Opt-in settings for ActiveX controls. Determine whether users are prompted for Opt-In the first time they encounter an ActiveX control not excepted by ActiveX Opt-in.
ActiveX Installer Service	Approved Installation Sites for ActiveX controls	Computer Configuration> Administrative Templates>Windows Components>Internet Explorer> Internet Control Panel>Security Page>*ZoneName*	Manage a list of URLs from which users can install ActiveX controls without the Administrator token.
Phishing Filter	Turn Off Managing Phishing Filter	Computer Configuration>Administrative Templates>Windows Components> Internet Explorer	Enable and disable the Phishing Filter, as well as determine how much control the user has over Phishing Filter settings.
Add-on Management	Add-on List	Computer Configuration>Administrative Templates>Windows Components> Internet Explorer>Security Features> Add-on Management	Manage a list of add-ons to be allowed or denied by Internet Explorer.
Add-on Management	All Processes	Computer Configuration>Administrative Templates>Windows Components> Internet Explorer>Security Features> Add-on Management	Determine whether user preferences affect processes (as reflected in the Add-On Manager) or policy settings.
Add-on Management	Deny all add-ons unless specifically allowed in the Add-on list	Computer Configuration>Administrative Templates>Windows Components> Internet Explorer>Security Features> Add-on Management	Deny all add-ons unless specifically allowed in the Add-on list.
Add-on Management	Process List	Computer Configuration>Administrative Templates>Windows Components> Internet Explorer>Security Features> Add-on Management	Determine whether user processes affect the listed processes (as listed in the Add-On Manager) or policy settings.

(continued)

Table 5-2 *(continued)*

SECURITY AREA	GROUP POLICY SETTING	LOCATION	DESCRIPTION
Binary Behavior Security Restriction	All Processes	Computer Configuration>Administrative Templates>Windows Components> Internet Explorer>Security Features> Binary Behavior Security Restriction	Enable or disable binary behaviors for rendering of HTML elements for all processes (including Internet Explorer and Windows Explorer processes).
Binary Behavior Security Restriction	Internet Explorer Processes	Computer Configuration>Administrative Templates>Windows Components> Internet Explorer>Security Features> Binary Behavior Security Restriction	Enable or disable binary behaviors for Windows Explorer and Internet Explorer processes.
Binary Behavior Security Restriction	Process List	Computer Configuration>Administrative Templates>Windows Components> Internet Explorer>Security Features> Binary Behavior Security Restriction	Manage a list of applications for which you can enable or disable binary behaviors.
Binary Behavior Security Restriction	Admin-approved behaviors	Computer Configuration>Administrative Templates>Windows Components> Internet Explorer>Security Features> Binary Behavior Security Restriction	Manage a list of behaviors permitted for each zone for which Script and Binary Behaviors is set to admin-approved.
Consistent Mime Handling	All Processes	Computer Configuration>Administrative Templates>Windows Components> Internet Explorer>Security Features> Consistent Mime Handling	Determine whether Internet Explorer requires that all file information provided by Web servers is consistent.
Consistent Mime Handling	Internet Explorer Processes	Computer Configuration>Administrative Templates>Windows Components> Internet Explorer>Security Features> Consistent Mime Handling	Determine whether Internet Explorer requires consistent MIME data for all received files.
Consistent Mime Handling	Process List	Computer Configuration>Administrative Templates>Windows Components> Internet Explorer>Security Features> Consistent Mime Handling	Manage a list of applications for which this security feature is either enabled or disabled.
Information Bar	All Processes	Computer Configuration> Administrative Templates>Windows Components>Internet Explorer> Security Features>Information Bar	Determine whether the Information Bar displays for all processes.
Information Bar	Internet Explorer Processes	Computer Configuration> Administrative Templates>Windows Components>Internet Explorer> Security Features>Information Bar	Determine whether the Information Bar displays for all Internet Explorer Processes.
Information Bar	Process List	Computer Configuration>Administrative Templates>Windows Components> Internet Explorer>Security Features> Information Bar	Manage a list of processes for which the Information Bar displays or does not display when file or code installs are restricted.

(continued)

Table 5-2 (*continued*)

Security Area	Group Policy Setting	Location	Description
Local Machine Zone Lockdown Security	All Processes	Computer Configuration>Administrative Templates>Windows Components> Internet Explorer>Security Features> Local Machine Lockdown Security	Determine whether Local Machine zone security applies to all local files and content processed by any process other then Internet Explorer or those defined in a process list.
Local Machine Zone Lockdown Security	Internet Explorer Processes	Computer Configuration>Administrative Templates>Windows Components> Internet Explorer>Security Features> Local Machine Lockdown Security	Determine whether Local Machine zone security applies to all local files and content processed by Internet Explorer.
Local Machine Zone Lockdown Security	Processes List	Computer Configuration>Administrative Templates>Windows Components> Internet Explorer>Security Features> Local Machine Lockdown Security	Manage a list of processes for which Local Machine Zone security applies or does not apply.
MIME Sniffing Safety Feature	All Processes	Computer Configuration>Administrative Templates>Windows Components> Internet Explorer>Security Features> MIME Sniffing Safety Feature	Determine whether the MIME Sniffing Safety Feature is enabled for all processes.
MIME Sniffing Safety Feature	Internet Explorer Processes	Computer Configuration>Administrative Templates>Windows Components> Internet Explorer>Security Features> MIME Sniffing Safety Feature	Determine whether Internet Explorer processes will enable a MIME sniff promoting of a file of one type to a more dangerous file type.
MIME Sniffing Safety Feature	Process List	Computer Configuration>Administrative Templates>Windows Components> Internet Explorer>Security Features> MIME Sniffing Safety Feature	Manage a list of applications for which to apply or not apply this security feature.
MK Protocol Security Restriction	All Processes	Computer Configuration>Administrative Templates>Windows Components> Internet Explorer>Security Features> MK Protocol Security Restriction Settings	Determine whether the MK Protocol is blocked for all processes and all uses.
MK Protocol Security Restriction	Internet Explorer Processes	Computer Configuration>Administrative Templates>Windows Components> Internet Explorer>Security Features> MK Protocol Security Restriction Settings	Determine whether applications can use the MK protocol application programming interface (API) and whether resources hosted on the MK protocol will work for the Windows Explorer and Internet Explorer processes.
MK Protocol Security Restriction	Process List	Computer Configuration>Administrative Templates>Windows Components> Internet Explorer>Security Features> MK Protocol Security Restriction Settings	Manage a list of applications for which to apply or not apply this security feature.

(*continued*)

Table 5-2 (*continued*)

Security Area	Group Policy Setting	Location	Description
Network Protocol Lockdown	All Processes	Computer Configuration>Administrative Templates>Windows Components> Internet Explorer>Security Features> Network Protocol Lockdown	Determine whether restricting content obtained through restricted protocols is allowed for all processes other than Windows Explorer or Internet Explorer.
Network Protocol Lockdown	Internet Explorer Processes	Computer Configuration>Administrative Templates>Windows Components> Internet Explorer>Security Features> Network Protocol Lockdown	Determine whether restricting content obtained through restricted protocols is allowed for Windows Explorer and Internet Explorer processes.
Network Protocol Lockdown	Process List	Computer Configuration>Administrative Templates>Windows Components> Internet Explorer>Security Features> Network Protocol Lockdown	Manage a list of applications for which to apply or not apply this security feature.
Restricted Protocols Per Security Zone	Internet Zone Restricted Protocols	Computer Configuration>Administrative Templates>Windows Components> Internet Explorer>Security Features> Network Protocol Lockdown>Restricted Protocols Per Security Zone	Manage a list of protocols that are restricted for the Internet zone.
Restricted Protocols Per Security Zone	Intranet Zone Restricted Protocols	Computer Configuration>Administrative Templates>Windows Components> Internet Explorer>Security Features> Network Protocol Lockdown>Restricted Protocols Per Security Zone	Manage a list of protocols that are restricted for the Intranet zone.
Restricted Protocols Per Security Zone	Local Machine Zone Restricted Protocols	Computer Configuration>Administrative Templates>Windows Components> Internet Explorer>Security Features> Network Protocol Lockdown>Restricted Protocols Per Security Zone	Manage a list of protocols that are restricted for the Local Machine zone.
Restricted Protocols Per Security Zone	Restricted Sites Zone Restricted Protocols	Computer Configuration>Administrative Templates>Windows Components> Internet Explorer>Security Features> Network Protocol Lockdown> Restricted Protocols Per Security Zone	Manage a list of protocols that are restricted for the Restricted Sites zone.
Restricted Protocols Per Security Zone	Trusted Sites Zone Restricted Protocols	Computer Configuration>Administrative Templates>Windows Components> Internet Explorer>Security Features> Network Protocol Lockdown>Restricted Protocols Per Security Zone	Manage a list of protocols that are restricted for the Trusted Sites zone.
Object Caching Protection	All Processes	Computer Configuration>Administrative Templates>Windows Components> Internet Explorer>Security Features> Object Caching Protection	Determine whether object reference is retained when navigating within or across domains in the Restricted Zone sites.

(*continued*)

Table 5-2 (*continued*)

SECURITY AREA	GROUP POLICY SETTING	LOCATION	DESCRIPTION
Object Caching Protection	Internet Explorer Processes	Computer Configuration>Administrative Templates>Windows Components> Internet Explorer>Security Features> Object Caching Protection	Determine whether an object reference is no longer accessible when navigating within or across domains for Internet Explorer processes.
Object Caching Protection	Process List	Computer Configuration>Administrative Templates>Windows Components> Internet Explorer>Security Features> Object Caching Protection	Manage a list of applications for which to apply or not apply this security feature.
Protection from Zone Elevation	All Processes	Computer Configuration>Administrative Templates>Windows Components> Internet Explorer>Security Features> Protection From Zone Elevation	Determine whether you can protect any zone from zone elevation for all processes, or if processes other than Internet Explorer or those listed in the Process List receive protection.
Protection from Zone Elevation	Internet Explorer Processes	Computer Configuration>Administrative Templates>Windows Components> Internet Explorer>Security Features> Protection From Zone Elevation	Determine whether any zone can be protected from zone elevation by Internet Explorer processes.
Protection from Zone Elevation	Process List	Computer Configuration>Administrative Templates>Windows Components> Internet Explorer>Security Features> Protection From Zone Elevation	Manage a list of applications for which to apply or not apply this security feature.
Restrict ActiveX install	All Processes	Computer Configuration>Administrative Templates>Windows Components> Internet Explorer>Security Features> Restrict ActiveX Install	Determine whether applications hosting the Web Browser Control block automatic prompting of ActiveX control installation.
Restrict ActiveX install	Internet Explorer Processes	Computer Configuration>Administrative Templates>Windows Components> Internet Explorer>Security Features> Restrict ActiveX Install	Determine whether there is blocking of ActiveX control installation prompts for Internet Explorer processes.
Restrict ActiveX install	Process List	Computer Configuration>Administrative Templates>Windows Components> Internet Explorer>Security Features> Restrict ActiveX Install	Manage a list of executables for which to apply or not apply this security feature.
Restrict File Download	All Processes	Computer Configuration>Administrative Templates>Windows Components> Internet Explorer>Security Features> Restrict File Download	Determine whether applications hosting the Web Browser Control block automatic prompting of file downloads that are not user initiated.
Restrict File Download	Internet Explorer Processes	Computer Configuration>Administrative Templates>Windows Components> Internet Explorer>Security Features> Restrict File Download	Determine whether there is blocking of file download prompts that are not user initiated.

(*continued*)

Table 5-2 (*continued*)

Security Area	Group Policy Setting	Location	Description
Restrict File Download	Process List	Computer Configuration>Administrative Templates>Windows Components> Internet Explorer>Security Features> Restrict File Download	Manage a list of executables for which to apply or not apply this security feature.
Scripted Windows Security Restrictions	All Processes	Computer Configuration>Administrative Templates>Windows Components> Internet Explorer>Security Features> Scripted Windows Security Restrictions	Determine whether scripted windows are restricted for all processes.
Scripted Windows Security Restrictions	Internet Explorer Processes	Computer Configuration>Administrative Templates>Windows Components> Internet Explorer>Security Features> Scripted Windows Security Restrictions	Determine whether restrictions on pop-up windows and other restrictions apply for Windows Explorer and Internet Explorer processes.
Scripted Windows Security Restrictions	Process List	Computer Configuration>Administrative Templates>Windows Components> Internet Explorer>Security Features> Scripted Windows Security Restrictions	Manage a list of applications for which to apply or not apply this security feature.

SUMMARY SKILL MATRIX

In this lesson you learned:
Internet Explorer 7 security is improved compared to previous versions. And it is raised further by Internet Explorer Protected Mode, which is available only on Windows Vista.
Protected Mode protects against unsolicited installation of software and modification of data.
How to enable or disable Protected Mode.
Security zones divide URL namespaces and enable you to vary security according to where the content is coming from.
How to configure zone security settings.
ActiveX Opt-in limits exposure to malicious ActiveX controls by disabling most ActiveX controls by default and requiring permission from a user with administrator credentials before installing any of the remaining ActiveX controls.
The ActiveX Installer Services enable administrators to specify a list of ActiveX controls that users can install without administrator credentials.
How to enable or disable ActiveX Opt-in.
How to configure the ActiveX Installer Service.
Add-ons extend the functionality of Internet Explorer, but they can also be malicious or cause instability or poor performance.
How to manage add-ons using the Manage Add-ons dialog box.
How to run Internet Explorer without add-ons.

(*continued*)

SUMMARY SKILL MATRIX (*continued*)

IN THIS LESSON YOU LEARNED:
Certificates identify the owner of Internet entities, such as websites. They also enable you to communicate with other users through public key encryption.
The Phishing filter monitors websites and alerts you when it suspects that you have encountered a phishing website.
How to enable or disable the Phishing Filter.
How to configure the Phishing Filter.
How to simultaneously reset many Internet Explorer settings by using REIS to restore the browser to a more uncorrupted state in an attempt to remedy instability.

■ Knowledge Assessment

Fill in the Blank

Complete the following sentences by writing the correct word or words in the blanks provided.

1. A(n) Sercuity zone is a URL namespace division for which you can configure security settings in Internet Explorer 7.
2. Certificates are used in Internet Explorer 7 to identify the owner of web entities, as well as to secure communication with users by offering a public encryption key.
3. The Phishing filters in Internet Explorer 7 helps to reduce the incidence of users providing personal information to fraudulent websites masquerading as legitimate organizations.
4. A quick way to restore almost all local Internet Explorer 7 Security settings to their default values is by using ~~REIS~~ RIES.
5. ActiveX controlls are downloaded to browsers to extend the functionality of web pages.
6. If an administrator locates ActiveX controls in an approved installation site for ActiveX controls, then the ActiveX controls can be installed without Admistrator. cerdencaids
7. The Active x Installer service service is required to achieve the functionality described in question 6.
8. The answer to question 2 is issued by an entity called a(n) Certificate. Athourity
9. Active x optin requires users to approve installation of ActiveX controls that are not already installed or specified as exceptions.
10. The Local machine Security zone is configurable through Group Policy but not through the Internet Explorer interface.

Multiple Choice

Select the best response for the following questions.

1. The ActiveX Installer Service is not available in which of the following combinations?
   a. Windows Vista Ultimate and Internet Explorer 6
   b. Windows Vista Business and Internet Explorer 5
   c. Windows Vista Enterprise and Internet Explorer 6
   d. Windows Vista Home Premium and Internet Explorer 7
2. Internet Explorer Protected Mode is not compatible with which of the following?
   a. Internet Explorer 6
   b. Windows XP Professional and Internet Explorer 7
   c. Windows Vista Ultimate and Internet Explorer 7
   d. All of the above
3. Internet Explorer Protected Mode makes browsing more secure by:
   a. Protecting users from phishing attacks by notifying the user when a known phishing web page is encountered.
   b. Withholding privileges needed to silently install programs or modify sensitive system data.
   c. Answers a and b.
   d. None of the above.
4. REIS does all of the following except:
   a. Resets Group Policy security settings for Internet Explorer 7 to their default settings.
   b. Resets all user-defined browser settings to Internet Explorer 7 defaults. This includes security settings, privacy settings, and zone settings.
   c. Prevents any extensions that you have added, such as toolbars, from running automatically.
   d. Resets ActiveX Opt-in so that any ActiveX controls that have been allowed to run by the user will require user permission to run again.
5. By default, Protected Mode is not enabled in the following zones:
   a. The Restricted Sites zone in Internet Explorer 7 on a Windows XP Professional system
   b. Local Machine zone in Internet Explorer 6 on a Windows Vista Enterprise system
   c. Trusted Sites zone in Internet Explorer 7 on Windows Vista Home system
   d. Local Intranet zone in Internet Explorer 7 on a Windows Vista Enterprise system
6. Which of the following are the five security zones in Internet Explorer?
   a. Internet, Local Intranet, Trusted Sites, Untrusted Sites, Local Machine
   b. Internet, Local Intranet, Trusted Sites, Restricted Sites, Remote Machine
   c. Internet, Local Intranet, Trusted Sites, Restricted Sites, Local Machine
   d. None of the above. There are only four Internet security zone in Internet Explorer 7.
7. A user disables Protected Mode for the Restricted Sites zone. An administrator, using Group Policy, enables it for the Restricted Sites zone and disables it for the Local Machine zone. The administrator then uses REIS to reset Internet Explorer on the user's computer. Which of the following is true?
   a. Protected Mode is disabled for the Restricted Sites zone because the administrator used REIS to reset Group Policy settings for Internet Explorer Security settings.
   b. Protected Mode is enabled for the Restricted Sites zone and for the Local Machine zone.
   c. Protected Mode is enabled for the Restricted Sites zone but is disabled for the Local Machine zone.
   d. None of the above.

8. Which of the following are not excepted from ActiveX Opt-in?
   a. ActiveX controls that are part of the pre-approved list
   b. ActiveX controls that are code-signed by a trusted certificate authority
   c. ActiveX controls that the user downloads and installs
   d. ActiveX controls that are listed in the Add-On Manager

9. The default zone security template for the Trusted Sites zone is the:
   a. Medium-low template.
   b. Medium template.
   c. Medium-high template.
   d. High template.

10. The default zone security template for the Internet zone is the:
   a. Medium-low template.
   b. Medium template.
   c. Medium-high template.
   d. High template.

Review Questions

1. Describe the relationship between IE7 security settings that are set locally and those that are set through Group Policy.

2. Name two new security features in IE7 and briefly describe them.

Case Scenarios

Scenario 1: Automated Install of ActiveX Controls

You have recently rolled out Windows Vista and IE7 to all workstations at Contoso. The call center at Contoso uses a custom web application that needs to install ActiveX controls to work properly. Because of ActiveX Opt-in, the users in the call center are asked if they want to install the control. They sometimes choose not to, in which case the application fails and IT receives a trouble ticket. How can you fix this problem?

Scenario 2: Recovering from Slow Internet Explorer Performance

A user has reported that Internet Explorer crashes frequently. How can you quickly undo almost any changes that the user has implemented while maintaining the security settings that you have applied through Group Policy?

Troubleshooting Security Issues

LESSON 6

OBJECTIVE DOMAIN MATRIX

Technology Skill	Objective Domain	Objective Domain Number
Understanding, Configuring, and Troubleshooting Software Restriction Policies	Troubleshoot software restrictions	5.2
How Software Restriction Policies Work	Troubleshoot software restrictions	5.2
Understanding Additional Rules	Troubleshoot software restrictions • Digital signing	5.2
Configuring Software Restriction Policies	Troubleshoot software restrictions • Digital signing	5.2
Monitoring and Troubleshooting with Event Viewer	Troubleshoot security configuration issues • Run Event Viewer tool	2.2
Getting Started with Event Viewer	Troubleshoot security configuration issues • Run Event Viewer tool	2.2
Sorting and Grouping Events	Troubleshoot security configuration issues • Run Event Viewer tool	2.2
Viewing Events	Troubleshoot security configuration issues • Run Event Viewer tool	2.2
Creating Filters and Custom Views	Troubleshoot security configuration issues • Run Event Viewer tool	2.2
Centralizing Event Data by Using Subscriptions	Troubleshoot security configuration issues • Run Event Viewer tool Configure and troubleshoot Event Forwarding • Monitor and respond to forwarded events	2.2 3.3
Using the Security Configuration and Analysis Snap-in	Troubleshoot security configuration issues • Run the Security Configuration and Analysis tool	2.2
Using the Security Configuration and Analysis Snap-in to Analyze Settings	Troubleshoot security configuration issues • Run the Security Configuration and Analysis tool	2.2
Using the Security Configuration and Analysis Snap-in to Configure Security Policy	Troubleshoot security configuration issues • Run the Security Configuration and Analysis tool	2.2

KEY TERMS

software restriction policies (SRP)
default security level
additional rules
hash rules
certificate rules
path rules
network zone rules
hash algorithm
file path rules
registry path rules
designated file types
Event Viewer
filters
custom views
collector
forwarder
subscription
Windows Event Collector service
Windows Remote Management service
Security Configuration and Analysis Snap-in
security templates

Contoso Incorporated, where you are a senior desktop support technician, has completed a pilot deployment of Windows Vista in the accounting department. As part of a new security initiative in the company, software restriction policies (SRP) are being tested in a laboratory environment before being rolled out to the enterprise. It is your task to troubleshoot these policies and ensure that they work before they are deployed through Group Policy. This may involve the use of Event Viewer, Group Policy Modeling, and Group Policy Results. A second part of the initiative involves creating new security templates by using the Security Configuration and Analysis Snap-in.

Understanding, Configuring, and Troubleshooting Software Restriction Policies

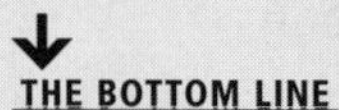

Software restriction policies provide a Group Policy mechanism by which the running of programs can be restricted.

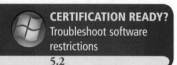

CERTIFICATION READY? Troubleshoot software restrictions 5.2

In an enterprise environment, ***software restriction policies*** are applied through Group Policy and restrict the running of software (including scripts) or define who can add trusted publishers to client computers. This section is primarily concerned with the how software restriction policies can be used to restrict the running of software, although the other purpose is briefly covered.

Software restriction policies can be set at the following levels:

- Computer
- Organizational unit (OU)
- Site
- Domain

TAKE NOTE*

Software restriction policies can be set at the computer level by using a Group Policy object (GPO) stored on the local computer (for computer configuration only; user configuration software restriction policies are not available on local GPOs). Because enterprises have large numbers of computers, it is most common in an enterprise to configure software restriction policies through a GPO in Active Directory.

Some common reasons for implementing software restriction policies are to:

- Fight malicious software (malware).
- Regulate what Microsoft ActiveX controls can be installed.
- Restrict running of scripts to digitally signed only.
- Allow only approved software to be installed or executed.
- Reduce the chance of software being installed or run that might conflict with other applications or change configuration information in a possibly undesirable way.
- Restrict users from adding untrusted publishers.

How Software Restriction Policies Work

Software restriction polices use a default rule and exceptions to that rule called additional rules to restrict how and if specified programs can run.

Software restriction policies define whether and with what access rights software is allowed to run. There are two fundamental parts to a software restriction policy: the default security level and additional rules.

The ***default security level*** defines behavior for all attempts to run software, whereas additional rules define exceptions to that default behavior.

The default security level can be one of three security levels:

- **Unrestricted:** The user is not prevented from running the software. The user can elevate the software from running with standard user privileges to running with administrator privileges.
- **Disallowed:** The user is prevented from running the software.
- **Basic User:** The user is not prevented from running the software, but she is prevented from elevating the software from running with standard user privileges to running with administrator privileges.

TAKE NOTE*

A basic user is the same thing as a standard user.

X REF

Privilege elevation and standard users are covered in the User Account Control–related sections in **Lesson 8: Troubleshoot Access, Authentication, and User Account Control Issues.**

By combining a default security level with additional rules, you can create complex schemes for preventing or allowing the running of software.

For example, you might create the following scheme to create a highly secure environment:

1. Set the default rule to Disallowed. All software started by the user is not allowed to run by default.
2. Provide additional rules to allow specified software to run with the Unrestricted security level. The user can run the specified software without restriction.
3. Provide more additional rules to allow specified software to run with the Basic User security level. The user can run the specified software with standard user privileges.

The diagram in Figure 6-1 shows an overview of how software restriction policies are implemented and used. The text following the figure explains the diagram.

Figure 6-1

Diagram of how software restriction policies work

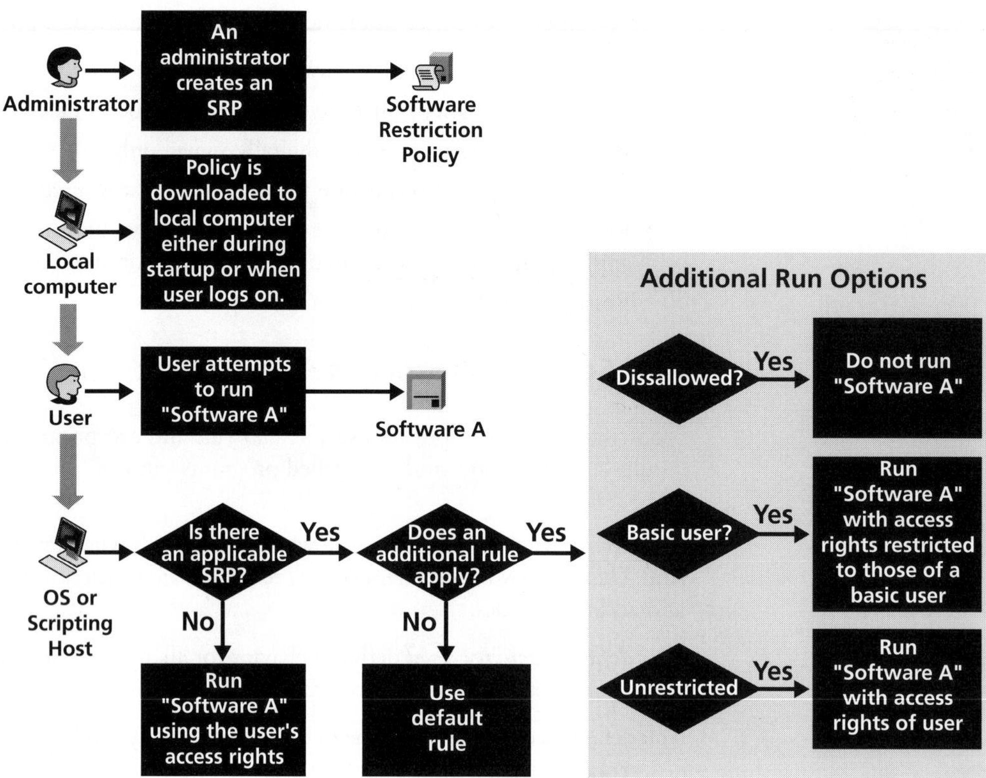

1. An administrator creates a software restriction policy through Group Policy.
2. The policies are applied to the local computer. This happens at startup for computer policies and logon for user policies.
3. The user attempts to run software.
4. The operating system (OS) checks to see if any software restriction policies apply. If not, the software runs using the user's access rights. If there is an applicable SRP, the SRP applies the default security level unless it is superseded by an additional rule. In either case, the end-result is that one of three policies applies:
   - **Unrestricted:** The user is not prevented from running the software. The user can elevate the software from running with standard user privileges to running with administrator privileges.
   - **Disallowed:** The user is prevented from running the software.
   - **Basic User:** The user is not prevented from running the software, but he is prevented from elevating the software from standard user privileges to administrator privileges.

Understanding Additional Rules

Additional rules are exceptions to a default rule and come in four varieties: hash rules, certificate rules, path rules, and network zone rules.

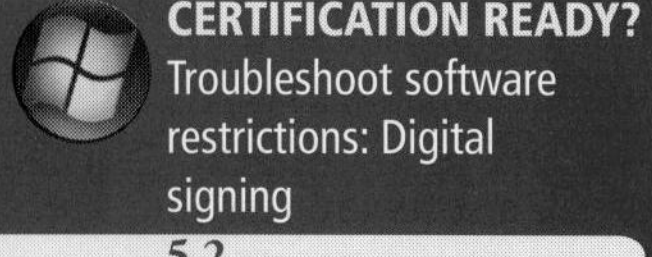

CERTIFICATION READY?
Troubleshoot software restrictions: Digital signing
5.2

Additional rules are used to identify software for the purpose of assigning a security level to the running of that software other than the security level defined by the default security level. Additional rules thus have two functions: identification of software and indication of security level. They are divided into four types according to how they achieve the first function (the identification of software):

- **Hash rules**: Identify programs by using a cryptographic hash. A cryptographic hash algorithm creates the hash.
- **Certificate rules**: Identify programs by digitally signed certificates.

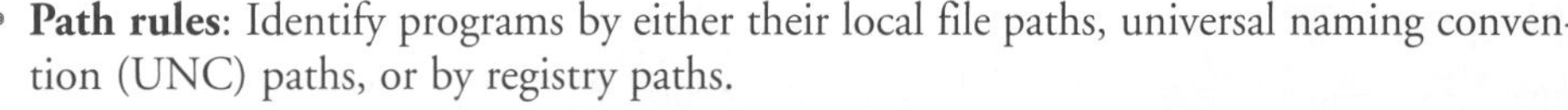

TAKE NOTE *

Certificate rules cannot use the Basic User security level.

- **Path rules**: Identify programs by either their local file paths, universal naming convention (UNC) paths, or by registry paths.
- **Network Zone rules**: Identify programs according to which network zone they belong.

For example, a default security level might be to run all software unrestricted, combined with a path rule that identifies programs that can run only at the Basic User security level, and a hash rule that disallows some software from running at all.

Understanding Hash Rules

Hash rules use hashes to identify program files so that the identified programs can be excepted in some way using additional rules or the default rule in a software restriction policy.

A hash is a cryptographic fingerprint that uniquely identifies a software program or executable file regardless of whether someone moves or renames that software or executable file. The hash algorithm does not base the hash on the name or location of the executable file or program, but instead on its contents.

A hash is the output of a hash algorithm. A ***hash algorithm*** takes a data string of any length as input and produces a fixed length string as output. In the case of a software restriction policy that uses a hash rule, a cryptographic hash algorithm creates a hash by using a program file as the input (in actuality, more than one hash is created for compatibility reasons; this is explained in a moment). The hash is then used to identify the program file (software), much like a fingerprint can be used to identify a person.

In Windows Vista, a new hash rule will contain two hashes:

- MD5 (Message-Digest algorithm) or SHA-1 (Secure Hash Algorithm)
- SHA-256

Hash types are determined according to the following rules:

- Files that are digitally signed will use the MD5 or SHA-1 according to which one is in their signature.
- Files that are not digitally signed and are on non–Windows Vista computers will use the MD5 hash.
- Files that are not digitally signed and that are on Windows Vista will use both the MD5 hash and the SHA-256 hash for compatibility reasons.

The SHA-256 hash is used in Windows Vista and Windows Server 2008 and is a security upgrade from previous hash rules.

The MD-5 or SHA-1 hash is meant to make the policy compatible with the previous generation of software restriction policies in Windows XP and Windows Server 2003 (software restriction policies were introduced in those operating systems). For example, by including the SHA-1 hash, Group Policy created on Windows Server 2008 will apply correctly to an XP client; whereas a Windows Server 2003 SRP policy can apply to a Windows Vista client. The more secure hash (SHA-256) will be used only if all participants are of the Windows Vista/Windows Server 2008 generation.

Because hash rules are based on a computation that is independent of the program file location or name, hash algorithms produce the same hashes for a program file regardless of its location or name.

Understanding Certificate Rules

Certificate rules use certificates to identify program files so that the identified programs can be excepted in some way using additional rules or the default rule in a software restriction policy.

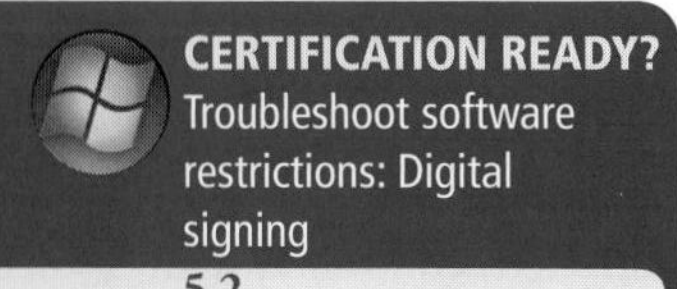

CERTIFICATION READY?
Troubleshoot software restrictions: Digital signing
5.2

A ***certificate rule*** identifies software according to its signing by a certificate. Certificates used in a certificate rule can be issued from a commercial certificate authority such as Verisign, by a Windows Server 2008 or Server 2003 Public Key Infrastructure (PKI) certificate server, or they can be self-signed certificates. Identifying software by using certificates is comparatively robust because of the built-in security provisions of certificates.

TAKE NOTE*

When troubleshooting software restriction policies based on certificate rules, remember that hashes are a common way to define exceptions to certificate rules.

Windows Vista does not enable Certificate rules by default; they must be enabled in the Enforcement Options dialog box. In addition, Certificate rules can only assign a security level of Unrestricted or Disallowed; Basic User is not an option.

Enforcement options are covered in the **Configure enforcement options** procedure later in this lesson.

Understanding Path Rules

Path rules use file paths or registry paths to identify program files so that the identified programs can be excepted in some way using additional rules or the default rule in a software restriction policy.

There are two types of ***path rules***: file path rules and registry path rules.

TAKE NOTE*

You can view and edit environment variables by clicking Environment Variables on the Advanced tab of the System Properties dialog box.

File path rules can specify a folder or a fully-qualified path to a program file. In the case of a folder, file path rules identify all software in the folder and subfolders recursively.

Registry path rules identify programs according to the paths that the programs specify in the registry as their install locations. Not all programs create such an entry in the registry.

File path rules can use environment variables (for example, %*WINDIR*% for the Windows installation folder) in their path definitions. This enables an administrator to specify paths that will match on computers with different folder structures so long as the environment variables on the different computers point to the same folders.

Environment variables are not secure because access control lists (permissions) do not protect them. Therefore, users can redefine environment variables to point wherever they want, thereby circumventing software restriction policies that use environment variables.

File path rules can be defined using the wildcards *?* and *. The *?* wildcard substitutes for any character, and the * wildcard character substitutes for zero or more characters.

Table 6-1 contains example path definitions using wildcards and example matches.

Table 6-1

Example path definitions using wildcards

PATH DEFINITION	EXAMPLE MATCHES
\\DC-xx\login$	\\DC-01\login$, \\DC-02\login$
*\Windows	c:\Windows, d:\Windows, e:\Windows
c:\win*	c:\winnt, c:\windows, c:\windir

Path rules can be easy to circumvent because they rely on paths to identify programs, and paths are easily changed by such actions as changing environment variables or moving programs.

In the context of software restriction policies, a registry path is the install folder path of a program as recorded in the registry on installation of the program. Only some programs record their install path in the registry during install.

Registry path rules identify programs according to their registry paths. Using registry path rules is a simple way to identify the location of an install path (wherein the program file generally resides) without having to worry about installation settings that modified the install path from the default during installation. This is because any modifications to the install path are reflected in the registry path.

Registry path rules are enclosed in the *%* character and can be defined using the wildcards *?* and ***. The *?* wildcard substitutes for any character, whereas the *** wildcard character substitutes for zero or more characters.

The following is an example of a registry path using the *** wildcard:

```
%HKEY_CURRENT_USER\Software\Microsoft\Windows\CurrentVersion\Explorer\
Shell Folders\Cache%OLK*
```

The following are example matches for the above registry path definition:

```
%HKEY_CURRENT_USER\Software\Microsoft\Windows\CurrentVersion\Explorer\
Shell Folders\Cache%OLK4
```

```
%HKEY_CURRENT_USER\Software\Microsoft\Windows\CurrentVersion\Explorer\
Shell Folders\Cache%OLK Example
```

```
%HKEY_CURRENT_USER\Software\Microsoft\Windows\CurrentVersion\Explorer\
Shell Folders\Cache%OLK41
```

When more than one path rule is used in a software restriction policy, path rules are applied in order, from most specific to most broad. The following is a list of generic file path definitions, in order from most specific to most broad:

1. `Drive:\folder1\folder2\Filename.extension`
2. `Drive:\folder1\folder2\*.extension`
3. `*.extension`
4. `Drive:\Folder1\Folder2\`
5. `Drive:\Folder1\`

Understanding Network Zone Rules

> Network zone rules use the network zone from where you downloaded the software as criteria for creating software restriction policies.

A ***network zone rule*** identifies a program according to which network zone it was downloaded from. The five network zones are:

- Internet
- Local Intranet
- Restricted Sites
- Trusted Sites
- Local Computer

X REF

Network zones, also called security zones, are covered in **Lesson 5: Configuring Windows Internet Explorer 7 Security.**

Using Additional Rules

Additional rules enable you to configure nondefault behavior for software restriction policies. In other words, additional rules are the exceptions to a default rule.

Table 6-2 contains examples of when you might use each additional rule in a software restriction policy.

Table 6-2

Examples of when to use various additional rules

PURPOSE	RULE	EXAMPLE
Allow or disallow a specific version of a program	Hash rule	NA
Identify a program that is always installed in the same place	Path rule with environment variables	%ProgramFiles%\Internet Explorer\iexplore.exe
Identify a program that can be installed in different locations registers its installation path in the registry	Registry path rule	%HKEY_LOCAL_MACHINE\SOFTWARE\ComputerAssociates\InoculateIT\6.0*Path*\and HOME%
Identify a set of scripts on a central server	Path rule	*SERVER_NAME**Share*
Identify a set of scripts on a set of servers: DC01, DC02, and DC03	Path rule with wildcards	*DC??*\Share
Disallow all.vbs files, except those in a login script directory	Path rule with wildcards	*.VBS set to Disallowed and \\LOGIN_SRV*Share**.VBS set to Unrestricted
Disallow running a file called flcss.exe (which a virus installs)	Path rule	*Location*\flcss.exe set to Disallowed
Identify a set of digitally signed scripts that you want to be allowed to run anywhere	Certificate rule	All scripts with the correct certificate set to unrestricted
Allow software to be installed from trusted Internet zone sites	Zone rule	Trusted Sites set to Unrestricted

Understanding Precedence Rules for Additional Rules

When there is a conflict between two or more additional rules, there are precedence rules to determine which additional rule is applied.

Rule precedence can be key to troubleshooting SRP issues. When more than one type of SRP additional rule is matched in a software restriction policy scheme, the most specific takes precedence, and then any ties are resolved according to the following precedence:

1. Hash rule
2. Certificate rule
3. Path rule
4. Internet zone rule
5. Default security level

For example, if a program is run and a software restriction policy scheme matches the program with both a certificate rule and a path rule, the certificate rule takes precedence.

The remainder of this section presents scenarios that explore rules precedence based on the SRP described in Table 6-3.

Table 6-3

Example settings for a software restriction policy

Rule type	Rule definition	Rule setting
Default security level		Unrestricted
Hash Rules		
Hash Rule 1	Hash of Undesirable.vbs	Basic User
Certificate Rules		
Certificate Rule 1	*ExampleCompany* Certificate	Unrestricted
Path Rules		
Path Rule 1	%*WINDIR*%\SYSTEM32*.vbs	Unrestricted
Path Rule 2	*.vbs	Disallowed
Path Rule 3	%*WINDIR*%	Unrestricted

Scenario 1: Table 6-4 summarizes which rules would apply in the SRP if a user starts C:\WINDOWS\SYSTEM32\Configxyz.vbs.

Table 6-4

Applicable rule summary for scenario 1

Rule	Reason it is applied
Default security level	It is the default security level
Path Rule 1	It is a .vbs file in the %WINDIR%\System32\ folder
Path Rule 2	It has a .vbs extension
Path Rule 3	It is within a subfolder of the %WINDIR% folder

Scenario 1 explanation: Path rule precedence tells us that the most specific path rule takes precedence, which in this case is Path Rule 1. The security level of Path Rule 1 is unrestricted, and therefore `Configxyz.vbs` runs unrestricted.

Scenario 2: Table 6-5 summarizes which rules would apply in the SRP if a user starts C:\WINDOWS\SYSTEM32\Undesirable.vbs.

Table 6-5

Applicable rule summary for scenario 2

Rule	Reason it is applied
Default security level	It is the default security level
Hash Rule 1	The hash of the rule matches the hash of the file
Path Rule 1	It is a.vbs file in the %*WINDIR*%\System32\ folder
Path Rule 2	It has a.vbs extension
Path Rule 3	It is within a subfolder of the %*WINDIR*% folder

Scenario 2 explanation: SRP Additional Rules Precedence tells us that hash rules take precedence over path rules. Therefore, Hash Rule 1 takes precedence: `Undesirable.vbs` runs with standard user privileges.

Scenario 3: Table 6-6 summarizes which rules would apply in the SRP if a user starts C:\WINDOWS\SYSTEM32\freecell.exe.

Table 6-6

Applicable rule summary for scenario 3.

RULE	REASON IT IS APPLIED
Default security level	It is the default security level.

Scenario 3 explanation: Because no rules apply but the default security level, which allows programs to run unrestricted, `freecell.exe` runs unrestricted.

Configuring Software Restriction Policies

Software restriction polices are configured through Group Policy and can be configured for both users and computers.

CONFIGURE SOFTWARE RESTRICTION POLICIES THROUGH GROUP POLICY

1. Click **Start**. In the **Start Search** text box, key **gpmc.msc** and then press **Ctrl + Shift + Enter**. A User Account Control dialog box appears.
2. Provide administrator credentials and then click **OK**. The Group Policy Management console appears.
3. In the console tree, expand **Forest:** ***ForestName*>Domains>*DomainName*>Group Policy Objects**.
4. Right-click the Group Policy object for which you want to configure software restriction policies and then click **Edit**. The Group Policy Object Editor appears with the selected GPO loaded.
5. In the console tree, expand **User Configuration** to configure software restriction policies for all users in the selected GPO, or expand **Computer Configuration** to configure software restriction policies for all computers in the selected GPO.
6. Expand **Windows Settings>Security Settings>Software Restriction Policies**, as shown in Figure 6-2.

Figure 6-2

A Group Policy object with the Software Restriction Policies node expanded

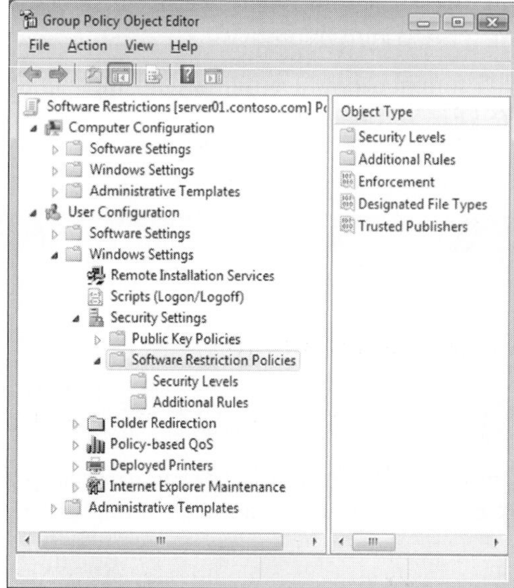

7. If no software restriction policies are defined, right-click **Software Restriction Polices** and then click **New Software Restriction Policies.**

The computer configuration software restriction policies affect computers for all users of those computers in the selected GPO (unless exceptions are defined), whereas the User Configuration policies affect all users on any computers in the selected GPO (again, unless exceptions are defined).

If a software restriction policy is defined for both a computer and a user using the computer, the policies are combined so that the most restrictive policies are enforced.

SET THE DEFAULT SECURITY LEVEL

The Default security level for a software restriction policy is set by designating one of the three security levels—Disallowed, Basic User, or Unrestricted—as the default.

OPEN the GPO you want to edit in the Group Policy Object Editor. Browse to the Software Restriction Policies node in either User Configuration or Computer Configuration.

1. In the Group Policy Object Editor, in the console tree, expand **Software Restriction Policies.**
2. Under Software Restriction Policies, select **Security Levels.** The details pane displays the security levels.
3. Right-click the security level that you want to designate as the default security level and then click **Properties.** The *SecurityLevel* Properties dialog box appears as shown in the example in Figure 6-3.

Figure 6-3

The *SecurityLevel* Properties dialog box

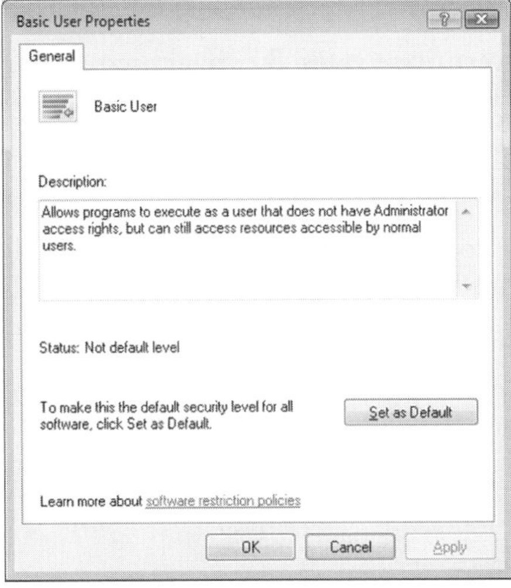

4. Click **Set as Default** (this option will be grayed-out if the security level is already designated as the default security level).
5. If you are moving to a more restrictive default security level, a message box will ask you to confirm the change. Click **Yes.**
6. Click **OK** to close the *SecurityLevel* Properties dialog box.

Configuring Enforcement Options

There are several enforcement options available for a software restriction policy:

- **Apply to all software files or to all software files except libraries (such as DLLs).** Most software consists of both an executable file and supporting libraries, usually DLLs (Dynamic Link Libraries). Libraries, including DLLs, are not by default restricted by software restriction policies because doing so causes performance degradation and is usually unnecessary because restricting the executable is sufficient to keep the software from running. Furthermore, if you restrict libraries and set the default security level to Disallowed, then to allow software to run you have to identify not only the program file using additional rules, but also each of the libraries that the software relies on. This can be cumbersome because most software uses many DLLs. So why would you want to restrict libraries? The reason is that malware can reside in DLLs, and therefore restricting libraries can increase security against malware. (A preferred protection method against malware is to use a set of hash rules that identifies both the executable and all of its required DLLs.) By default, software restriction policies do not enforce restrictions against libraries.

- **Apply software restriction policies to all users or to all users except local administrators**. By default, all users are subject to software restriction policies. Administrators can use an enforcement option to change this so that a software restriction policy applies to all users except local administrators. For example, it might make sense to restrict all but specific applications on a multi-user computer that has many users, but allow administrators to run all programs unrestricted.

In an enterprise environment, the preferred way to except administrators from a software restriction policy is not through the Enforcement Options dialog box, but rather by denying the Apply Group Policy permission for the administrators that you want to except, in the GPO defining the SRP.

This results in less network traffic and allows for a specific list of administrators that are excepted from the SRP. However, this method is not available if the SRP is located in a local security policy object rather than a GPO attached to a container in Active Directory.

- **Enforce or ignore certificate rules**. By default, certificate rules in software restriction policies are not enforced because of performance degradation.

CONFIGURE ENFORCEMENT OPTIONS

OPEN the GPO you want to edit in the Group Policy Object Editor. Browse to Software Restriction Policies in either User Configuration or Computer Configuration.

1. In the Group Policy Object Editor, in the console tree, select **Software Restriction Policies.**
2. In the details pane, right-click **Enforcement** and then click **Properties.** The Enforcement Properties dialog box appears, as shown in Figure 6-4.

Figure 6-4

The Enforcement Properties dialog box

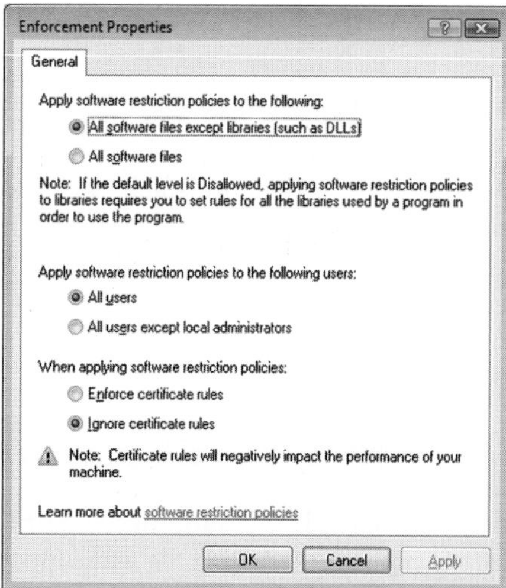

3. Configure the settings as desired.
4. Click **OK** to close the Enforcement Properties dialog box.

ADD OR REMOVE DESIGNATED FILE TYPES

Software restriction policies can only restrict the running of software if the extension of that software's executable program file is listed in the Designated File Types Properties dialog box.

OPEN the GPO you want to edit in the Group Policy Object Editor. Browse to Software Restriction Policies in either User Configuration or Computer Configuration.

1. In the Group Policy Object Editor, select **Software Restriction Policies.**
2. In the details pane, right-click **Designated File Types** and then click **Properties.** The Designated File Types Properties dialog box appears, as shown in Figure 6-5.

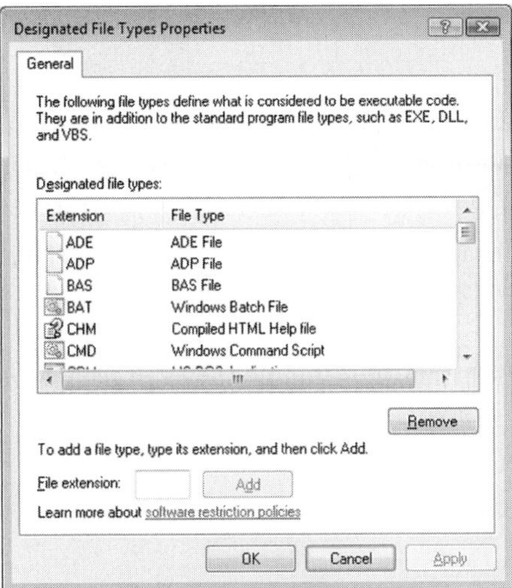

Figure 6-5

The Designated File Types Properties dialog box

3. To add a designated file type, key the extension in the **File extension** text box and then click **Add.**
4. To remove a designated file type, select it in the **Designated file types** list box and then click **Remove**. A Software Restriction Policies warning box appears. Click **Yes.**
5. Click **OK** to close the Designated File Types Properties dialog box.

CREATE A CERTIFICATE RULE

OPEN the GPO you want to edit in the Group Policy Object Editor. Browse to Software Restriction Policies in either User Configuration or Computer Configuration.

1. In the Group Policy Object Editor, under Software Restriction Policies, right-click **Additional Rules** and then click **New Certificate Rule.** The New Certificate Rule dialog box appears, as shown in Figure 6-6.

Figure 6-6

The New Certificate Rule dialog box

2. Click **Browse**. The Open dialog box appears.
3. Browse to and select the certificate you want to base the rule on and then click **Open**.
4. In the New Certificate Rule dialog box, in the **Security level** drop-down list, select one of the following:

   Unrestricted. Select Unrestricted to allow the user to run the software. The user can elevate the software from running with standard user privileges to running with administrator privileges.

   Disallowed. Select Disallowed to prevent the user from running the software.
5. In the **Description** text box, you can optionally type a description for the purpose of the rule.
6. Click **OK** to close the New Certificate Rule dialog box.

TAKE NOTE*

The Basic User security level is not available for certificate rules.

CREATE A HASH RULE

OPEN the GPO you want to edit in the Group Policy Object Editor. Browse to Software Restriction Policies in either User Configuration or Computer Configuration.

1. In the Group Policy Object Editor, under Software Restriction Policies, right-click **Additional Rules** and then click **New Hash Rule**. The New Hash Rule dialog box appears, as shown in Figure 6-7.

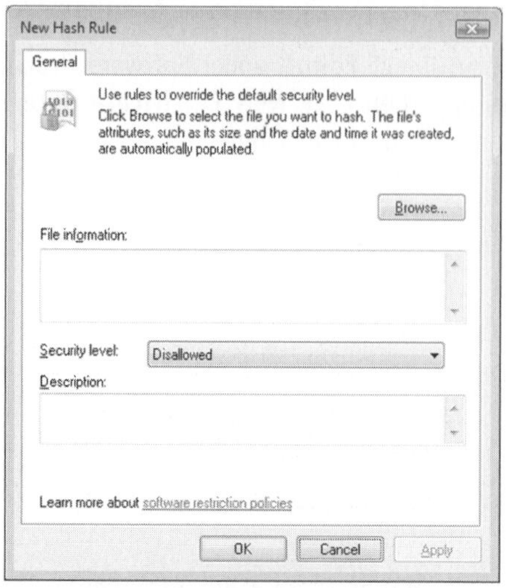

Figure 6-7

The New Hash Rule dialog box

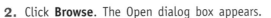

2. Click **Browse**. The Open dialog box appears.
3. Browse to and select the file that you want create a hash for in order to identify and restrict it. Usually, the file will be some sort of executable or script, but it could any file at all. Click **Open**.
4. In the New Hash Rule dialog box, in the **Security level** drop-down list, select one of the following:

   Unrestricted. Select Unrestricted to allow the user to run the software. The user can elevate the software from running with standard user privileges to running with administrator privileges.

   Disallowed. Select Disallowed to prevent the user from running the software.

   Basic User. Select Basic User to allow the user to run the software, but to prevent the user from elevating the software from running with standard user privileges to running with administrator privileges.
5. In the **Description** text box, you can optionally type a description for the purpose of the rule.
6. Click **OK** to close the New Hash Rule dialog box.

CREATE A NETWORK ZONE RULE

OPEN the GPO you want to edit in the Group Policy Object Editor. Browse to Software Restriction Policies in either User Configuration or Computer Configuration.

1. In the Group Policy Object Editor, under Software Restriction Policies, right-click **Additional Rules** and then click **New Network Zone Rule**. The New Network Zone Rule dialog box appears, as shown in Figure 6-8.

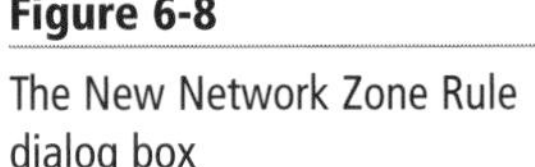

Figure 6-8

The New Network Zone Rule dialog box

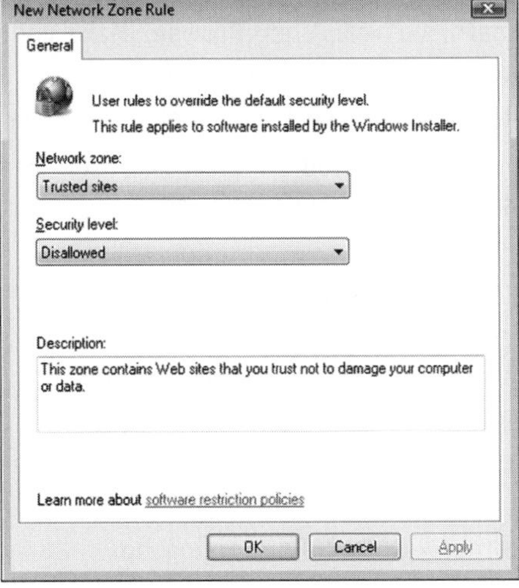

2. In the **Network zone** drop-down list, select the zone that you want to restrict.
3. In the **Security level** drop-down list, select one of the following:

   Unrestricted. Select Unrestricted to allow the user to run the software. The user can elevate the software from running with standard user privileges to running with administrator privileges.

   Disallowed. Select Disallowed to prevent the user from running the software.

   Basic User. Select Basic User to allow the user to run the software, but to prevent the user from elevating the software from running with standard user privileges to running with administrator privileges.
4. In the **Description** text box, you can optionally type a description for the purpose of the rule.
5. Click **OK** to close the New Network Zone Rule dialog box.

CREATE A PATH RULE

OPEN the GPO you want to edit in the Group Policy Object Editor. Browse to Software Restriction Policies in either User Configuration or Computer Configuration.

1. In the Group Policy Object Editor, under Software Restriction Policies, right-click **Additional Rules** and then click **New Path Rule**. The New Path Rule dialog box appears, as shown in Figure 6-9.

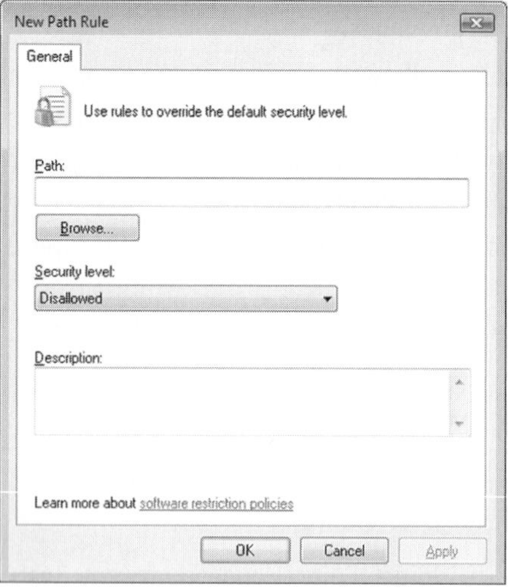

Figure 6-9

The New Path Rule dialog box

2. Enter a path in the **Path** text box. It can be a file path, UNC path, or registry path.

   To specify a file path, you can click **Browse**. Make your selection on the Browse for File or Folder dialog box and then click **OK**.

3. In the **Security level** drop-down list, select one of the following:

   Unrestricted: Select Unrestricted to allow the user to run the software. The user can elevate the software from running with standard user privileges to running with administrator privileges.

   Disallowed: Select Disallowed to prevent the user from running the software.

   Basic User: Select Basic User to allow the user to run the software, but to prevent the user from elevating the software from running with standard user privileges to running with administrator privileges.

4. In the **Description** text box, you can optionally type a description for the purpose of the rule.
5. Click **OK** to close the New Path Rule dialog box.

MODIFY AN ADDITIONAL RULE

OPEN the GPO you want to edit in the Group Policy Object Editor. Browse to Software Restriction Policies in either User Configuration or Computer Configuration.

1. In the Group Policy Object Editor, under Software Restriction Policies, select **Additional Rules**.
2. In the details pane, right-click the additional rule that you want to edit and then click **Properties**. Modify the rule as desired and then click **OK** to close the dialog box.
3. To delete an additional rule, right-click the rule in the details pane and then click **Delete**. A Software Restriction Warning box will open, asking you to confirm the delete. Click **Yes**.

■ Monitoring and Troubleshooting with Event Viewer

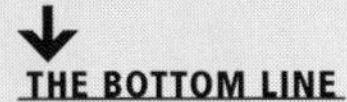

THE BOTTOM LINE

Event Viewer enables you to view recorded events in an organized way so that you can troubleshoot a wide range of issues by investigating related events.

CERTIFICATION READY?
Troubleshoot security configuration issues: Run Event Viewer tool
2.2

X REF

You can find more information on Task Scheduler in **Lesson 9: Configuring Task Scheduler.**

Event Viewer is an MMC Snap-in that enables you to view events. Events are any occurrence on a computer that is logged and recorded using the Windows Event Log service. Event Viewer also interfaces with the task scheduler to start tasks according to event occurrence.

Some of the primary reasons to use Event Viewer are:

- To troubleshoot problems that have occurred. For example, if Folder Redirection is failing for one computer but working for others, you might be able to diagnose why by finding related events.
- To prevent problems from occurring by monitoring computer systems. For example, you might find disk error events in the log that suggest a hard-drive is starting to fail.
- To find security breaches or attempts to breach security. For example, you might turn on auditing for a folder with sensitive information and use Event Viewer to watch attempts to access that folder.

Event Viewer has been re-designed for Windows Vista, and it includes the following new features:

- **Event subscriptions**. You can subscribe to events from multiple computers on a single computer and view the events with Event Viewer. This enables you to, for example, search for a specific error across multiple computers on the network.
- **Improved Event Filtering**. Event filtering is improved, and filter settings can be saved as ***views***, which can loaded for later use or emailed to a peer.
- **No log size limits**. Previously, your logs could not exceed 206 MB total, which meant you had to keep tabs on the size of various logs. Logs no longer have a size limit.
- **Additional logs**. There are now dozens of logs instead of four.
- **Critical event level**. There is a new event level called critical. Critical events are rare, and it is very important to pay attention when you see one.
- **Evtutil command line tool**. Enables you to archive logs so that log archiving can be scheduled using Task Scheduler.
- **Cross-log event viewing**. You can now view events across multiple logs simultaneously.
- **Added explanatory text**. Many events have more useful explanatory text.
- **Expanded details**. Most events contain more technical details.
- **XML data storage**. The detail data for an event is stored in XML. This makes it much more convenient for scripts or third-party applications to pull data from event details.

Getting Started with Event Viewer

You can use Event Viewer to browse logs and events on both the local computer and on remote computers.

START EVENT VIEWER

You can use Event Viewer to browse events on either the local computer or on a remote computer.

1. Click **Start**. In the **Start Search** text box, type **event viewer** and then press **Ctrl + Shift + Enter**. A User Account Control dialog box appears.
2. Provide administrator credentials and then click **OK.** The Event Viewer console appears, as shown in Figure 6-10.

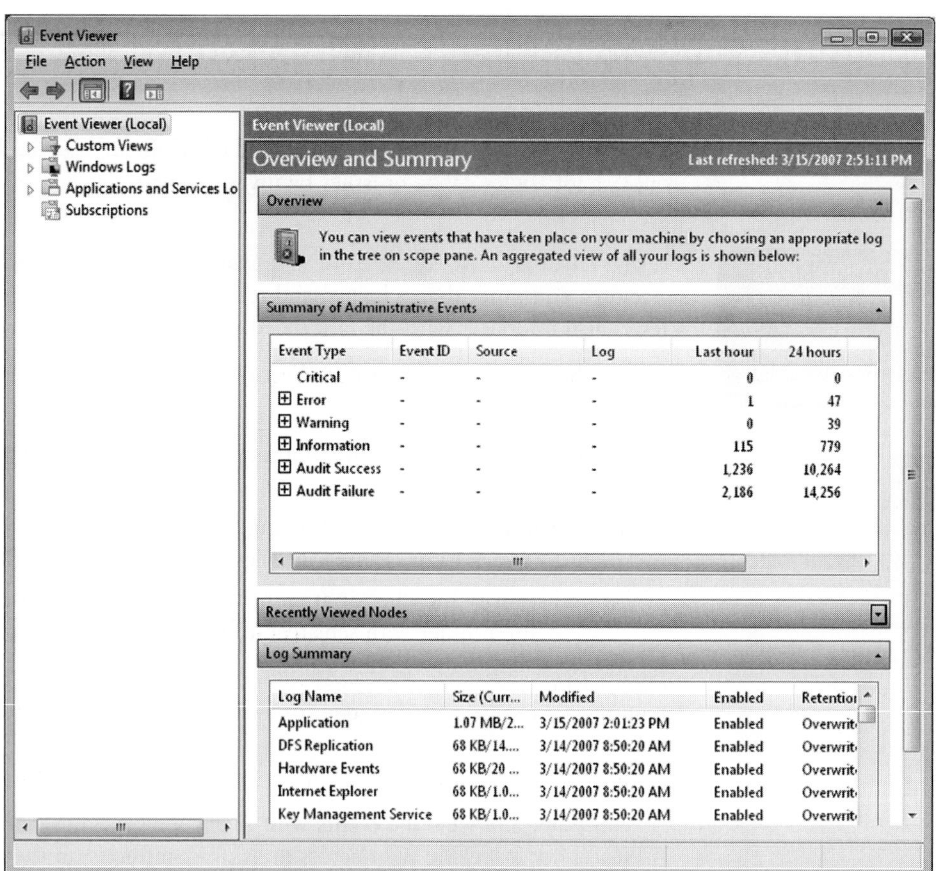

Figure 6-10

The Event Viewer console

3. To browse events on a remote computer, click **Connect to Another Computer** in the Action menu. The Select Computer dialog box appears, as shown in Figure 6-11.

   a. Select **Another computer** and then enter the computer name in the corresponding text box (you can browse to a computer by using the Browse button). To connect to the remote computer as another user, select the **Connect as another user** check box, click **Set User**, and then provide credentials when prompted. Click **OK**.

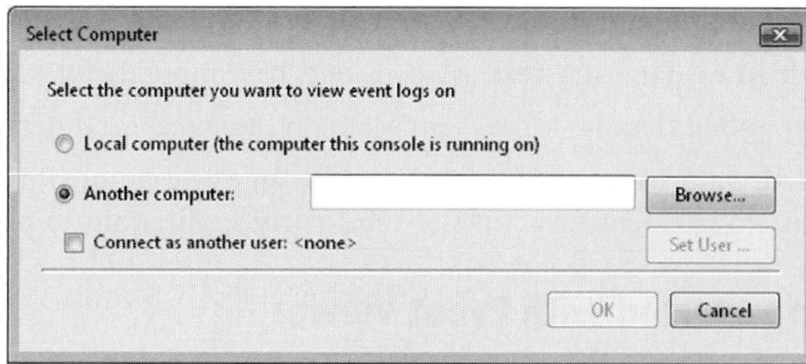

Figure 6-11

The Select Computer dialog box

4. To return to browsing on the local computer, click **Connect to Another Computer** in the Action menu.

   a. Select **Local Computer (the computer this console is running on)** and then click **OK**.

When the top-level node in the console tree is selected, the Overview and Summary is displayed in the details pane. The Overview and Summary section divided into three sections, each of which can be collapsed using the small black arrow on the right end of the title bars. The three sections are:

- **Summary of Administrative Events.** This section contains a custom view of events where the events are grouped according to event type. There are five common event types:
  - Error
  - Warning
  - Information
  - Audit Success
  - Audit Failure

To view events in any of the preceding five groups, expand the corresponding node. Figure 6-12 shows the Audit Failure node expanded. To view a list of all instances of an event that are currently in a log, double-click the event. The details pane will update and display a list of the events, and the preview pane will also be displayed.

Figure 6-12

The Summary of Administrative Events section of Event Viewer with the Audit Failure node expanded

Summary of Administrative Events

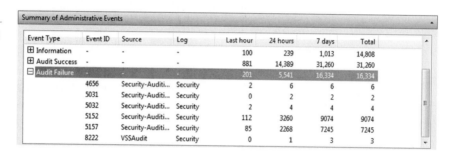

Event Type	Event ID	Source	Log	Last hour	24 hours	7 days	Total
⊞ Information	-	-	-	100	239	1,013	14,808
⊞ Audit Success	-	-	-	881	14,389	31,260	31,260
⊟ Audit Failure	-	-	-	201	5,541	16,334	16,334
	4656	Security-Auditi...	Security	2	6	6	6
	5031	Security-Auditi...	Security	0	2	2	2
	5032	Security-Auditi...	Security	2	4	4	4
	5152	Security-Auditi...	Security	112	3260	9074	9074
	5157	Security-Auditi...	Security	85	2268	7245	7245
	8222	VSSAudit	Security	0	1	3	3

- **Recently Viewed Nodes.** The Recently Viewed Node section contains a browsing history of the nodes you have recently visited in the console tree. This way you can quickly access the logs or views that you have recently viewed. To visit a node listed in the Recently Viewed Node section, double-click the listed node. The node will be selected in the console tree and corresponding information will be displayed in the details pane.
- **Log Summary.** The Log Summary section contains a summary of the different logs and contains information on whether the log is enabled, the log size, and the log retention policy. To view a log listed in the Log Summary section, double-click the listed log. The details pane will be populated with the log information, and your location in the console tree will be updated.

If you expand the Windows Logs node in the console tree, you will see five logs exposed, as shown in Figure 6-13.

Figure 6-13

The Event Viewer console tree with the Windows Logs node expanded

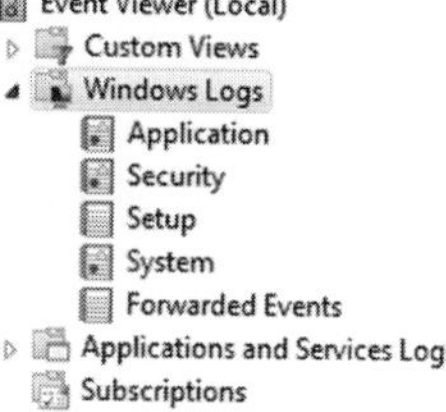

- **Application.** Contains events generated by applications. The application developers decide which application events are logged here, and which are logged in an application-specific log under *Application and Services logs.*

- **Security**. Contains events such as logon attempts and attempts to access or modify secured resources. You can determine what security events are logged by using the Local Security Policy Snap-in. Also, attempts to access objects that have object auditing configured are logged here.
- **Setup**. Contains events related to application installation.
- **System**. Contains events created by Windows and system components, such as device drivers.
- **Forwarded Events**. Contains events forwarded from other computers.

In addition to the logs in the Windows Logs folder, there is an Applications and Services Logs folder, which contains logs for events that are application or service specific. Also within the Applications and Services Logs folder is the Microsoft>Windows folder. In the Windows folders are many folders for various Windows components, each of which contains at least one log. Some of these logs are exposed in Figure 6-14.

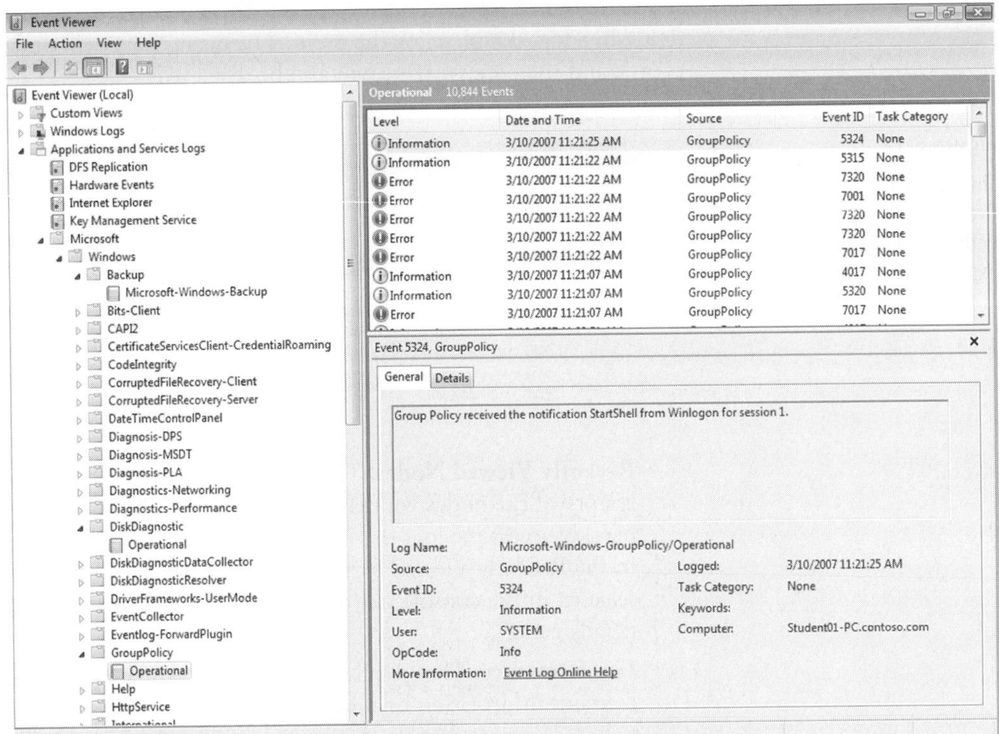

Figure 6-14

The Event Viewer with the Applications and Services log node expanded and the Group Policy Operational log selected

BROWSE LOGS IN EVENTS VIEWER

OPEN Event Viewer.

In Event Viewer, in the console tree, expand nodes as necessary to access the log that you want to browse. For example, to access the Group Policy Operational log, expand **Applications and Services Logs>Microsoft>Windows>Group Policy**, as shown in Figure 6-14. Events recorded in the log are displayed in the details pane, and summary information about the selected event is displayed below the details pane in the preview pane.

Sorting and Grouping Events

You can sort and group Events around many pivots to more easily find the events that you are looking for.

When events are displayed, event-related information is also displayed in columns. The default column headings are:

- **Level**. The level represents the severity of the event and can be one of three values: Information, Warning, or Error. The term *level* is used interchangeably with the term *event type*.
- **Date and Time**. The date and time the event occurred. It is given in the time-zone of the computer on which Event Viewer is running.
- **Source**. The source is the application, component, service, or other entity that created the event.
- **Event ID**. Each event is identified by a number. There is no required system by which event IDs are assigned. There is also no requirement that each event have a unique event ID.
- **Task Category**. Some event sources categorize events in to task categories that indicate what task the event calls for if any.

By default, events are sorted by Date and Time, from most recent event to least recent event. However, you can sort events by any column heading, and you can also group them by column heading by right-clicking the column heading and then selecting *Sort events by this column* or *Group Events by this column* respectively.

SORT BY AND CONFIGURE COLUMN HEADINGS

OPEN Event Viewer.

1. To sort events in the selected log according to a column heading, click the column heading in the details pane. For example, if you want to sort according to EventID, click **EventID.** Click it again to reverse the order. The Group Policy Operational Log is sorted by Event ID in Figure 6-15. Note that Event ID is highlighted and that a small arrow indicates whether it is sorted in ascending order (up arrow) or descending order (down arrow).

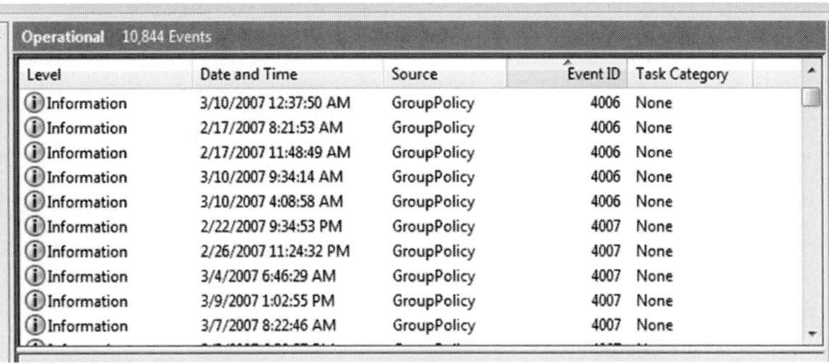

Level	Date and Time	Source	Event ID	Task Category
Information	3/10/2007 12:37:50 AM	GroupPolicy	4006	None
Information	2/17/2007 8:21:53 AM	GroupPolicy	4006	None
Information	2/17/2007 11:48:49 AM	GroupPolicy	4006	None
Information	3/10/2007 9:34:14 AM	GroupPolicy	4006	None
Information	3/10/2007 4:08:58 AM	GroupPolicy	4006	None
Information	2/22/2007 9:34:53 PM	GroupPolicy	4007	None
Information	2/26/2007 11:24:32 PM	GroupPolicy	4007	None
Information	3/4/2007 6:46:29 AM	GroupPolicy	4007	None
Information	3/9/2007 1:02:55 PM	GroupPolicy	4007	None
Information	3/7/2007 8:22:46 AM	GroupPolicy	4007	None

Figure 6-15

The Group Policy Operational Log sorted by EventID

2. To configure column headings, click **Add/Remove** columns in the **View** menu. The Add/Remove Columns dialog box appears, as shown in Figure 6-16.

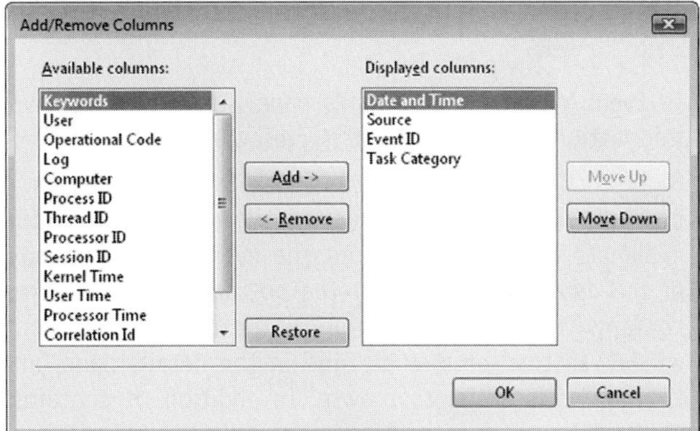

Figure 6-16

The Add/Remove Columns dialog box

To add a column heading, select the column heading in the **Available columns** list box and then click **Add.**

To remove a column heading, select the column heading in the **Displayed columns** list box and then click **Remove.**

To re-order the columns, select a column to move in the **Displayed columns** list box and then click **Move Up** or **Move Down.**

To restore the columns to the default, click **Restore.**

3. Click **OK** to close the Add/Remove Columns dialog box.

GROUP BY COLUMN HEADINGS

Grouping by column heading is a quick way to organize event data and can be useful for troubleshooting. For example, you can quickly group all the events having to do with Event ID so that you can inspect those instances more easily.

OPEN Event Viewer.

1. In Event Viewer, in the **View** menu, point to **Group by** and then click the column heading by which you want to group events. For example, to group by Event ID, point to **Group by** in the **View** menu and then click **Event ID**. The events are grouped according to the selected column heading, and you can expand or collapse each group by using the arrow to the right of the group name, as shown in Figure 6-17.

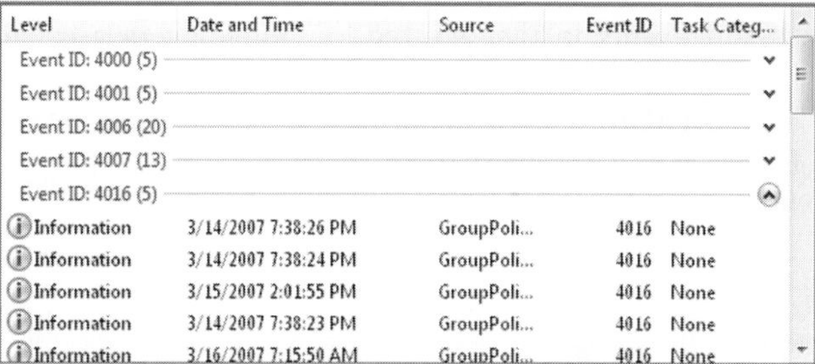

Figure 6-17

The Group Policy Operational Log grouped by EventID

2. After grouping events, several more options are available:

To collapse all groups, click **Collapse All Groups** in the **View** menu.

To expand all groups, click **Expand All Groups** in the **View** menu.

To remove grouping, click **Remove grouping of events** in the **View** menu.

Viewing Events

Events details are stored in XML and can be viewed in XML or in a more readable format.

VIEW EVENT DATA IN EVENT VIEWER

OPEN Event Viewer.

1. In Event Viewer, in the details pane, select the event you want to view. Note that information about the event is presented in the preview pane below the details pane.
2. Right-click the event and then click **Event Properties**. The Event Properties dialog box opens to the General tab, as shown in Figure 6-18. The General tab contains explanatory information about the event in the list box at the top, and a summary of the detail information at the bottom. The Event Properties dialog box actually contains the same information as the preview pane, but it puts each event in one window instead of a single line in the details pane, and therefore the information it contains is easier to browse. In addition, it contains added functionality in its ability to copy event data to the clipboard.

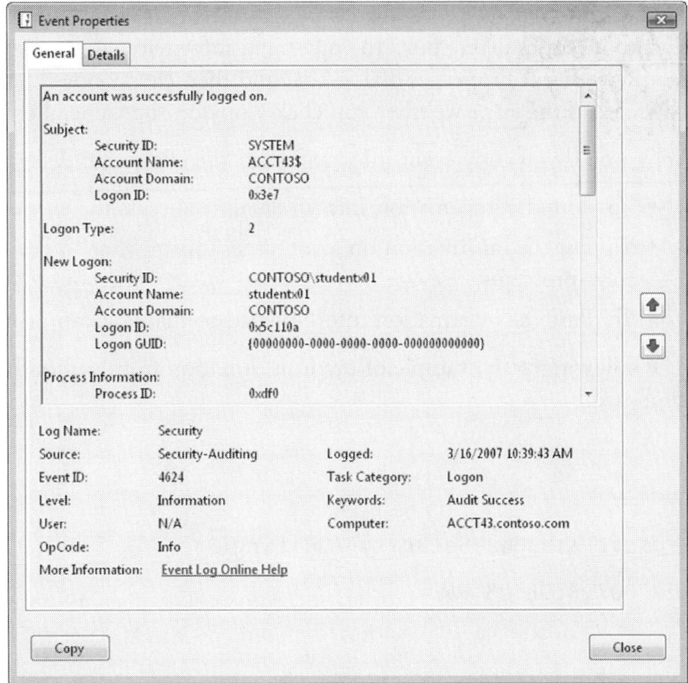

Figure 6-18

The General tab of the Event Properties dialog box

3. To access the events full detail information, click the **Details** tab, as Figure 6-19 shows.

   To view the details information in Friendly View, select **Friendly View**.

   To view the details information in XML View, select **XML View**.

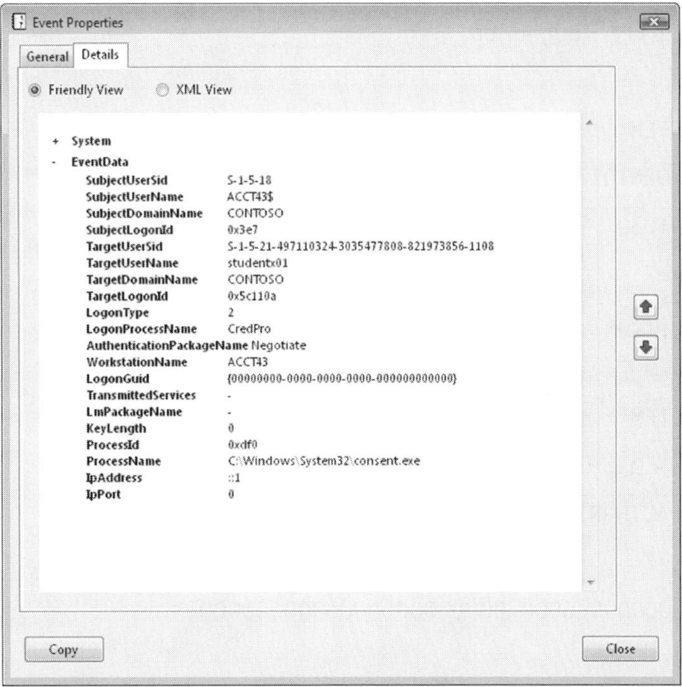

Figure 6-19

The Details tab of the Event Properties dialog box in Friendly View mode

The details information for all events is stored in XML. This makes it easy for scripts or third-party applications to pull data from an event. To make event detail easier to read, Event View offers the Friendly View. The Friendly View is simply a tree representation of the XML data. You can expand and collapse nodes in the tree just as you can in the console tree of an MMC Snap-in.

As mentioned in the procedure, you can copy event information to the clipboard by using the Event Properties dialog box. To copy event information, access either the General or Details tab of the Event Properties dialog box, and then click Copy. The information copied to the clipboard is the same whether you click Copy on the General or Details tab.

Why would you copy event information to the clipboard? A few reasons are:

- To paste the information into an email to discuss the event with a colleague.
- To post the information on an Internet forum where other IT professionals help users to solve problems.
- To paste the information into Notepad so that you can print it for closer examination.

The following is an example of event information from successful logon event copied to the clipboard:

```
Log Name:          Security
Source:            Microsoft-Windows-Security-Auditing
Date:              3/11/2007 3:06:05 AM
Event ID:          4624
Task Category:     Logon
Level:             Information
Keywords:          Audit Success
User:              N/A
Computer:          Student01-PC.contoso.com
Description:
An account was successfully logged on.
Subject:
    Security ID:     SYSTEM
    Account Name:    STUDENT01-PC$
    Account Domain:  CONTOSO
    Logon ID:        0x3e7
Logon Type:        5
New Logon:
    Security ID:     SYSTEM
    Account Name:    SYSTEM
    Account Domain:  NT AUTHORITY
    Logon ID:        0x3e7
    Logon GUID:      {00000000-0000-0000-0000-000000000000}
Process Information:
    Process ID:      0x25c
    Process Name:    C:\Windows\System32\services.exe
```

```
Network Information:
    Workstation Name:
    Source Network Address:-
    Source Port:      -
Detailed Authentication Information:
    Logon Process:   Advapi
    Authentication Package:Negotiate
    Transited Services:    -
    Package Name (NTLM only):     -
    Key Length:      0
This event is generated when a logon session is created. It is generated on the computer
that was accessed.
The subject fields indicate the account on the local system which requested the logon. This
is most commonly a service such as the Server service, or a local process such as Winlogon.
exe or Services.exe.
The logon type field indicates the kind of logon that occurred. The most common types are
2 (interactive) and 3 (network).
The New Logon fields indicate the account for whom the new logon was created, i.e. the
account that was logged on.
The network fields indicate where a remote logon request originated. Workstation name is
not always available and may be left blank in some cases.
The authentication information fields provide detailed information about this specific logon
request.
        - Logon GUID is a unique identifier that can be used to correlate this event with a
KDC event.
        - Transited services indicate which intermediate services have participated in this
logon request.
        - Package name indicates which sub-protocol was used among the NTLM protocols.
        - Key length indicates the length of the generated session key. This will be 0 if no
session key was requested.
Event Xml:
```


```
<Event xmlns="http://schemas.microsoft.com/win/2004/08/events/event">
  <System>
    <Provider Name="Microsoft-Windows-Security-Auditing" Guid="{54849625-5478-4994-a5ba-
    3e3b0328c30d}" />
  <EventID>4624</EventID>
  <Version>0</Version>
  <Level>0</Level>
  <Task>12544</Task>
  <Opcode>0</Opcode>
  <Keywords>0x8020000000000000</Keywords>
  <TimeCreated SystemTime="2007-03-11T10:06:05.259Z" />
```

```
  <EventRecordID>1084557</EventRecordID>
  <Correlation />
  <Execution ProcessID="620" ThreadID="3764" />
  <Channel>Security</Channel>
  <Computer>Student01-PC.contoso.com</Computer>
  <Security />
</System>
<EventData>
  <Data Name="SubjectUserSid">S-1-5-18</Data>
  <Data Name="SubjectUserName">STUDENT01-PC$</Data>
  <Data Name="SubjectDomainName">CONTOSO</Data>
  <Data Name="SubjectLogonId">0x3e7</Data>
  <Data Name="TargetUserSid">S-1-5-18</Data>
  <Data Name="TargetUserName">SYSTEM</Data>
  <Data Name="TargetDomainName">NT AUTHORITY</Data>
  <Data Name="TargetLogonId">0x3e7</Data>
  <Data Name="LogonType">5</Data>
  <Data Name="LogonProcessName">Advapi </Data>
  <Data Name="AuthenticationPackageName">Negotiate</Data>
  <Data Name="WorkstationName">
  </Data>
  <Data Name="LogonGuid">{00000000-0000-0000-0000-000000000000}</Data>
  <Data Name="TransmittedServices">-</Data>
  <Data Name="LmPackageName">-</Data>
  <Data Name="KeyLength">0</Data>
  <Data Name="ProcessId">0x25c</Data>
  <Data Name="ProcessName">C:\Windows\System32\services.exe</Data>
  <Data Name="IpAddress">-</Data>
  <Data Name="IpPort">-</Data>
</EventData>
</Event>
```

ATTACH A TASK TO AN EVENT

You can attach a task to an event so that task scheduler will launch a task when a particular event occurs. For example, you may want to receive an email if a critical event occurs related to an important server, or you may want to launch a script when a particular event occurs.

OPEN Event Viewer.

1. In Event Viewer, right-click an example of the event to which you want to attach a task and then click **Attach Task To This Event**. The Create Basic Task Wizard appears, as shown in Figure 6-20.

Figure 6-20

The Create Basic Task Wizard

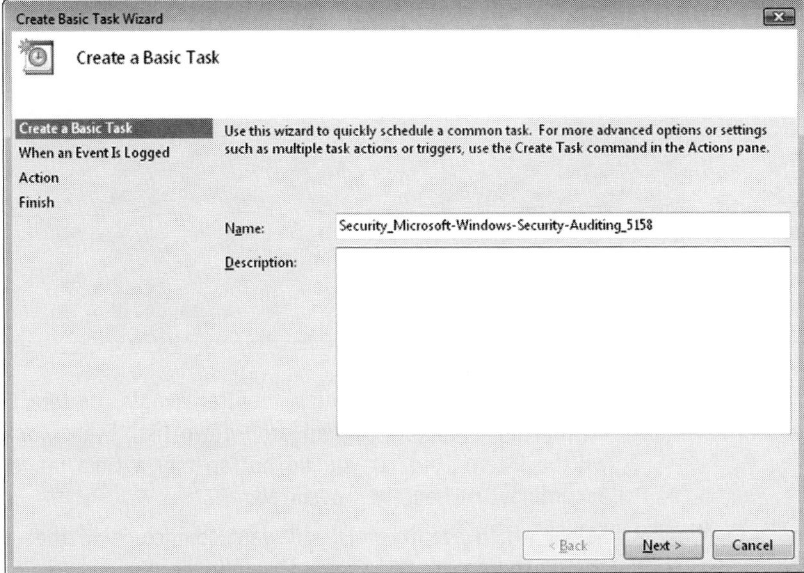

X REF

Creating tasks is covered in **Lesson 9**.

2. Follow the instructions in the wizard to create the task.

Creating Filters and Custom Views

> Filters and custom views enable you to filter large numbers of events according to custom criteria.

Event Viewer contains a formidable amount of data. To help you sort through the data, it is organized into different logs, such as the Security log and the Setup log, or the Group Policy Operational log. You have been shown how to sort and group data using column headings such as Event ID.

However, sorting and grouping does not remove events from the event list that you are not interested in, leaving only those that you are interested in. To do that, you use filters. ***Filters*** enable you to specify criteria by which events are filtered out of the event list.

FILTER A LOG

OPEN Event Viewer.

1. In Event Viewer, expand **Windows Logs** and then with the log that you want to filter selected, click **Filter Current Log** in the **Action** menu. The Filter Current Log dialog box appears, as shown in Figure 6-21.

Figure 6-21

The Filter Current Log dialog box

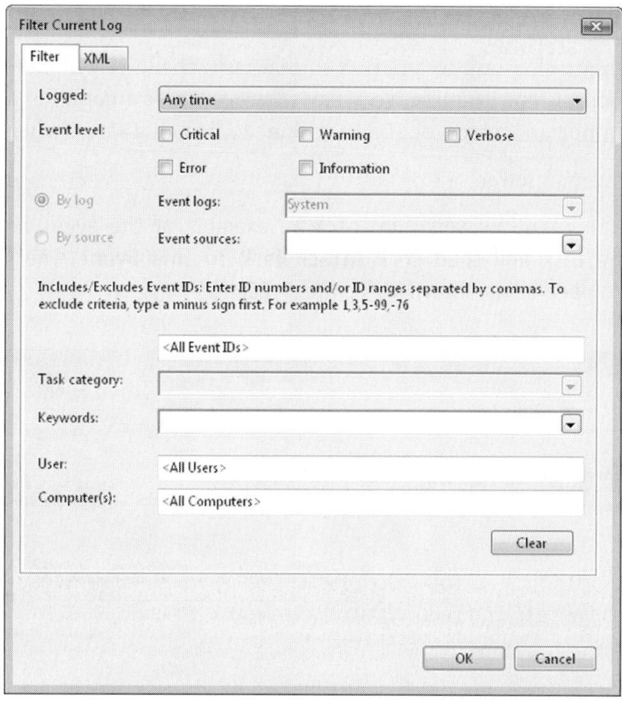

2. Select a time range by which to filter events, or select **Custom range** to specify a custom range in the **Logged** drop-down list. Events outside of the range specified will be filtered out. If you do not specify a time range, no events will be filtered according to when they occurred.
3. Select which event levels you want to include in the event list by selecting the corresponding check box for the following:

   Critical. Critical events indicate that there is a serious problem, and you should take action immediately.

   Warning. Warning events indicate that there may be a problem. You should pay attention to warnings, but you may not need to take any actions.

   Verbose. Verbose events are informational only.

   Error. There is an error. You most likely should address the error.

   Information. Information events are informational only.

TAKE NOTE* Another way of thinking about step three is that leaving a check box empty will filter out events with the corresponding event level.

4. In the **Event sources** drop-down list, select the check boxes for all of the event sources that you want to include in the event list. Selecting no check boxes is the same as selecting all check boxes (in other words, no events will be filtered out of the event list). You can also key event sources in the text box.
5. In the **Includes/Excludes Event IDs** text box, key events IDs that you want to include in the events list. To filter out events from the list by event ID, type the event ID preceded by the minus sign. To indicate a range, type the first event ID followed by a dash followed by the last event ID. Use commas to separate entries. For example, to filter out events with IDs between 1000 and 1500, include all events with event ID 7036, and include events between 8000 and 9000, key -1000-1500, 7036, 8000-9000.

6. In the **Task Category** drop-down list, select the check boxes for all of the task categories that you want to use to identify events to include in the events list. You can also key task categories in the text box. This drop-down list is not available for all event sources.
7. In the **Keywords** drop-down list, select the check boxes for all of the keywords that you want to use to identify events to include in the events list. You can also key keywords in the text box.
8. In the **User** text box, key the users associated with the events that you want to include in the events list, separated with commas. Leaving this blank will include all users.
9. In the **Computers** text box, key the computer names associated with the events that you want to include in the events list, separated by commas. Leaving this blank will include all computers.
10. To clear all of your selections, click **Clear**.
11. Click **OK** to close the Filter Current Log dialog box.

TAKE NOTE*

The filtering criteria you are providing is internally stored as a query in XML. You can click the XML tab to view the query, and you can select the Edit query manually check box to edit the query in XML. However, once you manually edit the query, you can no longer use the Filter tab interface to modify it.

Event filtering only enables you to filter the current log, and the filter cannot be saved.

Custom views address both these issues. ***Custom views*** are just like filters except:

- You can apply the filtering across multiple logs.
- You can save the filtering settings as a view, which can be loaded at a later date.

CREATE AND SAVE A CUSTOM VIEW

OPEN Event Viewer.

1. In Event Viewer, click **Create Custom View** in the **Action** menu. The Create Custom View dialog box appears, as shown in Figure 6-22.

Figure 6-22

The Create Custom View dialog box

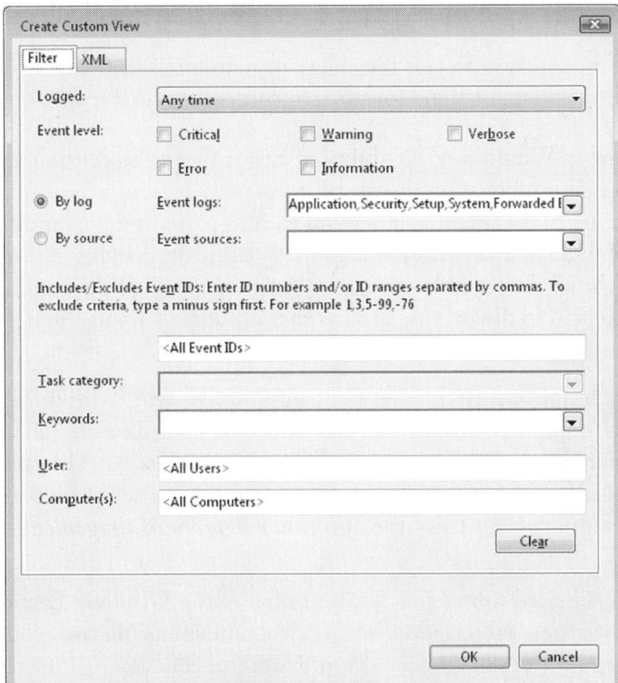

2. Configure the custom view just as you would a filter, except in the **Event logs** drop-down list, expand the nodes and then select the check boxes for all the logs that you want to include in the filtering.
3. Click **OK**. The Save Filter to Custom View dialog box appears, as shown in Figure 6-23.

Figure 6-23

The Save Filter to Custom View dialog box

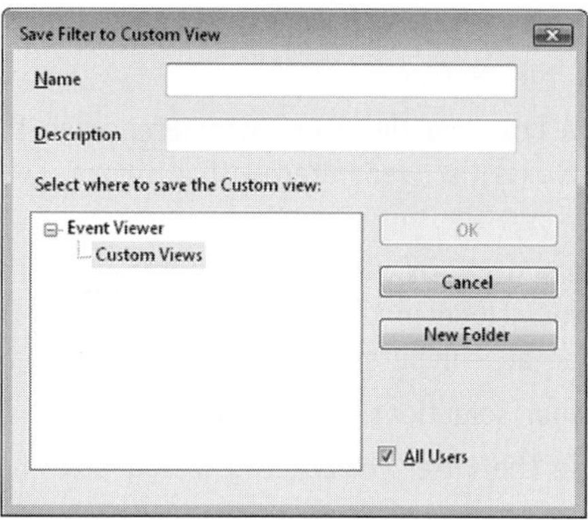

4. In the **Name** text box, key a name for the filter.
5. In the **Description** text box, key a description (you might want to list some of the key criteria or identify the purpose of the view, for example, "failed folder redirection events").
6. Select a folder in the tree in which to save the view. To create a new folder, click **New Folder**.
7. To make the filter available to all users, select the **All Users** check box. To make it available only to you, clear the **All Users** check box.
8. Click **OK**.

The custom view will appear in the console tree under the folder to which you saved it. To use the view, you don't need to load it, you only need to locate it in the console tree and select it. However, you can import a custom view by clicking Import Custom View in the Action menu. This option can be useful to share custom views with colleagues or other IT professionals.

CERTIFICATION READY?
Configure and troubleshoot Event Forwarding: Monitor and respond to forwarded events
3.3

Centralizing Event Data by Using Subscriptions

New in Windows Vista is the ability to centralize event data by creating subscriptions between a collector computer and forwarders (computers that forward events to the collector).

The new to Windows Vista ability of Event Viewer to centralize data from multiple computers is a major innovation. It can be immensely helpful when troubleshooting in a networked environment, because it enables you to find patterns across multiple computers. For example, if some users in a department are having difficulty logging into the domain, you might want to look at all the failed logon attempt events across all the computers in the department. It can also help in discovering attacks that are spread across the network and not concentrated on a single computer.

When centralizing event data, the computer on which you centralize data is called the ***collector***. The computers from which the collector pulls data are called ***forwarders***. You create a ***subscription*** when you create a collector/forwarders set. The collector must run the ***Windows Event Collector service***, whereas each machine in the subscription—both the collector and the forwarders—must run the ***Windows Remote Management service***.

TAKE NOTE*

You do not need to independently configure the Windows Event Collector service. When you configure a subscription for the first time on a collector, you are asked if you want to install and start the Windows Event Collector service.

The overall steps for configuring a subscription are:

1. Configure the forwarding computers using the winrm quickconfig command, which does the following:
   - Sets the startup type for the Windows Remote Management (WinRM) service to Automatic (Delayed Start).
   - Starts the WinRM service.
   - Enables an exception in Windows Firewall for Windows Remote Management.
2. Add the collector's MACHINE account to the Even Log Readers group on the forwarders.
3. Configuring the subscription on the collector computer.

CONFIGURE THE FORWARDING COMPUTERS

1. Click **Start**. In the **Start Search** box, type **cmd** and then press **Ctrl + Shift + Enter**. A User Account Control dialog box appears.
2. Provide administrator credentials and then click **OK**. A command prompt window appears.
3. Key **winrm quickconfig** and then press **Enter**. The following is output to the command prompt window:

```
C:\Windows\system32>winrm quickconfig
WinRM is not set up to allow remote access to this machine for
management.
The following changes must be made:
Set the WinRM service type to delayed auto start.
Start the WinRM service.
Create a WinRM listener on HTTP://* to accept WS-Man requests to any
IP on this
machine.
Enable the WinRM firewall exception.
Make these changes [y/n]?
```

4. Key **y** and then press **Enter**. The following is output to the command prompt window:

```
Make these changes [y/n]? y
WinRM has been updated for remote management.
WinRM service type changed successfully.
WinRM service started.
Created a WinRM listener on HTTP://* to accept WS-Man requests to
any IP on this machine.
WinRM firewall exception enabled.
```

5. Close the command prompt window.
6. Click **Start**, **Control Panel**. The Control Panel appears.
7. Click **User Accounts**. The User Accounts window appears.
8. Click **User Accounts**. The User Accounts window appears (this is not a typographical error: there are two User Account windows, one right after the other).
9. Click **Manage User Accounts**. A User Account Control dialog box appears.

Steps 6 through 9 can be accomplished by clicking Start, keying control userpassword2, and pressing Ctrl + Shift + Enter.

10. Provide administrator credentials and then click **OK**. The User Accounts dialog box appears, as shown in Figure 6-24.

Figure 6-24

The User Accounts dialog box

TAKE NOTE*

The dollar sign at the end of the machine account name was added in Windows 2000 as a work-around for a bug that occurred when a user had the same name as a computer.

11. Click **Add**. The Add New User wizard appears.
12. In the **User name** text box, key the machine account name of the collector. The machine account name is the computer name with a $ appended. For example, if the name of the forwarder is WS2543, then key WS2543$.
13. In the **Domain** text box, type the name of your domain.
14. Click **Next**. The next page of the wizard appears.
15. On the *What level of access do you want to grant this user?* page select **Other**.
16. In the **Other** drop-down list, select **Event Log Readers**, as shown in Figure 6-25.

Figure 6-25

Selecting Event Log Readers in the Add New User Wizard

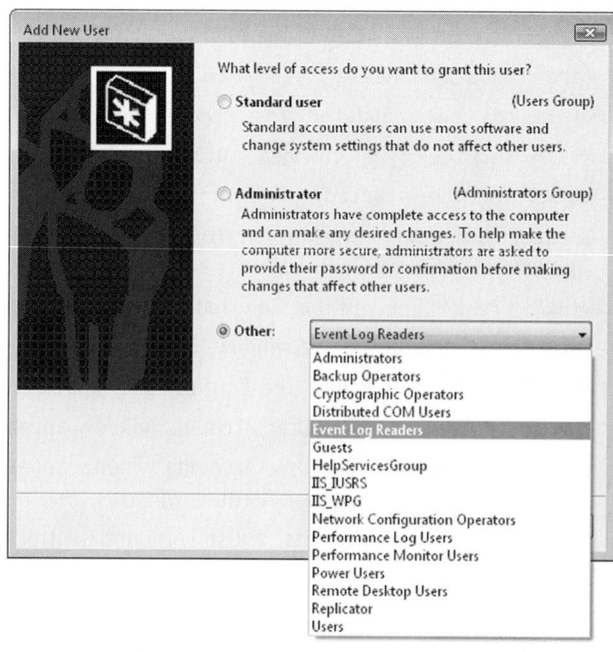

17. Click **Finish**.
18. Repeat the process for each event forwarder.

CONFIGURE THE COLLECTOR COMPUTER

CONTINUE from the previous procedure.

1. In Event Viewer, in the console tree, right-click **Subscriptions** and then click **Create Subscription.** If this is the first time you have configured a subscription on your computer, an Event Viewer message box will open, as shown in Figure 6-26.

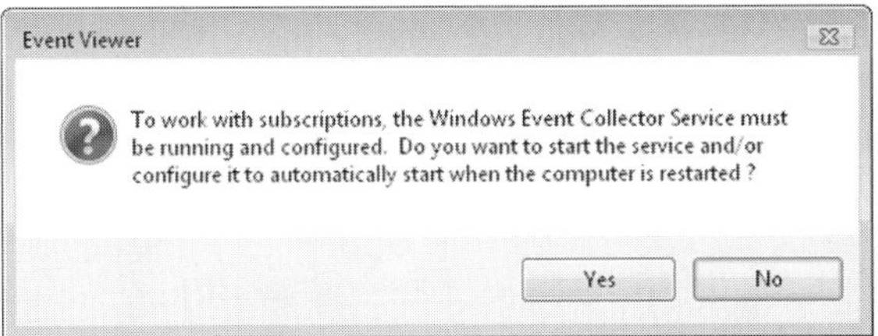

Figure 6-26

Event Viewer message box asking for confirmation to start and configure the Windows Event Collector service

2. Click **Yes.** The Subscription Properties dialog box appears, as shown in Figure 6-27.

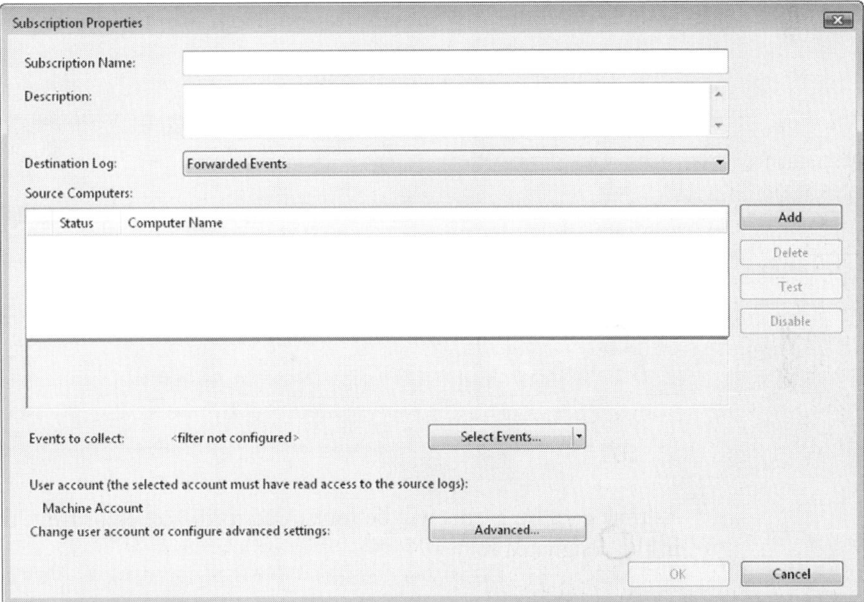

Figure 6-27

The Subscription Propertied dialog box

3. In the **Subscription Name** text box, key a name for the subscription. For example, **Logon Events for Accounting Workstations.**
4. In the **Description** text box, type a description for the subscription. For example, **Tracking of logon events in the accounting department to discover hacking attempts.**
5. In the **Destination Log** drop-down list, select a log in which to record the forwarded events. By default, the Forwarded Events log is selected, but you can choose any log. Whatever log you choose, be sure to display the Computer column so that you can distinguish from which computer an event originated.
6. In the Source Computers section, click **Add.** The Select Computer dialog box appears.
7. In the **Enter the object name to select** text box, type the computer name of each forwarder separated by semi-colons. For example: WRKSTN242;WRKSTN243; WRKSTN244.
8. Click **OK.**

9. In the Subscriptions Properties dialog box, in the **Select Events** drop-down list, click one of the following:
    - **Edit.** Click this to create a filter that will define the events to collect. The interface that appears when you click this is identical to that of the Create Custom View dialog box. When you are done configuring Filter settings, click **OK.**
    - **Copy from existing Custom View.** Click this to capture the same events that a custom view captures. After you copy the filter settings from the existing custom view, you can modify them. When you are done configuring filter settings, click **OK.**
10. Click **OK.**

TAKE NOTE* You can also configure some advanced options by clicking Advanced. These include which account to use to collect the forwarded events, and how the events are delivered (including protocol, port, and optimization settings).

If connectivity and access are configured correctly, when you select Subscriptions in the console tree, your new subscription will appear in the details pane with Active in the status column, as shown in Figure 6-28.

Figure 6-28

The example subscription is active, as indicated in the Status column

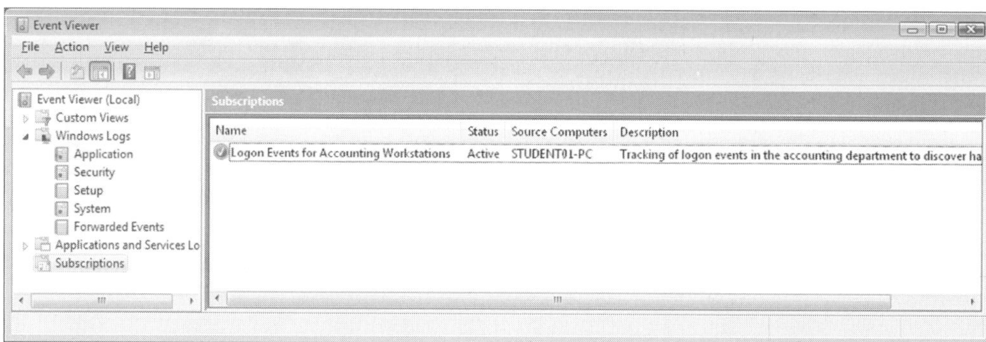

As time goes by, events will be forwarded to the collector from the forwarders, and will appear in the designated folder.

■ Using the Security Configuration and Analysis Snap-In

THE BOTTOM LINE

The Security Configuration and Analysis Snap-in is used to compare your security configuration settings to those contained in a security template, export settings that you configure in a database to a security template, and apply the security settings in a database to the local computer.

CERTIFICATION READY?
Troubleshoot security configuration issues: Run the Security Configuration and Analysis tool
2.2

The ***Security Configuration and Analysis Snap-in*** enables you to compare and configure security policies against those in security templates loaded into a database. ***Security templates*** contain policy settings for Windows Vista security policies. You can replace your system's security policies with those in the database as a whole or individually. Once you have your security settings the way you want them, you can use the Snap-in to export them for use on other computers.

The Security Configuration and Analysis Snap-in uses the following icons in its reports:

- **Red X.** The setting is defined in the database and on the system, but the values between the two do not match.
- **Green check mark.** The setting is defined in the database and on the system, and the values match.
- **Question mark.** The setting is not defined in the database and was therefore not analyzed, or, the user does not have sufficient permissions to perform the analysis.
- **Exclamation point.** The setting is defined in the database, but not on the system.
- **No icon.** The setting is not defined in the database or on the system.

The Security Configuration and Analysis Snap-in is used for both configuration and analysis. You can use it to heighten system security by selective application of settings in the database, and to export security settings to a security template for use elsewhere. You can also use it to analyze the current security settings on a system by comparing them to those of a baseline security template or templates.

MORE INFORMATION

The Windows Vista Security Guide download comes with several security templates, and contains thorough descriptions of them. You can download it by searching here: www.microsoft.com/downloads/.

Using the Security Configuration and Analysis Snap-in to Analyze Settings

One of the main purposes of the Security Configuration and Analysis Snap-in is to give you a quick report on how a particular system's security settings match up to those in pre-configured security templates.

CREATE A NEW DATABASE AND ANALYZE YOUR SYSTEMS SECURITY SETTINGS

1. Click **Start.**In the **Start Search** text box, type **mmc** and then press **Ctrl + Shift + Enter.** A User Account Control dialog box appears.
2. Provide administrator credentials and then click **OK.** The Microsoft Management console appears.
3. In the File menu, click **Add/Remove Snap-in.** The Add or Remove Snap-ins dialog box opens, as shown in Figure 6-29.

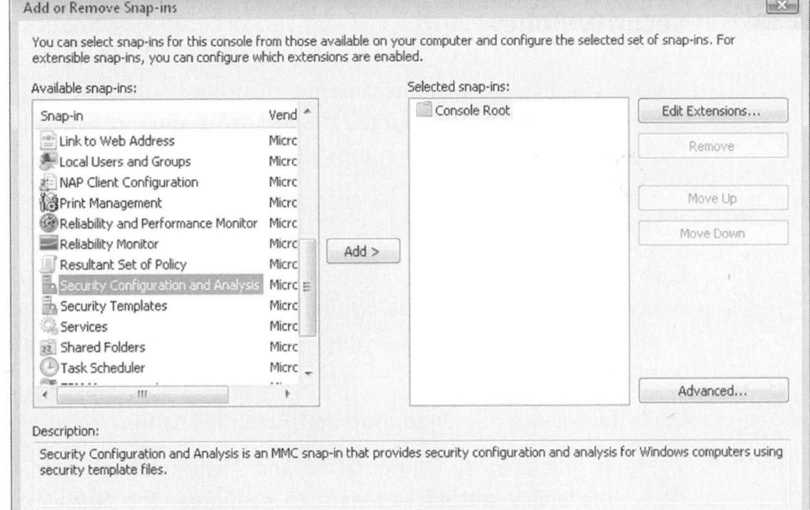

Figure 6-29

The Add or Remove Snap-ins dialog box

4. In the Available Snap-ins list box, select **Security Configuration and Analysis** and then click **Add.**
5. Click **OK.** The Snap-in is added.
6. In the console tree, right-click **Security Configuration and Analysis** and then click **Open Database.**
7. Key ***DatabaseName*** in the **File name** text box and then click **Open.** This will create a new database named *DatabaseName*. The Import Template dialog box appears.
8. Select a template to import. This could be in the Security Templates folder that opens by default, or someplace else. The remainder of this procedure uses the VSG EC Desktop.inf security template as an example. The EC stands for Enterprise Configuration.
9. If you are using an existing database and want to clear it before importing the template, select the **Clear this database before importing** check box.
10. After selecting a template, click **Open.** The template is loaded into the database. The details pane now displays instructions on how to configure and analyze your computer against the database.
11. If you want to add more templates to the database, right-click **Security Configuration and Analysis** in the console tree, click **Import template**, and then select the desired template. Repeat until all desired templates are added.
12. Right-click **Security Configuration and Analysis** in the console tree and then click **Analyze Computer Now.** The Perform Analysis dialog appears and displays the default location for the log file.
13. Specify an alternate location for the log file if desired and then click **OK.** The Analyze System Security message box indicates progress until the analysis completes.

Once the Security Configuration and Analysis Snap-in completes the analysis, the console tree under Security Configuration and Analysis becomes populated with nodes. Each of these nodes can be expanded to reveal either more nodes or security settings, which are displayed in the Policy column in the details pane.

Also displayed in the details pane are two other columns, Database Setting and Computer Setting, which contain information on how each policy is configured in the database versus on the local computer. Each policy can be tagged by an icon, the meanings of which were described in the previous section.

Using the Security Configuration and Analysis Snap-in to Configure Security Policy

Once you have decided on security settings using by loading and modifying settings from security templates, you can use the Security Configuration and Analysis Snap-in to apply those settings to the local computer.

CONFIGURE AN ANALYZED POLICY

Each setting listed in the details pane of the Security Configuration and Analysis Snap-in can be configured in the database by double-clicking it. This way you can adjust the policy setting in preparation to export the settings in the database to a template for application on other computers.

OPEN the Security Configuration and Analysis Snap-in.

1. In the Security Configuration and Analysis Snap-in, in the details pane, double-click the policy setting you want to configure. The *PolicyName* Properties dialog box appears, as shown in Figure 6-30.

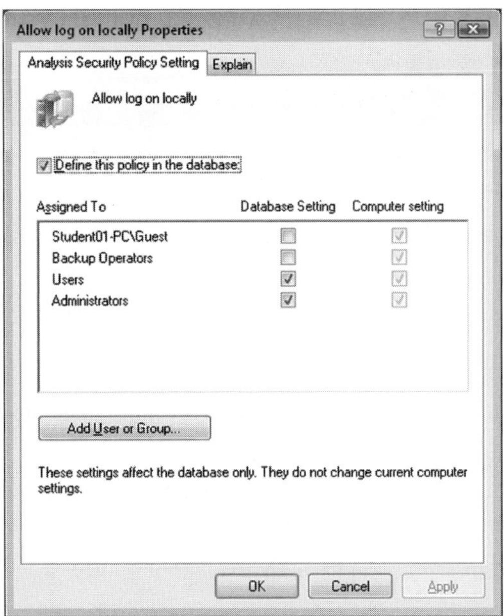

Figure 6-30

The Allow log on locally Properties dialog box

2. If you don't want the policy defined in the database, clear the **Define this policy in the database** check box and then click **OK.**
3. If you want the policy defined in the database, ensure that the **Define this policy in the database** check box is selected.
4. Configure the Database Setting and the Computer Setting as desired.
5. When you are finished, click **OK** to close the policy's dialog box.

CONFIGURE SECURITY POLICY BASED ON THE DATABASE POLICY SETTINGS

OPEN the Security Configuration and Analysis Snap-in, load a database, and make any desired modifications to the security policies in the database.

WARNING Completing this procedure will change the security settings on your computer to those in the database! This can change the behavior of your computer drastically depending on the security settings.

1. In the Security Configuration and Analysis Snap-in, in the console tree, right-click **Security Configuration and Analysis** and then click **Configure Computer Now.** The Configure System dialog box appears and displays the default location for the log file.
2. Specify an alternate location for the log file if desired and then click **OK.** The Configure System Security message box indicates progress until the configuration is complete.

EXPORT DATABASE SECURITY SETTINGS TO A SECURITY TEMPLATE

OPEN the Security Configuration and Analysis Snap-in and ensure that there is a database loaded from with to export settings to a template.

1. In the Security Configuration and Analysis Snap-in, in the console tree, right-click **Security Configuration and Analysis** and then click **Export Template.** The Export Template To dialog box appears.
2. Browse to the location where you want to save the template, and in the **File name** text box, key a name for the template and then click **Save.**
3. Close the console.

SUMMARY SKILL MATRIX

IN THIS LESSON YOU LEARNED:
Software restriction policies provide a Group Policy mechanism by which the running of programs can be restricted.
Additional rules in software restriction policies are exceptions to a default rule and come in four varieties: hash rules, certificate rules, path rules, and network zone rules.
Hash rules use hashes to identify program files in software restriction policies.
Certificate rules use certificates to identify program files in software restriction policies.
Path rules use file paths or registry paths to identify program files in software restriction policies.
Network zone rules use downloaded from locations to identify program files in software restriction policies.
Software restriction polices can be configured for both users and computers.
How to set the default security level for software restriction polices.
How to configure enforcement options for software restriction polices.
How to add or remove designated file types for software restriction polices.
How to create certificate, hash, network zone, and path rules for software restriction polices.
Event Viewer enables you to view recorded events in an organized way so that you can troubleshoot a wide range of issues by investigating related events.
How to use Event Viewer to view events on the local computer and on remote computers.
How to sort and group events around pivots to more easily find the events that you are looking for.
Events details are stored in XML, and can be viewed in XML or in a more readable format.
Filters and custom views enable you to filter large amounts of events according to custom criteria.
How to filter a log and how to create and save a custom view.
How to centralize event data by creating subscriptions between a collector computer and forwarders (computers that forward events to the collector).
The Security Configuration and Analysis Snap-in is used to: compare your security configuration settings to those contained in a security template; export settings that you configure in a database to a security template; and to apply the security settings in a database to the local computer.
How to create a new database and analyze your systems security settings using the Security Configuration and Analysis Snap-in.
How to apply security settings using the Security Configuration and Analysis Snap-in to the local computer.
How to export database security settings to a security template using the Security Configuration and Analysis Snap-in.

■ Knowledge Assessment

Fill in the Blank

Complete the following sentences by writing the correct word or words in the blanks provided.

1. Environment variables are not subject to access control lists, which make ________ within software restrictions polices vulnerable to circumvention.
2. ________ in software restriction policies are files that are considered to be executable code.
3. ________ rules in software restriction policies restrict access to programs based on their location on the network.
4. A(n) ________ is a collector/forwarders set created in Event Viewer for the purpose of centralizing recorded events onto a single computer.
5. The default rule in a software restriction policy can be overruled by any number of ________ rules.
6. The ________ service must be started on every computer within a subscription for an Event Viewer subscription to work properly.
7. ________ are like filters in Event Viewer but they can filter events across multiple logs.
8. A(n) ________ algorithm takes a data string of any length as input and produces a fixed length string as output.
9. A(n) ________ rule in a software restriction policy uses an encrypted signing of the file for identification.
10. ________ can be loaded into a database in the Security Configuration and Analysis Snap-in to be compared to the local computers security settings.

Multiple Choice

Select all answers that apply for the following questions.

1. Software restriction policies serve the following purpose:
   a. Allow only approved software to be installed or executed.
   b. Reduce the chance of software being installed or run that might conflict with other applications or change configuration information in a possibly undesirable way.
   c. Regulate what Microsoft ActiveX controls can be installed.
   d. Restrict running of scripts to digitally signed only.
2. The default security level in a software restriction policy can have the following values:
   a. unrestricted, disallowed, standard user
   b. unrestricted, disallowed, Basic User
   c. restricted, unrestricted, Basic User
   d. restricted, unrestricted, standard user
3. A hash rule in a software restriction policy can be circumvented by:
   a. Moving the restricted file to a different location.
   b. Altering the registry path for the restricted file.
   c. Modifying the code within the file so that it isn't really the same program as the one restricted.
   d. None of the above.

4. Which of the following software restriction policy rules can be defeated merely by moving a program from one location to another?
   a. Path rule
   b. Folder rule
   c. Hash rule
   d. Certificate rule

5. The Windows Event Collector service:
   a. Must be running on all forwarders within a subscription.
   b. Must be running on all computers in a subscription.
   c. Is not required for subscriptions—only the Windows Remote Management service is required.
   d. Must be running on the collector in a subscription.

6. Which of the following is not a possible default security level in software restriction policies?
   a. Unrestricted
   b. Standard user
   c. Basic user
   d. Disallowed

7. The question mark icon in Security Configuration and Analysis Snap-in reports could indicate which of the following?
   a. The setting cannot be analyzed because it has conflicting values in different GPOs.
   b. The setting cannot be analyzed because the user running the Snap-in doesn't have sufficient privileges.
   c. The setting cannot be analyzed because the target machine is unreachable.
   d. The setting is not defined in the database and was therefore not analyzed.

8. You can use wildcards in the following software restriction policy additional rules:
   a. Path rules
   b. Certificate rules
   c. Hash rules
   d. Network zone rules

9. You can export security settings from the following tool for use on other computers:
   a. Group Policy Results Wizard
   b. Security Configuration and Analysis Snap-in
   c. Event Viewer
   d. Security Template Export Wizard

10. A software restriction policy restricts the same software according to a path rule and a certificate rule. The path rule disallows the use of the software, whereas the certificate rule allows it to be run using a Basic User account. Which of the following statements is true?
   a. The certificate rule takes precedence and the software is allowed to run as using a Basic User account.
   b. The path rule takes precedence and the software is not allowed to run.
   c. It is not a valid question: certificate rules cannot specify the Basic User security-level.
   d. The certificate rule takes precedence and the software is allowed to run using the users account.

Review Questions

1. Describe the method by which a hash rule works and why it is not susceptible to circumvention by alteration of its path.

2. You can use Security and Analysis to compare, export, and apply. Describe what you can compare, what you can export, and what you can apply using the Snap-in. Give an example of when you might do each.

Case Scenarios

Scenario 1: Using Software Restriction Polices to Prevent Execution of Malware

Many computer viruses and other malware are scripts. The IT department uses scripts for many administrative tasks, and therefore disallowing all scripts is not a good solution for preventing malicious scripts from running. Describe a scheme using path rules and hash rules to prevent .VBS, .VBE, .JS, .JSE, .WSF, and .WSH script files from running while allowing scripts of any type from the IT department to run.

Scenario 2: Controlling Software Installation

Many roles for computers in an enterprise do not require that users be able to install any software. Limiting their ability to install software can greatly enhance security.

Describe a software restriction policy scheme where:

1. all .msi files are prevented from being installed except those digitally signed by the IT department.
2. .msi files in \\SoftServer2\safeinstall are allowed to install without digital signing.

Using Windows Firewall and Windows Defender

OBJECTIVE DOMAIN MATRIX

Technology Skill	Objective Domain	Objective Domain Number
Understanding Windows Firewall	Troubleshoot Windows Firewall issues	2.3
Configuring Windows Firewall	Troubleshoot Windows Firewall issues	2.3
Configuring Windows Firewall Basic Settings	Troubleshoot Windows Firewall issues • Configure system exceptions	2.3
Configuring Windows Firewall with Advanced Security and Group Policy Settings	Troubleshoot Windows Firewall issues • Configure system exceptions	2.3
Understanding Windows Defender	Troubleshoot Windows Defender issues	2.4
Using Windows Defender	Troubleshoot Windows Defender issues	2.4
Configure Windows Defender Options Locally	Troubleshoot Windows Defender issues	2.4
Using Software Explorer	Troubleshoot Windows Defender issues	2.4
Scanning Your System Manually	Troubleshoot Windows Defender issues	2.4
Configuring Windows Defender Group Policy	Troubleshoot Windows Defender issues	2.4

KEY TERMS

firewall
host firewall
Windows Firewall
Windows Firewall Settings dialog box
Domain profile
Private profile
Public profile
firewall rules
connection security rules
inbound rule
outbound rule
custom rule
program rule
port rule
pre-defined rule
spyware
Software Explorer

Contoso Incorporated, where you are a senior desktop support technician, uses a third-party perimeter firewall along with Windows Firewall on each workstation as a host firewall. In addition, the perimeter firewall does not protect some kiosk machines that are not connected to the domain. Your task is to configure Windows Firewall through Group Policy for the domain computers, and configure it locally on the kiosk computers.

Understanding Windows Firewall

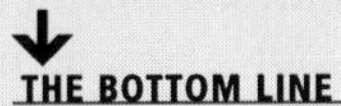
THE BOTTOM LINE

Windows Firewall is a host firewall that can run on each computer in a network to help prevent attacks.

CERTIFICATION READY?
Troubleshoot Windows Firewall issues
2.3

A ***firewall*** is a software device (and sometimes has software and hardware components) that limits inbound and sometimes outbound data connections in an attempt to strengthen security. ***Windows Firewall*** is a ***host firewall*** (as opposed to a perimeter firewall), which means that it can run on each computer inside the network, and that it provides local protection against attacks originating from inside the local network, or from outside the network when perimeter defenses have failed.

Windows Firewall filters all packets for Internet Protocol version 4 (IPv4) and IP version 6 (IPv6) traffic according to rules that you can create and modify. By default, Windows Firewall blocks inbound traffic unless it is a response to a request by the host or it is specifically unblocked. You can configure rules to unblock inbound traffic by specifying a port number, application name, service name, or other criteria. You can also configure rules to regulate outbound traffic, a feature new to Windows Firewall in Windows Vista. By default, Windows Firewall allows all outbound traffic unless it is excepted by a rule. Rules that are combined to unblock a particular communication type are called an exception. All exceptions are comprised of one or more rules.

Configuring IPsec in Windows Firewall is covered in **Lesson 11: Understanding, Configuring, and Securing TCP/IP Networks.**

In addition to normal firewall duties, Windows Vista integrates the IP security (IPsec) protocol into Windows Firewall. This enables you to selectively require or request that computers authenticate with each other before communicating, and that they use data integrity or encryption while communicating.

In previous versions of Windows Firewall, you accomplished local configuration primarily through the Windows Firewall Settings dialog box. In Windows Vista, this interface still exists, but new advanced functionality—along with some legacy functionality—is now configured in the Windows Firewall with Advanced Security Snap-in. This Snap-in has a nearly identical counterpart in Group Policy that you use to apply settings in a domain environment to many computers simultaneously.

Features new to or enhanced in Windows Firewall in Windows Vista are:

- **Windows Firewall with Advanced Security Snap-in**. This Microsoft Management Console (MMC) Snap-in exposes many new advanced Windows Firewall Settings. The same settings can be configured in Group Policy by expanding Computer Configuration>Windows Settings>Security Settings>Windows Firewall with Advanced Security.
- **IPsec integration**. Windows Firewall now integrates firewall filtering and Internet Protocol Security (IPsec) rule configuration. IPsec is a suite of protocols for securing Internet Protocol (IP) communications by authenticating or encrypting all IP packets in an IP data stream.
- **Expanded authenticated bypass**. With IPsec authentication, you can configure bypass rules for specific computers so that connections from those computers bypass other rules. This enables you to block a particular type of traffic while allowing authenticated computers to bypass the block.
- **Windows Service Hardening network restrictions**. Windows Service Hardening helps prevent critical Windows services from being misused to attack the file system, registry, or network. Windows Firewall will block behavior that the Windows Service Hardening network rules deem abnormal.
- **Outbound filtering**. Windows Firewall now provides outbound filtering in addition to inbound filtering.

- **Detailed rules.** You can configure rules for both inbound and outbound connections. Windows Firewall also supports filtering of any Internet Assigned Numbers Authority (IANA) protocol numbers, whereas previous versions of Windows Firewall supported filtering only User Datagram Protocol (UDP), Transmission Control Protocol (TCP), and Internet Control Message Protocol (ICMP) protocols. Windows Firewall now supports configuration of Active Directory domain service accounts and groups, application names, TCP, UDP, ICMPv4, ICMPv6, local and remote IP addresses, interface types and protocols, and ICMP type and code filtering.
- **Location-aware profiles.** You can configure different rules and settings for the following firewall profiles:

  Domain profile. Used when a computer is authenticated to an Active Directory domain of which the computer is a member. The Domain profile is active when all interfaces can authenticate to a domain controller.

  Private profile. Used when a computer is connected to a private network behind a private gateway or router. Only a user with administrative privileges can designate a network as private.

  Public profile. Used when a computer is connected directly to an unidentified network in a public location. The Public profile is active when there is at least one public network or unidentified connection.

  When a user connects to a network that is not part of the domain, Windows Vista asks the user to identify the network as either Public or Private. The user must be a local administrator of the computer to identify the network as Private.
- **Support for Active Directory users, computers, and groups.** You can create firewall rules that filter connections by Active Directory users, computers, and groups.
- **Support for IPv6.** Fully supports native IPv6, IPv6 to IPv4 (6to4), and a new method of Network Address Translation (NAT) traversal for IPv6, called Teredo.

■ Configuring Windows Firewall

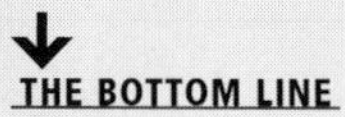

You can configure the most basic settings for Windows Firewall through the Windows Firewall Settings dialog box. More advanced settings can be configured using the Windows Firewall with Advanced Security Snap-in and Group Policy.

You can configure Windows Firewall through six interfaces including those in Group Policy. Table 7-1 describes each and when to use it.

Table 7-1

Windows Firewall interfaces and when to use each

INTERFACE	LOCATION	DESCRIPTION	APPLICATIONS
Windows Firewall Settings dialog box	Start>Control Panel>Security>Windows Firewall>Change Settings	This is the legacy interface.	Primarily for use on stand-alone computers or in small networks. Can be used in an enterprise environment to configure exceptions for an individual client computer, if such exceptions are allowed by Group Policy settings.

(continued)

Table 7-1 *(continued)*

Interface	Location	Description	Applications
Windows Firewall with Advanced Security Snap-in	Snap-in for the Microsoft Management console	A more complex interface that enables the creation and sorting of rules that can be combined to form exceptions.	Primarily for use on stand-alone computers or in small networks. Can be used in an enterprise environment to configure inbound and outbound rules and IPsec configuration for an individual client computer, if allowed by Group Policy settings. Can also be used to configure a specific remote computer on the network.
Windows Firewall with Advanced Security Group Policy settings	Computer Configuration>Windows Settings>Security Settings>Windows Firewall with Advanced Security	The interface and functionality are nearly identical to those of the Windows Firewall with Advanced Security Snap-in.	Used for configuring inbound and outbound rules and IPsec configuration for computers within a container in an Active Directory environment.
Windows Firewall Domain Profile Group Policy settings	Computer Configuration> Administrative Templates> Network>Network. Connections> Windows Firewall>Domain Profile	Contains Group Policy settings pertaining to Windows Firewall. These settings are applied to computers within the scope of the Group Policy Object (GPO) when the computers have network access to domain controllers for the domain.	Used in an Active Directory environment, such as an enterprise, to configure Group Policy settings.
Windows Firewall Standard Profile Group Policy settings	Computer Configuration> Administrative Templates> Network>Network Connections>Windows Firewall>Standard Profile	Contains Group Policy settings pertaining to Windows Firewall. These settings are applied to computers within the scope of the GPO when the computers do not have network access to domain controllers for the domain.	Used in an Active Directory environment, such as an enterprise, to configure Group Policy settings.
Netsh command-line tool	Runs in a command prompt	Enables administrators to configure local settings, or settings on a remote computer, in a command-line interface. It is amenable to scripting.	Primarily for use on stand-alone computers or in small networks. You can use it in an enterprise environment to configure inbound and outbound rules and IPsec configuration for an individual client computer, if allowed by Group Policy settings. Can also be used to configure a remote computer on the network. Also used when you want to take advantage of scripting to apply settings to one or more computers.

Configuring Windows Firewall Basic Settings

The basic settings for Windows Firewall can be configured using the Windows Firewall Settings dialog box.

The ***Windows Firewall Settings dialog box*** exposes many of the controls you are familiar with from Windows Firewall in XP SP2. This is where you can set the most basic settings and configure exceptions.

OPEN THE WINDOWS FIREWALL SETTINGS DIALOG BOX

1. Click **Start**. In the Start Search text box, key **Windows Firewall**, right-click **Windows Firewall** in the Programs list, and then click **Open**. The Windows Firewall window appears.
2. Click **Change settings**. A User Account Control dialog box appears.
3. Provide administrator credentials and then click **OK**. The Windows Firewall Settings dialog box appears, as shown in Figure 7-1.

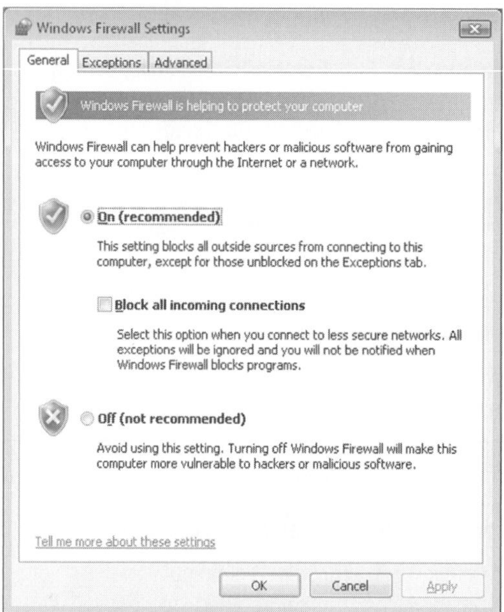

Figure 7-1

The Windows Firewall Settings dialog box

CONFIGURE THE GENERAL TAB OF THE WINDOWS FIREWALL SETTINGS DIALOG BOX

The General tab enables you to turn Windows Firewall on and off, and to block all inbound connections even if they are excepted on the Exceptions tab.

OPEN the Windows Firewall Settings dialog box.

In the Windows Firewall Settings dialog box, on the General tab (shown in Figure 7-1), select one of the following:

On. Select this option to block all incoming connections except those unblocked in the Exceptions tab. If you select this option, select Block all incoming connections if you want to block those incoming connections even if they are unblocked on the Exceptions tab.

Off. Select this option to disable the firewall. You should select this option only if you are using a third-party firewall.

CONFIGURE THE EXCEPTIONS TAB OF THE WINDOWS FIREWALL SETTINGS DIALOG BOX

The Exceptions tab is where you configure exceptions (creating exceptions is covered in the next two procedures). This procedure covers disabling, enabling, deleting, and editing exceptions. It also covers how to enable or disable blocking notification.

OPEN the Windows Firewall Settings dialog box.

1. In the Windows Firewall Settings dialog box, click the **Exceptions** tab, shown in Figure 7-2.

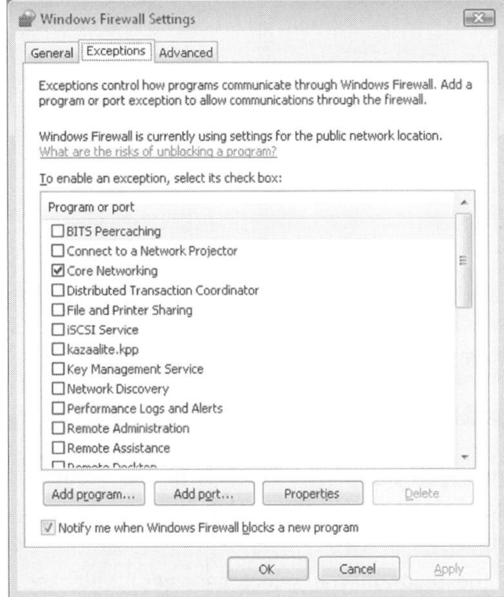

Figure 7-2

The Exceptions tab of the Windows Firewall Settings dialog box

2. Do one of the following:

   To enable an exception: Select the check box for the exception in the Program or port list box.

   To disable an exception: Clear the check box for the exception in the Program or port list box.

   To edit an exception: Select the exception in the Program or port list box and then click **Properties.** A different dialog box appears depending on what exception you are editing. When you are done editing the options, click **OK.**

   To delete an exception: Select the exception in the Program or port list box and then click **Delete** (some exceptions cannot be deleted)**.** In the message box asking for confirmation to proceed with the deletion, click **Yes.**

   To enable or disable blocking notification: Select the *Notify me when Windows Firewall blocks a program* check box (default setting), or clear the check box to disable blocking notification.

UNBLOCK A PROGRAM IN THE WINDOWS FIREWALL SETTINGS DIALOG BOX

There are three ways to create an exception for an inbound connection request from a program:

Click **Unblock** on the Windows Security Alert dialog box when Windows Firewall blocks a program and then asks you if you want it to keep blocking that program.

Configure a program exception on the Exceptions tab (covered in this procedure).

Open the appropriate port on the Exceptions tab (covered in the next procedure). This method is not recommended for individual programs because it is less secure than the other methods, due to the fact that the port is open to other applications.

OPEN the Windows Firewall Settings dialog box.

1. In the Windows Firewall Settings dialog box, click the **Exceptions** tab.
2. If the program you want to unblock appears in the Program or port list box, select the corresponding check box and then click **OK.** If not, continue to step 3.
3. To add a program that is not in the list box, click **Add program**. The Add a Program dialog box appears, as the example in Figure 7-3 shows.

Figure 7-3

Example programs in the Add a Program dialog box

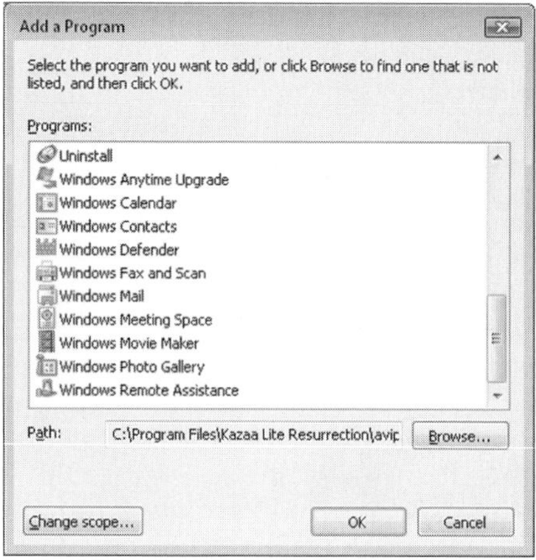

4. If the program you want to unblock is in the Programs list box, select it. If not, click **Browse.** To select the executable file for the program, use the Browse dialog box that appears.
5. By default, the program you select becomes unblocked for all computers. To control for which computers the specified program is unblocked, click **Change Scope**. The Change Scope dialog box appears.
6. Select one of the following:

   Any computer (including those on the Internet). Select this option to unblock the specified program for all computers.

   My network (subnet) only. Select this option to unblock the specified program for your subnet (your subnet is defined by your IP address combined with your subnet mask).

   Custom List. Select this option to specify the IP addresses of the computers for which you want to unblock the specified program. If you select this option, key the IP addresses (or subnets) in the corresponding text box, as the example in Figure 7-4 shows.

Figure 7-4

An example IP address specified in the Change Scope dialog box

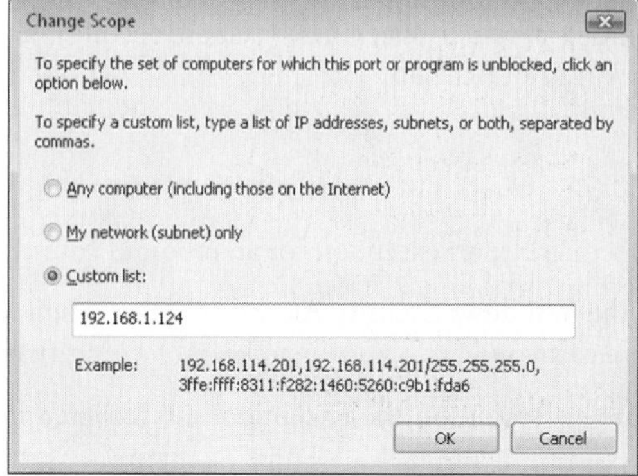

7. Click **OK** in the Change Scope dialog box.
8. Click **OK** in the Add a Program dialog box. The exception is added to the Program or port list box, and its check box is selected.

UNBLOCK A PORT IN THE WINDOWS FIREWALL SETTINGS DIALOG BOX

OPEN the Windows Firewall Settings dialog box.

1. In the Windows Firewall Settings dialog box, click the **Exceptions** tab.
2. In the Program or port list box, select the port that you want to unblock if it is in the list box.
3. To add a port that is not in the list box, click **Add port**. The Add a port dialog box appears, as shown in Figure 7-5.

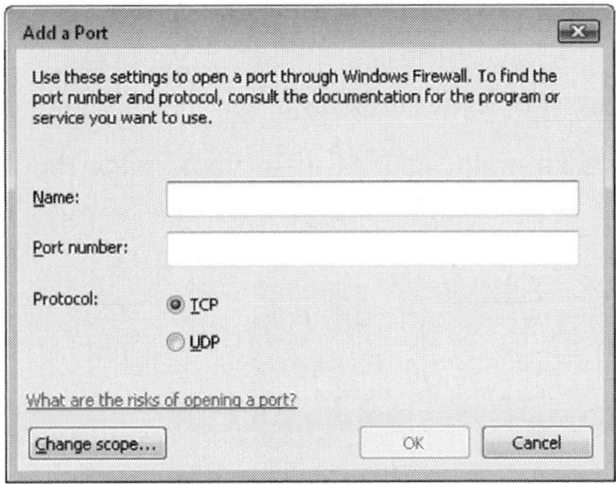

Figure 7-5

The Add a Port dialog box

4. In the Name text box, key a name for the port.
5. In the Port number text box, key a port number.
6. Select either the **TCP** or **UDP** Protocol option depending on what protocol you want to unblock on the port you specify.
7. By default, the port you select is unblocked for all computers. To control for which computers the specified port is unblocked, click **Change Scope**. The Change Scope dialog box appears.
8. Select one of the following:

   Any computer (including those on the Internet). Select this option to unblock the specified port for all computers.

   My network (subnet) only. Select this option to unblock the specified port for your subnet (your subnet is defined by your IP address combined with your subnet mask).

   Custom List. Select this option to specify the IP addresses of the computers for which you want to unblock the specified port. If you select this option, key the IP addresses (or subnets) in the corresponding text box, as the example in Figure 7-6 shows.

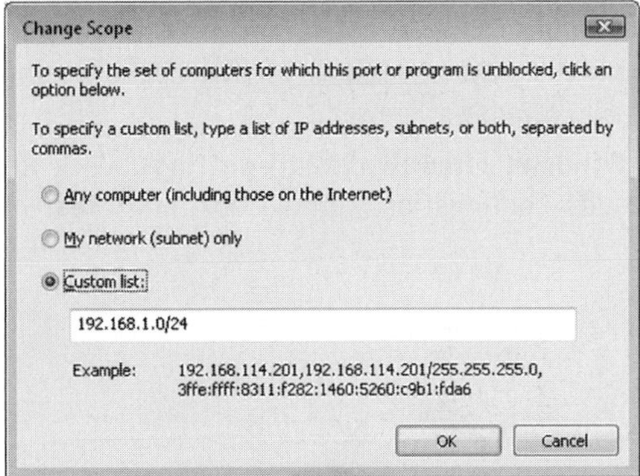

Figure 7-6

An example subnet specified in the Change Scope dialog box

9. Click **OK** in the Change Scope dialog box.
10. Click **OK** in the Add a Port dialog box. The exception is added to the Program or port list box and its check box is selected.

CONFIGURE THE ADVANCED TAB OF THE WINDOWS FIREWALL SETTINGS DIALOG BOX

On the Advanced tab, you can specify on which network connections Windows Firewall is enabled, and you can restore the default settings of Windows Firewall.

TAKE NOTE*

You may note that the settings available on the Advanced settings tab are not very advanced. This is because the advanced settings that used to reside here have been moved to the Windows Firewall with Advanced Security Snap-in (specifically ICMP and logging settings). The Windows Firewall with Advanced Security Snap-in is covered later in this lesson.

OPEN the Windows Firewall Settings dialog box.

1. In the Windows Firewall Settings dialog box, click the **Advanced** tab, as shown in Figure 7-7.

Figure 7-7

Advanced tab of the Windows Firewall Settings dialog box, showing an example configuration

2. Do one of the following:

   To enable Windows Firewall on a network connection: In the Network connections list box, select the check box for the network connection for which you want to enable Windows Firewall.

   To disable Windows Firewall on a network connection: In the Network connections list box, clear the check box for the network connection for which you want to disable Windows Firewall.

   To restore Windows Firewall default settings: Click **Restore Defaults**. In the Restore Defaults Confirmation warning box, click **Yes** to continue.

Configuring Windows Firewall with Advanced Security and Group Policy Settings

Windows Firewall with Advanced Security can be set through Group Policy or locally (Group Policy settings supersede local settings).

X REF

Configuring connection security rules is covered in **Lesson 11.**

This section covers configuring settings through the Windows Firewall with Advanced Security Snap-in and its counterpart in Group Policy. It also covers configuring Windows Firewall Group Policy settings for Domain and Standard Profiles.

You use the Windows Firewall with Advanced Security Snap-in (and its Group Policy counterpart) to configure two types of rules: ***firewall rules***, which control how Windows Firewall responds to incoming and outgoing traffic, and ***connection security rules***, which determine how Windows Firewall secures traffic between computers.

OPEN THE WINDOWS FIREWALL WITH ADVANCED SECURITY SNAP-IN

The Windows Firewall with Advanced Security Snap-in is where you can set advanced settings for Windows Firewall locally.

1. Click **Start.** In the Start Search text box, key **Windows Firewall**, right-click **Windows Firewall with Advanced Security** in the Programs list, and then click **Run as administrator.** A User Account Control dialog box appears.
2. Provide administrator credentials and then click **OK.** The Windows Firewall with Advanced Security Snap-in appears, as shown in Figure 7-8. We cover configuring Firewall rules later in this lesson.

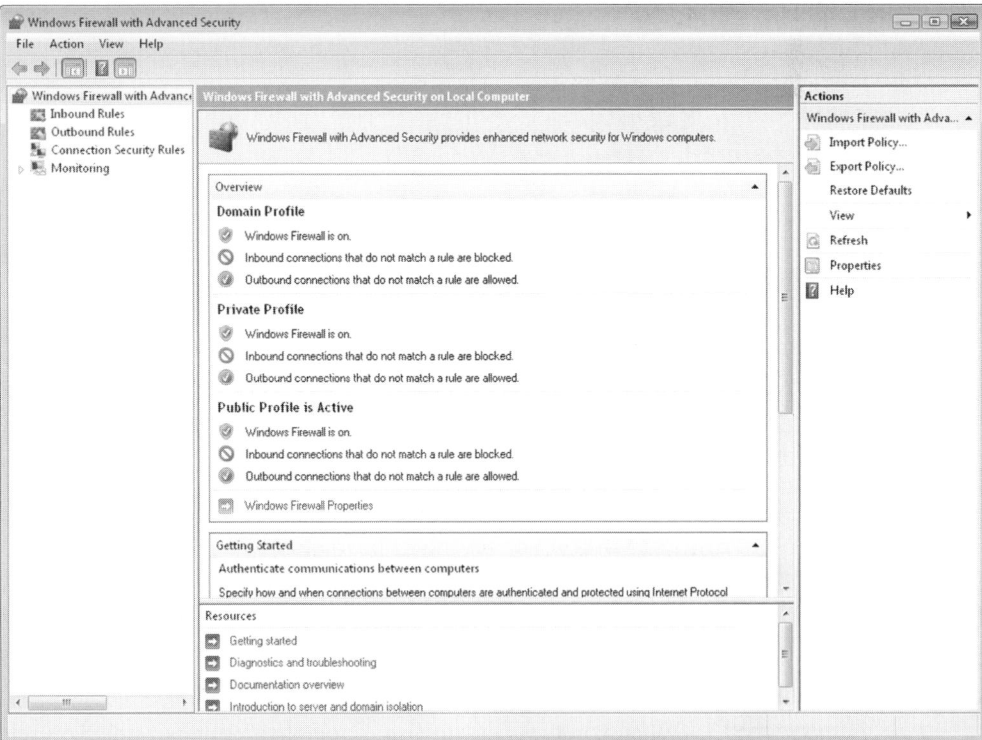

Figure 7-8

The Windows Firewall with Advanced Security Snap-in

OPEN WINDOWS FIREWALL WITH ADVANCED SECURITY IN GROUP POLICY

The Windows Firewall with Advanced Security interface in Group Policy is where you set advanced settings for Windows Firewall through Group Policy.

1. Click **Start.** In the **Start Search** text box, key **gpmc.msc** and then press **Ctrl + Shift + Enter.** A User Account Control dialog box appears.

2. Provide administrator credentials and then click **OK**. The Group Policy Management Console opens.
3. In the console tree, expand **Forest: *Forest Name*>Domains>*Domain Name*>Group Policy Objects**.
4. Right-click the Group Policy object for which you want to configure Windows Firewall with Advanced Security and then click **Edit**. The Group Policy Object Editor opens with the selected GPO loaded.
5. In the console tree, expand **Computer Configuration>Windows Settings>Security Settings>Windows Firewall with Advanced Security** and then select **Windows Firewall with Advanced Security**. The Windows Firewall with Advanced Security settings appear in the details pane, as shown in the example in Figure 7-9. The following sections describe configuring Windows Firewall rules.

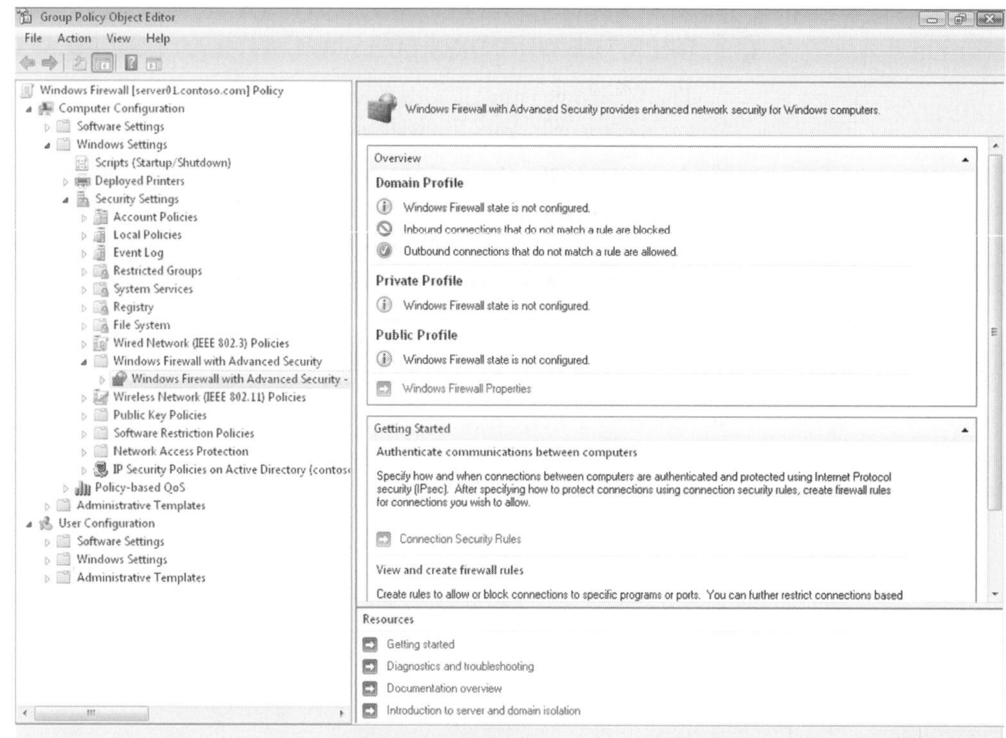

Figure 7-9

Windows Firewall with Advanced Security Group Policy settings

Creating and Configuring Firewall Rules

> Firewall Rules are the building blocks of exceptions. You can configure them for both inbound and outbound connections.

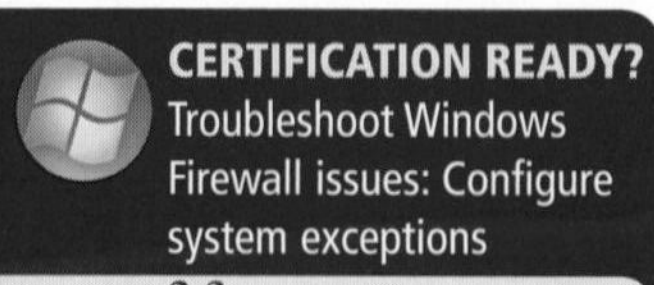

CERTIFICATION READY?
Troubleshoot Windows Firewall issues: Configure system exceptions
2.3

Firewall Rules come in two varieties: inbound and outbound. The former are created using the New Inbound Rule Wizard, and the latter are created using the New Outbound Rule Wizard. The interfaces and settings for these wizards are nearly identical. Once you create a rule, you can change its settings or modify its functionality.

When you create a rule using one of the rule wizards, you select a rule type and then configure settings in a maximum of seven areas (each on a different page in the wizard). Table 7-2 summarizes the rule types, when you should use them, and what pages you will need to configure.

Table 7-2

Firewall rule types and when to use them

Rule type	When to use	Pages in wizard to configure
Custom	You use a custom rule when the other rule types are not sufficient to do what you want, or when you want maximum control over creation settings. You also use a custom rule when you want to create a rule based on a service.	Rule Type, Program, Protocol and Ports, Scope, Action, Profile, Name
Program	You use a program rule to allow or block a connection based on the program that is attempting to create a connection.	Rule Type, Program, Action, Profile, Name
Port	You use a port rule when you want to allow or block a connection based on which UDP or TCP port the connection is attempting to use.	Rule Type, Protocol and Ports, Action, Profile, Name
Predefined	You use a predefined rule when one exists that will accomplish what you want to accomplish with the rule. There are predefined rules you select from the Predefined drop-down list that provide the appropriate network connectivity for most of the well-known Windows services and programs available in both Windows Vista and Windows Server code named Longhorn (not released at the time of the writing of this book).	Rule Type, Predefined Rules, Action

TO CREATE A CUSTOM INBOUND OR OUTBOUND RULE

You use a ***custom rule*** when the other rule types are not sufficient to do what you want, or when you want maximum control over creation settings. You also use a custom rule when you want to create an exception based on a service. The following procedure covers using both the inbound and outbound rules wizards. The figures use the Inbound Rules Wizard as an example.

OPEN either the Windows Firewall with Advanced Security Snap-in or the Windows Firewall with Advanced Security node in Group Policy.

1. In the console tree, select one of the following:

   Inbound Rules. Select this option to configure a rule to control inbound connections.

   Outbound Rules. Select this option to configure a rule to control outbound connections.

2. On the Action menu, click **New Rule.** The New [Inbound/Outbound] Rule Wizard appears. The example in Figure 7-10 shows the Rule Type page of the New Inbound Rule Wizard.

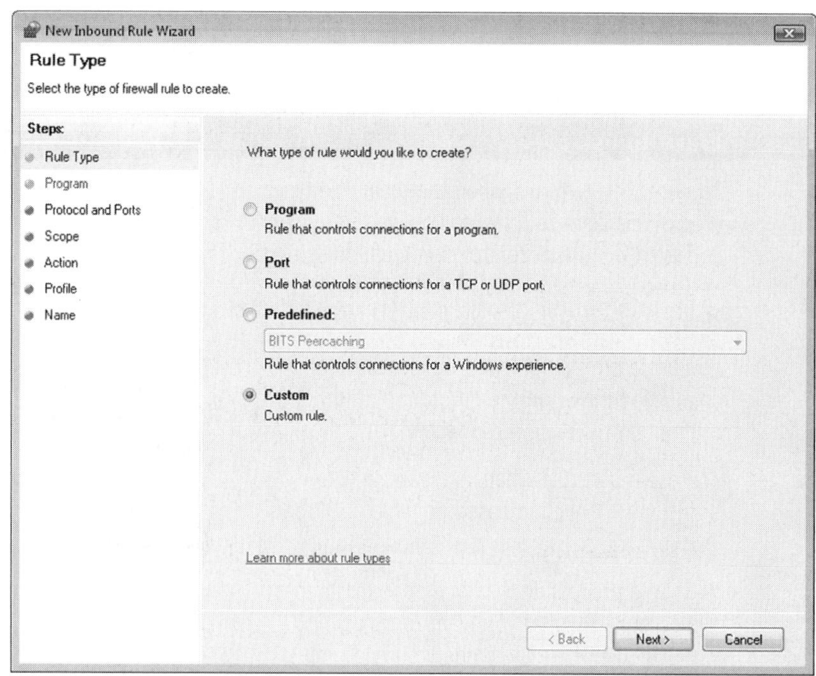

Figure 7-10

The Rule Type page of the New Inbound Rule Wizard

3. Select **Custom** and then click **Next**. The Program page appears, as shown in Figure 7-11.

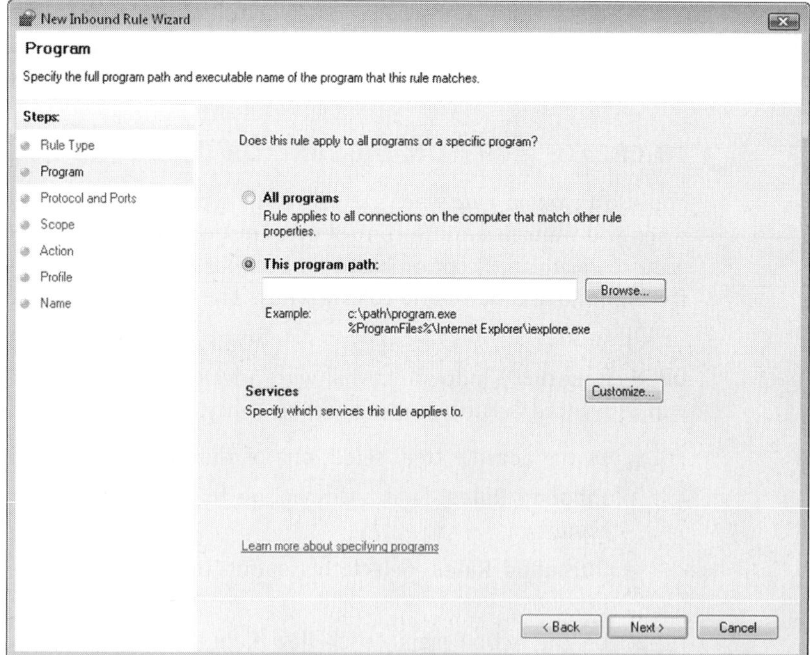

Figure 7-11

The Program page of the New Inbound Rule Wizard

4. Select one of the following:

   All programs. Select this option to apply the rule to all programs.

   This program path. Select this option to apply the rule to a specific program that you can specify by path (including environment variables) or by browsing to the .exe file and selecting it.

5. To specify services to which the rule applies, click **Customize**. The Customize Service Settings dialog box appears, as shown in Figure 7-12.

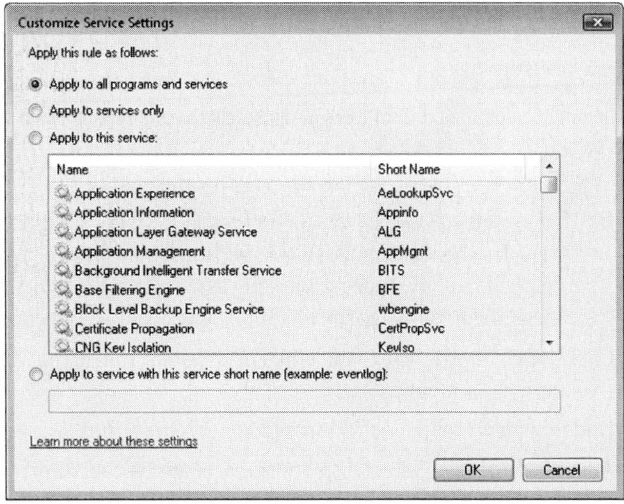

Figure 7-12

The Customize Service Settings dialog box

a. Select one of the following:

Apply to all programs and services. Select this option to apply the rule to all processes.

Apply to services only. Select this option to apply the rule only to services.

Apply to this service. Select this option to select the service in the associated list box to which you want to apply the rule.

Apply to service with this service short name. Select this option to select the service to which you want to apply the rule by specifying its short name, which you can find in the above list box. You can specify a short name even if it is not in the list box. Short names that do not match a service will be ignored.

b. Click **OK** to close the Customize Service Settings dialog box.

6. On the Program page, click **Next**. The Protocol and Ports page appears, as shown in Figure 7-13.

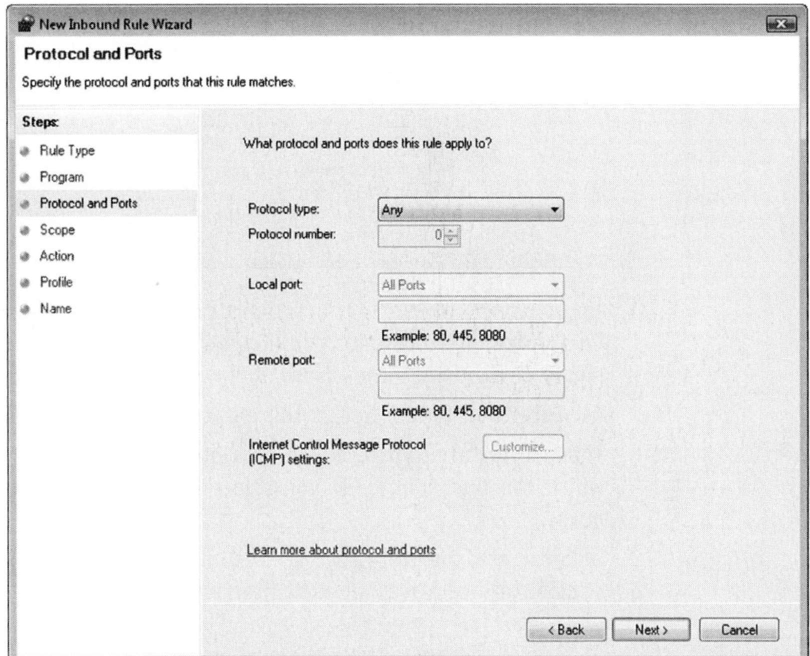

Figure 7-13

The Protocol and Ports page of the New Inbound Rule Wizard

7. In the **Protocol type** drop-down list, select a protocol type.
   a. If you select TCP or UDP as your protocol type, you can specify the local and remote port by using the Local port drop-down list and the Remote port drop-down list. You can specify specific ports by using the corresponding text boxes.

MORE INFORMATION

For more information on the protocol types available, click *Learn more about protocols and ports* on the Protocol and Ports page.

   b. If you select ICMPv4 or ICMPv6, you can click **Customize** to configure ICMP settings. In the Customize ICMP Settings dialog box, you can select All ICMP types or Specific ICMP types from the associated list box, or you can click **Add** to add a new ICMP type to the list box. Click **OK** when you are finished.
8. Click **Next** on the Protocol and Ports page. The Scope page appears, as the example in Figure 7-14 shows.
9. Under *Which local IP addresses does this rule match*, select one of the following:

   Any IP Address. Select this option to apply the rule regardless of the host IP address.

   These IP Addresses. Select this option to specify specific IP addresses, IP address ranges, or subnets. If you select this option, click Add to specify what you want to include. An example of an added IP address is shown in Figure 7-14.

Figure 7-14

The Scope page of the New Inbound Rule Wizard with example settings

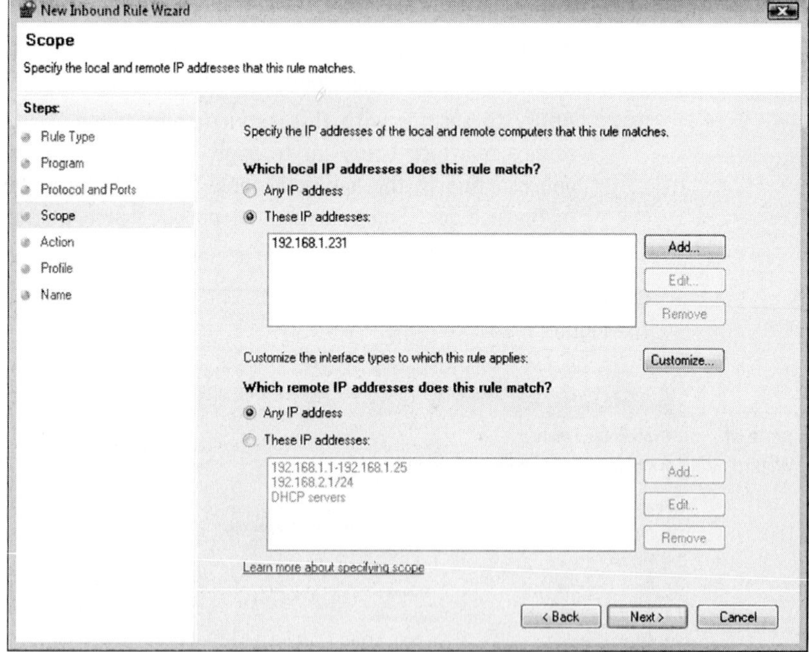

10. To specify to which interface types on the host computer the rule applies, click **Customize**. The Customize Interface Types dialog box appears, as shown in Figure 7-15. Select one of the following:

    All Interface types. Select this option to apply the rule to all interface types.

    These interface types. Select this option to specify the type of interface to which the rule applies. If you select this option, configure the following check boxes.

    - **Local area network**. Select this check box to apply the rule to connections using a local area network interface.

- **Remote access.** Select this check box to apply the rule to connections using remote access.
- **Wireless.** Select this check box to apply the rule to connections using wireless interfaces.

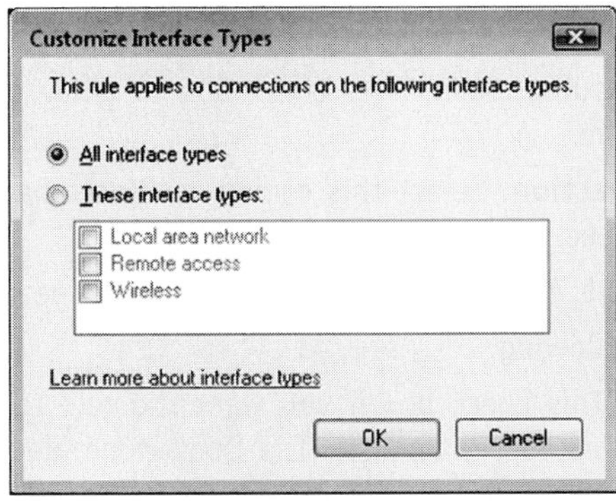

Figure 7-15

The Customize Interface Types dialog box

11. On the Scope page, under *Which remote IP address does this rule match*, select one of the following:

    Any IP Address. Select this option to apply the rule regardless of the remote IP address.

    These IP Addresses. Select this option to specify specific IP addresses, IP address ranges, subnets, or a predefined set of computers. If you select this option, click **Add** to add an IP address, subnet, range, or a predefined set of computers that you want to include. An example of an added IP address range, subnet, and set of computers is shown in Figure 7-14.

12. Click **Next** on the Scope page. The Action page appears, as shown in Figure 7-16.

TAKE NOTE

Predefined sets of computers are converted to IP addresses at runtime.

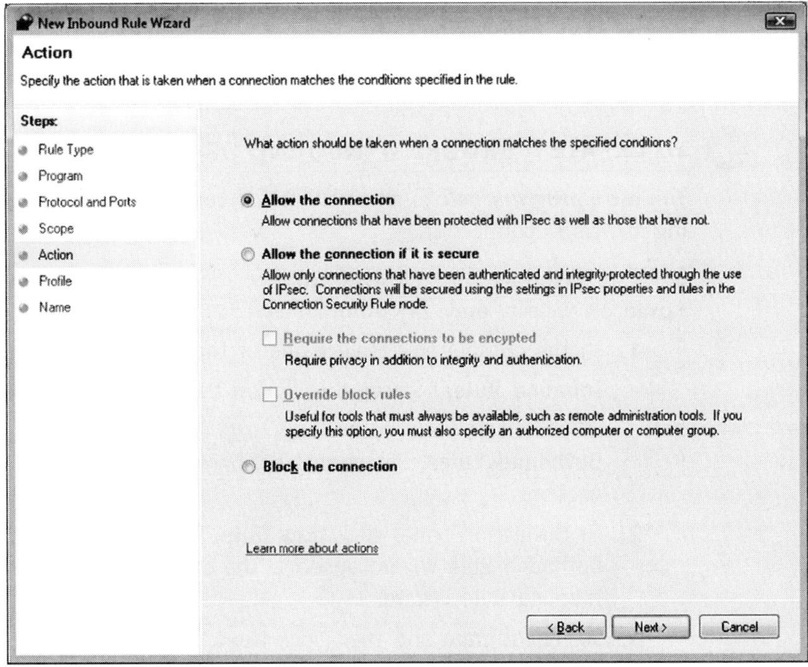

Figure 7-16

The Action page of the New Inbound Rule Wizard

13. Select one of the following:

    Allow the connection. Allows the connection regardless of whether it is secure.

    Allow the connection if it is secure. Allows the connection only if it is secured using IPsec. If you select this option, configure the following:

    Require the connections to be encrypted. Select this check box to require encryption in addition to integrity checking and authentication.

    Override block rules. Select this check box to allow the connection even if it is blocked elsewhere.

    Block the connection. Select this option to block the connection even if it is secured with IPsec.

14. Click **Next** on the Action page. The Profile page appears.
15. Configure the following:

    Domain. Select this check box if you want the rule to be applied when a computer is connected to the domain. The Domain profile tends to have the least restrictions on communications because the computer is presumed to be less open to attack from outside threats.

    Private. The rule is applied when the computer is attached to a private network. The Private profile tends to have more restrictions on communication than the Domain profile because the threat level on the private network is unknown.

    Public. The rule is applied when the computer is attached to a public network. The Public profile tends to have the most restrictions on communications because the computer is attached to a public network where security vulnerabilities are more common.

16. Click **Next** on the Profile page. The Name page appears.
17. In the **Name** text box, key a name for the rule. Use a descriptive name that will be useful if you need to troubleshoot rules.
18. In the **Description** text box, key a detailed description of the rule.
19. Click **Finish.** The rule is added to the Inbound Rules list or the Outbound Rules list as appropriate.

TO CREATE A PROGRAM INBOUND OR OUTBOUND RULE

You use a ***program rule*** to allow or block a connection based on the program that is attempting to create a connection.

OPEN the Windows Firewall with Advanced Security Snap-in or the Windows Firewall with Advanced Security node in Group Policy.

1. In the console tree, select one of the following:

   Inbound Rules. Select this option to configure a rule to control inbound connections.

   Outbound Rules. Select this option to configure a rule to control outbound connections.

2. In the action pane, click **New Rule.** The New Inbound Rule Wizard or the New Outbound Rule Wizard appears. The example in Figure 7-10 shows the New Inbound Rule Wizard.
3. Select **Program** and then click **Next.** The Program page appears, as shown in Figure 7-17.

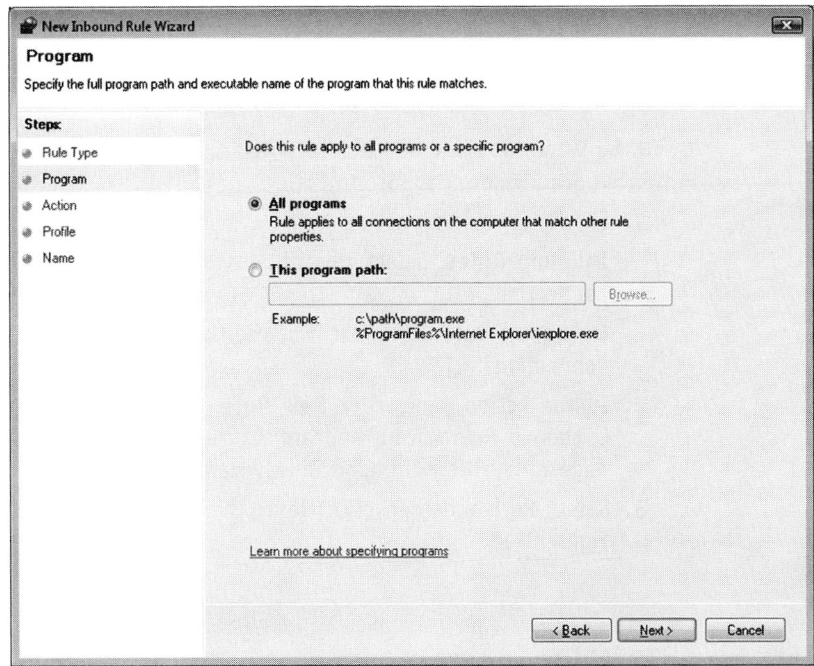

Figure 7-17

The Program page of the New Inbound Rule Wizard

4. Select one of the following:

   All programs. Select this option to apply the rule to all programs.

   This program path. Select this option to apply the rule to a specific program that you can specify by path (including environment variables) or by browsing to the .exe file and selecting it.

5. Click **Next.** The Action page appears, as shown in Figure 7-16.
6. Select one of the following:

   Allow the connection. Allows the connection regardless of whether it is secure.

   Allow the connection if it is secure. Allows the connection only if it is secured using IPsec. If you select this option, configure the following:

   Require the connections to be encrypted. Select this check box to require encryption in addition to integrity checking and authentication.

   Override block rules. Select this check box to allow the connection even if it is blocked elsewhere.

   Block the connection. Select this option to block the connection even if it is secured with IPsec.

7. Click **Next.** The Profile page appears. Configure the following:

   Domain. Select this check box if you want the rule to be applied when a computer is connected to the domain.

   Private. The rule is applied when the computer is attached to a private network.

   Public. The rule is applied when the computer is attached to a public network.

8. Click **Next.** The Name page appears.
9. In the **Name** text box, key a name for the rule. Use a descriptive name that will be useful if you need to troubleshoot later.
10. In the **Description** text box, key a detailed description of the rule.
11. Click **Finish.** The rule is added to the Inbound Rules list or the Outbound Rules list as appropriate.

TO CREATE A PORT INBOUND OR OUTBOUND RULE

You use a ***port rule*** when you want to allow or block a connection based on which UDP or TCP port the connection is attempting to use.

OPEN the Windows Firewall with Advanced Security Snap-in or the Windows Firewall with Advanced Security node in Group Policy.

1. In the console tree, select one of the following:

   Inbound Rules. Select this option to configure a rule to control inbound connections.

   Outbound Rules. Select this option to configure a rule to control outbound connections.

2. In the Action pane, click **New Rule.** The New Inbound Rule Wizard or the New Outbound Rule Wizard appears. The example in Figure 7-10 shows the Rule Type page of the New Inbound Rule Wizard.
3. Select **Port** and then click **Next.** The Protocol and Ports page appears, as shown in Figure 7-18.

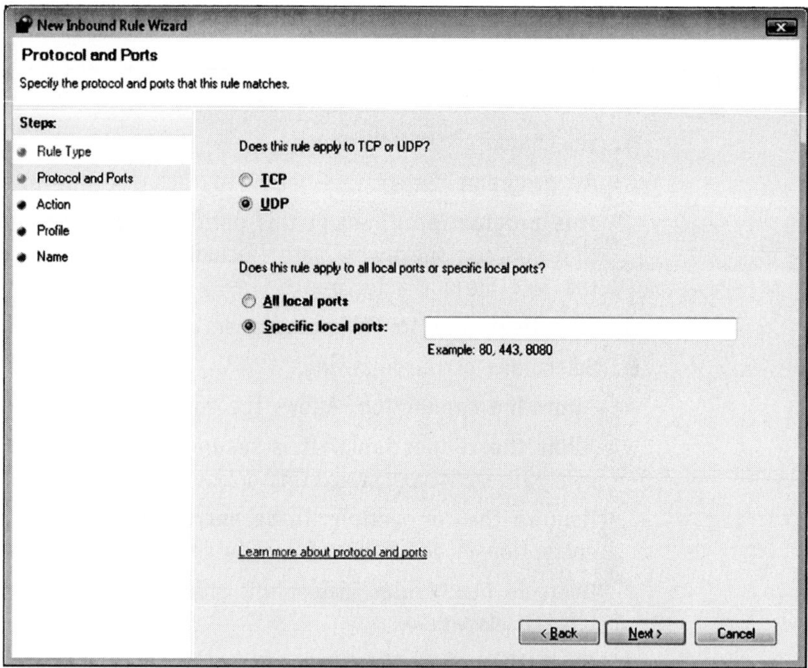

Figure 7-18

The Protocol and Ports page of the New Inbound Rule Wizard

4. Under *Does this rule apply to TCP or UDP*, select either TCP or UDP as appropriate.
5. Under *Does this rule apply to all local ports or specific local ports*, select one of the following:

   All local ports. Select this option if you want the rule to apply to all local ports for the specified protocol.

   Specified local ports. Select this option if you want the rule to apply only to specified ports. If you select this option, specify the port numbers separated by commas in the corresponding text box.

6. Click **Next.** The Action page appears.
7. Select one of the following:

   Allow the connection. Allows the connection regardless of whether it is secure.

   Allow the connection if it is secure. Allows the connection only if it is secured using IPsec. If you select this option, configure the following:

Require the connections to be encrypted. Select this check box to require encryption in addition to integrity checking and authentication.

Override block rules. Select this check box to allow the connection even if it is blocked elsewhere.

Block the connection. Select this option to block the connection even if it is secured with IPsec.

8. Click **Next.** The Profile page appears. Configure the following:

   Domain. Select this check box if you want the rule to be applied when a computer is connected to the domain.

   Private. The rule is applied when the computer is attached to a private network.

   Public. The rule is applied when the computer is attached to a public network.

9. Click **Next.** The Name page appears.
10. In the **Name** text box, key a name for the rule. Use a descriptive name that will be useful if you need to troubleshoot later.
11. In the **Description** text box, key a detailed description of the rule.
12. Click **Finish.** The rule is added to the Inbound Rules list or the Outbound Rules list as appropriate.

TO CREATE A PREDEFINED INBOUND OR OUTBOUND RULE

You use a predefined rule when one exists that will accomplish what you want to accomplish with the rule. Predefined rules provide the appropriate network connectivity for most of the well-known Windows services and programs available in both Windows Vista and Windows Server Longhorn (not released at the time of the writing of this book).

OPEN the Windows Firewall with Advanced Security Snap-in or the Windows Firewall with Advanced Security node in Group Policy.

1. In the console tree, select one of the following:

   Inbound Rules. Select this option to configure a rule to control inbound connections.

   Outbound Rules. Select this option to configure a rule to control outbound connections.

2. In the Action pane, click **New Rule.** The New Inbound Rule Wizard or the New Outbound Rule Wizard appears. The example in Figure 7-10 shows the Rule Type page of the New Inbound Rule Wizard.
3. Select **Predefined.** In the corresponding drop-down list, select a predefined rule. Figure 7-19 shows the possible choices, with Windows Meeting Space selected.

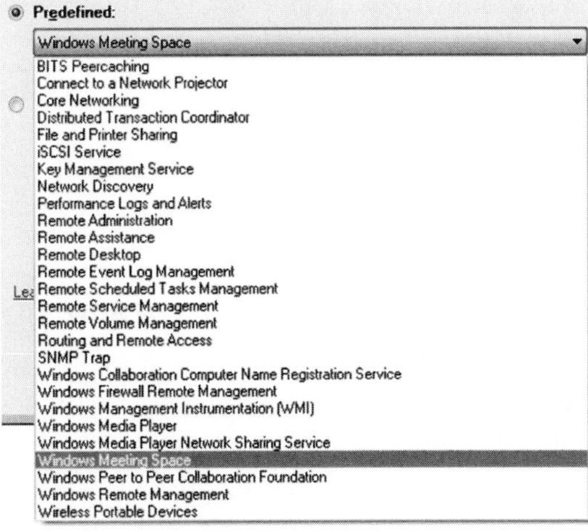

Figure 7-19

Possible choices for predefined rules with Windows Meeting Space selected

TAKE NOTE* When you select a predefined rule, you are actually selecting a group of rules that form an exception.

4. Click **Next.** The Predefined Rules page appears, as shown in the example in Figure 7-20.

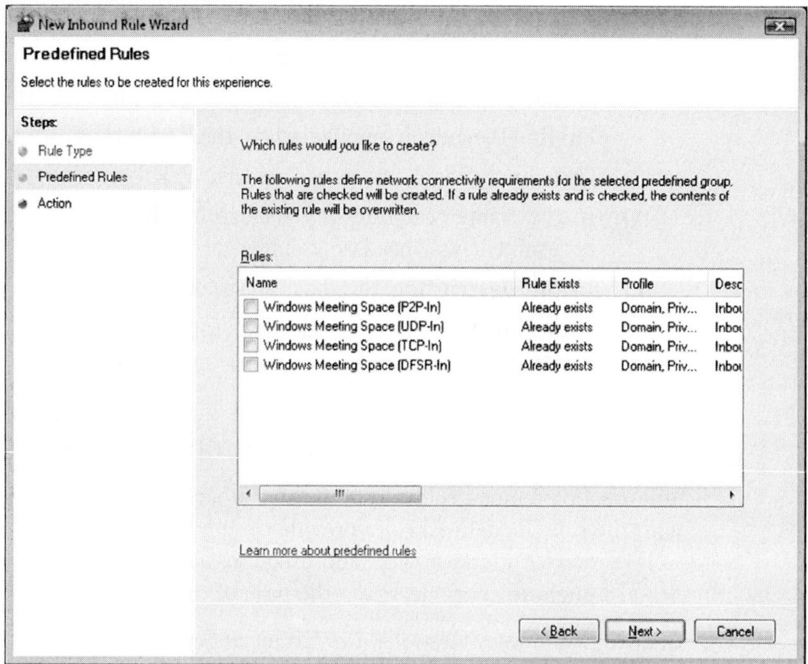

Figure 7-20

The Predefined Rules page for the Windows Meeting Space predefined rule

5. In the Rules list box, select the check boxes of the rules that you want to include in the group (by default, all check boxes are selected). Your options will vary depending on the predefined rule that you selected in the Predefined drop-down list.
6. Click **Next.** The Action page appears, as shown in Figure 7-16.
7. Select one of the following:

   Allow the connection. Allows the connection regardless of whether it is secure.

   Allow the connection if it is secure. Allows the connection only if it is secured using IPsec. If you select this option, configure the following:

   Require the connections to be encrypted. Select this check box to require encryption in addition to integrity checking and authentication.

   Override block rules. Select this check box to allow the connection even if it is blocked elsewhere.

   Block the connection. Select this option to block the connection even if it is secured with IPsec.
8. Click **Finish.** The group of rules is added to the Inbound Rules list or the Outbound Rules list as appropriate.

BROWSE RULES IN WINDOWS FIREWALL WITH ADVANCED SECURITY

Many inbound and outbound rules are preconfigured, and it can be difficult to easily find exactly what rule you are looking for. Windows Firewall with Advanced Security offers filtering to make finding rules easier.

OPEN the Windows Firewall with Advanced Security Snap-in or the Windows Firewall with Advanced Security node in Group Policy.

1. In the console tree, select one of the three rules nodes:

   Inbound Rules

   Outbound Rules

   Connection Security Rules

2. In the action pane, you can choose from three filters with which you can filter the list (two for Connection Security Rules):

   Filter by Profile. Use this drop-down menu to limit the list according to what profile the rules affect.

   Filter by State. Use this drop-down menu to show all the rules that are enabled or all the rules that are disabled.

   Filter by Group (Outbound Rules and Inbound Rules only). Use this drop-down menu to view all the rules in a particular group. For example, filtering by the Routing and Remote access group is shown in Figure 7-21.

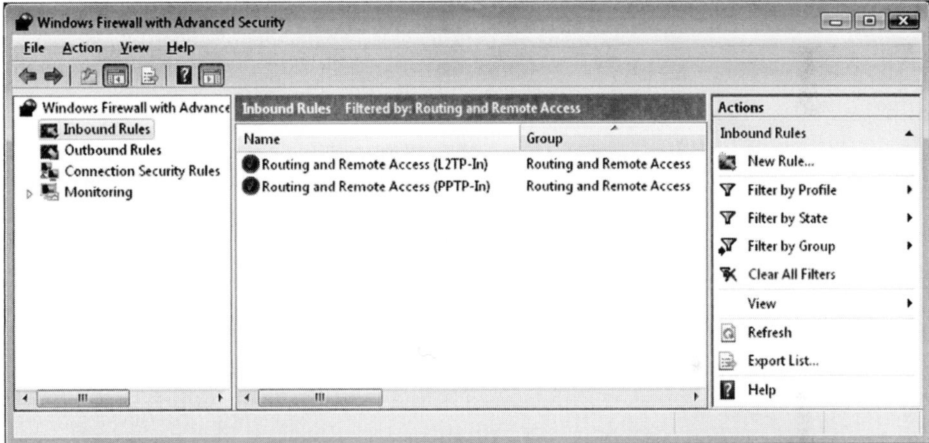

Figure 7-21

Inbound Rules filtered by the Routing and Remote access group

Configuring Windows Firewall Group Policy Settings

Windows Firewall Group Policy settings enable you to configure settings that simultaneously control Windows Firewall behavior for many computers through Group Policy.

Group Policy has three primary locations where you configure Windows Firewall settings:

- Computer Configuration>Windows Settings>Security Settings>Windows Firewall with Advanced Security
- Computer Configuration>Administrative Templates>Network>Network Connections>Windows Firewall>Domain Profile
- Computer Configuration>Administrative Templates>Network>Network Connections>Windows Firewall>Standard Profile

The first location contains the same settings that are available locally in the Windows Firewall with Advanced Security Snap-in.

The second and third locations are very similar and have the same Windows Firewall parent folder. The settings within the two locations are identical; they only differ in the circumstances in which they are applied. A computer uses the ***Domain Profile settings*** when that computer is connected to a network where domain controllers are available. A computer uses the ***Standard Profile settings*** if domain controllers are not available to that computer.

If you do not configure Standard Profile settings, the default values of Not configured are applied if the computer is not connected to the domain. This means that the policies set locally will be in effect. Therefore, it is recommended that you configure both the Domain Profile settings and the Standard Profile settings so that you can control settings for all domain computers regardless of whether they are currently connected to the domain.

Standard Profile settings should typically be more restrictive, because the Domain Profile settings have to accommodate applications and services that are only used in a domain environment, and the Standard Profile settings do not.

You'll find 14 Group Policy settings in the Standard and Domain profiles. Table 7-3 summarizes the settings.

Table 7-3

Windows Firewall Group Policy Standard Profile and Domains Profile settings

Group Policy Setting	Description
Windows Firewall: Allow local program exceptions	Allows administrators to use the Windows Firewall Settings dialog box to define a local program exceptions list. Administrators can also use the *Windows Firewall: Define inbound program exceptions* policy setting to define a program exceptions list through Group Policy. • **Enabled**: Allows administrators to use the Windows Firewall Settings dialog box to define a local program exceptions list. • **Disabled**: Prevents administrators from using the Windows Firewall Settings dialog box to define a local program exceptions list. • **Not Configured**: The ability of administrators to define a local program exceptions list depends on the configuration of the *Windows Firewall: Define inbound program exceptions* policy setting. If that setting is not configured, administrators can define a local program exceptions list. If it is enabled or disabled, administrators cannot define a local program exceptions list.
Windows Firewall: Define inbound program exceptions	Allows you to manage the program exceptions list defined by Group Policy. • **Enabled**: You can manage the program exceptions list defined by Group Policy. The listed programs are exceptions to Windows Firewall Rules. • **Disabled**: If you disable this policy setting, the program exceptions list defined by Group Policy is deleted. • **Not Configured**: The Group Policy exceptions list is not used.
Windows Firewall: Protect all network connections	Turns on or off Windows Firewall. • **Enabled**: Windows Firewall is turned on, and Windows Firewall ignores the *Prohibit use of Internet Connection Firewall on your DNS domain network* policy setting. • **Disabled**: Windows Firewall does not run. This is the only way to ensure that Windows Firewall does not run, and administrators who log on locally cannot start it. • **Not Configured**: Administrators can turn Windows Firewall on or off locally, unless the *Prohibit use of Internet Connection Firewall on your DNS domain network* policy setting is enabled.
Windows Firewall: Do not allow exceptions	Causes Windows Firewall to block all unsolicited incoming messages. This policy setting overrides all other settings that might allow unsolicited messages. • **Enabled**: The Don't allow exceptions check box is selected in the Windows Firewall Settings dialog box, and it cannot be cleared. If you enable this policy setting, you should also enable the *Windows Firewall: Protect all network connections* policy setting. If you don't, administrators can circumvent the setting by turning off the firewall locally. • **Disabled**: Whether unsolicited incoming messages are blocked is controlled by other policy settings. The Don't allow exceptions check box is cleared in the Windows Firewall Settings dialog box and cannot be selected. • **Not Configured**: Same as disabled.

(continued)

Table 7-3 (*continued*)

Group Policy Setting	Description
Windows Firewall: Allow inbound file and printer sharing exception	Allows inbound file and printer sharing by opening UDP ports 137 and 138, and TCP ports 139 and 445 in Windows Firewall. • **Enabled**: Windows Firewall opens UDP ports 137 and 138, and TCP ports 139 and 445 to receive print jobs and requests for access to shared files. You must specify the IP addresses or subnets from which these incoming messages are allowed. The File and Printer Sharing check box is selected in the Windows Firewall Settings dialog box, and it can not be cleared. • **Disabled**: Windows Firewall blocks UDP ports 137 and 138, and TCP ports 139 and 445, which prevents the computer from sharing files and printers. The File and Printer Sharing check box is cleared in the Windows Firewall Settings dialog box, and it cannot be selected. • **Not Configured**: Windows Firewall does not open UDP ports 137 and 138, and TCP ports 139 and 445. Therefore, the computer cannot share files or printers unless an administrator uses other policy settings to open the required ports. The File and Printer Sharing check box is cleared in the Windows Firewall Settings dialog box, and administrators can clear or select it.
Windows Firewall: Allow ICMP exceptions	Defines the set of Internet Control Message Protocol (ICMP) message types that Windows Firewall allows. Utilities can use ICMP messages to determine the status of other computers. For example, Ping uses the echo request message. If you do not enable the "Allow inbound echo request" message type, Windows Firewall blocks echo request messages sent by Ping running on other computers, but it does not block outbound echo request messages sent by Ping running on the local computer. • **Enabled**: You must specify which ICMP message types Windows Firewall allows the local computer to send or receive. • **Disabled**: Windows Firewall blocks all unsolicited incoming ICMP message types and the listed outgoing ICMP message types. Therefore, utilities that use the blocked ICMP messages will not be able to send those messages to or from the local computer. Administrators cannot use the Windows Firewall Settings dialog box to enable any message types. If you enable this policy setting and allow certain message types and then later disable this policy setting, Windows Firewall deletes the list of message types that you had enabled. • **Not Configured**: Windows Firewall behaves as if you had disabled it, except that administrators can use the Windows Firewall Settings dialog box to enable or disable message types. **Note**: If any policy setting opens TCP port 445, Windows Firewall allows inbound echo requests, even if the *Windows Firewall: Allow ICMP exceptions* policy setting would block them. Policy settings that can open TCP port 445 include *Windows Firewall: Allow file and printer sharing exception, Windows Firewall: Allow remote administration exception,* and *Windows Firewall: Define inbound port exceptions.*

(*continued*)

Table 7-3 *(continued)*

Group Policy Setting	Description
Windows Firewall: Allow logging	Allows Windows Firewall to record information about the unsolicited incoming messages that it receives. • **Enabled**: Windows Firewall writes information about unsolicited incoming messages to a log file. You must provide the name, location, and maximum size of the log file, and whether to record information about incoming messages that the firewall blocks (drops) and information about successful incoming and outgoing connections. Windows Firewall does not provide an option to log successful incoming messages. • **Disabled**: Windows Firewall does not record information in the log file. If you enable this policy setting, and Windows Firewall creates the log file and adds information, then upon disabling this policy setting, Windows Firewall leaves the log file intact. The Security Logging settings in the Windows Firewall Settings dialog box are cleared and administrators cannot select them. • **Not Configured**: Windows Firewall behaves as if the policy setting were disabled, except that administrators can configure the Security Logging settings in the Windows Firewall Settings dialog box.
Windows Firewall: Prohibit notifications	Prevents Windows Firewall from displaying notifications to the user when a program requests that Windows Firewall add the program to the program exceptions list. • **Enabled**: Windows Firewall prevents the display of these notifications. • **Disabled**: Windows Firewall does not prevent the display of these notifications. The Display a notification when Windows Firewall blocks a program check box in the Windows Firewall Settings dialog box is selected and cannot be cleared. • **Not Configured**: Windows Firewall behaves as if the policy setting were disabled, except that the Display a notification when Windows Firewall blocks a program check box is cleared in the Windows Firewall Settings dialog box, and administrators can clear or select it.
Windows Firewall: Allow local port exceptions	Allows administrators to use the Windows Firewall Settings dialog box to define a local port exceptions list. Windows Firewall uses two port exceptions lists; the other is defined by the *Windows Firewall: Define inbound port exceptions* policy setting. • **Enabled**: The Windows Firewall Settings dialog box enables administrators to define a local port exceptions list. • **Disabled**: The Windows Firewall Settings dialog box does not allow administrators to define a local port exceptions list. However, local administrators will still be allowed to create firewall rules in the Windows Firewall with Advanced Security Snap-in. If you wish to prevent all locally created rules from applying, use the Group Policy Object Editor and configure Computer Configuration\Windows Settings\Security Settings\Windows Firewall with Advanced Security to specify that local firewall rules should not apply. • **Not Configured**: The ability of administrators to define a local port exceptions list depends on the configuration of the *Windows Firewall: Define inbound port exceptions* policy setting. If that setting is not configured, administrators can define a local port exceptions list. If it is enabled or disabled, administrators cannot define a local port exceptions list.

(continued)

Table 7-3 (*continued*)

Group Policy Setting	Description
Windows Firewall: Define inbound port exceptions	Allows you to manage the inbound port exceptions list defined by Group Policy. Administrators can also define a local list of inbound port exceptions in the Windows Firewall Settings dialog box. • **Enabled**: You can manage an inbound port exceptions list applied by Group Policy. To allow administrators to add ports to the local port exceptions list in the Windows Firewall Settings dialog box, enable the *Windows Firewall: Allow local port exceptions* policy setting. • **Disabled**: The port exceptions list defined by Group Policy is deleted, but other policy settings can continue to open or block ports. Also, if a local port exceptions list exists, it is ignored unless you enable the *Windows Firewall: Allow local port exceptions* policy setting. • **Not Configured**: Windows Firewall uses only the local port exceptions list that administrators define by using the Windows Firewall Settings dialog box. Other policy settings can continue to open or block ports.
Windows Firewall: Allow inbound remote administration exception	Allows remote administration of the computer using administrative tools such as the Microsoft Management Console (MMC) and Windows Management Instrumentation (WMI) by opening TCP ports 135 and 445 in Windows Firewall. Services typically use these ports to communicate using remote procedure calls (RPC) and Distributed Component Object Model (DCOM). • **Enabled**: Windows Firewall allows the computer to receive unsolicited incoming messages associated with remote administration. You must specify the IP addresses or subnets from which these incoming messages are allowed. • **Disabled**: Windows Firewall does not open TCP port 135 or 445. • **Not Configured**: Same as Disabled.
Windows Firewall: Allow inbound Remote Desktop exceptions	Opens TCP port 3389 to enable the computer to receive inbound Remote Desktop requests. • **Enabled:** Windows Firewall opens TCP port 3389 so that the computer can receive Remote Desktop requests. You must specify the IP addresses or subnets from which these incoming messages are allowed. The Remote Desktop check box is selected in Windows Firewall Settings dialog box and cannot be cleared. • **Disabled:** Windows Firewall blocks TCP port 3389, which prevents the computer from receiving Remote Desktop requests. If an administrator attempts to open this port by adding it to a local port exceptions list, Windows Firewall does not open the port. The Remote Desktop check box in the Windows Firewall Settings dialog box is cleared and cannot be selected. • **Not Configured**: Windows Firewall does not open TCP port 3389. Therefore, the computer cannot receive Remote Desktop requests unless an administrator uses other policy settings to open the port. The Remote Desktop check box in the Windows Firewall Settings dialog box is cleared, and administrators can clear or select it.

(*continued*)

Table 7-3 (*continued*)

Group Policy Setting	Description
Windows Firewall: Prohibit unicast response to multicast or broadcast requests	Prevents the computer from receiving unicast responses to its outgoing multicast or broadcast messages. • **Enabled**: If the computer sends multicast or broadcast messages to other computers, Windows Firewall blocks the unicast responses sent by those other computers. • **Disabled**: If the computer sends a multicast or broadcast message to other computers, Windows Firewall waits up to three seconds for unicast responses from the other computers and then blocks all later responses. • **Not Configured**: Same as Disabled. **Note**: This policy setting has no effect if the unicast message is a response to a Dynamic Host Configuration Protocol (DHCP) broadcast message sent by the computer. Windows Firewall always permits those DHCP unicast responses. However, this policy setting can interfere with the NetBIOS messages that detect name conflicts.
Windows Firewall: Allow inbound UPnP framework exceptions	By opening TCP port 2869 and UDP port 1900, allows the computer to receive unsolicited inbound Plug and Play messages sent by network devices, such as routers with built-in firewalls. • **Enabled:** Windows Firewall opens TCP port 2869 and UDP port 1900 so that the computer can receive Plug and Play messages. You must specify the IP addresses or subnets from which these incoming messages are allowed. The UPnP framework check box is selected in the Windows Firewall Settings dialog box and cannot be cleared. • **Disabled:** Windows Firewall blocks TCP port 2869 and UDP port 1900, which prevents the computer from receiving Plug and Play messages. The UPnP framework check box in the Windows Firewall Settings dialog box is cleared and cannot be selected. • **Not Configured**: Windows Firewall does not open TCP port 2869 and UDP port 1900. Therefore, the computer cannot receive Plug and Play messages unless an administrator uses other policy settings to open the required ports or enable the required programs. The UPnP framework check box in the Windows Firewall Settings dialog box is cleared, and administrators can select or clear it.

CONFIGURE WINDOWS FIREWALL THROUGH GROUP POLICY

OPEN the Group Policy Object Editor for the Group Policy Object in which you want to configure firewall settings.

1. In the Group Policy Object Editor, in the console tree, expand **Computer Configuration>Administrative Templates>Network>Network Connections>Windows Firewall.**
2. In the console tree, select one of the following:

   Domain Profile. Select this folder if you want to configure Windows Firewall Group Policy settings for when the affected computers are connected to a network where domain controllers in which the computer's domain account resides are available. The example in Figure 7-22 shows the Domain Profile folder selected.

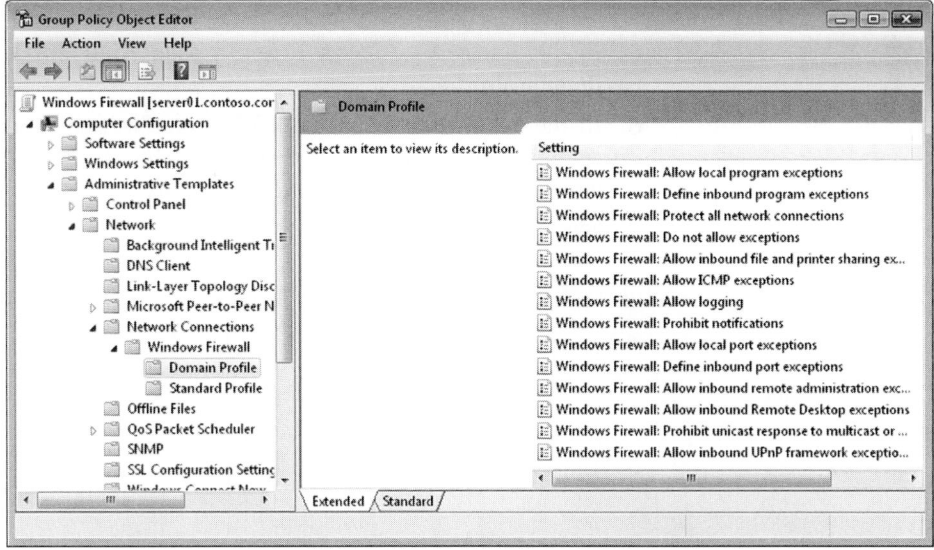

Figure 7-22

The Windows Firewall GPO (an example GPO) with the Domain Profile folder selected. The Windows Firewall Group Policy settings appear in the details pane.

Standard Profile. Select this folder if you want to configure Windows Firewall Group Policy settings for when the affected computers are not connected to a network where domain controllers in which the computer's domain account resides are available.

3. In the details pane, right-click the policy that you want to configure and then click **Properties.** The Explain tab describes configuration choices.

DISABLE WINDOWS FIREWALL THROUGH GROUP POLICY

If you use a third-party firewall in place of Windows Firewall, then you will want to disable Windows Firewall on all computers protected by the third-party firewall. You can do this through Group Policy.

OPEN the Group Policy Object Editor for the Group Policy Object in which you want to configure firewall settings.

1. In the Group Policy Object Editor, in the console tree, expand **Computer Configuration>Administrative Templates>Network.** Then select **Network Connections**.
2. In the details pane, right click **Prohibit use of Internet Connection Firewall on your DNS domain network** and then click **Properties.** The Prohibit use of Internet Connection Firewall on your DNS domain network Properties dialog box appears.
3. Select **Enabled**, as shown in Figure 7-23.

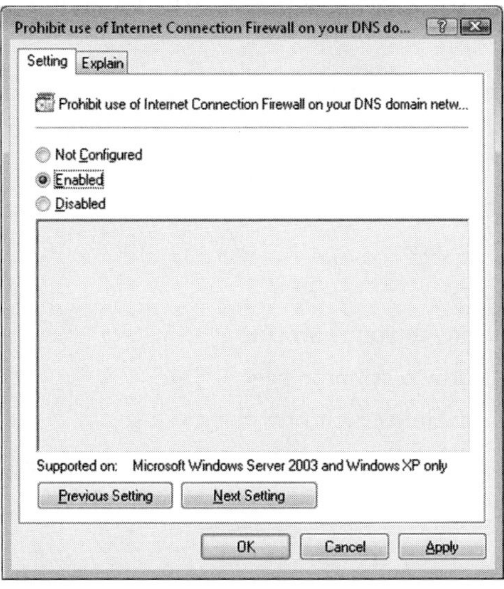

Figure 7-23

The Prohibit use of Internet Connection Firewall on your DNS domain network Properties dialog box with Enabled selected

4. Click **OK.**
5. In the Group Policy Object Editor, expand **Windows Firewall** and then select **Domain Profile.**
6. In the details pane, right-click **Windows Firewall: Protect all network connections** and then click **Properties.** The Windows Firewall: Protect all network connections Properties dialog box opens.
7. Select **Disabled**, as shown in Figure 7-24.

Figure 7-24

The Windows Firewall: Protect all network connections Properties dialog box with Disabled selected

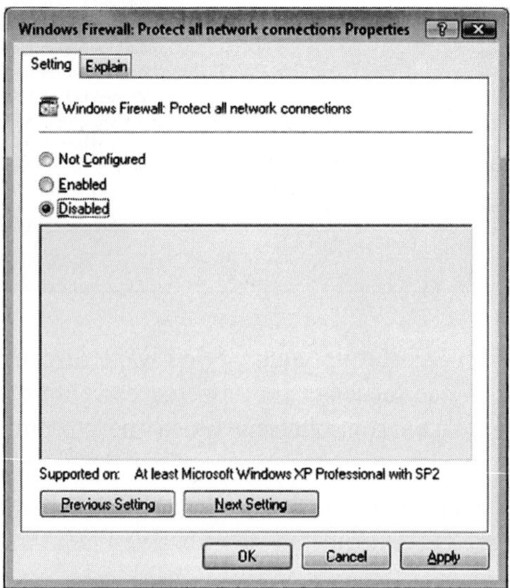

8. Click **OK.**
9. In the Group Policy Object Editor, select **Standard profile.**
10. In the details pane, right click **Windows Firewall: Protect all network connections** and then click Properties. The Windows Firewall: Protect all network connections Properties dialog box opens.
11. Select **Disabled** and then click **OK.**

Understanding Windows Defender

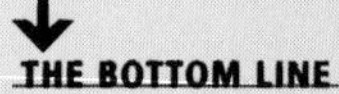

Windows Defender is Windows Vista's front-line defense against spyware and other unwanted software.

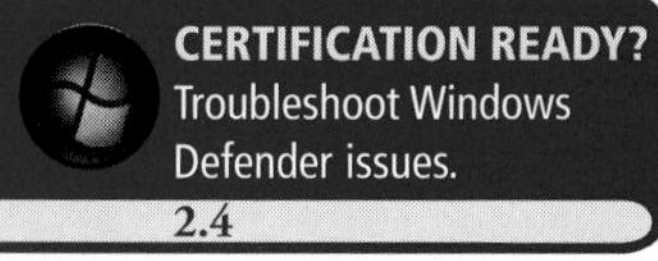

The definition of ***spyware*** has come to include a large variety of undesirable programs, from pop-up advertisements to applications that gather data from your computer and send it across the Internet. Such data can contain personal or financial information, your browsing habits, or anything else stored on your computer.

Symptoms of spyware include:

- Unexpected toolbars
- Unexpected additions to your Favorites
- Changing of your browser's home page
- Changing of your default search provider
- A sudden increase in computer crashes or a decrease in performance, especially while running Internet Explorer.

Windows Defender is Microsoft's front-line defense against spyware for individual computers. It defends against spyware by:

- Looking for and quarantining or removing known malicious programs as they are encountered.
- Looking for and providing guidance when programs bordering on spyware status are encountered.
- Scanning your computers files periodically to look for known spyware.
- Providing information on and tools to control programs that start during the startup process.

TAKE NOTE* Windows Defender is a good solution for spyware in small business networks or on home installations. For spyware protection in an enterprise environment, consider using a product such as Microsoft Forefront Client Security (*www.microsoft.com/forefront/default.mspx*).

Software Explorer is covered in the **Using Software Explorer** section later in this lesson.

Windows Defender runs as a service, which means that it can do its scans without requesting administrator privileges no matter which user is logged on. The interface, however, runs in the context of the current user, and so User Account Control elevation is required for some actions.

Windows Defender also provides the Software Explorer tool. ***Software Explorer*** enables you to view detailed information about software that can affect privacy and security, and to control startup programs (programs that are started when you start Windows Vista).

Using Windows Defender

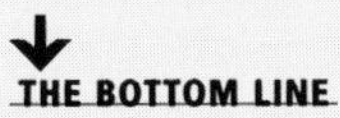

The Windows Defender interface enables you to configure options, schedule scanning, launch manual scans, and more. You can also configure settings for Windows Defender through Group Policy.

Configure Windows Defender Options Locally

Windows Defender local options control such things as when automatic scans take place, as well as what is scanned. Settings in Group Policy supersede local settings.

CONFIGURE WINDOWS DEFENDER OPTIONS

1. Click **Start**. In the Start Search text box, type **Windows Defender** and then press **Ctrl + Shift + Enter**. A User Account Control message box appears.
2. Provide administrator credentials and then click **OK**. Windows Defender opens, as shown in Figure 7-25.

Figure 7-25

Windows Defender

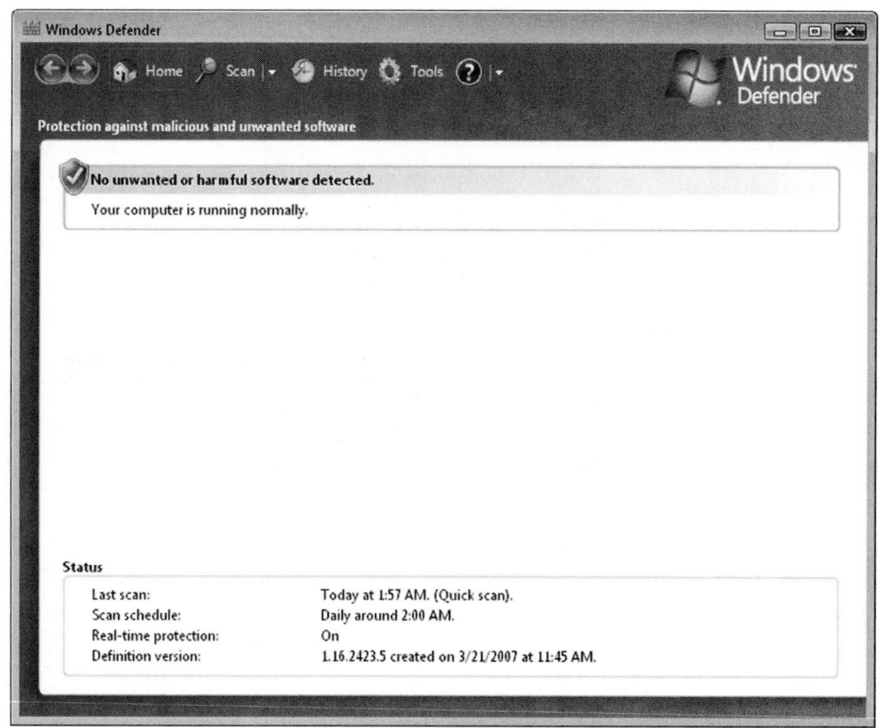

3. Click **Tools**. The Tools and Settings page appears, as shown in Figure 7-26.

Figure 7-26

The Tools and Settings page of Windows Defender

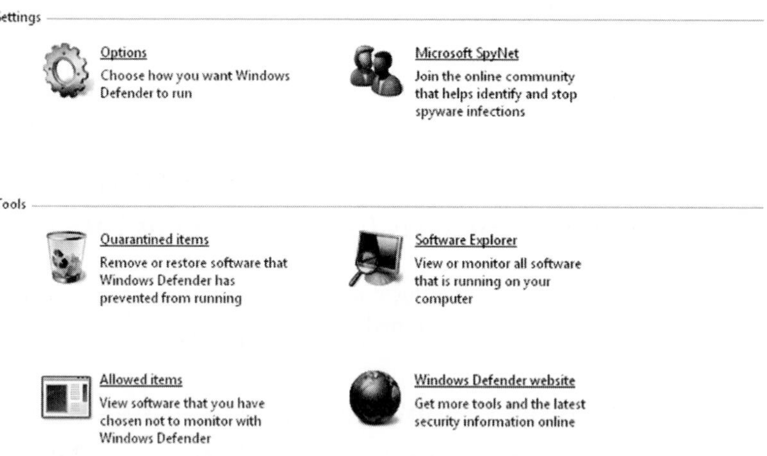

4. In the Settings section, click **Options**. The Options page appears, as shown in Figure 7-27. You can configure the following sets of options on the Options page of Windows Defender:

   Automatic scanning

   Default actions

   Real-time protection options

   Advanced options

   Administrator options

   Options in each of these settings are covered in the procedures that follow.

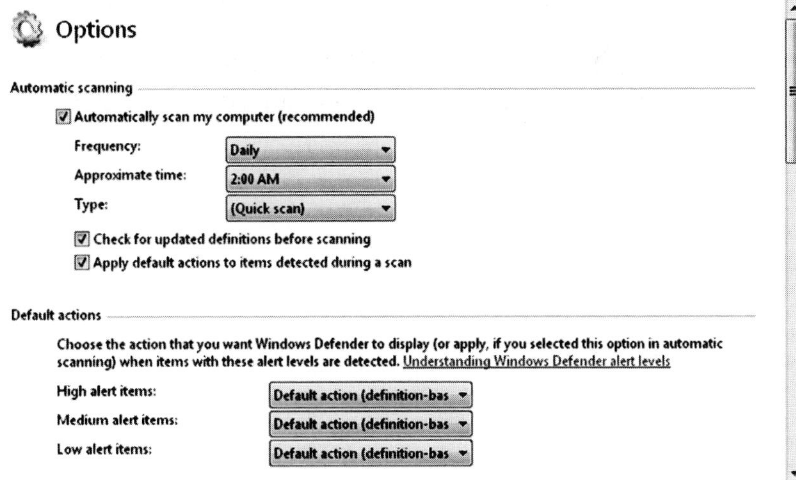

Figure 7-27

The Options page of Windows Defender

5. When you finish configuring Windows Defender options, click **Save**.

CONFIGURE AUTOMATIC SCANNING OPTIONS

OPEN the Options page of Windows Defender.

1. In the Automatic scanning section, if you want to enable automatic scanning, select the *Automatically scan my computer (recommended)* check box. To disable automatic scanning, clear the check box.
2. In the **Frequency** drop-down list, select one of the following:

   Daily. Select this option to scan each day.

   Sunday – Monday. Select a day between Sunday and Monday to scan on that day only (once per week).
3. In the **Approximate time** drop-down list, select a time. The start time for the scan is approximate because if you choose to update definitions before the scan starts, the definitions update begins before the actual scan. The time the update takes depends on the number of updated definitions Windows Defender needs to install.
4. In the Type drop-down list, select one of the following:

   (**Quick scan**). Select this option to scan the most critical areas.

   (**Full system scan**). Select this option to scan all areas.
5. To check for updated definitions before beginning an automatic scan, select the *Check for updated definitions before scanning* check box.
6. To apply default actions (configured in the next procedure) when Windows Defender detects a malicious program during a scan, select the *Apply default actions to items detected during a scan* check box.

CONFIGURE DEFAULT ACTIONS

OPEN the Options page of Windows Defender.

In the Default actions section, select one of the following options in the **High alert items**, **Medium alert items**, and **Low alert items** drop-down lists:

Default action (definition-based). Select this option to do what the virus definition recommends doing. This is the recommended setting.

Ignore. Select this option to ignore the detected program. This is not recommended, especially for high and medium alert items.

Remove. Select this option to remove the detected item automatically.

CONFIGURE REAL-TIME PROTECTION OPTIONS

OPEN the Options page of Windows Defender.

1. On the Options page, scroll to the Real-time protection options section, as shown in Figure 7-28.

Figure 7-28

Real-time protection options on the Options page of Windows Defender

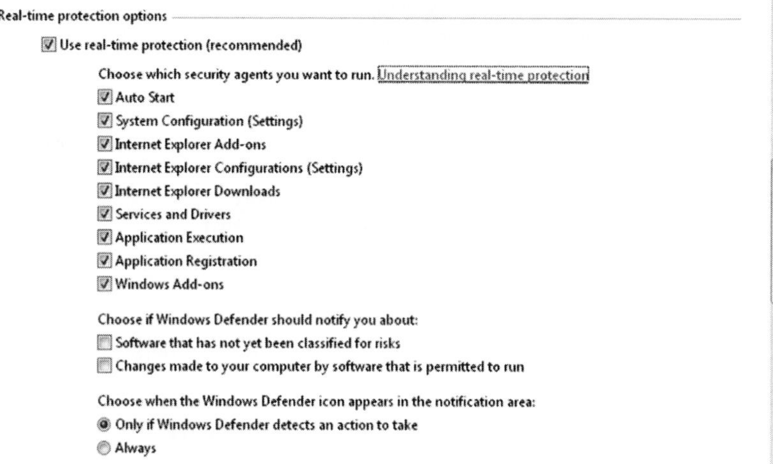

2. To use real-time protection (which is highly recommended), select the *Use real-time protection (recommended)* check box.
3. To configure what is protected, under *Choose which security agents you want to run*, select or clear the check boxes described in Table 7-4.

Table 7-4

Real-time protection security agents and their descriptions

CHECK BOX NAME	DESCRIPTION
Auto Start	Monitors lists of programs that are allowed to automatically run when you start your computer. Malicious individuals can set spyware and other unwanted software to run automatically when Windows starts. This can result in malicious individuals collecting confidential information from your computer, as well as computer performance degradation.
System Configuration (Settings)	Monitors security-related settings in Windows. Spyware and other unwanted software can change hardware and software security settings in an attempt to further undermine your computer's security.
Internet Explorer Add-ons	Monitors programs that automatically run when you start Internet Explorer. Spyware and other unwanted software can masquerade as Web browser add-ons and run without your knowledge.
Internet Explorer Configurations (Settings)	Monitors browser security settings because spyware and other unwanted software may try to change these settings.
Internet Explorer Downloads	Monitors files and programs that are designed to work with Internet Explorer, such as ActiveX controls and software installation programs. These files can be downloaded, installed, or run by the browser itself. Spyware and other unwanted software can be included with these files and installed without your knowledge.
Services and Drivers	Monitors services and drivers as they interact with Windows and your programs. Because services and drivers perform essential computer functions (such as allowing devices to work with your computer), they have access to important areas in the operating system.
Application Execution	Monitors when programs start and any operations they perform while running. Unwanted software can use vulnerabilities in programs to run malicious code. For example, spyware can run itself in the background when you start a program that you frequently use. Windows Defender monitors your programs and alerts you if suspicious activity is detected.

(continued)

Table 7-4 (*continued*)

Check box name	Description
Application Registration	Monitors tools and files in the operating system where programs can register to run at any time, not just when you start Windows or another program. Unwanted software can register a program to start without notice and run, for example, at a scheduled time each day. This could enable the program to collect information about you or your computer, or to gain access to important areas of the operating system without your knowledge.
Windows Add-ons	Monitors add-on programs (also known as software utilities) for Windows. Add-ons are designed to enhance your computing experience in areas such as security, browsing, productivity, and multimedia. However, add-ons can also install programs that can collect information about you or your online activities and expose sensitive, personal information to third parties.

4. Under *Choose if Windows Defender should notify you about*, configure the following:

   Software that has not yet been classified for risks. Select this option to be notified about software that has not been classified for risks. You can select this option if you are weary of being attacked by malicious software before it has been identified as such.

   Changes made to your computer by software that is permitted to run. Select this option to be notified about software that makes changes even if that software is permitted to run. You can select this option if you are worried that approved software might make unwanted changes.

5. Under *Choose when the Windows Defender icon appears in the notification area*, select one of the following:

   Only if Windows Defender detects an action to take. Select this option to display the Windows Defender icon in the notification area only when Windows Defender is going to take an action against something it detected.

   Always. Select this option to always display the Windows Defender icon in the notification area.

CONFIGURE ADVANCED OPTIONS

OPEN the Options page of Windows Defender.

1. On the Options page, scroll to the Advanced options section, as shown in Figure 7-29.

Figure 7-29

Advanced options on the Options page of Windows Defender

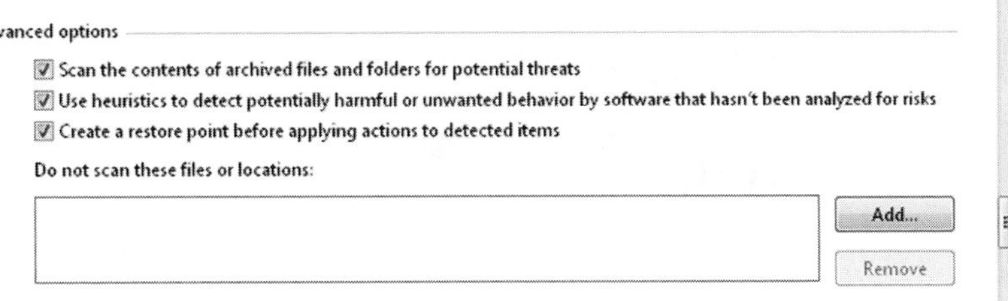
Advanced options
Scan the contents of archived files and folders for potential threats
Use heuristics to detect potentially harmful or unwanted behavior by software that hasn't been analyzed for risks
Create a restore point before applying actions to detected items
Do not scan these files or locations:
Add...
Remove

2. Configure the following check boxes:

   Scan the contents of the archived files and folders for potential threats.

   Use heuristics to detect potentially harmful or unwanted behavior by software that hasn't been analyzed for risks. Microsoft recommends this option because it enables Windows Defender to look for behavior that is bad regardless of whether the application has been analyzed before.

Create a restore point before applying actions to detected items. Select this option if you are concerned you may need to roll back a change made by Windows Defender.

3. To specify files or locations that you do not want to scan, click **Add**. The Browse for Files or Folders dialog box appears. Select the file or folder that you do not want to scan and then click **OK.**
4. To remove a folder or file from the Do not scan these files or locations list box, select the item, and then click **Remove.**

CONFIGURE ADMINISTRATOR OPTIONS

OPEN the Options page of Windows Defender.

1. On the Options page, scroll to the Administrator options section, as shown in Figure 7-30.

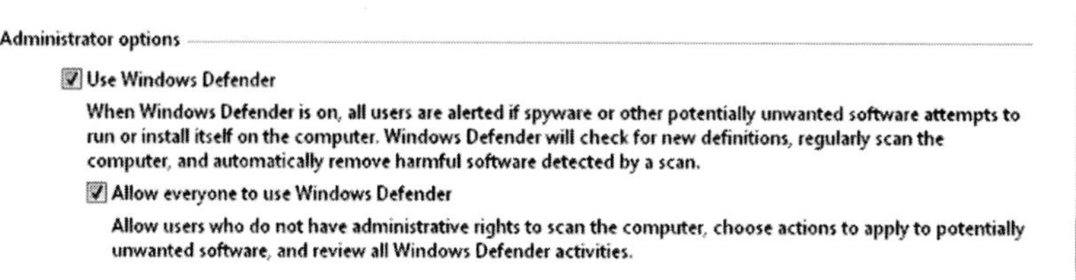

Administrator options
Use Windows Defender
When Windows Defender is on, all users are alerted if spyware or other potentially unwanted software attempts to run or install itself on the computer. Windows Defender will check for new definitions, regularly scan the computer, and automatically remove harmful software detected by a scan.
Allow everyone to use Windows Defender
Allow users who do not have administrative rights to scan the computer, choose actions to apply to potentially unwanted software, and review all Windows Defender activities.

Figure 7-30

Administrator options on the Options page of Windows Defender

2. If you want to turn Windows Defender on, select the **Use Windows Defender** check box. If you do not want to use Windows Defender, clear the check box.
3. If you choose to use Windows Defender, if you want to limit its use to administrators, clear the **Allow everyone to use Windows Defender** check box. If you select this check box, standard users will be able to scan the computer, choose actions to perform on unwanted software, and review all Windows Defender activities.

Using Software Explorer

Software Explorer is a component of Windows Defender that enables you to view detailed information and control software (including configuring startup options) on your computer that may have a negative impact on performance, privacy, or security.

Software Explorer enables you to view detailed information about software that can affect privacy and security, and to control startup programs (programs that are started when you start Windows Vista). You can explore the following categories of software in Software Explorer:

- **Startup programs.** Programs that run automatically with or without your knowledge when you start Windows.
- **Currently running programs.** Programs or processes currently running.
- **Network-connected programs.** Programs or processes that can connect to the Internet or to your home or office network.
- **Winsock service providers.** Programs that perform low-level networking and communication services and often have access to important areas of the operating system.

Some of the important information that Software Explorer can display is shown in Table 7-5.

Table 7-5

Some of the important information that Software Explorer displays for a given software product

INFORMATION TITLE	DESCRIPTION
Auto Start	Indicates if the program is registered to start automatically when Windows starts.
Startup Type	Indicates what causes the program to start on startup, for example, a registry setting or the All Users Startup folder.
Ships with Operating System	Indicates if the program was installed as part of Windows.
Classification	Identifies if the program has been analyzed for risks to your privacy and the security of the computer.
Digitally Signed By	Indicates if the software has been signed and, if so, if the publisher listed has signed it.

EXPLORE SOFTWARE USING SOFTWARE EXPLORER

OPEN the Tools and Settings page of Windows Defender.

1. In the Tools section of the Tools and Settings page, click **Software Explorer**. The Software Explorer page appears, as shown in Figure 7-31.

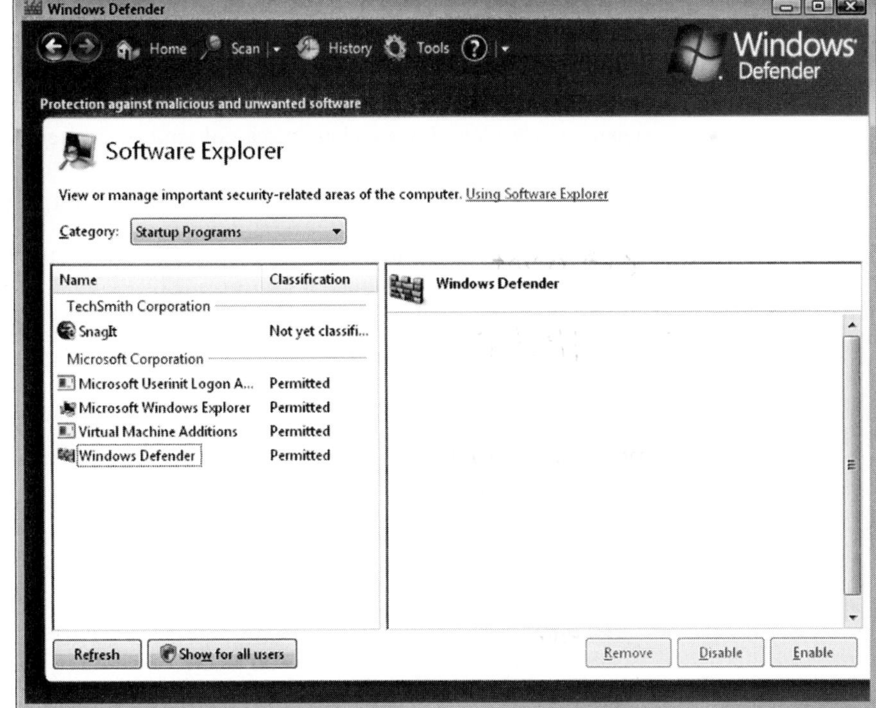

Figure 7-31

Software Explorer in Windows Defender

2. To monitor software that is used by all users on the computer, click **Show for all users**. A User Account Control dialog box appears. Provide administrator credentials and then click **OK**.
3. To change the category of software that you are exploring, select one of the following categories in the Category drop-down list:

   Startup Programs. Startup programs run automatically when you start Windows. Information is provided for each startup program such as the startup type, location, and file version. If you select this category, you can, depending on the selected software and its state, click the following:

Remove. Click this to remove the program from the startup folder.

Disable. Click this to disable the program from starting at startup.

Enable. Click this to enable the program to start at startup.

Currently Running Programs. This category lists all currently running programs; those that you started and those running in the background. Information is provided for each currently running program such as the publisher, digital signer, and file type. If you select this category, you can, depending on the selected software and its state, click the following:

Task Manager. Click this to start Task Manager.

End Process. Click this to end the selected process.

Network Connected Programs. This category lists all programs and processes that connect your computer to the Internet or to your network. Information for each network-connected program is provided such as the location of the program, its version, and the services it uses. If you select this option, you can, depending on the selected software and its state, click the following:

End Process. Click this to end the selected process.

Block Incoming Connections. Click this to block incoming connections to the selected program or process.

Winsock Service Providers. This category provides information (such as the publisher, SpyNet voting, and its file type) about programs that perform low-level services for the Windows operating system and for programs that run on Windows.

Scanning Your System Manually

You can launch a Windows Defender scan of your computer at any time.

SCAN YOUR SYSTEM AND TAKE ACTION WITH WINDOWS DEFENDER

If you want to scan your system before the next scheduled scan because you suspect malicious programs are active, you can launch a scan manually. If any actionable items are found, you can take the prescribed or other action.

OPEN Windows Defender.

1. In Windows Defender, click the small downward arrow to the right of Scan in the menu bar (as shown in Figure 7-32), and then click one of the following:

   Quick Scan. Select this option to scan the most likely areas where unwanted software resides.

   Full Scan. Select this option to scan the entire computer.

   Custom Scan. Select this option to specify the files and folders that you want to scan. You can use this option if you suspect a particular piece of undesirable software and know where it usually resides.

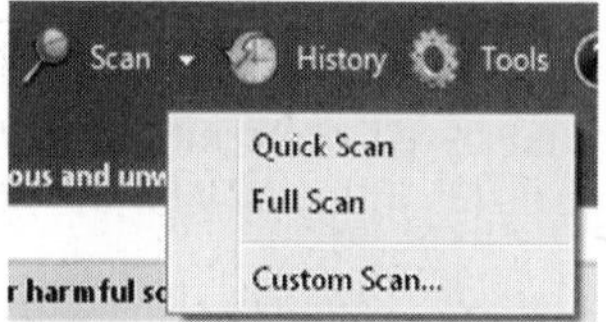

Figure 7-32
Manual scanning options

2. When the scan is complete, click **Review items detected by scanning** (available only if items were found). The Scan Results page appears, as shown in the example in Figure 7-33.

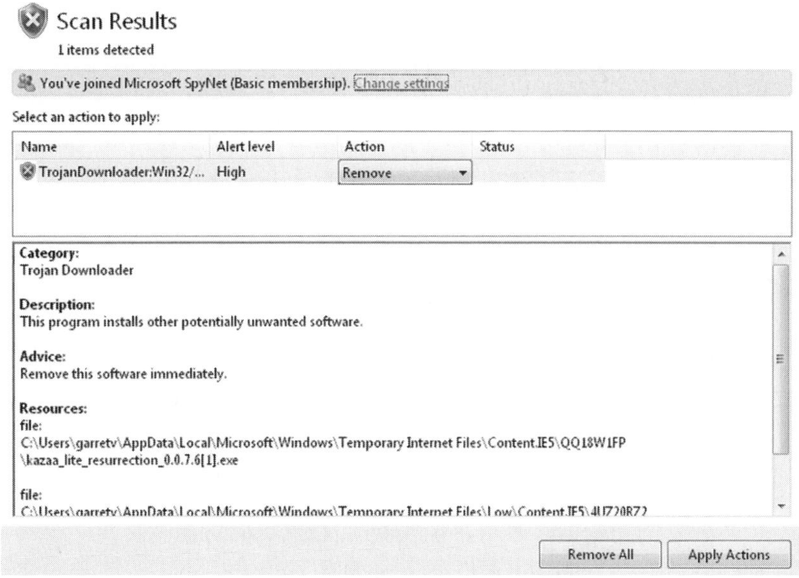

Figure 7-33

Reviewing example scan results in Windows Defender after a full system scan

3. For each item, select an action in the Action drop-down list. You should consult the advice given in the item description when choosing an action.
4. Click **Apply Actions**.

Configuring Windows Defender Group Policy

Windows Defender can be configured using Group Policy.

You can configure the behavior and many settings of Windows Defender for computers in an Active Directory directory services environment using Group Policy.

Windows Defender Group Policy settings are located in the Computer Configuration> Administrative Templates>Windows Components>Windows Defender folder of GPOs.

Table 7-6 summarizes the Group Policy settings available.

Table 7-6

Windows Defender Group Policy settings

POLICY SETTING	DESCRIPTION
Turn on definition updates through both WSUS and Windows Update	Enables you to configure Windows Defender to install definition updates from Windows Update when a local Windows Update Services (WSUS) server is not available. • **Enabled**: By default, Windows Defender will check for definition updates from Windows Update, if connections to a locally managed WSUS server fail. • **Disabled**: Windows Defender will check for definition updates only on a locally managed WSUS server, if the Automatic Updates client is configured to do so. • **Not Configured**: Same as Enabled.

(continued)

Table 7-6 (*continued*)

POLICY SETTING	DESCRIPTION
Check for New Signatures Before Scheduled Scans	Checks for new signatures before running scheduled scans. • **Enabled**: The scheduled scan checks for new signatures before it scans the computer. • **Disabled**: The scheduled scan begins without downloading new signatures. • **Not Configured**: Same as Disabled.
Turn off Windows Defender	Turns off Windows Defender Real-Time Protection. • **Enabled**: Windows Defender will not run. • **Disabled**: Windows Defender can run. • **Not Configured**: Same as Disabled.
Enable Logging Known Good Detections	Enables logging detection data during Real-time Protection when Windows Defender detects known good files. Logging detections provides you with detailed information about the programs that run on the computers you monitor. • **Enabled**: Known good files are logged. • **Disabled**: Known good files are not logged. • **Not Configured**: Same as Disabled.
Enable Logging Unknown Detection	Enables logging detections during Real-time Protection when Windows Defender detects unknown files. Logging detections provides you with detailed information about the programs that run on the computers you monitor. • **Enabled**: Unknown files are logged. • **Disabled**: Unknown files are not logged. • **Not Configured**: Same as Enabled.
Turn off Real-Time Protection Prompts for Unknown Detection	Turns off Real-Time Protection prompts for detection of unknown items. • **Enabled**: Windows Defender does not prompt users to allow or block unknown activity. • **Disabled**: Windows Defender prompts users to allow or block unknown activity. • **Not Configured**: Same as Disabled.
Download Entire Signature Set	Downloads the full signature set, rather than only the signatures that have been updated since the last signature download. Downloading the full signature set can help to solve problems with signature installations, but doing so takes longer because there is more to download. • **Enabled**: The full signatures set is downloaded each time Windows Defender downloads signatures. • **Disabled**: Only updated signatures are downloaded each time Windows Defender downloads signatures. • **Not Configured**: Same as Disabled.
Configure Microsoft SpyNet Reporting	Microsoft SpyNet is an online community that helps you choose how to respond to potential threats, and it helps stop the spread of new spyware. When Windows Defender detects software or changes by software not yet classified for risks, you can see how other SpyNet members responded to the alert and other members can see how you responded. Your actions also help Microsoft choose which software to investigate for potential threats. You can choose to send basic or additional information about detected software. Additional information helps improve how Windows Defender works. It can include, for example, the location of detected items on your computer if harmful software has been removed.

(*continued*)

Table 7-6 ***(continued)***

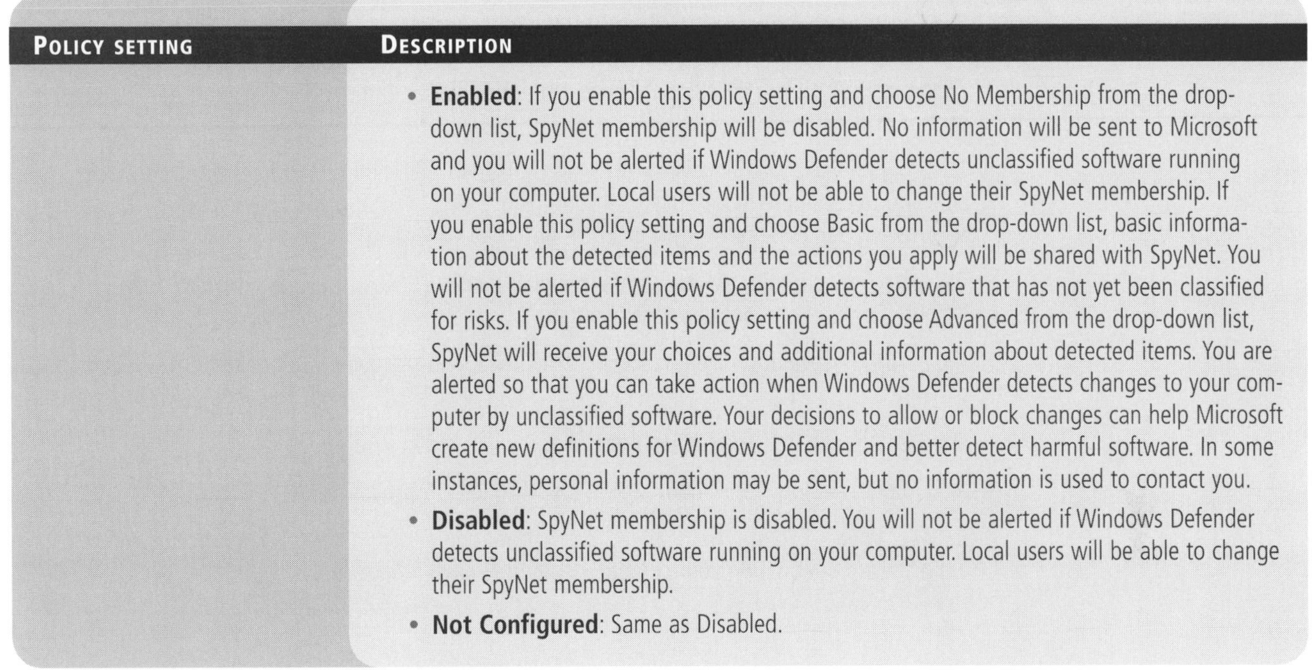

POLICY SETTING	DESCRIPTION
	• **Enabled**: If you enable this policy setting and choose No Membership from the drop-down list, SpyNet membership will be disabled. No information will be sent to Microsoft and you will not be alerted if Windows Defender detects unclassified software running on your computer. Local users will not be able to change their SpyNet membership. If you enable this policy setting and choose Basic from the drop-down list, basic information about the detected items and the actions you apply will be shared with SpyNet. You will not be alerted if Windows Defender detects software that has not yet been classified for risks. If you enable this policy setting and choose Advanced from the drop-down list, SpyNet will receive your choices and additional information about detected items. You are alerted so that you can take action when Windows Defender detects changes to your computer by unclassified software. Your decisions to allow or block changes can help Microsoft create new definitions for Windows Defender and better detect harmful software. In some instances, personal information may be sent, but no information is used to contact you. • **Disabled**: SpyNet membership is disabled. You will not be alerted if Windows Defender detects unclassified software running on your computer. Local users will be able to change their SpyNet membership. • **Not Configured**: Same as Disabled.

ACCESS WINDOWS DEFENDER GROUP POLICY SETTINGS

OPEN the Group Policy Object for which you want to configure Group Policy settings in the Group Policy Object Editor.

1. In the Group Policy Object Editor console tree, expand **Computer Configuration>Administrative Templates>Windows Components** and then select **Windows Defender**, as shown in Figure 7-34.

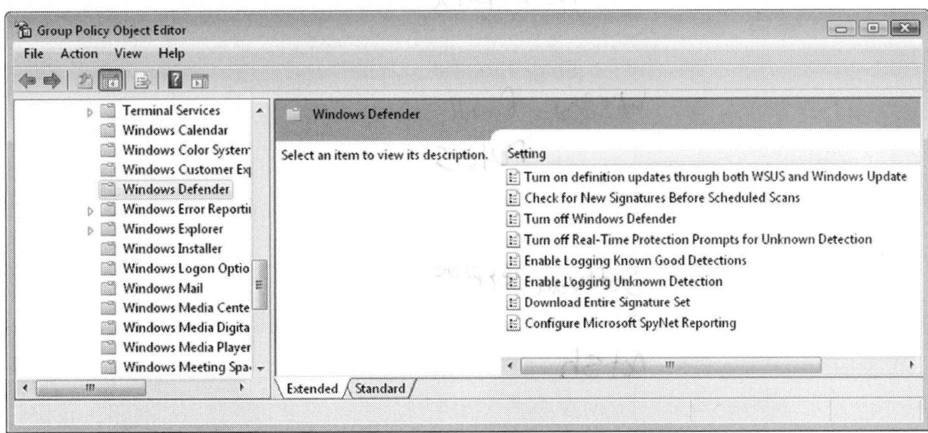

Figure 7-34

Group Policy settings for Windows Defender in an example GPO

2. In the details pane, right-click the policy setting that you want to configure. Then click **Properties**.

SUMMARY SKILL MATRIX

IN THIS LESSON YOU LEARNED:
Windows Firewall is a host firewall that can run on each computer in a network to help prevent attacks.
To configure basic Windows Firewall settings through the Windows Firewall Settings dialog box, and to configure more advanced settings by using the Windows Firewall with Advanced Security Snap-in, whether locally or in Group Policy.
To create Firewall Rules, which are the building blocks of exceptions and can be configured for both inbound and outbound connections.
The purpose of Windows Defender is to block, find, and remove malicious software, including spyware.
To schedule scanning and launch manual scans in Windows Defender.
To configure settings for Windows Defender through Group Policy.
To use Software Explorer to view detailed information and control software (including configuring startup options) on your computer that may have a negative affect.

■ Knowledge Assessment

Fill in the Blank

Complete the following sentences by writing the correct word or words in the blanks provided.

1. Out bount ______ rules are new to Windows Firewall in Windows Vista and control communication from your computer to other computers.
2. A(n) Host base ______ firewall is a firewall that resides on workstations or other computers to defend against attacks that originate behind the perimeter firewall or circumvent the perimeter firewall.
3. Windows firewall ______ is a host firewall that comes with Windows Vista.
4. Firewall rules ______ are combined to make exceptions.
5. Unexpected toolbars and unexpected additions to your Favorites in Internet Explorer are both indications that you may want to scan your computer by using Defender ______.
6. Software explore ______ in Windows Defender can be used to view which applications are configured to start when your computer starts.
7. netsh ______ is a command-line tool that can be used to configure Windows Firewall.
8. You can restrict application of a Firewall rule according to its subnet, which is a function of its IP address and Subnet mask ______.
9. ______ is Microsoft's online community that helps you choose how to respond to potential threats. It also helps stop the spread of new spyware.
10. A(n) Firewall ______ is a software or hardware device that limits inbound and sometimes outbound data connections in an attempt to strengthen security.

Multiple Choice

Select all answers that apply for the following questions.

1. The default behavior of Windows Firewall is to:
   a. block all incoming and outgoing traffic.
   b. block all incoming traffic unless it is solicited or it matches a configured rule, allow all outgoing traffic unless it matches a configured rule, and secure all traffic to domain controllers using IPsec.
   c. block all incoming traffic unless it is solicited, and block all outgoing traffic unless it is allowed by a configured rule.
   d. block all incoming traffic unless it is solicited or it matches a configured rule, and to allow all outgoing traffic unless it matches a configured rule.

2. The following profile is used for a computer that is authenticated to Active Directory:
   a. Domain profile
   b. Private profile
   c. Public profile
   d. Active Directory profile

3. The following are new to Windows Firewall in Windows Vista:
   a. control over outbound traffic
   b. integration of IPsec
   c. Windows Firewall with Advanced Security Snap-in
   d. all of the above

4. For which of the following is there *not* a Windows Defender security agent?
   a. Services and Drivers
   b. Application Execution
   c. Application Registration
   d. Outlook Add-ons

5. In Windows Firewall, connection security rules:
   a. consist of outbound and inbound traffic rules.
   b. determine how traffic between the host computer and other computers is secured.
   c. are required for each port not in the trusted ports list.
   d. are used to secure traffic using the encrypting file system (EFS).

6. When not on the domain network, Windows Vista determines whether it is on a public or private network by:
   a. checking the IP address of the DHCP Server.
   b. authenticating with the ISP.
   c. asking the user.
   d. using network heuristics.

7. Typically, you will configure the most restrictive settings for Windows Firewall in which profile?
   a. the Domain profile
   b. the Public profile
   c. the Private profile
   d. the User profile

8. You need to create an inbound rule for Remote Administration. You figure that this must be a fairly common task among administrators, and you suspect a rule might already exist that will accomplish this. In the New Inbound Rule Wizard, on the Rule Type page, which of the four rule types should you select?
   a. Program
   b. Port
   c. Predefined
   d. Custom

9. Typically, you will configure the least restrictive settings for Windows Firewall in which profile?
   a. the Domain profile
   b. the Public profile
   c. the Private profile
   d. the User profile

10. Software Explorer enables you to view programs that belong to which of the following classifications (select all that apply)?
    a. startup programs
    b. signed programs
    c. Winsock service providers
    d. shell programs

Review Questions

1. Contoso Inc, has just bought Woodgrove bank. You are an IT technician at Contoso and have been tasked with monitoring the computers on the network of Woodgrove before they are added to the Contoso domain to identify any security vulnerabilities. As part of this effort, you would like to know what programs are regularly run on the computers on the Woodgrove network. How can you use Windows Defender to accomplish this?
2. Outline the purpose of a host firewall as compared to a perimeter firewall.

■ Case Scenarios

Scenario 1: Protecting Laptops on Public Networks by Using Windows Firewall

Currently laptop and desktop computers for the Contoso domain are contained within the same organizational unit (OU) in Active Directory. You want to harden the security settings in Windows Firewall for laptops, which are often connected to public networks, while leaving the settings the same for the desktops, which are connected exclusively to the domain network.

Describe two different solutions to this problem. One should involve altering the Active Directory structure to accommodate a new OU and GPO, and the other should keep Active Directory structure the same and simply modify Group Policy settings.

Scenario 2: Safeguarding a TCP Port Used by an Application

A custom application used by 15 employees in the IT development department uses TCP port 591 to communicate. You have configured an exception in Windows Firewall by using Group Policy for all domain computers to allow incoming traffic for the custom application using port 591. The 15 computers are on their own subnet. Using the same port, a recent Internet worm exploits a security weakness. How can you most easily lock down the port so that it can only be used between those 15 computers and be blocked for all other computers in the domain?

Troubleshooting Access, Authentication, and User Account Control Issues

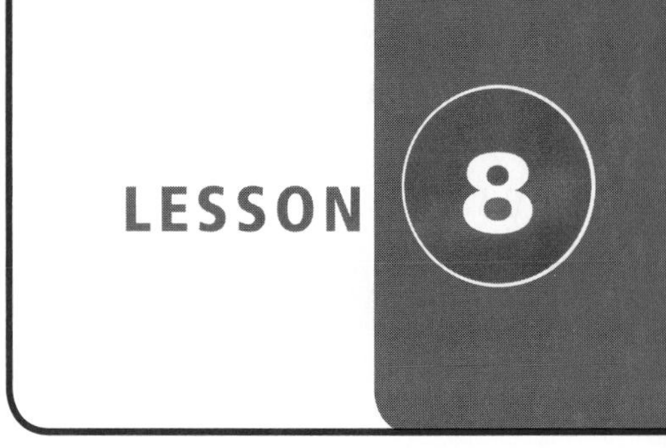

OBJECTIVE DOMAIN MATRIX

Technology Skill	Objective Domain	Objective Domain Number
Understanding User Account Control	Configure and troubleshoot User Account Control	2.8
Understanding the Principle of Least Privilege	Configure and troubleshoot User Account Control	2.8
Understanding the Consent UI	Configure and troubleshoot User Account Control • Configure credential prompts	2.8
Understanding the Secure Desktop	Configure and troubleshoot User Account Control	2.8
Understanding Admin Approval Mode	Configure and troubleshoot User Account Control • Administrator vs. Standard User	2.8
Understanding File and Registry Virtualization	Configure and troubleshoot User Account Control • Resolve UAC virtualization issues	2.8
Troubleshooting UAC Application Compatibility Issues	Troubleshoot deployment issues • Resolve application compatibility issues Configure and troubleshoot User Account Control • Troubleshoot application issues	1.5 2.8
Configuring UAC Group Policy	Configure and troubleshoot User Account Control • Configure credential prompts • Troubleshoot policy settings	2.8
Configuring and Troubleshooting Access to Encrypted Resources	Configure and troubleshoot access to resources	2.6

(continued)

OBJECTIVE DOMAIN MATRIX *(continued)*

TECHNOLOGY SKILL	OBJECTIVE DOMAIN	OBJECTIVE DOMAIN NUMBER
Understanding EFS	Configure and troubleshoot access to resources • EFS and BitLocker	2.6
Using the Encrypting File System Wizard	Configure and troubleshoot access to resources • EFS and BitLocker	2.6
Troubleshooting EFS	Configure and troubleshoot access to resources • EFS and BitLocker	2.6
Configuring EFS Group Policy Settings	Configure and troubleshoot access to resources • EFS and BitLocker	2.6
Understanding BitLocker	Configure and troubleshoot access to resources • EFS and BitLocker	2.6
Configuring BitLocker Group Policy	Configure and troubleshoot access to resources • EFS and BitLocker	2.6
Troubleshooting Authentication Issues	Troubleshoot authentication issues	2.7
Troubleshooting User Name and Password	Troubleshoot authentication issues • User name and password	2.7
Understanding and Renewing Smart Card Certificates	Troubleshoot authentication issues • Certificates • Smart cards	2.7

KEY TERMS

User Account Control (UAC)
principle of least privilege
Consent User Interface (Consent UI)
Secure Desktop
token
split token
administrator token (AT)
standard user token (SUT)
privilege
Admin Approval Mode
Program Compatibility Assistant
Sysmain.sdb
file and registry virtualization
Group Policy Software Installation (GPSI)
Encrypting File System (EFS)
transparency
BitLocker
Trusted Platform Module (TPM)
smart card
certificate autoenrollment

Contoso Incorporated, where you are a senior desktop support technician, has upgraded to Windows Vista. User Account Control (UAC) could potentially prevent some custom applications from running correctly, and you need to be ready to troubleshoot that issue. Also, the Contoso IT department has launched a Certificate Authority, which supplies certificates for Encrypting File System (EFS) to users across the domain. You need to understand the EFS process so that you can help employees to share EFS files, and so that you can troubleshoot EFS certificate issues.

Finally, you need to deploy BitLocker on some executives' laptops that contain highly sensitive data so that even if one of the laptops falls into the wrong hands, the data will be secured.

Understanding User Account Control

THE BOTTOM LINE

User Account Control increases security by helping to enforce the principle of least privilege.

CERTIFICATION READY?
Configure and Troubleshoot User Account Control.
2.8

User Account Control (UAC) is primarily an effort to reduce the exposure and attack surface of the operating system by requiring that all users run in standard user mode unless it is necessary to do otherwise. Essentially, User Account Control enforces the principle of least privilege.

Understanding the Principle of Least Privilege

The principle of least privilege limits exposure to security threats by limiting user privileges to the minimum required to complete required tasks.

TAKE NOTE*

You can control UAC behavior through Group Policy (Group Policy for UAC is covered in this lesson). The behaviors of UAC described in this lesson are the default behaviors unless specified otherwise.

The principle of least privilege is an important principle in IT security. The Department of Defense (DoD) Trusted Computer System Evaluation Criteria (TCSEC; DOD-5200.28-STD), also called the Orange Book, is an accepted standard for computer security in the United States. It defines the ***principle of least privilege*** as follows:

"[The principle of least privilege] requires that each subject in a system be granted the most restrictive set of privileges (or lowest clearance) needed for the performance of authorized tasks. The application of this principle limits the damage that can result from accident, error, or unauthorized use."

UAC removes from user prerogative some amount of freedom in choosing whether to apply the principle of least privilege. To understand the relationship between UAC and the principle of least privilege, you first need to understand what UAC does and how it does it.

CERTIFICATION READY?
Configure and Troubleshoot User Account Control: Configure credential prompts
2.8

Understanding the Consent UI

The Consent UI consist of UAC dialog boxes that prompt for consent or administrator credentials when you attempt a task that requires elevated privileges.

Anybody that spends any time with Vista will encounter, sometimes frequently, User Account Control dialog boxes. These dialog boxes appear when a task requires administrator privileges, and either ask for your consent (if you are logged on as an administrator) or for administrator credentials (if you are not).

The dialog boxes are part of UAC and are collectively called the ***Consent UI*** (Consent User Interface). All tasks in Windows Vista have been separated into two categories: those that require administrator privileges and those that don't. Whenever you attempt to complete a task that does requires administrative privileges, you will be presented with the Consent UI.

The Consent UI has three primary types of dialog boxes, each of which has two versions: one for administrators (sometimes called a consent prompt) and one for standard users (sometimes called a credentials prompt). The three credential prompts that can appear when you are logged on as a standard user are shown in Figures 8-1, 8-2, and 8-3.

Figure 8-1

Consent UI for a signed Microsoft application. The title bar is teal.

Figure 8-2

Consent UI for a signed third-party application. The title bar is gray.

Figure 8-3

Consent UI for an unsigned application. The title bar is orange.

Very similar dialog boxes (consent prompts) appear when you are logged on as an administrator, except that they do not request credentials; they only request consent. If you do not respond to a consent UI dialog box within two minutes, it closes as if you had clicked Cancel.

TAKE NOTE* In addition to the three primary Consent UI dialog boxes, there is a fourth less common dialog box with a red title bar for applications that are blocked.

As discussed, Windows Vista lets you know after you have started a task through the consent UI that it requires administrator privileges. But how about before you start a task? If you are launching the task from an icon or a button in an interface such as a dialog box, the icon or button is marked with a small Windows shield icon if the task being launched requires administrator privileges. Figure 8-4 shows an example of an application icon marked with the shield icon, whereas Figure 8-5 shows two examples of buttons marked with the Windows shield icon.

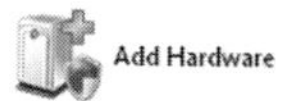

Figure 8-4

The Add Hardware icon in the classic view of the Control Panel is marked with a Windows shield icon because it requires administrator privileges.

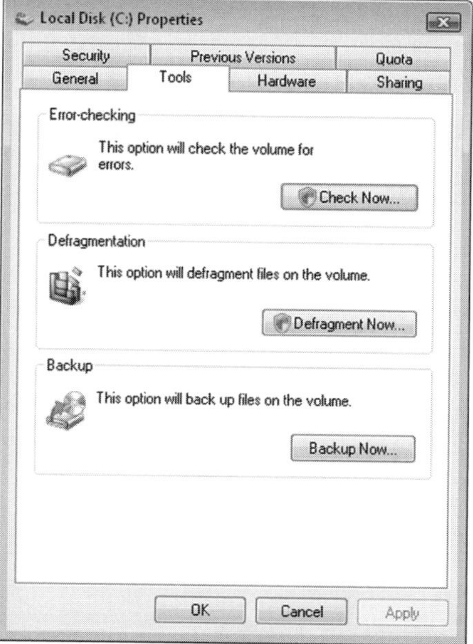

Figure 8-5

The Check Now and the Defragment Now buttons in the Local Disk (C:) Properties dialog box are marked with a Windows shield icon because clicking them launches tasks that require administrator privileges.

Understanding the Secure Desktop

The Secure Desktop helps to prevent hackers from circumventing the UAC Consent UI.

You will notice that when a Consent UI dialog box appears, the background turns gray and dims, and any animations appear to halt (they actually continue, but Windows Vista is not updating the screen).

This is called the Secure Desktop. The ***Secure Desktop*** is a desktop that Windows Vista uses to alter the user interface (UI) to provide protection against malware fooling users into selecting an option that they do not mean to accept. For example, malware could alter your mouse so that where you think you are clicking is actually not where you are clicking. Therefore, an apparent click on Cancel could actually be an actual click on OK. The Secure Desktop prevents this type of attack.

Just before a Consent UI appears, Secure Desktop takes a picture of the desktop, converts it to grayscale, dims it, and replaces your background with it. Then Windows Vista launches an instance of terminal services, which displays the Consent UI! That's right, when a Consent UI appears, it is not using the same session of Windows, but a new session that you access through terminal services. This way nothing (or very little) that a hacker does in the original session can corrupt the Consent UI and your interaction with it.

Understanding Admin Approval Mode

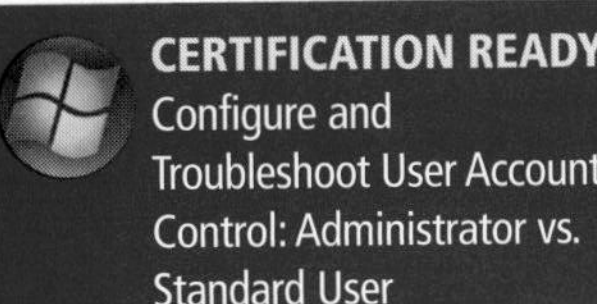

CERTIFICATION READY? Configure and Troubleshoot User Account Control: Administrator vs. Standard User
2.8

Admin Approval Mode is a mode in which administrators must give consent for applications to use the administrator token.

When you log into a pre–Windows Vista computer, you are issued a token. A ***token*** contains information that identifies you to the computer (tokens are based on your Security identifier, also called a SID) and details what privileges you have. Each process that you start (such as an application) requires a token to interact with the operating system. In previous versions of Windows, any process that you started received your token so that if you were logged on as an administrator, any process you started would use your administrator token and have the corresponding administrative privileges. If you were logged on as a standard user, the process would use your standard user token and have its privileges. Thus, any process you started would receive your privileges.

MORE INFORMATION
For more information on tokens, see *msdn2.microsoft.com/en-us/library/aa374909.aspx.*

TAKE NOTE*
By using the Run As command in previous versions of Windows you can start a process with a token other than the one created when you logged on.

UAC in Windows Vista implements a ***split token*** when you log on as an administrator, which means that you are issued two tokens: an ***administrator token (AT)*** and a ***standard user token (SUT)***. The AT is filtered to create the SUT by removing privileges. A ***privilege*** is the right of an account, such as a user or group account, to perform various system-related operations on the local computer, such as shutting down the system, loading device drivers, or changing the system time. All privileges except those listed in Table 8-1 are filtered from the AT to create the SUT.

Table 8-1
When you are issued a split token, all but these privileges are filtered from your AT to create your SUT.

PRIVILEGE	DESCRIPTION
SeShutdownPrivilege	Shuts down the system
SeChangeNotifyPrivilege	Bypasses traverse checking
SeUndockPrivilege	Removes computer from docking station
SeIncreaseWorkingSetPrivilege	Increases a process working set
SeTimeZonePrivilege	Changes the time zone

TAKE NOTE*
The privileges in Table 8-1 are listed with their real names. They also have friendly names that are used in most user interfaces.

Windows Vista decides whether you are an administrator and should therefore be issued a split token at logon by examining your privileges and group memberships. If you have any privileges or belong to any groups listed in Table 8-2, then you are issued a split token.

Table 8-2

If you have any of these privileges or belong to any of these groups, you will be issued a split token when you log on.

PRIVILEGES	GROUPS
SeCreateTokenPrivilege	Built-In Administrators
SeTcbPrivilege	Power Users
SeTakeOwnershipPrivilege	Account Operators
SeLoadDriverPrivilege	Server Operators
SeBackupPrivilege	Printer Operators
SeRestorePrvilege	Backup Operators
SeImpersonatePrivilege	RAS Servers Group
SeRelablePrivilege	Windows NT 4.0 App Compat Group
SeDebugPrivilege	Network Configuration Operators
	Domain Administrators
	Domain Controllers
	Certificate Publishers
	Schema Administrators
	Enterprise Administrators
	Group Policy Administrators

With UAC, when you are logged on as an administrator, any process that you start by default receives your SUT. If a process you start requests an AT, then the process is issued your AT only *after* you grant consent through the consent UI. Using the SUT by default, and requiring consent if the AT is requested, is called ***Admin Approval Mode***.

As stated earlier, when you start a process (application), Windows Vista issues the SUT by default. A process can be excepted from the default if one or more of the following is true:

- You right-clicked an applications icon to start the process and selected Run as administrator.
- You used the Ctrl + Shift + Enter shortcut to start an application with elevated credentials.
- The Run this program as an administrator check box on the Compatibility tab of the program properties dialog box is selected (or the properties dialog box of a shortcut for the program).
- Windows Vista guesses the process is an installer. Windows Vista uses the following rules to guess if it is an installer:

  a. Filename includes keywords like *install, setup, update*, etc.

  b. Keywords in the following Versioning Resource fields: Vendor, Company Name, Product Name, File Description, Original Filename, Internal Name, and Export Name

  c. Keywords in the manifest embedded in the executable

  d. Keywords in specific StringTable entries linked in the executable

  e. Key attributes in the RC data linked in the executable

  f. Targeted sequences of bytes within the executable

- The Program Compatibility Assistant has marked the process as requiring administrative privileges. The ***Program Compatibility Assistant*** is an application that will sometimes intervene when a program is not running correctly and ask if you want to try running it as an administrator. If you answer yes and the application then works, that application will—from that time forward—be run with administrator privileges.

- The application has a Windows Vista manifest that indicates it requires administrative privileges. A Windows Vista manifest is code in the executable file that indicates if the application requires administrator privileges.
- The Sysmain.sdb database file has the process marked as requiring administrative privileges. The ***Sysmain.sdb*** file contains a very large list of legacy applications that require administrator privileges to run correctly.
- The application is started by a process that is running with elevated privileges. In this case, no Consent UI is presented.

Understanding Changes to User Accounts

The Power Users group has been removed, and standard users have increased privileges.

In Windows Vista, the Power Users group has been removed. This means that Windows Vista has only two account types: standard user and administrator.

One reason that the principle of least privilege was commonly violated in previous versions of Windows is that it was not convenient to run Windows as a non-administrator, because many common tasks required administrator privileges.

As part of UAC, Windows Vista enables some tasks that used to be able to be completed by administrators only to be completed by standard users. This is another way in which UAC enforces the principle of least privilege: by not requiring administrator privileges for tasks that shouldn't require them. The first column in Table 8-3 lists the privileges that are new to the standard user in Windows Vista. For reference, the second column lists other important standard user privileges, and the third column lists administrator only privileges.

Table 8-3

In Windows Vista, standard users have privileges that they did not formerly have, which reduces the incentive to log on as an administrator.

Privileges New to the Standard User	Other Important Standard User Privileges	Important Administrator-Only Privileges
View system clock and calendar	Establish a Local Area Network (LAN) connection	Install and uninstall applications
Change time zone	Establish and configure a wireless connection	Install a driver for a device (e.g., a digital camera driver)
Install Wired Equivalent Privacy (WEP) to connect to secure wireless networks	Modify display settings	Install Windows updates
Change power management settings	Play CD/DVD media (configurable with Group Policy)	Configure Parental Controls
Add printers and other devices that have the required drivers installed on the computer or have been allowed by an IT administrator in Group Policy	Burn CD/DVD media (configurable with Group Policy)	Install an ActiveX control
Install ActiveX controls from sites approved by an IT administrator	Change the desktop background for the current user	Open the Windows Firewall Control Panel
Create and configure a Virtual Private Network connection	Change user's own account password	Change a user's account type
Install critical Windows Updates	Configure Accessibility options	Modify UAC settings in the Security Policy Editor Snap-in (Secpol.msc)

(*continued*)

Table 8-3 (*continued*)

PRIVILEGES NEW TO THE STANDARD USER	OTHER IMPORTANT STANDARD USER PRIVILEGES	IMPORTANT ADMINISTRATOR-ONLY PRIVILEGES
	Use Remote Desktop to connect to another computer	Configure Remote Desktop access
	Restore user's backed-up files	Add or remove a user account
	Set up computer synchronization with a mobile device (smart phone, laptop, or PDA)	Copy or move files into the Program Files or Windows directory
	Connect and configure a Bluetooth device	Schedule Automated Tasks
	Configure battery power options	Restore system backed-up files
		Configure Automatic Updates
		Browse to another user's directory

TAKE NOTE* Although standard users do not have the privileges required to defragment disks, disk defragmentation is now an automatically scheduled event, so users will not have a need to start it.

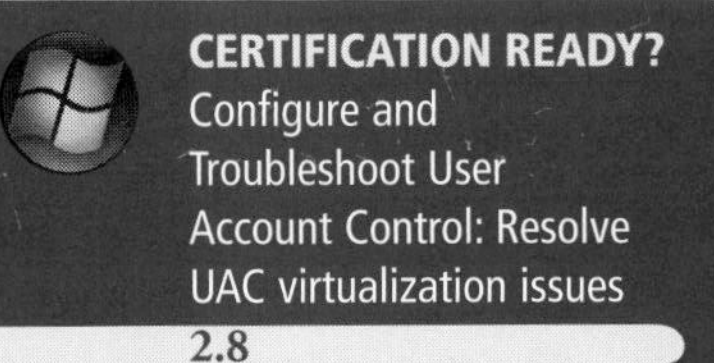

CERTIFICATION READY?
Configure and Troubleshoot User Account Control: Resolve UAC virtualization issues
2.8

Understanding File and Registry Virtualization

File and registry virtualization increases compatibility with legacy applications by redirecting reads and writes to sensitive areas of the hard drive and registry.

If you are logged on as a standard user, some legacy applications that read and write data to sensitive areas of the hard drive and registry will not work properly in Windows Vista without the help of file and registry virtualization.

File and registry virtualization is the redirecting of attempts by an application to write data to secure areas to instead write to other, stand-in areas. This applies both to the file system and the registry.

TAKE NOTE* Microsoft has announced that Windows Vista will be the last version of Windows to support file and registry virtualization.

For example, when an application attempts to write data to the Program Files folder (which requires administrator privileges), the writing is redirected to a location in the user's profile. When the application attempts to read data from the Program Files folder, it is redirected to the alternate user profile location and only resorts to reading directly from the Program Files folder if that fails. A similar scheme is used for registry writes and reads. Because the application wants to read and write to the secure areas, this enables a standard user to run applications that would normally require administrative credentials.

By enabling some programs that otherwise might need to run with administrator credentials to run with standard user credentials, file and registry virtualization helps to enforce the principle of least privilege.

Table 8-4 shows which read and write attempts are redirected by file and registry virtualization and to where they are redirected.

Table 8-4

File and registry virtualization enables you to run some applications— that would normally require an administrative token—with a standard user token. It does this by redirecting reads and writes from secure areas to non-secure areas.

ATTEMPTED READ/WRITE LOCATION	REDIRECTED READ/WRITE LOCATION
\Windows	\Users*UserName*\AppData\Local\Virtual Store\Windows
\Program Files	\Users*UserName*\AppData\Local\Virtual Store\Program Files
\Program Files (x86)	\users*UserName*\AppData\Local\Virtual Store\Program Files (x86)
HKLM\SOFTWARE	HKEY_CURRENT_USER\Software\Classes\VirtualStore\MACHINE\SOFTWARE\etc

TAKE NOTE*

The \Program Files (x86) folder exists only in 64-bit versions of Windows Vista.

CERTIFICATION READY?
Troubleshoot deployment issues: Resolve application compatibility issues
Configure and Troubleshoot User Account Control: Troubleshoot application issues
1.5, 2.8

Troubleshooting UAC Application Compatibility Issues

UAC, like many security innovations, can cause compatibility issues with legacy applications.

UAC can cause compatibility issues with legacy applications and custom applications.

The ideal way to solve compatibility issues for custom applications is to update the applications themselves so that they are compatible. Of course, this is not always practical.

The following are some manifestations of compatibility issues caused by UAC:

- Windows Vista may not correctly detect an installer, uninstaller, or updater, and therefore may not request elevation.
- Applications that require administrative privileges but are run using a SUT token may have tasks that fail or are not available.
- If a user attempts to perform a task that he does not have permission to perform, the application may fail.
- Control Panel applications that perform administrative tasks and make global changes may not function properly.
- DLL applications that run using RunDLL32.EXE may not function properly if they perform global operations.

Most installers will request elevation because Windows Vista has detected that they are an installer. When Windows Vista fails to recognize installers, you can manually elevate them using the Run as administrator option, or by selecting the Run this program as an administrator check box on the Compatibility tab of the application or its shortcut.

However, in an enterprise, you most often don't want to install applications on a per-machine basis. And you certainly don't want to give normal users administrative credentials so that they can respond to installers requesting elevation.

To avoid this problem, you can use application installation solutions that don't require the user to provide administrator credentials. The most readily available solution is to use Windows Installer files (.msi) to create install packages, and ***Group Policy Software Installation (GPSI)*** to install them. MSI files can also be used to update custom applications without requiring the user to provide administrator credentials.

Other solutions include using a system management tool such as Microsoft System Center Operations Manager 2007.

CERTIFICATION READY?
Configure and Troubleshoot User Account Control:
- Configure credential prompts
- Troubleshoot policy settings

2.8

Configuring UAC Group Policy

You can use Group Policy to configure the behavior of UAC.

UAC group policy is configured in Computer Configuration>Windows Settings>Security Settings>Local Policies>Security Options.

Group Policy settings for UAC are described in Table 8-5.

Table 8-5

Group Policy settings for UAC

POLICY SETTING	DESCRIPTION
User Account Control: Admin Approval Mode for the Built-in Administrator account	Determines the behavior of Admin Approval Mode for the Built-in Administrator account. • **Enabled**: The Built-in Administrator will log on in Admin Approval Mode. UAC will invoke the consent prompt for any operation that requires elevation. • **Disabled**: The Built-in Administrator will log on in XP compatible mode, which means that all applications will run by default with full administrative privileges. This is the default setting.
User Account Control: Behavior of the elevation prompt for administrators in Admin Approval Mode	Determines the behavior of the Consent UI for administrators. • **Prompt for consent**: UAC will invoke the consent prompt for any operation that requires elevation. If the administrator selects Permit, the operation will continue with their highest available privilege. This is the default setting. • **Prompt for credentials**: UAC will invoke the credentials prompt for any operation that requires elevation. • **Elevate without prompting**: UAC does not invoke the Consent UI for operations that require elevation. This option is not recommended.
User Account Control: Behavior of the elevation prompt for standard users	Determines the behavior of the elevation prompt for standard users. • **Prompt for credentials**: UAC will invoke the credentials prompt for any operation that requires elevation. This is the default setting for home installations. • **Automatically deny elevation requests**: An access denied error message is returned when a standard user tries to perform an operation that requires elevation. Most enterprises running desktops as standard users will configure this policy to reduce help desk calls. This is the default setting for enterprise installations.
User Account Control: Detect application installations and prompt for elevation	Determines the behavior of application installation detection for the entire system. • **Enabled**: UAC will attempt to determine if the operation that started is an installer. If UAC concludes that it is, UAC will invoke the Consent UI. This is the default setting for home installations. • **Disabled**: UAC will not attempt to determine if the started operation is an installer. This is the default setting for enterprise installations because enterprises will usually elect to use an installation technology such as GPSI or System Center Operations Manager.
User Account Control: Only elevate executables that are signed and validated	Enforce public key infrastructure (PKI) signature checks on any interactive application that requests elevation.

(continued)

Table 8-5 ***(continued)***

Policy Setting	Description
	This enables administrators to control which applications can be elevated through the list in the local computer's Trusted Publisher Store. • **Enabled**: Enforces the PKI certificate chain validation of a given executable before it is permitted to run. • **Disabled**: Does not enforce PKI certificate chain validation before a given executable is permitted to run. This is the default setting.
User Account Control: Only elevate UIAccess applications that are installed in secure locations	Enforces the requirement that applications that request execution with a UIAccess integrity level (which means their application manifest specifies that UIAccess=true) must reside in a secure location on the file system. Secure locations are limited to the following directories: ...\Program Files\, including subdirectories ...\Windows\system32\ ...\Program Files (x86)\, including subdirectories for 64-bit versions of Windows UAC enforces a PKI signature check on any interactive application that requests execution with UIAccess integrity level regardless of the state of this security setting. • **Enabled**: An application will only launch with UIAccess integrity if it resides in a secure location in the file system. This is the default setting. • **Disabled**: An application will launch with UIAccess integrity even if it does not reside in a secure location in the file system.
User Account Control: Run all administrators in Admin Approval Mode	Determines the behavior of all UAC policies. Changes to this setting will not take effect until the system reboots. • **Enabled**: Enables Admin Approval Mode and all related UAC policies. This is the default setting. • **Disabled**: Admin Approval Mode and all related UAC policies will be disabled. The Security Center will notify you that the overall security of the operating system has been reduced.
User Account Control: Switch to the Secure Desktop when prompting for elevation	Determines whether UAC will use the Secure Desktop when the Consent UI is invoked. • **Enabled**: UAC will use the Secure Desktop for all Consent UIs. This is the default setting. • **Disabled**: UAC will use the interactive desktop for all Consent UIs.
User Account Control: Virtualizes file and registry write failures to per-user locations	Determines whether file and registry virtualization is used. • **Enabled**: File and registry virtualization is enabled. This is the default setting. • **Disabled**: File and registry virtualization is disabled.

CONFIGURE UAC GROUP POLICY SETTINGS

Group policy settings are configured in Configuration>Windows Settings>Security Settings>Local Policies>Security Options.

1. Click **Start**.
2. In the **Start Search** text box, key **gpmc.msc** and then press **Ctrl** + **Shift** + **Enter**. A User Account Control dialog box appears.

3. Provide administrator credentials and then click **OK**. The Group Policy Management console appears.
4. In the console tree, expand **Forest: *ForestName*>Domains>*DomainName*>Group Policy Objects**.
5. Right-click the Group Policy Object (GPO) for which you want to configure UAC Group Policy settings and then click **Edit**. The Group Policy Object Editor appears with the selected GPO loaded.
6. In the console tree, expand **Computer Configuration>Windows Settings>Security Settings>Local Policies** and then select **Security Options**. All of the UAC Group Policy settings start with *User Account Control*. Figure 8-6 shows an example Group Policy Object with the UAC Group Policy settings exposed in the details pane.

Figure 8-6

An example GPO with the User Account Control Group Policy settings exposed

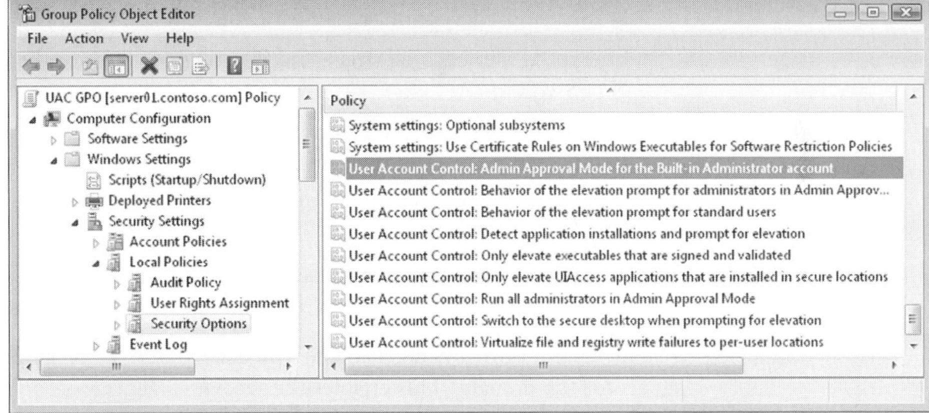

7. In the details pane, double-click the policy setting that you want to configure and then click **OK** when you are finished.

Configuring and Troubleshooting Access to Encrypted Resources

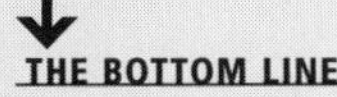

Encrypting File System and BitLocker are used to encrypt data. Part of an administrator's job is to ensure that those who should have access to encrypted resources do, and to make encryption as transparent to users as possible.

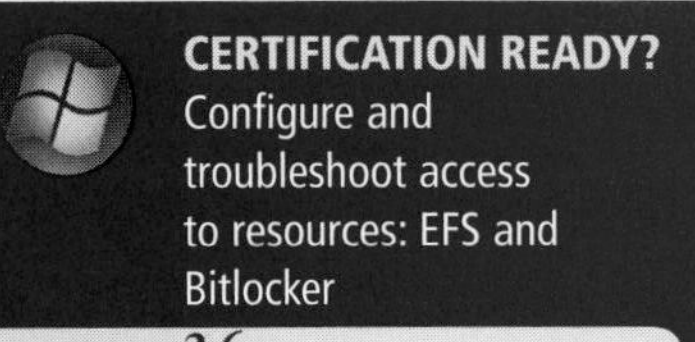

CERTIFICATION READY?
Configure and troubleshoot access to resources: EFS and Bitlocker
2.6

This section covers configuring and troubleshooting access to resources that are encrypted in one of two ways: with BitLocker, which is used to encrypt entire volumes, and ***Encrypting File System (EFS)***, which is used to encrypt files and folders.

Understanding EFS

The Encrypting File System enables you encrypt folders and files. Encrypting a folder encrypts all the files within the folder.

Files or folders encrypted with EFS are first decrypted when being sent over the network. To secure network traffic, you can use IPsec, which is covered in **Lesson 12: Configuring and Troubleshooting Access**.

You can use EFS to encrypt or decrypt any file or folder that you own. To decrypt a file for reading or editing, you must have the private key for that file. If you don't have it, EFS will deny you access. If you do have it, you can open and edit the file as you normally would, without any extra actions. This is called ***transparency***.

EFS has the following characteristics:

- Only files and folders on NTFS volumes can be encrypted.
- EFS uses strong public key-based cryptography. The file encryption keys are encrypted using a public key from the users' X.509 v3 Certificate. The encrypted encryption keys are stored within the file and are decrypted with a private key.
- Users with roaming profiles or redirected folders cannot use EFS unless the files being encrypted are stored locally.
- You can use EFS to encrypt and decrypt files on remote systems, but not to encrypt transmission of files across the network.
- Files or folders that are compressed cannot be encrypted. If you mark a compressed file or folder for encryption, that file or folder will be uncompressed and then encrypted.
- Encrypted files become decrypted if you copy or move them to a volume that is not an NTFS volume.
- Moving unencrypted files into an encrypted folder will automatically encrypt those files. However, the reverse operation will not automatically decrypt files.
- Files marked with the System attribute cannot be encrypted, nor can files in the systemroot directory.
- Anyone with the appropriate permissions can delete or list encrypted folders or files. For this reason, using EFS in combination with NTFS permissions is recommended.

The file encryption keys are also encrypted separately with the private keys of any recovery agents for the domain. This enables the recovery agents to decrypt files in case a user loses his private key. A recovery agent is a user that can decrypt encrypted data in the domain.

Using the Encrypting File System Wizard

The Encrypting File System Wizard can help users to manage their encrypted files and their EFS certificates.

Windows Vista introduces the Encrypting File System Wizard in the Control Panel, which helps users to manage their encryption certificates. You can use the wizard to do the following:

- Select an EFS certificate and key to use for EFS
- Create a new EFS certificate and key
- Back up an EFS certificate and key
- Restore an EFS certificate and key
- Set EFS to use an EFS certificate and key located on a smartcard
- Put an EFS certificate and key on a smartcard
- Update previously encrypted files to use a different certificate and key

The advantage to storing your EFS certificate and key on a smartcard is that you can move from computer to computer and use your smartcard for all of your encryption needs.

START THE ENCRYPTING FILE SYSTEM WIZARD

This procedure covers starting the Encrypting File System Wizard and selecting a task. To complete any particular task, follow the wizard's instructions.

1. Click **Start** and then click **Control Panel**. The Control Panel window appears.
2. Click **User Accounts**. The User Accounts window appears.
3. Click **User Accounts** again. Another User Accounts window appears.

4. In the left navigation bar, click **Manage your file encryption certificates.** The Encrypting File System Wizard appears.
5. Click **Next.** The Select or create a file encryption certificate page appears.
6. From this page, you can use the wizard to start the following tasks:

   Select the **Use this certificate** option and then click **Next** to back up the certificate. You may want to back up the certificate so that you can access the files should the certificate become corrupt or lost.

   Click **Select certificate** to change the certificate used for encryption. For example, you could select a certificate on a smart card.

   Click **View certificate** to view the details of the selected certificate.

   Select **Create a new certificate** and then click **Next** to create a new EFS certificate.

Troubleshooting EFS

The primary problems you will encounter with EFS are lost certificates and file sharing of encrypted files.

Table 8-6 lists common EFS problems and solutions. Details of the solutions can be found in the procedures that follow.

Table 8-6

Common EFS problems and their solutions

EFS Problem	Solution
Access is denied because the encrypted file was transferred from another computer.	1. Export the applicable certificate and private key from the source computer to a floppy or other media accessible by the destination computer. 2. Import the applicable certificate and private key in the Personal certificate store on the destination computer.
Access is denied because the encrypted file was given to you by another user on another (or the same) computer.	This solution assumes that you (User A) want to have access to an encrypted file provided by User B. 1. Log on and export your EFS certificate to a floppy or other media accessible to the source computer. 2. Have User B Log on and import your EFS certificate into her Trusted People certificate store. 3. Add the certificate to the encrypted file. Transfer the encrypted file to your computer.
Access is denied because your private key and/or certificate is missing (perhaps you recovered the file from a disaster but did not properly restore the certificate and private key). You have a backup of the encryption key and the related certificate on a floppy or other media.	Import the backed-up EFS certificate and private key to the Personal certificate store on your computer.
Encryption failed and the following message was displayed: "Recovery policy configured for this system contains invalid recovery certificate."	This most often means that one or more of the recovery agents for the domain have expired certificates. Renew any outdated EFS recovery agent certificates.

EXPORT AN EFS CERTIFICATE

This procedure exports only the selected EFS certificate and not the associated key. Use this procedure if you want to share an encrypted file between users.

1. Log on as the user for which you want to export a certificate.
2. Click **Start**.
3. In the Start Search text box, key **certmgr.msc** and then press **Enter**. The Microsoft Management Console (MMC) appears with the Certificate Manager Snap-in loaded, as shown in Figure 8-7.

Figure 8-7

The Certificate Manager Snap-in

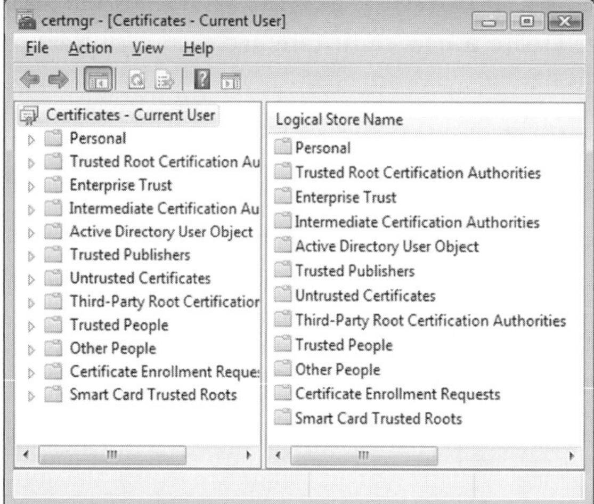

4. In the console tree, expand **Personal** and then select **Certificates.**
5. In the details pane, right-click the certificate that you want to export, point to **All Tasks**, and then click **Export.** The Certificate Export Wizard appears.

TAKE NOTE*

If you are not sure which certificate to export, right-click each certificate and then click Properties. The General tab lists the purposes of the certificate (for EFS, the purpose listed is Encrypting File System). You can also search for certificates by choosing Find Certificates in the Action menu.

6. Click **Next.** The Export Private Key page appears. Select **No, do not export the private key.**
7. Click **Next.** The Export File Format page appears. Select the format you want to use.
8. Click **Next.** The File to Export page appears.
9. In the **File name** text box, enter a path and filename, or click **Browse** to browse for the file.
10. Click **Next.** The Completing the Certificate Export Wizard page appears. Click **Finish.**
11. In the Certificate Export Wizard message box confirming the export, click **OK.**

EXPORT AN EFS CERTIFICATE AND THE ASSOCIATED PRIVATE KEY

This procedure exports both the selected EFS certificate and associated private key. Use this procedure if you want to share an encrypted file between computers with the same user, or if you want to back up the certificate and key.

START the Certificate Export Wizard for the certificate you want to export (see steps 1–5 of the previous procedure).

1. In the Certificate Export Wizard, click **Next.** The Export Private Key page appears.

2. Select **Yes, export the private key**.
3. Click **Next**. The Export File Format page appears. Select the format you want to use.
4. Click **Next**. The Password page appears.
5. Type and confirm a password in the appropriate text boxes. The password can be—but should not be—the same as your user account password. Click **Next**. The File to Export page appears.
6. In the **File name** text box, enter a path and filename, or click **Browse** to browse for the file.
7. Click **Next**. The Completing the Certificate Export Wizard page appears. Click **Finish**.
8. In the Certificate Export Wizard message box announcing the successful export, click **OK**.

IMPORT A CERTIFICATE FROM A TRUSTED PERSON

This procedure covers importing a certificate from a trusted person. Use this procedure if you are trying to give another user access to an encrypted file by adding that user's certificate to the file.

OPEN certmgr.msc.

1. In the Certificate Manager Snap-in, in the console tree, right-click **Trusted People**, point to **All Tasks**, and then select **Import**. The Certificate Import Wizard appears.
2. Click **Next**. The File to Import page appears.
3. In the **File name** text box, enter the path and filename of the certificate that you want to import, or click **Browse** to locate it.
4. Click **Next**. The Certificate Store page appears.
5. The wizard selects the Place all certificates in the following store option by default. Ensure that Trusted People is present in the Certificate store text box and then click **Next**.
6. The Completing the Certificate Import Wizard page appears. Verify that the wizard lists the correct settings and then click **Finish**.
7. In the Certificate Import Wizard message box announcing the successful import, click **OK**.

IMPORT OR RESTORE FROM BACKUP AN EFS CERTIFICATE AND PRIVATE KEY

This procedure can be used if you are attempting to access an EFS-encrypted file from two different computers. This can happen, for example, when a file is encrypted on a portable USB drive that you access with both your laptop and desktop computer. You can also use this procedure to restore an EFS certificate and private key that you backed up earlier.

OPEN certmgr.msc.

1. In the Certificate Manager Snap-in, in the console tree, right-click **Personal**, point to **All Tasks**, and then select **Import**. The Certificate Import Wizard appears.
2. Click **Next**. The File to Import page appears.
3. In the **File name** text box, enter the path and filename of the certificate that you want to import, or click **Browse** to locate the file.
4. Click **Next**. Depending on what type of certificate you are importing, the remaining pages of the wizard will vary. Follow the onscreen prompts to complete the import.

ADD A CERTIFICATE TO AN EFS-ENCRYPTED FILE

You can use this procedure to give access to an encrypted file to another user by adding the other user's EFS certificate to the encrypted file. You can also use it to give yourself access to an encrypted file by using a different EFS certificate, for example, one on a laptop.

1. Locate the file to which you want to add an EFS certificate.
2. Right-click the file and then select **Properties**. The *FileName* Properties dialog box appears for the file or folder.
3. Click the **General** tab and then click **Advanced**. The Advanced Attributes dialog box appears.
4. Click **Details**. The User Access to *Path* dialog box appears, as shown in the example in Figure 8-8.

Figure 8-8

The User Access to *Path* dialog box for an example file and user

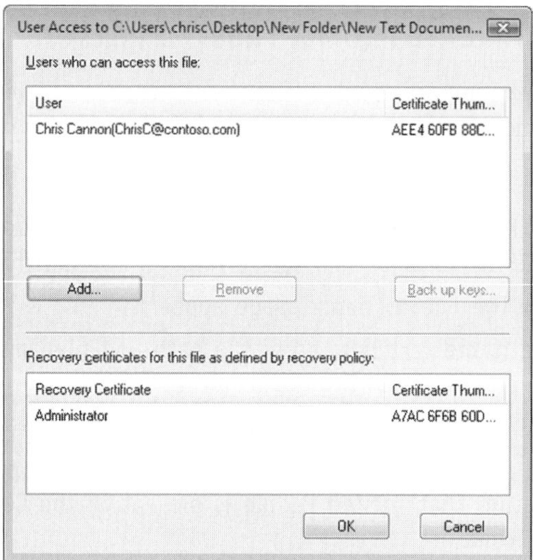

5. Click **Add**. The Encrypting File System dialog box appears, as shown in the example in Figure 8-9.

Figure 8-9

The Encrypting File System dialog box enables you to select a certificate to add to the file

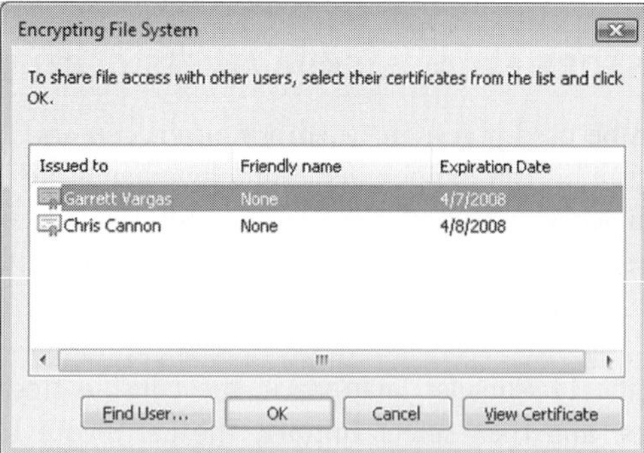

6. Select the certificate that you want to add and then click **OK**.

RENEW A CERTIFICATE FOR A RECOVERY AGENT

As stated in Table 8-6, if encryption failed and you receive the "Recovery policy configured for this system contains invalid recovery certificate" message, it is likely that you need to renew one or more certificates for recovery agents.

OPEN certmgr.msc.

1. In the Certificates console, in the console tree, expand personal and then select **Certificates**.
2. In the details pane, right-click the certificate that you want to renew, point to **All Tasks**, point to **Advanced Operations**, and then select **Renew this certificate with the same key**. The Certificate Enrollment Wizard appears.
3. Click **Next**. The Request Certificates page appears. Click **Enroll**. The new certificate is issued, and the Certificate Installation Results page appears.
4. Click **Finish**.

Configuring EFS Group Policy Settings

You can configure EFS behavior by using Group Policy.

EFS group policy settings are configured in Computer Configuration>Windows Settings> Security Settings>Public Key Policies>Encrypting File System. Policy settings are configured through the Encrypting File System Properties dialog box.

CONFIGURE EFS GROUP POLICY SETTINGS

OPEN the Group Policy Object for which you want to configure Group Policy settings in the Group Policy Object Editor.

1. In the Group Policy Object Editor, in the console tree, expand **Computer Configuration>Windows Settings>Security Settings>Public Key Policies**.
2. Right-click **Encrypting File System** and then click **Properties**. The Encrypting File System Properties dialog box appears, as shown in Figure 8-10. From this dialog box, you can configure any of the settings in Table 8-7.

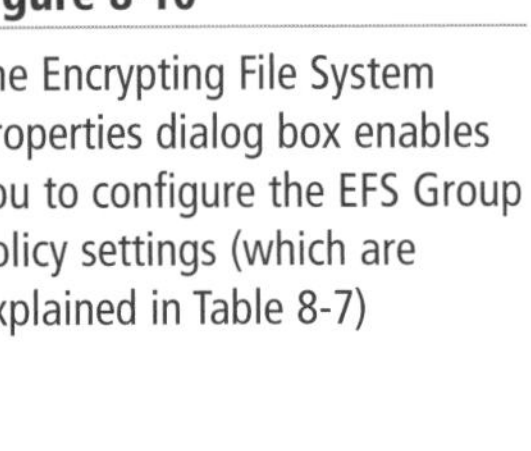

Figure 8-10

The Encrypting File System Properties dialog box enables you to configure the EFS Group Policy settings (which are explained in Table 8-7)

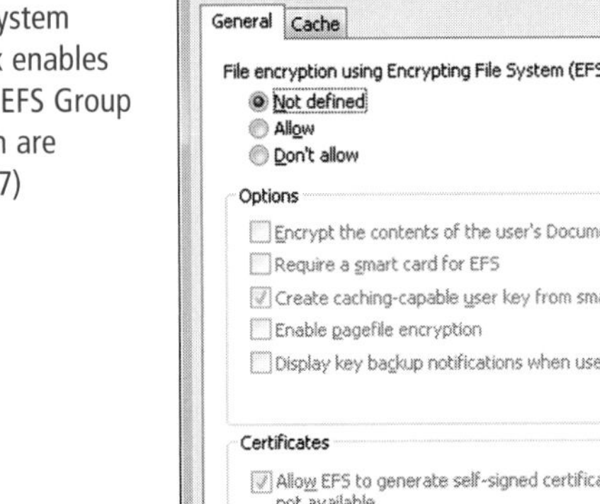

Table 8-7

EFS Group Policy settings in the Encrypting File System Properties dialog box. All of these settings are on the General tab except for the last row.

POLICY SETTING	DESCRIPTION
Not defined option button Allow option button Don't allow option button	You can select one of these three options: disallow EFS, allow it, or leave it up to local policy (not defined).
Encrypt the contents of the user's Documents folder check box	If you select this check box, then all documents in the Documents folder for each affected user will be encrypted.
Require a smart card for EFS check box	If you select this check box, all encryption for EFS will use the EFS certificates and encryption keys on users' smartcards.
Create caching-capable user key from smart card check box	Selecting this option will enable users to remove their smart cards during a logon session and still encrypt and decrypt using the certificate and key on the smart card by caching them.
Enable pagefile encryption check box	When you edit an encrypted document, that document may be saved temporarily to the hard-drive decrypted in a page file (a page file is essentially the use of the hard disk as RAM). Selecting this option encrypts the page file so as to remove this security vulnerability.
Display key backup notifications when user key is created or changed check box	Selecting this option will cause warnings about backing up EFS certificates and keys when a user encryption key is created or changed.
Allow EFS to generate self-signed certificates when a certification authority is not available check box	This will enable a computer to issue its own certificate for EFS purposes if no certificate authority (CA) is available.
Key size for self-signed certificates drop-down list	The larger the key size, the more secure the key.
EFS template for automatic certificate requests text box	You can select which certificate template to use when requesting a certificate from the CA. This enables you to use custom certificates. You can use the Browse button to browse for the template.
Cache tab	The settings in this tab enable you to determine how long an EFS certificate is cached, and whether to clear the cache when a user locks his workstation.

Understanding BitLocker

BitLocker encrypts all the data stored on the Windows operating system volume, and it works in conjunction with Trusted Platform Modules.

BitLocker is a new security feature that encrypts all data stored on the Windows operating system volume. The volume must be a simple volume, which means that the volume is the only volume on the partition.

BitLocker is available in Windows Vista Enterprise and Windows Vista Ultimate, and will be available in Server 2008.

CERTIFICATION READY? Configure and troubleshoot access to resources. 2.6

BitLocker can work in conjunction with a ***Trusted Platform Module (TPM)*** version 1.2 or higher, which is a hardware component used to store cryptographic information, such as encryption keys, and to perform other security duties. When you start your computer, the TPM compares a hash of a subset of operating system files to a hash calculated earlier of the same operating system files. Only if the two hashes are exactly equal does your computer boot normally (equal hashes means that the operating system files have not been tampered with or changed). If they are not equal, then TPM withholds the encryption keys on the suspicion that the operating system has been maliciously tampered with. Because the TPM processes instructions on its own, it does not rely upon the operating system and cannot be compromised through external software execution.

TAKE NOTE*

A hash is the output of a hash function. A hash function takes a data string of any length as input and produces a fixed length string as output. A hash can be used to identify whatever the hash was made from, kind of like a fingerprint.

BitLocker can also be used without a TPM, in which case the encryption keys are stored on a USB flash drive that is required to decrypt the data stored on a volume secured with BitLocker.

Because BitLocker encrypts the entire volume independent of the operating system, even if hacker has physical access to the hard drive the encryption is not easily compromised.

BitLocker requires at least two partitions on the hard disk. The first partition can be small, is unencrypted, and contains the boot information. The second partition contains the volume that is to be encrypted by BitLocker. To assist in preparing a drive for BitLocker, you can use the BitLocker Drive Preparation Tool, which will help you to:

- Create the second volume that BitLocker requires
- Migrate the boot files to the new volume
- Make the new volume an active volume

DOWNLOAD For more information on how to download and install the BitLocker Drive Preparation tool, go to *support.microsoft.com/kb/930063.*

If the TPM ever changes or cannot be accessed, or there are changes to key system files, or someone tries to start the computer from another disk to circumvent the operating system, the computer will switch to recovery mode. Recovery mode is s mode before Windows has started where you can provide credentials to cause BitLocker to allow the operating system to boot. You will need to supply the recovery password to leave recovery mode and boot normally.

PREPARE A DRIVE FOR BITLOCKER BY USING THE BITLOCKER DRIVE PREPARATION TOOL

BEFORE YOU BEGIN. Install the BitLocker Drive Preparation Tool. If there is valuable data on your computer, consider backing it up before you start. The BitLocker Drive Preparation Tool creates a new partition, from which it creates a new disk called Local Disk (S:). The new partition is set as the active partition, meaning that your computer will boot from it.

1. Log on with an administrator account.
2. Click **Start>All Programs>Accessories>System Tools>BitLocker>BitLocker Drive Preparation Tool.** A User Account Control dialog box appears.
3. Click **Continue.** The BitLocker Drive Preparation Tool Wizard appears. Click **I Accept** if you accept the terms of the license agreement.
4. The Preparation Drive for BitLocker page appears. Read the cautions and then click **Continue.**
5. The tool will prepare your drive, which can take substantial time. When the process is complete, click **Finish.**
6. In the BitLocker Drive Encryption message box, click **Restart Now.**

ACCESS THE MANAGE BITLOCKER KEYS WIZARD

Windows Vista provides a wizard that you can use to manage your BitLocker keys.

1. Click **Start**, click **Control Panel**, click **Security**, and then click **Manage BitLocker keys** under BitLocker Drive Encryption. A User Account Control dialog box appears.
2. Provide administrator credentials and then click **OK**. The Manage BitLocker Keys Wizard appears. Follow the instructions in the wizard.

MORE INFORMATION

You can find more information and links to additional resources on implementing BitLocker at *technet.microsoft.com/en-us/windowsvista/aa905065.aspx.*

Configuring BitLocker Group Policy

You can configure the behavior of BitLocker by using Group Policy.

BitLocker Group Policy settings are located in Computer Configuration>Administrative Templates>Windows Components>BitLocker Drive Encryption. Table 8-8 lists the Group Policy settings for BitLocker.

Table 8-8

BitLocker Group Policy settings

Policy Setting	Description
Turn on BitLocker backup to Active Directory Domain Services	Enables the Active Directory Domain Services (AD DS) to back up the BitLocker Drive Encryption recovery information. BitLocker recovery information includes the recovery password and some identification data. You can optionally include a package that contains a BitLocker-protected volume's encryption key. This key package is secured by one or more recovery passwords and may help perform specialized recovery when the disk is damaged or corrupted. • **Enabled**: BitLocker recovery information will be automatically and silently backed up to AD DS when BitLocker is turned on for a computer. • **Require BitLocker backup to AD DS**: You can select this check box if the policy setting is enabled. Select this check box to only turn on BitLocker provided that the backup to AD DS succeeds first. • **Not Configured** or **Disabled**: BitLocker will not back up recovery information to AD DS.
Control Panel Setup: Configure recovery folder	Enables you to specify the default path when the BitLocker Drive Encryption setup wizard prompts the user to enter the location of a folder in which to save the recovery password. Regardless of this policy setting, the user can specify any path. • **Enabled**: If you enable this setting, specify the default folder path. You can specify either a fully-qualified path or include environment variables in the path. If the path is not valid, the BitLocker setup wizard will use the computer's top-level folder view in its place. • **Not Configured** or **Disabled**: The BitLocker setup wizard will use the computer's top-level folder as the default path.
Control Panel Setup: Configure recovery options	Enables you to configure whether the BitLocker Drive Encryption setup wizard will ask the user to save BitLocker recovery options. If you disable all recovery options, you must back up the recovery options to AD DS, or there will be an error. • **Enabled**: If you enable this setting, select which options the user can select in the BitLocker Drive Encryption Wizard. • **Require recovery password (default)**: Select this option to require that the user specify a numerical, 48-digit recover password.

(continued)

Table 8-8 ***(continued)***

POLICY SETTING	DESCRIPTION
	• **Disallow recovery password**: Select this option to disallow the user from specifying a recovery password. This will prevent users from being able to save or print a recovery password. • **Require recovery key (default)**: Select this option to require that the user be given a recovery key. • **Disallow recovery key**: Select this option to disallow the user from generating a recovery key. • **Not Configured** or **Disabled**: The settings will be set to the default values as specified previously.
Control Panel Setup: Enable advanced startup options	Enables you to configure whether the BitLocker Drive Encryption setup wizard will ask the user to set up an additional authentication that is requested each time the computer starts. On a computer with a compatible TPM, two different startup authentication procedures can provide more protection for encrypted data. When the computer starts, it can require users to insert a USB flash drive containing a startup key, and it can also require users to enter a 4 to 20 digit startup personal identification number (PIN). A USB flash drive is mandatory for computers without a compatible TPM. **Enabled**: If you enable this policy setting, the wizard will enable the user to configure advanced startup options for BitLocker. You can further configure setting options for computers with and without a TPM. **Not Configured** or **Disabled**: If you disable or do not configure this policy setting, the BitLocker setup wizard will display basic steps that allow users to enable BitLocker on computers with a TPM. No additional startup key or startup PIN can be configured.
Configure encryption method	BitLocker will use the default encryption method of AES 128 bit with Diffuser or the encryption method specified by a local administrator's setup script.
Prevent memory overwrite on restart	Controls whether Windows will overwrite memory on restarts. Preventing overwriting memory on restart increases performance, but at the risk of exposing sensitive BitLocker information. **Enabled**: If you enable this policy setting, Windows will not instruct the computer to overwrite memory on restarts. **Not Configured** or **Disabled**: If you disable or do not configure this policy setting, Windows will overwrite memory on restarts, thus strengthening security around BitLocker.
Configure TPM platform validation profile	Enables you to configure what boot components the TPM will validate before unlocking access to the BitLocker encrypted OS volume. **Enabled**: If you enable this policy setting before turning on BitLocker, you can configure the boot components that the TPM will validate before unlocking access to the BitLocker encrypted OS volume. If any of these components change while BitLocker protection is in effect, the TPM will not release the encryption key to unlock the volume, and the computer will enter into recovery mode during boot. Changing from the default profile affects the security and manageability of your computer. BitLocker's sensitivity to platform modifications (malicious or authorized) is increased or decreased depending on inclusion or exclusion (respectively) of the PCRs. **Not Configured or Disabled**: If you disable or do not configure this policy setting, the TPM uses the default platform validation profile or the platform validation profile specified by a local administrator's setup script. The default platform validation profile secures the encryption key against changes to the Core Root of Trust of Measurement (CRTM), BIOS, Platform Extensions (PCR 0), the Option ROM Code (PCR 2), the Master Boot Record (MBR) Code (PCR 4), the NTFS Boot Sector (PCR 8), the NTFS Boot Block (PCR 9), the Boot Manager (PCR 10), and the BitLocker Access Control (PCR 11).

Troubleshooting Authentication Issues

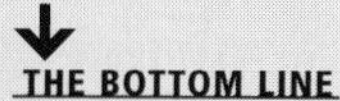

THE BOTTOM LINE

Most authentication issues concern user names and passwords. Other common authentication issues involve authentication by using smart cards.

CERTIFICATION READY?
Troubleshoot authentication issues.
2.7

Troubleshooting User Name and Password

CERTIFICATION READY?
Troubleshoot authentication issues: User name and password
2.7

Probably the most common issues with authentication concern user names or passwords.

The most common authentication method by which users authenticate with the domain is by using user names and passwords. You use a user name and password when you log on, of course, but also in other circumstances where you need to be authenticated either with the domain or the local computer (e.g., when UAC requests elevated credentials).

Troubleshooting user name and password problems primarily involves telling users what their user names are in the event they forget, or resetting their passwords.

FINDING A USER'S USER NAME

1. Log on to a domain server.
2. Click **Start**, point to **Administrative Tools**, and then click **Active Directory Users and Computers.** The Active Directory Users and Computers console appears.
3. In the console tree, right-click the domain name and then click **Find.** The Find Users, Contacts, and Groups dialog box appears, as shown in Figure 8-11.

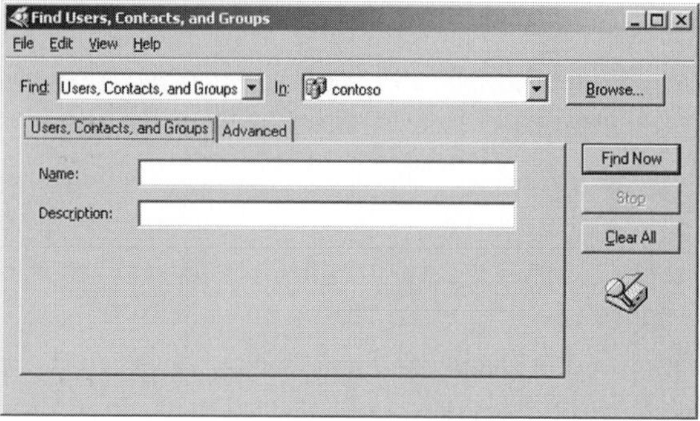

Figure 8-11

The Find Users, Contacts, and Groups dialog box enables you to find Active Directory objects such as users

4. In the Name text box, key the user's name (for example, Garrett Vargas). Or, you can use wildcards. For example, you could key t*, which would list all the users whose names start with *t*. Alternatively, you can click **Find Now** to search for the user.
5. Once you have searched for the user, in the Search results section, double-click the user. The Properties dialog box for the user appears.
6. Click the **Account** tab. The user's logon name is in the *User logon name* text box.

RESETTING A USER PASSWORD

When you reset a user's password, make sure that you require the user to change the password to a secure password at the next logon.

FIND the user (see steps 1–4 in the previous procedure).

1. In the Find Users, Contacts, and Groups dialog box, right-click the user in the search results pane and then click **Reset Password**. The Reset Password dialog box appears, as shown in Figure 8-12.

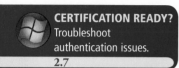

Figure 8-12

The Reset Password dialog box

2. In the New password and Confirm password text boxes, key the password that you want to reset the user's password to.
3. Select the **User must change password at next logon** check box.
4. Click **OK.** An Active Directory message box appears, confirming that the password has been changed.
5. Click **OK.**

Understanding and Renewing Smart Card Certificates

Smart card certificates are used in conjunction with a PIN to authenticate a user to the domain.

Certificates can be used to identify users (or other entities) for various purposes. For example, EFS uses certificates to determine who can decrypt files.

Certificates can also be used in user authentication. The most common way is by using smart cards. A ***smart card*** is a plastic card about the size of a credit card that has electronic logic embedded in it for a data smart card, or a microprocessor in the case of smart cards with processing ability. Smart cards are commonly used to store digital signatures, authenticate users, and store encryption keys to encrypt or decrypt data. The user is issued a certificate that is stored on the smart card. When the smart card is inserted into the smart card reader, and the personal identification number (PIN) for the card is entered, the user is authenticated to the domain by using the certificate on the smart card. Issuing of certificates for smart cards is often performed using kiosk computers in a secure location where users are required to produce valid picture IDs prior to issuance.

The most likely issue you will need to troubleshoot regarding certificates and smart cards is renewing certificates. The expiration date of the certificate on a smart card depends on the certificate template that was used to create the certificate. Typical lifetimes are from six months to two years. The renewal process uses the information in the current certificate to create a renewal request. You can then renew the certificate with either the existing key or a new key.

Many enterprise environments will use certificate autoenrollment. ***Certificate autoenrollment*** is a feature of Windows Server 2003, Enterprise Edition that automatically uses the existing certificate to sign a renewal request for a new certificate before the existing certificate expires. Depending on your policies, an administrator may need to approve each certificate renewal manually, or it may be automated.

You can find more information on certificate autoenrollment by searching at *www.microsoft.com/technet/prodtechnol/windowsserver2003/technologies/security/autoenro.mspx.* Also, you can find information on complete smart card implementations here: *www.microsoft.com/technet/security/guidance/networksecurity/securesmartcards/default.mspx.*

RENEW A CERTIFICATE

OPEN the Certificate Manager console.

1. In the Certificate Manager console, in the console tree, expand **Personal** and then select **Certificates.**
2. In the details pane, right click the certificate that you want to renew, point to **All Tasks**, and then do one of the following:
   - Click **Renew Certificate with New Key.**
   - Point to **Advanced Operations.** Click **Renew this certificate with the same key.**

   The Certificate Enrollment Wizard appears.
3. Click **Next.** The Request Certificate page appears.
4. Click **Enroll.** The certificate is renewed and the Certificate Installation Results page appears. Click **Finish.**

APPROVE A CERTIFICATE REQUEST

Some certificate templates require that an administrator approve certificate requests before the certificates are issued.

LOG ON to the issuing certificate authority and **OPEN** the Certification Authority console.

1. In the Certification Authority console, expand the certificate authority and then select **Pending Requests**, as shown in Figure 8-13.

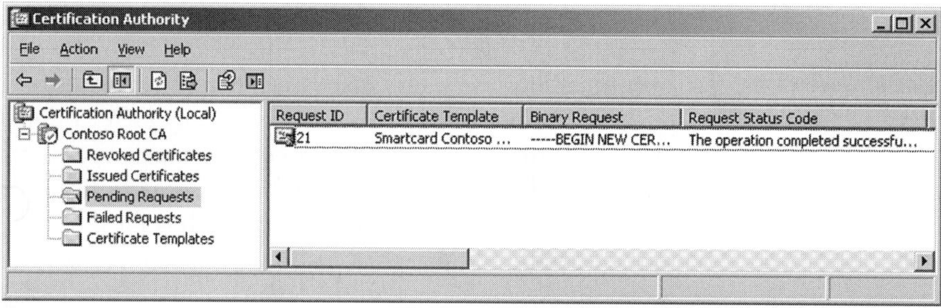

Figure 8-13

The Certification Authority console connected to the Contoso Root CA certificate authority. The Pending Requests node is selected, and the pending requests are listed in the details pane.

2. In the details pane, right-click the pending certificate that you want to issue, point to **All Tasks**, and then click **Issue.** The certificate is issued.

SUMMARY SKILL MATRIX

IN THIS LESSON YOU LEARNED:
User Account Control increases security by helping to enforce the principle of least privilege.
The principle of least privilege limits exposure to security threats by limiting user privileges to the minimum required to complete required tasks.
The Consent UI is a collection of UAC dialog boxes that prompt for consent or for administrator credentials when you attempt a task that requires elevated privileges.
The Secure Desktop helps to prevent hackers from circumventing the UAC Consent UI.
Admin Approval Mode is a mode in which administrators must give consent for applications to use the administrator token.
The Power Users group has been removed, and standard users have increased privileges.

(continued)

SUMMARY SKILL MATRIX (*continued*)

IN THIS LESSON YOU LEARNED:
File and registry virtualization increases compatibility with legacy applications by redirecting reads and writes to sensitive areas of the hard drive and registry.
UAC, like many security innovations, can cause compatibility issues with legacy applications.
You can simultaneously centrally manage the behavior of UAC for many computers by using Group Policy.
Encrypting File System and BitLocker are used to encrypt data. Part of an administrator's job is to ensure that those that should have access to encrypted resources do, and to make encryption as transparent to users as possible.
The Encrypting File System Wizard can help users to manage their encrypted files and their EFS certificates.
The primary troubleshooting issues you will encounter with EFS are lost certificates and how to help users share encrypted files.
How to export an EFS certificate and an associated private key.
How to import a certificate from a trusted person.
How to import or restore from backup an EFS certificate and private key.
How to add a certificate to an EFS-encrypted file.
How to renew a certificate for a Recovery Agent.
How to configure EFS Group Policy settings.
BitLocker encrypts all the data stored on the Windows operating system volume and works in conjunction with Trusted Platform Modules.
How to prepare a drive for BitLocker by using the BitLocker Drive Preparation Tool.
How to access the Manage BitLocker Keys Wizard.
You can configure the behavior of BitLocker by using Group Policy.
Most authentication issues concern user names and passwords. Other common authentication issues involve authentication by using smart cards.
How to find a user's user name and reset a user's password.
Smart card certificates are used in conjunction with a PIN to authenticate a user to the domain.
How to renew a certificate and approve a certificate request.

Knowledge Assessment

Fill in the Blank

Complete the following sentences by writing the correct word or words in the blanks provided.

1. Because ________________ causes a SUT to be used more often than an AT, it can be seen as an implementation of the principle of least privilege.
2. The ________________ helps to prevent hackers from circumventing the Consent UI by altering your mouse cursor.
3. A(n) ________________ is issued to you upon logon and identifies you to the computer.

4. The SUT is created by filtering an ________.
5. Limiting the privileges users have to those necessary to complete the tasks they need to complete is an application of the principle ________
6. A(n) ________ is the right of an account to perform various system-related operations on the local computer.
7. The ________ is an application that will sometimes intervene when an application is not running correctly to ask if you want to try running it as an administrator.
8. ________ is used to encrypt an entire volume.
9. ________ is used to encrypt individual files and folders.
10. A(n) ________ is a hardware component used to store cryptographic information, such as encryption keys.

Multiple Choice

Select all answers that apply for the following questions.

1. Admin Approval Mode does the following:
   a. Uses the AT token by default and requests your permission to use the SUT when necessary
   b. Uses the SUT by default and requests your consent if the AT is requested
   c. Makes Windows Vista require administrator consent to launch any application not in the safe applications list
   d. Creates a split token where the AT is created from a filtered version of the SUT
2. A UAC consent prompt with a gray title bar appears. This means that the application you are trying to start:
   a. Is a signed Microsoft application.
   b. Is an unsigned application.
   c. Is a third-party signed application.
   d. Has been blocked by an administrator.
3. Secure Desktop does the following (select each that applies):
   a. Dims the desktop, takes a picture of it, and displays it
   b. Starts an instance of terminal services
   c. Starts an instance of Remote Desktop
   d. Starts a new session of Windows separate from the current session
4. The sysmain.sdb file contains:
   a. A list of applications that require file and registry virtualization to run correctly.
   b. A list of applications that require a split token to run correctly.
   c. A list of applications that are allowed to launch applications without invoking the Consent UI.
   d. A list of legacy applications that require administrative privileges to run correctly.
5. Which group in Windows Vista has been removed?
   a. Power Users
   b. Standard Users
   c. Guests
   d. Anonymous Users
6. Disabling which Group Policy setting will turn UAC off?
   a. User Account Control: Behavior of the elevation prompt for standard users
   b. User Account Control: Run all users, including administrators, as standard users
   c. User Account Control: Behavior of the elevation prompt for administrators in Admin Approval Mode
   d. User Account Control: Only elevate executables that are signed and validated

7. Why shouldn't you use EFS to encrypt files that are accessed across a network?
   a. Because TCP/IP doesn't support the transport of EFS-encrypted files
   b. Because when the user accesses an encrypted file across the network, it is decrypted on the local machine and sent across the network unencrypted
   c. Because encrypted files are significantly larger than unencrypted files and network performance will suffer
   d. Because user's cannot decrypt a file that is stored remotely

8. When you move a file from an EFS-encrypted folder to an unencrypted folder:
   a. Windows Vista returns an error because you can only move files in an encrypted folder to another encrypted folder.
   b. The file is decrypted.
   c. The file remains encrypted.
   d. Windows Vista asks if you want the file to remain encrypted.

9. You can use the Encrypting File System Wizard to do all of the following except:
   a. Select which certificate to use for EFS.
   b. Create a new EFS certificate and key.
   c. Configure the compression level that EFS uses.
   d. Set EFS to use an EFS certificate on a smart card.

10. When you use Windows compression to compress an EFS-encrypted file:
    a. There is little effect because EFS also compresses files.
    b. The file compresses normally and remains encrypted.
    c. The file is decrypted and then compressed.
    d. Compressing encrypted files weakens the encryption and is therefore not recommended.

Review Questions

1. Explain how you could determine if an application was using file virtualization.
2. Explain how split tokens in Windows Vista enforce the principle of least privilege.

■ Case Scenarios

Scenario 1: Hardening User Account Control

You have been tasked with hardening the security on a set of kiosk computers that are not attached to the domain. As part of this hardening, you are going to modify the default behavior of UAC in the following ways.

1. For normal non-administrator users, you want UAC to refuse requests to start tasks that require elevated privileges (in other words, you don't want them prompted for administrator credentials).
2. For administrators, UAC should behave according to default settings.
3. For your own local standard user account, you want to be able to run administrative tasks. In other words, for your standard user account, you want UAC to use default settings.

Scenario 2: Sharing EFS files on Network Share

A small group of five users in the accounting department at Contoso stores sensitive files on a file server in a share. You have implemented IPSec so that the files are encrypted when accessed over the network. How can you use EFS to ensure that the files are encrypted, while still allowing each of the five users access?

Configuring Task Scheduler

OBJECTIVE DOMAIN MATRIX

Technology Skill	Objective Domain	Objective Domain Number
Understanding Task Scheduler	Configure and manage the Task Scheduler	3.2
Using Task Scheduler	Configure and manage the Task Scheduler	3.2
Managing Tasks	Configure and manage the Task Scheduler	3.2
Creating a Task	Configure and manage the Task Scheduler	3.2
Configuring General Task Settings	Configure and manage the Task Scheduler	3.2
Configuring Task Triggers	Configure and manage the Task Scheduler	3.2
Configuring Task Actions	Configure and manage the Task Scheduler	3.2
Configuring Task Conditions	Configure and manage the Task Scheduler	3.2
Configuring Task Settings	Configure and manage the Task Scheduler	3.2
Using the Create Basic Task Wizard	Configure and manage the Task Scheduler	3.2

KEY TERMS

Task Scheduler
task
triggers
conditions
settings
actions
schtasks.exe

Contoso Incorporated uses Task Scheduler for many purposes, from running routine maintenance tasks such as backup and disk defragmentation, to custom applications that further their business goals. Among the tasks that Contoso automates using Task Scheduler is the publishing of a newsletter via a custom application that pulls together XML articles and composites them into a PDF file.

■ Understanding Task Scheduler

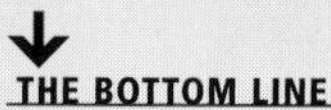

Task Scheduler enables administrators to automate the completion of tasks on individual computers.

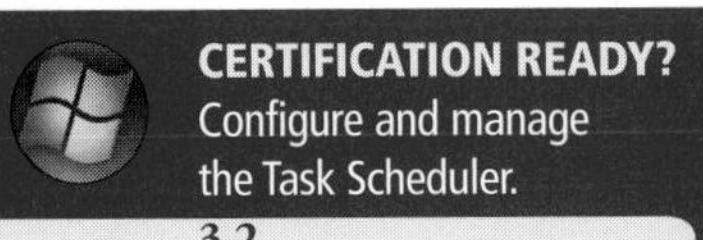

CERTIFICATION READY?
Configure and manage the Task Scheduler.
3.2

Task Scheduler is a Microsoft Management Console Snap-in that administrators can use to schedule tasks according to a schedule, event occurrence, or a change in the system state.

A ***task*** is composed of triggers, conditions, settings, and actions.

- ***Triggers*** are criteria that when met cause the computer to start actions. For example, you can set a time each week to be a trigger.
- ***Conditions*** are criteria that can override a trigger based on the state of the machine. For example, you can set a condition so that a task will run only if the computer is connected to an AC power source (in other words, if it is not running on battery power).
- ***Settings*** are execution options. For example, you can use settings to determine how many times a task is retried if it fails for some reason.
- ***Actions*** are activities the computer starts when a trigger is activated. For example, an action might be to email an administrator when a trigger event occurs (such as a write failure to a hard drive).

Task Scheduler enables administrators to save time by automating common tasks. For example, you can configure Task Scheduler to back up data, launch a virus scanner, or defragment disks. Task Scheduler can also be used to notify you if an important event occurs, such as a write failure to a hard drive (which might indicate that the hard drive is failing).

X REF

Group Policy is covered in **Lesson 4: Using Group Policy.**

Task Scheduler in Windows Vista is improved in many ways over the versions included in previous editions of Windows. Areas of improvement include increased functionality, integration with Event Viewer, and better reliability and security. Table 9-1 details limitations of previous versions and how Windows Vista addresses them.

Table 9-1

Task Scheduler in Windows Vista is much improved and expanded over previous versions

TASK SCHEDULER IN PREVIOUS EDITIONS	TASK SCHEDULER IN WINDOWS VISTA
Credentials for task execution are stored locally, so changes in domain or local passwords can cause tasks that previously worked to fail.	In most cases, credentials are no longer stored locally. Encryption is used to store passwords in the Credentials Manager (CredMan) service.
When Microsoft hardened the security for Server 2003, they were compelled by security vulnerabilities to restrict the use of the Task Scheduler service to administrators only, which reduces its usefulness.	Because of more secure handling of credentials, the Task Scheduler service is no longer limited to use only by administrators.
No task history is maintained, so the only error an administrator sees (unless continually monitoring the machine) is the last error to occur.	Task Scheduler logs its execution status in the Event Log, including errors. You can also monitor task execution in real-time by using the Task Scheduler interface.
Only a single action can be part of a task, so super-tasks that require more than one action must be constructed of multiple tasks scheduled to occur in sequence. The scheduled sequencing can cause failure of a set of tasks if any one task takes more than its allotted time, thus decreasing reliability. Adding buffers of time can increase reliability, but at the expense of adding time to the overall completion.	A task can contain multiple actions that are completed in sequence. This removes the unreliable and burdensome workaround you had to use in previous versions.
The set of triggers that can launch a task is limited.	Triggers have been vastly expanded, including an expansion of system state criteria and the ability to trigger a task by event.

In Windows Vista, Task Scheduler has been integrated with Event Viewer in two ways. You can trigger tasks based on event occurrence, and task history is logged by Event Viewer. Event Viewer is covered in **Lesson 6: Troubleshooting Security Issues.**

As in previous versions of Task Scheduler, you can use a command-line tool to create tasks: ***schtasks.exe***. This tool can be handy because there is no simple way to push tasks to many computers simultaneously through Group Policy. You can, however, create scripts that configure tasks and push them out through Group Policy.

Using Task Scheduler

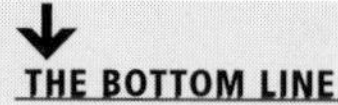

You can use Task Scheduler to manage, create, and monitor tasks.

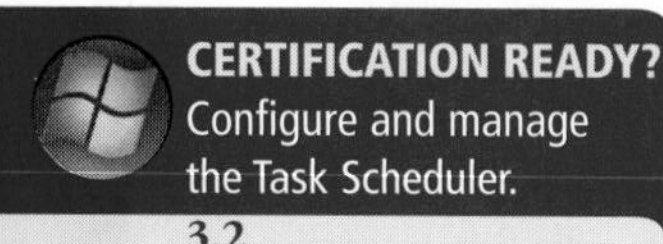

CERTIFICATION READY? Configure and manage the Task Scheduler. 3.2

Managing Tasks

Managing tasks includes starting, ending, disabling, and enabling tasks, as well as viewing task history.

When Task Scheduler opens, the details pane by default contains three sections (two of which are visible in Figure 9-1).

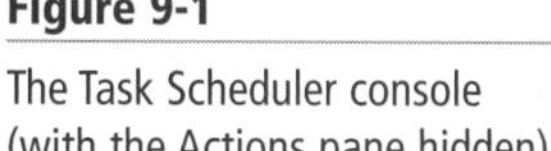

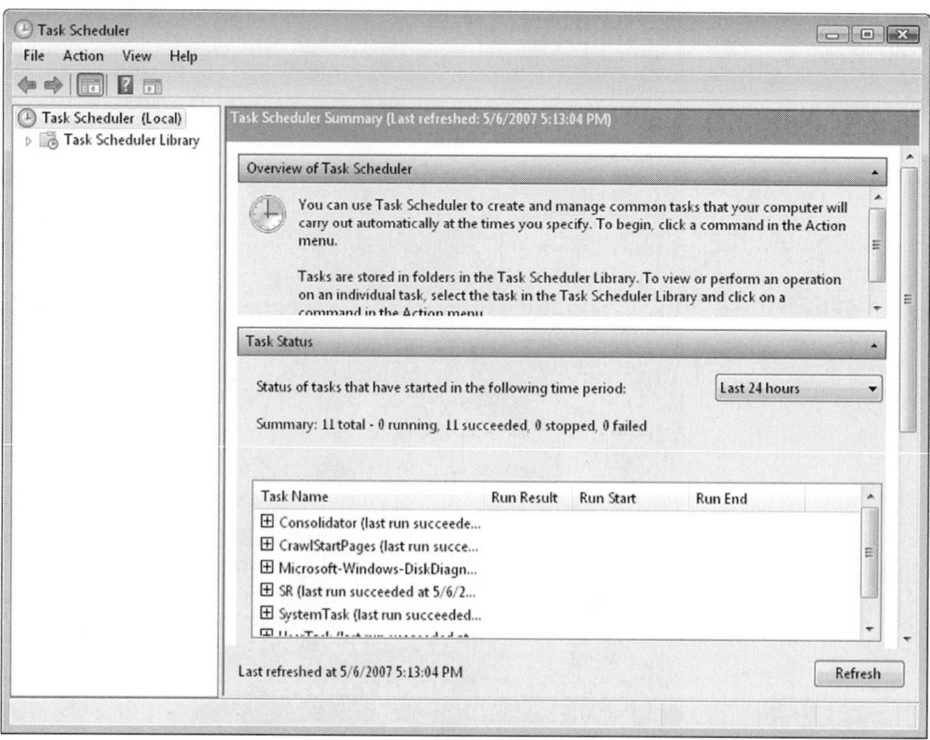

Figure 9-1

The Task Scheduler console (with the Actions pane hidden)

- **Overview of Task Scheduler.** This section gives a description of Task Scheduler. It has no functional elements, and you may want to minimize it (click the up arrow in the upper right corner) after reading the description.

- **Task Status.** This section contains a list of tasks that have started in a specified time period. You can alter the time period by using the drop-down list in the Task Status section's upper right corner.
- **Active Tasks.** This section contains a list of all tasks that are currently enabled and have not expired. You can double-click any of the tasks in the list box to open it in the details pane and then view its settings. The meaning of each setting is described in Tables 9-2 through 9-10. Figure 9-2 shows the IPAddressConflict1 task open in the details pane.

Figure 9-2

The details pane displays the IPAddressConflict1 task settings

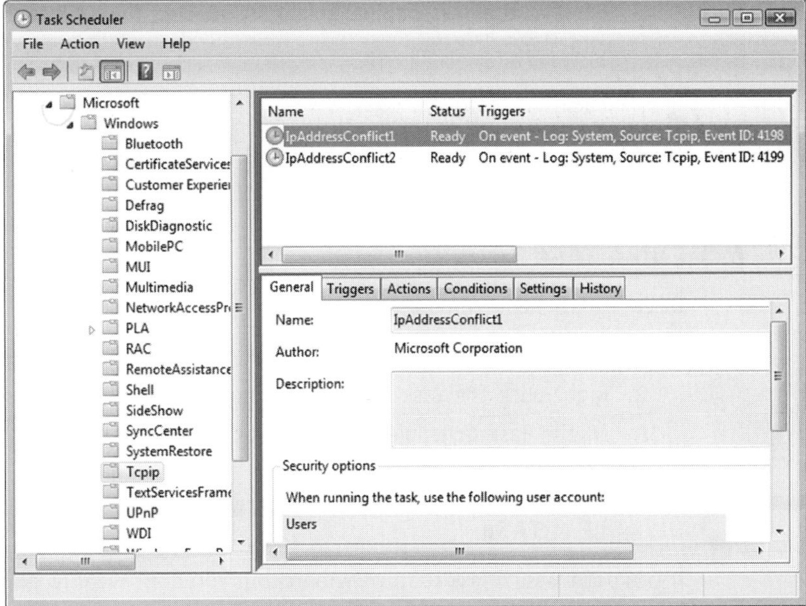

The console tree on the left enables you to browse the Task Scheduler Library, which is a library of both active and inactive tasks on your computer. You can use it to run, disable, modify, and delete tasks. When you browse to a task in the library, the details pane contains a tabbed browser where you can view the task's properties. To modify a task, browse to it in the library, right-click it, and then click Properties. The *TaskName* Properties dialog box appears, as shown in Figure 9-3. Use the dialog box to edit the settings, which Tables 9-2 through 9-10 describe.

Figure 9-3

The ScheduledDefrag Properties dialog box

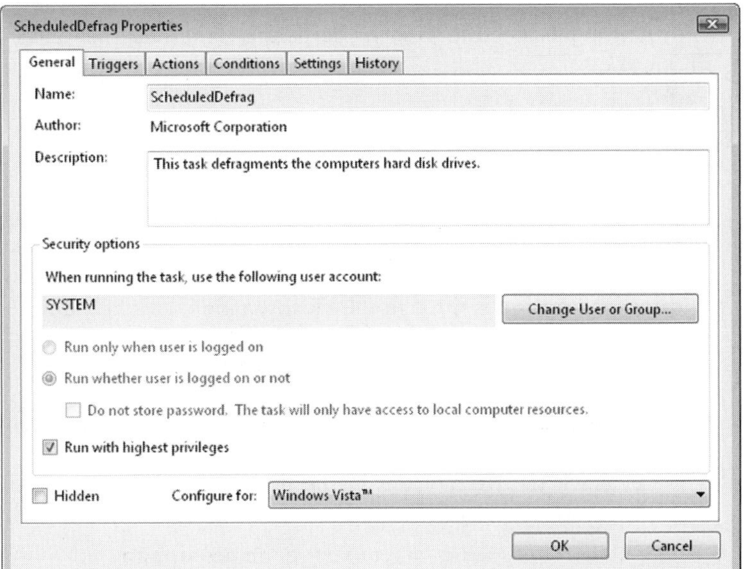

START A TASK

You can start a task manually if you want to run the task immediately. One reason you might want to do this is to see if the task is working properly.

1. Click **Start**. In the Start Search text box, key **Task Scheduler** and then press **Ctrl + Shift + Enter**. A User Account Control dialog box appears.
2. Provide administrator credentials and then click **OK**. The Task Scheduler console appears, as shown in Figure 9-1.
3. Look in the Task Scheduler Library to find the task you want to start, right-click it, and then click **Run**.

TAKE NOTE* To run a task manually, you need to select the Allow task to be run on demand check box on the Settings tab. This setting is covered in Table 9-10.

END A TASK

OPEN Task Scheduler.

1. In Task Scheduler, locate the task folder in the console tree.
2. Right-click the task in the details pane and then click **End**.
3. In the Task Scheduler message box, click **Yes** to end all instances of the task.

DISABLE A TASK

If you don't want a task to run anymore, but you don't want to delete it either, you can disable it.

OPEN Task Scheduler.

1. In Task Scheduler, locate the task folder in the console tree.
2. Right-click the task in the details pane and then click **Disable**.

ENABLE A TASK

OPEN Task Scheduler.

1. In Task Scheduler, locate the task folder in the console tree.
2. Right-click the task in the details pane and then click **Enable**.

VIEW TASK HISTORY

Event Viewer records log entries for task successes, failures, and other task-related events. You can view this information in Event Viewer directly by navigating in the Event Viewer console tree to Applications and Services Logs\Microsoft\Windows\TaskScheduler\Operational and then applying a filter to show only the task history that you want. An easier way to access the same information is through the History tab in Task Scheduler.

X REF Viewing a task's history is the same as viewing events. You can find more information on viewing events in **Lesson 6.**

OPEN Task Scheduler.

1. In Task Scheduler, locate the task folder in the console tree.
2. Select the task in the details pane.
3. Click the **History** tab in the details pane. Figure 9-4 shows the History tab of the SystemDataProviders task.

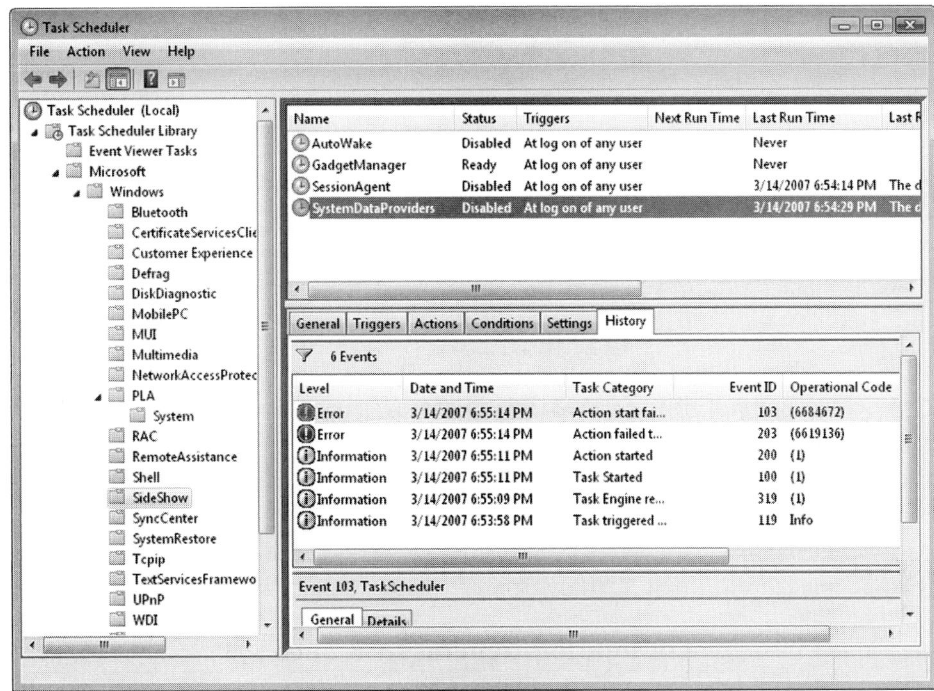

Figure 9-4

The History tab of an example task

Creating a Task

Creating a task consists of configuring general settings, triggers, actions, conditions, and task settings.

Most procedures in this book are described in a list of steps. Because there are so many options to consider when creating a task in Task Scheduler, providing a list procedure is not sufficient. Therefore, the list procedure that follows is supplemented by the following five sections, which describe the available options for a task:

- Configuring General Task settings
- Configuring Task Triggers
- Configuring Task Actions
- Configuring Task Conditions
- Configuring Task Settings

CREATE A TASK BY USING TASK SCHEDULER

The sections that follow this procedure detail the options for creating a task.

OPEN Task Scheduler.

1. In Task Scheduler, in the Action menu, click **Create Task**. The Create Task dialog box appears, as shown in Figure 9-5.
2. The Create Task dialog box contains five tabs: General, Triggers, Actions, Conditions, and Settings. Configure each tab as desired and then click **OK** to create the task. Tables 9-2 through 9-10 provide information for each setting on each tab.

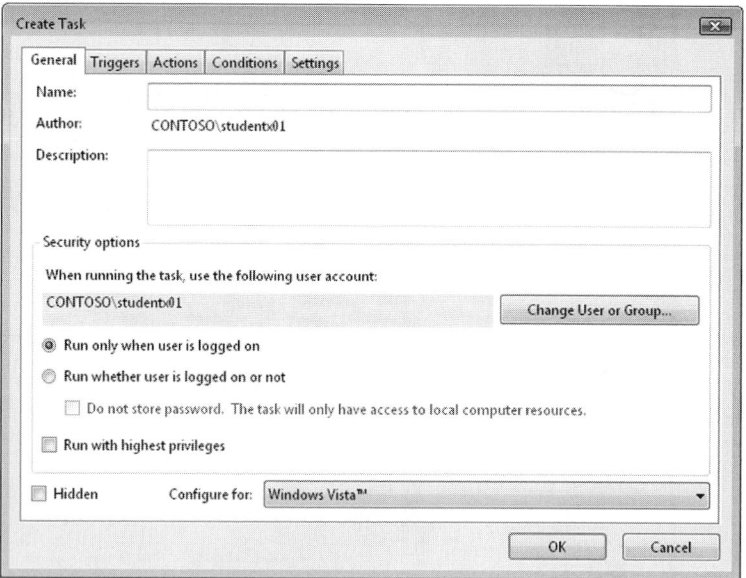

Figure 9-5

The Create Task dialog box with the General tab selected

Configuring General Task Settings

General task settings include such settings as the task name and description.

General task settings are configured on the General tab, which is shown in Figure 9-5. Table 9-2 describes the settings in the General tab.

Table 9-2

Settings for the General tab of the Create Task dialog box in Task Scheduler

SETTING	DESCRIPTION
Name text box	Use the Name text box to specify a name for the task. For example, *weekly backup.*
Description text box	Use the Description text box to provide a description for the task. Verbose descriptions can be helpful. You may want to wait until you have configured the other tabs before filling in the description so that you can provide details, such as the triggers and schedule.
Change User or Group button	You can use this button to specify what account should be used to complete that task. For example, you might create a user with backup privileges to back up data and then specify that account to create a backup task.
Run only when user is logged on option button Run whether user is logged on or not option button	• Select Run only when user is logged on if you only want to execute the task if the specified user is logged on. Select this option if you want the task to run interactively. • Select Run whether user is logged on or not if you want to execute the task whether or not the specified user is logged on. The task will not run interactively if you choose this option. If you select this option, you can select the *Do not store password. This task will only have access to local computer resources* check box. If you do so, Task Scheduler will not store the credentials supplied on the local computer and will discard them after authenticating the user. If necessary, the Task Scheduler service will use the Service-for-User (S4U) extensions to the Kerberos authentication protocol to retrieve the user's token. Regardless of whether you select the *Do not store password. This task will only have access to local computer resources* check box, Task Scheduler may prompt you to supply the credentials of the specified account when saving the task.

(*continued*)

Table 9-2 (*continued*)

SETTING	DESCRIPTION
Run with highest privileges check box	Select the Run with highest privileges check box to run the task using the administrative token rather than the standard user token (see Lesson 8: Troubleshoot Access, Authentication, and User Account Control Issues).
Hidden check box	Select the Hidden check box to hide the execution of the task from users.
Configure for drop-down list	You can select what operating system you are configuring the task for by using the Configure for drop-down list. This is useful if you want to create a script for another operating system and then export the task.

Configuring Task Triggers

Task triggers are criteria that when met cause the computer to start actions.

Tables 9-3 through 9-7 cover settings related to configuring triggers. The settings are accessed through the New Trigger dialog box or the Edit Trigger dialog box. As stated earlier, triggers are criteria that when met cause the computer to start actions. For example, you can set a trigger to activate a backup session for your computer at a certain time each week.

Triggers for a task are listed on the Triggers tab, shown in Figure 9-6. Table 9-3 describes the settings on the Triggers tab.

Figure 9-6

The Triggers tab of the Create Task dialog box

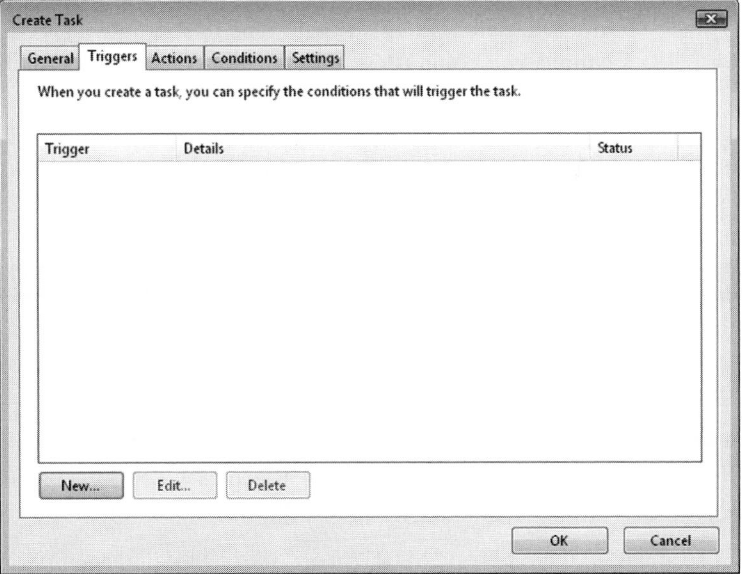

Table 9-3

Settings for the Triggers tab of the Create Task dialog box in Task Scheduler

SETTING	DESCRIPTION
New	Click New to open the New Trigger dialog box to create a new trigger.
Edit	In the list box, select the existing trigger you need to edit and then click Edit to open the Edit Trigger dialog box.
Delete	Click Delete to delete a trigger after selecting the trigger in the list box.

When you click New to create a new trigger, or you click Edit to edit an existing trigger, the New trigger dialog box or the Edit trigger dialog box appears as appropriate. Both dialog boxes contain the same settings. Figure 9-7 shows the New Trigger dialog box.

Figure 9-7

The New Trigger dialog box. The Edit Trigger dialog box is identical except for the title bar.

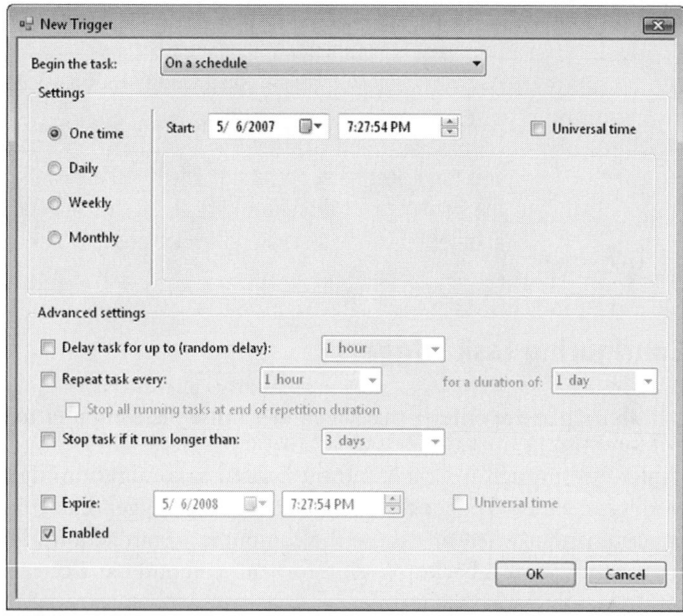

You select the trigger type by using the Begin the task drop-down list. You can trigger a task by using the following trigger types:

- **On a schedule**. Use this trigger type to schedule a task according to a schedule. For example, you could use it to schedule a regular backup. This trigger is covered in Table 9-4 and shown in Figure 9-8.

Table 9-4

Settings for scheduling a task by using the On a schedule trigger type (settings in the Advanced settings section are covered in Table 9-7)

SETTING	DESCRIPTION
One time	Select One time to run the task only once. If you select the One time setting, in the Start date drop-down list select a date, and in the time spin box, select a time to complete the task.
Daily	Select Daily to run a task using days to define the frequency. If you select Daily, then specify a number in the Recur every *numeral* days text box. For example, to complete the task ever other day, specify 2 in the Recur every numeral days text box. Also, in the Start date drop-down list and in the time spin box, specify a date and time for the first iteration of the task.
Weekly	Select Weekly to run a task by using weeks to define the frequency. If you select Weekly, select a check box for the day of the week (Monday, Tuesday, etc.) and then specify a number in the Recur every *numeral* weeks on text box. For example, to run the task on Thursday once every three weeks, select the Thursday check box and specify 3 in the Recur every *numeral* weeks on text box. Also, in the Start date drop-down list and in the time spin box, specify a date and time for the first iteration of the task.
Monthly	Select Monthly to run a task by using months to define the frequency. If you select Monthly, then in the Months drop-down list, select a check box for each of the months in which you want to run the task. Select one of the following: **Days**. In the Days drop-down list, select a check box for each day of the month on which you want to schedule the task. For example, to schedule the task on the 5th and the 8th, select the 5 and 8 check boxes in the Days drop-down list.

(continued)

Table 9-4 (*continued*)

SETTING	DESCRIPTION
	On. In the first drop-down list, select one or more positions within the month (first, second, third, etc.). In the second drop-down list, select one or more days of the week (Monday, Tuesday, etc.). For example, to schedule a task for the first and third Mondays and Thursdays of each month, select the First and Third check boxes in the first drop-down list, and the Monday and Thursday check boxes in the second. Finally, in the Start date drop-down list and in the time spin box, specify a date and time for the first iteration of the task.
Universal time	Select the Universal time check box to specify the iteration of the first scheduled task in the series in universal time. This can be useful if you have computers in multiple time zones and want to specify time uniformly.

Figure 9-8

New Trigger dialog box with the On a schedule trigger type selected

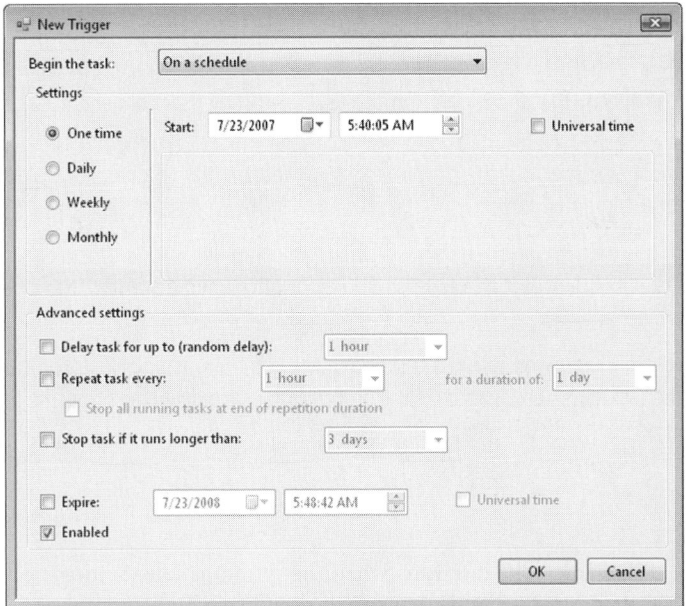

- **At log on**. Use this trigger type to run a task at each logon. For example, you could use this task to start a program that you want to start automatically for users when they log on. This trigger is covered in Table 9-5.
- **At startup**. Use this trigger type to start a task at startup. For example, you could use it to start a program that defends against malware.

Table 9-5

The settings for scheduling a task by using the At log on, On connection to user session, On disconnect from user session, On workstation lock, and On workstation unlock trigger types are very similar. When to use each is covered here.

TRIGGER TYPE	DESCRIPTION
At log on	Select this trigger type to run a task when a user logs on to the computer. You can specify that the trigger run the task when any user logs on, or only when a specific user or a user in a specific group logs on.
On connection to user session	Select this trigger type to run a task when someone connects to a user session either from the local computer or from a remote desktop connection.

(continued)

Table 9-5 (*continued*)

Trigger Type	Description
	For example, you can use this trigger type to start a task when the user is switched on the local computer (because a new user connects to a user session). Another example is to run a task when a user connects to a user session by using the Remote Desktop Connection program from a remote computer. You can specify that the trigger run the task when any user connects to a user session, or only when a specific user or a user in a specific group connects to a user session. You must also specify if the connection that triggers the task is from a remote computer or the local computer.
On disconnect from user session	Select this trigger type to run a task when a user session is disconnected from the local computer or from a remote desktop computer. For example, you can use this trigger type to start a task when a user session on the local computer is disconnected by switching users on the computer. Another example of when to use this trigger is if you want to run a task when a user disconnects from a user session by using the Remote Desktop Connection program from a remote computer. You can specify that the trigger run the task when any user connects to a user session, or only when a specific user or a user in a specific group connects to a user session. You must also specify if the disconnected connection that triggers the task is from a remote computer or the local computer.
On workstation lock	Select this trigger type to run a task when the computer is locked. You can specify that the trigger run the task when any user locks the computer, or only when a specific user or a user in a specific group locks the computer.
On workstation unlock	Select this trigger type to run a task when the computer is unlocked. You can specify that the trigger run the task when any user unlocks the computer, or only when a specific user or a user in a specific group unlocks the computer.

For more information on the Conditions tab, see Table 9-9.

- **On idle**. The task runs when the system is idle. Settings for what idle means are configured on the Conditions tab of the Create Task dialog box (or, after the task is created, in its Properties dialog box). For example, you could use this trigger to launch a program that takes advantage of idle computer time to work on some sort of problem. Some such programs, for example, work collaboratively with other computers to calculate pi to ever more decimal places.
- **On an event**. You can use this trigger to, for example, send an email to yourself when a hard disk registers an error. This trigger is covered in Table 9-6.
- **At task creation/modification**. Use this trigger to cause the task to run immediately after you create or modify it. This way you can test to see if it is working. If it is, then you can re-configure how it is triggered if necessary.
- **On connection to user session**. You can, for example, use this trigger to run a task when a user connects to a user session by using the Remote Desktop Connection program from a remote computer. This trigger is described in Table 9-5.
- **On disconnect from user session**. You can use this trigger, for example, to run a task when a user disconnects from a user session by ending a Remote Desktop Connection. This trigger is described in Table 9-5.
- **On workstation lock**. Select this trigger type to run a task when the computer is locked. This trigger is described in Table 9-5.
- **On workstation unlock**. Select this trigger type to run a task when the computer is unlocked. This trigger is described in Table 9-5.

Table 9-6

Settings for scheduling a task by using the On an event trigger type

SETTING	DESCRIPTION
Basic option button	Select Basic to run a task based on an event occurring. If you select Basic, in the Log drop-down list, select the event log in which the event will be recorded. Specify the event publisher in the Source drop-down list (the available publishers depend on the log selected) and then specify the event's identification number in the Event ID text box (you can find the event's ID in Event Viewer). For more information on Event Viewer, see Lesson 6.
Custom option button	Select Custom to run a task based on an event filter. Click New Event Filter to display the New Event Filter dialog box.

The following trigger types have similar settings:

- At log on
- On connection to user session
- On disconnect from user session
- On workstation lock
- On workstation unlock

Each of these settings has similar settings and identical settings in the Advanced settings section (covered in Table 9-7). Each of the five trigger types is shown in Figures 9-9 through 9-13, and when to use each is explained in Table 9-5.

Table 9-7

Advanced settings for triggers in the New Trigger dialog box and the Edit Trigger dialog box

SETTING	DESCRIPTION
Delay task for check box Delay task for up to (random delay) check box	This setting will be displayed as Delay task for with any trigger type selected except On a schedule, in which case it will be displayed as Delay task for up to (random delay). Select this check box to specify an amount of time to delay the task from running, after the task is triggered. For example, if you are starting the task because an event has occurred, you may want to wait 15 minutes for the event to complete. If you are using the On a schedule trigger type, the delay time will be a random time between the time the task is triggered and the time specified by using the drop-down list. For example, If a task is scheduled to be triggered at 1:00 pm, and 5 minutes is selected in the drop-down list, then the task will run sometime between 1:00 pm and 1:05 pm.
Repeat task every check box	Select this check box to set a task to repeat over a specified duration. You select the frequency of repetition in the Repeat task every *numeral* drop-down list, and the duration in the for a duration of *numeral* drop-down list. You can optionally select the Stop all running tasks at end of repetition duration check box to end all tasks, finished or not, at the end of the specified duration. You might do this if you expect that some tasks might not ever finish because they fall into an endless loop.
Stop task if it runs longer than check box	Select this check box to stop a task by selecting a duration period in the corresponding drop-down list.

(continued)

Table 9-7 (*continued*)

Setting	Description
Activate check box	Select this check box to specify a date and time when the trigger will become active. Prior to the specified date, the trigger will not start the task. Select the Universal time check box to make the time relative to Coordinated Universal Time (UTC) instead of the time zone that is set on the computer that runs the task. This is useful if you want to coordinate tasks on computers in different time zones. Note that this setting is not available if the On a schedule trigger type is selected.
Expire check box	Select this check box to specify a date and time when the trigger will become inactive. After the specified date, the trigger will not start the task. Select the Universal time check box to make the time relative to Coordinated Universal Time (UTC) instead of the time zone that is set on the computer that runs the task. This is useful if you want to coordinate tasks on computers in different time zones.
Enabled check box	To disable the trigger for the task, clear the enabled check box. The selected trigger will not run the task if this check box is cleared. Other triggers can still start the task.

Figure 9-9

New Trigger dialog box with the At log on schedule trigger type selected

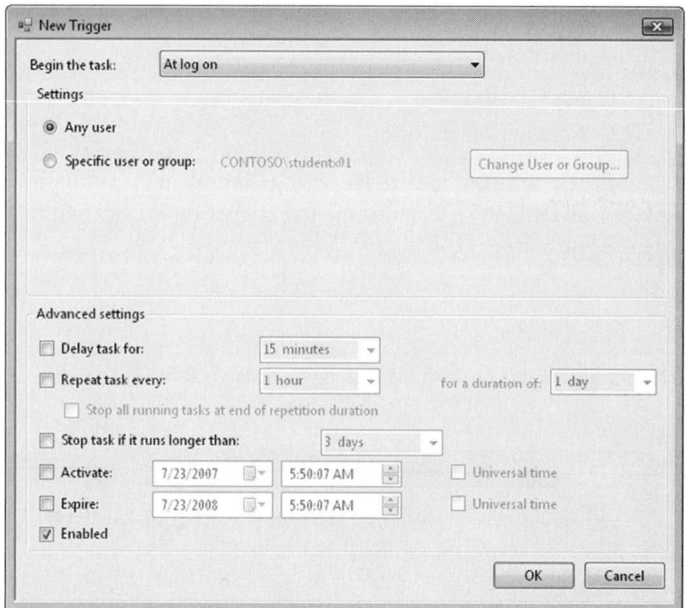

Figure 9-10

New Trigger dialog box with the On connection to user session trigger type selected

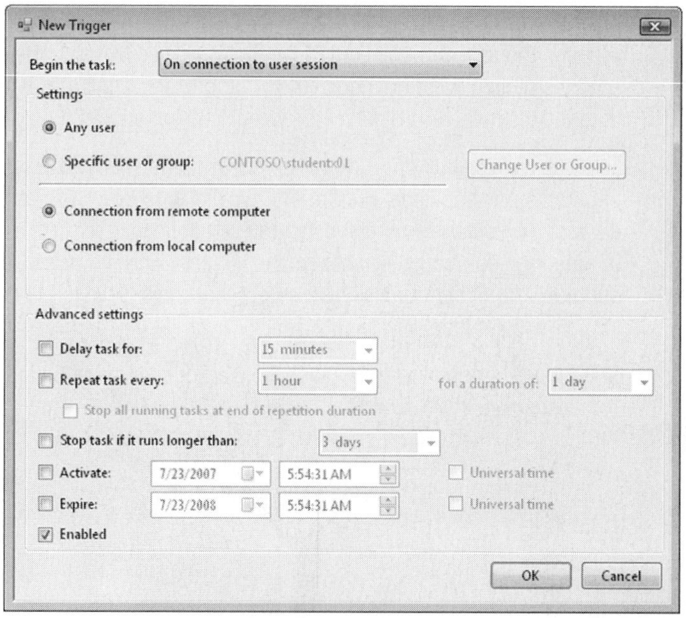

Figure 9-11

New Trigger dialog box with the On disconnect from user session trigger type selected

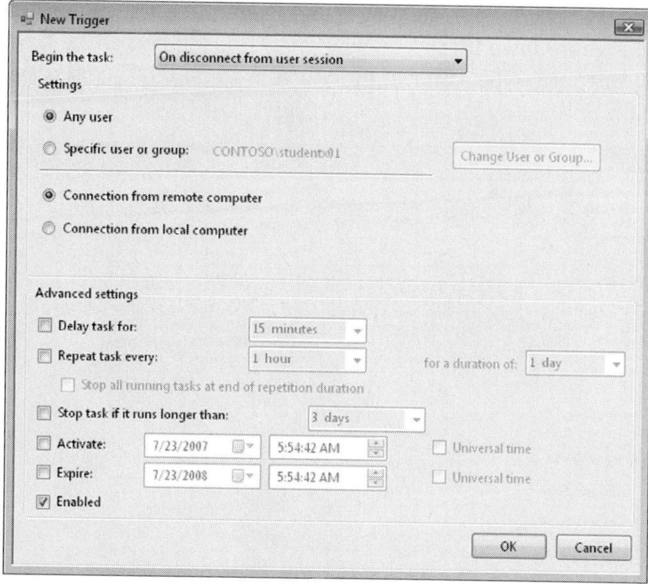

Figure 9-12

New Trigger dialog box with the On workstation lock trigger type selected

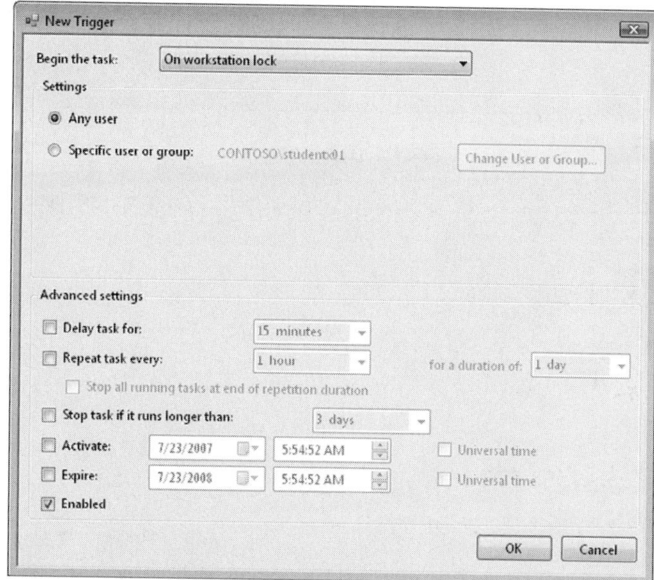

Figure 9-13

New Trigger dialog box with the On workstation unlock trigger type selected

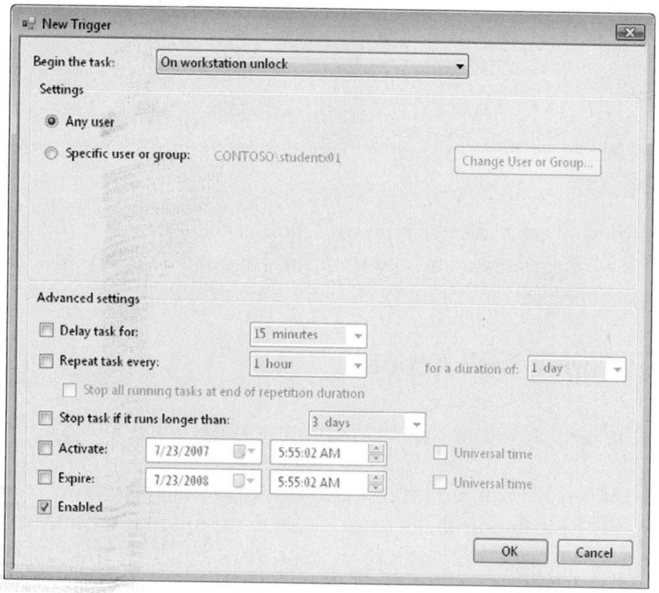

To create a trigger that activates when a specified event occurs, select On an event in the Begin the task drop-down list in the New Trigger dialog box or the Edit Trigger dialog box. The On an event trigger type is shown in Figures 9-14 and 9-15 and is explained in Table 9-6.

Figure 9-14

New Trigger dialog box with the On an event trigger type selected and the Basic option button selected

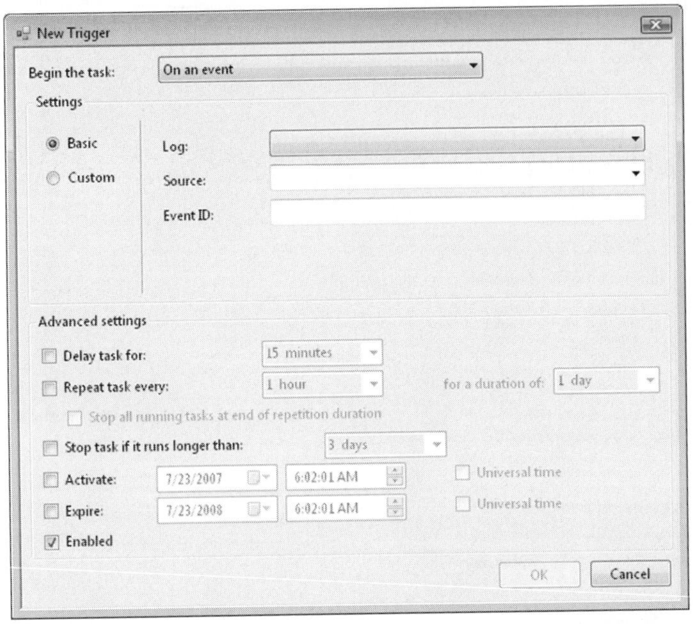

Figure 9-15

New Trigger dialog box with the On an event trigger type selected and the Custom option selected

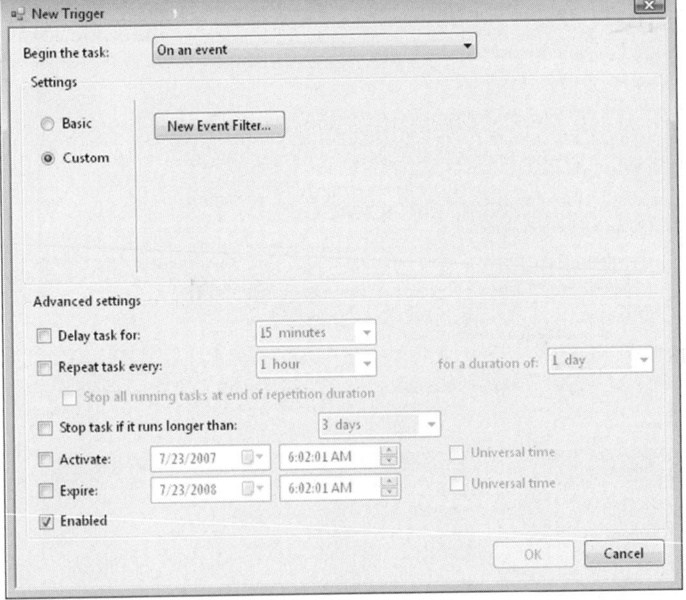

Events and event filters are covered in **Lesson 6.**

Regardless of what trigger type you choose, the settings in the Advanced settings section of the New Trigger dialog box or the Edit Trigger dialog box will be the same (and are shown in many of the previous figures). Table 9-7 describes the advanced trigger settings.

Configuring Task Actions

Actions are activities that the computer starts when a trigger is activated.

Task actions are configured in the New Action dialog box for a new task and are modified using the Edit Action dialog box for an existing task. Actions, as stated earlier, are activities the computer starts when a trigger is activated. For example, an action might be to email an administrator when a trigger event occurs (such as a write failure to a hard drive).

The Actions tab for a task can contain more than one action. The actions are run in sequence.

Figure 9-16 shows the Actions tab with two actions listed, while Figure 9-17 shows the Edit Action dialog box. Table 9-8 explains each of the actions available in the Edit Action dialog box or the Create Action dialog box.

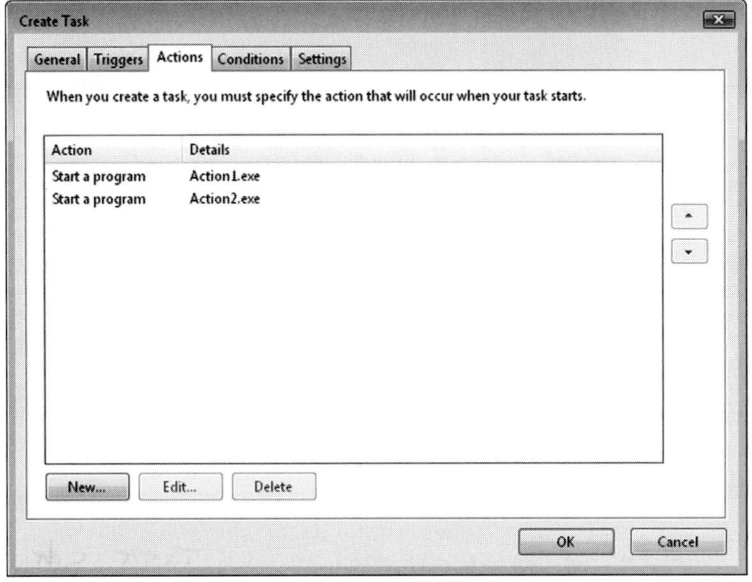

Figure 9-16

The Actions tab of the Create Task dialog box. The Actions tab can also be accessed through the Task Properties dialog box.

Figure 9-17

The Edit Action dialog box. The Create Action dialog box is identical except for the title bar.

Table 9-8

Actions a trigger can start in the Edit Action and Create Action dialog boxes

Action	Description
Start a program	Select Start a program in the Action drop-down list if you want the computer to run a program or script when the task is triggered. If you select this option, enter the program or script name in the Program/script text box. If the program accepts arguments, you can specify them in the Add arguments (optional) text box. You can specify the working directory for the program or script in the Start in (optional) text box. This would typically be either the path to the program or script file or the path to the files that are used by the program or script file.
Send an email	Select Send an email in the Action drop-down list if you want the computer to send an email when the task is triggered. If you select this option, configure the From, To, Subject, Text, and Attachment text boxes just as you would a normal email. In the SMPT server text box, specify the server that will handle sending an email (for example, smtp.contoso.com).
Display a message	Select Display a message in the Action drop-down list if you want the computer to display a message when a task is triggered.
	If you select this option, enter a title for the message in the Title text box and enter message text in the Message text box.

Configuring Task Conditions

Conditions are criteria that can override a trigger based on the state of the machine.

Task conditions are configured on the Conditions tab of the Create Task dialog box or the Task Properties dialog box. As stated earlier, conditions are criteria that can override a trigger based on the state of the machine. For example, you can set a condition so that a task will run only if the computer is connected to an AC power source (in other words, if it is not running on battery power).

Figure 9-18 shows the Conditions tab. Table 9-9 explains each of the settings available on the Conditions tab.

Figure 9-18

The Conditions tab of the Create Task dialog box. The Conditions tab for the Task Properties dialog box is identical.

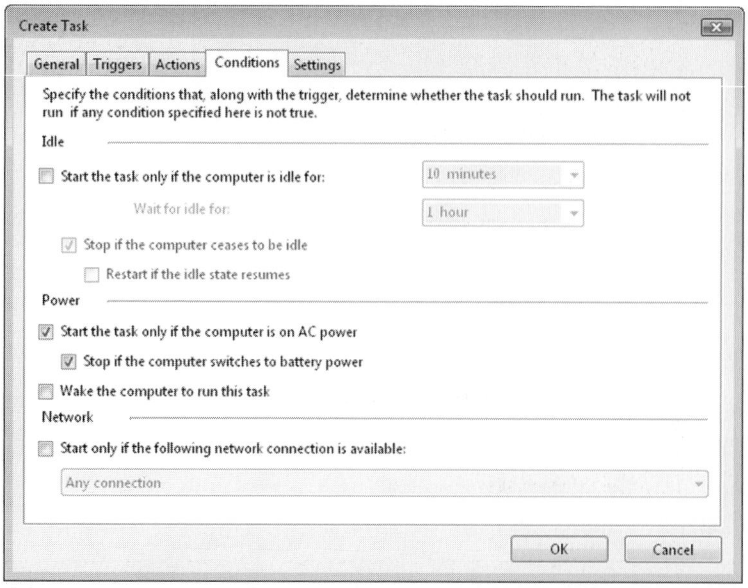

Table 9-9

You configure conditions for a task by using settings on the Conditions tab.

SETTING	DESCRIPTION
Start the task only if the computer is idle for check box	Select this check box if you want to start the task only if the computer has been idle for an amount of time you specify using the corresponding drop-down list. If you select this option, select how long to wait for the specified idle period in the Wait for idle for *numeral* drop-down list. If you want the task to stop if the computer ceases to be idle, select the Stop if the computer ceases to be idle check box. If you select this option, you can optionally select the Restart if the idle states resumes check box to resume the task if the computer becomes idle again. A computer is considered to be in an idle state either when a screen saver is running or if there is 0% CPU usage, and 0% disk input or output for 90% of the past 15 minutes and if there is no keyboard or mouse input during the same period of time. Once the Task Scheduler service detects that the computer is in an idle state, only user input can end the designation as idle. If a task is set to start only if the computer is idle for 30 minutes, and the task waits for the computer to be idle for 10 minutes, then the task will launch in 5 minutes only if the computer has been idle for 25 minutes prior to the time the trigger was activated. The task will not start if the computer enters an idle state 5 minutes after the trigger is activated.
Start the task only if the computer is on AC power check box	Select this check box if you want to start the task only if the computer is connected to an AC power source (in other words, it isn't using battery power). If you select this option, you can optionally select the Stop if the computer switches to battery power check box.
Wake the computer to run this task check box	Select this check box to wake the computer from hibernation to run the task.
Start only if the following network connection is available check box	Select this check box to run the task only if a specified network connection is available or if any network connection is available. If your task action requires a network connection to execute, set this condition and then select the desired connection in the associated drop-down list.

Configuring Task Settings

Task settings are execution options for the tasks.

You configure task settings on the Settings tab of the Create Task dialog box or the Task Properties dialog box. As stated earlier, settings are execution options for tasks. For example, you can use settings to determine how many times a task is retried if it fails for some reason.

Figure 9-19 shows the Settings tab. Table 9-10 explains each of the settings available on the Settings tab.

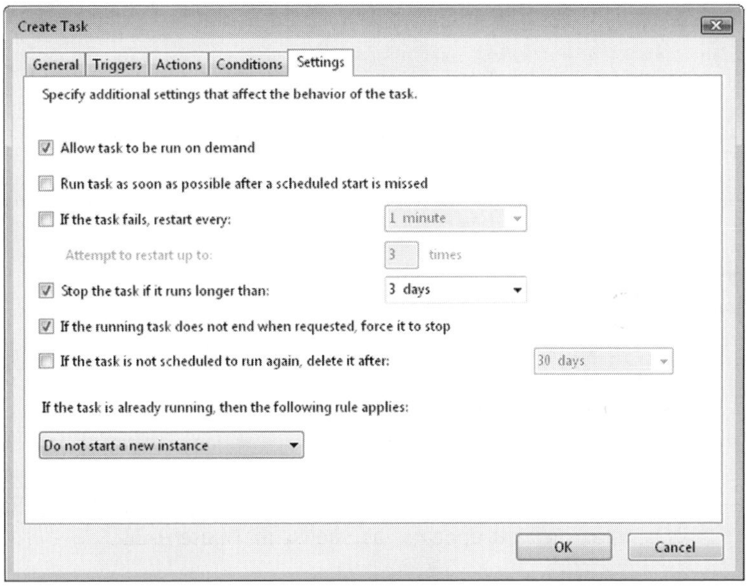

Figure 9-19

The Settings tab of the Create Task dialog box. The Settings tab for the *Task* Properties dialog box is identical.

Table 9-10

You configure settings for a task in the Settings tab.

Setting	Description
Allow task to be run on demand check box	Select this check box if you want to be able to run the task manually at any time. The default setting enables users to run the task at any time on demand.
Run task as soon as possible after a scheduled start is missed check box	Select this check box to start the task if the task was scheduled to run but for some reason was unable to (for example, if the task settings required the computer to be on AC power and it was on battery power). By default, the Task Scheduler service waits 10 minutes after the blocking condition is overcome before starting the missed task.
If the task fails, restart every check box	Select this check box to retry the task if it fails. If you select this check box, use the corresponding drop-down list to specify the time interval between retries. In the Attempt to restart up to *numeral* times text box, you need to specify the number of retry attempts to make. For example, to retry a task up to 8 times every 5 minutes, select 5 minutes in the drop-down list and type 8 in the Attempt to restart up to *numeral* times text box. If the task succeeds, then it will stop retrying even if there are retry attempts remaining.
Stop the task if it runs longer than check box	Select this check box to limit the time a task is allowed to run. If you select this check box, select a time period in the corresponding drop-down list. You can use this setting to limit tasks that might take a long time to complete if you think it could inconvenience the user.
If the running task does not end when requested, force it to stop check box	Select this option to force a task to stop if the task does not respond to a request to stop.
If the task is not scheduled to run again, delete it after check box	Select this option to delete a task after a specified period of time if the task is not scheduled to run again. If you select this option, in the corresponding drop-down list, select a time period to wait before deleting the task. For this setting to be active, the task must include at least one trigger with an expiration date.
If the task is already running, then the following rule applies drop-down list	Use this setting to specify what Task Scheduler should do if another instance of the same task is already running. • **Do not start a new instance**. Task Scheduler will not run the new instance of the task and will not stop the instance that is already running. • **Run a new instance in parallel**. Task Scheduler will run the new instance of the task in parallel with the instance that is already running. • **Queue a new instance**. Task Scheduler will add the new instance of the task to the queue of tasks to run and will not stop the instance of the task that is already running. • **Stop the existing instance**. Task Scheduler will stop the instance of the task that is already running and then run the new instance of the task.

Using the Create Basic Task Wizard

You can use the Create Basic Task Wizard to create a simple task. You can then use the task as is or make changes to it through the task's properties dialog box.

CREATE A BASIC TASK

You can quickly create a simple task by using the Create Basic Task Wizard. After completing the wizard, you can use the task as is or you can edit it through its Properties dialog box to configure additional settings.

OPEN Task Scheduler.

1. In Task Scheduler, on the Action menu, select **Create Basic Task.** The Create Basic Task Wizard appears, as shown in Figure 9-20.

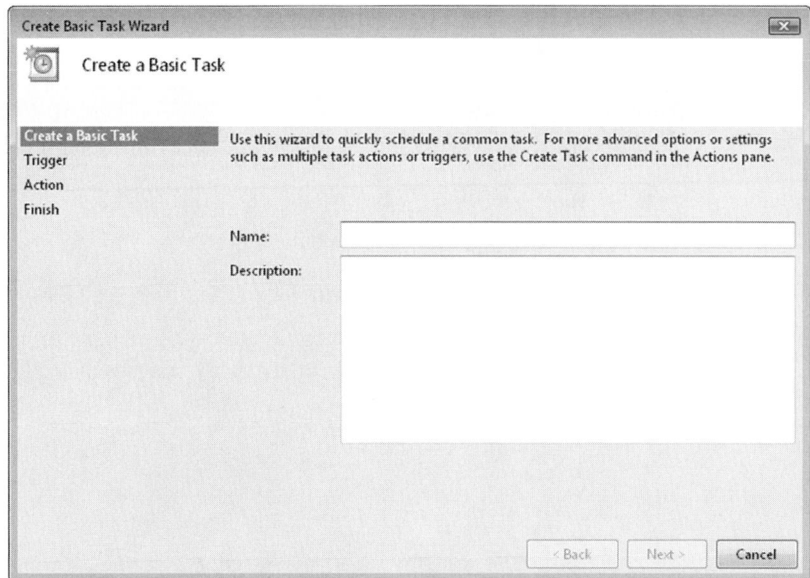

Figure 9-20

The Create Basic Task Wizard with the Create a Basic Task page active.

2. In the **Name** text box, provide a name for the task.
3. In the **Description** text box, you can optionally provide a description.
4. Click **Next**. The Task Trigger page appears.
5. Select when you want the trigger task to start and then click **Next**. Depending on your selection, the wizard will behave differently. You can find information on the settings in Tables 9-3 through 9-7. Follow the onscreen instructions until the Action page appears. Then continue to step 6.
6. Select one of the following actions that you want the task to perform:
   - Start a program
   - Send an email
   - Display a message

   The wizard will behave differently depending on your selection. See Table 9-8 for information on each option. Follow the onscreen instructions until the Summary page appears and then continue to step 7.
7. The Summary page summarizes your selections. You can select the *Open the Properties dialog for this task when I click Finish* check box if you want to make changes to the task.
8. Click **Finish**. You should see the new task listed in the details pane in the Active Tasks section.

SUMMARY SKILL MATRIX

IN THIS LESSON YOU LEARNED:
Task Scheduler enables administrators to automate the completion of tasks on individual computers.
You can use Task Scheduler to manage, create, and monitor tasks.
Managing tasks includes starting, ending, disabling, and enabling tasks, as well as viewing task history.
How to start, end, disable, or enable a task.
How to view a tasks history.

(continued)

SUMMARY SKILL MATRIX (*continued*)

IN THIS LESSON YOU LEARNED:
Tasks consist of general settings, triggers, actions, conditions, and task settings.
Task triggers are criteria that when met cause the computer to start actions.
Actions are activities that the computer starts when a trigger is activated.
Conditions are criteria that can override a trigger based on the state of the machine.
You can use the Create Basic Task Wizard to create a simple task. You can then use the task as is or make changes to it through the task's Properties dialog box.

Knowledge Assessment

Fill in the Blank

Complete the following sentences by writing the correct word or words in the blanks provided.

1. ______________ are criteria in a task that determine if a task is started.
2. The activities that a task performs are called ______________.
3. You can browse the tasks available in the ______________.
4. You can find the Start the task only if the computer is on AC power check box on the ______________ tab.
5. You can configure the account that a task uses by configuring the ______________ tab.
6. ______________ is a command-line tool that you can use for managing tasks.
7. Microsoft has integrated the Task Scheduler Snap-in in Windows Vista with the ______________ Snap-in.
8. When the top node in the console tree is selected, the details pane of Task Scheduler lists tasks that are enabled and not expired in the ______________ section.
9. Task-related events can be accessed in the ______________ tab of an event's properties dialog box.
10. If you want to create a basic task by using a wizard, you can use the ______________.

Multiple Choice

Select all answers that apply for the following questions.

1. Credentials provided to Task Scheduler to complete tasks in Windows Vista are:
   a. Stored locally so that if network connectivity fails the tasks that require user authentication can still run.
   b. Stored remotely using CredMan so that changes in domain passwords will be recognized and cannot cause the task to fail.
   c. Not necessary because of User Account Control.
   d. Stored locally but encrypted using CredMan for security purposes.

2. In previous versions of Task Scheduler, tasks could complete only one action. In Windows Vista:
   a. You can combine nest tasks, thus putting one task inside another so that it completes more than one action.
   b. The behavior is the same; you can only complete one action per task.
   c. Tasks can contain multiple actions that are run serially.
   d. None of the above apply.

3. To run a task manually:
   a. You must be logged on as an administrator.
   b. The Allow task to be run on demand check box must be selected.
   c. You must start the task locally from the computer that the task is to run on; you cannot start a task manually from a remote computer.
   d. All of the above.

4. Task histories can be located in Event Viewer in:
   a. Applications and Services Logs\Microsoft\Windows\Task Scheduler\History.
   b. Applications and Services Logs\Microsoft\Windows\Administrative tools\Task History.
   c. Applications and Services Logs\Windows\Task Scheduler\Operational.
   d. Applications and Services Logs\Microsoft\Windows\TaskScheduler\Operational.

5. To preserve battery power on laptop computers, you can configure tasks to:
   a. Run only if the laptop computer is connected to AC power.
   b. Run only if the battery is at 80% of capacity or higher.
   c. Run only if the computer is idle.
   d. Only run if the task on average takes longer than a specified amount of time.

6. The setting you set to accomplish the goal stated in question 5 is located on which tab of the Create Task dialog box?
   a. Settings
   b. Actions
   c. Triggers
   d. Conditions

7. A task is configured to use an administrator account. You want to ensure that it uses only the standard user token. You should edit the properties for the task and:
   a. Disable the administrator token for the administrator on the General tab.
   b. Provide credentials for the standard user token but not for the administrator token on the General tab.
   c. Clear the Run with highest privileges check box on the General tab.
   d. Disable the administrator account for the task on the Settings tab.

8. The three types of actions available for tasks are:
   a. Start a program, send an email, and display a message
   b. Start a program, start a script, and display a message
   c. Start a program, log an event, and display a message
   d. Start a program, send an email, and forward an event

9. A task is composed of:
   a. A trigger, conditions, settings, and an action.
   b. Triggers, conditions, settings, and actions.
   c. Triggers, conditions, settings, and an action.
   d. A trigger, conditions, settings, and actions.

10. To create a task that is triggered when a user logs off a Remote Desktop session, select the following trigger type:
    a. On an event
    b. On disconnect from remote connection
    c. At log off
    d. On disconnect from user session

Review Questions

1. Explain how allowing multiple actions in a single task alleviates synchronization problems present in previous versions of Task Scheduler for jobs that require multiple actions.
2. Explain how Microsoft has integrated Task Scheduler with Event Viewer. Include in your answer how Event forwarding expands the set of possible triggers for a computer.

■ Case Scenarios

Scenario 1: Sending an Email When a Task Fails

It is standard operating procedure after rolling a task out to workstations at Contoso to have an email sent to selected administrators if the task fails. However, there is no provision within a task for doing this. Outline a solution to this problem.

Scenario 2: Creating a Task to Run a Program on a Schedule

Contoso publishes a weekly newsletter for its employees. Contributors create their articles in an XML format and save them to a share by Monday at 11 p.m. Developers in the company have created a program that automatically retrieves each of the articles from the network share, composes them into a PDF file, and then mails them to subscribers. The program is in beta testing and will be released in its final version on October 8, 2008, at 8 a.m.

Outline a task that:

1. Starts the program each week on Tuesday morning at 2 a.m.
2. Does not begin running until after the developers release the final version of the program (the first Tuesday after the release date is on October 14).
3. Starts only if connectivity to the network is verified (the program requires connectivity to email the newsletter).

In your answer, address requirements 1–3 separately and mention the specific settings required.

Updating Windows Vista

LESSON 10

OBJECTIVE DOMAIN MATRIX

Technology Skill	Objective Domain	Objective Domain Number
Understanding Updates	Apply security patches and updates	2.5
	Apply and troubleshoot updates • Troubleshoot restart manager	3.4
Understanding Windows Server Update Services	Apply security patches and updates Apply and troubleshoot updates	2.5 3.4
Configure Windows Server Update Services Clients	Apply and troubleshoot updates • Configure Windows Update Agent	3.4
Configure Automatic Updating	Apply and troubleshoot updates • Configure Windows Update Agent	3.4
Monitoring Performance and Reliability	Apply and troubleshoot updates • Troubleshoot performance and reliability issues • Establish and monitor performance baselines by using built-in tools	3.4
Using the Reliability and Performance Monitor	Apply and troubleshoot updates • Troubleshoot performance and reliability issues • Establish and monitor performance baselines by using built-in tools	3.4
Understanding Windows Diagnostic Infrastructure	Apply and troubleshoot updates • Use Windows Diagnostic Infrastructure to collect and troubleshoot issues	3.4
Configure WDI Through Group Policy	Apply and troubleshoot updates • Use Windows Diagnostic Infrastructure to collect and troubleshoot issues	3.4

KEY TERMS

Microsoft Update
Windows Update
Microsoft Office Update
Automatic Updating
Automatic Updates
hidden updates
Windows Server Update Services 3.0 (WSUS 3.0)
Restart Manager
Windows Server Update Services server
WSUS 3.0 Administration console
System Information tool
Windows Reliability and Performance Monitor
Performance Monitor
performance counters
Reliability Monitor
Windows Diagnostic Infrastructure (WDI)

Contoso Incorporated was previously using Group Policy to configure workstations to download updates directly from Microsoft. IT management has decided to deploy internal Windows Server Update Services (WSUS) servers to provide updates to computers so that each update can be vetted in a lab environment before deploying the WSUS servers. Your task is to configure Group Policy to cause workstations to request updates from internal WSUS servers, and to test updates by using built-in performance tools before deploying them.

■ Understanding Updates

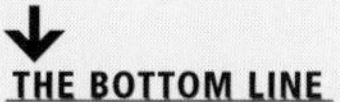

Automatic Updating automates the process of downloading, either from an internal update server or from Microsoft, and installing updates.

CERTIFICATION READY?
Apply security patches and updates
Apply and troubleshoot updates
2.5, 3.4

Microsoft provides updates through three websites for its operating systems and other software products. Updates are provided frequently to mitigate security vulnerabilities, fix bugs, and occasionally add features or improve functionality. The three update websites are:

- ***Microsoft Update***. This website provides updates for Microsoft Windows Vista, Microsoft Office, and other current Microsoft applications. It supports Windows Vista, Windows XP, Windows 2000 SP4 or later, and Windows Server 2003. It also provides updates for Microsoft Office 2007, Microsoft Office XP, Microsoft Office 2003, Microsoft SQL Server, and Microsoft Exchange Server.
- ***Windows Update.*** This website provides updates for current Windows operating systems (therefore, it overlaps with Microsoft Update) and the following earlier versions of Windows: Windows 2000 SP3 or earlier, Windows Me, Windows 98, Windows 95, and Windows NT Workstation 4.0. It also provides updates for applications that come with Windows, such as Internet Explorer.
- ***Microsoft Office Update***. This website provides updates for all the programs in the Microsoft Office suite. This site overlaps with the Microsoft Update site that also offers updates for Microsoft Office 2007, Microsoft Office 2003, and Microsoft Office XP.

To help you keep your updates current, Microsoft provides ***Automatic Updating*** (called ***Automatic Updates*** in previous versions of Windows), which enables you to automate the downloading and installation of updates from Windows Update and Microsoft Update (or from internal update servers, such as Windows Server Update Services 3.0 servers, which are discussed later in this lesson).

In previous versions of Windows, if you wanted to access the Windows Updates site, you simply browsed to it in a web browser such as Internet Explorer. You did this in Windows XP, for example, by clicking Windows Update in All Programs in the Start menu. In Windows Vista, you access Windows Update by using the Windows Update control panel. From there, you can:

- Manually check for updates.
- Configure Automatic Updating settings.
- View update history (a list of what updates have been installed and
- Restore hidden updates. ***Hidden updates*** are updates you've asked Windo... you about or to install automatically. You can restore these updates and install them later if needed.

For a home user, all that you really need to do is configure Automatic Updating through the Windows Update control panel. In an enterprise environment, however, you probably want to centrally manage the application of updates to client computers. This can be done using various tools offered by Microsoft and third parties. Two prominent tools Microsoft offers that can centrally manage update deployment are System Center Configuration Manager 2007 (which does other things as well) and Windows Software Update Server 3.0 (WSUS).

X REF

ACT 5.0 is covered in **Lesson 1: Preparing to Deploy Windows Vista.**

Enterprises need to be careful deploying updates because updates can cause software to stop working or to behave differently, thus disrupting operations (sometimes with severe consequences). Therefore, it is normal to first assess the effects of an update before deploying it to many workstations or servers. This can be done by testing updates in a lab on workstations and servers designed to mimic those used in the enterprise, and by using compatibility assessment tools such as the Application Compatibility Toolkit 5.0 (ACT 5.0).

CERTIFICATION READY?
Apply and troubleshoot updates: Troubleshoot restart manager
3.4

New to Windows Vista is Restart Manager. ***Restart Manager*** limits the number of restarts needed after updates or installations by checking if the part of the system that needs to be updated can be cleared and updated without adversely affecting the system. If this is the case, it does so and a restart is not required. If a restart is required, Restart Manager takes a snapshot of the system state. It then restarts and returns the system to the state it was in before the restart.

CERTIFICATION READY?
Apply security patches and updates
Apply and troubleshoot updates
2.5, 3.4

Understanding Windows Server Update Services

Windows Server Update Services enables you to manage the deployment of updates by directing workstations to download updates from internal WSUS servers.

After updates have been vetted, the next task is to deploy them to workstations and track their status to ensure that they are installed correctly and are not causing issues. Among the tools you can use to do this is the ***Windows Server Update Services 3.0 (WSUS)***, which manages the distribution of updates to workstation computers and enables you to track their deployment.

TAKE NOTE*

Most enterprises are going to use a comprehensive software deployment solution that integrates deploying updates, such as System Center Configuration Manager 2007 (previously called System Management Server). This lesson and the corresponding Lab Manual lesson use WSUS as a means to cover exam 70-622 objective domains 2.5 Apply security patches and updates and 3.4 Apply and troubleshoot updates.

To use WSUS, you:

- Install WSUS server on one or more servers on your network.
- Configure WSUS server to download updates from Microsoft or from another WSUS server.
- Decide which updates you want to deploy and then configure WSUS servers to make them available to clients.
- Configure your workstations (WSUS clients) to get updates from the WSUS servers rather than from Windows Update.
- Use WSUS to track the deployment of updates.

In essence, WSUS intercedes in the middle of the update transfer process from Microsoft Update to client computers, enabling you to control which updates are pushed to workstations in your network.

WSUS can be divided into two components:

- ***Windows Server Update Services server***. This component is installed on a Windows Server 2003 SP1 or later server inside the enterprise firewall. The WSUS server enables administrators to manage and distribute updates by using the ***WSUS 3.0 Administration console***, which can be installed on any Windows computer in the domain. A WSUS server can also serve as the source for updates for other WSUS servers. At least one WSUS server on the network must connect to Microsoft Update to download updates directly.
- **Automatic Updating** (also called Automatic Updates). This component (mentioned earlier) is the client application that enables workstations to receive updates, whether from Microsoft Update directly or from a WSUS server. Automatic Updating is part of Windows Server 2008, Windows Vista, Windows Server 2003, Windows XP, and Windows 2000 SP4.

Configure Windows Server Update Services Clients

WSUS clients download updates from WSUS servers rather than directly from Microsoft.

CERTIFICATION READY?
Apply and troubleshoot updates: Configure Windows Update Agent
3.4

Configuring computers in your network to be WSUS clients and receive updates from an internal WSUS server is a matter of configuring the appropriate Group Policy settings.

An example scheme for configuring WSUS clients through Group Policy is as follows:

1. Enable the Configure Automatic Updates Group Policy setting. This will prevent users from disabling Automatic Updating.
2. Schedule updates to install on a schedule by using the Configure Automatic Updates Group Policy setting. This way the burden does not fall to users or administrators to install updates.
3. Enable the Specify intranet Microsoft update service location Group Policy setting and specify a WSUS server. This will point the WSUS clients to an internal WSUS server rather than directly to Microsoft update sites.
4. Enable the Automatic Updates detection frequency Group Policy setting and configure a frequency for detecting updates. This will configure the WSUS clients to ask the WSUS server for available updates on an interval. There is some randomness added to the interval to prevent the WSUS server from being overloaded by many WSUS clients simultaneously. If you skip this step, the interval will default to 22 hours.
5. Enable the Reschedule Automatic Updates scheduled installations Group Policy setting so that if a computer misses a scheduled update installation (e.g., it is turned off), the installation takes place the next time the computer is started.
6. Enable the Enabling Windows Update Power Management to automatically wake up the system to install scheduled updates Group Policy setting. This will rouse laptops that are hibernating if updates are scheduled to install.

The following procedure provides the steps for implementing this example scheme.

CONFIGURE WSUS CLIENTS THROUGH GROUP POLICY

OPEN the Group Policy Object Editor with the Group Policy object in which you want to configure Automatic Updating settings loaded.

1. In the Group Policy Object Editor console tree, expand **Computer Configuration>Windows Settings>Administrative Templates>Windows Components** and then select **Windows Update**.
2. In the details pane, right-click **Configure Automatic Updates** and then click **Properties**. The Configure Automatic Updates Properties dialog box appears.
3. Select **Enabled**, as shown in Figure 10-1. Enabling this setting will prevent users from disabling Automatic Updates.

Figure 10-1
Configure Automatic Updates Properties dialog box

4. In the Configure automatic updating drop-down list, select **4 - Auto download and schedule the install**.
5. Use the **Schedule install day** and **Schedule install time** drop-down lists to configure when to install updates. The default settings of 0 - everyday and 03:00 are good options that will install updates each morning at 3 a.m.
6. Click **OK**.
7. In the details pane, right-click **Specify intranet Microsoft update service location** and then click **Properties**. The Specify intranet Microsoft update service location Properties dialog box appears.
8. Select **Enabled**.
9. In the *Set the intranet update service for detecting updates* text box, type the Hypertext Transfer Protocol (HTTP) path to the WSUS server (e.g., **http://wsus1**).
10. In the *Set the intranet statistics server* text box, type the HTTP path to the server where update statistics are stored. These statistics are used to track the deployment of updates. Often, this will be the same server as the server specified in step 9. Example settings are shown in Figure 10-2.

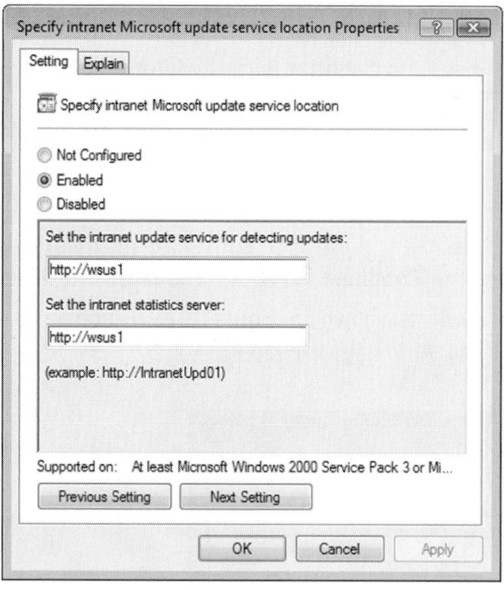

Figure 10-2

The Specify intranet Microsoft update service location Properties dialog box with example settings

11. Click **OK**.
12. In the details pane, right-click **Automatic Updates detection frequency** and then click **Properties**. The Automatic Updates detection frequency Properties dialog box appears.
13. Select **Enabled**.
14. In the Check for updates at the following interval spin box, select the interval (hours) that you want to check for updates. If you want the interval to be 22 hours, then you do not need to configure this setting (the default is 22 hours).
15. Click **OK**.
16. In the details pane, right-click **Reschedule Automatic Updates scheduled installations** and then click **Properties**. The Reschedule Automatic Updates scheduled installations Properties dialog box appears.
17. Select **Enabled**.
18. In the Wait after system startup (minutes) spin box, enter how many minutes to wait before installing updates after startup when a scheduled update install was missed. The default setting of 1 is a reasonable choice, and it is shown in Figure 10-3.

Reschedule Automatic Updates scheduled installations Prope...
Setting
Explain
Reschedule Automatic Updates scheduled installations
Not Configured
Enabled
Disabled
Wait after system startup (minutes): 1
Supported on: At least Microsoft Windows 2000 Service Pack 3 or Mi...
Previous Setting
Next Setting
OK
Cancel
Apply

Figure 10-3

The Reschedule Automatic Updates scheduled installations Properties dialog box with example settings

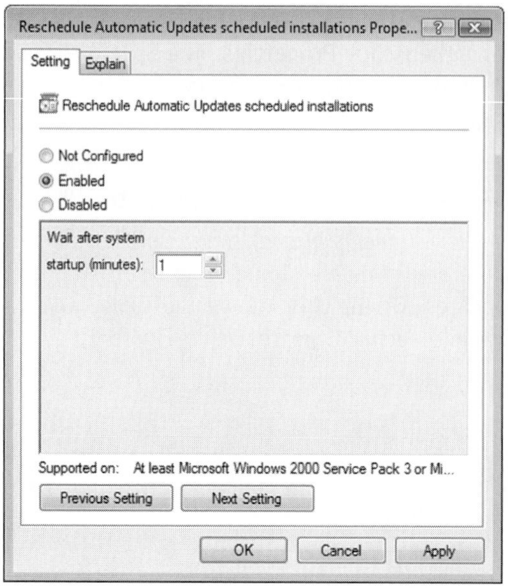

19. Click **OK**.
20. In the details pane, right-click **Enabling Windows Update Power Management to automatically wake up the system to install scheduled updates** and then click **Properties**. The Enabling Windows Update Power Management to automatically wake up the system to install scheduled updates Properties dialog box appears.
21. Select **Enabled**.

Configure Automatic Updating

CERTIFICATION READY?
Apply and troubleshoot updates: Configure Windows Update Agent
3.4

You can configure Automatic Updating locally, or you can centrally manage Automatic Updating by using Group Policy.

You can configure Automatic Updating locally or through Group Policy. In a domain, you will most likely configure Automatic Updating through Group Policy. You might, however, need to configure Automatic Updating locally on computers that are not part of the domain but are still part of the network.

CONFIGURE AUTOMATIC UPDATING LOCALLY

1. Click **Start**. In the **Start Search** text box, type **windows update** and then press **Ctrl + Shift + Enter**. A User Account Control dialog box appears.
2. Provide administrator credentials and then click **OK**. The Windows Update control panel appears.
3. In the task list, click **Change Settings**. The Windows Update>Change Settings control panel appears.
4. Select one of the following:

   Install updates automatically (recommended). If you select this option, configure the Install new updates drop-down lists to choose an installation schedule.

   Download updates but let me choose whether to install them. You can select this option to have the convenience of downloading updates automatically, while maintaining the freedom of deciding whether to install them.

   Check for updates but let me choose whether to download and install them. This option checks for updates, but lets you decide whether to download and install them.

   Never check for updates (not recommended). Select this option if you want to check for updates manually, or if you don't want to install updates.
5. If you don't want to be notified about or automatically download recommended updates, clear the **Include recommended updates when downloading, installing, or notifying me about updates** check box.

UNINSTALL UPDATES

If an update is causing problems, or you suspect that it is, you can uninstall it.

OPEN the Windows Update control panel.

1. In the Windows Update task list, under See also, click **Installed Updates**. The Installed Updates control panel appears, as shown in Figure 10-4.

Figure 10-4

The Installed Updates control panel

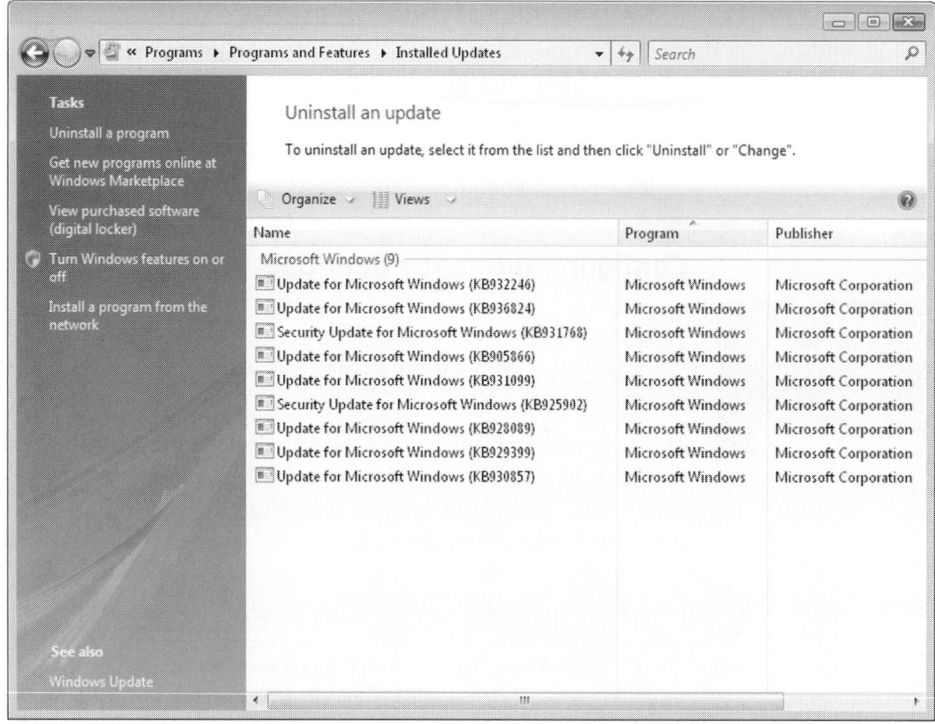

2. Right-click the update that you want to uninstall and then click **Uninstall.** A message box appears asking if you want to uninstall the updates.
3. Click **Yes**. A User Account Control dialog box appears.
4. Provide administrator credentials and then click **OK**. The update is uninstalled, which may take a few minutes.
5. You may be required to restart your computer before the update is entirely uninstalled.

Using Group Policy is covered in **Lesson 4: Using Group Policy**.

You can use Group Policy to centrally manage Automatic Updating settings for many computers simultaneously.

Automatic Updating–related Group Policy settings are configured in the Computer Configuration>Windows Settings>Administrative Templates>Windows Components>Windows Update folder of Group Policy objects.

Group Policy settings for Automatic Updates are described in Table 10-1.

Table 10-1

Group Policy settings for Automatic Updating

Group Policy Setting	Description
Do not display 'Install Updates and Shut Down' option in Shut Down Windows dialog box	Determines whether the Install Updates and Shut Down option is displayed in the Shut Down Windows dialog box. • **Enabled**: The Install Updates and Shut Down option will not appear in the Shut Down Windows dialog box. Enable this policy setting if you want to control when updates are installed using other Group Policy settings. • **Disabled**: The Install Updates and Shut Down option will appear in the Shut Down Windows dialog box. • **Not Configured**: Same as Disabled.

(continued)

Table 10-1 (*continued*)

Group Policy Setting	Description
Do not adjust default option to 'Install Updates and Shut Down' in Shut Down Windows dialog box	Determines whether the Install Updates and Shut Down option is allowed to be the default option in the Shut Down Windows dialog box. This setting has no effect if the preceding setting is enabled. • **Enabled**: The user's last shut down choice (Hibernate, Restart, etc.) is the default option in the Shut Down Windows dialog box, regardless of whether the Install Updates and Shut Down option is available. • **Disabled**: The Install Updates and Shut Down option will be the default option in the Shut Down Windows dialog box if updates are available for installation. • **Not Configured**: Same as Disabled.
Enabling Windows Update Power Management to automatically wake up the system to install scheduled updates	Determines if Windows Update will wake systems from hibernation to install scheduled updates. Windows Update will wake machines only if there are updates to be applied. If a system is on battery power when Windows Update wakes it up, Windows Update will not install updates and the system will return to hibernation in 2 minutes. • **Enabled**: Windows Update will wake systems to install scheduled updates. • **Disabled**: Windows Update will not wake systems to install scheduled updates. • **Not Configured**: Same as Disabled.
Configure Automatic Updates	Determines if the computer will receive updates through Windows updating. • **Enabled**: The computer will receive updates through Windows Update. Select one of the following: ○ **2 - Notify for download and notify for install**. When updates are available, an icon appears in the status area with a message that updates are ready to be downloaded. Clicking the icon or message provides the option to select specific updates to download. Selected updates are downloaded in the background. When the download is complete, the icon appears in the status area again, along with a notification message that the updates are ready to be installed. Clicking the icon or message enables you to select which updates to install. ○ **3 - Auto download and notify for install**. Windows downloads updates in the background automatically. When the updates are downloaded, an icon appears in the status area along with a notification message that the updates are ready to be installed. Clicking the icon or message provides the option to select which updates to install. This is the default setting. ○ **4 - Auto download and schedule the install**. The setting enables you to download the updates automatically, as in option 3, and then specify a schedule for installing them. If you select this option, configure the Schedule install day (the options are every day, or any one particular day of the week) and Scheduled install time. The default is to install each day at 3 am. If any of the updates require a restart to complete the installation, Windows will restart the computer automatically. If a user is logged on to the computer when Windows is ready to restart, the user will be notified and given the option to delay the restart. ○ **5 - Allow local admin to choose setting**. The enables the local administrator for the computer to select the setting through the Control Panel, but not to select whether Automatic Updating is on.

(*continued*)

Table 10-1 (*continued*)

GROUP POLICY SETTING	DESCRIPTION
	• **Disabled**: Updates that are available on Windows Update must be downloaded and installed manually. • **Not Configured**: Automatic Updating settings are not affected by Group Policy and can be set at the local level by using the Control Panel.
Specify intranet Microsoft update service location	Specifies an intranet server to host updates. For example, use this setting if you have configured WSUS servers in your domain. Enabling this setting means affected users don't have to go through a firewall to get updates. It also gives you the opportunity to test updates before deploying them. If the Configure Automatic Updates policy is disabled, then this policy has no effect. • **Enabled**: The Windows Update client on the computer will look to the specified server for updates. If you select this option, configure the Set the intranet update service for detecting updates setting with the internal update server. Configure the Set the intranet statistics server with the server responsible for gathering update deployment data. This is often the same server. • **Disabled**: Automatic Updating clients connect directly to Microsoft for updates. • **Not Configured**: Same as Disabled.
Automatic Updates detection frequency	Determines the interval between checking for updates when the Windows Update server is internal. This setting is used in conjunction with the preceding setting, and it has no effect if that setting is not enabled. The interval is determined using the specified number of hours and then subtracting a random amount between 0 and 20% of the specified number of hours. The randomization ensures that the internal server is not overwhelmed with computers looking for updates, and it ensures that if you are using an internal server it is not overwhelmed. • **Enabled**: Windows will check for available updates at the specified interval minus a random amount. If you select this option, configure the Check for updates at the following interval (hours) setting. The default is 22 hours. • **Disabled**: Windows will check for updates at the default interval of 22 hours. • **Not Configured**: Same as Disabled.
Allow non-administrators to receive update notifications	Specifies whether, when logged on, non-administrative users will receive update notifications when they are available. If the Configure Automatic Updates policy is disabled, this policy has no effect. • **Enabled**: Automatic Updates will include non-administrators when determining which user should receive notification.
	• **Disabled**: Automatic Updates will notify only administrators. • **Not Configured**: Same as Disabled.
Allow Automatic Updates immediate installation	Determines whether Automatic Updates immediately installs updates that neither interrupt Windows services nor restart Windows. If the Configure Automatic Updates policy is disabled, this policy has no effect. • **Enabled**: Automatic Updates immediately installs these updates that neither interrupt Windows services nor restart Windows. • **Disabled**: Updates that neither interrupt Windows services nor restart Windows are installed normally. • **Not Configured**: Same as Disabled.

(*continued*)

Table 10-1 (*continued*)

GROUP POLICY SETTING	DESCRIPTION
Turn on recommended updates via Automatic Updates	Determines whether to download both important as well as. recommended updates. • **Enabled**: Automatic Updates will install recommended updates as well as important updates. • **Disabled**: Automatic Updates will install important updates but not recommended updates. • **Not Configured**: Same as Disabled.
No auto-restart for scheduled Automatic Updates installations	Determines whether Automatic Updates will wait for the computer to be restarted by any user who is logged on, instead of causing the computer to restart automatically. This policy applies only when Automatic Updates is configured to perform scheduled installations of updates. If the Configure Automatic Updates policy is disabled, this policy has no effect. • **Enabled**: Automatic Updates will wait for the user to restart the computer. • **Disabled**: Automatic Updates will notify the user that the computer will automatically restart in 5 minutes to complete the installation. • **Not Configured**: Same as Disabled.
Re-prompt for restart with scheduled installations	Determines the amount of time Automatic Updates waits before prompting again with a scheduled restart. This policy applies only when Automatic Updates is configured to perform scheduled installations of updates. If the Configure Automatic Updates policy is disabled, this policy has no effect. • **Enabled**: A scheduled restart will occur the specified number of minutes after the previous prompt for restart was postponed. If you select Enabled, configure the Wait for the following period before prompting again with a schedule restart (minutes) spin box. • **Disabled**: A default interval of 10 minutes is used. • **Not Configured**: Same as Disabled.
Delay Restart for scheduled installations	Determines the amount of time for Automatic Updates to wait before proceeding with a scheduled restart. This policy applies only when Automatic Updates is configured to perform scheduled installations of updates. If the Configure Automatic Updates policy is disabled, this policy has no effect. • **Enabled**: A scheduled restart will occur the specified number of minutes after the installation is finished. If you select this option, configure the Wait for the following period before proceeding with a scheduled restart (minutes) spin box. • **Disabled**: A default interval of 5 minutes is used. • **Not Configured**: Same as Disabled.
Reschedule Automatic Updates scheduled installations	Determines the amount of time for Automatic Updates to wait, following startup, before proceeding with a scheduled installation that was missed. This policy applies only when Automatic Updates is configured to perform scheduled installations of updates. If the Configure Automatic Updates policy is disabled, this policy has no effect. • **Enabled**: A missed scheduled installation will occur the specified number of minutes after the computer is next started. If you select this option, specify the interval in the Wait after system startup (minutes) spin box. • **Disabled**: Missed scheduled installations will occur at the next scheduled installation. • **Not Configured**: A missed scheduled installation will occur 1 minute after the computer is next started.

(*continued*)

Table 10-1 (*continued*)

GROUP POLICY SETTING	DESCRIPTION
Enable client-side targeting	Determines the target group name that should be used to receive updates from an intranet Microsoft update service. This policy applies only when the intranet Microsoft update service this computer is directed to is configured to support client-side targeting. If the Specify intranet Microsoft update service location policy is disabled or not configured, this policy has no effect. • **Enabled**: The specified target group information is sent to the intranet Microsoft update service, which uses it to determine which updates should be deployed to this computer. • **Disabled**: No target group information will be sent to the intranet Microsoft update service. • **Not Configured**: Same as Disabled.

Monitoring Performance and Reliability

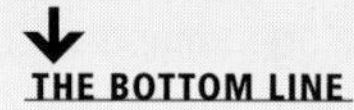

You can use built-in tools such as the Reliability and Performance monitor to analyze the reliability and performance of Windows Vista workstations.

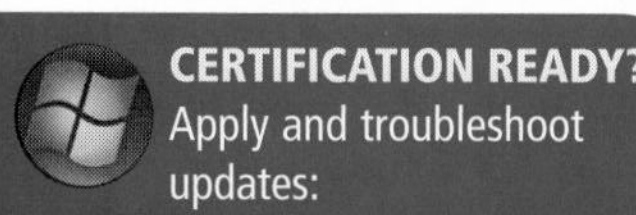

CERTIFICATION READY? Apply and troubleshoot updates:
- Troubleshoot performance and reliability issues
- Establish and monitor performance baselines using built-in tools

3.4

There are many reasons that you might want to monitor the performance of an individual workstation. Some examples are:

- A user complains that the performance of his machine has degraded.
- To test updates in a lab environment before deploying them.
- You want to see if the application of an update affects performance.
- Degraded performance can be an indication of the presence of malware or the failing of hardware.

Windows Vista provides several built-in tools that you can use to monitor performance. These can be accessed in the Advanced Tools control panel.

CERTIFICATION READY? Apply and troubleshoot updates.

3.4

From the Advanced Tools control panel you can perform the following performance-related actions:

- View performance details in Event Log (covered later in this lesson).
- Open Reliability and Performance Monitor (covered later in this lesson).
- Open Task Manager.
- View advanced system details in System Information (covered later in this lesson).
- Adjust the appearance and performance of Windows.
- Open Disk Defragmenter.
- Generate a system health report (covered later in this lesson).

OPEN THE ADVANCED TOOLS CONTROL PANEL

1. Click **Start** and then click **Control Panel**. The Control Panel appears.
2. Click **System and Maintenance.** The System and Maintenance control panel appears.
3. Click **Performance Information and Tools.** The Performance Information and Tools control panel appears.
4. In the left navigation bar, click **Advanced tools.** The Performance Information and Tools>Advanced Tools control panel appears, as shown in Figure 10-5.

Figure 10-5

The Advanced Tools control panel

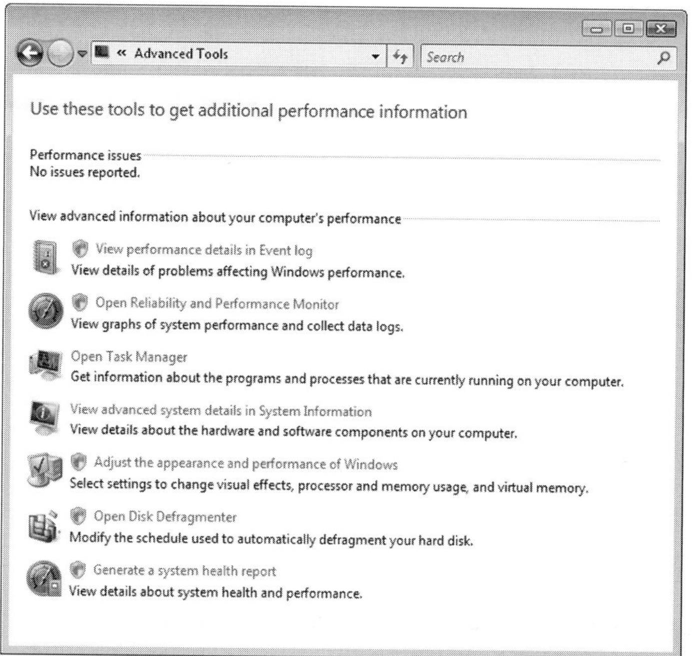

VIEW PERFORMANCE-RELATED EVENTS IN EVENT VIEWER

You can easily access an Event Viewer log on performance-related events using the Advanced Tools control panel. The same log is accessible using Event Viewer directly.

Event Viewer is covered in **Lesson 6: Troubleshooting Security Issues.**

If you are experiencing performance issues, or just want to check to see if there are any problems hindering system performance, browsing performance-related events is a good place to start.

OPEN the Advanced Tools control panel.

1. In the Advanced Tools control panel, click **View performance details in Event log.** A User Account Control dialog box appears.
2. Provide administrator credentials and then click **OK.** After a moment, Event Viewer appears with the Applications and Services Logs>Microsoft>Windows>Diagnostics-Performance>Operational log open. You can browse performance-related events in the details pane, as shown in Figure 10-6.

Figure 10-6

The Event Viewer console opened to the Diagnostics-Performance Operation log

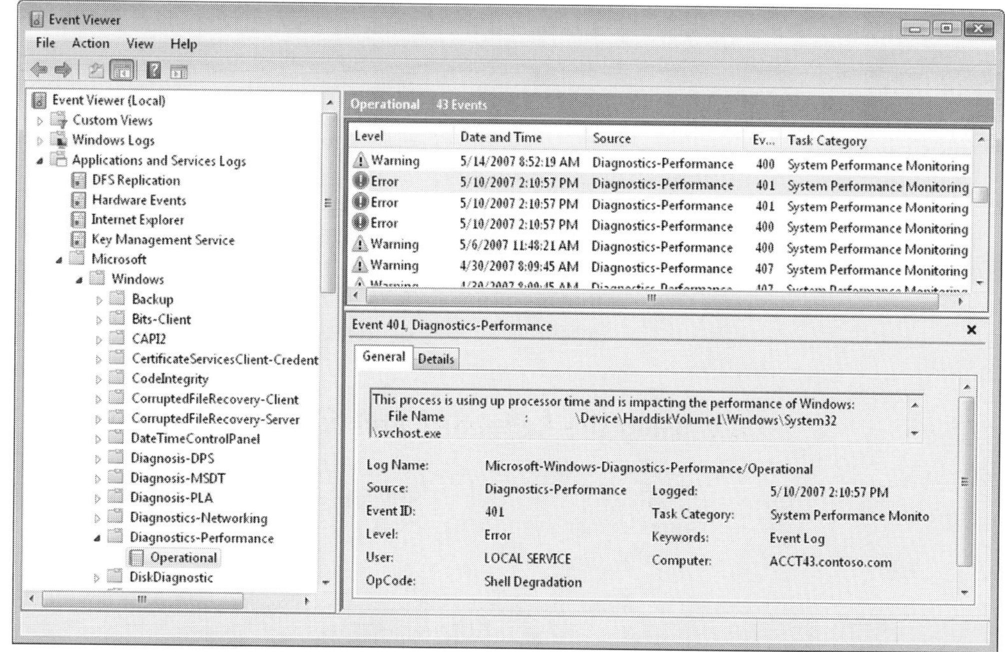

VIEW SYSTEM INFORMATION IN THE SYSTEM INFORMATION TOOL

Did you ever want a list of all the hardware, devices, and software on a system along with important information about each? The ***System Information tool*** provides oodles of information on a system, including details on hardware resources, hardware components (from optical drives to ports and input devices), and the software environment (e.g., drivers, print jobs, and running services).

For performance-related issues, you can, for example, use the System Information tool to find out how much RAM a computer has, what clock rate the processor runs at, and the capacity of its hard drives.

OPEN the Advanced Tools control panel.

1. Click **View advanced system details in System Information**. The System Information tool appears.
2. Expand the details pane as desired to view various hardware resources, hardware components, or software information. For example, to view hard disks and their capacities, expand **Components>Storage** and then select **Disks**. You can then view the disks in the details pane, as shown in the example in Figure 10-7.

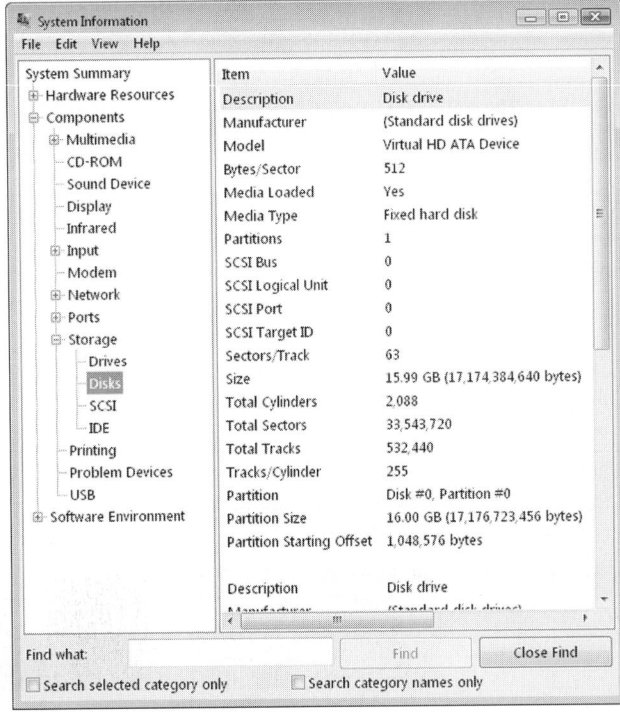

Figure 10-7

Information for a hard disk viewed using the System Information tool

3. To do a keyword search, type the word in the **Find what** text box and then click **Find**. You can select the Search selected category only check box to search only items within the category selected in the console tree. You can select Search category names only to search not for items, but for categories (which can contain categories or items).

Using the Reliability and Performance Monitor

The Reliability and Performance Monitor enables you to monitor and analyze system performance and reliability.

The ***Windows Reliability and Performance Monitor*** enables you to monitor and analyze system performance and reliability.

The monitor is useful in a number of circumstances. The most obvious is to analyze the performance of a computer simply to see why it is performing how it is performing. You can find out if its performance is bound by lack of RAM or processor speed, or you can see what applications are taking the most resources.

Another reason to use the monitor is to test updates before you deploy them to enterprise workstations. This way you can assess any negative or positive effects that updates might have on performance or reliability before deploying them. This enables you to weigh performance costs or benefits against whatever advantage installing the update might have.

The monitor is a combination and expansion of the following tools, available in previous versions of Windows:

- Performance Logs and Alerts (PLA)
- Server Performance Advisor (SPA)
- System Monitor

OPEN THE WINDOWS RELIABILITY AND PERFORMANCE MONITOR

1. Click **Start**. In the **Start Search** text box, type **perfmon.msc** and then press **Ctrl + Shift + Enter**. A User Account Control dialog box appears.
2. Provide administrator credentials and then click **OK**. The Reliability and Performance Monitor appears.
3. The Reliability and Performance Monitor appears with the root selected in the console tree and displays a use summary of four system resources: CPU, Disk, Network, and Memory usage. Clicking the small arrows on the right expands each corresponding section to reveal more details. For example, in Figure 10-8, the Memory section has been expanded, and a list of processes and their memory use is exposed. Clicking the graphs at the top has the same effect as clicking the arrows; if you click the CPU graph, the CPU section is expanded, and if you click it again, the section is contracted.

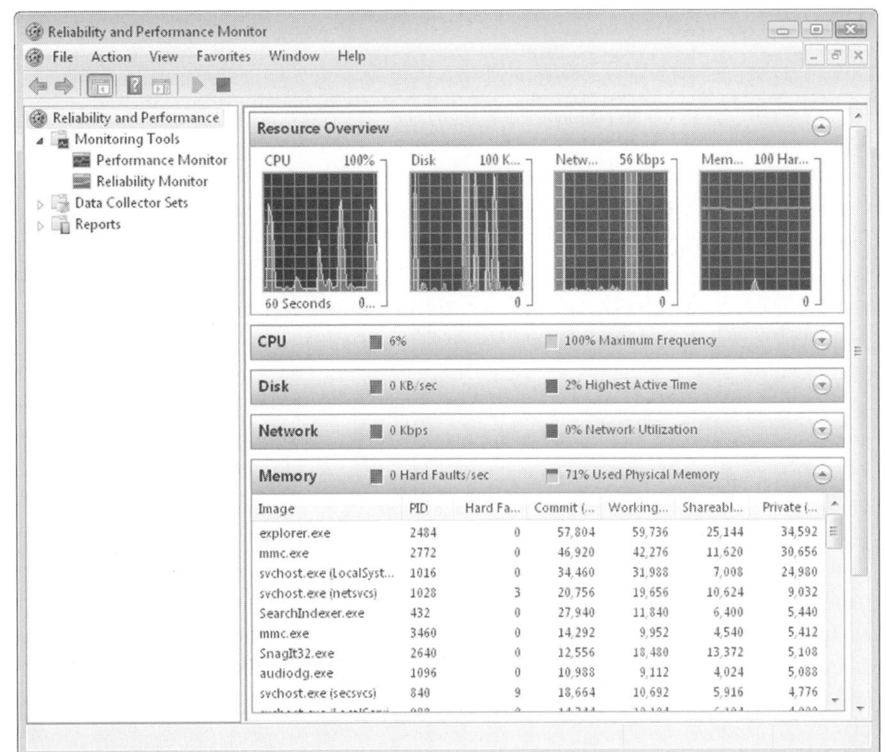

Figure 10-8

The Reliability and Performance Monitor with the root selected in the console tree

CONNECT TO ANOTHER COMPUTER WITH THE RELIABILITY AND PERFORMANCE MONITOR

You can use the Reliability and Performance Monitor to monitor remote computers as well as the local computer.

OPEN the Reliability and Performance Monitor.

1. In the Reliability and Performance Monitor, select **Reliability and Performance** in the console tree.
2. In the **Action** menu, click **Connect to another computer**. The Select Computer dialog box appears.
3. In the Remote computer text box, enter the computer name to which you want to connect, for example, \\Acct42. You can also click **Browse** to browse for a computer.
4. Click **OK**.

Using Performance Monitor

The Performance Monitor is a component of the Reliability and Performance Monitor that enables you to analyze system performance.

The ***Performance Monitor*** in the Reliability and Performance Monitor console enables you to view various historical or real-time data of performance counters. ***Performance counters*** are measurements of system state or activity, for example, CPU utilization as a percentage.

When you first select the Performance Monitor in the Reliability and Performance Monitor console tree, it displays a line graph showing a 1-minute and 40-second range of a processor performance counter. If you hover the mouse over the line in the line graph, a pop-up will tell you what the underlying performance counter is. An example is shown in Figure 10-9.

Figure 10-9

The Performance Monitor graphing CPU utilization

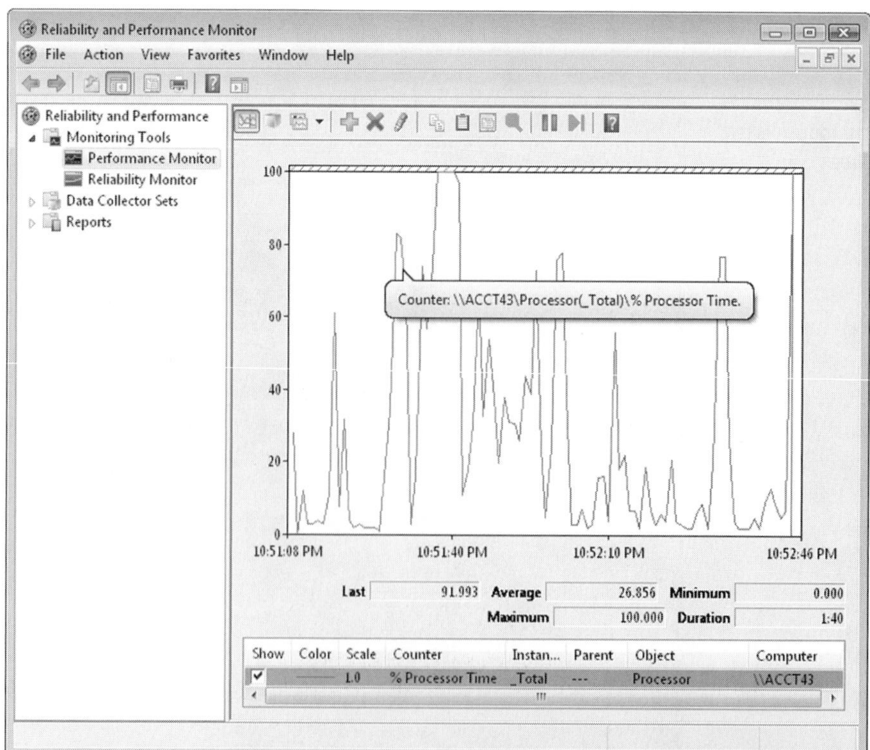

The example in Figure 10-9 shows a graph of one performance counter, but you can configure Performance monitor to graph as many performance counters as you like.

It is often useful to view more than a single counter at the same time. For example, you may want to see if an application is bound in performance by memory or CPU resources. You can also add counters from different computers and view them from Performance Monitor. For example, you could simultaneously look at the CPU utilization of all the file servers on your network.

This procedure and the next few break with the normal format of this text book and lead you through examples. In the first example, you will:

- Add the *% Processor Time* performance counter from a remote computer (your domain server).
- Add the *% Committed Bytes In Use* performance counter for your local computer.
- Add all performance counters in the physical disk category.

ADD PERFORMANCES COUNTERS

OPEN the Reliability and Performance Monitor.

1. In the Reliability and Performance Monitor, in the console tree, expand **Monitoring Tools** and then select **Performance Monitor**.
2. In the details pane, click the green plus sign in the menu bar at the top, or press **Ctrl + I**. The Add Counters dialog box appears.
3. In the **Select counters from computer** combo box, type ***DomainControllerUNCPath***. In the example, the UNC path of the domain controller is //Server01.
4. In the list box of performance counters, expand **Processor** and then select **% Processor Time**.
5. Click **Add**. The *% Processor Time* is added to the Added counters list box. Click **OK**.
6. In Reliability and Performance Monitor, press **Ctrl + I** to add more counters. The Add Counters dialog box appears.
7. In the list box of performance counters, expand **Memory** and then select **% Committed Bytes In Use**.
8. Click **Add**. The *% Committed Bytes In Use* performance counter is added to the Added counters list box.
9. In the list box of performance counters, select the **Physical Disk** category (do not expand it) and in the **Instances of selected object** list box, select **<All instances>**. Then click **Add**. This action adds all the performance counters in the Physical Disk category. This is represented in the Added counters list box by an asterisk in the counter column. Your Add Counters dialog box should look like the example in Figure 10-10.

Figure 10-10

The Add Counters dialog box with counters added

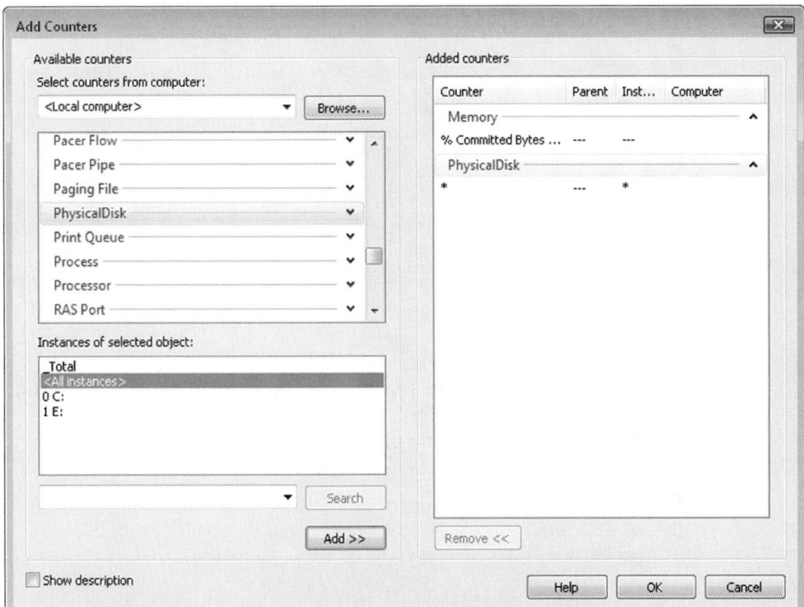

10. Click **OK**.

Suppose that after adding the entire category of Physical Disk performance counters, you decide that you want to remove the following:

- Avg. Disk Read Queue Length
- Avg. Disk Write Queue Length
- Split IO/Sec

REMOVE PERFORMANCE COUNTERS

CONTINUE from the previous procedure.

1. In the Reliability and Performance Monitor, in the details pane, press the **Ctrl** key and click the following performance counters in the performance counters list box to select each of them:
   a. Avg. Disk Read Queue Length
   b. Avg. Disk Write Queue Length
   c. Split IO/Sec
2. Click the red X in the menu bar at the top of the details pane, or press **Delete**.

Even with the removed counters, the Performance Monitor line graph is still quite crowded with lines and therefore nearly incomprehensible, as shown in Figure 10-11.

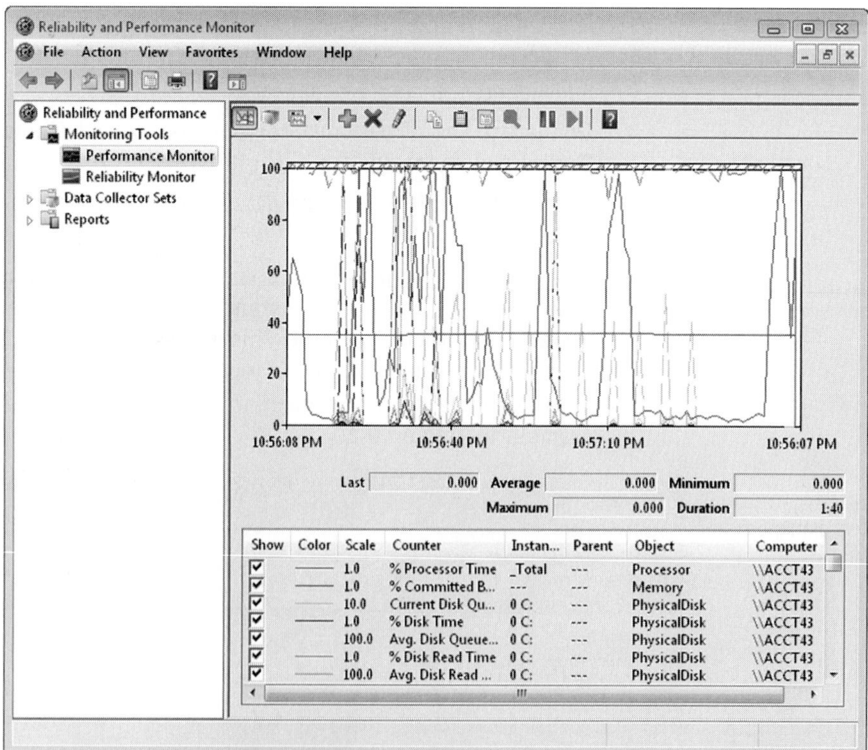

Figure 10-11

Graphing many performance counters simultaneously. The graph becomes incomprehensible, which can be remedied by hiding performance counters or by highlighting the one you want to study.

There are a number of ways to modify display settings so that you can see the data that you want to see more clearly. The most obvious way is to limit which performance counters are represented in the graph.

SHOW OR HIDE PERFORMANCE COUNTERS

CONTINUE from the previous procedure.

1. In the Reliability and Performance Monitor, in the details pane, in the list box of performance counters, clear the **Current Disk Queue Length** check box.
2. Click **Avg. Disk Queue Length** to select it and then press and hold the **Shift** key. Scroll to the last performance counter and click it to select all performance counters between the **Avg. Disk Queue length** and the last performance counter.
3. Right-click any selected performance counters and then click **Hide-Selected Counters**.

HIGHLIGHT A PERFORMANCE COUNTER

If you want to make one counter standout in the graph, you can highlight it.

CONTINUE from the previous procedure.

1. In the Reliability and Performance Monitor, in the details pane, in the list box of performance counters, select the **Avg. Disk Bytes/Transfer** performance counter and then click the highlighter icon in the menu bar at the top of the details pane, as shown in Figure 10-12.

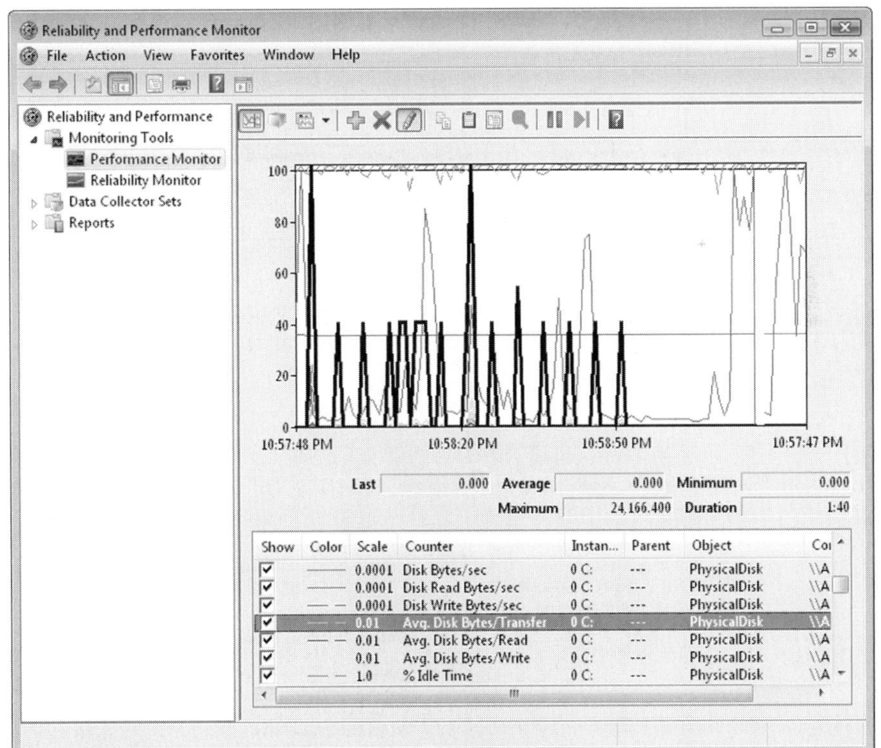

Figure 10-12

Highlighting a performance counter in the Performance Monitor

FREEZE THE DISPLAY

You can freeze the display if you want to study it without having it change.

CONTINUE from the previous procedure.

1. In the Reliability and Performance Monitor, in the details pane, click the pause button (it has a standard pause icon on it). To unfreeze the display, press the play button (it replaces the pause button).

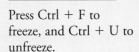

> **ANOTHER WAY**
>
> Press Ctrl + F to freeze, and Ctrl + U to unfreeze.

You can also change the type of graph that Performance Monitor displays to one of three types:

- **Line**. Shows a line graph of performance counters as they vary over the specified duration. An example is shown in Figure 10-12. Line graphs are useful for seeing performance change over time.

- **Histogram Bar**. Represents the real-time value of performance counters in a vertical bar. Histogram bars are useful for visualizing performance at a point in time. An example is shown in Figure 10-13.

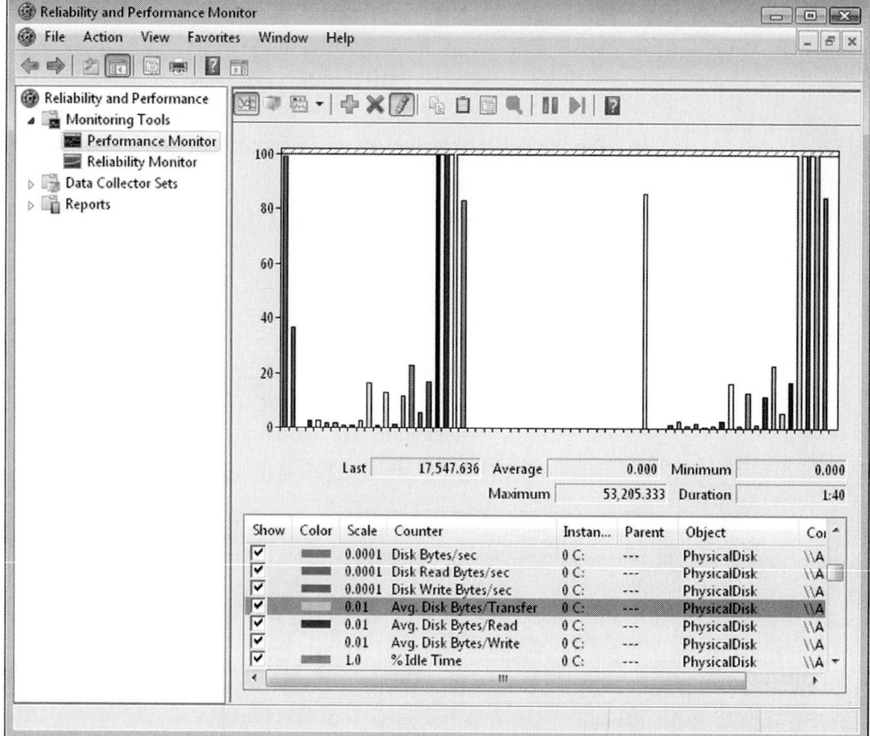

Figure 10-13

Performance Monitor displaying histogram bars

- **Report**. Displays text showing the real-time values of the performance counters. Reports are useful if you want to see actual numbers instead of graphs. An example is shown in Figure 10-14.

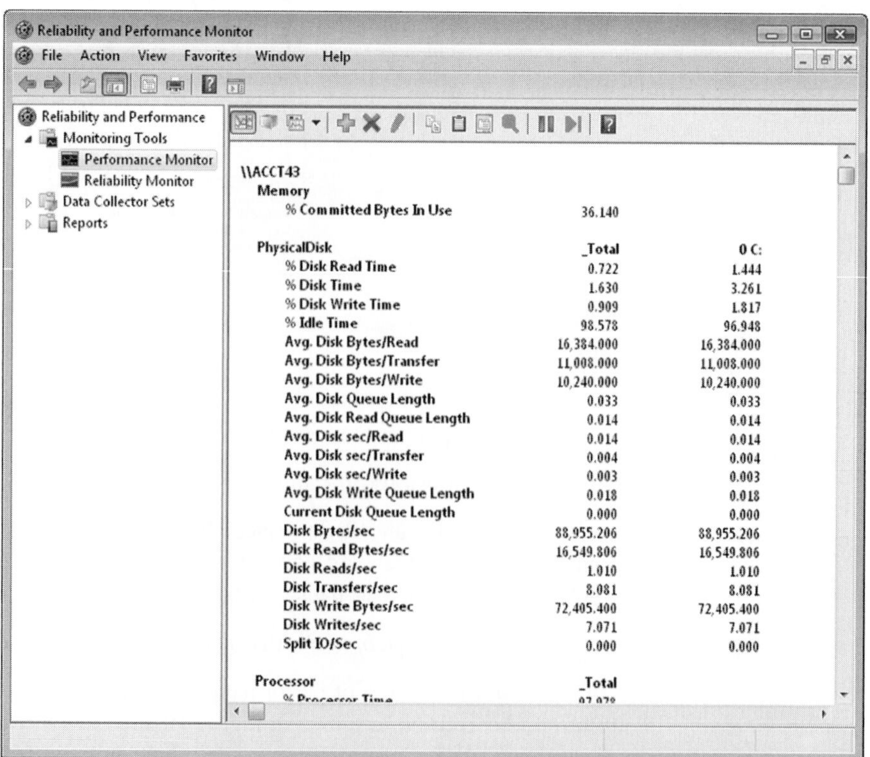

Figure 10-14

Performance Monitor displaying a text report

CHANGE GRAPH TYPE

CONTINUE from the previous procedure.

1. In the Reliability and Performance Monitor, in the details pane menu bar, click the arrow next to the Change graph type icon (see Figure 10-15) and select one of the following:
   - Line
   - Histogram bar
   - Report

Figure 10-15

The Change graph type button

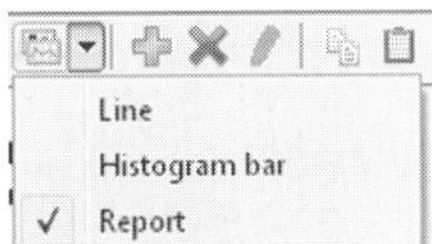

The Performance Monitor Properties dialog box contains many settings that you can modify. The following procedure shows how to access the settings, and Table 10-2 describes what some of the settings do (the most obvious settings are not covered in the table).

CONFIGURE PERFORMANCE MONITOR PROPERTIES

ANOTHER WAY

Press Ctrl + G to toggle through the three graph types.

OPEN the Reliability and Performance Monitor and select Performance Monitor in the console tree.

1. In the Reliability and Performance Monitor, in the **Action** menu, click **Properties.** The Performance Monitor Properties dialog box appears.
2. Configure the properties as desired, according to the explanations in Table 10-2.

Table 10-2

Settings in the Performance Properties dialog box

Tab in the Performance Monitor Properties Dialog Box	User Interface Interface Elements	Description
General		This tab contains five options. The options determine what the Histogram tab and Report display types display. • **Default**. The default value for the performance counter is displayed. For example, if the performance counter is an average, then that average is displayed. • **Current**: The current value of the performance counter is displayed. • **Minimum**: The minimum value of the computer over the given duration is displayed. • **Maximum**: The maximum value of the computer over the given duration is displayed. • **Average**: The average (mean) of the computer over the given duration is displayed.

(continued)

Table 10-2 ***(continued)***

TAB IN THE PERFORMANCE MONITOR PROPERTIES DIALOG BOX	USER INTERFACE INTERFACE ELEMENTS	DESCRIPTION
General	Sample automatically> Sample every text box	This text box enables you to specify the sample frequency in seconds. The sample frequency is how often Performance Monitor gets the current value of a computer.
General	Sample automatically> Duration text box	This text box enables you to specify the duration, which is used, for example, to calculate averages or as a range for determining the minimum or maximum value of a computer.
Source	All	The Source tab enables you to specify log files or a database as a source for data rather than using the current activity as data. Once you select log files or database, you can specify a time range by using the Time Range button.
Data	All	The Data tab enables you to add or remove counters by using Add and Remove. You can also change the appearance of the graph.
Graph	All	On the Graph tab you can change the view type (Line, Histogram bar, or Report). You can also adjust graphing parameters such as scale.
Appearance	All	The Appearance tab contains more controls over the graph appearance, such as background color and font.

Using the Reliability Monitor

The Reliability Monitor is a component of the Reliability and Performance Monitor that enables you to analyze system reliability.

The ***Reliability Monitor*** gives you a current snapshot and a historical analysis of system reliability. It bases its analysis on data gathered in the event log by the Windows Diagnostic Infrastructure (WDI), which is covered later in this lesson.

USE THE RELIABILITY MONITOR

OPEN the Reliability and Performance Monitor.

1. In the Reliability and Performance Monitor, in the console tree, expand **Monitoring Tools** and then select **Reliability Monitor.** The Reliability Monitor appears in the details pane, as shown in Figure 10-16.

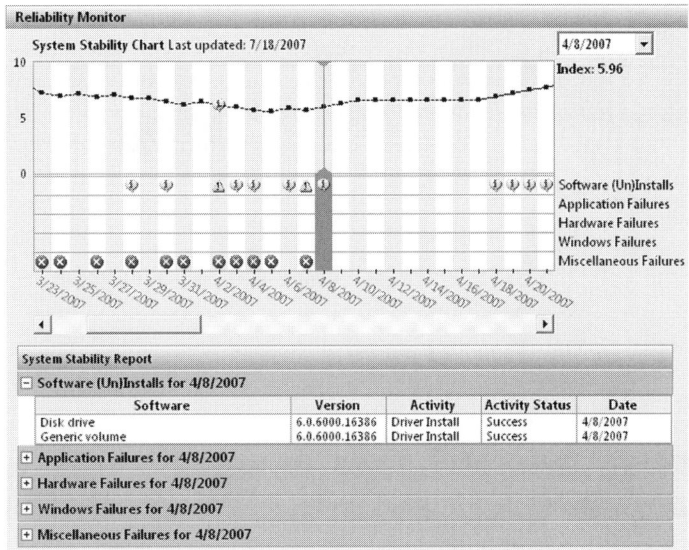

Figure 10-16

Reliability Monitor displaying a text report

The following describes each element in the diagram in Figure 10-16.

1. Reliability Monitor creates a line graph of a system' stability rating over time.
2. The system stability rating is graphed on the vertical axis and ranges from 0 (very unstable) to 10 (very stable).
3. Below the graph of system stability over time are stability-related event indicators. They come in three types:
   - **Red circle with white x.** This represents an error event. For example, a Disruptive Shutdown event (the computer was not shut down properly).
   - **Yellow triangle with black exclamation mark.** This represents a warning event. For example, a failed software installation.
   - **White balloon text icon with small i.** This represents an information-only event. For example, a successful driver installation.

If a system becomes unstable, the Reliability Monitor can be an excellent diagnostic tool. You can use it to pinpoint the day the problem started and then look at any suspicious events listed in the System Stability Report in Event Viewer. You may find, for example, that a hardware driver was updated that day, or that a new application was installed. The Reliability Monitor can be an excellent tool to use before deploying updates that you suspect might compromise system stability.

1. The type of stability-related event is indicated by which horizontal row it appears in. There are five rows:
   - Software (Un)Installs
   - Application Failures
   - Hardware Failures
   - Windows Failures
   - Miscellaneous Failures
2. Time is measured across the horizontal access in increments of a day. You can click in the area above a day to select that day, which will move the selected day indicator (number 6). When you select a day, the corresponding events are revealed in the System Stability Report section (number 8).
3. The selected day indicator moves to any date you click in the area above the dates on the horizontal axis.
4. You can also select a day in the date drop-down list.

5. Stability-related events can be viewed in the System Stability Report section. When you select a day, the stability-related events for that day are revealed. You can also select a day and manually expand or contract event types by using the + and − buttons to the left of the event type names. Stability-related events are divided into five sections (what these sections contain is evident from their titles):

   - Software (Un)Installs
   - Application Failures
   - Hardware Failures
   - Windows Failures
   - Miscellaneous Failures

■ Understanding Windows Diagnostic Infrastructure

THE BOTTOM LINE

The Windows Diagnostic Infrastructure is a wide-ranging set of built-in monitoring tools, diagnostic logic, and solutions that help users and administrators resolve computer problems.

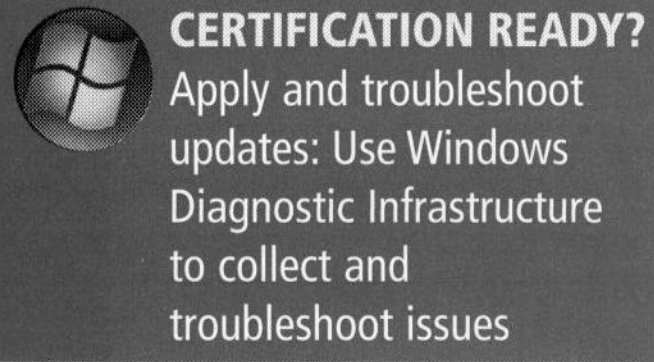

CERTIFICATION READY?
Apply and troubleshoot updates: Use Windows Diagnostic Infrastructure to collect and troubleshoot issues
3.4

The ***Windows Diagnostic Infrastructure (WDI)*** is a set of built-in monitoring tools, diagnostic logic, and solutions that help users and administrators to diagnosis and resolve computer problems. Various components of WDI provide logging, which can be viewed in Event Viewer and used for troubleshooting. One such troubleshooting application is testing updates in a lab environment before they are deployed to workstations.

WDI covers many areas, all of which can be controlled centrally using Group Policy. Some of the components of WDI are:

- **Application Compatibility Diagnostics**. These diagnostics can help to solve application compatibility issues. For example, application compatibility diagnostics will detect if a program attempts to load a deprecated dynamic link library (.dll) file.
- **Disk Diagnostics**. Keeps an eye on disk performance and reliability.
- **Windows Boot Performance Diagnostics**. Just about every Windows user has experienced a computer that takes a very long time to boot. This WDI component can often diagnose why.
- **Windows Resource Exhaustion Detection and Resolution**. This WDI component can help to tell you where performance bottlenecks are occurring on a computer. What is slowing you down? Is it lack of memory? Processor speed? Disk access?
- **Network diagnostics and troubleshooting**. Probably destined to be the most used component of WDI, at least by home users. This can help you to determine why a network connection is failing.

Users are most often exposed to WDI through dialog boxes that appear when a problem or solution has been encountered. The user is given options to solve the problem if there is a ready solution, and often is also pointed to the relevant portion of online help. You can limit WDI from giving users advice on how to solve problems, restricting it to simply diagnosing and logging. You can then review the results in Event Viewer or the Performance and Reliability Console.

Configure WDI Through Group Policy

You can manage WDI centrally by using Group Policy.

Table 10-3 covers WDI-related group policy settings. Each setting is located in the Computer Configuration>Administrative Templates>System>Troubleshooting and Diagnostics folder and subfolders of Group Policy objects.

Table 10-3

Windows Diagnostic Infrastructure Group Policy settings

GROUP POLICY SETTING	DESCRIPTION
Diagnostics: Configure scenario retention	Determines the data retention limit for Diagnostic Policy Service (DPS) scenario data. This setting of policy will take effect only when the Diagnostic Policy Service is in the running state. When the service is stopped or disabled, diagnostic scenario data will not be deleted. • **Enabled**: Enables you to specify the maximum size of the Diagnostic Policy Service scenario data. If you select this option, configure the Scenario data size limit (in MB) spin box. • **Disabled**: A default value of 128 MB is used. • **Not Configured**: Same as Disabled.
Diagnostics: Configure scenario execution level	Determines the execution level for DPS scenarios. The execution level determines if users are provided with resolutions when WDI diagnoses a problem. This policy setting takes precedence over any scenario-specific policy settings when it is enabled or disabled. Scenario-specific settings take effect only if this policy is not configured. This policy setting will take effect only when the Diagnostic Policy Service is in the running state. • **Enabled**: If you enable this policy setting, select one of the following in the Scenario Execution Level: ○ **Detection and Troubleshooting only**. The DPS will detect problems and attempt to determine their root causes. These root causes will be logged to the event log when detected, but no corrective action will be taken. ○ **Detection, Troubleshooting and Resolution**. The DPS will attempt to automatically fix problems it detects or indicate to the user that assisted resolution is available. • **Disabled**: Windows will not be able to detect, troubleshoot, or resolve any problems that are handled by the DPS. • **Not Configured**: DPS will enable all scenarios for resolution by default, unless you configure separate scenario-specific policy settings.
Application Compatibility Diagnostics> Notify blocked drivers	Determines whether the Program Compatibility Assistant (PCA) will diagnose drivers blocked due to compatibility issues. Disabling the Turn off Program Compatibility Assistant policy setting will cause this policy setting to have no effect. The DPS and Program Compatibility Assistant Service must be running for the PCA to execute. • **Enabled**: the PCA will notify the user of blocked driver issues with an option to check the Microsoft website for solutions. • **Disabled**: PCA will not notify the user of blocked driver issues and will present solutions to blocked driver issues. • **Not Configured**: Same as Enabled.

(continued)

Table 10-3 (*continued*)

Group Policy Setting	Description
Application Compatibility Diagnostics> Detect application failures caused by deprecated Windows DLLs or COM objects	Determines whether the PCA will diagnose DLL load or COM object creation failures in programs. Disabling the Turn off Program Compatibility Assistant policy setting will cause this policy setting to have no effect. The DPS and Program Compatibility Assistant Service must be running for the PCA to execute. • **Enabled**: The PCA detects programs trying to load legacy Microsoft Windows DLLs or creating legacy COM objects that are not part of Windows Vista. When this failure is detected, after the program is terminated, PCA will notify the user about this problem and provide an option to check the Microsoft website for solutions. • **Disabled**: The PCA does not detect programs trying to load legacy Windows DLLs or creating legacy COM objects. • **Not Configured**: Same as Enabled.
Application Compatibility Diagnostics> Detect application install failures	Determines whether the PCA diagnoses failures with application installations. Disabling the Turn off Program Compatibility Assistant policy setting will cause this policy setting to have no effect. The DPS and Program Compatibility Assistant Service must be running for the PCA to execute. • **Enabled**: The PCA is configured to detect failures in the execution of application installers through heuristics. When potential failures are detected, the PCA will provide the user with an option to restart the installer with Microsoft Windows XP compatibility mode. • **Disabled**: The PCA is not configured to detect failures in execution of program installers. • **Not Configured**: Same as Enabled.
Application Compatibility Diagnostics> Detect application installers that need to be run as administrator	Determines whether the PCA will diagnose failures with application installers that are not detected to run as administrator. Disabling the Turn off Program Compatibility Assistant policy setting will cause this policy setting to have no effect. The DPS and Program Compatibility Assistant Service must be running for the PCA to execute. • **Enabled**: The PCA will detect application installers that do not have privileges to run as administrator and are therefore prohbited by User Access Control (UAC) from running. When potential failures are detected, the PCA will provide the user with an option to restart the installer as administrator. • **Disabled**: The PCA will not detect application installers that do not have privileges to run as administrator and are therefore prohibited by UAC from running. • **Not Configured**: Same as Enabled.
Application Compatibility Diagnostics> Detect applications unable to launch installers under UAC	Determines whether the PCA diagnoses failures with programs under User Account Control (UAC). Disabling the Turn off Program Compatibility Assistant policy setting will cause this policy setting to have no effect. The DPS and Program Compatibility Assistant Service must be running for the PCA to execute. • **Enabled**: The PCA detects programs that failed to launch child processes that are installers (typically updaters). When this failure is detected, the PCA will apply the ELEVATECREATEPROCESS compatibility mode, which enables the program to successfully launch the installer with administrator privileges the next time the program is run. • **Disabled**: The PCA will not detect applications that fail to launch installers run under UAC. • **Not Configured**: Same as Enabled.

(continued)

Table 10-3 (*continued*)

GROUP POLICY SETTING	DESCRIPTION
Corrupted File Recovery>Configure Corrupted File Recovery Behavior	Enables you to configure the recovery behavior for corrupted files. • **Enabled**: If you select enabled, then select one of the following: ○ **Troubleshooting only**. Detection and troubleshooting of corrupted files will automatically start without gaining user consent. Recovery is not attempted automatically. Windows will log an administrator event with instructions if manual recovery is possible. ○ **Regular**. Detection, troubleshooting, and recovery of corrupted files will automatically start with minimal information conveyed to the user. Windows will attempt to present a dialog box when a system restart is required. This is the default recovery behavior for corrupted files. ○ **Silent**. Detection, troubleshooting, and recovery of corrupted files will automatically start with no notification to the user. Windows will log an administrator event when a system restart is required. • **Disabled**: The recovery behavior for corrupted files will be disabled. No troubleshooting or resolution will be attempted. • **Not Configured**: Same as enabled with Regular selected.
Disk Diagnostics>Disk Diagnostic: Configure execution Level	Determines the execution level for SMART-based disk diagnostics. This policy setting will take effect only when the Diagnostic Policy Service is in the running state. When the service is stopped or disabled, diagnostic scenarios will not be executed. This policy setting takes effect only if the diagnostics-wide scenario execution policy is not configured. • **Enabled**: If you select enabled, then users will we be warned when SMART reports a fault, and Windows will take corrective action. SMART stands for self-monitoring and reporting technology and is a standard method that storage devices use to report faults to Windows. The DPS will detect and log SMART faults to the event log when they occur. • **Disabled**: SMART faults will still be detected and logged, but no corrective action will be taken. • **Not Configured**: Same as Enabled.
Disk Diagnostics>Disk Diagnostic: Configure custom alert text	Enables you to specify custom alert text in the disk diagnostic message shown to users when a disk reports a SMART fault. This policy setting will take effect only when the Diagnostic Policy Service is in the running state. When the service is stopped or disabled, diagnostic scenarios will not be executed. • **Enabled**: Windows will display custom alert text in the disk diagnostic message. If you select enabled, provide the text for the alert message in the Custom alert text text box. • **Disabled**: Windows will display the default alert text in the disk diagnostic message. • **Not Configured**: Same as Disabled.
Microsoft Support Diagnostic Tool> Microsoft Support Diagnostic Tool: Restrict tool download	Restricts the tool download policy for Microsoft Support Diagnostic Tool. The Microsoft Support Diagnostic Tool (MSDT) gathers diagnostic data for analysis by administrators. For some problems, MSDT may prompt the user to download additional tools for troubleshooting. These tools are required to completely troubleshoot some problems. This policy setting will take effect only when the DPS is in the running state. When the service is stopped or disabled, diagnostic scenarios will not be executed. This policy setting will take effect only when MSDT is enabled.

(*continued*)

Table 10-3 (*continued*)

Group Policy Setting	Description
	• **Enabled**: MSDT will prompt the user to download additional tools to diagnose problems on remote computers only. If the setting is enabled for local and remote troubleshooting, MSDT will always prompt for additional tool download. • **Disabled**: MSDT will never download tools and will be unable to diagnose problems on remote computers. • **Not configured**: MSDT will prompt the user before downloading any additional tools.
Microsoft Support Diagnostic Tool: Configure execution Level	Determines the execution level for Microsoft Support Diagnostic Tool. The MSDT gathers diagnostic data for analysis by administrators. This policy setting will take effect only when the DPS is in the running state. When the service is stopped or disabled, diagnostic scenarios will not be executed. This policy setting takes effect only if the diagnostics-wide scenario execution policy is not configured. • **Enabled**: Administrators will be able to use MSDT to collect and send diagnostic data to a support professional to resolve a problem. • **Disabled**: MSDT will not be enabled to gather diagnostic data. • **Not Configured**: Same as Enabled.

Windows Boot Performance Diagnostics>Configure Scenario Execution Level	Determines the execution level for Windows Boot Performance Diagnostics. This policy setting will take effect only when the Diagnostic Policy Service is in the running state. When the service is stopped or disabled, diagnostic scenarios will not be executed. This policy setting takes effect only if the diagnostics-wide scenario execution policy is not configured.
	• **Enabled**: If you enable this setting, then select one of the following:
	  ○ **Detection and Troubleshooting Only**: The DPS will detect Windows Boot Performance problems and attempt to determine their root causes. These root causes will be logged to the event log when detected, but no corrective action will be taken.
	  ○ **Detection, Troubleshooting and Resolution**: The DPS will detect Windows Boot Performance problems and indicate to the user that assisted resolution is available.
	• **Disabled**: Windows will not be able to detect, troubleshoot, or resolve any Windows Boot Performance problems that are handled by the DPS.
	• **Not Configured**: Same as Enabled with Detection, Troubleshooting and Resolution selected.

Windows Memory Leak Diagnosis> Configure Scenario Execution Level	This policy setting determines whether DPS will diagnose memory leak problems. This policy setting will take effect only when the Diagnostic Policy Service is in the running state. When the service is stopped or disabled, diagnostic scenarios will not be executed. This policy setting takes effect only if the diagnostics-wide scenario execution policy is not configured. • **Enabled**: The DPS sill diagnoses memory leak problems. • **Disabled**: The DPS will not diagnose memory leak problems. • **Not Configured**: Same as Enabled.

(*continued*)

Table 10-3 (*continued*)

<table>
<tr><th>Group Policy Setting</th><th>Description</th></tr>
<tr><td>Windows Resource Exhaustion Detection and Resolution>Configure Scenario Execution Level</td><td>Determines the execution level for Windows Resource Exhaustion Detection and Resolution. This policy setting will take effect only when the Diagnostic Policy Service is in the running state. When the service is stopped or disabled, diagnostic scenarios will not be executed. This policy setting takes effect only if the diagnostics-wide scenario execution policy is not configured.
• Enabled: If you enable this setting, then select one of the following in the Scenario Execution Level drop-down list:
❍ Detection and Troubleshooting only. The DPS will detect Windows Resource Exhaustion problems and attempt to determine their root causes. These root causes will be logged to the event log when detected, but no corrective action will be taken.
❍ Detection, Troubleshooting and Resolution. The DPS will detect Windows Resource Exhaustion problems and indicate to the user that assisted resolution is available.
• Disabled: Windows will not detect, troubleshoot, or resolve any Windows Resource Exhaustion problems that are handled by the DPS.
• Not Configured: Same as Enabled with Detection, Troubleshooting and Resolution selected.</td></tr>
<tr><td>Windows Shutdown Performance Diagnostics>Configure Scenario Execution Level</td><td>Determines the execution level for Windows Shutdown Performance Diagnostics. This policy setting will take effect only when the Diagnostic Policy Service is in the running state. When the service is stopped or disabled, diagnostic scenarios will not be executed. This policy setting takes effect only if the diagnostics-wide scenario execution policy is not configured.
• Enabled: If you enable this setting, then select one of the following in the Scenario Execution Level drop-down list:
❍ Detection and Troubleshooting only. The DPS will detect Windows Shutdown Performance problems and attempt to determine their root causes. These root causes will be logged to the event log when detected, but no corrective action will be taken.
❍ Detection, Troubleshooting and Resolution. The DPS will detect Windows Shutdown Performance problems and indicate to the user that assisted resolution is available.
• Disabled: Windows will not detect, troubleshoot, or resolve any Windows Shutdown Performance problems that are handled by the DPS.
• Not Configured: Same as Enabled with Detection, Troubleshooting and Resolution selected.</td></tr>
<tr><td>Windows Standby/Resume Performance Diagnostics>Configure Scenario Execution Level</td><td>Determines the execution level for Windows Standby/Resume Performance Diagnostics. This policy setting will take effect only when the Diagnostic Policy Service is in the running state. When the service is stopped or disabled, diagnostic scenarios will not be executed. This policy setting takes effect only if the diagnostics-wide scenario execution policy is not configured.
• Enabled: If you enable this setting, then select one of the following in the Scenario Execution Level drop-down list:
❍ Detection and Troubleshooting only. The DPS will detect Windows Standby/Resume Performance problems and attempt to determine their root causes. These root causes will be logged to the event log when detected, but no corrective action will be taken.</td></tr>
</table>

(*continued*)

Table 10-3 ***(continued)***

Group Policy Setting	Description
	○ **Detection, Troubleshooting and Resolution**. The DPS will detect Windows Standby/Resume Performance problems and indicate to the user that assisted resolution is available. • **Disabled**: Windows will not detect, troubleshoot, or resolve any Windows Standby/Resume Performance problems that are handled by the DPS. • **Not Configured**: Same as Enabled with Detection, Troubleshooting and Resolution selected.
Windows System Responsiveness Performance Diagnostics>Configure Scenario Execution Level	Determines the execution level for Windows System Responsiveness Diagnostics. This policy setting will only take effect when the Diagnostic Policy Service is in the running state. When the service is stopped or disabled, diagnostic scenarios will not be executed. This policy setting takes effect only if the diagnostics-wide scenario execution policy is not configured. • **Enabled**: If you enable this setting, then select one of the following in the Scenario Execution Level drop-down list: ○ **Detection and Troubleshooting only**. The DPS will detect Windows System Responsiveness problems and attempt to determine their root causes. These root causes will be logged to the event log when detected, but no corrective action will be taken. ○ **Detection, Troubleshooting and Resolution**. The DPS will detect Windows System Responsiveness problems and indicate to the user that assisted resolution is available. • **Disabled**: Windows will not detect, troubleshoot, or resolve any Windows System Responsiveness problems that are handled by the DPS. • **Not Configured**: Same as Enabled with Detection, Troubleshooting and Resolution selected.

SUMMARY SKILL MATRIX

In this lesson you learned:
Automatic Updating automates the process of downloading—either from an internal update server or from Microsoft—and installing updates.
Windows Server Update Services enables you to manage the deployment of updates by directing workstations to download updates from internal WSUS servers.
How to configure WSUS clients through Group Policy.
How to configure Automatic Updating either locally or using Group Policy.
You can use built-in tools such as the Windows Reliability and Performance Monitor to analyze the reliability and performance of Windows Vista workstations.
How to open the Advanced Tools control panel.
How to view performance-related events in Event Viewer.
How to view system information in the System Information tool.
The Reliability and Performance Monitor enables you to monitor and analyze system performance and reliability.

(continued)

SUMMARY SKILL MATRIX (*continued*)

IN THIS LESSON YOU LEARNED:
How to use the Windows Reliability and Performance Monitor.
How to connect to a remote computer with the Reliability and Performance Monitor.
The Performance Monitor is a component of the Reliability and Performance Monitor that enables you to analyze system performance.
How to add and remove performances counters in the Performance Monitor.
How to configure viewing settings in the Performance Monitor.
How to configure Performance Monitor properties.
The Reliability Monitor is a component of the Reliability and Performance Monitor that enables you to analyze system reliability.
How to use the Reliability Monitor to view reliability data.
The Windows Diagnostic Infrastructure (WDI) is a wide-ranging set of built-in monitoring tools, diagnostic logic, and solutions that help users and administrators resolve computer problems.
How to manage WDI centrally by using Group Policy.

■ Knowledge Assessment

Fill in the Blank

Complete the following sentences by writing the correct word or words in the blanks provided.

1. ________________ enables Windows clients to update automatically using updates provided online by Microsoft.
2. ________________ provides updates for current Windows operating systems and current Microsoft Office applications.
3. ________________ appears displaying usage summaries of four system resources: CPU, disk, network, and memory.
4. You can install the ________________ on any workstation and use it to configure WSUS.
5. ________________ is a set of built-in monitoring tools, diagnostic logic, and solutions that help users and administrators to diagnosis and resolve computer problems.
6. You can browse all of the hardware, devices, and software on a system along with important information about each by using the ________________.
7. The ________________ Group Policy setting controls the execution level for the WDI component that monitors shutdown performance.
8. The ________________ in Windows Vista replaces Performance Logs and Alerts (PLA).
9. There is a client component and a server component in WSUS. The server component is called the ________________.
10. ________________ is the legacy name for Automatic Updating.

Multiple Choice

Select all answers that apply for the following questions.

1. The Microsoft Update site does not provide updates for the following:
   a. Windows Vista
   b. Microsoft Office 2003
   c. Windows 2000 SP 2
   d. Microsoft SQL server
2. The Windows Update site does not provide updates for the following:
   a. Internet Explorer
   b. Microsoft Office 2003
   c. Windows Firewall
   d. Windows Vista
3. Select which of the following tools can be used to centrally manage the deployment of updates:
   a. Windows Software Update Server 3.0 (WSUS)
   b. Reliability and Performance Monitor
   c. Automatic Updating
   d. System Center Configuration Manager 2007
4. Restart Manager does the following:
   a. Limits the number of restarts required by checking to see if the part of the system that needs to be updated can be cleared and updated without affecting the current Windows session. If so, it does so and a restart is averted.
   b. Limits the number of restarts required by waiting until a set number of updates that require a restart have been deployed, and only then restarts.
   c. Informs users that a restart will occur in a set number of minutes after a schedule install of updates has occurred. It then saves the system state and restarts the computer when the set number of minutes has expired.
   d. Enables centralized management of Restart-related settings by using Group Policy.
5. To set an update schedule using Group Policy, you:
   a. Cannot create an update schedule by using Group Policy; you must use a tool such as WSUS.
   b. Use the Windows Update control panel, select the Install updates automatically (recommended) setting, and then specify a schedule.
   c. Enable the Configure Automatic Updates Group Policy setting, enable the Install Updates on a Schedule Group Policy setting, and configure the schedule in the latter.
   d. Enable the Configure Automatic Updates Group Policy setting and specify a schedule within that setting.
6. The Windows Reliability and Performance Monitor is a combination of which legacy tools?
   a. Task Manager, Performance Logs and Alerts (PLA), Server Performance Advisor
   b. Performance Logs and Alerts (PLA), Server Performance Advisor (SPA), System Monitor
   c. Event Viewer, Server Performance Advisor (SPA), System Monitor
   d. Performance Logs and Alerts (PLA), Task Manager, System Monitor
7. If a system becomes unstable, you can use this tool to view its stability history and to view events that might give an indication of how it became unstable?
   a. Event Viewer
   b. Stability Monitor
   c. Performance Monitor
   d. Reliability Monitor

8. Which of the following are not part of WDI?
   a. Application compatibility diagnostics
   b. Peripheral performance diagnostics
   c. Disk diagnostics
   d. Windows resource exhaustion Detection and Resolution

9. The Reliability Monitor displays all of the following event categories except:
   a. Update Failures
   b. Application Failures
   c. Hardware Failures
   d. Windows Failures

10. You set the Automatic Updates detection frequency to 24 hours by using Group Policy. However, in testing, you find that the actual interval was only 22 hours and 18 minutes. The most likely explanation for this discrepancy is:
    a. The Group Policy setting had no effect and the default value of 22 hours was used, but it was delayed by some other factor.
    b. Network latency caused the update to occur earlier than scheduled.
    c. A random amount is automatically subtracted from the specified interval.
    d. The WSUS server starts updates 2 hours before the specified interval and completes them 2 hours after to avoid being overloaded.

Review Questions

1. Describe how you would configure Group Policy to create the following updates scheme:

   a. Download both important and recommended updates.

   b. Notify the user when updates are downloaded and when they are installed.

2. Give three reasons and explain in each why you might use the Reliability and Performance console.

■ Case Scenarios

Scenario 1: Laptops Do Not Update Correctly

You have configured Automatic Updating through Group Policy, thus disabling local settings. You have configured Automatic Updates to occur on a schedule, with updates being downloaded and installed at 3 a.m. each morning.

However, when users leave their laptops turned on and connected to the network, the laptops are not updating consistently at around 3 a.m.

What is the likely problem, and how can you fix it?

Scenario 2: Safeguarding a TCP Port Used by an Application

You have configured the Automatic Updates Detection frequency setting to 10 hours by using Group Policy and the Configure Automatic Updates setting. You have not configured any other settings. However, updates schedules have not changed to occur according to your specified frequency of 10 hours. You run the Group Policy Results Wizard and find that the policy is being applied. What is most likely the problem?

Understanding, Configuring, and Securing TCP/IP Networks

OBJECTIVE DOMAIN MATRIX

Technology Skill	Objective Domain	Objective Domain Number
Introducing TCP/IP	Configure and troubleshoot network protocols	4.1
Understanding IP Addresses	Configure and troubleshoot network protocols • IPv6 • IPv4	4.1
Understanding Subnetting and Subnet Masks	Configure and troubleshoot network protocols • IPv4	4.1
Understanding DNS	Configure and troubleshoot network services at the client level • DNS	4.2
Understanding DHCP	Configure and troubleshoot network services at the client level • DHCP	4.2
Configuring TCP/IP Network Settings	Configure and troubleshoot network protocols • Auto vs. manual configuration	4.1
Understanding and Configuring Wireless Networking and Security	Configure and troubleshoot wireless networking • Configure wireless network security • WPA • WEP	4.5
Configuring Wireless Networking in Group Policy	Configure and troubleshoot wireless networking • Configure policy settings	4.5
Understanding and Securing Data with IPsec by Using Windows Firewall	Configure network security • IPSec	4.6
Using Windows Firewall with Advanced Security to Implement IPsec	Configure network security • IPSec • Windows Firewall	4.6

KEY TERMS

- Transmission Control Protocol/Internet Protocol (TCP/IP)
- IP address
- octet
- loopback address
- public facing IP addresses
- subnetting
- subnets
- network ID
- host ID
- subnet masks
- gateway
- routers
- default subnet masks
- AND
- NOT
- Classless Inter-Domain Routing (CIDR) notation
- Domain Name System (DNS)
- fully qualified domain names (FQDNs)
- Top-Level Domain names (TLDs)
- DNS name server
- resolving
- DNS caching
- Dynamic Host Control Protocol (DHCP)
- DHCP client
- DHCP server
- DHCP lease duration
- DHCP options
- DHCP lease
- DHCPDISCOVER
- DHCPOFFER
- DHCPREQUEST
- DHCPACK
- alternate IP address
- Wired Equivalent Policy (WEP)
- Wi-Fi Protected Access (WPA)
- Wi-Fi Protected Access 2 (WPA2)
- enterprise single sign-on (SSO)
- wireless network profiles
- Internet Protocol Security (IPsec)
- data integrity
- encryption
- authentication
- key exchange

Wireless networking is becoming increasingly popular, even for non-portable computers, because routing cables can be a nuisance and expensive. Contoso is deploying wireless networks on its 33rd and 34th floors, and you will need to configure TCP/IP settings and wireless network policies accordingly.

Introducing TCP/IP

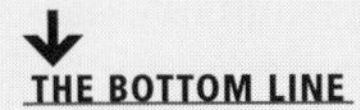
THE BOTTOM LINE

TCP/IP is the most commonly used network communications protocol in use today. It is used on the Internet and in most other networks, for example, enterprise networks.

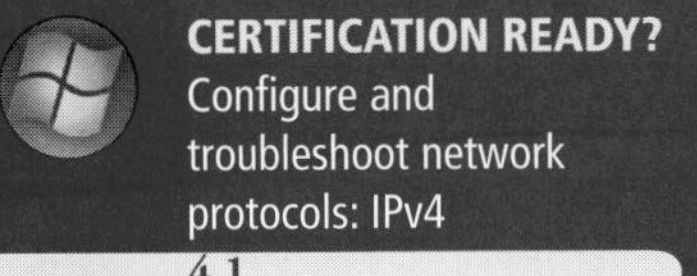
CERTIFICATION READY?
Configure and troubleshoot network protocols: IPv4
4.1

Transmission Control Protocol/Internet Protocol (TCP/IP) is the most commonly used protocol for communication on computer networks, and it is the network communications protocol that is the basis for the Internet.

TCP/IP is an open standard (in other words, it has no proprietary components), which is steered by such bodies as the Internet Society (ISOC), the Internet Architecture Board (IAB), and the Internet Engineering Task Force (IETF).

The *IP* in TCP/IP is the primary component of TCP/IP communications. It provides the addressing scheme (IP addresses) and supports the routing of messages across networks.

Computers running Windows Vista are by default TCP/IP hosts, meaning that they have all the software required for taking part in a TCP/IP network. Most modern computers have a network interface integrated into the motherboard. For older computers, network interface expansion cards are available.

Understanding IP Addresses

Hosts in a TCP/IP network identify each other via IP addresses.

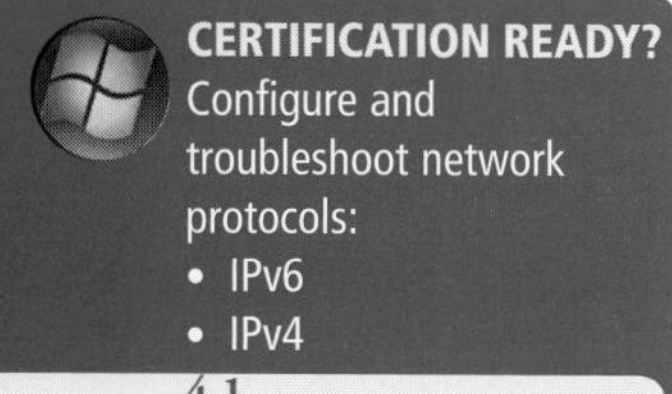
CERTIFICATION READY?
Configure and troubleshoot network protocols:
• IPv6
• IPv4
4.1

TCP/IP hosts such as computers running Windows Vista are identified on TCP/IP networks with an ***IP address***. Other network entities such as printers or routers can also be identified with an IP address. Just as a house's address identifies a house, an IP address identifies a host, for example, a computer. IP addresses are 32 bits in length and are expressed in four octets separated from one another with a dot (the "." character). Each ***octet*** is 8 bits long (32 bits for each address divided by 4 octets = 8 bits), which is why they are called octets. An example IP address is 10.23.132.23.

TAKE NOTE*

When you hear or read IP address, think IPv4, not IPv6, unless the context is for IPv6. This book refers to IPv4 IP addresses as *IP addresses*, and IPv6 as *IPv6 addresses*.

The octets are expressed as values between 0 and 255 (with some restrictions). The first octet determines the class of the address. Classes divide the IP address space into sections that are used for different purposes. Table 11-1 summarizes the classes.

Table 11-1

IP address classes

IP ADDRESS CLASS	FIRST OCTET RANGE	PURPOSE
Class A	1-126	Very large networks
Class B	128-191	Medium to large networks
Class C	192-223	Small networks
Class D	224-239	Multicasting (sending messages to more than one host at a time)
Class E	240-255	Reserved for experimental purposes

XREF

Troubleshooting networking is covered in **Lesson 12: Configuring and Troubleshooting Access.**

If you examine the preceding table closely, you may ask "What about 127?" IP addresses with a first octet of 127 are called loopback addresses and are reserved for troubleshooting purposes. A ***loopback address*** points back to the host rather than to another host.

TCP/IP hosts that are directly exposed to the Internet must receive their IP addresses from the Internet Corporation for Assigned Names and Numbers (ICANN) or some other authority. These IP addresses are called ***public facing IP addresses***. Enterprises usually obtain public facing IP addresses from their Internet service provider (ISP).

Almost all organizations today use private networks, in which the IP addresses internal to the organization are hidden from hosts external to the organization. This means that hosts within different organizations can have the same IP addresses, because hosts in one network are unable to see hosts on the other. Hosts that are directly connected to the Internet, however, must have unique IP addresses, which is why governing authorities like ICANN are necessary.

Understanding Subnetting and Subnet Masks

Subnetting enables you to split a network into multiple networks by using a subnet mask.

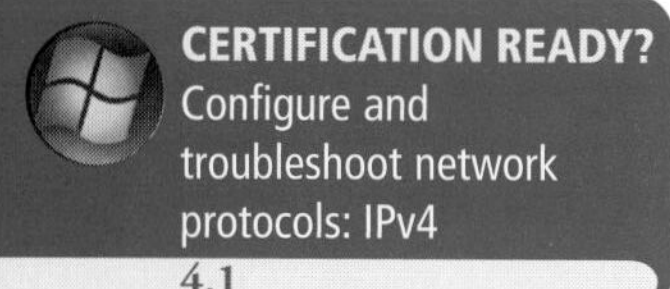
CERTIFICATION READY?
Configure and troubleshoot network protocols: IPv4
4.1

Subnetting is using subnet masks (see definition in the following paragraph) to partition a network into smaller networks called ***subnets***. Subnetting uses a subnet mask to divide an IP address into a network ID and a host ID. The ***network ID*** identifies the subnet, and the ***host ID*** identifies the host within that subnet.

Subnet masks divide IP addresses into network IDs and host IDs, and can be used to partition networks into subnets. Like IP addresses, subnet masks are composed of 4 octets. The most common values of the octets in a subnet mask are 255 and 0. An example of a subnet mask for the IP address 10.23.132.23 is 255.0.0.0.

The purpose of subnetting is to organize a large network into smaller networks so that you can more easily customize each network according to its requirements and so that you can optimize your network for the TCP/IP traffic flow. When you subnet a larger network, hosts within the subnets can communicate with each other with minimal configuration. But to communicate outside of the subnet, hosts have to first contact a ***gateway***, which is a TCP/IP host that can translate communications between TCP/IP networks (the most common use of a gateway is to translate messages between a local network and the Internet). Typically, routers serve as the gateways. ***Routers*** route TCP/IP traffic between TCP/IP networks.

For example, consider a situation where you have four departments, all of which mostly communicate with other hosts in the same department. You might want to divide your network into four subnets—one for each department. Consider that all your IP address all start with 192.168.255. The subnet mask 255.255.255.192 will divide the network into the following subnets:

192.168.255.1 to 192.168.255.62

192.168.255.65 to 192.168.255.126

192.168.255.129 to 192.168.255.190

192.168.255.193 to 192.168.255.254

How does this work? To understand requires doing a little binary arithmetic. Though this may sound daunting (and perhaps it is if it is unfamiliar to you), the rules are actually fairly simple:

1. Convert the octets in the IP address and the subnet mask from decimal to binary.
2. To find the network ID, you combine the IP address with the subnet mask using a logical ***AND***. You then convert back to decimal.
3. To find the host ID, you combine the IP address with the logical ***NOT*** of the subnet mask using a logical AND. You then convert back to decimal.

To make this more clear, let's go through how to convert from binary to decimal and vice versa and how to apply logical ANDs and NOTs by using Windows Calculator. After that, we will complete the entire subnetting process on a couple of examples and look at the resulting network IDs and host IDs.

CONVERT OCTETS FROM DECIMAL TO BINARY

1. Click **Start**. In the **Start Search** text box, key **calc** and then press **Enter**. Calculator appears.
2. In the View menu, click **Scientific**. The calculator expands to include more advanced features.
3. Key the decimal octet.
4. In the upper left, just below the text box, select **Bin**. The number is displayed in binary. Add zeros to the left side until there are eight digits. This last step of adding zeroes is not necessary to express the value, but it is necessary later to perform the AND operation.

CONVERT OCTETS FROM BINARY TO DECIMAL

OPEN Calculator and then select the Scientific view.

1. In Calculator, select **Bin** in the upper left.
2. Key the binary value excluding leading 0s.
3. Select **Dec** in the upper left. The value is displayed in decimal.

COMBINE OCTETS BY USING A LOGICAL AND

1. Compare the first digit of each octet and follow these rules:
   1 AND 1 = 1
   0 AND 0 = 0
   0 AND 1 = 0
2. Do the same for the remaining 7 digits.

APPLY A LOGICAL NOT TO AN OCTET

Replace each 1 with a 0, and each 0 with a 1.

Let's do an example all the way through. Consider the Class A IP address 192.168.0.22 and the subnet mask 255.255.255.0.

First, to find the host ID, you convert the IP address and the subnet mask to binary and combine with the logical AND:

192.168.0.22 in binary 11000000.10101000.00000000.00010110
AND
255.255.255.0 in binary 11111111.11111111.11111111.00000000
=
192.168.0.0 in binary 11000000.10101000.00000000.00000000

192.168.0.0 is therefore the network ID.

The host ID is determined in a similar way, except that you apply a logical NOT to the subnet mask first:

192.168.2.22 = 11000000.10101000.00000010.00010110
AND
NOT 255.255.255.0 = 00000000.00000000.00000000.11111111
=
0.0.0.22 = 00000000.00000000.00000000.00010110

0.0.0.22 is the host ID. In other words, this is host .22 in network 192.168.2.

The subnet mask 255.255.255.0 is an example of a default subnet mask. ***Default subnet masks*** are subnet masks that do not create any subnets; they are the most commonly used subnet masks. Table 11-2 lists the default subnet masks for each network class.

Table 11-2

IP address classes

IP ADDRESS CLASS	DEFAULT SUBNET MASK	PURPOSE
Class A	255.0.0.0	Very large networks
Class B	255.255.0.0	Medium to large networks
Class C	255.255.255.0	Small networks

The following is an example of a Class C address with 2 subnets.

Consider the IP address 192.168.0.54 and the subnet mask 255.255.255.128.

The network ID is calculated as shown in Table 11-3.

Table 11-3

Calculating a network ID. The 1s that are preserved with the logical AND operation are bolded.

	Decimal octets	Binary octets
IP Address	192.168.0.54	11000000.10101000.00000000.00110110
Subnet mask	255.255.255.128	11111111.11111111.11111111.10000000
Network ID (IP address AND subnet mask)	192.168.0.0	11000000.10101000.00000000.00000000

The host ID is calculated as shown in Table 11-4.

Table 11-4

Calculating a host ID. The 1s that are preserved with logical AND are bolded.

	Decimal octets	Binary octets
IP address	192.168.0.54	11000000.10101000.00000000.00110110
NOT subnet mask	0.0.0.127	00000000.00000000.00000000.01111111
Host ID (IP address AND NOT subnet mask)	0.0.0.54	00000000.00000000.00000000.00110110

The results in Tables 11-5 and 11-6 are very similar to the previous example. But now consider the same subnet mask with the IP address 192.168.0.135. The network ID is calculated as shown in Table 11-5.

Table 11-5

Calculating a network ID. The 1s that are preserved with the logical AND logical are bolded.

	Decimal octets	Binary octets
IP address	192.168.0.135	11000000.10101000.00000000.10000111
Subnet mask	255.255.255.128	11111111.11111111.11111111.10000000
Network ID (IP address AND subnet mask)	192.168.0.128	11000000.10101000.00000000.10000000

The host ID is calculated as shown in Table 11-6.

Table 11-6

Calculating a host ID. The 1s that are preserved with the AND logical operation are bolded.

	Decimal octets	Binary octets
IP address	192.168.0.135	11000000.10101000.00000000.10000111
NOT subnet mask	0.0.0.127	00000000.00000000.00000000.01111111
Host ID (IP address AND NOT subnet mask)	0.0.0.7	00000000.00000000.00000000.00000111

Note that the network ID for IP address 192.168.0.54 is different than the network ID for IP address 192.168.0.135 when the subnet mask of 255.255.255.128 is applied. This means that the IP addresses exist on different subnets. Also note that the host ID for 192.168.0.135 is not simply the last octet lead by zeroes as was the case in previous examples, but is instead a 7 (you can think of it as the 7th host on the 2nd subnet).

Tables 11-7, 11-8, and 11-9 cover the possible subnetting that you can accomplish using subnet masks for Class A, B, and C networks.

Table 11-7

Subnet masks for subnetting Class A networks

Subnet Mask	Number of Subnets	Number of Hosts per Subnet	CIDR Notation
255.0.0.0	1	16,777,214	/8
255.128.0.0	2	8,388,606	/9
255.192.0.0	4	4,194,302	/10
255.224.0.0	8	2,097,150	/11
255.240.0.0	16	1,048,574	/12
255.248.0.0	32	524,286	/13
255.252.0.0	64	262,142	/14
255.254.0.0	128	131,070	/15
255.255.0.0	256	65,534	/16
255.255.128.0	512	32,766	/17
255.255.192.0	1024	16,382	/18
255.255.224.0	2048	8190	/19
255.255.240.0	4096	4094	/20
255.255.248.0	8192	2046	/21
255.255.252.0	16,384	1022	/22
255.255.254.0	32,768	510	/23
255.255.255.0	65,536	254	/24
255.255.255.128	131,072	126	/25
255.255.255.192	262,144	62	/26
255.255.255.224	524,288	30	/27
255.255.255.240	1,048,576	14	/28
255.255.255.248	2,097,152	6	/29
255.255.255.252	4,194,304	2	/30

Table 11-8

Subnet masks for subnetting Class B networks

SUBNET MASK	NUMBER OF SUBNETS	NUMBER OF HOSTS PER SUBNET	CIDR NOTATION
255.255.0.0	1	65,534	/16
255.255.128.0	2	32,766	/17
255.255.192.0	4	16,382	/18
255.255.224.0	8	8190	/19
255.255.240.0	16	4094	/20
255.255.248.0	32	2046	/21
255.255.252.0	64	1022	/22
255.255.254.0	128	510	/23
255.255.255.0	256	254	/24
255.255.255.128	512	126	/25
255.255.255.192	1024	62	/26
255.255.255.224	2048	30	/27
255.255.255.240	4096	14	/28
255.255.255.248	8192	6	/29
255.255.255.252	16,384	2	/30

Table 11-9

Subnet masks for subnetting Class C networks

SUBNET MASK	NUMBER OF SUBNETS	NUMBER OF HOSTS PER SUBNET	CIDR NOTATION
255.255.255.0	1	254	/24
255.255.255.128	2	126	/25
255.255.255.192	4	62	/26
255.255.255.224	8	30	/27
255.255.255.240	16	14	/28
255.255.255.248	32	6	/29
255.255.255.252	64	2	/30

TAKE NOTE*

The CIDR notation column in each of the three previous tables contains information that is explained in the next section, Understanding CIDR notation.

X REF

Troubleshooting networking is covered in **Lesson 12.**

All of this is very laborious, so what is the point? Part of troubleshooting TCP/IP problems is understanding subnetting, because hosts on different subnets cannot communicate with each other without a go-between that translates from one subnet to the other (the go-between is called a gateway).

Understanding Classless Inter-Domain Routing Notation

CIDR notation is a different way of expressing an IP address and a subnet mask.

Classless Inter-Domain Routing (CIDR) notation is a common way of expressing a subnetted network address, from which you can derive the IP addresses and subnet mask for the hosts on each network. An example is 192.168.255.0/26. The number after the forward slash indicates how many bits are allocated to the network address, which also determines how many subnets there are. The remaining bits are available for identifying hosts within each subnet.

For example, 192.168.255.0/26 indicates that 26 of the 32 bits are used to identify the network. From this, you can determine that the subnet mask for the network will be 255.255.255.192. Because this is a Class C address, you know that the original network ID is 24 bits long, which leaves two bits for subnetting. A 2-bit subnet ID enables you to create 4 subnets (because $2^2 = 4$). The 6 ($32 - 26$) remaining bits form the host ID, meaning that each subnet can have 62 ($2^6 - 2$) hosts.

Therefore, the four subnets for this particular network are as follows:

- 192.168.255.0/26
- 192.168.255.64/26
- 192.168.255.128/26
- 192.168.255.192/26

From these network addresses, you can derive the range of IP addresses for each subnet, which are as follows:

- 192.168.255.1 to 192.168.255.62
- 192.168.255.65 to 192.168.255.126
- 192.168.255.129 to 192.168.255.190
- 192.168.255.193 to 192.168.255.254

Here is another example. Imagine that you want 16 subnets in a Class B network. Sixteen subnets require 4 bits dedicated to identifying the subnet ($2^4 = 16$ subnets). Therefore, to use CIDR notation to express a subnet on this network, you would append a network address with /20, which is the 16 Class B bits plus the 4 subnet bits, as in the example 128.32.32.0/20.

■ Understanding DNS

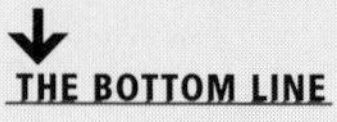

Domain Name System (DNS) is a user-friendly naming convention. DNS names, called fully qualified domain names, are converted into IP addresses by DNS name servers so that TCP/IP hosts can communicate.

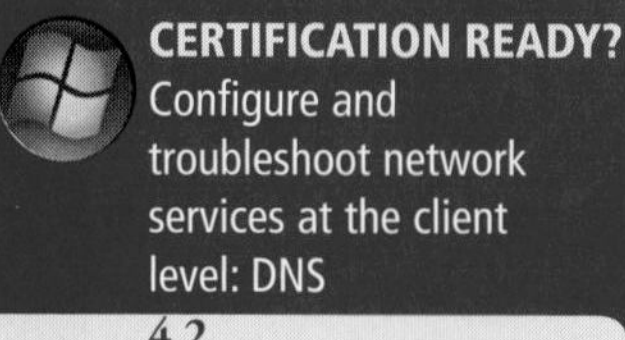

CERTIFICATION READY?
Configure and troubleshoot network services at the client level: DNS
4.2

Domain Name System (DNS) is a hierarchical naming convention for identifying TCP/IP hosts on a network. In DNS, IP addresses are mapped to ***fully qualified domain names (FQDNs)***, which are user-friendly names. An example of an FQDN is client42.northwind.contoso.com. Essentially, the purpose of DNS is to provide user-friendly names that can be used, in some circumstances, instead of IP addresses.

FQDNs are hierarchical, with each level of the hierarchy separated by a dot (the "." character). The hierarchy from left to right goes from the most specific to the most broad. For example, consider the following FQDN: client42.northwind.contoso.com.

To move from most general to most specific, move from right to left:

1. com: the top-level domain (TLD).
2. contoso: second-level domain, belongs to Contoso corporation.
3. northwind: third-level domain. Northwind is a fictitious subsidiary of Microsoft.
4. client42: TCP/IP host name. This is the name of the host, most often a computer (but it could be a printer or any other TCP/IP host).

There is one other level of the hierarchy that is not shown in an FQDN: the root domain. The root domain sits above the top-level domain.

Also, there can be an arbitrary number of levels between the TLD and the host name. Table 11-10 summarizes the DNS hierarchy.

Table 11-10

DNS hierarchy

LEVEL	EXAMPLES	NOTES
root	(.)	The root domain is represented by the "." character. It is not expressed in FQDNs.
Top-level domain	net, org, com, uk, gov	There are many other TLDs, most of them country codes.
Second-level domain	microsoft, contoso	Typically, the second-level domain is a good indication of who owns the FQDN.
Additional domain levels	Northwind	There can be any number of additional levels in an FQDN.
Host name	client42, www	Yes, www is a host name. Most FQDNs with www designated as the host resolve to the IP address of one or more web servers.

Top Level Domain names (TLDs) are used to identify broad classes of areas within the Internet. TLDs are controlled by the Internet Corporation for Assigned Names and Numbers (ICANN).

You can find a complete and up-to-date list of TLDs at *www.icann.org/registries/top-level-domains.htm.*

DNS is the naming system used by the Internet. Whenever you enter a web address into a web browser, such as www.contoso.com, it is converted into an IP address. This conversion is done by ***DNS name servers*** (often abbreviated to name servers) and is called ***resolving***.

Besides being the naming convention used on the Internet, DNS is also integral to Active Directory domains. In an enterprise, you will have at least one DNS server that is responsible for resolving internal DNS names. Resolution of external DNS names (such as www.microsoft.com) is performed by external DNS name servers. Often, however, your DNS clients won't contact the external DNS name servers directly. Instead, the internal DNS servers will forward external DNS name resolution requests from DNS clients to external DNS name servers, which in turn can forward the requests to other external DNS name servers.

In an enterprise, most if not all computers will be DNS clients, meaning that they will make DNS queries to DNS servers. A few of the DNS clients will be DNS servers, which will answer DNS queries from the DNS clients.

Both DNS clients and servers also can cache DNS name resolutions. This means that after they find the answer to a resolution, they store it locally for some time in case they need it. This way, they don't have to look it up again which increases performance. This is call ***DNS caching***.

To tie this all together, consider the following example:

1. You log onto the domain at Contoso and then open Internet Explorer.
2. You have invested your life savings in penny stocks and want to log on to your brokerage account to see if you can retire yet. You type *http://www.woodgrovebank.com* into the Address text box and then press Enter. Your computer checks to see if the IP address for www.woodgrovebank.com is cached. It is not.
3. Your computer sends a DNS name resolution request for www.woodgrovebank.com to the DNS name server specified in its TCP/IP network settings. The DNS name server is internal to Contoso.
4. The DNS name server checks its cache, and finds that www.woodgrovebank.com is not in it. It then forwards the DNS name resolution request to an external DNS name server.
5. That DNS server forwards the request as required until it gets an IP address back.
6. The IP address makes its way back to your computer, at which point Internet Explorer connects to that IP address, which identifies a host that is a web server for Woodgrove Bank. Internet Explorer displays the Woodgrove Bank website. You log onto your account, check your penny stocks, and then cancel your plans for a vacation in November.

■ Understanding DHCP

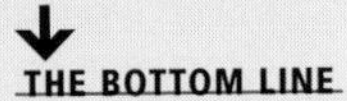

Dynamic Host Control Protocol (DHCP) is a protocol by which TCP/IP hosts can automatically obtain IP addresses and supporting information.

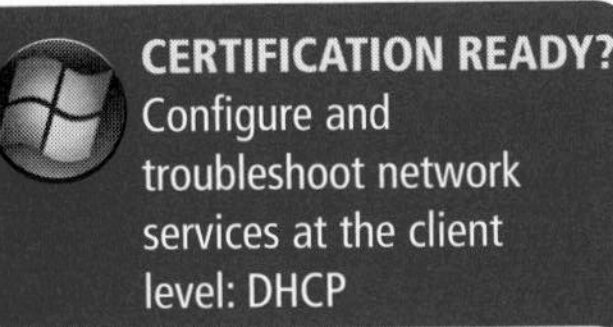

CERTIFICATION READY?
Configure and troubleshoot network services at the client level: DHCP
4.2

Dynamic Host Control Protocol (DHCP) is a protocol that DHCP clients, such as computers running Windows Vista, can use to request and lease IP addresses from a DHCP server. The client can also use DHCP to request DHCP options.

The preceding definition uses some terms with which you might not be familiar:

DHCP client. A DHCP client is a machine that uses DHCP to request an IP address lease and other information called DHCP options. In an enterprise network, there are many DHCP clients, including printers and workstations, but also sometimes servers, routers, and other networked devices.

DHCP server. A DHCP server allocates IP addresses from a pool of IP addresses to DHCP clients and can optionally offer supporting information—called DHCP options—to the DHCP clients. The IP addresses are given out for a specified period of time called a ***DHCP lease duration.***

DHCP options. A DHCP option is a piece of information that DHCP servers can optionally offer to DHCP clients. DHCP options include default gateway IP addresses, and IP addresses for DNS name servers. There are other DHCP options that are not relevant for this lesson.

DHCP lease. A DHCP lease is the entire package that a DHCP client receives from a DHCP server.

In an enterprise, most computers will be DHCP clients. The process of a DHCP client requesting and receiving a DHCP lease from a DHCP server is completed in the following four steps:

1. ***DHCPDISCOVER:*** the DHCP client broadcasts a request for a DHCP lease.
2. ***DHCPOFFER:*** DHCP servers on the network offer DHCP leases of specific IP addresses to the DHCP client.
3. ***DHCPREQUEST:*** The DHCP client chooses from which DHCP server to obtain a DHCP lease and broadcasts that it has chosen that server in a broadcast message. The other offering DHCP servers receive the DHCPREQUEST message and return the IP addresses they offered to their pools of available IP addresses for lease.
4. ***DHCPACK:*** The chosen DHCP server also receives the DHCPREQUEST message and sends an acknowledgement to the DHCP client and assigns it any configured DHCP options. The client configures its TCP/IP settings with the IP address and DHCP options supplied by the DHCP server.

As the term *DHCP lease* implies, IP addresses obtained through DHCP can expire. Expiration of IP addresses enables IP addresses that were leased and then vacated to be returned to the pool of available IP addresses. If IP addresses never expired, even when computers and other clients were removed, then the IP address pool would eventually be depleted. Very long expiration times also can result in depleted IP address pools. Also, by assigning fairly short leases (a day or two, for example), administrators can change DHCP options and be assured that the changes will be adopted reasonably quickly through DHCP lease renewals. There is no hard and fast rule on when DHCP leases should be configured to expire; it really depends on how many workstations, laptops, and so on request IP addresses each day.

Leased IP addresses are not, however, fated for expiration. DHCP clients will make automatic renewal requests. These renewal requests occur when the lease is half expired, and, if that renewal fails, when the lease is 87.5 percent expired. DHCP clients also make renewal requests each boot. DHCP renewal requests consist of the last two steps in the DHCP IP address lease process: the DHCPREQUEST and DHCPACK.

The following is an example of a DHCP client requesting and receiving a DHCP lease: A new Windows Vista laptop has been connected to the network for the first time. As it boots, Windows Vista detects that it is configured to *Obtain an IP address automatically*, which means that it is configured to use DHCP to obtain an IP address. It broadcasts a DHCPDISCOVER message over the network by using the DHCP protocol. Two DHCP servers are on the network, and each one receives the DHCPDISCOVER message. Each DHCP server offers an IP address from its pool of available IP addresses by using a DHCPOFFER message. The workstation receives the DHCPOFFER messages, chooses one of the offers, and broadcasts a DHCPREQUEST message that contains an IP address that identifies the chosen DHCP server. The DHCP server that was not chosen returns the IP address it offered back to its pool of available IP addresses. The chosen DHCP server sends a DHCPACK message and also provides three DHCP options: a subnet mask of 255.255.0.0, a default gateway IP address of 192.168.100.101, and a primary DNS server address of 192.168.100.10. The DHCP client configures its TCP/IP network settings accordingly.

Now consider that the IP address in the preceding example is set to expire after 72 hours (3 days). Let's say that the IP address is assigned at 12 noon on Tuesday. On Wednesday, the user takes the laptop home (without turning it off), plugs it in to power but not a network, and does some work until 1 a.m. At 12 midnight, the DHCP client for the laptop makes a DHCP lease renewal request (because half the lease has expired), which fails, because the computer cannot contact either DHCP server. The user gets to work late the next day, plugs the laptop into the network, and logs onto the domain. At 3 p.m. (or after 87.5% of the lease has expired), the laptop sends a second DHCP renewal request and this time DHCP server renews the lease. On Tuesday, the IT department brought a second DNS server online and configured the DHCP servers to offer its IP address as the secondary DNS server DHCP option. The DNS client configures its TCP/IP network settings as before, with the addition of the secondary DNS server IP address.

TAKE NOTE*

Another scheme for assigning IP addresses automatically is Automatic Private IP Addressing (APIPA). APIPA is a part of Windows operating systems. If you configure a computer to automatically obtain an IP address and no DHCP server is available, you will receive an APIPA address. APIPA addresses always start with the octets 169.254.

Configuring TCP/IP Network Settings

THE BOTTOM LINE

You need to configure TCP/IP networks settings so that they can communicate with other TCP/IP hosts.

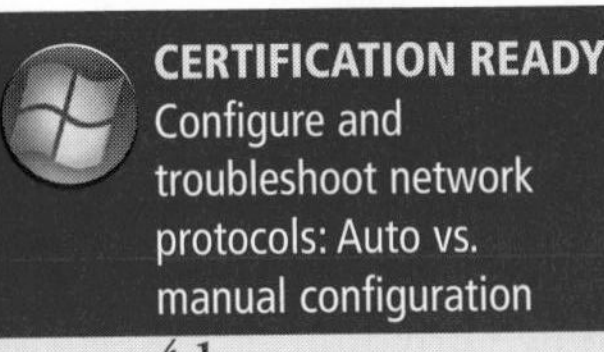

CERTIFICATION READY?
Configure and troubleshoot network protocols: Auto vs. manual configuration
4.1

Each network adapter has IPv4 and IPv6 settings. At this time (2007), there is usually no need to configure the IPv6 settings because almost all networks, including the Internet, use IPv4 exclusively. This is likely to be the case for at least several more years.

CONFIGURE IPv4 TCP/IP NETWORK SETTINGS MANUALLY

1. Click **Start** and then click **Control Panel**. The Control Panel appears.
2. Under Network and Internet, click **View network status and tasks**. The Network and Sharing Center control panel appears.
3. Click **Manage network connections** in the task list. The Network Connections control panel appears.
4. Right-click the connection for which you want to configure TCP/IP settings and then click **Properties**. A User Account Control dialog box appears.
5. Provide administrator credentials and then click **OK**.
6. The *ConnectionName* Properties dialog box appears, as shown in Figure 11-1.

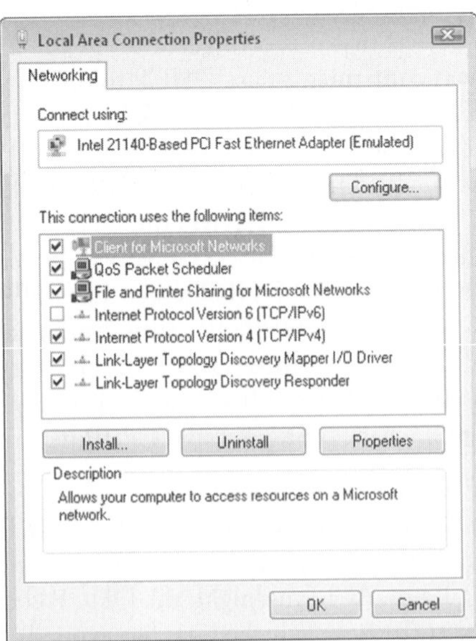

Figure 11-1

The Properties dialog box for an example connection

7. In the **This connection uses the following items** list box, select Internet Protocol Version 4 (TCP/IPv4) and then click **Properties**. The Internet Protocol Version 4 (TCP/IPv4) Properties dialog box appears.
8. Select **Use the following IP address** and then configure the following settings:
   - **IP address.** Specify the IP address of the host.

- **Subnet mask.** Specify the subnet mask of the network.
- Default Gateway. Specify the default gateway. The default gateway is the IP address of a host that can connect the computer to other networks, most commonly the Internet.

9. In the Use the following DNS server addresses section, configure the following:
   - **Preferred DNS server.** This is the IP address of the first DNS name server that the host should contact to resolve DNS names into IP addresses. Enterprises will have internal DNS name servers that take care of the internal DNS name resolution requests required by Active Directory. They will also forward external DNS name resolution for requests to external DNS name servers.
   - **Alternate DNS server.** If the preferred DNS name server is unavailable or cannot resolve an IP address, the host will send the same request to the alternate DNS server. The alternate DNS server is optional.
10. Click **OK**. Example settings for a Class C private network with 64 subnets are shown in Figure 11-2.

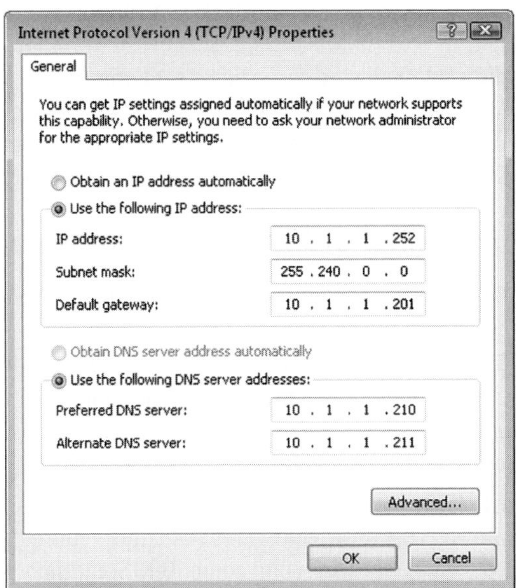

Figure 11-2

Example settings for a Class C private network with 64 subnets

USE DHCP TO CONFIGURE IPv4 TCP/IP SETTINGS AUTOMATICALLY

OPEN the Properties dialog box for the connection you want to configure.

1. In the *ConnectionName* Properties dialog box, select **Internet Protocol Version 4 (TCP/IPv4)** and then click **Properties**. The Internet Protocol Version 4 (TCP/IPv4) Properties dialog box appears.
2. Select **Obtain an IP address automatically**.
3. Select one of the following:
   - **Obtain DNS server addresses automatically.** Select this option if your DNS servers provide at least one DNS server as part of DHCP options.
   - **Use the following DNS server addresses.** Select this option to manually specify DNS name servers. This setting is unlikely in an enterprise environment. If you select this option, specify the IP address of a preferred DNS server and, optionally, the IP address of an alternate DNS server.
4. Click **OK**.

You can configure an ***alternate IP address*** for when a DHCP server is not available. The most common scenario for this is when a portable computer is used on a work network and on a home network. You can configure the computer to use DHCP to get an IP address at work and to use a static IP address (or an APIPA address) at home. When the computer is attached to the home network, it will get no response to its DHCPDISCOVER broadcast message and will instead use the alternate configuration.

TAKE NOTE* Many home networks use routers or modems that host DHCP servers. In this case, you won't need to configure an alternate IP address, because the DHCP client on the portable computer will receive a DHCPOFFER from the local DHCP server.

CONFIGURE AN ALTERNATE IP ADDRESS

OPEN the Internet Protocol Version 4 (TCP/IPv4) Properties dialog box for the connection for which you want to configure an alternate IP address.

1. In the Internet Protocol Version 4 (TCP/IPv4) Properties dialog box, ensure that **Obtain an IP address automatically** is selected and then click the **Alternate Configuration** tab.
2. Select one of the following:
   - **Automatic private IP address.** Select this option to use an APIPA address. The computer will be able to communicate with other hosts configured with APIPA addresses.
   - **User configured.** Select this option to configure an IP address manually. This option is preferred because when an APIPA address is assigned, the DHCP client in Windows Vista continues send out DHCPDISCOVER messages, desperately looking for a DHCP server. If you select this option, configure the following:
   - **IP address.** Specify the IP address of the host. On most home networks this will begin with 192.168.0 or 192.168.1.
   - **Subnet mask.** Specify the subnet mask of the network. For almost all home networks this will be 255.255.255.0.
   - **Default Gateway.** Specify the default gateway. The default gateway is the IP address of a host that can connect the computer to other networks, most commonly the Internet. For most home networks this will be the IP address of your router or modem.
   - **Preferred DNS server.** For most home networks, this will be the same as the default gateway, because that host (usually a router or modem) will forward DNS requests on behalf of your computer. Sometimes, however, it will be the IP address of an external DNS name server.
   - **Alternate DNS server.** For most home networks this will be blank.
3. Example alternate IP address settings for a Class A private network are shown in Figure 11-3.

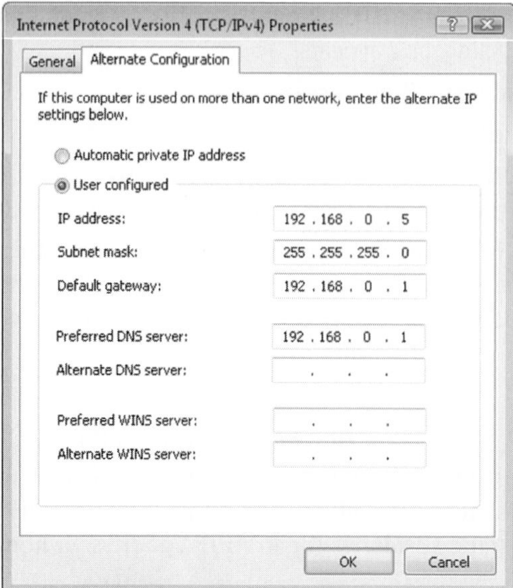

Figure 11-3

Example alternate IP address settings for a Class A private network

You can configure network settings through Group Policy in the Computer Configuration> Windows Settings>Security Settings>Wired Network (IEEE 802.3) Policies folder of Group Policy Objects (GPOs).

CONFIGURE WINDOWS VISTA WIRED NETWORK POLICY THROUGH GROUP POLICY

OPEN the Group Policy Object for which you want to configure wired network polices.

1. In the Group Policy Object Editor, in the console tree, expand **Computer Configuration>Windows Settings>Security Settings**, right-click **Wired Network (IEEE 802.3) Policies**, and then click **Create a New Windows Vista Policy**. The New Vista Wired Network Policy Properties dialog box appears.
2. In the **Policy Name** text box, key a policy name.
3. In the **Description text** box, key a description for the policy. Provide a detailed description to assist with troubleshooting later if it is necessary.
4. Select the Use Wired Auto Config Service for clients check box to automatically configure and connect clients running Windows Vista. The Wired Auto Config service performs authentication on network cards when they are connected to a network. In almost all circumstance, you want to enable this service.

TAKE NOTE*

Authentication is the act of an entity identifying itself to another entity. For example, when you log on to a domain, you have authenticated yourself to the domain by providing your user name and password. Authentication often consists of two parts: a statement of identity, and proof of that identity (e.g., a user name and password).

5. Click the **Security** tab, which is shown in Figure 11-4.

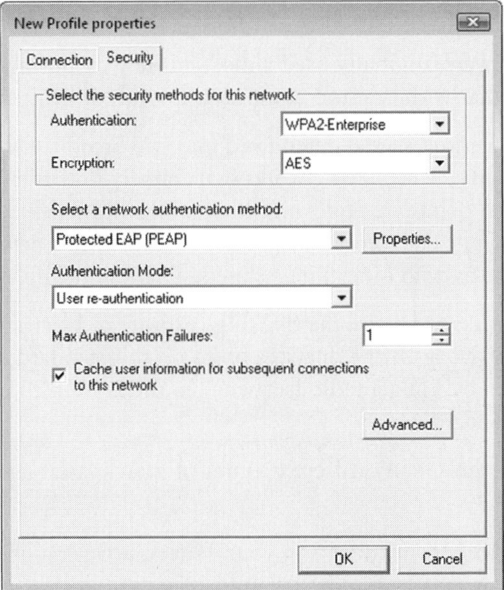

Figure 11-4

The Security tab of the *WiredNetworkPolicyName* Properties dialog box

6. In the **Select a network authentication method** drop-down list, select one of the following:
   - **Smart Card or other certificate.** Select this option if you want wireless users to authenticate with a smart card.
   - **Protected EAP (PEAP).** Protected Extensible Authentication Protocol. User names and passwords fall into this authentication category.

7. In the **Authentication Mode** drop-down list, select one of the following:
   - **User re-authentication.** Authentication uses the computer's credentials when a user is not logged on. When a user logs on, re-authentication using the user's credentials is performed. This is the recommended and default setting.
   - **Computer authentication.** Authentication uses the computer's credentials.
   - **User authentication.** Authentication uses the computer's credentials until a new wireless access point is connected to (usually because the user has moved), at which time re-authentication takes place with the user's credentials.
   - **Guest authentication.** All connections to the network are regulated by the settings for the Guest user account. This is the least restrictive and most flexible. It is recommended when you are creating a wireless policy for a network on which guests are welcome.
8. In the **Max Authentication Failures** spin box, specify the number of authentication requests to make before giving up. The default for wired networks is 1.
9. To cache user information for subsequent logons, ensure that the Cache user information for subsequent connections to this network check box is selected. This will result in faster connections to the network after the initial connection, but may lightly decrease security.
10. To configure the 802.1X timeouts in Advanced settings, select the Enforce advanced 802.1X settings check box.

■ Understanding and Configuring Wireless Networking and Security

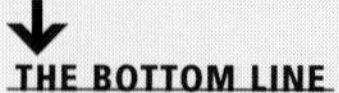
THE BOTTOM LINE

Security is very important in wireless networks because anybody with a receiver can potentially log on to the network if security is weak.

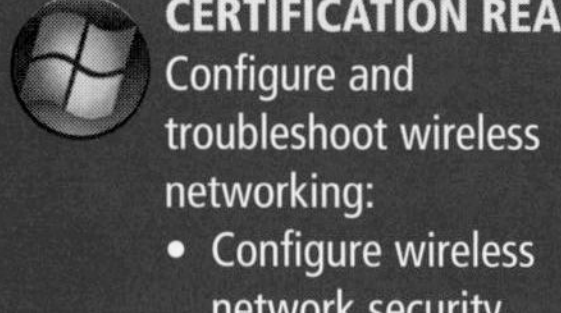
CERTIFICATION READY?
Configure and troubleshoot wireless networking:
• Configure wireless network security
• WPA
• WEP
1.5

Wireless networks were originally used almost entirely by portable computers, but they have become more popular with desktop computers because it is often inconvenient to run cables.

In Windows Vista, networks are differentiated into two broad classes. The first class is Infrastructure networks, which are networks that connect to wireless access points on your network. Wireless access points are nodes on the network with wireless transceivers where you can connect to the network. The second class of networks is ad-hoc networks, which are networks that you can form on the fly with other wireless users. This lesson emphasizes infrastructure networks.

Most wireless networks today use the 802.11g Institute of Electrical and Electronics Engineers (IEEE) standard (802.11g IEEE). Devices based on this standard are capable of transferring 54 megabits per second by using a radio frequency in the 2.4 GHz range. Some older networks will use the 802.11b standard.

Hackers can perpetrate many different types of attacks that against wireless networks. They include:

- **Theft of service**. An intruder uses your wireless access point to gain access to the Internet.
- **Denial of service**. An intruder floods your wireless access point with connection requests, which can bog it down to near zero performance.
- **Privacy violations**. An intruder can monitor your data transfers, thus seeing which Internet sites you visit and any user names or passwords that you transmit.
- **Data theft or destruction**. Intruders who connect to your network may be able to browse shared printers and folders and, depending on permissions, may be able to copy or delete that data.
- **System compromise**. An intruder may be able to install malware or alter permissions, thus compromising the system.

Windows Vista offers three primary technologies to defeat these types of attacks. You can configure only one of them per access point, so you want to make sure that all the wireless devices that access that wireless access point are compatible with the security technology. The technologies are:

- ***Wired Equivalent Policy (WEP)***. This is the least secure of the three. It encrypts data between any device and its access point. It requires a WEP key, which you supply to the wireless devices that connect to the access point. The key can be either 60 bits long or 128 bits long (5 or 13 characters). WEP has known vulnerabilities that enable hackers to crack it with retail hardware. WEP is not recommended for enterprise use.
- ***Wi-Fi Protected Access (WPA)***. WPA was designed to eliminate the known security flaws of WEP. Wireless devices and the access point use a pre-shared key (PSK) that can be either a 256 bit number or an alphanumeric password between 8 and 63 characters long.
- ***Wi-Fi Protected Access 2*** (WPA2): WPA2 is undoubtedly the preferred security technology for enterprise wireless networks. It uses 802.1X-based authentication and Advanced Encryption Standard (AES) encryption. This ensures that the data is from who it says it is from, and that the data cannot be easily decrypted or altered. There are two versions of WPA2: WPA2-personal and WPA2-enterprise. WPA2-enterprise requires that a user authenticate on the network before wireless connectivity is granted. Since 2006, all network devices that bear the Wi-Fi Certified designation are WPA2 capable.

Enterprise single sign-on enables users to authenticate to the wireless network access point and the domain in a single step. In other words, users don't have to enter credentials once to authenticate for wireless network access and an additional time to log onto the domain.

Using Group Policy is covered in **Lesson 4: Using Group Policy.**

In Enterprise Single Sign-on, 802.1X authentication to the wireless network precedes logon to the domain, and users are only prompted for wireless credential information if needed. With a wireless connection established prior to logon, client computers can receive Group Policy updates, run logon scripts, download updates, and perform other network-reliant tasks. Single sign-on works with both user name/password authentication and with smart card authentication. It is configured through Group Policy.

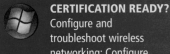

TAKE NOTE*

To use the new Windows Vista wireless settings in Group Policy, you must extend the Active Directory scheme on Server 2003 domain controllers. For more information, go to *www.microsoft.com/technet/network/wifi/vista_ad_ext.mspx*.

You can configure Group Policy to automatically connect users to designated, protected wireless networks whenever they are available. This ability, combined with SSO, means that wireless users can turn on their computer and connect to a wireless network without any actions required, all before they are logged on.

Some users are going to want to connect to wireless networks outside of your organization, such as at home or in public places such as coffee houses (you can use Group Policy to prevent this, as discussed later). Users can manually connect to wireless networks the same way that they make other connections, such as virtual private network (VPN) connections, by using the Connect to a network Wizard—click Start and then click Connect To.

CERTIFICATION READY?
Configure and troubleshoot wireless networking: Configure policy settings
4.5

Configuring Wireless Networking in Group Policy

You can configure wireless policy for many computers simultaneously by using Group Policy.

You can configure wireless networking in Group Policy in the Computer Configuration> Windows Settings>Security Settings>Wireless Network (IEEE 802.11) Policies node in Group Policy Objects.

To configure Windows Vista wireless policy, you must first create a new Windows Vista wireless policy in a GPO. You can have only one Windows Vista policy per GPO, but you can configure polices for multiple wireless networks in the single policy. You can also have a separate wireless policy for XP clients.

Though configuring polices for ad-hoc networks is not covered in this lesson, the settings are just a subset of the settings for creating infrastructure networks.

The options for configuring wireless policy are vast, and therefore we present them in tables after the procedure for accessing the interface.

TAKE NOTE*

If you configure a Windows XP wireless policy but no Windows Vista policy, Windows Vista clients will use the Windows XP wireless policy. However, XP clients cannot use a Windows Vista policy.

CONFIGURE WINDOWS VISTA WIRELESS POLICY FOR INFRASTRUCTURE NETWORKS

Using Group Policy is covered in **Lesson 4.**

OPEN the Group Policy Object in which you want to configure Windows Vista wireless settings in the Group Policy Object Editor.

1. In the Group Policy Object Editor console tree, expand **Computer Configuration>Windows Settings>Security Settings**, right-click **Wireless Network (IEEE 802.11) Policies** and then click **Create A New Windows Vista Policy.** The New Vista Wireless Network Policy Properties dialog box appears.
2. Use Tables 11-11 through 11-14 to help you configure the settings as required.

Table 11-11

Settings on the General tab of the *WirelssPolicyName* Properties dialog box.

SETTING	DESCRIPTION
Vista Policy Name text box	A name for the wireless policy. Providing a good name will make it easier for you or another administrator to troubleshoot later.
Description text box	A description for the wireless policy. Providing a good description will make it easier for you or another administrator to troubleshoot later.
Use Windows WLAN Autoconfig service for clients check box	Select this check box to use the WLAN Autoconfg service. This enables wireless cards in clients to automatically configure themselves. You should enable this setting (default) unless you are using a third-party application from the wireless card manufacturer.
Connect to available networks in the order of profiles listed below list box	This list box is a list of the available wireless networks (called **wireless network profiles**), listed in order of preference. A client will connect to the most preferred, available network. You can reorder the list by selecting network and clicking the up and down arrows on the right of the list box. Ad-hoc networks cannot be listed higher than infrastructure networks.
Add button	Click to add a wireless network profile. When you click Add, a context menu appears from which you can select Infrastructure or Ad hoc, depending on what type of network profile you want to add. See Table 11-12 for information on what to do after clicking Add.
Edit button	Click to edit a wireless network profile. See Table 11-12 for information on the settings that you can edit.
Remove button	Select a wireless profile and then click Remove to remove it.
Import button	Click to import an XML-based wireless profile. Use when you have a similar wireless profile elsewhere that you can export and import here to save time. After importing, modify any settings as needed.
Export button	Click to export the selected wireless profile. Choose this option if you want to use this profile on another wireless network. You can then import the settings there.

You can use the General tab of the *WirelessPolicyName* Properties dialog box to configure general settings such as name and description, as well as to manage wireless network profiles.

The New Profile properties dialog box differs for Infrastructure and Ad-hoc network profiles. Table 11-12 covers the dialog box's settings for the Connection tab when you are adding an infrastructure wireless network profile. The same settings are exposed when you edit an existing infrastructure wireless network profile. The settings when you add or edit an ad-hoc wireless network profile are a subset of the settings covered here. Figure 11-5 shows the Connection tab of the New Profile properties dialog box for an infrastructure wireless network profile.

Table 11-12

Settings in the New Profile properties dialog box (the same settings appear when you edit and existing wireless network profile)

Setting	Description
Profile name text box	A name for the wireless network profile. Providing a good name will make it easier for you or another administrator to troubleshoot later.
Network name(s) (SSID) text box and Add button	Use this text box to type the SSIDs of the wireless network you want to add to the wireless network profile. Once you key the name in the text box, click Add to add it to the profile. Repeat to add additional networks.
Connect automatically when this network is in range check box	Select this check box to connect to the specified network when it is in range.
Connect to a more preferred network if available	Select this check box to connect to a more preferred network than this one if it is available.
Connect even if the network is not broadcasting	Some wireless access points are configured to not broadcast their existence for security purposes. Select this check box to attempt to connect to such network access points.

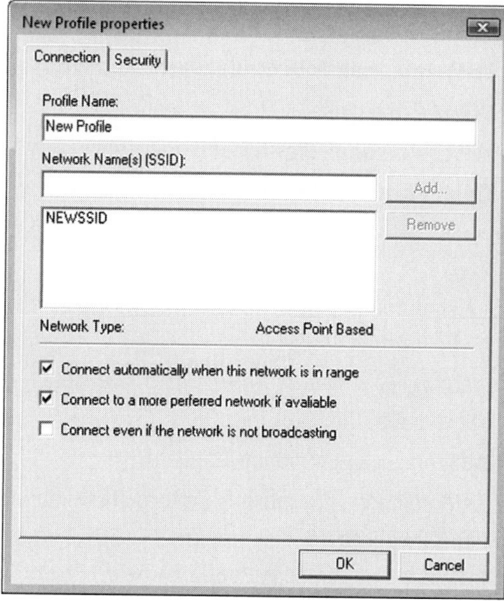

Figure 11-5

The Connection tab of the New Profile properties dialog box for an infrastructure wireless network profile

The Security tab in the New Profile properties dialog box enables you to configure security for the wireless profile that you are adding. Figure 11-6 shows the Security tab, and Table 11-13 covers the settings.

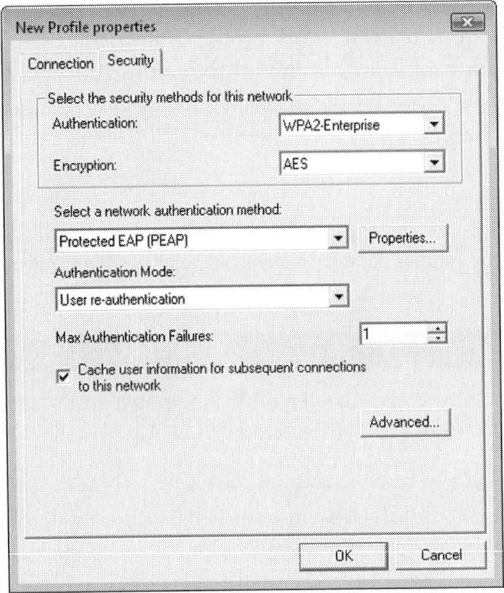

Figure 11-6

The Security tab of the New Profile properties dialog box

Table 11-13

Security tab in the New Profile properties dialog box (the same settings appear when you edit an existing wireless network profile)

Setting	Description
Authentication drop-down list	Select one of the following: • **Open**. No authentication. • **Shared**. Pre-shared key authentication. • **WPA-Enterprise**. 802.1X authentication. • **WPA-Personal**. WPA personal authentication is used (pre-shared key). • **WPA2-Enterprise**. 802.1X authentication. • **WPA2-Personal**. Pre-shared key authentication. • **Open with 802.1X.** 802.1X authentication. If you select any of the three 802.1X variants, more settings are exposed (discussed in this table). This setting automatically defaults to the most secure setting supported by the wireless hardware and drivers.
Encryption drop-down list	For WPA-Enterprise, WPA-Personal, WPA2-Enterprise, or WPA2-Personal authentication, select one of the following: • **AES**. American Encryption Standard. • **TKIP**. Temporal Key Integrity Protocol. TKIP improves upon WEP without requiring hardware upgrades. For Open, Shared, or Open with 802.1X, select one of the following: • **WEP**. Wired Equivalent Privacy. • **Disabled**. Select this option to not use encryption. This is not recommended, even on home networks.

(continued)

Table 11-13 (*continued*)

SETTING	DESCRIPTION
Select a network authentication method drop-down list	Use this drop-down list to specify the network authentication method to use. Select one of the following: • **Smart Card or other certificate**. Select this option if you want wireless users to authenticate with a smart card. • **Protected EAP (PEAP)**. Protected Extensible Authentication Protocol. User names and passwords fall into this authentication category.
Properties button	Click to modify the properties of the selected authentication method. Actions you can take include: • Modifying certificate settings. • Selecting trusted root certificate authorities. • Configuring further authentication settings.
Authentication Mode drop-down list	Use this drop-down list to specify how credentials are used to authenticate. Select one of the following: • **User re-authentication**. Authentication uses the computer's credentials when a user is not logged on. When a user logs on, re-authentication using the user's credentials is performed. This is the recommended and default setting. • **Computer authentication**. Authentication uses the computer's credentials. • **User authentication**. Authentication uses the computer's credentials until a new wireless access point is connected to (usually because the user has moved), at which time re-authentication takes place with the user's credentials. • **Guest authentication**. All connections to the network are regulated by the settings for the Guest user account. This is least restrictive and most flexible. It is recommended when you are creating a wireless policy for a network on which guests are welcome.
Max Authentication Failures numeral box	Use this numeral box to specify how many times to re-try authentication before giving up and displaying a message to the user. The default is three for wireless networks.
Cache user information for subsequent connections to this network check box	Select this option to store user information for subsequent connections to this network. This can save time, but may decrease security.
Advanced button	Click this button to access advanced security settings. These settings include: • 802.1X configuration options, such as timeouts. • Single Sign-On (SSO) settings, including enabling SSO. • Fast roaming options. Fast roaming can enable users to more quickly log onto wireless networks.

The Network Permissions tab of the *WirelessPolicyName* Properties dialog box enables you to configure a list of networks for which you can either deny or allow access. An example of this tab is shown in Figure 11-7. Networks that are in the preferred networks list on the General tab of the *WirelssPolicyName* Properties dialog box are automatically listed as allowed. You can also configure other access settings on the Network Permissions tab. All the settings are covered in Table 11-14.

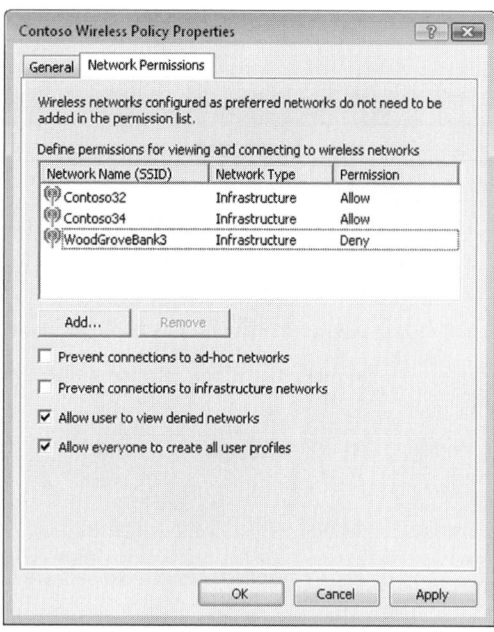

Figure 11-7

The Network Permissions tab of the *WirelssPolicyName* Properties dialog box with example settings configured

Table 11-14

Settings on the Network Permissions tab of the *WirelssPolicyName* Properties dialog box

SETTING	DESCRIPTION
Add button	Click to add a network to the list box of networks. When you click Add, you can configure the network name (SSID), network type (infrastructure or ad-hoc), and permission (Deny or Allow). Select Deny to prevent users from accessing the network, and Allow to allow them to access the network.
Remove button	Click to remove the network selected in the list box of networks.
Prevent connections to ad-hoc networks	Select this check box to prevent users from connecting to any of the ad-hoc networks listed in the network list box, even networks with the allow permission.
Prevent connections to infrastructure networks	Select this check box to prevent users from connecting to any of the infrastructure networks listed in the network list box, even networks with the allow permission.
Allow user to view denied networks	Clear this check box to prevent users from viewing denied networks.
Allow everyone to create all user profiles	Clear this check box to prevent anyone with an account on the computer from creating an all user profile. All user profiles are used to connect to any wireless network. If you clear this check box, only Network Administrators or Network Operators can create an all user profile.

■ Understanding and Securing Data with IPsec by using Windows Firewall

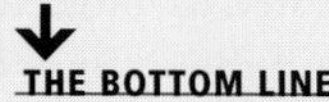

IP security protocol in Windows Vista can be implemented using Windows Firewall with Advanced Security. You can configure custom IP security policies to fit a variety of requirements.

CERTIFICATION READY?
Configure network security: IPSec
4.6

Internet Protocol Security (IPsec) is a suite of protocols for securing communication between two TCP/IP hosts.

IPsec provides for both data integrity and encryption. ***Data integrity*** is ensuring that the data that is transmitted is identical to the data received. ***Encryption*** is making the data unreadable by anybody but the intended reader. IPsec also validates the identity of both hosts in an IPsec session, which is called ***authentication***.

The two hosts an IPsec session must share a common key with which to decrypt the encrypted data. The challenge is letting each other know what this key is without compromising it.

The solution that Windows Vista uses is not to actually exchange the key, but instead to exchange information that each host uses to generate identical keys locally. The algorithm used to do this is called the Diffie-Hellman algorithm (DH). This exchange of key-generating data and identical key creation is called a ***key exchange***.

Only after the DH key exchange takes place do the hosts authenticate with one another. They can do this by using a variety of authentication methods, which are tried in the order that they are presented in the following list. To authenticate, the hosts must have an authentication method in common. Authentication methods offered by Windows Vista and commonly used in IPsec include:

- **Kerberos V5**. Used for computers in the same domain, or computers in different domains when the domains have a trust relationship.
- **NTLMv2**. A Microsoft authentication method using a challenge and response. One host sends a challenge consisting of a string of characters, and the other host must return the correct response.
- **Certificate**. You can specify that a certificate from a particular certificate authority is required to authenticate. Certificates are electronic documents that identify entities such as users or computers.
- **Pre-shared key**. This authentication method is less secure than the other methods. Each host must share a key before the IPsec session.

Using Windows Firewall with Advanced Security to Implement IPsec

CERTIFICATION READY?
Configure network security:
- IPSec
- Windows Firewall

1.5

You can use Windows Firewall with Advanced Security, either locally or through Group Policy, to implement IPsec on your network or between networks.

You can implement IPsec in Vista using the Windows Firewall with Advanced Security by using a Connection Security Rule. Connection Security Rules enable you to specify IPsec parameters for an IPsec session between hosts.

You can use the New Connection Security Rule Wizard to help you create connection security rules. The wizard offers five rule types:

- **Isolation**. This type of rule uses authentication criteria that you supply to restrict connections and thus isolate computers from other computers, such as those outside your domain. For example, you could require all computers in your domain to authenticate using IPsec before communicating.
- **Authentication exemption**. This type of rule is actually used to exempt computers from IPsec connection restrictions rather than to subject them to IPsec connection restrictions. It is often used to grant access to infrastructure computers such as domain controllers and DHCP servers that computers need to communicate with before authenticating.
- **Server-to-server**. This type of rule is used to authenticate communications between two specific computers, between two groups of computers, between two subnets, or between a specific computer and a group of computers or a subnet. For example, you can use this type of rule to authenticate between infrastructure computers to decrease the chance of an imposter infrastructure computer.

- **Tunnel**. This type of rule is for securing communications between two peer computers through tunnel endpoints, such as virtual private networking (VPN). An example of Virtual Private Networking is a computer on a distant network using the Internet to connect and authenticate to a domain.
- **Custom**. You can use this type of rule to create custom IPsec configurations.

There are two interfaces where you can configure IPsec through Windows Firewall with Advanced Security. One is local, using the Windows Firewall with Advanced Security snap-in. The other is through Group Policy. The former creates settings that apply only to the local computer, whereas the latter creates settings that can be applied to groups of computers through Group Policy.

You can find more information on Windows Firewall with Advanced Security in **Lesson 7: Using Windows Firewall and Windows Defender.** You can find more information on using Group Policy in **Lesson 4.**

CREATE A CUSTOM CONNECTION SECURITY RULE

OPEN the Windows Firewall with Advanced Security settings (either locally or through Group Policy; see Lesson 7 for more information).

1. In Windows Firewall with Advanced Security settings, in the console tree, right-click **Connection Security Rules** and then click **New Rule.** The Rule Type page of the New Connection Security Rule Wizard appears as shown in Figure 11-8.

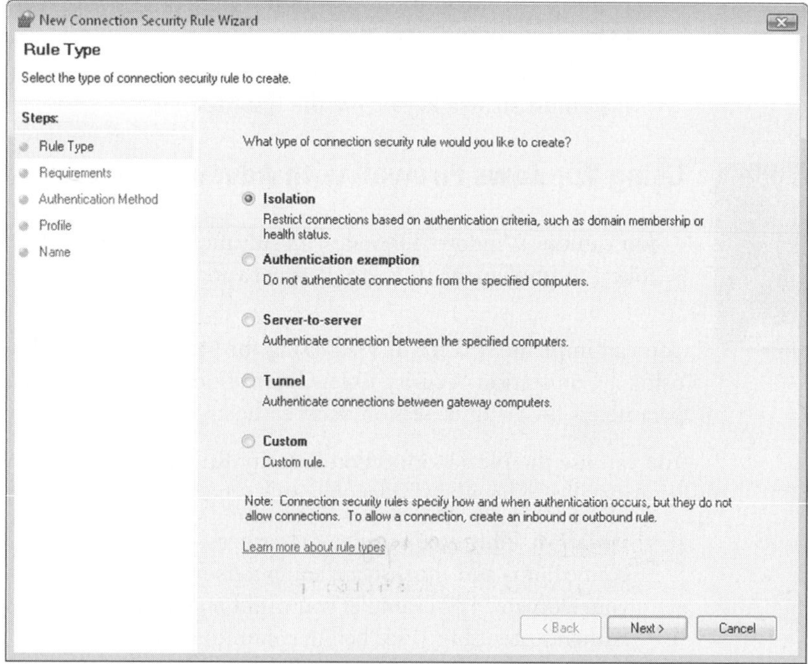

Figure 11-8

The New Connection Security Rule Wizard

2. Select **Custom** and then click **Next.** The Endpoints page appears.
3. Under Which computers are in Endpoint 1, select one of the following:

   Any IP address. Select this option to create a rule that applies to any host for Endpoint 1. For example, if you were creating a rule through Group Policy for a group of computers and you wanted them all to use this connection security rule, you would select Any IP address.

   These IP addresses. Select this option to specify IP addresses, IP address ranges, subnets, or predefined computers such as DNS servers or DHCP servers. For example, if you wanted to create a rule that applied only to the local computer for Endpoint 1, you could select this option and add the local IP address. An example of an added IP address is shown in Figure 11-9.

Figure 11-9

The Endpoints page of the New Security Connection Wizard with example settings

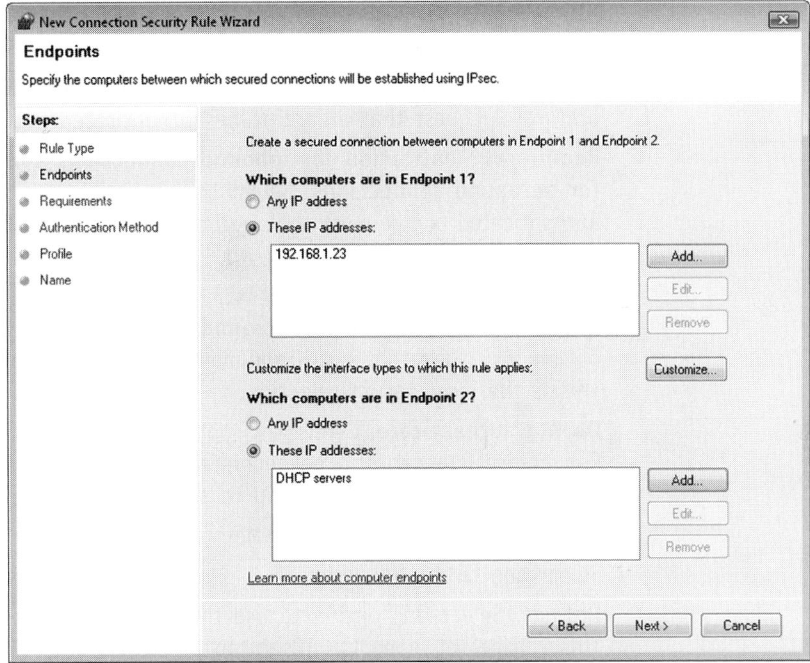

4. To specify to which interface types on the Endpoint 1 host(s) the rule applies, click **Customize**. The Customize Interface Types dialog box appears, as shown in Figure 11-10. Select one of the following:

   All Interface types. Select this option to apply the rule to all interface types.

   These interface types. Select this option to specify the type of interface to which the rule applies. If you select this option, configure the following check boxes:

   - **Local area network.** Select this check box to apply the rule to connections using a local area network interface.
   - **Remote access.** Select this check box to apply the rule to connections using remote access.
   - **Wireless.** Select this check box to apply the rule to connections using wireless interfaces.

Figure 11-10

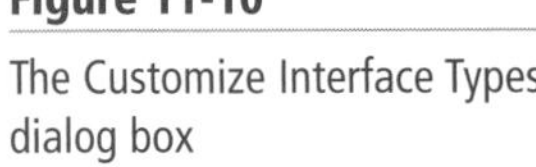

The Customize Interface Types dialog box

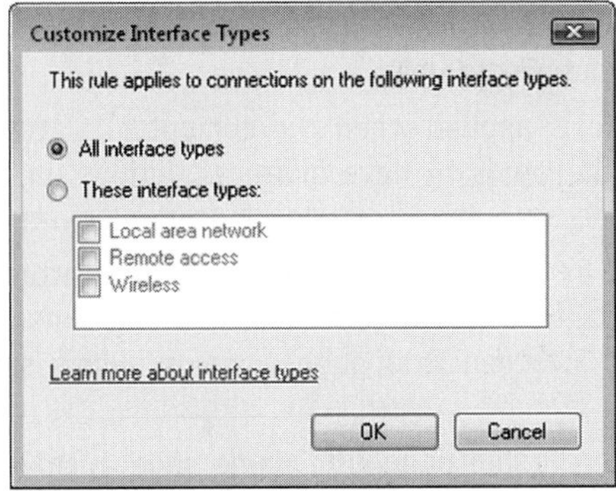

5. On the Endpoints page, under Which computers are in Endpoint 2, configure the same settings for Endpoint 2 that you did for Endpoint 1. For example, you might be creating a rule to except all communications to DHCP servers. In this case, select **These IP addresses**, click **Add**, and then select **DHCP servers**.
6. Click **Next**. The Requirements page appears.
7. Select one of the following:

   Request authentication for inbound and outbound connections. Select this option to request that all traffic be authenticated but proceed if it is not.

   Require authentication for inbound connections and request authentication for outbound connections. Select this option to require that inbound traffic be authenticated and request that outbound traffic be authenticated. In other words, you're saying, "I need to know who you are before we communicate, but you don't need to know who I am."

   Require authentication for inbound and outbound connections. Select this option to require that both inbound and outbound traffic be authenticated. This is the most secure selection.

   Do not authenticate. Select this option if authentication is not important to you. Communications can still be encrypted if you select this option. If you select this option, click Next and then skip to step 11.
8. Click **Next**. The Authentication Method page appears.
9. Select one of the following:

   Default. Select this option to use the default authentication method for the host. This can be set using the IPsec tab of the Windows Firewall with Advanced Security Properties dialog box.

   Computer and user (Kerberos V5). Select this option to authenticate both the host and the user using Kerberos V5.

   Computer (Kerberos V5). Select this option to authenticate the host computer only, not the user, using Kerberos V5.

   Computer certificate. Select this option to authenticate using a certificate. Your domain must have a certificate authority to use this option.

   Advanced. Select this option to configure a method not available in the other options, and to specify a First Authentication and Second Authentication. First Authentication methods include Computer Kerberos, computer certificate, and a pre-shared key. Second Authentication methods include User Kerberos, User NTLM, user certificates, and computer health certificates.
10. Click **Next**. The Profile page appears.
11. Configure the following:

    Domain. Select this check box if you want the rule to be applied when a computer is connected to the domain. The Domain profile tends to have the least restrictions on communications because the computer is presumed to be less open to attack from outside threats.

    Private. The rule is applied when the computer is attached to a private network. The Private profile tends to have more restrictions on communication than the Domain profile because the threat level on the private network is unknown.

    Public. The rule is applied when the computer is attached to a public network. The Public profile tends to have the most restrictions on communications because the computer is attached to a public network where security vulnerabilities are more common.
12. Click **Next** on the Profile page. The Name page appears.
13. In the **Name** text box, key a name for the rule. Use a descriptive name that will be useful if you need to troubleshoot rules.

14. In the **Description (optional)** text box, key a detailed description of
15. Click **Finish**. The rule is added to the Connection Security Rules list.

Creating rules of the remaining types is similar to creating a custom rule, and usually simp because you have fewer options to choose from. Table 11-17 shows the remaining rule types when to use them, and it provides notes on how configuring them is different from configuring a custom rule.

Table 11-17

Settings on the Network Permissions tab of the *WirelssPolicyName* Properties dialog box

RULE TYPE	WHEN TO USE	COMPARED TO A CREATING A CUSTOM RULE
Isolation	An isolation rule is a rule that requires authentication to communicate. You can use it, for example, to isolate a computer from other domains or to isolate a group of servers from other computers.	The configuration is nearly identical except there is no Endpoints page to configure (because isolation rules are about isolating a single computer), and you must select an Authentication scheme on the Requirements page (Do not authenticate is not an available option as it is in other rules).
Authentication exemption	Authentication exemption has the reverse purpose of all the other rule types; its purpose is to exempt computers from IPsec authentication requirements. It is commonly used to grant access to infrastructure computers. For example, if your DNS servers, domain controllers, and DHCP servers all had IP addresses in a particular range, you could exempt that range of addresses.	You do not configure the Endpoints, Requirements, or Authentication method pages. There is, however, an additional page you must configure: Exempt computers. On this page you specify the exempt computers by IP address, IP address range, or predefined set of computers (e.g., DNS servers).
Server-to-server	The name says it all—this rule is designed to create rules for communicating between servers. It is almost as flexible as a custom rule, however, so you can use it to configure IPsec between subnets, IP address ranges, etc.	You must select an authentication scheme on the Requirements page (Do not authenticate is not an available option as it is in other rules).
Tunnel	Tunnel rules are for configuring IPsec between tunnel endpoints (e.g., two computers communicating using a virtual private networking connection across the Internet. Virtual private networks are covered in **Lesson 12**.	You do not configure the Requirements page, because it is assumed that in a tunneling scenario both endpoints must authenticate both incoming and outgoing traffic. The Endpoints page is replaced with the Tunnel Endpoints page, which is slightly more complex. In addition to configuring endpoints (which can be individual computers or groups according subnet, IP address range, etc.), you configure the local tunnel computers by IP address. These are the computers that the computers in the endpoints use to communicate with computers outside the local network (in other words, they are the gateway computers).

SUMMARY SKILL MATRIX

IN THIS LESSON YOU LEARNED:
TCP/IP is the most commonly used network communications protocol in use today. It is used on the Internet and in most other networks such as enterprise networks.
IP addresses are how hosts in a TCP/IP network identify each other.
Subnetting enables you to split a network into multiple networks by using a subnet mask.
How to convert decimal octets into binary octets, and vice-versa.
How to perform AND and NOT operations on binary octets.
Domain Name System is a user-friendly naming convention. DNS names, called fully qualified domain names, are converted into IP addresses by DNS name servers so that TCP/IP hosts can communicate.
Dynamic Host Control Protocol is a protocol by which TCP/IP hosts can automatically obtain IP addresses and supporting information.
How to configure IPv4 TCP/IP network settings manually.
How to use DHCP to configure IPv4 TCP/IP settings automatically.
How to configure an alternate IP address.
How to configure Windows Vista wired network policy through Group Policy.
The importance of wireless network security and how to implement it.
How to configure Windows Vista wireless policy for infrastructure networks.
IP security protocol in Vista can be implemented using Windows Firewall with Advanced Security. You can configure custom IP security policies to fit a variety of requirements.
How to create connection security rules.

■ Knowledge Assessment

Fill in the Blank

Complete the following sentences by writing the correct word or words in the blanks provided.

1. A DHCP server can provide supporting information along with an IP address, such as a default gateway, or preferred DNS server. These pieces of supporting information in the context of DHCP are called Options.
2. DNS names are called FQDM.
3. Data Integraty indicates that the data sent by one computer to another is the same when it arrives as when it left.
4. When you apply a subnet mask to an IP address, you are left with a network ID and Host.
5. Single Signon -SSO enables you to log on to a wireless network and a domain with a single act of signing on.
6. Dividing a network into subnets using a subnet mask is called Subnetting.
7. Identifying yourself with a user name and password when logging onto a domain is an example of Athenication.

8. A(n) ________________ is used to resolve DNS names into IP addresses.

9. The protocol that TCP/IP hosts use to request IP addresses from servers is called ________________.

10. The storing of mappings between fully qualified domain names and IP addresses for later use is called ________________.

Multiple Choice

Select all answers that apply for the following questions.

1. The underlying communications protocol for the Internet and most networks is:
- **a.** Hyper Text Transfer Protocol (HTTP)
- **b.** Transmission Control Protocol/Internet Protocol (TCP/IP)
- **c.** Dynamic Host Control Protocol (DHCP)
- **d.** Domain Name System (DNS)

2. Which of the following are not valid Class C IP addresses?
- **a.** 237.168.0.1
- **b.** 192.168.0.1
- **c.** 192.168.0.127
- **d.** 127.192.168.121

3. How many subnets do you get on a class B network with the subnet mask 255.255.0.0?
- **a.** 0
- **b.** 1
- **c.** 2
- **d.** 4

4. A DHCP server returns an offered IP address to its pool of available IP address after receiving which of the following:
- **a.** A DHCPACK message stating that another DHCP server had been chosen to supply the IP address
- **b.** A DHCPREQUEST message identifying another DHCP server as the server chosen to supply the IP address
- **c.** A DHCPOFFER message stating that another IP address has been accepted
- **d.** A DHCPOFFER message identifying the DHCP server as the server chosen to supply the IP address

5. A host receives a DHCP lease with a duration of 24 hours. The host will attempt to renew the lease at each startup and:
- **a.** 6, 12, 18, and 24 hours after the lease begins.
- **b.** 12, 21, and 24 hours after the lease begins.
- **c.** 24 hours after the lease begins.
- **d.** 12 and 21 hours after the lease begins.

6. Which of the following is the most secure?
- **a.** WEP protected wireless network
- **b.** WPA2 protected wireless network
- **c.** WPA protected wireless network
- **d.** DNS protected wireless network

7. 10.21.2.123 is an example of a(n):
- **a.** Class A IP address.
- **b.** Class B IP address.
- **c.** Class C IP address.
- **d.** invalid IP address.

8. A laptop user turns off her laptop, takes it home, and attaches it to her home network. The next day, she removes it from her home network, but does not turn it off. She takes it in to work and connects it to the enterprise network. She finds that she cannot access her email. You investigate and find that the IP address for the laptop is 192.168.0.3. The enterprise network uses Class A IP addresses. Which of the following (you can select more than one) are plausible explanations for what happened?
   a. The laptop configured itself with an APIPA address on the home network. The address was not changed to a Class A IP address because the user did not reboot after connecting to the enterprise network.
   b. The laptop used its alternate IP address when attached to the home network. The laptop configured itself with an APIPA address on the home network. The address was not changed to a Class A IP address because the user did not reboot after connecting to the enterprise network.
   c. 192.168.0.3 is a Class A IP address; the problem is not with the IP address.
   d. The laptop was given the IP address 192.168.0.3 by a DHCP server on the home network when it attempted to renew its old IP address lease. The laptop configured itself with an APIPA address on the home network. The address was not changed to a Class A IP address because the user did not reboot after connecting to the enterprise network.
9. Which of the following connection security rules do not require you to configure two endpoints?
   a. Tunnel
   b. Authentication exemption
   c. Server-to-server
   d. Isolation
10. On the Contoso wireless network, you want to use computer authentication until a user logs on, at which point you want to switch to user authentication. Which authentication mode should you use?
    a. Computer authentication
    b. User authentication
    c. User re-authentication
    d. Guest authentication

Review Questions

1. Describe the DHCP communications process between a DHCP client and server for renewing an existing lease in comparison to the process for requesting a new lease.
2. From right-to-left, identify each level of the FQDN northwind.woodgrovebank.com. Include the implied, but not expressed, level.

■ Case Scenarios

Scenario 1: Creating Wireless Policies

Contoso is adding wireless networks on two floors of a building in a branch office. It is your job to create wireless policies through Group Policy for both networks. The settings for each wireless network are going to be nearly the same, except for a couple of settings. How can you most efficiently create the policies?

Scenario 2: Alternate IP Address for Mobile Computers

A laptop user works from home as much as she does from work. She does not have a DHCP server on her home network. How can you configure her laptop so that she can easily connect to her home network? Where is the interface for doing so? Use an example to explain how the solution will work.

Configuring and Troubleshooting Access

LESSON 12

OBJECTIVE DOMAIN MATRIX

Technology Skill	Objective Domain	Objective Domain Number
Understanding and Configuring Remote Assistance	Configure and troubleshoot remote access • Remote Assistance	4.3
Configure Remote Assistance Through Group Policy	Configure and troubleshoot remote access • Remote Assistance	4.3
Using Remote Desktop	Configure and troubleshoot remote access • Remote Desktop	4.3
Configuring Remote Desktop Through Group Policy	Configure and troubleshoot remote access • Remote Desktop	4.3
Understanding and Configuring Virtual Private Networks	Configure and troubleshoot remote access • VPN connections	4.3
Configuring VPN Users	Configure and troubleshoot remote access • VPN connections	4.3
Accessing Local and Network Resources	Configure and troubleshoot access to resources Troubleshoot access to network resources	2.6 4.7
Understanding Permissions	Configure and troubleshoot access to resources • Files and folders	4.7
Configuring NTFS Permissions	Configure and troubleshoot access to resources • Files and folders	4.7
Configuring Network Sharing	Configure and troubleshoot access to resources • Printers • Configure Network Discovery and Sharing	4.7
Troubleshooting Networking	Troubleshoot connectivity issues Configure and troubleshoot wireless networking Troubleshoot access to network resources	4.4 4.5 4.7
Troubleshooting networking with command-line tools	Troubleshoot connectivity issues	4.4
Using Windows Network Diagnostics	Troubleshoot connectivity issues • Use the Network Connections Diagnostics tool	4.4

KEY TERMS

Remote Assistance
Terminal Services
Remote Desktop
Terminal Services (TS) Gateway server
virtual private network (VPN)
VPN servers
Local resources
network resources
NTFS
NTFS permissions
Special permissions
Standard permissions
effective permissions
Network Access Protection (NAP)
Ping
IPConfig
Net view
TraceRt
Pathping
NSlookup
DNS resolver cache
Windows Network Diagnostics (WND)

Understanding and Configuring Remote Assistance

Remote Assistance enables support technicians to help clients remotely by viewing and controlling users' desktops. Because technicians don't have to travel to the computer's location, enterprises can see substantial gains in support efficiency by implementing Remote Assistance.

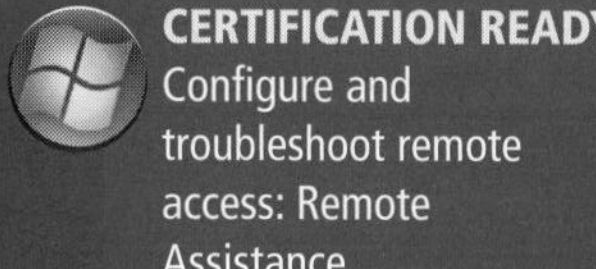
CERTIFICATION READY? Configure and troubleshoot remote access: Remote Assistance 4.3

Remote Assistance enables a technology professional or other user to connect to your computer remotely. The connected user (herein called the assistant, also called an expert) can view your computer screen, and chat using text messages. With your permission, the assistant can control your computer with his mouse and keyboard.

For just a moment consider yourself a user needing assistance. To request Remote Assistance, you invite the assistant using an email or instant message (or by re-using an old invitation). After the assistant accepts the invitation, Windows Remote Assistance creates an encrypted connection between your computer and the assistant's computer. The assistant's computer can but does not need to be on the local network.

An assistant can also extend an offer of assistance, rather than relying on an invitation. You then can accept the offer, at which point Windows Remote Assistance will establish the encrypted connection.

The assistant can perform only actions that require elevated credentials when you grant permission through User Account Control (UAC) consent user interface (UI), or explicitly enable him to do so by selecting the Allow *AssistantName* to respond to User Account Control prompts check box. If you grant permission through a Consent UI, your user name and password will not be visible to the assistant.

User Account Control is covered in **Lesson 8: Troubleshooting Access, Authentication, and User Account Control Issues.**

Remote Assistance is implemented using ***Terminal Services***, which is a set of services that give you access applications or data stored on a remote computer over a network connection.

In an enterprise environment, you will most often configure Remote Assistance settings through Group Policy. However, you can configure Remote Assistance locally when required.

CONFIGURE REMOTE ASSISTANCE SETTINGS LOCALLY

1. Click **Start**, right-click **Computer**, and then click **Properties.** The System control panel appears.
2. Click **Remote settings** in the task list. A User Account Control dialog box appears.
3. Provide credentials and then click **OK**. The System Properties dialog box appears.
4. Click the **Remote** tab, which is shown in Figure 12-1.

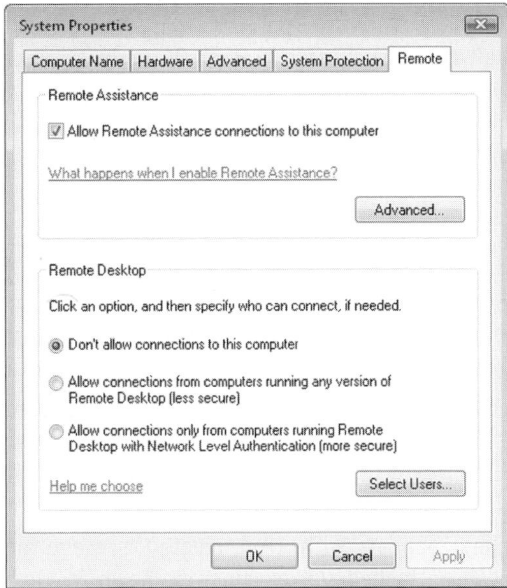

Figure 12-1

The Remote tab of the System Properties dialog box

5. To enable Remote Assistance, ensure that the **Allow Remote Assistance connections to this computer** check box is selected.
6. Click **Advanced.** The Remote Assistance Settings dialog box appears, as shown in Figure 12-2.

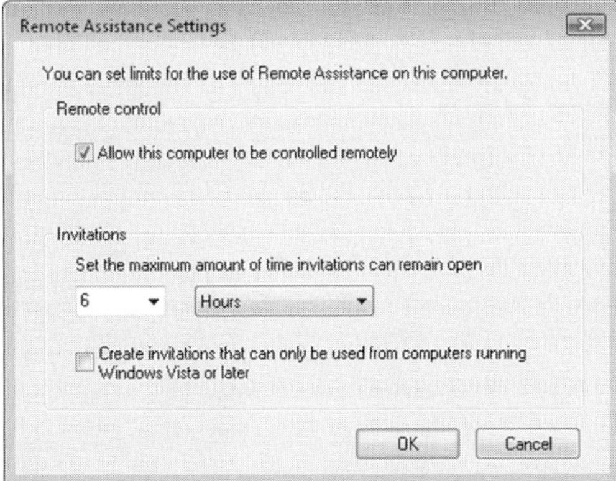

Figure 12-2

The Remote Assistance Settings dialog box

7. To enable an assistant to control your computer (rather than just see your desktop), select the **Allow this computer to be controlled remotely** check box.
8. In the Invitations section, in the corresponding drop-down lists, configure how long it takes for an invitation to expire. When choosing a setting, remember that open invitations can be a security risk.
9. To allow your computer to create invitations that can only be used by computers running Windows Vista or later, select the **Create invitations that can only be used by Windows Vista or later** check box. The reason for doing this is that Windows Vista invitations are more secure.
10. Click **OK**.

INVITE REMOTE ASSISTANCE

This procedure assumes you are a user requesting help from an assistant.

ANOTHER WAY

Click Start> All Programs> Maintenance>Windows Remote Assistance.

1. Click **Start**. In the **Start Search** text box, key **msra** and then press **Enter**. The Windows Remote Assistance Wizard appears.
2. Click **Invite someone you trust to help you**. The How do you want to invite someone to help you? page appears.
3. Click one of the following:

   Use e-mail to send an invitation. This is the easiest option if you have configured an email client such as Microsoft Outlook. If you select this option, continue to step 4.

   Save this invitation as a file. You can select this option if you want to attach the invitation to an email and mail it manually. For example, you can choose this option to use web email to send an invitation. If you select this option, follow the instructions in the wizard, save the file to any location, and then get it to the assistant one way or another. The most common way is to attach it to an email that you send to the assistant. Continue to step 7.

   Click an existing invitation. You can also resend an existing invitation by clicking it. Existing invitations are listed under the heading Or use a previous invitation again.
4. On the Choose a password for connecting to your computer page, key a password in the **Password (at least 6 characters)** text box and the **Retype the password** text box. Click **Next**. If you have not configured a mail client, the wizard will walk you through that task. Follow the instructions and continue to step 5.
5. Your mail client appears with a pre-created message and subject. The invitation file is automatically attached. An example is shown in Figure 12-3. In the **To** text box, key the assistant's email address. Send the email.

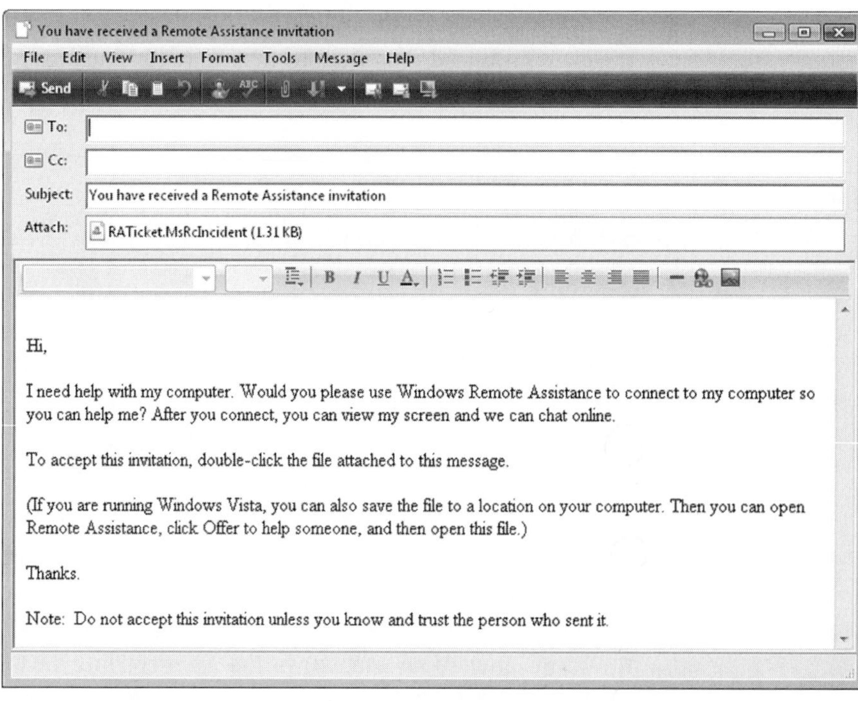

Figure 12-3

An email client with an invitation file attached. The invitation should be sent to the assistant.

6. The Windows Remote Assistance control window appears, as shown in Figure 12-4.

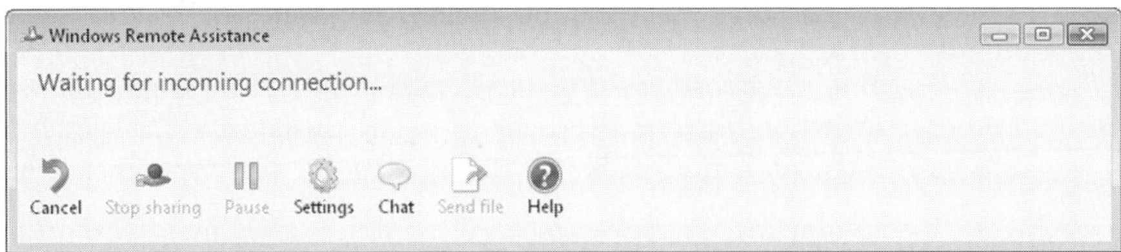

Figure 12-4

You can control the Remote Assistance session by using the Windows Remote Assistance control window

7. Before the assistant can accept the invitation, you must convey the password to the assistant. If you can, you should do this by phone to provide an additional safeguard if computer communications have been compromised.
8. Once the assistant accepts the invitation, a Windows Remote Assistance message box appears asking if you want to enable the assistant to connect, as shown in Figure 12-5. Click **Yes**.

Figure 12-5

Windows Remote Assistance message box asking if you want to enable the assistant to connect to your computer

9. Windows Remote Assistant creates an encrypted session between your computer and the assistant's. You can control the session by using the buttons in the control window. Table 12-1 provides more information on each button.

Table 12-1

You can control a Remote Assistance session by using the following buttons.

Button	Description
Cancel	Click this button to cancel the assistance session.
Stop sharing	Click this button to stop sharing control of your desktop. This button is not available until you have given control of your desktop to the assistant.
Pause Continue	This is a toggle button that toggles between a Pause button and a Continue button. Click Pause to pause sharing. Click Continue to continue sharing.
Settings	Click this button to adjust settings, which include a slider that determines how much network bandwidth is used. Adjust it higher if there are no performance problems, and lower if there are. You can also configure the Use ESC key to stop sharing control and Save a log of this session check boxes. If you are logged on as an administrator, you can also select the Allow helper to respond to User Account Control prompts check box (it doesn't appear if you are logged in as a standard user). If you select this check box, the assistant can respond to UAC consent user interfaces (UIs) directly. Select this check box only if you know for certain that you can trust the assistant.
Chat	Click to start a text chat session with the assistant.
Send file	Click to send a file to the assistant.
Help	Click to get additional help on using Remote Assistance.

10. Before the assistant can control your desktop, she must request to do so by clicking the Request control button in the Windows Remote Assistance–Helping *User name* control window. You then can respond Yes or No to her request.

You may have guessed that the email or instant message options are just ways of getting the invitation file from the user who needs assistance to the assistant. As long as the assistant gets the invitation, regardless of the method, she can respond and the user can start the session.

In some circumstances, especially with less savvy users, you (in the role of an assistant) may want to initiate a session rather than relying on the user to send you an invitation.

To successfully offer Remote Assistance to a user, three conditions must be met:

- You must be added to the list of helpers in the Offer Remote Assistance Group Policy setting. This can be through a local or Active Directory Group Policy Object (GPO).
- Windows Firewall must except `msra.exe` and `raserver.exe`.
- Windows Firewall must allow communication on DCOM port 135 (TCP).

To meet the first condition, you need to configure the Offer Remote Assistance Group Policy setting for either the local machine, or in an Active Directory Group Policy Object that controls policy for the target computer. See the last row in Table 12-2 for more information on this setting.

You can configure a computer locally to meet the latter two conditions through the Windows Firewall control panel. On the Exceptions tab, select the Remote Assistance check box and then click OK. This single action will meet both of the Windows Firewall conditions in the preceding list.

Windows Firewall exceptions are covered in **Lesson 7: Using Windows Firewall and Windows Defender.**

In an enterprise, you will typically meet all three conditions though Group Policy so that you don't have to configure target computers individually. Instructions on configuring Group Policy for Remote Assistance are given later in this lesson.

OFFER REMOTE ASSISTANCE

This procedure assumes that you are a support professional offering to assist a user.

1. Click **Start**. In the **Start Search** text box, key **msra** and then press **Enter**. The Windows Remote Assistance Wizard appears.
2. Click **Offer to help someone**. The Choose a way to connect to the other person's computer page appears.
3. Do one of the following:

   Use the Enter an invitation file location text box. You can do this if you have an invitation from the person you want to offer assistance to. For example, if you frequently help the same people, you can collect invitations and use them when necessary. You can use the Browse button to find the invitation file.

   Select an existing invitation. Existing invitations are listed under the heading Or use a previous connection. To use one of these, click the invitation.

   Use the Type a computer name or IP address option. This is a very common option in an enterprise environment in which you are helping people in your domain. You can enter a computer name (e.g., acct43), or an Internet Protocol (IP) address (e.g., 10.1.2.123).
4. Click **Finish**. The user on the identified computer is presented with a Windows Remote Assistance message box asking if they want you to connect.
5. If the user accepts the assistance offer, click **Request control** to request control of the user's desktop.

Configure Remote Assistance through Group Policy

You can simultaneously centrally manage Remote Assistance for many computers by using Group Policy.

You access Remote Assistance Group Policy settings in the Windows Settings>Administrative Templates>System>Remote Assistance node in Group Policy Objects. Table 12-2 offers information about each setting.

Table 12-2

You can configure Remote Assistance by using Group Policy.

GROUP POLICY SETTING	DESCRIPTION
Allow only Vista or later connections	Causes Remote Assistance invitations to be generated with improved encryption so that only computers running Windows Vista or later can connect. This setting does not affect Remote Assistance connections that are initiated by instant messaging contacts or the unsolicited Offer Remote Assistance. • **Enabled**: Only computers running Windows Vista or later can connect to the computer. • **Disabled**: Computers running previous versions of Windows can connect to the computer. • **Not Configured**: Same as Disabled.
Turn on session logging	Turns logging on or off. Log files are located in the user's Documents folder under Remote Assistance. • **Enabled**: Logging is turned on and log files will be created. Logging can be useful for users if they want to see how you did something. They can also be useful for troubleshooting if actions during a Remote Assistance session cause problems. • **Disabled**: Logging is turned off and log files are not created. • **Not Configured**: Logging will be controlled by the application.
Turn on bandwidth optimization	Enables you to adjust bandwidth use. You can use this setting to reduce bandwidth usage of you are worried about too much traffic on the network, or if Remote Assistance sessions run too slowly. Higher bandwidth sessions, however, provide a more pleasing and complete connected experience. This setting is incrementally scaled from No optimization to Full optimization. Each incremental setting includes the previous optimization setting. • **Enabled**: If you enable this policy setting, bandwidth optimization will occur at the level specified. • **Disabled**: Bandwidth use is controlled by the application. • **Not Configured**: Same as Disabled.
Customize Warning Messages	Enables you to specify a custom message to display before a user shares control of his computer. • **Enable**: You can specify a custom message to display before a user shares control of his computer. • **Disabled**: The default message is used. • **Not configured**: Same as Disabled.

(*continued*)

Table 12-2 (*continued*)

Group Policy Setting	Description
Solicited Remote Assistance	Determines whether users can solicit Remote Assistance from the computer. If you enable this policy you should also enable appropriate firewall exceptions to allow Remote Assistance communications. It is recommended that you enable this policy setting so that users can request Remote Assistance. Remote Assistance can save time and resources because technicians don't have to travel to the computer. If you do not enable this policy setting, consider enabling the Offer Remote Assistance policy setting. If you enable this policy you should also enable appropriate firewall exceptions to allow Remote Assistance communications. • **Enabled**: Users can solicit Remote Assistance. The Select the method for sending e-mail invitations setting specifies which email standard to use to send Remote Assistance invitations. Depending on your email program, you can use either the Mailto standard (the invitation recipient connects through an Internet link) or the SMAPI (Simple MAPI) standard (the invitation is attached to your email message). This setting is not available in Windows Vista because SMAPI is the only method supported. • **Disabled**: Users cannot solicit Remote Assistance from the computer. • **Not Configured**: Local settings on the Remote tab of the System Properties dialog box determine whether or not users can solicit Remote Assistance from the computer.
Offer Remote Assistance	Determines whether technicians can offer Remote Assistance on computer. It is recommended that you enable this policy so that technicians can offer assistance to users remotely. If you enable this policy you should also enable appropriate firewall exceptions to allow Remote Assistance communications. • **Enabled**: Users can receive and accept offers of Remote Assistance from support technicians. • **Disabled**: Users cannot receive and accept offers of Remote Assistance from support technicians. • **Not Configured**: Local settings on the Remote tab of the System Properties dialog box determine whether users can receive offers of Remote Assistance.

Using Remote Desktop

THE BOTTOM LINE

Remote Desktop enables you to connect to a computer from another computer over a network, such as a local area network or a virtual private network.

CERTIFICATION READY? Configure and troubleshoot remote access: Remote Desktop 4.3

Remote Desktop enables you to connect to a computer (Computer A) from a remote computer (Computer B) over a network (such as a virtual private network over the Internet, or a local area network). You can control Computer A by using the mouse and keyboard on Computer B, and you can see the contents of Computer A's screen on Computer B's screen.

Remote Desktop can be an excellent tool for working from home when you cannot take your work computer with you. It can also be a great tool for remote administration of servers and infrastructure computers. You can reduce the chance of physical damage to infrastructure computers such as domain controllers (and increase security) by requiring administrators to log onto them remotely.

Before you can use Remote Desktop to connect to a computer, you must first:

1. Add the user account with which you want to connect to the target computer to the Remote Desktop Users group of the target computer. Administrators are members of this group by default.

You can find more information on configuring exceptions in Windows Firewall in **Lesson 7.**

2. Configure the firewall to allow Remote Desktop connections. You can do this locally by enabling the Remote Desktop exception in the Windows Firewall control panel or you can do it through Group Policy.
3. Ensure that the target computer allows Remote Desktop connections. You can do this either through Group Policy or locally.

When you use Remote Desktop to connect to a computer that isn't on the local network (e.g., if you want to connect to your work computer from your home computer), you need to either make use of a virtual private network connection (VPN; covered later in this lesson) to connect to the target computer's network, or connect to a ***Terminal Services Gateway server (TS Gateway server)***. A TS Gateway server is a computer that enables authorized users to connect to a remote computer on a corporate network from anywhere on the Internet. You can specify a TS Gateway server by using the Remote Desktop Connection dialog box, or through Group Policy (both are covered later in this section).

Similar to Remote Assistance, Remote Desktop is implemented using Terminal Services.

Use this procedure to configure your computer to allow Remote Desktop connections and to add users to the Remote Desktop Users group.

CONFIGURE REMOTE DESKTOP SETTINGS LOCALLY

OPEN the System Properties dialog box.

1. In the System Properties dialog box, click the **Remote** tab.
2. In the Remote Desktop section, select one of the following:

   Don't allow connections to this computer. Select this option to prevent any Remote Desktop connections.

   Allow connections from computers running any version of Remote Desktop (less secure). Select this option to allow any version of Remote Desktop to connect to this computer.

   Allow connections only from computers running Remote Desktop with Network Level Authentication (more secure). Network Level Authentication (NLA) is a reordering of the normal authentication process. Ordinarily, to authenticate to a server you contact the server and then provide your credentials. This is a security risk because limited contact exists with the entity to which you are authenticating well before authentication. In NLA, you provide your user name and password first and only after that is the server contacted for authentication. NLA is included with all versions of Windows Vista.
3. Click **Select Users**. The Remote Desktop Users dialog box appears.
4. To enable a user or group to connect to this computer remotely, click **Add**. This is one way to add users to the Remote Desktop Users group. The Select Users or Groups dialog box appears.

   In the **Enter the object names to select** text box, key the user or group name (e.g., garrett vargas) and then click **Check Names.** If the name is not found, the Name not found dialog box appears. If the name is found then it is underlined.

   To search for a user instead of keying the user, click **Advanced**.

   Add as many users and groups as you want and then click **OK.** Figure 12-6 shows example users added.

Figure 12-6

Example users in the Remote Desktop Users dialog box

TAKE NOTE*

Administrators can connect whether or not they are listed.

5. To prevent a user or group listed in the Remote Desktop Users dialog box from connecting remotely to this computer, select the user or group and then click **Remove**.
6. When you are done adding and removing users or groups, click **OK** in the Remote Desktop Users dialog box.
7. Click **OK** in the System Properties dialog box.
8. Close the Control Panel.

In addition to the settings you configured in the preceding procedure, you can also configure settings in the Remote Desktop Connection dialog box. These settings center mostly around how a Remote Desktop session behaves. The following procedure and tables explain the settings in the Remote Connection Desktop dialog box.

CONFIGURE REMOTE DESKTOP SESSION SETTINGS LOCALLY

1. Click **Start**. Type **Remote Desktop** and then press **Enter**. The Remote Desktop Connection dialog box appears, as shown in Figure 12-7.

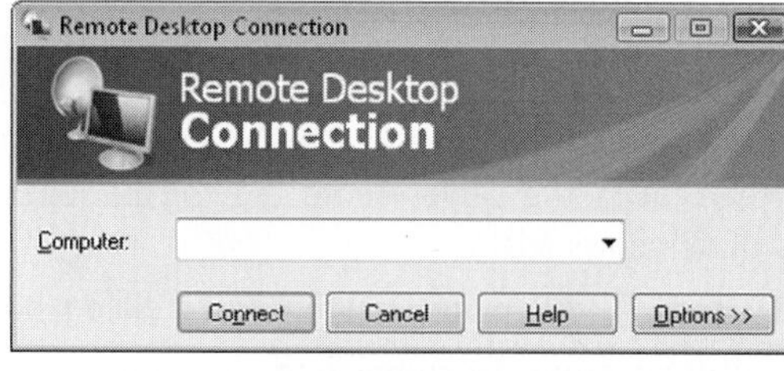

Figure 12-7

The Remote Desktop Connection dialog box

ANOTHER WAY

Click Start>All Programs>Accessories>Remote Desktop Connection.

2. Click **Options**. The dialog box is transformed to include additional settings and tabs, as shown in Figure 12-8. Tables 12-3 through 12-7 cover the settings on each tab. You may be disallowed from changing some settings; this is because an administrator has configured them through Group Policy, which is covered later in this section.

You can configure basic settings on the General tab of the Remote Desktop Connection dialog box, as shown in Figure 12-8.

Figure 12-8

Settings on the General tab of the Remote Desktop Connection dialog box

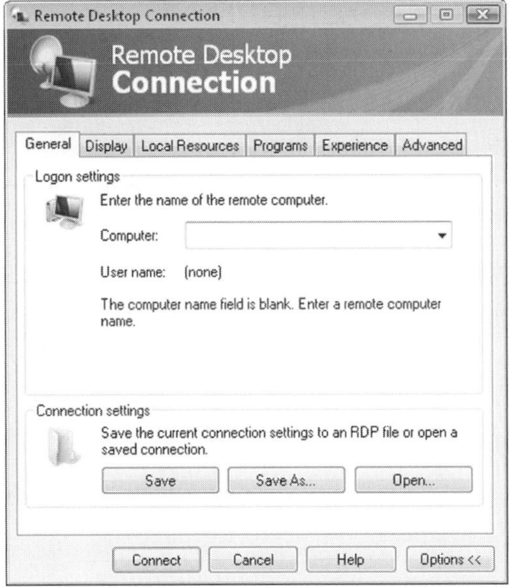

Table 12-3

Configure these settings on the General tab of the Remote Desktop Connection dialog box

Setting	Description
Computer drop-down list	This is a combination drop-down list and text box. You can type the target computer fully qualified domain name (FQDN) or IP address to identify the computer to connect to. You can also use the drop-down list to select a computer.
Save button Save As button	Click to save the current settings for this connection to a Remote Desktop Protocol (RDP) file in a location of your choice. You can then open the settings for later use. Saving enables you to save the settings on all of the tabs, not just the General tab.
Open button	Click to open an existing RDP file.

You can configure display-related settings on the Display tab, as shown in Figure 12-9 and explained in Table 12-4.

Figure 12-9

Settings on the Display tab of the Remote Desktop Connection dialog box

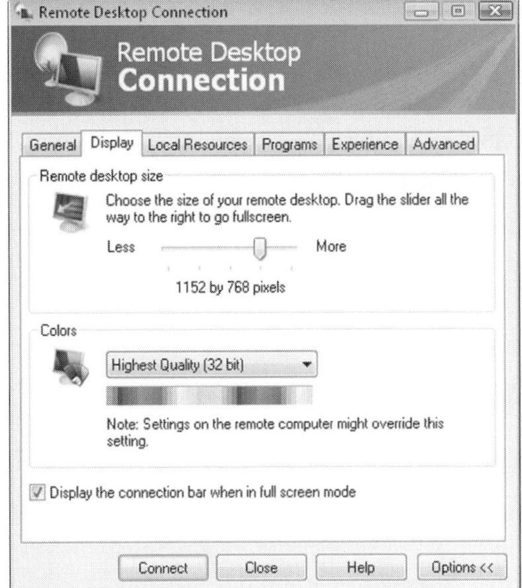

Table 12-4

Configure these settings on the Display tab of the Remote Desktop Connection dialog box.

SETTING	DESCRIPTION
Remote desktop size Resolution slider	Use the slider to set the resolution of your Remote Desktop window. Set it to the far right for full-screen viewing.
Colors drop-down list	Use this drop-down list to select the color depth to display on our Remote Desktop.
Display the connection bar when in full screen mode check box	Select this check box to display the connection bar, which enables you to close the connection or change the Remote Desktop window size, when in full-screen mode.

You can configure resource redirection by using the Local Resources tab, as shown in Figure 12-10. For example, you can redirect audio output to the local sound card rather than to the target computer's sound card. This way sound will play at your Remote Desktop and not at the target computer. Settings on this tab are described in Table 12-5.

Figure 12-10

Settings on the Local Resources tab of the Remote Desktop Connection dialog box

Table 12-5

Configure these settings on the Local Resources tab of the Remote Desktop Connection dialog box

SETTING	DESCRIPTION
Remote computer sound drop-down list	Use this drop-down list to select to where audio output is heard. Select one of the following: • **Bring to this computer** • **Do not play** • **Leave at remote computer**
Apply Windows key combinations (for example ALT + TAB) drop-down list	When you press Ctrl + Alt + Del, do you mean for it to apply to the local computer or to the remote computer? You use this list box to determine that. Select one of the following: • **On the local computer** • **On the remote computer** • **In full screen mode only**. Select this option to apply key combinations to the remote computer if you are in full-screen mode.

(continued)

Table 12-5 (*continued*)

Setting	Description
Select the devices and resources you want to use in your remote sessions check boxes	Select which local devices you want to use in your remote session. You can select one of the following check boxes: • **Printers** • **Clipboard** To specify other devices or resources, click More.

Using the Programs tab (shown in Figure 12-11), you can configure a program to run automatically whenever you connect. For example, perhaps you only connect remotely to use a specific application, and you want that application to launch automatically when you connect. Administrators can also assign a program to start through Group Policy. To specify a program to run, select the Start the following program on connection check box and then use the Program path and file name text box to specify which program to run. You can also supply a working directory for the program by using the Start in the following folder text box.

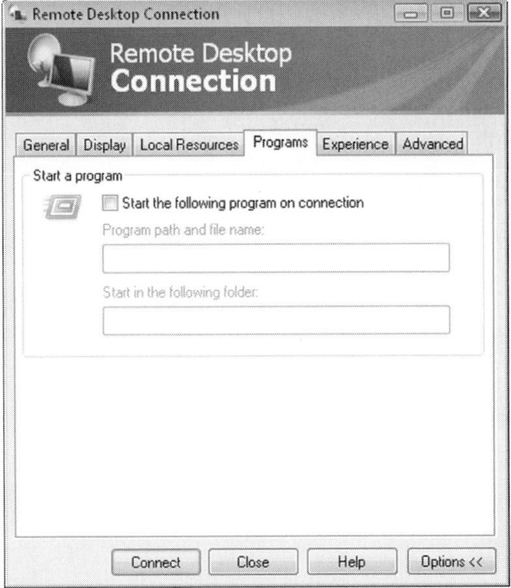

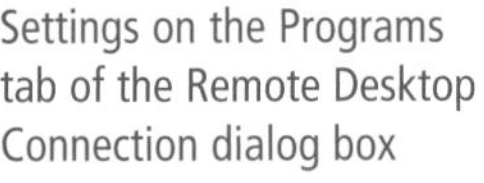

Figure 12-11

Settings on the Programs tab of the Remote Desktop Connection dialog box

You can configure the session experience by using the Experience tab, shown in Figure 12-12. For example, you can specify whether menus and windows are animated. By limiting the experience, you can limit bandwidth use. Table 12-6 describes each setting on the Experience tab.

Figure 12-12

Settings on the Experience tab of the Remote Desktop Connection dialog box

Table 12-6

Configure these settings on the Experience tab of the Remote Desktop Connection dialog box

Setting	Description
Choose your connection speed to optimize performance drop-down list	When you select one of the connection methods in this drop-down list, Remote Desktop Connection configures the check boxes in the Allow the following section in a way that is reasonable for the connection speed you select. Select one of the following speeds from the drop-down list: • **Modem (28.8 Kbps)** • **Modem (56 Kbps)** • **Broadband (128 Kbps – 1.5 Mbps)** • **LAN (10 Mbps or higher)** • **Custom**
Experience check boxes	You can configure the session experience by selecting or clearing the following check boxes: • **Desktop background** • **Font smoothing** • **Desktop composition** • **Show contents of window while dragging** • **Menu and window animation** • **Themes** • **Bitmap caching**
Reconnect if connection is dropped check box	Select this check box to reconnect automatically if a connection is dropped.

You can configure advanced settings on the Advanced tab, which is shown in Figure 12-13 and explained in Table 12-7.

Figure 12-13

Settings on the Advanced tab of the Remote Desktop Connection dialog box

Table 12-7

Configure these settings on the Advanced tab of the Remote Desktop Connection dialog box

SETTING	DESCRIPTION
Authentication options drop-down list	In an enterprise environment, an administrator usually controls this setting through Group Policy. Select one of the following: • **Always connect, even if authentication fails**. This is not a recommended setting when the target computer is a Windows Vista computer, because Windows Vista computers should be able to identify themselves for authentication. • **Warn me if authentication fails**. • **Do not connect if authentication fails**. This is the recommended setting for a secure environment.
Settings button	To start a Remote Desktop session when logging on from a remote location not on the network (e.g., over the Internet), you need to either connect to the network first (e.g., by using a VPN connection) or log into a TS server. Click Settings to configure how to connect to a TS Gateway server (see the next row in this table).
Gateway Server Settings	You can access these setting by clicking Settings (see the preceding row). Select one of the following: • **Automatically detect TS Gateway server settings**. Select this option to automatically detect settings provided by the TS Gateway server. • **Use these TS Gateway server settings**. If you select this option, configure the Server name text box and the Logon method drop-down list. • **Do not use a TS Gateway server**. If you select this option, the session will not attempt to use a TS Gateway server.

CONNECT TO A COMPUTER USING REMOTE DESKTOP

OPEN the Remote Desktop Connection dialog box.

1. On the General tab, in the **Computer** combo box, type the FQDN (e.g., acct42.contoso.com) or the IP address (e.g., 10.10.21.34) of the computer to which you want to connect.

TAKE NOTE* To establish a Remote Desktop connection, your local computer needs to be able to communicate with the remote computer. If you want to connect over the Internet, you can first establish a VPN or other connection to the remote computer's network.

2. Click **Connect.** The Windows Security dialog box appears and asks for credentials (assuming you are using Windows authentication and not a smart card or other method).
3. In the **User Name** text box, key the user name of the user that you want to use to connect to the target computer in the form *domain/user name* (e.g., contoso\jenr). Click **OK.**
4. If the connection is successful, a window will open over the full screen, showing the desktop of the remote computer. You can resize and adjust this window just like any other. Close the window and click **OK** in the resulting message box to end the session.

Configuring Remote Desktop through Group Policy

You can centrally manage Remote Desktop settings for many computers simultaneously by using Group Policy.

Because Terminal Services implements Remote Desktop, Remote Desktop Group Policy is configured through Terminal Services Group Policy settings. When configuring policies remember that a Remote Desktop session is a type of Terminal Services session.

More than 50 Group Policy settings are related to Terminal Services. Rather than cover each individually, Table 12-8 summarizes the settings according to their location in GPOs. You can configure Terminal Services Group Policy settings in the Computer Configuration>Administrative Templates>Windows Components>Terminal Services folder and subfolders of GPOs.

Table 12-8

Summary of policy settings in the Terminal Services Group Policy Object folder and subfolders. Remote Desktop is implemented through Terminal Services, and you therefore configure Remote Desktop policies through Terminal Services policies.

LOCATION IN GPO STARTING FROM TERMINAL SERVICES FOLDER	SUMMARY
Remote Desktop Connection Client	Contains a single setting: Do not allow passwords to be saved. You can use this setting to prevent users from saving passwords when they are connected using Terminal Services.
Terminal Server>Connections	This folder contains eight policy settings related to Terminal Services connections. Paramount among the settings is the Allow users to connect remotely using Terminal Services setting. If you enable this policy setting, users who are members of the Remote Desktop Users group on the target computer can connect remotely to the target computer by using Terminal Services. If you disable it, they cannot, and if you do not configure it, local settings take precedence.

(*continued*)

Table 12-8 ***(continued)***

Location in GPO starting from Terminal Services folder	Summary
	Policy settings in this folder include: • Automatic reconnection. • Allow users to connect remotely using Terminal Services. • Deny logoff of an administrator logged in to the console session. • Configure keep-alive connection interval. • Limit number of connections. • Set rules for remote control of Terminal Services user sessions. This setting enables you to control whether users in a Terminal Services session can just see the desktop, or if they can have full control. • Allow reconnection from original client only. • Restrict Terminal Services users to a single remote session.
Terminal Server>Device and Resource Redirection	If you are connected to a target computer miles away via Remote Desktop, and you want to hear audio produced from the target computer, you need to either turn up the volume very loud on the remote computer or redirect the audio to your local computer. You can use the policies in this folder to allow or restrict the redirection of remote resources to local resources. Policy settings in this folder include: • Allow audio redirection. • Do not allow clipboard redirection. • Do not allow COM port redirection. • Do not allow drive redirection. • Do not allow LPT port redirection. • Do not allow supported Plug and Play device redirection. • Do not allow smart card device redirection. • Allow time zone redirection.
Terminal Server>Licensing	Remote Desktop can conflict with software licensing because Remote Desktop enables multiple users to connect to a single machine. The policy settings in this folder control how Terminal Services (TS) communicates with licensing servers. Policy settings in this folder include: • Use the specified Terminal Server license servers. • Display notifications about TS licensing problems that affect the Terminal Server. • Set the Terminal Server licensing mode.
Terminal Server>Printer Redirection	The policy settings in this folder control how users can redirect print jobs on remote computers to print devices on the local computer. Policy settings in this folder include: • Do not set default client printer to be default printer in a session. • Do not allow client printer redirection. • Terminal Server Fallback Printer Driver Behavior.

(continued)

… 12-8 (*continued*)

Location in GPO starting from Terminal Services folder	Summary
Terminal Server>Profiles	The two policy settings in this folder control how Terminal Services store user profiles. Policy settings in this folder include: • Set TS User Home Directory. • Set path for TS Roaming Profiles.
Terminal Server>Remote Session Environment	These settings control, in part, what the user sees and can do in a Terminal Services session. For example, you can control the maximum color depth that the local computer uses. Policy settings in this folder include: • Limit maximum color depth. • Enforce Removal of Remote Desktop Wallpaper. • Remove "Disconnect" option from Shut Down dialog. • Remove Windows Security item from Start menu. • Start a program on connection. • Always show desktop on connection.
Terminal Server>Security	These policy settings cover how security is implemented in Terminal Services sessions. Policy settings in this folder include: • Server Authentication Certificate Template. • Set client connection encryption level. • Always prompt client for password upon connection. • Require Secure RPC communication. • Require use of specify security layer for remote (RDP) connections. • Do not allow local administrators to customize permissions. • Require user authentication using RDP 6.0 for remote connections.
Terminal Server>Session Directory	These policy settings enable you to control whether and how Windows Vista uses a session directory to log and track user terminal services sessions. Policy settings in this folder include: • Join Session Directory. • Session Directory Cluster Name. • Terminal Server IP Address Redirection. • Session Directory Server.
Terminal Server>Session Time Limits	These policy settings enable you to control how sessions time out. Making sessions time out more quickly increases security because each connection to a computer is a security risk. Policy settings in this folder include: • Set time limit for disconnected sessions. • Set time limit for active but idle Terminal Services sessions. • Set time limit for active Terminal Services sessions. • Terminate session when time limits are reached.

(*continued*)

Table 12-8 (*continued*)

Location in GPO starting from Terminal Services folder	Summary
Terminal Server>Temporary folders	These settings control how temporary folders are used in a remote session. Policy settings in this folder include: • Do not delete temp folder upon exit. • Do not use temporary folders per session.

Understanding and Configuring Virtual Private Networks

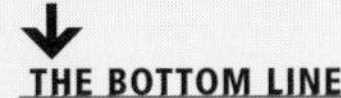

THE BOTTOM LINE Virtual private networks are private networks established on public networks such as the Internet. They can connect branch offices of large organizations, or can enable users to log onto your domain from remote computers through the Internet.

CERTIFICATION READY? Configure and troubleshoot remote access: VPN connections 4.3

A ***virtual private network (VPN)*** is a private network established within a public network, most frequently the Internet. In an enterprise, the most frequent users are those logging in from remote locations, such as their homes, to the enterprise domain through the Internet.

To emulate point-to-point links (when in fact the link travels through who-knows how many hosts across the Internet), VPNs encapsulate data in a package that contains both a header with routing information and a payload of encrypted data.

TAKE NOTE* VPNs are also used to connect branch locations of large networks.

Enterprises typically have one or more ***VPN servers***, that is, servers that users can use to create a VPN by connecting through the Internet.

As work environments become more decentralized in the information age, with branch offices crossing the globe and workers telecommuting, VPNs will become more and more common.

From an implementation standpoint, there are three basic requirements for establishing a VPN:

- **User Authentication and auditing**. You need to be able to identify users who wish to use a VPN to connect to your domain. You must also log who connects and when they do so that you can detect or investigate attacks, and so that you can optimize performance by allocating bandwidth and server use appropriately.
- **IP Address assignment**. Each VPN client must be assigned an IP address on the network.
- **Data Encryption**. Data carried on the public network must be encrypted.

Before a Windows Vista VPN client can connect to your network via a VPN connection, you must first configure VPN server-side settings.

Configuring VPN Users

You can grant users permission to connect to a VPN server either through the Active Directory Users and Computers console, or by using the Routing and Remote Access console.

Users need to be explicitly enabled to connect to a VPN server. You can enable users to connect individually using the Active Directory Users and Computers console, or in groups using the Routing and Remote Access console.

ALLOW A USER TO CONNECT TO A VPN SERVER BY USING THE ACTIVE DIRECTORY USERS AND COMPUTERS CONSOLE

1. Log on to a domain server.
2. Click **Start**, point to **Administrative Tools**, and then click **Active Directory Users and Computers**. The Active Directory Users and Computers console appears.
3. In the console tree, right-click the domain name and then click **Find**. The Find Users, Contacts, and Groups dialog box appears, as shown in Figure 12-14.

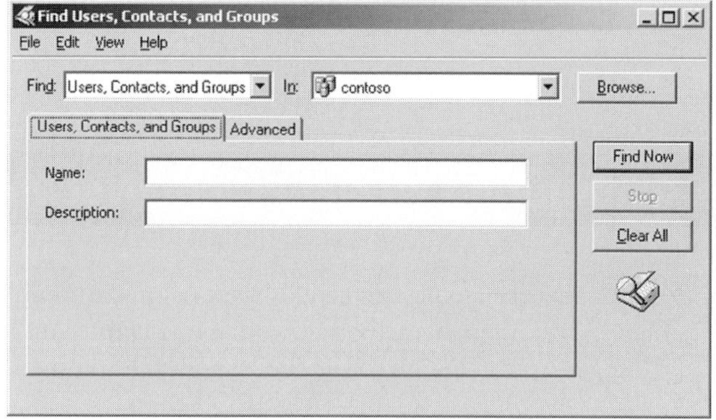

Figure 12-14

The Find Users, Contacts, and Groups dialog box enables you to find Active Directory objects such as users

4. In the **Name** text box, key the user's name (e.g., Garrett Vargas). Or, you can use wildcards in the Name text box. E.g., you could key t* to get a list of all the users whose names start with *T*. Alternatively, you can click **Find Now** to search for the user.
5. Once you have searched for the user, in the Search results list box, double-click the user. The Properties dialog box for the user appears.
6. Click the **Dial-in** tab, as shown in Figure 12-15.

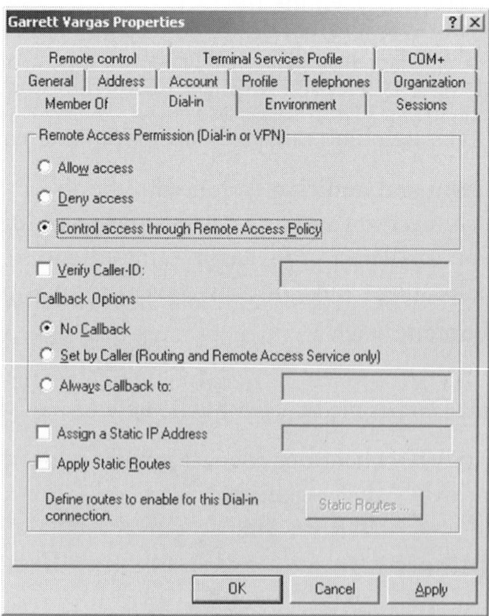

Figure 12-15

The Dial-in tab of an example user's Properties dialog box

7. In the Remote Access Permission (Dial-in or VPN) section, select **Allow access**. Click **OK**.

ALLOW A USER OR GROUP TO CONNECT TO A VPN SERVER THROUGH THE ROUTING AND REMOTE ACCESS CONSOLE

This procedure assumes that you are using Routing and Remote Access to enable VPN connections.

1. Log on to a domain controller.
2. Click **Start**, point to **Administrative Tools**, and then click **Routing and Remote Access**. The Routing and Remote Access console appears.
3. In the console tree, expand ***ServerName***, right-click **Remote Access Policies**, and then click **New Remote Access Policy**. The New Remote Access Policy Wizard appears with the Welcome to the New Remote Policy Wizard page open.
4. Click **Next**. The Policy Configuration Method page appears.
5. Ensure that **Use the wizard to set up a typical policy for a common scenario** is selected.
6. In the Policy name text box, key a name for the policy (e.g., Authenticate Sales Department VPN connections).
7. Click **Next**. The Access Method page appears.
8. Select one of the following options:

   VPN. Select this option to authenticate all VPN connections from the specified user or group. This is the most common selection for VPN connections for remote users.

   Dial-up. Select this option to authenticate only phone-line or Integrated Services Digital Network (ISDN) connections.

   Wireless. Select this option to authenticate only wireless local area network (LAN) connections.

   Ethernet. Select this option to authenticate only Ethernet connections.
9. Click **Next**. The User or Group Access page appears.
10. Select one of the following:

    User. Select this option to accept users according to the settings for each user (see previous procedure to configure access for users individually).

    Group. Select this option to add a group to the list of groups to authenticate. Then click **Add**. You can add more than one group.

> **WARNING** If you add a group, but a user in the group is denied access in the Properties dialog box for the user, then the user will be denied access.

11. Click **Next**. The Authentication Methods page appears.
12. Select one of the following to choose which authentication scheme to use:

    Extensible Authentication Protocol (EAP). EAP is typically used for wireless network authentication, but is falling out in favor of WEP and WEP2. Do not use EAP unless you have some compelling reason to do so.

    Microsoft Encrypted Authentication version 2 (MS-CHAPv2). This is the default and recommended authentication method.

    Microsoft Encrypted Authentication (MS-CHAP). This authentication method is available for backward-compatibility reasons. It is less secure, so there is no good reason to choose this method with Windows Vista clients.
13. Click **Next**. The Policy Encryption Level page appears.
14. Configure the following check boxes according to which encryption methods you want to support:

    Basic encryption (IPSec 56-bit DES or MPPE 40-bit)

    Strong encryption (IPSec 56-bit DES or MPPE 56-bit)

    Strongest encryption (IPSec Triple DES or MPPE 128-bit). Clear all but this check box to allow only the most strongly encrypted connections. The number of bits allocated to the encryption key (40, 56, and 128 bits respectively) partly determines the strength of the encryption.

15. Click **Next.** The Completing the New Remote Access Policy Wizard page appears.
16. Review the summary of the policy and then click **Finish.**

From a Windows Vista VPN client standpoint, configuring and connecting to a VPN server is a simple matter.

CONFIGURE A VPN CLIENT CONNECTION

1. Click **Start** and then click **Connect To**. The Connect to a network Wizard appears.
2. Click **Set up a connection or network**. The Choose a connection option page appears.
3. Select **Connect to a workplace** and then click **Next.**
4. On the How do you want to connect page, click **Use my Internet connection (VPN)**. The Type the Internet address to connect to page appears.
5. In the Internet address text box, key the IP address of your VPN server (e.g., 10.21.23.54), or its fully qualified domain name (FQDN; e.g., vpn12.contoso.com).
6. In the **Destination** name text box, key the name you want to use to identify the connection. The following options are available:

   Use a smart card. Select this check box to authenticate using a smart card. If you select this check box, provide administrator credentials in the User Account Control dialog box that appears.

   Allow other people to use this connection. Select this check box to allow all users of the computer to use this VPN connection.

   Don't connect now; just set it up so I can connect later. Select this check box if you don't want to connect immediately after you complete the wizard.
7. Example settings are shown in Figure 12-16. Click Next. The Type your user name and password page appears.

TAKE NOTE*

You can also create a direct phone connection without going through the Internet by clicking Dial directly. But this is not strictly a VPN connection.

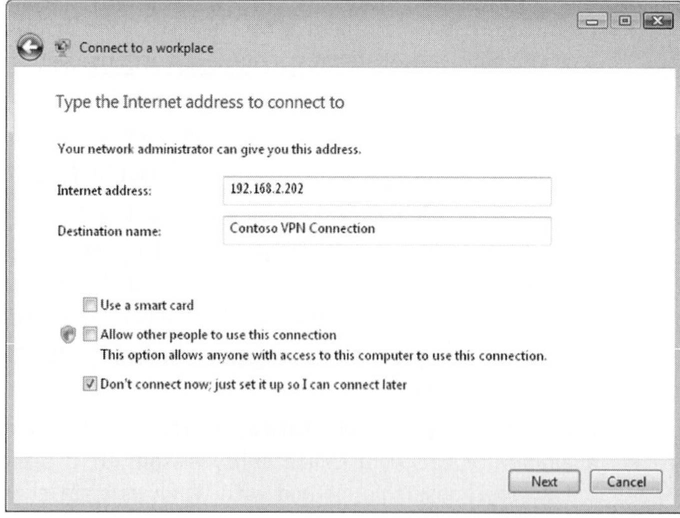

Figure 12-16

Example settings for configuring a VPN connection using the Connect to a workplace Wizard

8. Key your user name and password in the user name and password text boxes.
9. Select the **Show characters** check box if you want to be able to see your password. This decreases security.
10. Select the **Remember this password** check box if you want your computer to remember your password so that you don't have to enter it each time. This decreases security.
11. In the **Domain (optional)** text box, key your domain name (e.g., CONTOSO.COM). Click **Create**. After the connection is created, the Connection is ready to use page appears. Click **Close**.

CONNECT TO A DOMAIN BY USING A VPN CONNECTION

To connect to a domain by using a VPN connection, you must first create the connection (see the previous procedure).

1. Click **Start** and then click **Connect To**. The Connect to a network Wizard appears.
2. Select the VPN connection in the list of network connections and then click **Connect**.
3. A Connect *ConnectionName* Connection dialog box may appear. Provide your credentials and then click **Connect**.
4. If the connection is successful, the Successfully connected to *ConnectionName* Connection page appears. Click **Close**.

Accessing Local and Network Resources

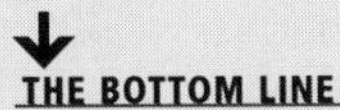

THE BOTTOM LINE

Users need to be able to access both local and network resources, while being restricted from accessing resources that they don't need to or shouldn't access. Access denied messages are a result of users being unable to access or modify a resource (usually a folder or file).

CERTIFICATION READY? Configure and troubleshoot access to resources: Troubleshoot Access Denied messages Troubleshoot access to network resources
2.6, 4.7

Resources in an enterprise come in two varieties: local and network. ***Local resources*** include anything on or connected to your computer that is not part of a network. For example, a USB drive or printer is local, as is the internal hard drive. There are a vast number of possible ***network resources***, including shared folders and files, printers, routers, gateways, DHCP servers, and many others.

Just about all users have seen an "Access is Denied" message. This section is on troubleshooting those messages, and troubleshooting and configuring access to resources in general.

Understanding Permissions

NTFS permissions control user access and level-of-control over files and folders. NTFS permissions are implemented using special permissions and standard permissions.

CERTIFICATION READY? Troubleshoot access to network resources: Files and folders
4.7

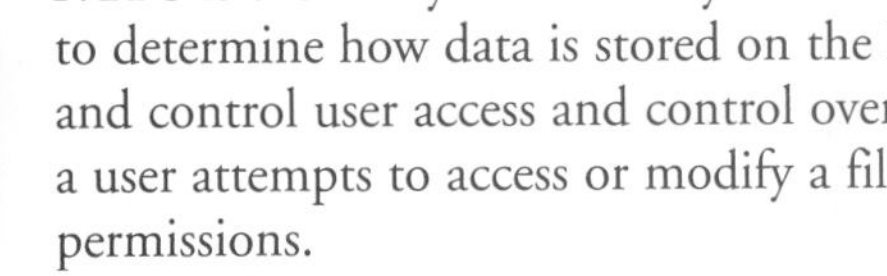

NTFS is the file system used by Windows Vista and other, more recent versions of Windows to determine how data is stored on the hard drives. ***NTFS permissions*** are a part of NTFS and control user access and control over files and folders. Access denied messages result when a user attempts to access or modify a file or folder in a way for which they do not have NTFS permissions.

Each file or folder in NTFS has separate permissions (although permissions can be inherited from parent objects—more on that later). The permissions are determined by access control entries (ACEs). For each user, for each permission on each object, there is an ACE. For example, if you have the read permission for a file, then that file has an ACE for the read permission for you. Files and folders can also have ACEs for groups as well as individual users.

You can control NTFS permissions at two levels of granularity. You can use NTFS permissions to configure the most granular permissions, called ***special permission***. Table 12-9 describes each special permission.

Table 12-9

Special permissions

NTFS PERMISSION	DESCRIPTION
Full Control	Selecting the full control permission is the same as selecting all the other permissions.
Traverse folder/execute file	• **Traverse Folder** allows or denies moving through folders to reach other files or folders, even if the user has no permissions for the traversed folders. Traverse folder takes effect only when the group or user is not granted the Bypass traverse checking user right in Group Policy (by default, the Everyone group is given the Bypass traverse checking user right). • Setting the Traverse Folder permission on a folder does not automatically set the Execute File permission on all files within that folder. • **Execute File** allows or denies running program files.
List folder/read data	• **List Folder** allows or denies viewing file names and subfolder names within the folder. List Folder only affects the contents of that folder and does not affect whether the folder you are setting the permission on will be listed. • **Read Data** allows or denies viewing data in files.
Read Attributes	Allows or denies viewing the attributes of a file or folder, such as read-only and hidden. Attributes are defined by NTFS.
Read extended attributes	Allows or denies viewing the extended attributes of a file or folder. Extended attributes are defined by programs and may vary by program.
Create files/write data	• **Create Files** allows or denies creating files within the folder. • **Write Data** allows or denies making changes to the file and overwriting existing content.
Create folders/append data	• **Create Folders** allows or denies creating folders within the folder. • **Append Data** allows or denies making changes to the end of the file but not changing, deleting, or overwriting existing data.
Write attributes	Allows or denies changing the attributes of a file or folder, such as read-only or hidden. Attributes are defined by NTFS.
Write extended attributes	Allows or denies changing the extended attributes of a file or folder. Extended attributes are defined by programs and may vary by program.
Delete	Allows or denies deleting the file or folder. If you do not have Delete permission on a file or folder, you can still delete it if you have been granted Delete Subfolders and Files on the parent folder permissions.
Read permissions	Allows or denies reading permissions of the file or folder, such as Full Control, Read, and Write.
Change permissions	Allows or denies changing permissions of the file or folder, such as Full Control, Read, and Write.
Take ownership	Allows or denies taking ownership of the file or folder. The owner of a file or folder can always change permissions on it, regardless of any existing permissions that protect the file or folder.

You can also configure less granular permissions, called ***standard permissions***, on the Security tab of the Permissions for *FolderName* dialog box of the file or folder (an example is shown in Figure 12-17). Standard permissions, described in Table 12-10, are combinations of special permissions. In other words, selecting one of them is the equivalent of selecting one or more of the more granular special permissions.

Figure 12-17

The permissions under Permissions for Garrett Vargas are examples of standard permissions

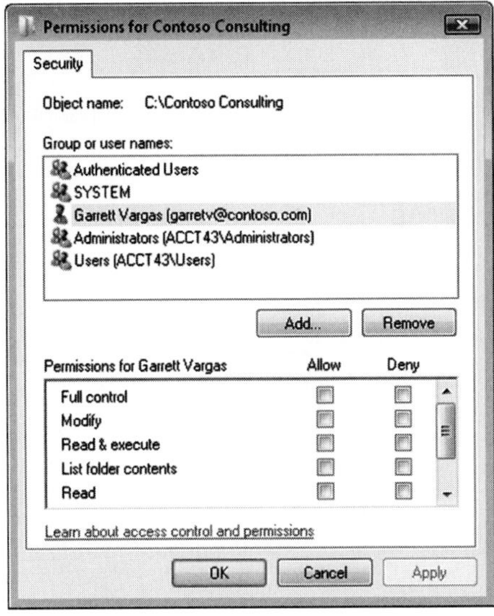

Table 12-10

Standard permissions and the special permissions of which they are composed

Permission	Actual NTFS permissions
Full control	Traverse folder/execute file, List folder/read data, Read attributes, Read extended attributes, Create files/write data, Create folders/append data, Write attributes, Write extended attributes, Delete subfolders and files, Delete, Read permissions, Change permissions, Take ownership
Modify	Traverse folder/execute file, List folder/read data, Read attributes, Read extended attributes, Create files/write data, Create folders/append data, Write attributes, Write extended attributes, Delete subfolders and files, Delete, Read permissions, Change permissions, Take ownership
Read & execute	Traverse folder/execute file, List folder/read data, Read attributes, Read extended attributes, Read permissions
List folder contents	Traverse folder/execute file, List folder/read data, Read attributes, Read extended attributes, Read permissions
Read	List folder/read data, Read attributes, Read extended attributes, Read permissions
Write	Create files/write data, Create folders/append data, Write attributes, Write extended attributes

Permissions for a file or folder can come from two sources: they can come from a file or folder's properties, or they can be inherited from parent folders. For example, if you configure permissions for a folder and put a file in that folder, the file can inherit the permissions of the folder. There are a number of ways to configure how folders and files inherit permissions, and how folders pass permissions on to their descendants. Table 12-11 covers the different settings you can use to configure permission inheritance.

Table 12-11

Permission inheritance settings

Setting	Description
Include inheritable permissions from this object's parent check box in the advanced security settings dialog box for the file or folder	Affects how this object inherits permissions. Selecting this check box means that the file or folder will inherit permissions, while clearing it means that it won't.
Replace all existing inheritable permissions on all descendants with inheritable permissions from this object check box in the advanced security settings dialog box for the file or folder	Affects how this object passes on permissions. Selecting this check box will replace all existing and inheritable permissions for all descendants with the permissions from this folder.
Apply to list box in the Permissions Entry dialog box for the file or folder	Affects how this object passes on permissions. This list box determines to which descendents a folder passes permissions. In other words, this setting determines which permissions are inheritable. You can select one of the following (the options are self-explanatory): • This folder only • This folder, subfolder and files • This folder and subfolders • This folder and files • Subfolder and files only • Subfolders only • Files only
Apply these permissions to objects and/or containers within this container only check box in the Permissions Entry dialog box for folder	Affects how this object passes on permissions. Selecting this check box limits the inheritance to the next generation of files and folders.

Configuring NTFS Permissions

NTFS permissions control access to folders and files.

This procedure covers defining the less granular permissions that are made of NTFS permissions.

CONFIGURE PERMISSIONS FOR A FOLDER

1. Right-click the folder for which you want to configure permissions and then click **Properties.** The *FolderName* Properties dialog box appears.
2. Click the **Security** tab, as shown in Figure 12-18.

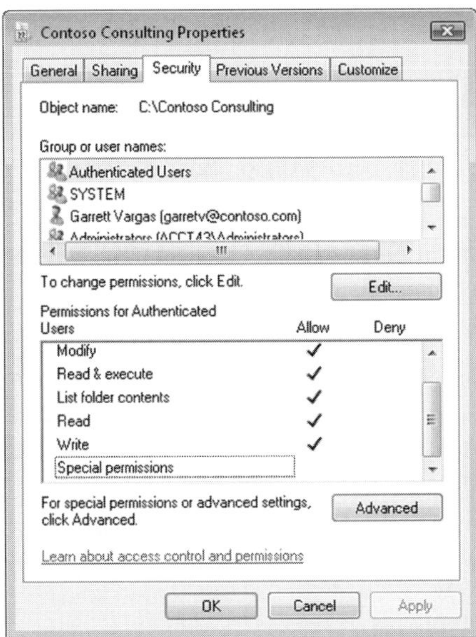

Figure 12-18

The Security tab in the Properties dialog box of an example folder

3. To see permissions for a user or group, click that user or group in the Group or user names list box.
4. Click **Edit**. The Permissions for *FolderName* dialog box appears, as shown in Figure 12-19.

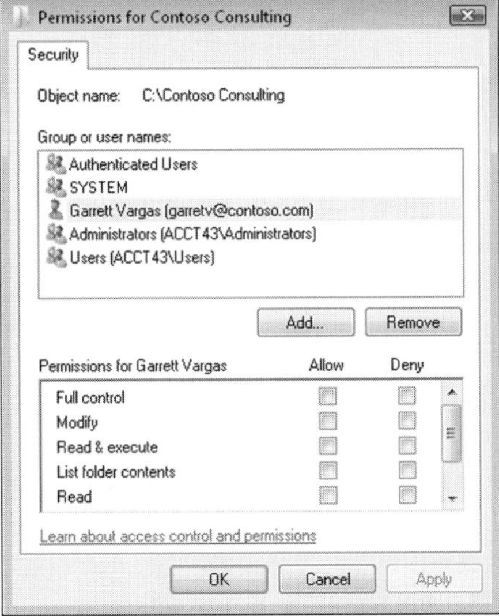

Figure 12-19

The Permissions dialog box of an example folder

5. In the Group or user names list box, select the user or group for which you want to configure permissions. If the user or group does not appear in the list box, click **Add** to add the user or group. You can remove a user or group by selecting it and then clicking **Remove**.
6. In the Permissions for *UserOrGroupName* list box, select or clear the Allow or Deny check box for each permission. Note that if you select a check box Windows Vista will select any check boxes implied by the one you selected. For example, if you select Read & execute, Windows Vista will automatically select List folder contents and Read.
7. Click **OK** three times to close the remaining dialog boxes.

This procedure covers configuring the most granular permissions: NTFS permissions.

CONFIGURE NTFS PERMISSIONS FOR A FOLDER

OPEN the Security tab of the Properties dialog box of the folder for which you want to configure permissions.

1. In the *FolderName* Properties dialog box, click **Advanced.** The Advanced Security Settings for *FolderName* dialog box appears.
2. Click **Edit.** Another Advanced Security Settings for *FolderName* dialog box appears.
3. In the Permissions entries list box, select the user or group that you want to configure permissions for and then click **Edit.** If the user or group does not appear in the list box, click **Add** to add the user or group. You can remove a user or group by selecting it and then clicking **Remove.**
4. In the Permission Entry for *FolderName* dialog box, shown in Figure 12-20, in the Apply to drop-down list, select one of the following to define the scope of the permissions:

   This folder only

   This folder, subfolders and files

   This folder and subfolders

   This folder and files

   Subfolders and files only

   Subfolders only

   Files only

Figure 12-20

The Permission Entry dialog box for an example folder

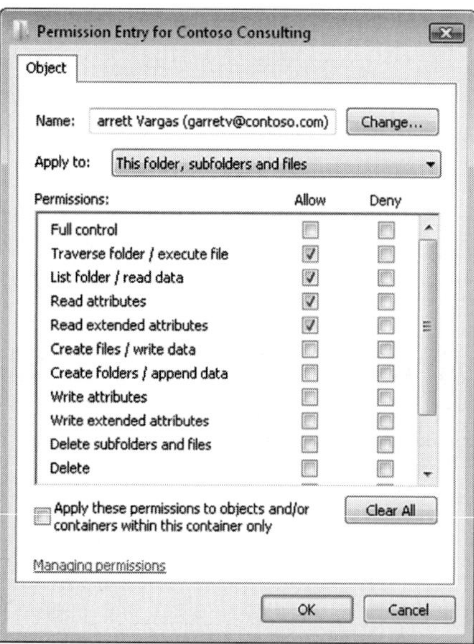

5. In the Permissions list box, select the Allow and Deny check boxes for each permission as desired. Also configure the *Apply these permissions to objects and/or containers within this container only* check box. Click **OK.**

CONFIGURE PERMISSION INHERITANCE FOR A FOLDER OR FILE

OPEN the Security tab of the Properties dialog box of the folder for which you want to determine permission inheritance.

1. On the Security tab of the *FolderName* Properties dialog box, click **Advanced.** The Advanced Security Settings for *FolderName* dialog box appears with the Permissions tab active.

2. Click **Edit**. Another Advanced Security Settings for *FolderName* dialog box appears.
   a. Configure the *Include inheritable permissions from this object's parent* check box. Selecting this check box means that the file or folder will inherit permissions. Clear the check box so that it won't.
   b. Configure the *Replace all existing inheritable permissions on all descendants with inheritable permissions from this object* check box. Selecting this check box will replace all existing and inheritable permissions for all descendants with the permissions from this folder.
3. Select the user or group for which you want to configure permission inheritance and then click **Edit**.
4. Select one of the following from the Apply to list box (this setting affects how permissions are passed-on by this folder):

   This folder only

   This folder, subfolder and files

   This folder and subfolders

   This folder and files

   Subfolder and files only

   Subfolders only

   Files only
5. Configure the *Apply these permissions to objects and/or containers within this container only* check box. This setting affects how this folder passes on permissions. Selecting this check box limits the inheritance to the next generation of files and folders.

DETERMINE EFFECTIVE PERMISSIONS

OPEN the Security tab for the Properties dialog box of the folder for which you want to determine effective permissions. ***Effective permissions*** are the permissions that a particular object has for a particular user.

1. On the Security tab of the *FolderName* Properties dialog box, click **Advanced**. The Advanced Security Settings for *FolderName* dialog box appears.
2. Click the **Effective Permissions** tab, shown in Figure 12-21.

Figure 12-21

The Effective Permissions tab for an example folder

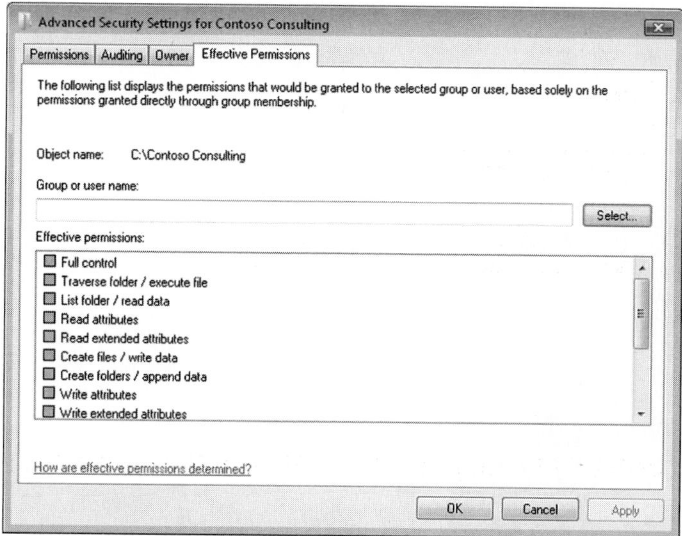

3. Click **Select** to select a user or group for which to determine effective permissions. The Select User, Computer, or Group dialog box appears. In the *Enter the object name to select* text box, key the name of the user or group and then click **Check**

Names. The user or group will be underlined if it is found. You can click **Advanced** to search for a user or group.

4. Click **OK.** On the Effective Permissions tab, examine the effective permissions for the user or group, as shown in Figure 12-22.

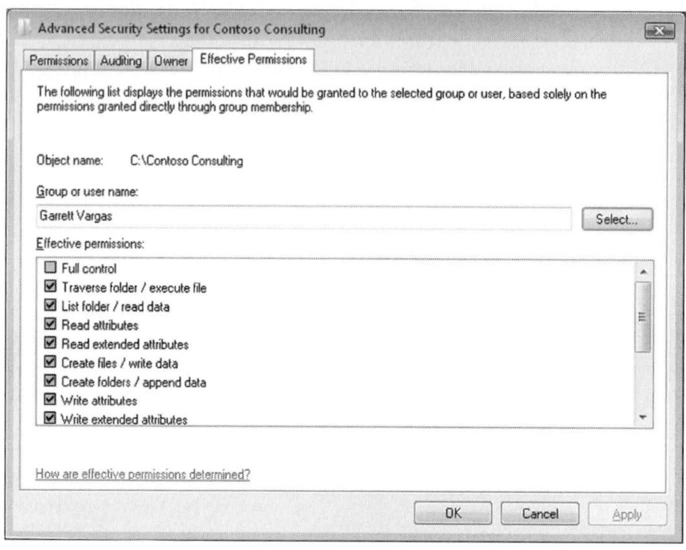

Figure 12-22

The Effective Permissions tab for an example folder with an example user selected

5. Close all open dialog boxes and windows.

Configuring Network Sharing

CERTIFICATION READY?
Troubleshoot access to network resources:
• Files and folders
• Printers
• Configure Network Discovery and Sharing
4.7

Network sharing controls network users' access to local resources.

Whether a user has access to network resources depends first on connectivity and then on permissions. These permissions can be NTFS permissions, or they can be shared permissions.

You can configure network sharing settings for Windows Vista clients locally in the Network and Sharing Center (shown in Figure 12-23).

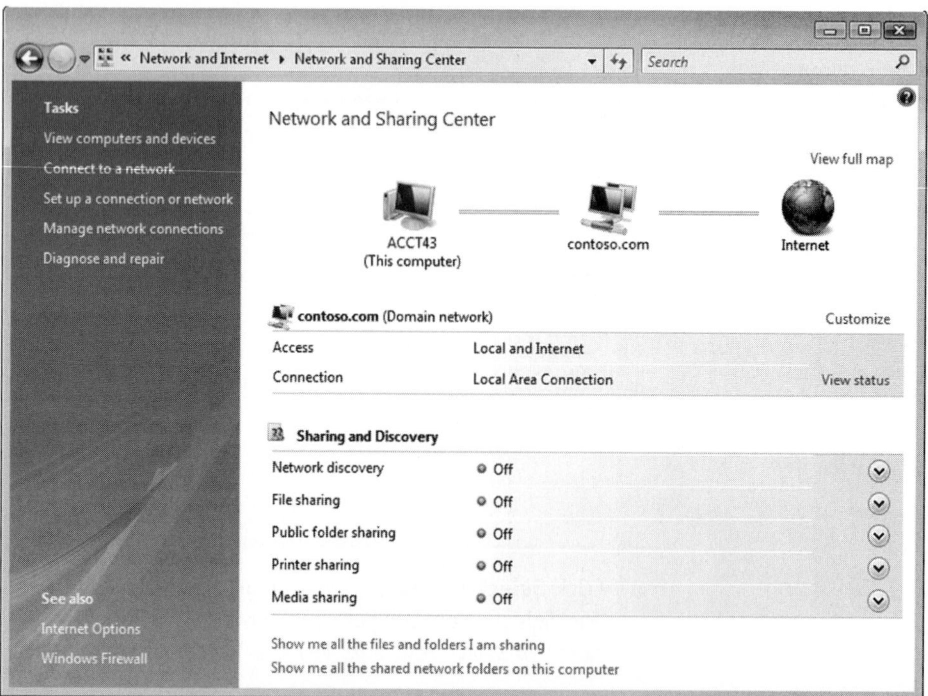

Figure 12-23

Network and Sharing Center

Network discovery is not typically used for workstation computers in an enterprise. It is used in small offices and home networks. By turning on network discovery, you are enabling other users to see your computer on the network. For other users to see shares on your computer, network discovery must be enabled.

ENABLE NETWORK DISCOVERY

1. Click **Start** and then click **Control Panel**. The Control Panel appears.
2. Click **Network and Internet**. The Network and Internet control panel appears.
3. Click **Network and Sharing Center**. The Network and Sharing Center control panel appears.
4. Under Sharing and Discovery, expand the **Network and discovery** section by clicking the down arrow on the right.
5. Click **Turn on network discovery** and then click **Apply**. A User Account Control dialog box appears.
6. Provide administrator credentials and then click **OK**.

Enabling file sharing lets you give users to access shared folders or files over the network.

ENABLE FILE SHARING

OPEN the Network and Sharing Center.

1. In the Network and Sharing Center, under Sharing and Discovery, Expand the **File sharing** section.
2. Click **Turn on file sharing** and then click **Apply**. A User Account Control dialog box appears.
3. Provide administrator credentials and then click **OK**.

By enabling Public folder sharing, you give network users access to the Public folder on the local machine. You can do this if you want users to be able to read documents in the Public folder, or if you want to create a collaboration space.

ENABLE PUBLIC FOLDER SHARING

OPEN the Network and Sharing Center.

1. In the Network and Sharing Center, under Sharing and Discovery, expand the **Public folder sharing** section.
2. Select one of the following and then click **Apply**:

   Turn on sharing so anyone with network access can open files. Select this option if you want network users to be able to open—but not change or create—files or folders in the Public folder. This is the best choice if there are documents that you want read but not changed.

   Turn on sharing so anyone with network access can open, change, and create files. Select this option if you want network users to be able to open, change, and create files and folders in the Public folder. This is the best choice for creating a collaboration space.

   Turn off sharing (people logged on to this computer can still access this folder). Select this option to allow users on the local computer to access the folder, and to deny remote users access to the folder.
3. In the User Account Control dialog box, provide credentials and then click **OK**.

A network share is a folder that is accessible by remote users. To create a network share, you share a folder and then configure permissions to limit access. You can complete both steps manually, or you can use the File Sharing Wizard, as explained in the following procedure.

CREATE A NETWORK SHARE USING THE FILE SHARING WIZARD

1. Right-click the folder that you want to share and then click **Share**. The File Sharing Wizard appears.
2. In the drop-down text box, do one of the following:

   To specify a particular user or group to share the folder with, type the user name or group name and then click **Add**. Repeat as necessary to add as many users or groups as desired.

   To share the folder with everyone (do this only if you are not concerned with security for the shared folder), click the down-arrow on the right, select **Everyone**, and then click **Add**.

   To browse for users or groups to share the folder with, click the down arrow on the right and then select **Find**. Use the Select Users or Groups dialog box to select the user or group. Repeat as necessary to add as many users or groups as desired.
3. For each group or user that you add, click the corresponding down arrow in the Permission Level column. Then select one of the following:

   Reader. The user or group is granted the following standard permissions: Read & execute, List folder contents, and Read. Select this option if the user or group needs to be able to read the documents in the share but not to modify them or create new documents.

   Contributor. The user or group is granted the following standard permissions: Modify, Read & execute, List folder contents, Read, and Write. Select this option if the user or group needs to be able to modify documents in the file share or create new documents.

   Co-owner. The user or group is granted all standard permissions but is not, as the name suggests, given co-ownership over the shared folder. Select this option if you want the user or group to have full control over the shared folder.
4. Click **Share**. A User Account Control dialog box appears.
5. Provide administrator credentials and then click **OK**. The Sharing Items page will appear briefly and then the Your folder is shared page appears.
6. Click **Done**.

By enabling printer sharing, you are allowing users to access shared printers on the network.

ENABLE PRINTER SHARING

OPEN the Network and Sharing Center.

1. In the Network and Sharing Center, under Sharing and Discovery, expand the **Printer sharing** section.
2. Click **Turn on printer sharing** and then click **Apply**. A User Account Control dialog box appears.
3. Provide administrator credentials and then click **OK**.

New to Windows Vista, ***Network Access Protection (NAP)*** is a platform that can restrict computers from connecting to a network if they do not meet minimum thresholds for security and system health. For example, you can use NAP to keep computers that do not have specified anti-virus protection from connecting to your network. NAP is supported by Windows Vista, Server 2008, and it will be in XP SP2 with the NAP Client for Windows XP added (now in beta testing). To fully use NAP, you need to have Server 2008 servers (this book was written assuming you are using Server 2003, because Server 2008 was not available at the time of writing).

Troubleshooting Networking

THE BOTTOM LINE

Troubleshooting networking is a common and important task for support technicians. A variety of tools are available to help you troubleshoot networking, including command-line tools and the Network Connections Diagnostic tool.

CERTIFICATION READY?
Troubleshoot connectivity issues
Configure and troubleshoot wireless networking
4.4, 4.5

Most network troubleshooting involves first determining where the network is failing. You should always check the simple stuff first, such as unplugged cables or out of range wireless connections.

Assuming that the problem is more involved than a disconnected cable, you can use many tools to diagnose network troubles, including a suite of command-line tools and the Network Connection Diagnostics Tool.

Troubleshooting Networking with Command-Line Tools

Command-line tools offer a quick way to diagnose and sometimes resolve network issues.

After checking the obvious, the first place you may want to go to diagnose network problem is the command line. Many command-line tools enable you to quickly diagnose and sometimes resolve network issues.

Table 12-12 summarizes some of the more useful command-line tools for diagnosing and resolving networking issues.

Table 12-12

Command-line tools you can use to diagnose and sometimes correct networking issues

Command-line tool	Description	When to use
Ping	***Ping*** enables you to check connectivity between TCP/IP clients. Ping sends Internet Control Message Protocol (ICMP) Echo Request messages to the specified TCP/IP client. You can specify the recipient either by IP address or by FQDN. If the ICMP echo requests are received, the recipient computer replies and the round-trip time for the message is displayed. To ping a TCP/IP client is to use the Ping command to send the client the ICMP echo request. Some firewalls are configured to block the ICMP Echo Request, which means that they block Ping. When you ping a computer behind such a firewall, you will get no response.	Ping is always one of the first tools to use in diagnosing connectivity issues. First, ping the loopback address (127.0.0.1), which points back to the TCP/IP client. This is a way of checking to see that TCP/IP is at least working locally. Then ping other TCP/IP hosts, local and perhaps remote (such as on the Internet). You can also ping infrastructure computers (such as DNS or DHCP servers) to see if the client can access them.
IPConfig	***IPConfig*** is a utility for displaying TCP/IP client settings. You can also use it for some configuration tasks, such as manually renewing an IP address from a DHCP server or clearing a DNS cache.	Use IPConfig when you want to find the TCP/IP settings quickly. Also use it when you want to renew an IP address from a DHCP server.

(*continued*)

	Description	When to use
[illegible]	You can use ***Net view*** to display a list of file and print shares on a TCP/IP client. You can identify the client by either IP address or FQDN.	Use Net view when you want to know what network resources are available on a computer. The computer can be remote.
TraceRt	***TraceRt*** can help you to determine where communication between two TCP/IP clients is failing. You can specify a recipient computer and use TraceRt to tell you where packets (data) are being lost on the way to the target computer.	Use TraceRt when you want to see where packets are being lost in a route.
Pathping	***Pathping*** combines aspects of Ping and TraceRt, and it has additional functionality as well. It sends packets to each router on the way to a target TCP/IP client, and then computes results based on which packets return when. Because Pathping shows the degree of packet loss at any specified router or link, you can pinpoint which routers or links might be causing network problems.	Use Pathping when you want to see detailed information on where packets are lost in a route. For example, if a network connection works but is very slow or unstable, use Pathping to see if the packets are being lost along the way in one or more places.
NSlookup	***NSlookup*** enables you to manually request DNS name resolution. You can either specify an FQDN and NSlookup will attempt to contact a DNS server and then return an IP address, or you can specify an IP address and NSlookup will attempt to contact a DNS server and then return an FQDN (this is called a reverse lookup). You can also specify which DNS name server to use. This way you can check to see which DNS name servers are answering your DNS queries.	Use NSlookup when you suspect that DNS name resolution is failing. You might suspect DNS name resolution failure when connectivity using IP addresses is working, but using FQDNs is not.

You can find syntax and parameters for each of these command-line tools by executing them with the /? switch. The following procedures outline examples of using each tool.

USE PING

You can ping any IP address that you want; whether that IP address is reachable is another matter. This procedure covers using Ping by supplying several examples of useful IP addresses to ping when troubleshooting networking.

1. Click **Start** and key **cmd** in the **Start Search** text box. Then press **Enter**. A command prompt window appears.
2. At the command prompt, key **ping 127.0.0.1** to check local TCP/IP functionality. The following is an example of the resulting text:

```
C:\Users\chrisc.ping 127.0.0.1

Pinging 127.0.0.1 with 32 bytes of data:
```

```
Reply from 127.0.0.1: bytes=32 time<1ms TTL=128
Reply from 127.0.0.1: bytes=32 time=6ms TTL=128
Reply from 127.0.0.1: bytes=32 time<1ms TTL=128
Reply from 127.0.0.1: bytes=32 time<1ms TTL=128
Ping statistics for 127.0.0.1:
    Packets: Sent = 4, Received = 4, Lost = 0 (0% loss),
Approximate round trip times in milli-seconds:
    Minimum = 0ms, Maximum = 6ms, Average = 1ms
```

3. At the command prompt, key **ping *DefaultGatewayIPAddress*** (e.g., 192.168.2.1). If the default gateway responds, then you know that any connectivity problems to outside resources are not a result of not being able to contact the default gateway. A successful ping will look similar to the following:

```
C:\Users\chrisc>ping 192.168.1.1
Pinging 192.168.1.1 with 32 bytes of data:
Reply from 192.168.1.1: bytes=32 time=6ms TTL=149
Reply from 192.168.1.1: bytes=32 time=3ms TTL=149
Reply from 192.168.1.1: bytes=32 time=3ms TTL=149
Reply from 192.168.1.1: bytes=32 time=23ms TTL=149
Ping statistics for 192.168.1.1:
Packets: Sent = 4, Received = 4, Lost = 0 (0% loss),
Approximate round trip times in milli-seconds:
Minimum = 3ms, Maximum = 23ms, Average = 8ms
```

4. At the command prompt, key ping **www.example.com**. Example.com is an example FQDN that you can use to check connectivity to the Internet. If the default gateway responds, then you know that any connectivity problems to outside resources are not a result of not being able to contact the default gateway. A successful ping will look similar to the following:

```
C:\Users\chrisc>ping www.example.com
Pinging www.example.com [208.77.188.166] with 32 bytes of data:
Reply from 208.77.188.166: bytes=32 time=46ms TTL=52
Reply from 208.77.188.166: bytes=32 time=103ms TTL=52
Reply from 208.77.188.166: bytes=32 time=41ms TTL=52
Reply from 208.77.188.166: bytes=32 time=41ms TTL=52
Ping statistics for 208.77.188.166:
Packets: Sent = 4, Received = 4, Lost = 0 (0% loss),
Approximate round trip times in milli-seconds:
Minimum = 41ms, Maximum = 103ms, Average = 57ms
```

TAKE NOTE*

Notice that the FQDN *www.example.com* was resolved into an IP address.

When troubleshooting networking, you often want to know basic TCP/IP settings for a computer, such as its IP address, subnet mask, default gateway, or DNS servers. For example, if you suspect that FQDNs are not being resolved correctly to IP addresses, you can use IPConfig to find out the DNS server IP address. You can then use Ping to see if the DNS server responds.

USE IPCONFIG TO DISPLAY TCP/IP SETTINGS

OPEN a command prompt window.

1. At the command prompt, key **IPConfig /all** and then press **Enter**. Text similar to the following is output:

   ```
   C:\Users\chrisc.ipconfig /all
   ```

TAKE NOTE* There is more information here than might normally appear because the example computer had a VPN connection configured (which is why information on tunnel adapters is displayed).

```
Windows IP Configuration
   Host Name............: ACCT43
   Primary Dns Suffix.......: contoso.com
   Node Type............: Hybrid
   IP Routing Enabled........: No
   WINS Proxy Enabled........: No
   DNS Suffix Search List......: contoso.com
Ethernet adapter Local Area Connection:
   Connection-specific DNS Suffix.: contoso.com
   Description...........: Intel 21140-Based PCI Fast Ethernet Adapt
   er (Emulated)
   Physical Address.........: 00-03-FF-AB-45-4E
   DHCP Enabled...........: Yes
   Autoconfiguration Enabled....: Yes
   Ipv4 Address...........: 192.168.2.10(Preferred)
   Subnet Mask...........: 255.255.255.0
   Lease Obtained..........: Sunday, June 24, 2007 2:53:25 PM
   Lease Expires..........: Monday, July 02, 2007 3:05:51 PM
   Default Gateway.........: 192.168.2.202
   DHCP Server...........: 192.168.2.202
   DNS Servers...........: 192.168.2.202
   NetBIOS over Tcpip........: Enabled
Tunnel adapter Local Area Connection* 6:
   Connection-specific DNS Suffix.:
   Description...........: Teredo Tunneling Pseudo-Interface
   Physical Address.........: 02-00-54-55-4E-01
   DHCP Enabled...........: No
   Autoconfiguration Enabled....: Yes
   Ipv6 Address...........: 2001:0:4136:e378:3c97:1d6f:3f57:fdf5(Pref
   erred)
   Link-local Ipv6 Address.....: fe80::3c97:1d6f:3f57:fdf5%10(Preferred)
   Default Gateway.........:::
   NetBIOS over Tcpip........: Disabled
Tunnel adapter Local Area Connection* 10:
   Connection-specific DNS Suffix.: contoso.com
   Description...........: Microsoft ISATAP Adapter #3
```

```
Physical Address.........: 00-00-00-00-00-00-00-E0
DHCP Enabled...........: No
Autoconfiguration Enabled....: Yes
Link-local Ipv6 Address.....: fe80::5efe:192.168.2.10%16(Preferred)
Default Gateway.........:
DNS Servers...........: 192.168.2.202
NetBIOS over Tcpip........: Disabled
```

Most enterprise workstations are dependent on DHCP servers for their IP addresses, subnet masks, default gateways, and DNS servers. If you suspect a problem with the IP address, you can use IPConfig to release the old IP address (so that it is returned to the pool of available addresses on the DHCP server) and to obtain a new IP address.

USE IPCONFIG TO RELEASE AND RENEW A DHCP IP ADDRESS

OPEN an elevated command prompt window.

1. At the command prompt, key **ipconfig /release** and then press **Enter**. Output similar to the following is displayed:

```
C:\Windows\system32>ipconfig /release

Windows IP Configuration
Ethernet adapter Local Area Connection:

  Connection-specific DNS Suffix.:
  Default Gateway.........:

Tunnel adapter Local Area Connection* 6:
  Media State...........: Media disconnected
  Connection-specific DNS Suffix.:
Tunnel adapter Local Area Connection* 7:
  Media State...........: Media disconnected
  Connection-specific DNS Suffix.:
```

2. At the command prompt, key **ipconfig /renew**. Output similar to the following is displayed:

```
C:\Windows\system32>ipconfig /renew

Windows IP Configuration

Ethernet adapter Local Area Connection:

  Connection-specific DNS Suffix.: contoso.com
  Ipv4 Address...........: 192.168.2.10
  Subnet Mask...........: 255.255.255.0
  Default Gateway.........: 192.168.2.202

Tunnel adapter Local Area Connection* 6:
  Media State...........: Media disconnected
  Connection-specific DNS Suffix.:
Tunnel adapter Local Area Connection* 7:
  Media State...........: Media disconnected
  Connection-specific DNS Suffix.:
```

Windows TCP/IP clients are equipped with a ***DNS resolver cache***, which caches resolved FQDNs. When your computer needs to resolve an FQDN to an IP address, it first checks to see if the resolution is cached. Only after that does it contact a DNS server.

In some instances, the cache can become corrupted, or a cached resolution can become obsolete. You can use IPConfig to clear the DNS resolver cache so that you can be assured when troubleshooting that the DNS resolver cache is not the problem.

USE IPCONFIG TO FLUSH THE DNS RESOLVER CACHE

OPEN an elevated command prompt window.

1. At the command prompt, key **Ipconfig /flushdns** and then press **Enter.** Output similar to the following is displayed:

```
C:\Windows\system32>ipconfig /flushdns
Windows IP Configuration
Successfully flushed the DNS Resolver Cache.
C:\Windows\system32>
```

You can use net view to view shared resources quickly on a computer.

USE NET VIEW

OPEN an elevated command prompt window.

1. At the command prompt, key **net view *Ipaddress*** and then press **Enter.** Output similar to the following is displayed:

```
C:\Windows\system32>net view 192.168.2.10
Shared resources at 192.168.2.10

Share name                          Type     Used as Comment
Contoso Consulting                  Disk
Contoso Corporate Graphics          Disk
The command completed successfully.
```

2. At the command prompt, key **net view *ComptuerName*.** Output similar to the following is displayed:

```
C:\Users\chrisc>net view acct43
Shared resources at acct43

Share name                          Type     Used as Comment
Contoso Consulting                  Disk
Contoso Corporate Graphics          Disk
Public Disk
Users Disk
The command completed successfully.
```

You can use traceRt to trace a rout from your computer to a target computer. TraceRt will gather and display statistics for each stop on the route.

USE TRACERT

OPEN an elevated command prompt window.

1. At the command prompt, key **tracert *FQDN*** and then press **Enter**. The following output uses the FQDN www.example.com as an example:

```
C:\Users\chrisc>tracert www.example.com
Tracing route to www.example.com [208.77.188.166]
over a maximum of 30 hops:
1    *       *         *       Request timed out.
2    12 ms   12 ms     *       ge-1-7-ur01.seattle.wa.seattle.comcast.net [68.86.99.65]
3    *       *         *       Request timed out.
4    *       27 ms     *       te-9-1-ar01.seattle.wa.seattle.comcast.net [68.86.96.102]
5    11ms    12 ms     21 ms   68.86.96.174
6    16 ms   93 ms     27 ms   68.86.90.217
7    31 ms   31 ms     31 ms   te-0-0-0-0-cr01.sacramento.ca.ibone.comcast.net [68.86.84.38]
8    *       *         35 ms   68.86.85.78
9    *       192.168.1.1 reports: Destination net unreachable.
Trace complete.
```

You can use Pathping to trace a route from your computer to a target computer. Pathping will gather and display statistics for each stop on the route (the statistics are more comprehensive than those returned by TraceRt, and they take longer to compute).

USE PATHPING

OPEN an elevated command prompt window.

1. At the command prompt, key **pathping *FQDN*** and then press **Enter**. The following output uses the FQDN www.example.com as an example:

```
C:\Users\chrisc.pathping www.example.com
Tracing route to www.example.com [208.77.188.166]
over a maximum of 30 hops:
0 ACCT43.contoso.com [192.168.2.10]
1    *        192.168.1.1
2    ge-1-7-ur01.seattle.wa.seattle.comcast.net [68.86.99.65]
3    te-9-3-ur02.seattle.wa.seattle.comcast.net [68.86.96.98]
4    *        *           te-9-1-ar01.seattle.wa.seattle.comcast.net [68.86.96.102]
5    68.86.96.174
6    68.86.90.217
7    te-0-0-0-0-cr01.sacramento.ca.ibone.comcast.net [68.86.84.38]
8    68.86.85.78
9    tengigabitethernet3-1.ar1.snv2.gblx.net [64.214.174.109]
10   icann.te1-3.1113.ar4.lax1.gblx.net [67.17.163.238]
11   www.example.com [208.77.188.166]
```

```
Computing statistics for 275 seconds...
   Source to Here     This Node/Link
Hop RTT Lost/Sent = Pct Lost/Sent = Pct Address
    0  ACCT43.contoso.com [192.168.2.10]
                                    33/ 100 = 33% |
    1  3ms 33/ 100 5 33% 0/ 100 5 0% 192.168.1.1
                                    7/ 100 5 7% |
    2  17ms 40/ 100 5 40% 0/ 100 5 0% ge-1-7-ur01.seattle.wa.seattle.com cast.net [68.86.99.65]
                                    0/ 100 5 0% |
    3  14ms 42/ 100 5 42% 2/ 100 5 2% te-9-3-ur02.seattle.wa.seattle.com cast.net [68.86.96.98]
                                    0/ 100 5 0% |
    4  18ms 41/ 100 5 41% 1/ 100 5 1% te-9-1-ar01.seattle.wa.seattle.com cast.net [68.86.96.102]
                                    0/ 100 5 0% |
    5  13ms 41/ 100 5 41% 1/ 100 5 1% 68.86.96.174
                                    0/ 100 5 0% |
    6  15ms 43/ 100 5 43% 3/ 100 5 3% 68.86.90.217
                                    0/ 100 5 0% |
    7  30ms 42/ 100 5 42% 2/ 100 5 2% te-0-0-0-0-cr01.sacramento.ca.ibone.comcast.net [68.86.84.38]
                                    0/ 100 5 0% |
    8  36ms 40/ 100 = 40% 0/ 100 5 0% 68.86.85.78
                                    0/ 100 = 0% |
    9  41ms 41/ 100 = 41% 1/ 100 5 1% tengigabitethernet3-1.ar1.snv2.gbl x.net [64.214.174.109]
                                    0/ 100 = 0% |
   10  41ms 44/ 100 = 44% 4/ 100 5 4% icann.te1-3.1113.ar4.lax1.gblx.net [67.17.163.238]
                                    0/ 100 5 = 0% |
   11  41ms 40/ 100 = 40% 0/ 100 5 0% www.example.com [208.77.188.166]
Trace complete.
```

You can use NSlookup to troubleshoot DNS issues. If you think that DNS is not working properly, use NSlookup to manually request DNS resolution of an example IP address. If the resolution fails, then DNS name resolution might be your problem.

USE NSLOOKUP

OPEN an elevated command prompt window.

1. At the command prompt, key **nslookup FQDN** and then press **Enter**. The following output uses the FQDN for www.example.com as an example:

```
C:\Users\chrisc>nslookup www.example.com
Server: UnKnown
Address: 192.168.2.202:53

Non-authoritative answer:
Name: www.example.com
Address: 208.77.188.166
```

Using Windows Network Diagnostics

Windows Network Diagnostics is part of the Windows Diagnostic Infrastructure (WDI) and can help users solve some wireless and other networking issues.

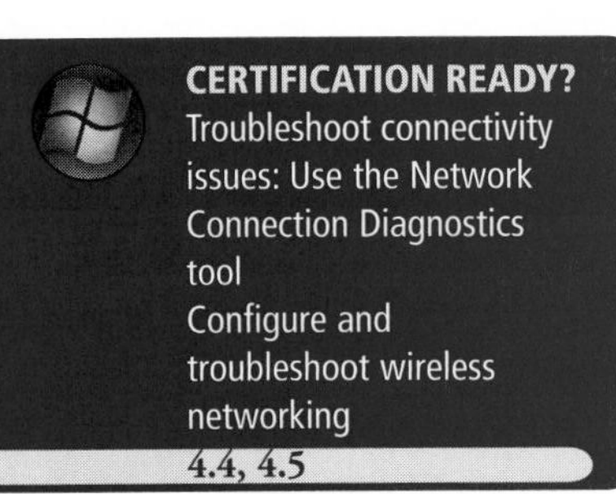

CERTIFICATION READY?
Troubleshoot connectivity issues: Use the Network Connection Diagnostics tool
Configure and troubleshoot wireless networking
4.4, 4.5

Windows Network Diagnostics (WND) is part of the Windows Diagnostic Infrastructure (WDI) and can help users solve some wireless and other networking issues. By helping users solve problems, WND can reduce calls to the help desk.

WDI is covered in **Lesson 10: Updating Windows Vista.**

Some of the common problems that WND can help users to solve are:

- Receiving a weak wireless signal.
- Having a disabled wireless card.
- Not receiving an IP address assignment.
- Typing an incorrect security key.
- Using invalid certificates when logging on.
- Experiencing hardware or driver issues.

Using Event Viewer is covered in **Lesson 6: Troubleshooting Security Issues.**

For wireless networking, WND logs the following events, which can be viewed in Event Viewer to troubleshoot networking issues:

- The wireless network adapter name and whether the driver is native to Windows Vista or is a legacy driver
- A list of detected wireless networks and the signal strength, channel, and protocol (such as 802.11b or 802.11g) for each
- The list of preferred wireless networks and each network's configuration settings
- Diagnostic conclusions, for example, "The Internet connection on the wireless router or access point might not be working correctly" and "The computer has a low signal strength from ContosoWLAN"
- Any repair options offered to users, for example, "Try moving the computer to a different location, eliminating any sources of possible interference, and then try connecting to ContosoWLAN again"
- Any repair options chosen by the user and whether the repair options solved the problem

START WINDOWS NETWORK DIAGNOSTICS

You can manually start WND to help troubleshoot networking issues.

1. Click **Start** and then click **Control Panel**. The Control Panel appears.
2. Under Network and Internet, click **View network status and tasks.**
3. In the tasks list, click **Diagnose and repair.** A Windows Network Diagnostics message box appears and indicates progress, as shown in Figure 12-24.

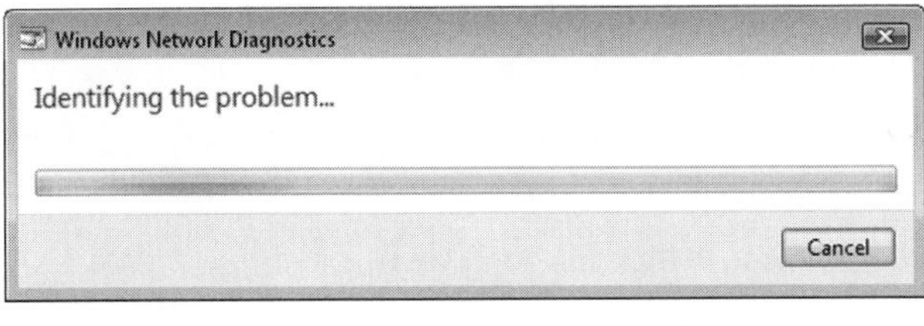

Figure 12-24
Windows Network Diagnostics attempts to identify a networking problem

4. After some time, WND will report either that it could not find a problem, or it will tell you that it did find a problem. In the latter case, you are often presented with options that can help you to solve the problem. For example, Figure 12-25 shows two possible solutions: Getting a new IP address, or resetting the network adapter:

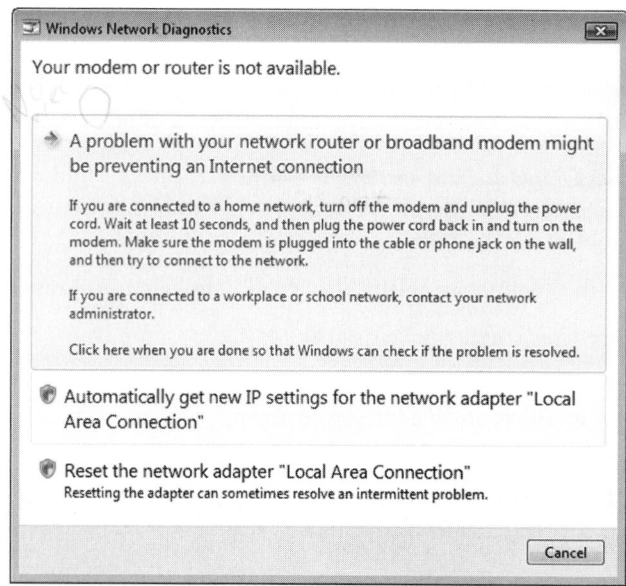

Figure 12-25

Windows Network Diagnostics identifies the problem and offers two possible solutions

SUMMARY SKILL MATRIX

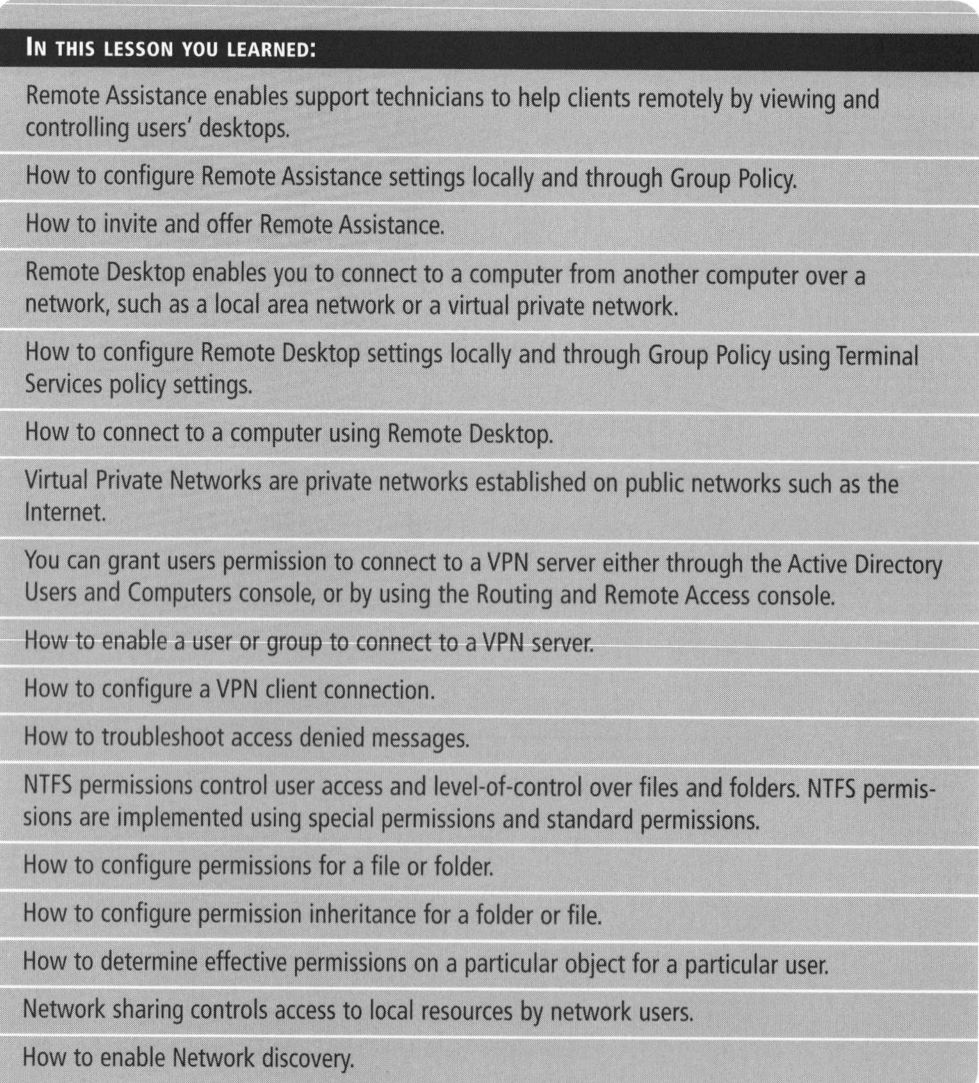

IN THIS LESSON YOU LEARNED:
Remote Assistance enables support technicians to help clients remotely by viewing and controlling users' desktops.
How to configure Remote Assistance settings locally and through Group Policy.
How to invite and offer Remote Assistance.
Remote Desktop enables you to connect to a computer from another computer over a network, such as a local area network or a virtual private network.
How to configure Remote Desktop settings locally and through Group Policy using Terminal Services policy settings.
How to connect to a computer using Remote Desktop.
Virtual Private Networks are private networks established on public networks such as the Internet.
You can grant users permission to connect to a VPN server either through the Active Directory Users and Computers console, or by using the Routing and Remote Access console.
How to enable a user or group to connect to a VPN server.
How to configure a VPN client connection.
How to troubleshoot access denied messages.
NTFS permissions control user access and level-of-control over files and folders. NTFS permissions are implemented using special permissions and standard permissions.
How to configure permissions for a file or folder.
How to configure permission inheritance for a folder or file.
How to determine effective permissions on a particular object for a particular user.
Network sharing controls access to local resources by network users.
How to enable Network discovery.

(continued)

SUMMARY SKILL MATRIX (*continued*)

IN THIS LESSON YOU LEARNED:
How to enable file sharing, public folder sharing, and printer sharing.
How to create a network share using the File Sharing Wizard.
How to troubleshoot networking using command-line tools and the Network Connections Diagnostic tool.
How to use `Ping`, `IPConfig`, `Net View`, `TraceRT`, `Pathping`, and `NSlookup`.

Knowledge Assessment

Fill in the Blank

Complete the following sentences by writing the correct word or words in the blanks provided.

1. A very common command-line tool that reports how long it takes to send and receive to a remote host, and that you can use to test connectivity is ________________.
2. You can use the ________________ switch with `IPConfig` to empty the DNS resolver cache.
3. The ________________ on a DNS client contains resolved FQDNs from name resolution requests.
4. ________________ are a part of the file system Windows Vista uses to control access to objects such as files and folders.
5. You can use the ________________ command-line tool to manually make DNS name resolution requests.
6. Both Remote Assistance and Remote Desktop are implemented using ________________ Services.
7. A private network established on a public network is called a(n) ________________.
8. When using Remote Desktop to connect to a remote computer not on the local network, you can connect using a VPN or by connecting to a(n) ________________
9. ________________ can prevent computers that lack antivirus software from authenticating to a network.
10. NTFS permissions being passed from parent folders to child objects is called ________________.

Multiple Choice

Select all answers that apply for the following questions.

1. Which of the following is not a prerequisite for offering a Remote Assistance session?
   a. You must be added to the list of helpers in the Offer Remote Assistance Group Policy setting.
   b. Windows Firewall on the target computer must except msra.exe and raserver.exe
   c. A security connection rule establishing IPsec between the target computer and the assistant's computer must be implemented.
   d. Windows Firewall on the target computer must allow communication on DCOM port 135 (TCP).

2. To prevent users from soliciting Remote Assistance through Group Policy:
   a. Enable Remote Assistance request messages in Windows Firewall on the target computer.
   b. Enable the Solicited Remote Assistance policy setting.
   c. Enable the Offer Remote Assistance policy setting.
   d. Enable the Terminal Services group policy setting.
3. Which of the following are prerequisites for establishing a Remote Desktop session within the same LAN?
   a. If the user account with which you want to connect to the target computer is not an administrator's, add the user account to the Remote Desktop Users group of the target computer.
   b. Configure Windows Firewall on the target computer to allow Remote Desktop connections.
   c. Establish a VPN connection between the remote and local computer.
   d. Ensure that policy for the target computer allows Remote Desktop connections.
4. You have established a Remote Desktop connection to a remote computer. You use Media Player to play an audio file on the remote computer, but you cannot hear it at your local computer. You should:
   a. Enable the Redirect Remote Audio Group Policy setting.
   b. Configure the Remote Audio setting on the Local Resources tab of the Remote Connections dialog box to Redirect audio.
   c. Turn up the volume on the remote computer loud enough so that you can hear it from the local computer.
   d. Configure the Remote computer sound setting on the Local Resources tab of the Remote Desktop Connections dialog box to Bring to this computer.
5. You can enable users to connect using a VPN connection in the following locations:
   a. Routing and Remote Access console
   b. Virtual Private Networking console
   c. In a GPO by using the Group Policy Object Editor console
   d. On the Users tab of the Virtual Private Networking properties dialog box

6. Selecting the Read & execute permission is the same as selecting the following NTFS permissions:
   a. Traverse folder/execute file, List folder/read data, Read attributes, Read extended attributes, Read permissions
   b. Traverse folder/execute file, List folder/read data, Read attributes, Read extended attributes, Read permissions
   c. List folder/read data, Read attributes, Read extended attributes, Read permissions
   d. Create files/write data, Create folders/append data, Write attributes, Write extended attributes
7. Which of the following is not an option when configuring permission inheritance on a folder?
   a. Files only
   b. Subfolders and files only
   c. All
   d. This folder and subfolders
8. When testing Group Policy, you can use the Group Policy Results Wizard to determine what the Group Policy is for a specific user on a specific computer. What is the equivalent of the Group Policy Results Wizard for NTFS permissions on a folder?
   a. NTFS Permissions Results Wizard
   b. Permissions Results tab in the Advanced Security Settings dialog box of the folder in question
   c. NTFS permissions analyzer
   d. Effective permissions tab in the Advanced Security Settings dialog box of the folder in question

9. When you enable Public folder sharing, you:
   a. Enable all local users on the local machine to access the Public folder.
   b. Enable users to create Public folders and share them with other users.
   c. Enable network users to access the Public folder on the local machine.
   d. Enable administrators to determine how the Public folder is shared.

10. If on a computer attached to a domain with a DNS server, you execute the command NSlookup 127.0.0.1, what is the response likely to include?
   a. The response will be an error because 127.0.0.1 is not a valid IP address.
   b. The response will be the FQDN of your computer.
   c. The response will be an error because no FQDN is associated with the loop-back address.
   d. The response will be the name of your domain.

Review Questions

1. Describe the requirements for requesting and receiving Remote Assistance.
2. Describe permission inheritance and give an example of how you could use permission inheritance to control access to files within a folder.

■ Case Scenarios

Scenario 1: NTFS Permissions

You need to create a folder in which users in the Accounting group can read and modify the files, and those in the Analysts group can only read. Outline what NTFS permissions to use for both.

Scenario 2: Using Ping to Diagnose Network Issues

A computer is having trouble connecting to Internet URLs. You use Ping to verify connectivity to the loop-back address. You then use Ping and find that you can reach the gateway server for the network adapter. Ping fails, however, on www.microsoft.com. But when you ping an IP address for www.microsoft.com, it is successful. What do you think the problem is, and what command-line tool or tools can you use to back up your suspicion?

Supporting and Maintaining Desktop Applications

OBJECTIVE DOMAIN MATRIX

Technology Skill	Objective Domain	Objective Domain Number
Software Deployment Overview	Support deployed applications	5.1
SMS Advanced Client	Support deployed applications	5.1
Using Group Policy To Deploy Software	Support deployed applications	5.1
Creating a Network Share for Distributing Software via Group Policy	Support deployed applications	5.1
Using Group Policy to Assign and Publish Packages	Support deployed applications	5.1
Using Group Policy to Upgrade or Replace an Existing Application	Maintain desktop applications	5.3
Upgrading Applications	Maintain desktop applications	5.3
Troubleshooting Group Policy Software Deployment	Maintain desktop applications	5.3
Deploying Software Using Systems Management Server 2003	Support deployed applications	5.1
Installing Systems Management Server 2003	Support deployed applications	5.1
Assigning the SMS Client to Windows Vista by Using Group Policy	Support deployed applications	5.1

KEY TERMS

Microsoft Installer
IntelliMirror
Management Point
Distribution Point
Distributed file system (DFS)
scope of management (SOM)

In this lesson, you are going to experiment with various methods for deploying and managing applications on a Windows-based network using Group Policy Software Installation (GPSI) and Systems Management Server 2003 (SMS 2003). The results of these experiments will help you to familiarize yourself with the two different technologies and make an informed decision about which is most suitable for your needs.

■ Software Deployment Overview

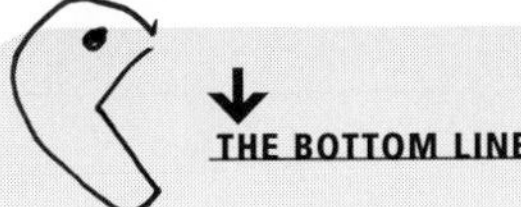

THE BOTTOM LINE

Microsoft offers two technologies for the purposes of installing and maintaining software on a Windows-based network: Group Policy Software Installation and Systems Management Server 2003 (SMS 2003).

Group Policy is included as part of Windows Server 2003 when Microsoft Active Directory directory service is installed. Group Policy Software Installation offers simple deployment features and management using Microsoft Installer technology (.msi file format). Group Policy Software Installation uses IntelliMirror, which is a group of technologies that enables users' data and programs to follow them around a network. GPSI is ideal for use in small environments where software is deployed occasionally on a local area network (LAN). Group Policy Software Installation lacks the sophisticated deployment, reporting, and scheduling features offered by Systems Management Server 2003 (SMS 2003).

You can use Group Policy to install, upgrade, and remove software packages on Windows Vista and other NT-based operating systems, from Windows 2000 onwards. The following features are supported:

- Software distribution using Microsoft Installer (MSI).
- Distribution of legacy applications using zap files. Zap files (Zero Administration for Windows down-level application packages) are non-MSI text files that contain a set of instructions for installing legacy applications using Group Policy.
- Removal of managed software.
- Customization of MSI-based application packages using transform files. Transform files have an .mst extension. Microsoft Office 2007 is customized using patch files that have an .msp extension. You can also edit MSI packages using a free tool from Microsoft called Orca.
- Upgrading of managed applications.
- Ability to assign or publish applications to specific users or computers.

Systems Management Server 2003 offers benefits over Group Policy such as the ability to utilize BITS (Background Intelligent Transfer Service) for distributing software packages over slow wide area networks (WANs), reporting and inventory services, scheduling, and flexible management of software deployment for large organizations.

Although SMS offers considerable advantages over Group Policy, you should note that it also introduces additional cost and complexity to your environment. Group Policy is included as part of Active Directory, but SMS is a server product that you must purchase separately. You should consider using SMS Server under the following circumstances:

- Software distribution needs to be managed for a large network with many physically dispersed sites
- Software deployments/upgrades need to be scheduled
- Reporting and inventory capabilities are required
- Packages are frequently deployed, removed, or upgraded

SMS Advanced Client

The SMS Advanced Client 2.5, which supports all operating systems from Windows 2000 to Windows Vista, has a number of benefits over Group Policy Software Installation especially in the area of supporting remote users on slow network links. Table 13-1 outlines the differences between software distribution using the SMS Advanced Client and Group Policy.

Table 13-1

The differences between Group Policy and SMS Advanced Client software distribution

	Software distribution	Scheduling	Inventory
Group Policy	NTFS/DFS Share	N/A Software that is assigned to a computer account using Group Policy will be installed the next time the target computer is rebooted.	N/A
Systems Management Server Advanced Client	BITS (Background Intelligent Transfer Service). See the detailed description of BITS that follows this table.	SMS can schedule the installation of software to occur at a specified time.	SMS Server can produce an inventory of all the applications installed on every machine on your network and store this information in the SMS database.

	Reporting	Status information	Wide area networks
Group Policy	N/A	Refer to the Event Log on every machine to view status information.	Although Group Policy does not directly support advanced features for distributing software over a WAN, it is possible. Using DFS (Distributed file system) shares, you can transparently direct the installation source to the closest file server. DFS provides replication of files across multiple servers and the ability to route users transparently to the nearest available replicated copy of a given file.
Systems Management Server Advanced Client	SMS Server can generate detailed reports based on inventory information that is stored in the database.	Using SMS, it's possible to determine if the software was successfully installed.	SMS Advanced Client now supports use of BITS for slow network links. However, it's recommended that you consider creating additional SMS sites for geographically separated locations.

BITS

The SMS Advanced Client makes use of BITS (Background Intelligent Transfer Service). BITS adjusts the rate at which software is transferred from a DP (Distribution Point) to a client according the available bandwidth. Using the Advanced Client also ensures that other network traffic gets priority so that important network services are not interrupted. BITS makes it possible to restart an interrupted software download from the point at which it stopped. These features are especially important when supporting laptop users over slow dial-up links. The downloaded application will remain in the client's cache until it's scheduled to be installed. An Advanced Client receives policy information from an SMS Management Point (MP).

TAKE NOTE*

Requirements for the procedures in this lesson:

- Windows Server 2003 (SP1 R2) Active Directory domain, which is the only domain in a single forest (contoso.com).
- A Windows Vista Enterprise workstation, named, for example, VISTA1, which is a member of the contoso.com domain.
- An administrative workstation or server on which you have installed the Group Policy Management Console (GPMC) and the Windows 2003 Server Administration Tools.
- Systems Management Server 2003 SP3 must be installed on a member server in the contoso.com domain with a working configuration.

Using Group Policy to Deploy Software

THE BOTTOM LINE

As discussed in the previous section, Group Policy provides a simple and effective means to distribute software to workstations in small- and medium-sized organizations.

This section covers the technologies involved in Group Policy Software Installation including Microsoft Installer and IntelliMirror.

Microsoft Installer A proprietary Microsoft system for installing applications on Windows Operating Systems. MSI is the file extension for Windows Installer packages.

IntelliMirror A group of technologies that allows users' data and programs to follow them around a network.

Scope of Management The Active Directory objects to which a Group Policy Object applies.

Distributed File System (DFS) Provides replication of files across multiple servers and the ability to route users transparently to the nearest available replicated copy of a given file.

Creating a Network Share for Group Policy Software Installation

This may sound like a relatively trivial task, but there are some points that you should consider before deploying software using Group Policy Software Installation.

The following section describes the procedures involved in publishing or assigning software by Group Policy. To use Group Policy Software Installation, you need to complete these steps:

- Create an NTFS or DFS network share for use as a software distribution point
- Add Microsoft Installer packages to the share
- Create an Organizational Unit (OU; optional)
- Create a new Group Policy Object (GPO) and link it to an Organizational Unit
- Configure new Software Installation settings in the Group Policy Object (GPO)
- Test the configuration

When Group Policy installs software that has been assigned to a computer account, it does so under the security context of the local computer account. Therefore, for the software to install successfully, computer accounts within the domain must have Read permission to the necessary MSI package(s) and associated files. This can be achieved by giving the Authenticated Users group Read permission on the Access Control List (ACL) for the shared folder.

Second, although it's not a requirement to use a DFS (Distributed file system) share when specifying the location of an MSI package during the configuration of a Group Policy Object if you specify a standard network share, it will not be possible to change the source path after the GPO has been created. The only way to specify a new location is to delete the software installation from the GPO and recreate it. The advantage of using a DFS share is that you can change the location of the shared files as many times as you like, and the changes will be completely transparent to the Group Policy Object or users.

Using a DFS share has additional benefits if your client machines are spread over geographically dispersed sites. Clients can read MSI packages from file servers that are located closest to them rather than across a WAN link, for example.

CREATE A FOLDER FOR GROUP POLICY SOFTWARE INSTALLATION

Create a folder on a file server for storing software packages that will be distributed using Group Policy.

LOG ON to a file server in the contoso.com domain as an administrator.

1. Create a folder called Software, in a suitable location on a file server that's a member of your Active Directory domain.
2. Right-click the new folder and then select **Properties**. The folder Properties dialog box appears.
3. Select the Security tab and then click **Add**. The Select Users, Computers, or Groups dialog box appears.
4. Key **authenticated users** in the Enter object names to select list box and then click **Check Names**. Authenticated Users will then be underlined.
5. Click **OK** to close the Select Users, Computers, or Groups dialog box.
6. Make sure that Authenticated Users is highlighted on the Security tab and that the following permissions are selected: Read & Execute, List Folder Contents, and Read.
7. Click **OK** to close the Properties dialog box.

CREATE A DFS ROOT

For ease of management, create a DFS share rather than a NTFS share for use with Group Policy Software Installation.

LOG ON to a file server in the contoso.com domain as an administrator.

1. From the Start Menu, select **Administrative Tools** and then **Distributed File System**.
2. Right-click **Distributed File System** in the Distributed File System console and then select **New Root**. The Welcome to the New Root Wizard page appears.
3. Click **Next**. The Root Type page appears.
4. Ensure that **Domain Root** is selected before clicking **Next**. The Host Domain page appears.
5. Select your domain to host the new root (in this case, contoso.com) and then click **Next**. The Host Server page appears.
6. Next to the Server name text box, click **Browse** to locate the server which will host the new DFS root. The Find Computers dialog box appears.
7. Select the server in the Search results list box and then click **OK**.

8. The server you selected should appear in the Server name text box. Click **Next.** The Root Name page appears.
9. In the Root name text box, give the new DFS root a name. You need to key only **software.** The full path for the new DFS root, which is \\contoso.com\software, appears in the Preview of UNC path to the root preview box. Click **Next.** The Root Share page appears.
10. Click **Browse** to locate the folder called Software that you created in the previous procedure. The Browse for Folder dialog box appears.
11. Highlight the folder name and then click **OK.**
12. In the Root Share page, the folder name you selected should appear in the Folder to share text box. Click **Next.** The Root Name page appears.
13. Click **Next.** The Completing the New Root Wizard page appears.
14. Review the settings and then click **Finish.**
15. Test the new DFS root by opening Windows Explorer, keying the path of the DFS root into the Address Box, and then clicking **Enter.** You should see the shared folder appear under Folders on the left side of the window.

In this example, there is only one DFS root target and no replication. It's possible to add DFS root targets to multiple file servers if required.

Figure 13-1 shows a completed DFS root.

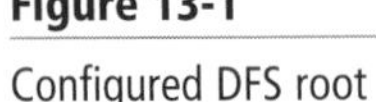

Figure 13-1

Configured DFS root

Using Group Policy to Assign and Publish Packages

Group Policy provides two methods for deploying software.

In software assignment, a package is essentially forced on a given computer or user, making the installation mandatory. In the case of assignment to a user account, although the software will appear as installed, the various components will only be set up on demand, as the user needs them.

You can use software publication only in conjunction with user accounts. Installation is not mandatory, and the user must look for the publication in the Add/Remove Programs control panel. If the user chooses to install the application, Vista will install the full application.

USER ASSIGNMENTS

Software packages that are assigned to users via Group Policy are advertised to a user on the Start menu when a user logs on to a computer. The application is not installed until the user clicks the icon on the Start menu. If, for instance, the user clicks the PowerPoint icon from Microsoft Office 2003, only PowerPoint will be installed, not the whole Microsoft Office suite. A user must log off and back on again for new assignments to appear on the Start menu.

COMPUTER ASSIGNMENTS

Windows Vista installs packages assigned to computers the next time the user reboots the machine. In this case, Vista installs the entire application.

PACKAGES PUBLISHED TO USERS

Packages published to users appear only in the Add/Remove Programs control panel and not in the Start menu. Therefore, users must check for new published applications. Additionally, the whole application is installed rather than only the code that's needed.

Table 13-2 summarizes the different methods for deploying applications via Group Policy and the results that end users will see.

TAKE NOTE*

By default, both Group Policy and Systems Management Server distribute software by means of unicast packets. This means that if you assign applications simultaneously to a large number of computers, it's possible that network bandwidth may become saturated.

For example, when deploying Microsoft Office 2007, Microsoft recommends that no more than 200 computers should have the software deployed at any one time. Systems Management Server can be extended by third-party products to support multicast packets to optimize the bandwidth consumed during the installation process. In addition, SMS supports scheduling, which you can use to limit the bandwidth used for software distribution.

Table 13-2

Summary of software distribution methods using Group Policy

	Published (Users Only)	Assigned (User Accounts)	Assigned (Computer Accounts)
Where can the user find the application?	Add/Remove Programs Control Panel	Start menu	Start menu
When or where is the application installed?	Add/Remove Programs Control Panel	At logon	At reboot
How is the application installed?	Full installation	As needed	Full installation

DOWNLOAD You can download the Group Policy Management console (GPMC) with Service Pack 1 here: *http://www.microsoft.com/downloads.* GPMC is an add-on component for Windows Server 2003 that delivers advanced functionality for managing Group Policy. GPMC can also be installed on Windows XP and is built into Windows Vista.

DOWNLOAD You can download a beta of Microsoft SharedView as an MSI package from the following URL: *http://www.connect.microsoft.com/site/sitehome.aspx?SiteID=94.* Copy the MSI package to the software distribution share created earlier in the lesson. You need to download this package to perform procedures later in this lesson.

To help users locate applications published via Group Policy, it is best practice to assign those application packages to predefined software categories. Let's define some software categories for use with GPSI.

When you define software categories by using the Group Policy Object Editor for a particular GPO, those categories are stored in Active Directory and become available for use with any new GPO that you create. Therefore, it's necessary to define the categories only once. From GPMC, let's create a new GPO to publish the SharedView MSI that you've just downloaded. Before defining the package, we'll create some categories.

CREATE A NEW GROUP POLICY OBJECT

To distribute software using Group Policy you must first create a new Group Policy Object (GPO).

LOG ON to your Windows Vista machine with your standard user account.

1. Click **Start.**
2. In the Start Search text box, key **mmc** and then press **Enter.** A User Account Control dialog box appears.
3. Provide administrator credentials and then click **OK.** An MMC console appears.
4. Click **File** and then click **Add/Remove Snap-in.**
5. In the Available snap-ins list box, select **Group Policy Management** and then click **Add.**
6. Click **OK** to close the Add or Remove Snap-ins dialog box.
7. In the console tree, expand Group Policy Management > Forest: contoso.com > Domains > contoso.com.
8. Right-click **Group Policy Objects** and then select **New.** The New GPO dialog box appears.
9. Key **SharedView** in the Name text box and then click **OK.** See the SharedView GPO listed in the details pane, as shown in Figure 13-2.

Figure 13-2

Create a new Group Policy Object

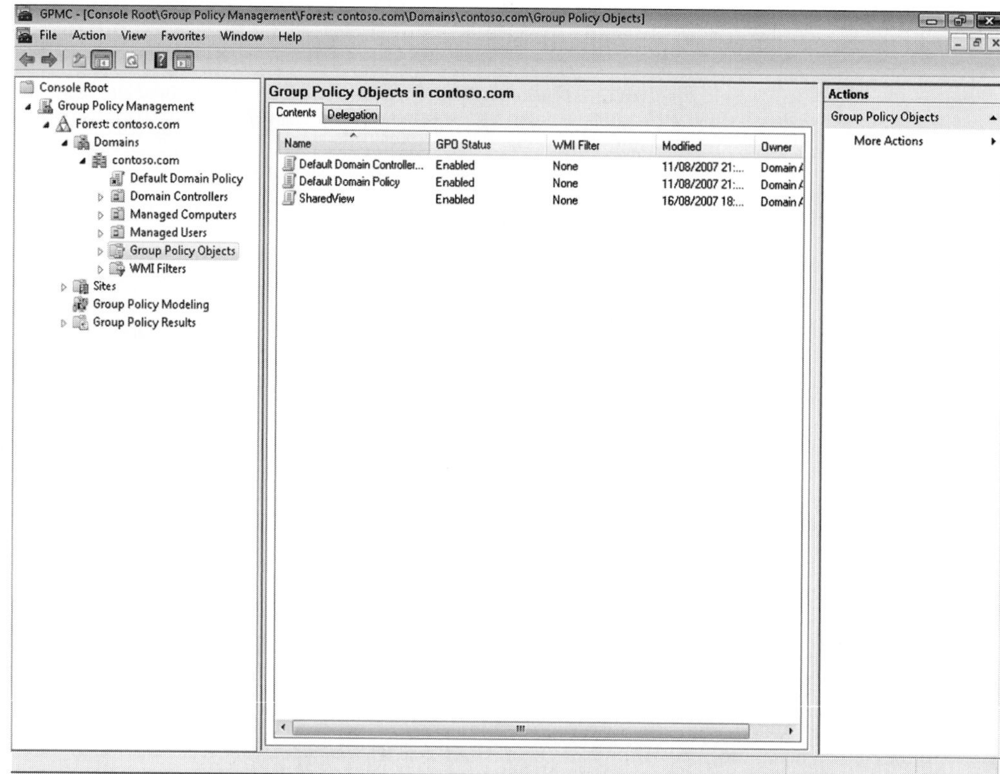

10. To save the console you just created, click **File** and then click **Save**. The Save as dialog box appears.
11. Under Save in column, click **Desktop.**
12. In the File name text box, key **GPMC SharedView.**
13. Click **Save.** The icon for this console now appears on the desktop.

CREATE TWO ORGANIZATIONAL UNITS FOR USE WITH GROUP POLICY SOFTWARE INSTALLATION

To control which users or computers the Group Policy Object applies to (otherwise known as Scope of Management) you need to create Organizational Units.

LOG ON to your Windows Vista machine with your standard user account.

1. Double-click the **GPMC SharedView** icon on the desktop. A User Account Control dialog box appears.
2. Provide administrator credentials and then click **OK.** The GPMC SharedView console appears.
3. Expand **Group Policy Management** > **Forest:contoso.com** > **Domains.**
4. Right-click **contoso.com** and then click **New Organizational Unit.** The New Organizational Unit dialog box appears.
5. Key **Managed Users** in the Name text box and then click **OK.**
6. Repeat steps 4 and 5 to create another OU called **Managed Computers.**
7. If you close the GPMC SharedView console, click **Yes** to save the console.

CREATE SOFTWARE CATEGORIES

Software Categories allow users to locate programs easily in the Add/Remove Programs control panel.

LOG ON to your Windows Vista machine with your standard user account.

1. Double-click the **GPMC SharedView** icon on the desktop. A User Account Control dialog box appears.
2. Provide administrator credentials and then click **OK**. The GPMC SharedView console appears.
3. Expand **Group Policy Management** > **Forest:contoso.com** > **Domains** > **contoso.com** > **Group Policy Objects**, and you'll see the SharedView GPO in the list.
4. Right-click **SharedView** and then click **Edit**. The Group Policy Object Editor appears.
5. Expand **User Configuration** > **Software Settings**.
6. Right-click **Software installation** and then select **Properties**. The Software installation Properties dialog box appears.
7. Select the Categories tab and then click **Add.** The Enter New Category dialog box appears.
8. Create two new categories, the first called Collaboration and the second Accounting, as shown in Figure 13-3.

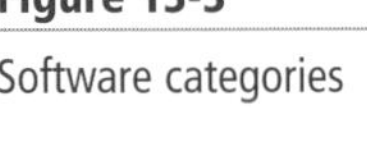

Figure 13-3

Software categories

9. Click **Apply**.
10. In the Software installation Properties dialog box, we can also set other defaults. Click the **Advanced** tab and then select **Uninstall the applications when they fall out of the scope of management** check box to be a default setting for new packages.
11. Click **OK** to close the Software installation Properties dialog box.
12. If you close the GPMC SharedView console, click **Yes** to save the console.

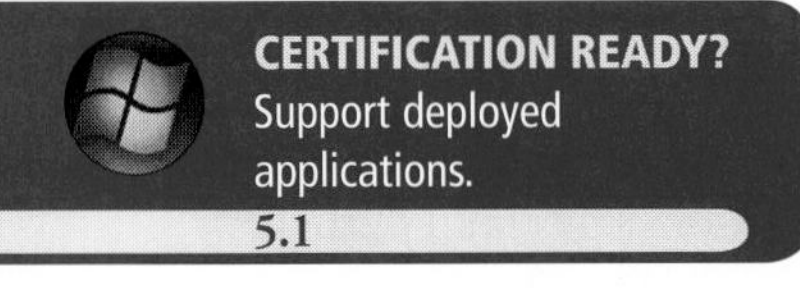

PUBLISH APPLICATION PACKAGES TO USERS VIA GROUP POLICY

Now that we have some categories assigned in Active Directory and we've modified the default settings for Software installation Properties we're ready to create a published package.

LOG ON to your Windows Vista machine with your standard user account.

1. Double-click the **GPMC SharedView** icon on the desktop. A User Account Control dialog box appears.
2. Provide administrator credentials and then click **OK.** The GPMC SharedView console appears.

3. In the details pane, under Group Policy Objects in contoso.com, right-click **SharedView** and then select **Edit**. The Group Policy Object Editor appears.
4. Expand **User Configuration > Software Settings**, right-click **Software installation**, and then select **New > Package.** The Open dialog box appears.
5. When selecting the MSI package to publish, it's important to use the DFS share that we created earlier. In the File name box, key **\\contoso.com\software** and then click **Open**. You should now see the folders for the MSI packages listed.
6. Select **SharedView** folder and then click **Open**.
7. Select **SharedView MSI package** and then click **Open**. The Deploy Software dialog box appears.
8. Verify that **Published** is selected as the default and then click **OK**.
9. Let's allocate this published application to a software category. Make sure that **Software installation** is highlighted under User Configuration and right-click the **Microsoft SharedView** package in the details pane. Then select **Properties**. The Microsoft SharedView (Beta) Properties dialog box appears.
10. Select the **Categories** tab.
11. In the Available categories list box, select **Collaboration** and then click **Select**. Collaboration now appears under the Selected categories list box.
12. Click **OK**.
13. Close Group Policy Object Editor.
14. Link the new GPO to the Managed Users OU by right-clicking the **Managed Users** OU in the console tree and then selecting **Link an Existing GPO**. The Select GPO dialog box appears.
15. In the Group Policy objects list box, select **SharedView** and then click **OK**. For the sake of simplicity, we'll leave the security filtering set to Authenticated Users.
16. Expand the **Managed Users** OU and then select the **SharedView** GPO. You'll see the links and security filtering for the GPO in the details pane, as shown in Figure 13-4.

Figure 13-4

SharedView GPO linked to the Managed Users OU

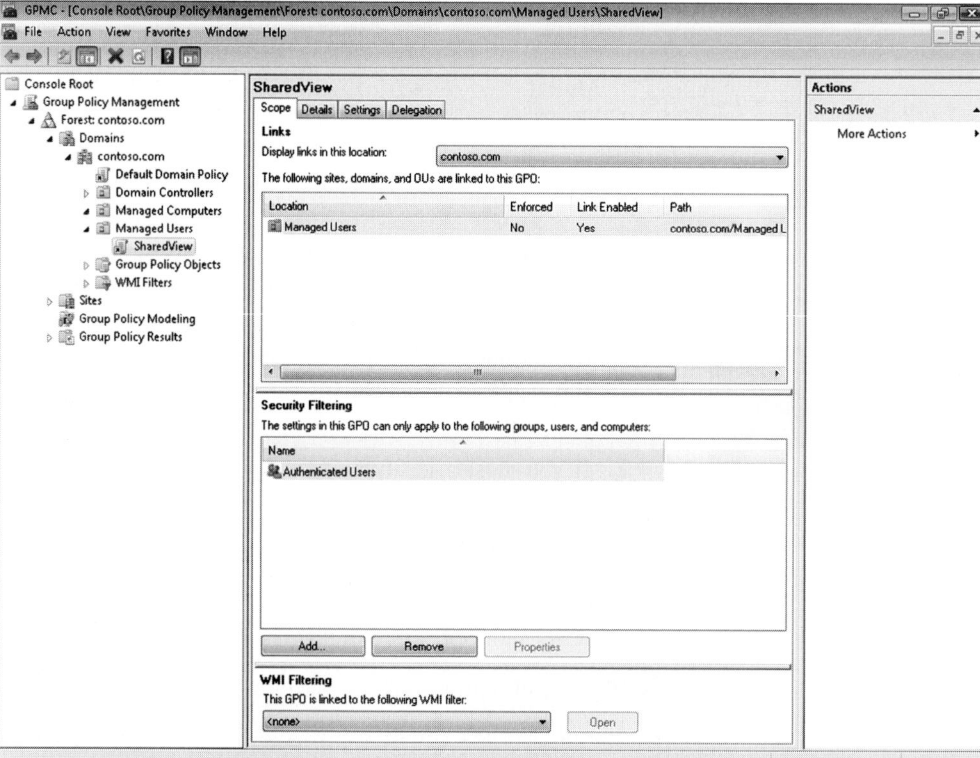

TEST A PUBLISHED APPLICATION

To test the new policy, **LOG ON** to Windows Vista with a user account that is located in the Managed Users OU.

1. From the Start menu, click **Control Panel.** The Control Panel appears.
2. Click **Programs**. The Programs control panel appears.
3. Under Get Programs, select **Install a program from the network**.
4. You should see Microsoft SharedView listed. Highlight the application and then click **Install**.

TAKE NOTE*

If you right-click a published package in the Group Policy Object Editor, you'll notice that Auto-install is checked by default in the menu. This option is the same as the Auto-install this application by file extension activation option on the Deployment tab. It gives the user the impression that the application is actually installed, but in fact the application is not installed until the user double-clicks a related file extension if the package is assigned or published to a user account.

Group Policy Objects by default apply to all child containers below the parent container to which they are linked. Therefore, it is efficient to link GPOs to containers high up the Active Directory hierarchy. To control to which users and computers software packages are assigned or published, you should consider filtering by security groups.

For instance, we can have an Organizational Unit called Managed Desktops under the root level of our domain contoso.com. This Organizational Unit can have many child objects including a hierarchy of additional OUs where Computer Accounts are placed.

Rather than linking Group Policy Objects that contain Software Installation settings at various levels of this hierarchy, all these GPOs should be linked to the top-level Managed Desktops OU.

If, for example, there's a GPO called Accounts Application that should be assigned only to computers within the accounts department, we can create a security group of which all those computer accounts are a member.

CREATE AN ACTIVE DIRECTORY SECURITY GROUP

To control which computers the Group Policy Object will apply to (Scope of Management) you first need to create an Active Directory group and populate it with computer account objects.

LOG ON to a Windows 2003 server in the contoso.com domain as an administrator.

1. From the Start menu, open **Administrative Tools** > **Active Directory Users and Computers**. The Active Directory Users and Computers console appears.
2. Under contoso.com, right-click **Users** and then select **New** > **Group**. The New Object–Group dialog box appears.
3. In the Group Name text box, key **Accounts Application** and then click **OK.**
4. Expand **Users** in the console tree, right-click **Accounts Application**, and then click **Properties**. The Accounts Application Properties dialog box appears.
5. Click the **Members** tab and then click **Add**. The Select Users, Contacts, or Computers dialog box appears.
6. Click **Object Types**. The Object Types dialog box appears.
7. Select the **Computers** check box and then click **OK.**
8. In the Select Users, Contacts, or Computers dialog box, key the name of your computer account and then click **Check Names.**
9. Verify that the computer name is underlined and then click **OK.**
10. Click **OK** to close the Accounts Application Properties dialog box.

FILTER A GROUP POLICY OBJECT BY SECURITY GROUP

Now we can use the security group created in the previous step to change the scope of management of the Group Policy Object.

LOG ON to your Windows Vista machine with a standard user account.

1. Double-click the **GPMC SharedView** icon on the desktop. A User Account Control dialog box appears.
2. Provide administrator credentials and then click **OK.** The GPMC SharedView console appears.
3. Expand **Forest:contoso.com** > **Domains** > **contoso.com** > **Group Policy Objects** and then highlight a GPO in the console tree. In the details pane, you will see Security Filtering in the bottom half of the console.
4. You can see that the Authenticated Users group is listed by default, ensuring that any user or computer account within the affected area of the Active Directory hierarchy will have this GPO applied. To change this behavior, click **Add.** The Select User, Computer, or Group dialog box appears.
5. Key **accounts application** in the Enter the object name to select list box and then click **Check Names**. Accounts application should become underlined.
6. Click **OK** to close the Select User, Computer, or Group dialog box.
7. Click **Authenticated Users** in the Security Filtering section and then click **Remove**. A Group Policy Management dialog box appears.
8. Click **OK** to remove this delegation privilege. You should now see only the Accounts Application group under Security Filtering, as shown in Figure 13-5.

Figure 13-5

Security Filtering for a GPO

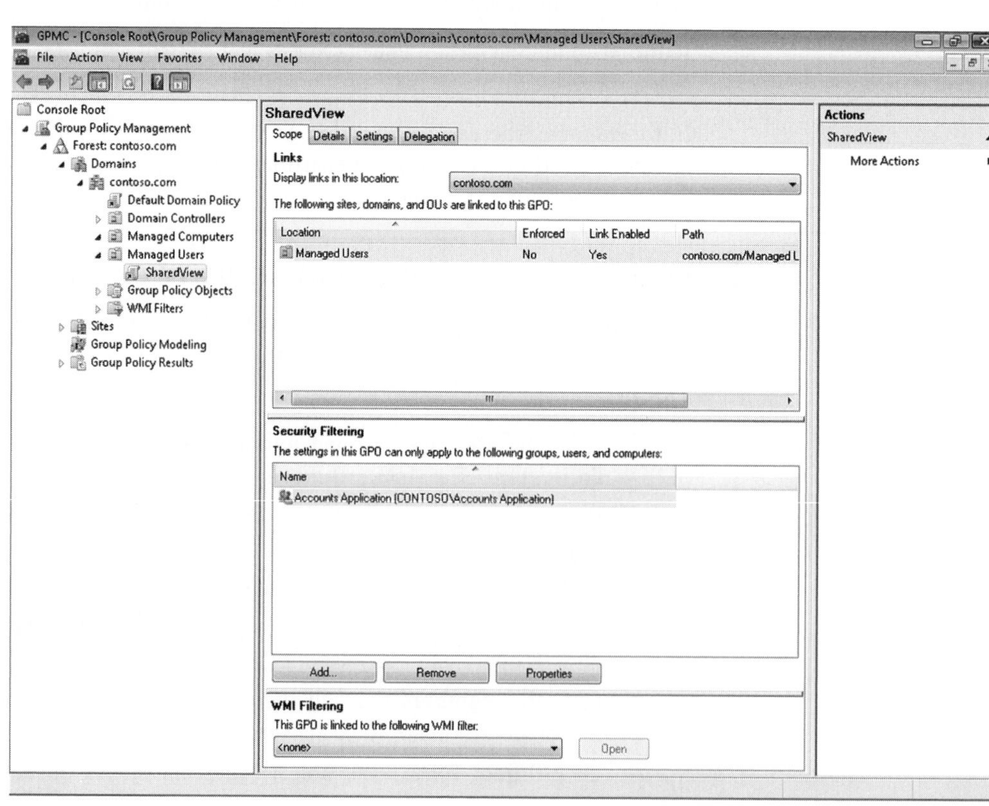

TAKE NOTE*

It's best practice to assign or publish only one application per Group Policy Object.

Using Group Policy to Upgrade or Replace an Existing Application

Group Policy can be used to upgrade a previously assigned or published application.

Group Policy can upgrade a previously assigned or published application in two ways:

- The existing application can be uninstalled and replaced with the upgrade package
- The upgrade package can be installed without removing the previously deployed version of the application

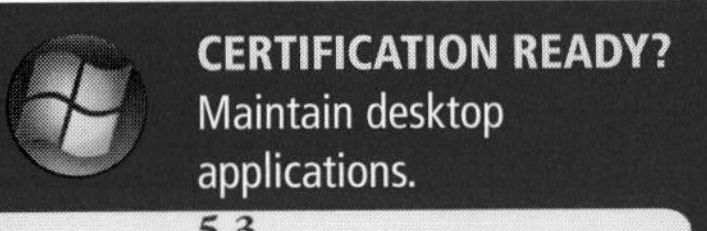
CERTIFICATION READY?
Maintain desktop applications.
5.3

Removing the existing version of an application and replacing it with a new version may be necessary in some scenarios or when you want to replace an application with one from a different vendor. You should test all upgrades in a lab environment to ensure that the process is successful.

Upgrading Applications

To upgrade an application, add a new package to an existing Group Policy Object.

You should follow the same procedure as for assigning or publishing any other package (as shown in the Packages published to users section), but you can add the upgrade package to the already existing GPO.

UPGRADE AN APPLICATION

LOG ON to your Windows Vista machine with your standard user account and then follow this procedure.

1. Double-click the **GPMC SharedView** icon on the desktop. A User Account Control dialog box appears.
2. Provide administrator credentials and then click **OK**. The GPMC SharedView console appears.
3. Expand **Forest:contoso.com** > **Domains** > **contoso.com** > **Group Policy Objects**.
4. Right-click **SharedView** and then click **Edit**. The Group Policy Object Editor appears. We will create a new publication where we'd previously deployed the software via Group Policy Object Editor.
5. Expand **User Configuration** > **Software Settings.**
6. Right-click **Software installation** and then select **New** > **Package**. The Open dialog box appears.
7. Browse to the software distribution share, select the upgrade package, and then click **Open**.
8. Select **Advanced** on the Deploy Software dialog box and then click **OK.**
9. Select the Upgrades tab, and you'll see that Group Policy already understands that this new package will upgrade the existing package configured in this policy, as shown in Figure 13-6.

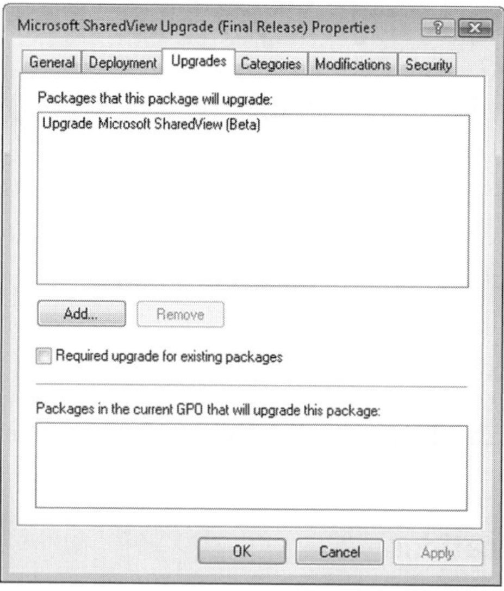

Figure 13-6

Upgrading an application by using Group Policy

TAKE NOTE*

If you want to control whether the original application will be uninstalled before the upgrade or whether this package will simply install on top of the existing install, you can highlight the package name under Packages that this package will upgrade and click Remove. Click Add and then select a package from the current GPO or browse for a package in a different GPO. Specify if the existing application should be removed prior to upgrading.

10. Click **OK** to close the dialog box.
11. Right-click the original SharedView package in the Group Policy Object Editor and then click **Properties.**
12. Click the **Upgrades** tab, and you'll see that the upgrade package is listed in the Packages in the current GPO that will upgrade this package list box, as shown in Figure 13-7.

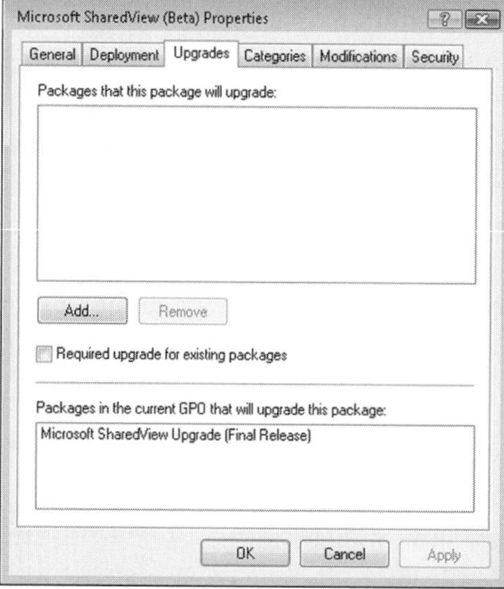

Figure 13-7

Upgrading an application by using Group Policy

TAKE NOTE*

It's best practice to perform required upgrades as opposed to optional upgrades. This is to help avoid compatibility problems in which two users might be using different versions of an application.

 REMOVING APPLICATIONS

If Uninstall this application when it falls out of the scope of management is selected on the Deployment tab, it's possible to manage the full life cycle of the application and use Group Policy to remove an application.

Scope of management (SOM) is related to the fact that any user or computer account in the Active Directory hierarchy is located in an Organizational Unit that may have Group Policy Objects linked to it. When a user or computer account is moved from one Organization Unit to another, the SOM changes, and potentially different settings are applied depending on the Resultant Set of Policy (RSoP). If Uninstall this application when it falls out of the scope of management is selected for a package deployed using Group Policy, when the user or computer account is moved to an OU where the GPO for the given package does not apply, the package is removed for that user or computer.

Microsoft recommends selecting the Uninstall this application when it falls out of the scope of management option so that Group Policy can be used to manage the full life cycle of the software and so that Microsoft Installer can roll back the deployment in the event of a problem during the installation process.

Consider, for example, a scenario in which you deploy a piece of software via Group Policy. If the target machine doesn't have enough disk space to complete the installation, to remove the corrupted software, you'll need to move the affected computer account out of the scope of management for the given Group Policy Object. When Uninstall this application when it falls out of the scope of management was selected, Microsoft Installer will then roll back the failed installation if the affected AD object is moved out of scope of management. In some cases, this might be the only way to roll back a failed installation.

The ability to uninstall an application by using Group Policy is also useful. You should ensure that all administrators understand the implications of this setting. For instance, moving computer or user accounts to different OUs without due consideration might result in software being automatically removed from users' computers.

TAKE NOTE* If you set the Uninstall this application when it falls out of the scope of management option for a package in Group Policy, you should make sure that all administrators are aware of the consequences of moving user or computer accounts around the Active Directory hierarchy. Applications may be removed because of such actions.

 REDEPLOY AN APPLICATION

You may want to redeploy an application if the application has stopped working correctly due to another change that has been made. Sometimes the easiest way to resolve such problems is to re-install the application. To redeploy an application that has been assigned or published using Group Policy, you should edit the Group Policy Object from GPMC.

LOG ON to a Windows Server 2003 machine in the contoso.com domain as an administrator and then follow these steps.

1. Open Group Policy Object Editor.
2. Expand **Computer Configuration** > **Software Settings** or **User Configuration** > **Software Settings**.
3. Click **Software installation**.
4. Right-click the installation package in the details pane and then select **All tasks** > **Redeploy application.**

TAKE NOTE* The application will be redeployed everywhere that it was previously assigned/published. This can cause considerable disruption to your network because the redeployment action cannot be scheduled. Therefore, it is recommended that the redeployment be run during off-peak hours.

Software installed using Microsoft Installer is identified in the system registry by means of product code. The product code for an application can be determined by taking the following steps once the package has been configured for distribution by Group Policy.

IDENTIFY PACKAGES BY PRODUCT CODE

Microsoft Installer Packages can be identified by a Global Unique Identifier (GUID) called the Product Code.

LOG ON to your Windows Vista machine with your standard user account.

1. Double-click the **GPMC SharedView** icon on the desktop. A User Account Control dialog box appears.
2. Provide administrator credentials and then click **OK**. GPMC SharedView console appears.
3. Locate the GPO where the package is configured for distribution under Group Policy Objects. Right-click the GPO and then select **Edit**. The Group Policy Object Editor appears.
4. Expand **User Configuration** > **Software Settings** or **Computer Configuration** > **Software Settings** and then click **Software installation**.
5. Right-click the package in the details pane and select **Properties**. The Properties dialog box appears.
6. Select the Deployment tab and then click **Advanced**. The Advanced Deployment Options dialog box appears.
7. Under the Advanced diagnostic information section, you'll see Product Code. This is the Global Unique Identifier (GUID) for the MSI package. See Figure 13-8.

Figure 13-8

MSI product code

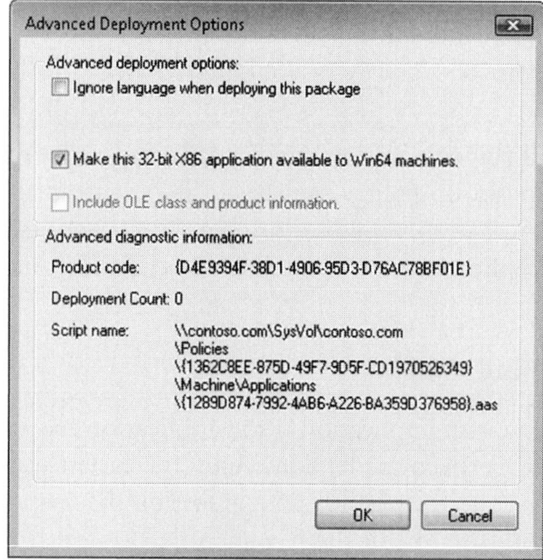

Troubleshooting Group Policy Software Deployment

There are many reasons why a package may not be successfully installed on a user's workstation.

The main source for troubleshooting information will be RSoP (Resultant Set of Policy), which is part of GPMC. RSoP enables you to scan either the local or a remote workstation for Group Policy events. It then compiles a report about which Group Policy Objects and settings have been successfully applied.

Before running RSoP, let's "create" a problem for a Windows Vista workstation that is under the scope of management of a GPO and that contains a software package assigned to computer accounts. This is easily achieved by removing Authenticated Users from the ACL on the software distribution share.

REMOVE AUTHENTICATED USERS FROM THE ACL

LOG ON to a file server in the contoso.com domain as an administrator.

1. Use Windows Explorer to browse to the folder called Software that you created earlier in this lesson.
2. Right-click the **Software** folder and then select **Properties**. The folder's Properties dialog box appears.
3. Select the **Security** tab and then click **Authenticated Users** in the Group or user names list box.
4. Click **Remove** and then click **OK.**

RUN RSoP AGAINST A WINDOWS VISTA WORKSTATION

The Resultant Set of Policy (RSoP) tool can be used to generate reports from client workstations detailing Group Policy processing events and what policy settings are applied to a user or machine.

LOG ON to your Windows Vista machine with a standard user account.

1. Double-click the **GPMC SharedView** icon on the desktop. A User Account Control dialog box appears.
2. Provide administrator credentials and then click **OK.** GPMC SharedView console appears.
3. Expand **Forest: contoso.com.**
4. Right-click **Group Policy Results** and then click **Group Policy Results Wizard.** The Welcome to the Group Policy Results Wizard page appears.
5. Click **Next.** The Computer Selection page appears.
6. For the purposes of this example, we will run RSoP locally, so select **This computer** and then click **Next.** The User Selection page appears.
7. Accept the default settings by clicking **Next.** The Summary of Selections page appears.
8. Review your selections and then click **Next.** The Completing the Group Policy Results Wizard page appears.
9. Click **Finish.** You should see the Group Policy Results report in the details pane.
10. On the Summary tab in the details pane of the GPMC SharedView console, Component Status might be highlighted with a yellow warning flag (see Figure 13-9). If the warning flag appears, click **Component Status** to view detailed information. It should state that the installation source is not available.
11. Click the **Policy Events** tab.
12. Look for Event ID 102. Double-click the event to view detailed information. If you do not see this event ID, open another event to view its detailed information. An Event Properties dialog box appears.
13. When you are finished, click **OK** to close the Event Properties dialog box.

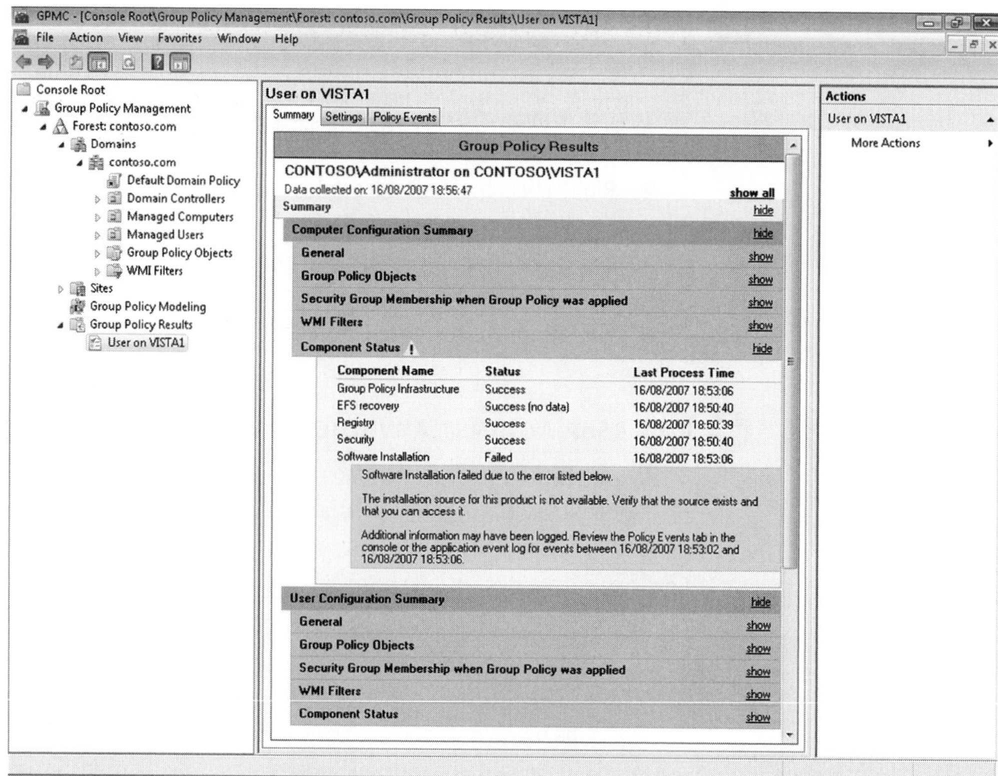

Figure 13-9

RSoP component status

■ Deploying Software using Systems Management Server 2003

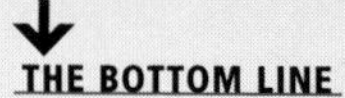

Systems Management Server 2003 offers more flexible and comprehensive deployment and management options for larger organizations.

Systems Management Server 2003 consists of two main components. SMS itself (which is supported by a back-end SQL database) and the Advanced Client. Before you can use SMS to deploy software to Windows Vista workstations, you must deploy the Advanced Client. The following procedures describe how to deploy the client (using Group Policy) and how to install the server.

SMS can be set up to provide a network of distribution points from which clients can install software. This allows for a lot of flexibility on large corporate networks. Such a setup is beyond the scope of this lesson, so we will install a single SMS server in a single site with all the possible roles hosted on one server. Below are some key terms related to Systems Management Server that you should be familiar with:

Management Point (MP): Advanced Clients communicate with Systems Management Server Management Points to retrieve Advanced Client Policy and check for advertisements

Distribution Point (DP): A Systems Management Server where software packages are stored for SMS Clients to download

Installing Systems Management Server 2003

> Systems Management Server 2003 requires SQL Server 2000/2005 to be installed either on the same or preferably on a different member server.

Systems Management Server 2003 should be installed on a member server in the contoso.com domain.

INSTALL SYSTEMS MANAGEMENT SERVER 2003

LOG ON to a member server in the contoso.com domain with Enterprise Administrator credentials.

1. Insert the SMS 2003 media and select **SMS 2003** from the Systems Management Server 2003 Setup window.
2. If you're installing SMS on Windows Server 2003, you'll be presented with a compatibility warning. For now, you can ignore this warning. Select the **Don't display this message again** option and then click **Continue.** The problem that this message refers to will be resolved when you apply Service Pack 3 (SP3) to SMS.
3. Click **Next** on the Welcome page.
4. Click **Next** again on the System Configuration page.
5. Under Setup Options, select **Install an SMS primary site** and then click **Next.**
6. On the Installation Options page, select **Custom Setup** and then click **Next.**
7. On the License Agreement page, select **I agree** to accept the license agreement and then click **Next.**
8. Key the Name, Organization, and CD Key and then click **Next.**
9. On the SMS Site Information page, enter a Site code of **001** and then click **Next.**
10. Select **Extend the Active Directory schema** and then click **Next.**
11. Select **Advanced security** and then click **Next.**
12. Under Number of SMS clients, enter **100** and then click **Next.**
13. On the Installation Options page, leave everything selected as default and click **Next.**
14. Enter the name of the computer running SQL Server and then select **Yes** for Windows Authentication Mode.
15. Click **Next.**
16. Select **Yes** to have the SMS installer automatically create the database on SQL Server. Then click **Next.**
17. Enter a database name of **SMS_001** and then click **Next.**
18. Leave the default path of c:\smsdata and then click **Next.**
19. On the Concurrent SMS Administrator Consoles page, leave everything as default and then click **Next.**
20. Click **Finish.**

UPGRADE SYSTEMS MANAGEMENT SERVER 2003 TO SERVICE PACK 3

Update SMS to the latest service pack to ensure compatibility with Windows Server 2003 and to apply the latest security patches.

LOG ON to the new Systems Management Server with Domain Administrator credentials.

1. Copy the Service Pack 3 installer package to SMS and run it by double-clicking the package.
2. Click **Next** on the Welcome page.

3. Select **I agree** and then click **Next.**
4. Select **Do not install Asset Intelligence**.
5. Click **Finish**.
6. Wait for the Service Pack to install. Then click **OK** on the confirmation screen.
7. Click **Finish**.

Assigning the SMS Client to Windows Vista Using Group Policy

The SMS Advanced Client replaces the Legacy Client.

Before using Systems Management Server to manage a Windows Vista-based workstation, it's necessary to install the SMS client software. You can do this manually by copying the necessary files from the SMS server and running them on the client machine, by using the Client Install method of SMS server, or by using Group Policy.

CREATE A NEW GROUP POLICY OBJECT

Before you can use SMS to distribute software to Windows Vista, you can install the Advanced Client, via Group Policy.

LOG ON to your Windows Vista machine with your standard user account.

1. Double-click the **GPMC SharedView** icon on the desktop. A User Account Control dialog box appears.
2. Provide administrator credentials and then click **OK**. GPMC SharedView console appears.
3. Expand **Group Policy Management** > **Forest: contoso.com** > **Domains** > **contoso.com**.
4. Right-click **Group Policy Objects** and then select **New**. The New GPO dialog box appears. Key **SMS Client 2.5** in the Name text box and then click **OK** to close the dialog box.
5. In the console tree, expand **Group Policy Objects**, right-click **SMS Client 2.5**, and then select **Edit**. The Group Policy Object Editor appears.
6. Expand **Computer Configuration** > **Software Settings**.
7. Right-click **Software installation** and then click **New** > **Package**. The Open dialog box appears.
8. Locate the client.msi file on your SMS server. The path will be something similar to *sms_server*\SMS_001\Client\i386.
9. Select **client.msi** and then click **Open**. The Deploy Software dialog box appears.
10. Select **Assigned** and then click **OK**. In the details pane, you should now see the SMS Advanced Client package.
11. Right-click the package and then select **Properties**. The Properties dialog box appears.
12. Select the Deployment tab and then select **Uninstall this application when it falls out of the scope of management**.
13. Click **OK** to close the dialog box.
14. Close the Group Policy Editor.

LINK THE GPO TO AN ORGANIZATIONAL UNIT

You must link the Group Policy Object you created in the last procedure to an OU in order to apply the new software installation settings to computers within your chosen scope of management.

LOG ON to your Windows Vista machine with your standard user account.

1. Double-click the **GPMC SharedView** icon on the desktop. A User Account Control dialog box appears.
2. Provide administrator credentials and then click **OK**. The GPMC SharedView console appears.
3. Right-click the **Managed Computers** Organizational Unit and then select **Link an Existing GPO**. The Select GPO dialog box appears.
4. In the Group Policy objects list box, select **SMS Client 2.5** and then click **OK**.
5. Make sure that the Managed Desktops Organizational Unit is highlighted in the console tree. You will see the SMS Client 2.5 GPO object listed under Managed Desktops in the details pane.

CONFIGURE THE SMS CLIENT

You must configure the Advanced Client to communicate with a specified SMS Site.

LOG ON to your Windows Vista machine with your standard user account.

1. Once the SMS Client has been successfully installed on Windows Vista, from the Start menu open the Control Panel.
2. Select **Systems Management** under System and Maintenance. The Systems Managements Properties dialog box appears.
3. Select the **Advanced** tab and then click **Discover** in the SMS Site section. If automatic site discovery is successful, a confirmation dialog box appears.

Figure 13-10

SMS Advanced Client

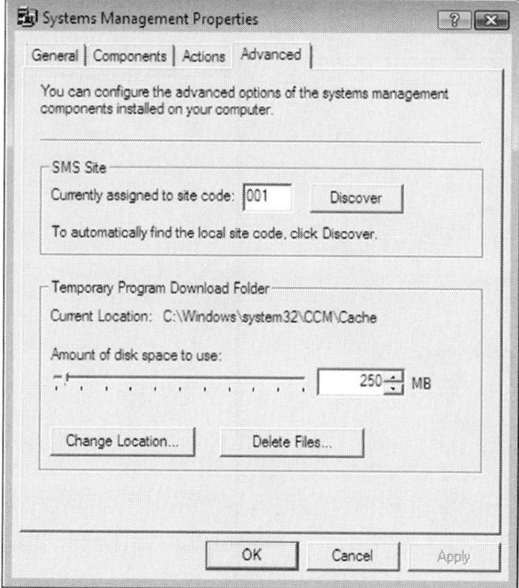

4. Click **OK**, and you should see the site number in the Currently assigned to site code text box (see Figure 13-10).
5. Click **OK** to close the Systems Managements Properties dialog box.

In addition to installing the client on the computers to be managed by SMS, it's also necessary to populate SMS collections with information about users and computer accounts in Active Directory. A collection is a folder in the SMS Administrator console that enables you to target software deployments to specific groups of computers based on the results of a query against the SMS site database.

Follow the steps in the next procedure to populate the default SMS Collections.

POPULATE THE SMS SERVER DATABASE WITH CLIENT INFORMATION

The SMS site database must contain information about workstations in the Active Directory domain.

LOG ON to SMS with SMS Administrator credentials and open the SMS Administrator console.

1. Expand **Site Database > Site Hierarchy > Site Settings** and then click **Discovery Methods.**
2. In the details pane, right-click **Active Directory System Discovery** and then select **Properties.** The Properties dialog box appears.
3. Select the **Enable Active Directory System Discovery** option.
4. Click **Add** on the right side of Active Directory Containers and then select **Local Domain or Forest for Location.**
5. Select **Recursive for Search** options to ensure that objects in child containers are also discovered.
6. Click **OK.**
7. Select a container or domain/forest and then click **OK.**
8. Click the Polling Schedule tab, click **Schedule** under Recurrence pattern section, and then change the polling interval to every five minutes.
9. Click **OK.**
10. Select the **Run discovery as soon as possible** check box and then click **OK.** Figure 13-11 shows a Windows Vista workstation discovered in the All Windows Vista Systems collection.

Figure 13-11

All Windows Vista Systems collection in SMS Server 2003

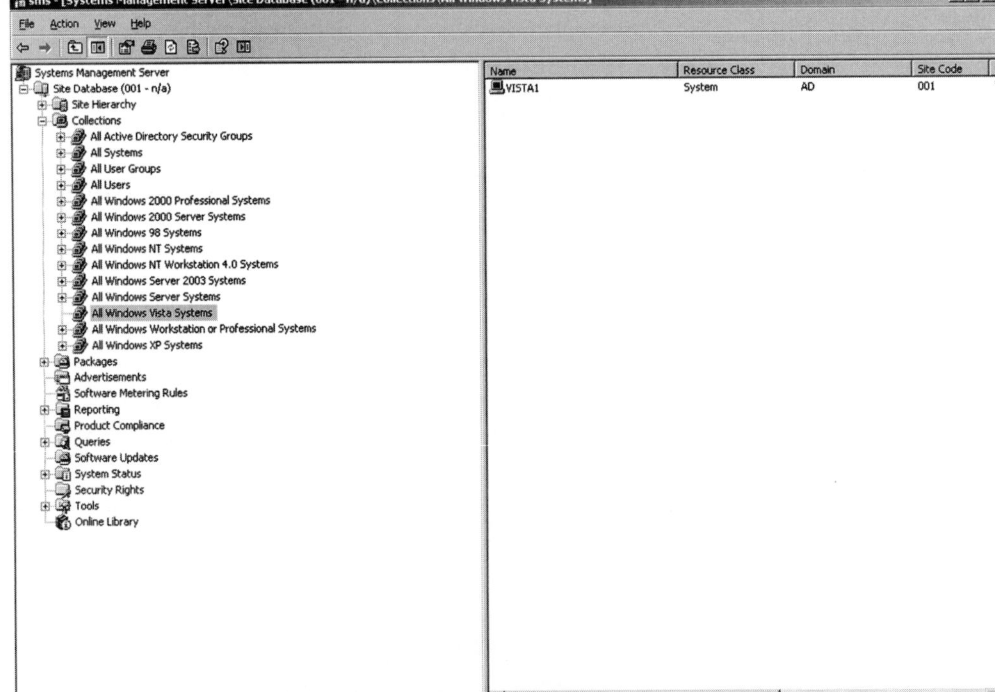

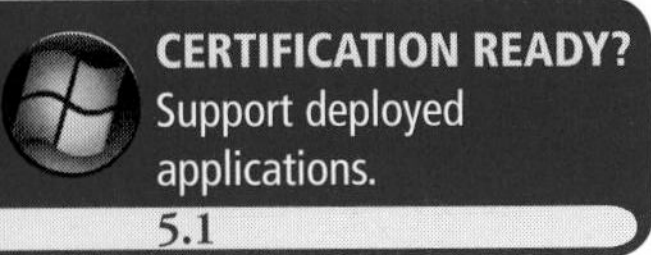

CERTIFICATION READY?
Support deployed applications.
5.1

CREATE AN SMS PACKAGE (MICROSOFT SHAREDVIEW)

You can generate SMS packages from MSI files.

LOG ON to SMS with SMS Administrator credentials.

1. Open the SMS Administrator console and then expand your site.
2. Right-click **Packages** and then select **New** > **Package From Definition.** The Welcome to the Create Package from Definition Wizard appears.
3. Browse for the Microsoft SharedView MSI package, click it, and then click **Next.**
4. On the Source Files screen, select **This package does not contain any files** and then click **Next.** Everything required to install SharedView is contained within this MSI package.
5. Click **Finish.**

ASSIGN A PACKAGE TO AN SMS DISTRIBUTION POINT (DP)

SMS sites can have multiple Distribution Points. You must select to which distribution point(s) each package will be assigned.

LOG ON to SMS with SMS Administrator credentials.

1. In the SMS Administrator console, expand **Packages** > **Microsoft Corporation Microsoft SharedView.**
2. Right-click **Distribution Points**, click **New**, and then click **Distribution Points.**
3. Click **Next** on the Welcome page.
4. Click **Next** on the Copy package page.
5. Select all the DPs (Distribution Points) where you want the package to be made available. (A Distribution Point is a Systems Management Server where software packages are stored for SMS clients to download.)
6. Click **Finish** to close the wizard.

ADVERTISE A PACKAGE TO A COLLECTION IN SYSTEMS MANAGEMENT SERVER

In the same way that Group Policy Objects are linked to Organizational Units to define scope of management, SMS packages are advertised to collections.

LOG ON to SMS with SMS Administrator credentials.

1. Right-click the collection you want to advertise a package to in the SMS Administrator console and select **All Tasks** > **Distribute Software.**
2. On the Welcome page, click **Next.**
3. Select the **Select an existing package** option and then highlight the required package under the Packages list box.
4. Click **Next.**
5. Select the install method. In this case, let's choose to install the package on every system in the collection without user interaction. Highlight **Per-system unattended** and then click **Next.**
6. Modify the Advertisement name and comment if required. Then click **Next.**
7. Choose whether to advertise the package to just this collection or to sub collections as well and then click **Next.**
8. On the Advertisement Schedule page, set the time from which the package will be advertised and if the advertisement should expire. Then click **Next.**
9. Let's choose to assign the package, because it's mandatory for our organization. Select **Yes. Assign the program.**

10. Set a date and time. Click **Next.**
11. Review the details on the Summary page and then click **Finish.**
12. Expand **System Status > Package Status**, and you'll see the SharedView package listed as shown in Figure 13-12. You can expand the package for more information.

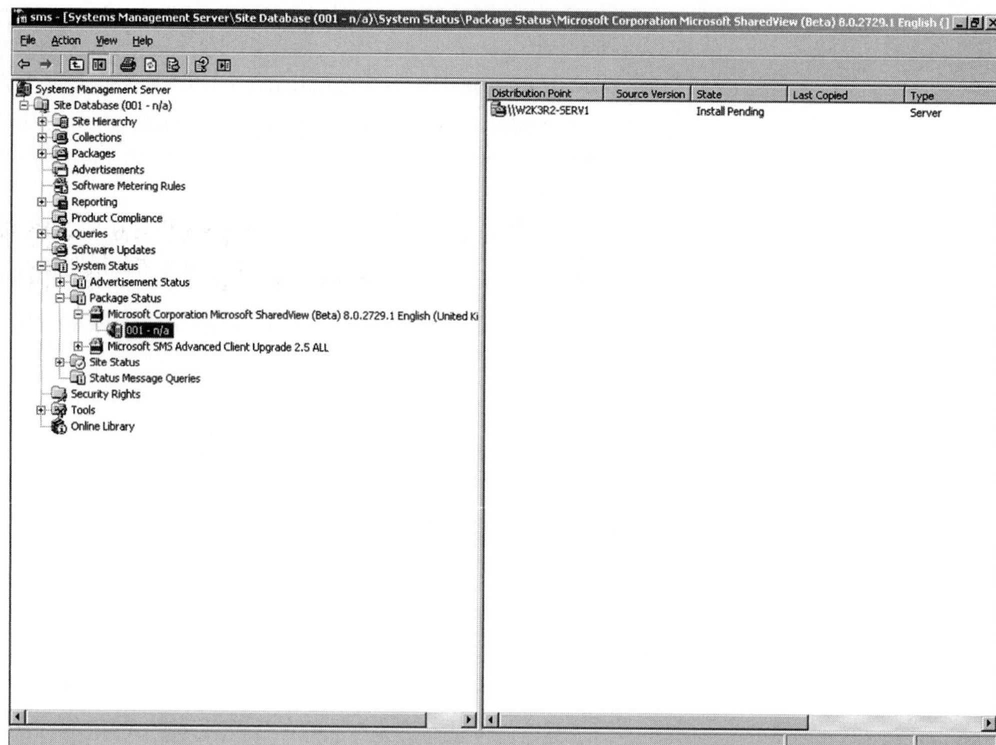

Figure 13-12

A configured package in SMS Server 2003

One of the advantages of SMS Server over Group Policy Software Installation is that you can perform an inventory on client machines to establish whether software has been successfully installed. This is just one example of how you could use SMS reporting.

REPORTING IN SMS SERVER 2003

LOG ON to SMS with SMS Administrator credentials.

1. To run a pre-defined report in SMS Server (it's possible to build your own reports too), highlight **Reports** in the SMS Administrator console under Reporting.
2. In the details pane, right-click the report that you want to run.
3. Select **All Tasks > Run > WIN2KR2**. Internet Explorer appears, showing you the results of the report.

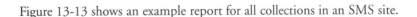

Figure 13-13 shows an example report for all collections in an SMS site.

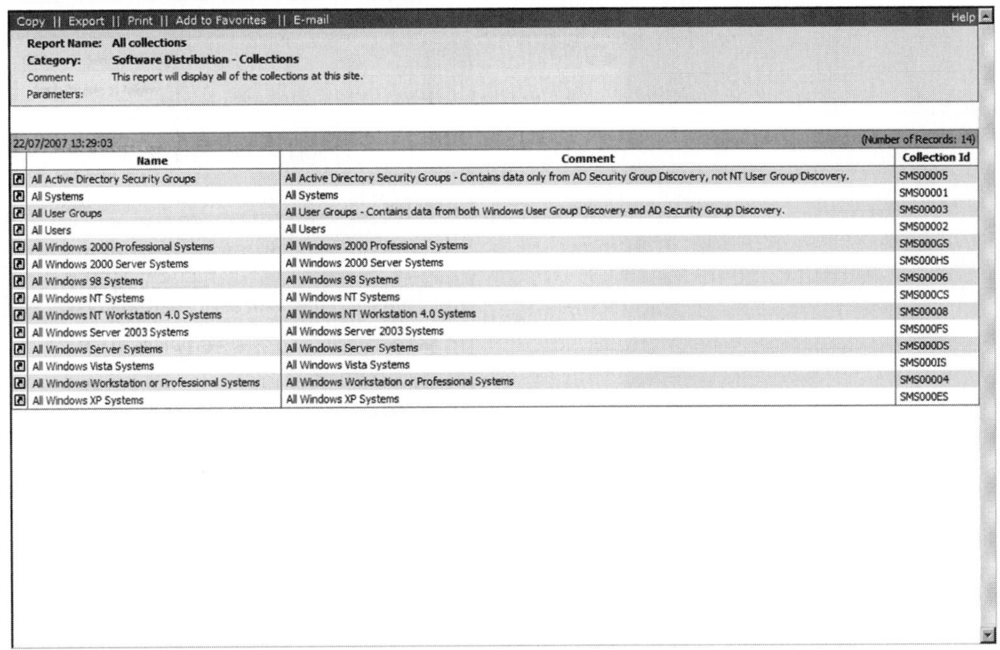

Copy || Export || Print || Add to Favorites || E-mail   Help

Report Name: **All collections**
Category: **Software Distribution - Collections**
Comment: This report will display all of the collections at this site.
Parameters:

22/07/2007 13:29:03   (Number of Records: 14)

Name	Comment	Collection Id
All Active Directory Security Groups	All Active Directory Security Groups - Contains data only from AD Security Group Discovery, not NT User Group Discovery.	SMS00005
All Systems	All Systems	SMS00001
All User Groups	All User Groups - Contains data from both Windows User Group Discovery and AD Security Group Discovery.	SMS00003
All Users	All Users	SMS00002
All Windows 2000 Professional Systems	All Windows 2000 Professional Systems	SMS000GS
All Windows 2000 Server Systems	All Windows 2000 Server Systems	SMS000HS
All Windows 98 Systems	All Windows 98 Systems	SMS00006
All Windows NT Systems	All Windows NT Systems	SMS000CS
All Windows NT Workstation 4.0 Systems	All Windows NT Workstation 4.0 Systems	SMS00008
All Windows Server 2003 Systems	All Windows Server 2003 Systems	SMS000FS
All Windows Server Systems	All Windows Server Systems	SMS000DS
All Windows Vista Systems	All Windows Vista Systems	SMS000IS
All Windows Workstation or Professional Systems	All Windows Workstation or Professional Systems	SMS00004
All Windows XP Systems	All Windows XP Systems	SMS000ES

Figure 13-13

A report in Systems Management Server 2003

DOWNLOAD You can download the SMS Toolkit for troubleshooting problems with Systems Management Server 2003 Toolkit 2 from the following link: *http://www.microsoft.com/downloads*. The kit contains many useful tools. SMS Trace can be used to read SMS log files. You can find the log files for the SMS Advanced Client on the Windows Vista workstation where the client is installed, under System32\ccm\logs.

SUMMARY SKILL MATRIX

IN THIS LESSON YOU LEARNED:
To create new assigned and published packages using Group Policy.
To create packages and advertisements using Systems Management Server.
To deploy and configure the SMS Advanced Client.
To run reports using Systems Management Server.
To upgrade packages using Group Policy.
To remove and redeploy packages using Group Policy.
That legacy applications can be deployed by Group Policy using zap files.
To identify MSI packages by product code.
To assign packages to Distribution Points in Systems Management Server.
To use software categories in Group Policy.

■ Knowledge Assessment

Fill in the Blank

Complete the following sentences by writing the correct word or words in the blanks provided.

1. A(n) _____________ file has the extension .mst and is used to customize Microsoft Installer packages.
2. A Microsoft Installer patch file has the extension _____________ and is used to make customizations to enterprise installations of Microsoft Office 2007.
3. _____________ is the free Microsoft tool used for creating or editing Microsoft Installer packages.
4. _____________ is a Windows service used by the SMS Advanced Client for downloading software packages over slow network links.
5. _____________ is the term used to refer the relationship between user/computer accounts and Organizational Units in the Active Directory hierarchy.
6. _____________ is a special file system that is part of Active Directory and that can be used for fault tolerance and making files available close to users who are working across a wide area network.
7. A(n) _____________ is a list of objects in Systems Management Server that is generated by performing an SQL query against the site database for the purposes of SMS operations.
8. The Group Policy _____________ option enables you to re-install software on all computers that the GPO applies to.
9. An application that is _____________ to a computer account via Group Policy is installed when the given computer boots.
10. An SMS Advanced Client receives policy information from an SMS Server via a(n) _____________ point.

Multiple Choice

Select the best response for the following scenarios.

1. After installing the SMS Advanced Client on a Windows Vista desktop, you discover that the components listed in the Control Panel are installed but not listed as enabled. What steps should you take to try to resolve the problem?
   a. Check the System and Application Event log on the Windows Vista desktop for errors
   b. Install SMS Trace from the SMS Toolkit and examine the logs under System32\ccm\logs on the Windows Vista desktop
   c. Check the System and Application Event logs on the SMS Server
   d. Reinstall SMS Server
2. You create a new package in SMS Server by right-clicking Packages and selecting New > Package from Definition. But the package is not being distributed to clients. You should:
   a. Configure one or more Distribution Points (DPs) for the package.
   b. Add the package source files to a DFS share.
   c. Configure one or more Distribution Points (DPs) for the package and create an Advertisement.
   d. Create a GPO to deploy the package.

3. You want a software package to be installed on every computer in an OU by means of Group Policy. You should:
   a. Assign the software under Computer Configuration.
   b. Publish the software under User Configuration.
   c. Publish the software under Computer Configuration.
   d. Assign the software under User Configuration.
4. You want to make software available to administrative users on your network through the Add/Remove Programs control panel and ensure that the software is fully installed when selected. You should:
   a. Assign the software under Computer Configuration.
   b. Publish the software under User Configuration.
   c. Publish the software under Computer Configuration.
   d. Assign the software under User Configuration.
5. You want to upgrade an existing package that has been deployed using Group Policy. You should:
   a. Delete the original GPO and create a new GPO for the upgrade.
   b. Create a new GPO and deploy the upgrade as any other package.
   c. Use a script to perform the upgrade.
   d. Create a new package in the same GPO in which the original application was deployed.
6. You configure a GPO to deploy a software package, but it is not being installed on the clients. You should:
   a. Check the Event Log on every client.
   b. Check the Event Log on a Domain Controller.
   c. Use RSoP in the Group Policy Management Console and check the Policy Events tab.
   d. Check the Event Log on a Member Server.
7. You want to use Group Policy to control which computer accounts a software package is assigned to. You should:
   a. Create an OU for those computer accounts only.
   b. Create a GPO for each computer account.
   c. Create a script to assign the software to selected computer accounts.
   d. Link the GPO at a high level in the Active Directory hierarchy and use security filtering to control which computer accounts the software is assigned to.
8. You want to ensure that if a user clicks a file extension for a particular software package the package will be installed on demand. You should:
   a. Ensure that Auto-install is configured in the Group Policy.
   b. Assign the package to the computer account.
   c. Create an upgrade package.
   d. Install the application by using a script.
9. You want an application to be available for a user to install from the Add/Remove Programs control panel. What kind of Group Policy software deployment should you use?
   a. Assign to a computer account
   b. Publish to a user account
   c. Assign to a user account
   d. Publish to a computer account
10. When you create a network share for storing software packages that will be deployed using Group Policy, you should ensure that which Active Directory group has Read and Execute NTFS permissions on the share?
    a. Everyone
    b. Authenticated Users
    c. Domain Users
    d. Domain Administrators

Review Questions

1. Describe the differences between assigning and publishing software packages to users and computers using Group Policy.
2. Describe the benefits of using a DFS share when configuring Group Policy Software Installation.

■ Case Scenarios

Scenario 1: Event 102

You publish a package in User Configuration using Group Policy, but the application is not being deployed to computers with scope of management. You run RSoP on an affected desktop and under Policy Events you see Error 102. The installation source for this product is not available. Verify that the source exists and that you can access it. What's the likely problem, and how can you resolve it?

Scenario 2: Software Not Being Deployed and No Errors

You publish a package in User Configuration using Group Policy, but the application is not being deployed. You see that the computer accounts are in the OU that the policy is linked to. What's the problem, and how can you resolve it?

Appendix A
Microsoft Certified IT Professional Exam 70-622 Objective Domain

MATRIX SKILL	SKILL NUMBER	LESSON NUMBER
Deploying Windows Vista		
Analyze the business environment and select an appropriate deployment method	1.1	1
Prepare a system for clean installation or upgrade	1.2	1
Deploy Windows Vista from a custom image	1.3	2
Perform post-installation tasks	1.4	1, 3
Troubleshoot deployment issues	1.5	1, 2, 3, 8
Managing Windows Vista Security		
Configure and troubleshoot security for Windows Internet Explorer 7+	2.1	5
Troubleshoot security configuration issues	2.2	4, 6
Troubleshoot Windows Firewall issues	2.3	7
Troubleshoot Windows Defender issues	2.4	7
Apply security patches and updates	2.5	10
Configure and troubleshoot access to resources	2.6	8, 12
Troubleshoot authentication issues	2.7	8
Configure and troubleshoot User Account Control	2.8	8
Managing and Maintaining Systems That Run Windows Vista		
Troubleshoot policy settings	3.1	4
Configure and manage the Task Scheduler	3.2	9
Configure and troubleshoot Event Forwarding	3.3	6
Apply and troubleshoot updates	3.4	10
Configuring and Troubleshooting Networking		
Configure and troubleshoot network protocols	4.1	11
Configure and troubleshoot network services at the client level	4.2	11
Configure and troubleshoot Remote Access	4.3	12
Troubleshoot connectivity issues	4.4	12
Configure and troubleshoot wireless networking	4.5	11, 12
Configure network security	4.6	11
Troubleshoot access to network resources	4.7	12
Supporting and Maintaining Desktop Applications		
Support deployed applications	5.1	13
Troubleshoot software restrictions	5.2	6
Maintain desktop applications	5.3	13

Appendix B

LAB SETUP GUIDE

Getting Started

The *Supporting and Troubleshooting Windows Vista Client* title of the Microsoft Official Academic Course (MOAC) series includes two books: a textbook and a Lab Manual. The exercises in the Lab Manual are designed for classroom use under the supervision of an instructor or a lab aide. In an academic setting, the computer classroom might be used by a variety of classes each day, so you must plan your setup procedure accordingly. For example, consider automating the classroom setup procedure and using removable fixed disks in the classroom. Use the automated setup procedure to rapidly configure the classroom environment and remove the fixed disks after teaching this class each day.

Classroom Setup

This course should be taught in a classroom containing networked computers where students can develop their skills through hands-on experience with Microsoft Windows Vista and Microsoft Windows Server 2003. The exercises in the Lab Manual require the computers to be installed and configured in a specific manner. Failure to adhere to the setup instructions in this document can produce unanticipated results when the students perform the exercises.

TAKE NOTE*

You can either use a pair of physical machines for each student, or you can install the server and client as virtual machines on a single physical machine using Microsoft Virtual PC. If you use Virtual PC, your physical machine must comply with the minimum requirements for both Windows Server 2003 and Vista Enterprise edition. Virtual PC also requires 1.6 GHz processor speed or faster and 640 MB RAM (1GB recommended) over and above the RAM required by the hosting operating system.

Depending on your network and hardware, setting up the server and client can take a great deal of time. Consider allowing enough time that you can initiate the installation, and then perform other tasks while your machine processes the most time-consuming installation steps, which are the Windows Server installation step just prior to the GUI mode phase of setup, and downloading and installing Windows Server 2003 Service Pack 2 (SP2).

WINDOWS SERVER 2003 REQUIREMENTS

The computers running Windows Server 2003 require the following hardware and software.

HARDWARE REQUIREMENTS

All hardware must be on the Microsoft Windows Server 2003 Hardware Compatibility List (HCL).

- One Pentium 133 CPU (Pentium 733 or greater recommended)
- 128 MB RAM (256 or greater recommended)
- 2 GB hard disk minimum (4 GB or greater recommended)
- One CD-ROM drive
- One mouse
- One VGA display adapter and monitor (SVGA display adapter and monitor capable of displaying 256 colors recommended)
- One Ethernet network interface adapter

SOFTWARE REQUIREMENTS

The software listed below is required for the course.

- Microsoft Windows Server 2003 (evaluation edition available as a free download from Microsoft's web site at http://technet.microsoft.com/. A CD containing a trial version of this software is also bundled within this text.

VISTA ENTERPRISE EDITION REQUIREMENTS

The computers running Microsoft Vista Enterprise Edition require the following hardware and software.

HARDWARE REQUIREMENTS

- 1 GHz 32-bit (x86) or 64-bit (x64) processor
- 512 MB of system memory (1 GB recommended)
- 80 GB hard drive
- DVD-ROM drive
- Network interface adapter
- For Windows Aero, support for DirectX 9 graphics with:
  - WDDM Driver
  - 128 MB of graphics memory (minimum)
  - Pixel Shader 2.0 in hardware
  - 32 bits per pixel

SOFTWARE REQUIREMENTS

The software listed below is required for the course.

- Windows Vista, Enterprise Edition

CLASSROOM CONFIGURATION AND NETWORK CONSIDERATIONS

The following configurations and naming conventions are used throughout the course and are required for completing the labs as outlined in the Lab Manual. You might wish to append a student number (01, 02, etc.) to the server, client, and domain names to isolate each student's server, client, and domain configuration. If you use this approach you might need to modify the way in which you configure the servers to avoid having multiple DHCP servers.

Alternatively, if you are using Virtual PC you can disconnect each physical machine from any network. Whether you use physical machines or Virtual PC, you must ensure that each student's client and server are isolated from duplicate servers and clients that might be visible in a lab network. Isolating the domains can be problematic if you allow Internet access. One approach is to disable Internet access. Be aware, however, that machines will not have Internet access, and you will have to make available any files that students would otherwise download. If you are using Virtual PC, the easiest way to make such files available is by including them in the Virtual PC machine images that you distribute or by including a subfolder in the host's Virtual Machines folder that students can access through the Shared Folder option of Virtual PC's Settings dialog box. Files that students will need to download (or that you will need to download for them) are noted in this document.

Each student's server is configured as a Windows Server 2003 domain controller. Use the following information for the server:

- Active Directory domain name: contoso.com
- Computer name: WinSrv03
- Fully qualified domain name (FQDN): WinSrv03.contoso.com

Each student's client computer is configured as a Windows Vista Enterprise client on an isolated classroom network, with the student's server configured as the domain controller in a domain separate from other students' networks and from the rest of the school network. The client computer in the domain is named Sales01.

Setup Instructions

Before you begin, do the following:

- Read this entire document.
- Make sure you have the Instructor CD provided with the course materials and the installation disks for Microsoft Windows Server 2003 and Microsoft Windows Vista Enterprise Edition.

TAKE NOTE*

Unless you are using Virtual PC, by performing the following setup instructions, your computer's hard disks will be repartitioned and reformatted. You will lose all existing data on these systems.

SERVER SETUP

Using the following setup procedure, install Windows Server 2003 on each server machine and configure it to function as a domain controller (DC) in the contoso.com domain.

INSTALLING WINDOWS SERVER 2003 USING AN ANSWER FILE

To use the unattended answer file setup for the server computer, your system must meet the following configuration requirements:

- The computer's basic input/output system (BIOS) and CD/DVD-ROM must be able to boot from a CD/DVD.
- The computer's BIOS must be configured to boot from the CD/DVD-ROM drive.
- You must have a floppy disk drive in the computer (or an external USB floppy drive.)

If your system meets these requirements, you can install Windows Server 2003 on the server machine by performing the following steps.

TAKE NOTE*

Depending on how your school's network is set up, you might need to go back and adjust settings, such as IP addresses, as appropriate for your environment after the unattended installation completes.

INSTALL WINDOWS SERVER 2003 USING AN ANSWER FILE

1. Copy the Winnt.sif file from the \Lab Setup Guide\SetupFiles\Server folder on the Instructor CD-ROM to a floppy disk.

TAKE NOTE*

If using Virtual PC, modify the IP address, subnet mask and DNS settings in the [params. MS_TCPIP.Adapter1] section of the winnt.sif file accordingly before performing your unattended installation. See step 10 of the following "Run the GUI Mode Phase of Windows Server 2003 Setup" section for details.

2. Insert the Windows Server 2003 Installation disk into the computer's DVD-ROM drive and restart the computer.
3. If prompted, press any key to boot from the CD/DVD-ROM drive.
4. As soon as the system begins to boot from the CD/DVD-ROM drive, insert the floppy disk with the Winnt.sif file into the floppy drive.
   If you don't insert the floppy disk fast enough, the system will begin to prompt you with questions. If this happens, restart the computer and try again.

TAKE NOTE*

If your system is configured to start from floppy, you might have to remove the floppy disk upon restart. Ensure that the computer's network cable is attached; otherwise, the automated installation of Active Directory directory service might fail.

The installation of Windows Server 2003 should be mostly automated. During the GUI mode phase of the installation, you will see the following message: Unattended Setup Is Unable To Continue Because A Setup Parameter Specified By Your System Administrator Or Computer Manufacturer Is Missing Or Invalid. Setup Must Therefore Ask You To Provide This Information Now. Once You Have Furnished The Required Information, Unattended Setup Will Continue.

5. Click **OK**.
6. Enter the Product Key for your copy of Windows Server 2003, and then click **Next** to continue. Automated setup should finish configuring your computer at this point.

After the installation is complete, you might have to adjust your computer's regional settings, such as the time zone. If you use the answer file setup method, you can skip to the "Complete Post-Installation Tasks on the Server" section of this document.

TAKE NOTE

You only need to perform a manual installation if you were unable to perform the answer file installation described in the previous section.

INSTALLING WINDOWS SERVER 2003 USING THE MANUAL METHOD

If your computer has an existing 32-bit operating system installed, start the computer as usual and insert the Windows Server 2003 Installation disk. The Microsoft Windows 2003 window opens automatically. In the left pane of the window, select Install Windows Server 2003. If the Microsoft Windows 2003 window does not open automatically, run Winnt32.exe, located in the \I386 folder on the disk. This will launch the Windows Server 2003 Setup program.

If your computer has an existing 16-bit operating system installed, start the computer as usual, and insert the Windows Server 2003 Installation disk. Run Winnt.exe, located in the \I386 folder on the disk. This will launch the Windows Server 2003 Setup program.

If your computer does not have an operating system installed, you might be able to boot your computer from the Windows Server 2003 Installation disk. When you boot from the disk, the Windows Server 2003 Setup program starts automatically.

If your computer will not boot from the disk, start your computer with any MS-DOS or Microsoft Windows startup floppy disk that has DVD-ROM support. Once you have started the computer and can navigate among the files on the Windows Server 2003 Installation disk, run \Winnt.exe, located in the \I386 folder on the disk. This will launch the Windows Server 2003 Setup program.

After Windows Server 2003 Setup is launched, follow the steps below to continue the installation.

INSTALLING WINDOWS SERVER 2003 USING THE MANUAL METHOD

TAKE NOTE

Depending on how your school's network is set up, throughout the following instructions you might need to use different values for settings, such as IP addresses, to match your actual networking environment.

1. If you are installing the evaluation version of Windows Server 2003, a setup notification window is displayed, informing you that you are about to install an evaluation version of Windows Server 2003. If this screen is displayed, press **Enter** to continue. The Welcome To Setup window is displayed.
2. Press **Enter** to continue the installation. The Windows Server 2003 Licensing Agreement window is displayed.
3. Select I Agree by pressing **F8**.
4. If another copy of Windows Server 2003 is detected, a Windows Server 2003 Setup window informs you that you can repair the installation. If another copy of Windows Server 2003 is detected, press **Esc** to continue. The Windows Server 2003 Setup window is displayed, prompting you to select an area of free space or an existing partition on which to install Windows Server 2003, create a partition, or delete a partition.
5. If any partitions exist, delete them by pressing the **D** key and following the on-screen instructions. When the disks contain only unpartitioned space, go to the next step.
6. Make sure that the unpartitioned space on Disk 0 is selected, and then press **Enter** to continue the installation.

7. Select **Format This Partition Using The NTFS File System**, and then press **Enter** to continue. If you are prompted to insert the disk, do so, and then press **Enter** to continue. The system will perform various installation tasks and then restart when complete. A Windows Setup message box is displayed and the installation continues.

TAKE NOTE*

If your computer supports booting from CD/DVD, then after Windows Server 2003 Setup restarts, the computer might try to boot from the Windows Server 2003 disk. If this happens, you should be prompted to press a key to boot from the disk. However, if Setup restarts automatically, simply remove the disk, and then restart the computer.

RUN THE GUI MODE PHASE OF WINDOWS SERVER 2003 SETUP

1. In the Regional And Language Options window, make sure that the settings are correct for your language and location, and then click **Next**. The Personalize Your Software window is displayed, prompting you for your name and organization name.
2. In the Name text box, key **Server01**; in the Organization text box, key the name of your school, and then click **Next**. The Your Product Key window is displayed.
3. Enter your Product Key, and then click **Next**. The Licensing Modes window is displayed, prompting you to select a licensing mode. By default, the Per Server option is selected.
4. Select the **Per Device Or Per User** option, and then click **Next**. The Computer Name And Administrator Password window is displayed.
5. In the Computer Name text box, key **WINSRV03**. Windows Server 2003 displays the computer name in all capital letters regardless of how it is entered.
6. In the Administrator Password and Confirm Password text boxes, key **p@ssw0rd** (where the "0" is a zero) and then click **Next**. The Date And Time Settings dialog box is displayed.
7. Select the appropriate date, time, and time zone, and then click **Next**. After a short time the Network Settings dialog box is displayed.
8. Select the **Custom Settings** option, and then click **Next**.
9. Highlight the **Internet Protocol (TCP/IP)** option by clicking it, and then click the **Properties** button. The Internet Protocol (TCP/IP) Properties dialog box is displayed.
10. In the General tab, select the **Use The Following IP Address** option and set the following parameters:
    - IP address: **10.1.1.200** (if using Virtual PC, use IP address of **192.168.1.200**)
    - Subnet mask: **255.255.0.0** (use **255.255.255.0** if using Virtual PC)
    - Default gateway: Leave this field blank. (If using Virtual PC enter **192.168.1.1.**)
    - Preferred DNS server: **10.1.1.200** (If using Virtual PC, use IP address of **192.168.1.200.**)
    - Alternate DNS server: Leave this field blank.
11. Click **OK** to close the Internet Protocol (TCP/IP) Properties dialog box.
12. Click **Next** to continue with setup. The Workgroup Or Computer Domain window is displayed, prompting you to join either a workgroup or a domain.
13. Verify that the **No, This Computer Is Not On A Network, Or Is On A Network Without A Domain** option is selected and that the workgroup name is Workgroup. Click **Next**.

TAKE NOTE*

At this point, if the network interface adapter is not detected, you will have to install it manually. You might have to return to these steps later when you are configuring.

TAKE NOTE*

Depending on your classroom setup, you may want to specify different IP address settings.

Windows Setup begins copying installation files. The installation should proceed uninterrupted. (If you are using an evaluation version of the software, you might be prompted to confirm the date and time settings.) Eventually the computer will restart.

COMPLETE POST-INSTALLATION TASKS ON THE SERVER

TAKE NOTE*

At some point the operating system will prompt you to activate the server. When that happens, follow the steps to activate the server.

1. After the installation is complete and the computer has restarted, you should see the Welcome To Windows dialog box. Press **Ctrl+Alt+Delete** and enter the username and password you specified earlier to log on (Administrator/p@ssw0rd). The Manage Your Server dialog box is displayed.
2. Select the **Don't Display This Page At Logon** checkbox, and then close the Manage Your Server dialog box.
3. If you are using Virtual PC, install Virtual Machine Additions. To do so, select **Install Or Update Virtual Machine Additions** from the Actions menu, and then follow the prompts. After the installation, you will be prompted to restart Windows Server 2003. After restarting, repeat step 1 of this section to log on.

INSTALLING ACTIVE DIRECTORY ON THE SERVER

You can use an automated installation file to install Active Directory. This file is named Dc.txt and is located on the Instructor CD-ROM under the \Lab Setup Guide\SetupFiles\Server folder. You can use this file to install Active Directory by typing dcpromo /answer: D:\Lab Setup Guide\SetupFiles\Server\dc.txt and then pressing Enter in the Run dialog box. If you would rather install Active Directory manually on the server machine, complete the following steps.

TAKE NOTE* The previous command assumes that drive D represents your CD-ROM drive. If your CD-ROM drive is referenced by a different drive letter, substitute that letter for D.

INSTALL ACTIVE DIRECTORY ON THE SERVER

1. Click **Start**, select **Run**, key **dcpromo**, and then press **Enter**. The Welcome To The Active Directory Installation Wizard is displayed.
2. Click **Next** to proceed with the Active Directory installation.
3. On the Operating System Compatibility page, click **Next.**
4. On the Domain Controller Type page, select **Domain Controller For A New Domain**, then click **Next.**
5. On the Create New Domain page, verify that **Domain In A New Forest** is selected, and then click **Next.**
6. On the New Domain Name page in the Full DNS Name For New Domain box, key **contoso.com** and then click **Next.** After a few moments, the NetBIOS Domain Name page is displayed.
7. Verify that **CONTOSO** is the default NetBIOS name, and then click **Next.**
8. On the Database And Log Folders page, click **Next.** This will leave the log files and database in their default locations.
9. On the Shared System Volume page, verify that the \Sysvol folder is on a volume formatted with the NTFS file system (this should already be done), and then click **Next.**
10. On the DNS Registration Diagnostics page, view the details of the diagnostic test. (Ignore a message, if it appears in the results, indicating that none of the DNS servers used by the server responded.) Verify that the **Install And Configure The DNS Server On This Computer And Set This Computer To Use This DNS Server As Its Preferred DNS Server** option is selected, and then click **Next.**
11. On the Permissions page, click **Next** to accept the default permissions setting.
12. On the Directory Services Restore Mode Administrator Password page, key **p@ssw0rd** as the restore mode password. Confirm the password by keying it again, and then click **Next.**
13. Review the information in the Summary dialog box, and then click **Next.**

14. When the Completing The Active Directory Installation Wizard page is displayed, click **Finish**, and then click **Restart Now.** The computer restarts.
15. Log in using the appropriate domain administrator name and password.
16. If the This Server Is Now A Domain Controller page is displayed, click **Finish.** Active Directory is now installed on the server.

INSTALL AND CONFIGURE THE DHCP SERVER

1. On WinSrv03, click **Start**, select **Control Panel**, and then click **Add Or Remove Programs.** The Add Or Remove Programs window is displayed.
2. In the left frame, click **Add/Remove Windows Components.** The Windows Components Wizard is displayed.
3. In the Components box, scroll down and highlight **Networking Services** by clicking it (without modifying the state of the checkbox), and then click **Details.** The Networking Services dialog box is displayed.
4. In the Subcomponents Of Networking Services box, select the **Dynamic Host Configuration Protocol (DHCP)** checkbox.
5. Click **OK.** The Windows Components page reappears.
6. Click **Next.** The Configuring Components page shows a progress indicator as the changes you requested are made. The Completing The Windows Components Wizard page is displayed.
7. Click **Finish.**
8. Close the Add Or Remove Programs window.
9. Click the **Start** menu, select **Administrative Tools**, and then select **DHCP.** The DHCP console is displayed and winsrv03.contoso.com is listed in the scope pane.
10. In the scope pane, expand the winsrv03.contoso.com node. A red down-arrow is displayed to the left of the server name.
11. Select **winsrv03.contoso.com**, and then select **Authorize** from the Action menu.
12. Select **WinSrv03.contoso.com**, and then select **New Scope** from the Action menu. The New Scope Wizard is displayed.
13. Click **Next.** The Scope Name page is displayed.
14. In the Name text box, key **Classroom Network** and then click **Next.** The IP Address Range page is displayed.
15. Key **10.1.1.201** in the Start IP Address text box, and then key **10.1.1.250** in the End IP Address text box. (If you are using Virtual PC, key **192.168.1.201** in the Start IP Address text box, and then key **192.168.1.254** in the End IP Address text box.)
16. In the Subnet Mask text box, key **255.255.0.0** (key **255.255.255.0** if using Virtual PC), and then click **Next.**
17. Click **Next** to skip the Add Exclusions page. The Lease Duration page is displayed.
18. Click **Next** to accept the default lease duration. The Configure DHCP Options page is displayed.
19. Click **Next** to accept the default **Yes, I Want To Configure These Options Now** option. The Router (Default Gateway) page is displayed.
20. In the IP Address text box, key **10.1.1.200** (key **192.168.1.1** if using Virtual PC), click **Add**, and then click **Next.** The Domain Name And DNS Servers page is displayed.
21. In the IP Address text box, key **10.1.1.200** (key **192.168.1.1** if using Virtual PC) and click **Add.** Click **Next.**
22. Click **Next** to bypass the WINS Servers page. The Activate Scope page is displayed.
23. Click **Next** to accept the default **Yes, I Want To Active This Scope Now** option.
24. Click **Finish** to complete the New Scope Wizard.
25. Close the DHCP console.

UPDATING WINDOWS SERVER 2003

If you installed Windows Server 2003 Service Pack 1 or earlier, you should update your server to Service Pack 2 level. To do this, click Start, click All Programs, and then select Windows Update. (Internet connectivity is needed.) If you are prompted with a blocked content message, click Add to add the Windows Update site to your Trusted Sites Zone. Use the Custom button on the Windows Update site and follow the on-screen prompts to install Windows Server 2003 Service Pack 2 (SP2).

After the Windows Server 2003 Service Pack 2 installation is complete, you will need to restart the server. Log back on with your administrator credentials and re-run Windows Update. Click the Custom button to install the following three updates. You might be presented with additional updates to install. However, installing updates other than those listed might produce unanticipated results when the students perform the exercises.

- Update For Windows Server 2003 Service Pack 2 (KB931836)
- Windows Internet Explorer 7.0 For Windows Server 2003
- Windows Malicious Software Removal Tool – March 2007 (KB890830)

DOWNLOADING OR CREATING FILES

If students will not have access to the Internet, you will need to download the following files for Labs 1 through 3. Note that these files are large.

- **USMT 3.0 install program**: Search www.microsoft.com/downloads for "Windows User State Migration Tool (USMT) Version 3.0.1".
- **WAIK**: Search www.microsoft.com/downloads for "Windows Automated Installation Kit (AIK)".

TAKE NOTE*

If you are using Virtual PC, you should perform the following task on the host machine so that students can easily burn the WAIK to a DVD or access it as a virtual DVD from the virtual machine on which the WAIK is to be installed.

1. Click Download on the Windows Automated Installation Kit (AIK) page.
2. In the File Download dialog box, click Save.
3. In the Save As dialog box, choose a location for the vista_6000.16386.061101-2205-LRMAIK_EN.img file and then click Save.
4. When the download is complete, close the Download File dialog box.
5. Close Internet Explorer.
6. Using Windows Explorer, navigate to the folder in which you saved the WAIK download file.
7. Right-click the vista_6000.16386.061101-2205-LRMAIK_EN.img file and then select Rename from the context menu.
8. Change the file extension from .img to .iso.
9. Close Windows Explorer.

- **Vista Upgrade Advisor**: Search www.microsoft.com/windows/products for "Download Windows Vista Upgrade Advisor".
- If you are using Virtual PC, you might also wish to provide students with a Windows XP image against which students can run the Vista Upgrade Advisor.
- You should also supply a wim image of a Vista client for use in Lab 2, which you can create after installing the Vista client. (Instructions for creating a wim image file are given in Lab 2.)

CREATE USER AND COMPUTER ACCOUNTS

1. Click **Start**, select **Administrative Tools**, and then click **Active Directory Users and Computers.** The Active Directory Users And Computers console is displayed.
2. Right-click the **Users** container, point to **New**, and select **User**. The New Object-User wizard is displayed.

3. Key **Chris** in the First Name text box. Key **Ashton** in the Last Name text box and key **chrisa** in the User Logon Name text box. Click **Next.**
4. In the Password and Confirm Password text boxes, key **p@ssw0rd.**
5. Clear the **User Must Change Password At Next Logon** checkbox and select the **Password Never Expires** checkbox. Click **Next.**
6. Click **Finish** to create the user account. The user chrisa should be given normal user privileges.
7. Repeat steps 2 through 6 to create a user account named *Network Administrator*, whose User Logon Name is *netadmin*. Again use the password *p@ssw0rd*. Assign this account full administrator privileges. (Double-click the user, select the **Member Of** tab, and click **Add.** Enter **Administrators**, click **Check Names**, and then click **OK** twice to close the dialog boxes.)
8. In the Active Directory Users And Computers console right-click the **Computers** container, point to **New**, and select **Computer.** The New Object-Computer wizard is displayed.
9. Key **Sales01** in the Computer Name text box and click **Next.** The Managed page is displayed.
10. Click **Next.**
11. Click **Finish** to create the computer account.
12. Close the Active Directory Users And Computers console.

CONSIDERING SERVER CONFIGURATION AND PERFORMANCE

At this point, the server is prepared for Labs 1 through 7. To improve performance, consider waiting to perform the remaining changes for your server until they are needed. Note that the configuration changes required for Labs 8 through 11 are not required for working through Labs 12 and 13. If you are using Virtual PC, you can configure the three images detailed in Table B-1. You will also want to provide a corresponding client image for use with the later server images. In the client image, you should have completed all exercises in Lab 1 and Labs 3 through 7 (you can skip Lab 2).

Table B-1

Server Configuration

Suggested Virtual PC Image Name	Used for These Labs	Server Configuration
Srv01-07.vmc	Labs 1 through 7	Server configurations through this point
Srv08-11.vmc	Labs 8 through 11	Srv01-07 plus: Install Internet Information Server (IIS) (for Lab 8) Install Windows Server 2003 Enterprise Certification Authority (for Lab 8) Install .NET Framework 2.0 (for Lab 10) Install Report Viewer 2005 (for Lab 10) Extend Active Directory Schema for Wired/Wireless Networking (for Lab 11)
Srv12-13.vmc	Labs 12 and 13	Srv01-07 plus (you do not need the changes configured for the Srv08-11 image): Configure as a Virtual Private Network (VPN) server

If you are using Virtual PC, you should consider creatir
disk. If you use a differencing disk, you can share the sa
the server images detailed in Table B-1.

To set up a differencing disk, in the settings for your virtu
1. Next create a new Hard Disk 1, telling Virtual PC to cre
compressed folder with the old Hard Disk 1 file as the pare
1 file as read-only. (You can also compress the folder contain
Enable the Undo Disks setting, which will give your students ...g
any changes they make during a session without having to sav ... the previous
image.

If you use differencing disks, it will be easiest for your students to coordinate the disks and virtual machines for clients and servers if you supply multiple images that point to the appropriate differencing disks, rather than have the students update their virtual machines images to point to the required differencing disk.

CONFIGURING THE SERVER FOR LAB 8

For Lab 8, you will need to install Internet Information Server (IIS) and Windows Server 2003 Enterprise Certification Authority.

INSTALL IIS

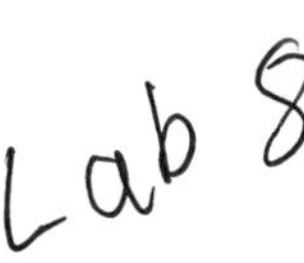

1. Click **Start**, select **Control Panel**, and then click **Add Or Remove Programs.**
2. Click **Add/Remove Windows Components**. The Windows Components Wizard is displayed.
3. In the Components list, select **Application Server**, and then click **Details**. The Application Server dialog box is displayed.
4. Select **Internet Information Services (IIS)**, and then click **Details.** The Internet Information Services (IIS) dialog box is displayed.
5. Select the following checkboxes, and then click **OK**.

   Common Files

   File Transfer Protocol (FTP) Service

   Internet Information Services Manager

   World Wide Web Service
6. Click **OK** to close the Application Server dialog box, and then click **Next.** After the installation is completed, the Completing The Windows Components Wizard appears.
7. Click **Finish**.

INSTALL WINDOWS SERVER 2003 ENTERPRISE CERTIFICATION AUTHORITY

For detailed information about installing a Certificate Authority, visit http://technet.microsoft.com and search for "Install a Windows Server 2003 Enterprise CA". Note that in most enterprises you would have a root authority and then subordinate authorities, but for the purposes of this book we will have just a root Certificate Authority that remains online. (Best practice would be to offline the root CA.) Name the root CA: "CONT-CA01".

1. Click **Start**, point to **Control Panel**, and then click **Add or Remove Programs.**
2. In the Add or Remove Programs window, click **Add/Remove Windows Components.**
3. Under Components in the Windows Components Wizard, select **Certificate Services.**
4. Read the warning about domain membership, and then click **Yes**.
5. Click **Next**. The CA Type page is displayed.

6. Click **Enterprise root CA**, and then click **Next**. The CA Identifying Information page is displayed.
7. In the Common Name For This CA box, key **CONT-CA01**, and then click **Next**. The Certificate Database Settings page is displayed.
8. Accept the defaults in the Certificate database box and the Certificate database log box, and then click **Next**.
9. When prompted to stop Internet Information Services, click **Yes**.
10. When asked if you want to enable Active Server Pages (ASP), click **Yes**.
11. After the wizard completes the installation, click **Finish**. After the CA has been installed, you might have to open the Certification Authority Snap-in on the server, right-click the **Revoked Certificates** node, choose **All Tasks**, select **Publish**, then select **New CRL**.

CONFIGURING THE SERVER FOR LAB 10

For Lab 10, you will need to install .NET Framework 2.0 and Report Viewer 2005.

INSTALLING .NET FRAMEWORK 2.0

On www.microsoft.com/downloads, search for "Microsoft .NET Framework Version 2.0 Redistributable Package (x86)". Download dotnetfx.exe and run it, following the onscreen prompts to install .NET Framework 2.0.

INSTALLING REPORT VIEWER 2005

On www.microsoft.com/downloads, search for "Microsoft Report Viewer Redistributable 2005". Download ReportViewer.exe and run it, following the onscreen prompts to install Report Viewer 2005.

If student machines will not have access to the Internet, download WSUSSetupx86.exe (about 80 MB) and make this file available to students. You can download this file by searching on http://technet.microsoft.com for "Microsoft Windows Server Update Services".

CONFIGURING THE SERVER FOR LAB 11

For Lab 11, you will need to extend the Active Directory Schema for wired/wireless networking.

EXTENDING THE ACTIVE DIRECTORY SCHEMA FOR WIRED/WIRELESS NETWORKING

Search www.microsoft.com for "Active Directory Schema Extensions for Windows Vista Wireless and Wired Group Policy Enhancements". Scroll to find the files listed as 802.11Schema.ldf and 802.3Schema.ldf. Copy and paste the file listings into Notepad and save them as files with the names *802.11Schema.ldf* and *802.3Schema.ldf* in a folder on the server, and then run the following commands at a command prompt on the server:

```
ldifde -i -v -k -f 802.11Schema.ldf -c DC=X DC=contoso,DC=com

ldifde -i -v -k -f 802.3Schema.ldf -c DC=X DC=contoso,DC=com
```

CONFIGURING THE SERVER FOR LABS 12 AND 13

For Lab 12, you will need to configure your server as a Virtual Private Network (VPN) server. For Lab 13, you will need to download a sample MSI package.

CONFIGURING THE SERVER AS A VIRTUAL PRIVATE NETWORK (VPN) SERVER

To use the Routing and Remote Access console to configure a VPN server, the server should have two networking interfaces installed. If your lab environment uses Virtual PC to host the server, you can configure two networking interfaces using a single physical network card.

If you are using a physical machine for the server, your server will need either two physical network cards or a custom configuration to configure it as a VPN server.

For detailed information about this procedure, search http://articles.techrepublic.com for "Configure a Windows Server 2003 VPN on the server side".

CONFIGURE THE SERVER AS A VIRTUAL PRIVATE NETWORK (VPN) SERVER

1. If you are using Virtual PC, add a second network adapter. (In VPC you can point both virtual adapters to the same physical adapter.)
2. Logged on to WinSrv03, click **Start**, point to **Administrative Tools**, and then click **Routing and Remote Access.**
3. In the Routing and Remote Access console tree, select **WINSRV03 (local)**. From the Action menu, select **Configure And Enable Routing And Remote Access.**
4. Click **Next** in the first screen of the wizard.
5. On the Configuration page, select the **VPN Access And NAT** option and click **Next.**
6. On the VPN Connection page, select the first network interface (which should be IP Address **192.168.1.200** if you are using Virtual PC), note the second IP address for future reference, clear the **Enable Security By Setting Up Basic Firewall** checkbox, and click **Next.**
7. Click **Next** twice, and click **Finish**.

INSTALL INTERNET AUTHENTICATION SERVICE

You will also need to install Internet Authentication Service.

1. Click **Start**, select **Control Panel**, and then select **Add Or Remove Programs.**
2. In the Add Or Remove Programs page of Control Panel, select **Windows Components**, highlight **Networking Services** by clicking it, click **Details**, and then select **Internet Authentication Service.**
3. Click **OK**.
4. Click **Next** in the Windows Components window and follow the on-screen prompts to complete the installation.

DOWNLOADING A SAMPLE MSI PACKAGE

If students will not have access to the Internet, you will need to download a sample MSI package. You can use the installation package for a beta version of SharedView.msi, which at the time of publication can be found by searching www.connect.microsoft.com for "Microsoft SharedView Beta download".

If the beta version is no longer available, you will need to provide a similar, alternate msi package. The beta version for Microsoft SharedView is about 3 MB in size.

SETTING UP VISTA ENTERPRISE EDITION CLIENT

Using the following setup procedure, install Windows Vista Enterprise Edition on each client machine.

SET UP VISTA ENTERPRISE EDITION CLIENT

1. If your BIOS allows you to boot from CD-ROM, set it to do so and boot the Windows Vista Enterprise Edition installation CD. If your computer will not boot from CD-ROM, start your computer with a floppy system disk that has CD-ROM support. At the command prompt, key **D:\setup.exe** (where D: is the drive letter of your CD-ROM) and then press **Enter.** Remove the floppy disk from the drive.
2. On the Windows Vista Install Windows screen, select appropriate language, locale, and keyboard settings. Click **Next.**

3. On the next screen, click **Install Now**. The Please Read The License Terms page is displayed.
4. Click the **I Accept The License Terms** checkbox and then click **Next**.
5. Click the **Custom (advanced)** option on the Which Type Of Installation Do You Want page.
6. Click **Next** in the Where Do You Want To Install Windows page. The Setup program completes the setup process. When installation is complete and the Set Up Windows screen is displayed, proceed to the next step.
7. Key **locadmin** in the Type A User Name text box and key **p@sswOrd** in the Type A Password and Retype Your Password text boxes. Click **Next**.
8. Key **Sales01** in the Type A Computer Name text box. Click **Next**.
9. In the Help Protect Windows Automatically screen, click the **Ask Me Later** option.
10. Adjust the date and time as necessary on the Review Your Time And Date Settings window and click **Next**.
11. On the Select Your Computer's Current Location window, click the **Work** option.
12. On the Thank You window, click the **Start** button.
13. When presented with a logon window for locadmin, key **p@sswOrd** in the text box and press **Enter**.

COMPLETING POST-INSTALLATION TASKS ON THE CLIENT

If you are using Virtual PC, install Virtual Machine Additions.

INSTALL VIRTUAL MACHINE ADDITIONS

1. Select **Install Or Update Virtual Machine Additions** from the Actions menu, then follow the prompts to run setup.exe.
2. After the installation, restart Vista when prompted. Make sure you remove the Vista installation disk before restarting.
3. After restarting, log back on as locadmin.

TAKE NOTE* At this point you might consider changing the screen resolution for the Vista client as appropriate for your students.

CREATE A LOCAL ADMINISTRATOR ACCOUNT

1. Click **Start**, then **Control Panel**.
2. Click **User Accounts**. Click **Add Or Remove User Accounts**.
3. In the User Account Control box, click **Continue**.
4. Click **Create A New Account**. In the New Account Name text box, key **locadmin**. Turn on the **Administrator** option and click **Create Account**.
5. On the Choose The Account You Would Like To Change window, click **locadmin**.
6. On the Make Changes To Locadmin's Account page, click **Create A Password**. Key **p@sswOrd** in both password textboxes and click **Create Password**.
7. Close Control Panel.

UPDATE WINDOWS VISTA

1. Click **Start**, click **All Programs**, and then click **Windows Update**.
2. Click **Turn On Now**.
3. In the User Account Control dialog box, click **Continue**.

4. If prompted to install new windows updating software, do so.
5. When prompted to download and install updates for your computer, click the **View Available Updates** link.

> **TAKE NOTE***
> If you choose to install Windows Vista with Service Pack 1 on your client machines, you should test all the lab procedures in this course before letting your students perform them because the labs for this course were tested on Windows Vista RTM with only these updates installed.

Using Windows Update, install the following components on each client machine. You might be presented with additional updates to install. However, installing updates other than those listed might produce unanticipated results when the students perform the exercises. (Alternatively, sort the available updates by date published and install all updates published before May 1, 2007.)

- Update for Windows Vista (KB932246)
- Update for Windows Vista (KB931573)
- Update for Windows Mail Junk E-mail Filter [March 2007] (KB905866)
- Update for Windows Vista (KB930857)
- Updates for Windows Media Format 11 SDK for Windows Vista (KB929399)
- Definition Update for Windows Defender – KB15597 (Definition 1.16.2428.7)
- Windows Malicious Software Removal Tool – March 2007 (KB890830)
- Update for Windows Vista (KB928089)
- Definition Update for Windows Defender – KB9155976 (Definition 1.16.2430.5)
- Security Update for Windows Vista (KB925902)
- Security Update for Windows Vista (KB930178)
- Definition Update for Windows Defender – KB15597 (Definition 1.17.2529.3)
- Security Update for Windows Vista (KB925902)
- Update for Windows Vista (KB929735)
- Update for Windows Vista (KB931099)
- Definition Update for Windows Defender – KB15597 (Definition 1.18.2533.5)

> **TAKE NOTE***
> After installing updates make sure your server is started before you restart the client.

MODIFY AUTOMATIC UPDATING SETTINGS

1. After installing the updates, restart the client when prompted and log back on as locadmin.
2. To turn off automatic updating, click **Start**, then **All Programs**, then **Windows Update**.
3. Click the **Change Settings** link.
4. On the Choose How Windows Can Install Updates page, select the **Never Check For Updates (Not Recommended)** option and click **OK**.
5. In the User Account Control dialog box, click **Continue**.
6. Close Control Panel.

PREPARE TO JOIN THE DOMAIN

Before joining the domain, adjust your network settings. The server must be started before you execute the following procedures.

1. Click **Start** and then click **Network**.
2. Click **Network And Sharing Center**.
3. Click the **Manage Network Connections** link.
4. Right-click the **Local Area Connection** icon and select **Properties**.
5. Click **Continue** in the User Account Control dialog box.
6. Clear the **Internet Protocol Version 6 (TCP/IPv6)** checkbox.
7. Highlight the **Internet Protocol Version 4 (TCP/IPv4)** by clicking it and click **Properties**.

8. In the Internet Protocol Version 4 (TCP/IPv4) Properties dialog box, select the **Use The Following DNS Server Addresses** option. Key **10.1.1.200** (key **192.168.1.200** if using Virtual PC) in the Preferred DNS Server box. Click **OK.**
9. Click **Close** in the Local Area Connection Properties dialog box.
10. Close all Control Panel windows.

Depending on your network environment, you might also need to make the following settings:

- Static IP = 192.168.1.201,
- Default Gateway = 192.168.1.1,
- Alternate DNS server = 12.189.32.61, or use an appropriate alternate DNS server IP address for your Internet Service Provider (ISP)

JOIN THE DOMAIN

Now, you can join the client to the domain.

1. Click **Start**, then **Control Panel**, then **System And Maintenance.**
2. Click **System.**
3. Under the Computer Name, Domain, And Workgroup Settings section, click **Change Settings.**
4. Click **Continue** in the User Account Control dialog box.
5. From the System Properties dialog box, click **Network ID.**
6. Click **Next**, click **Next** a second time, and then click **Next** again.
7. In the Join A Domain Or Workgroup page, key **netadmin** in the User Name text box and key **p@ssw0rd** in the Password text box. Key **CONTOSO.COM** in the Domain name text box. Click **Next.**
8. If a message box is displayed indicating an account for Sales01 has been found in the domain, click **Yes.**
9. On the Do You Want To Enable A Domain User Account On This Computer page, click **Next.**
10. On the Choose An Account Type page, select the **Administrator** option and click **Next.**
11. Click **Finish.**
12. Close all windows and restart the client machine. Log back on to the client as *netadmin*, with the password *p@ssw0rd*.

If you would like your students to be able to experiment with various Organizational Units, you can now optionally download and install the Windows Vista Security Guide. To download the file, search www.microsoft.com for "Windows Vista Security Guide". After installing the guide, execute the Windows Vista Security Guide's Task 1 of Chapter 1, steps 1–8 to create the EC Environment as described in the Windows Vista Security Guide. These steps are not required for the labs, however, so they are optional.

If you are using Virtual PC you might want to set up differencing disks and create images to correspond with the server images detailed in Table 1. The client images for Labs 8 through 11 and for Labs 12 through 13 should incorporate the results of all the exercises in Lab 1 and Labs 3 through 7 but need no other changes.

CREATE SALES.TXT

The following steps must be completed after the user johnt has been created in Lab 1. The files will be used in Lab 8. If you are using Virtual PC and you are supplying the client images for Labs 8 through 11, you can perform this step as part of creating that image. If you are using physical machines, you can have your students perform this step before they start Lab 8.

1. Log onto the client as johnt.
2. Use Windows Explorer to create the folder and file ***C:\Sales data\sales.txt*** with the contents "This file contains sensitive sales data."
3. Making sure you are logged on as johnt, use the file properties/Advanced button to encrypt the Sales data folder.

Glossary

A

actions Used in reference to Task Scheduler. Activities the computer starts when a trigger is activated. For example, an action might be to email an administrator when a trigger event occurs (such as a write failure to a hard drive).

Active Directory A Microsoft Windows database hosted on Windows Server computers. The database contains a directory of the objects in your network, combined with a service that interfaces with applications to enable you to manage the objects in the network.

ActiveX The set of ActiveX controls that are linked to a web page and can be downloaded and executed by an ActiveX compliant browser, such as Internet Explorer.

ActiveX controls Programs that expand the functionality of web pages in ActiveX compliant web browsers.

ActiveX Installer Service (AxIS) A service that enables administrators to install ActiveX on client computers.

ActiveX Opt-in A scheme in which most ActiveX controls are disabled by default, and users must opt in to them before they can run.

additional rules Part of software restriction policies. Rules that are exceptions to the default security level in a software restriction policy.

Admin Approval Mode Part of UAC. The mode in which tasks run on a computer use the standard user token by default and require user consent to use the administrative token.

administrator token (AT) Part of UAC. The administrative token in a split token pair.

Administrators LGPO A local Group Policy object (LGPO) that applies only to administrators.

All Users profile A profile in Windows operating systems prior to Windows Vista. Contains profile data applied to all users that log onto a workstation.

Allow Used in reference to permissions. When you allow a user or group a permission, you enable that user or group to perform the associated actions.

alternate IP address An IP address used by a DHCP client when a DHCP server is not available.

AND A logical operation. In the context of subnetting, it is used to combine a subnet mask and IP address to determine the host ID and the network ID.

Application Compatibility Toolkit 5.0 (ACT) A tool for assessing software compatibility with Windows Vista.

approved installation site for ActiveX Controls A URL for storing ActiveX Controls that are approved for installation by an administrator.

authentication The validating of the identities of entities to one another on a network. For example, when you log on to your computer, you are authenticating yourself to it. Computers also can authenticate with each other when communicating over a network.

Automatic Updates The name for Automatic Updating in previous versions of Windows.

Automatic Updating A tool that enables you to automate the downloading and installation of updates from Windows Update and Microsoft Update (or from internal update servers, such as Windows Server Update Services 3.0 servers).

B

BitLocker A system in Windows Vista by which entire hard drive volumes can be encrypted. Even if a malicious user has physical access to the disk, it is still protected.

C

certificate authority (CA) A trusted third party that issues certificates.

certificate autoenrollment A feature of Windows Server 2003, Enterprise Edition that automatically uses the existing certificate to sign a renewal request for a new certificate before the existing certificate expires.

certificate rules Part of software restriction policies. A rule in software restriction policies that uses a certificate to identify software.

certificates Electronic documents that certify the identity of an entity, such as a user or a file.

CIDR notation Classless Inter-Domain Routing (CIDR) notation is a common way of expressing an IP address and subnet mask. An example is 192.168.255.22/2. The number after the forward slash indicates how many bits are allocated to subnetting the network, which determines how many subnets there are. The remaining bits are available for identifying hosts within each subnet.

collector Used in reference to Event Forwarding. A collector is the computer in an event forwarding subscription that collects events.

color depth The number of colors each pixel can be in a graphics image.

compatibility layers Compatibility-related settings you can configure for individual applications on the Compatibility tab of the Properties dialog box for the application.

Component Manifests Part of USMT 3.0. Files that contain Windows Vista data and settings that determine which operating system and browser settings are migrated and how they are migrated.

conditions Used in reference to Task Scheduler. Criteria that can override a trigger based on the state of the machine. For example, you can set a condition so that a task will run only if the computer is connected to an AC power source (in other words, if it is not running on battery power).

Config.xml Part of USMT 3.0. A configuration file used in configuring settings for profile migrations.

connection security rules Determine how Windows Firewall secures traffic between computers.

Consent User Interface (Consent UI) Used in reference to User Account Control. The collection of user interfaces that requests elevation from users to complete tasks.

CRT monitor Cathode ray tube (CRT) monitors use a CRT to project the image on the screen. Similar in design to traditional television sets.

custom rule Used in reference to Windows Firewall. A firewall rule based on custom criteria.

custom views Unique specification of criteria by which events are filtered that can be applied across multiple logs.

D

data integrity The extent to which data that is transmitted is identical to data received.

default security level Part of software restriction policies. Defines the behavior for all attempts to run software.

Deny Used in reference to permissions. When you deny a user or group a permission, you prevent that user or group from performing the associated actions. Denied permissions supersede allowed permissions.

designated file types Used in reference to software restriction policies. A list of file types that can be restricted as programs in a software restriction policy.

device A hardware item that your computer interacts with.

device class GUIDs (globally unique identifiers) A text string that identifies a class of devices.

device driver A hardware-dependent, operating system specific program that enables a computer to interact with a device.

device installation restrictions The policies in Group Policy that enable administrators to restrict the installation of devices.

Device Manager A tool for managing devices and device drivers.

DHCP client A DHCP client is a machine that uses DHCP to request an IP address lease and other information called DHCP options. An enterprise network has many DHCP clients, including printers and workstations, but also sometimes servers, routers, and other networked devices.

DHCP lease A DHCP lease is the entire package that a DHCP client receives from a DHCP server.

DHCP lease duration The duration for which a DHCP client is given a DHCP lease.

DHCP options A DHCP option is a piece of information that DHCP servers can optionally offer to DHCP clients. DHCP options include default gateway IP addresses, subnet masks, and IP addresses for DNS name servers.

DHCP server A DHCP server allocates IP addresses from a pool of IP addresses to DHCP clients and can optionally offer supporting information to the DHCP clients, called DHCP options.

DHCPACK Part of the DHCP protocol. The fourth and final step in a DHCP lease. A DHCP server chosen by a DHCP client assigns it an IP address and supporting DHCP options.

DHCPDISCOVER Part of the DHCP protocol. The first step in a DHCP lease. The DHCP client requests an IP address.

DHCPOFFER Part of the DHCP protocol. The second step in a DHCP lease. DHCP servers respond to a DHCPDISCOVER message from a DHCP client with an offering of an IP address.

DHCPREQUEST Part of the DHCP protocol. The third step in a DHCP lease. The DHCP client chooses a DHCP server from which to accept an offered IP address.

distributed compatibility evaluators Small programs installed on each computer being evaluated to gather and send application compatibility data to a single, centralized store where it is organized and can be viewed. Part of ACT.

distributed file system (DFS) DFS provides replication of files across multiple servers and the ability to route users transparently to the nearest available replicated copy of a given file.

Distribution Point (DP) A Systems Management Server where software packages are stored for SMS clients to download.

DNS caching DNS clients sometimes contain a cache, where the IP address for a given domain name is stored for a limited amount of time to avoid having to resolve the name again against a DNS server.

Domain Name System (DNS) a user-friendly naming convention for naming TCP/IP hosts. DNS names, called fully qualified domain names (FQDNs), are converted into IP addresses by DNS name servers so that TCP/IP hosts can communicate.

Domain Name System (DNS) name server A server that accepts DNS name resolution requests from DNS clients. DNS name servers convert FQDNs to IP addresses and vice-versa so that TCP/IP hosts can communicate with each other.

Domain profile Part of Windows Firewall. Profiles in Windows Firewall enable different behavior depending on what type of network a computer is logged onto. The domain profile is used when a computer is authenticated to an Active Directory domain of which the computer is a member. The Domain profile is active when all interfaces can authenticate to a domain controller.

Downlevel Manifests Part of USMT 3.0. Files that list settings and data for Windows XP and Windows 2000. Determine which operating system and browser settings are migrated and how they are migrated.

Dynamic Host Control Protocol (DHCP) A protocol that DHCP clients, such as computers running Windows Vista, can use to request and lease IP addresses from a DHCP server. The client can also use DHCP to request DHCP options.

E

effective permissions The permissions for a particular user for a particular object.

Encrypting File System (EFS) A file system used to encrypt files and folders.

encryption Encoding of data to make it unreadable by anybody but the intended reader.

enterprise single sign-on (SSO) A technology that enables users to authenticate to a wireless network access point and a domain in a single step.

Event Viewer A tool for viewing logged events in Windows operating systems.

F

file and registry virtualization The redirecting of attempts by an application to write data to secure areas of the file system or registry to instead write to non–security sensitive areas of a user's profile or the registry, as appropriate.

file path rules Part of software restriction policies. A rule in software restriction policies that uses a file's location to identify software.

filters Used in reference to Event Viewer. Filters display events that match a set of parameters that you specify in Event Viewer.

firewall A software device (which sometimes has hardware components) that limits inbound and sometimes outbound data connections on a network in an attempt to strengthen security.

firewall rules Control how Windows Firewall responds to incoming and outgoing traffic.

Folder Redirection The process of redirecting the saving and loading of data from a user profile folder to another folder (almost always a network share).

forwarder Used in reference to Event Forwarding. A computer that forwards events to a collector computer.

fully qualified domain names (FQDNs) User-friendly names for TCP/IP hosts.

G

gateway A TCP/IP host that enables hosts on one TCP/IP network to communicate with hosts on another TCP/IP network. Most commonly used to connect computers on a local area network to the Internet.

Group Policy Results Wizard A wizard used to determine the resultant policy that a user or computer, or group of users or computers, is subject to through Group Policy.

Group Policy The collective set of policy settings for users, computers, and other entities within Active Directory as applied through Group Policy objects (Group Policy can also include policy settings local to a specific computer).

Group Policy Modeling The act of modeling Group Policy schemes.

Group Policy Modeling Wizard A wizard for modeling Group Policy schemes.

Group Policy Objects (GPOs) Collections of settings that are applied through Active Directory and edited using the Group Policy Object Editor.

Group Policy Object (GPO) link order The order in which GPOs are applied.

Group Policy Software Installation (GPSI) Installing software to client computers by using Group Policy.

H

hardware ID A text string that identifies a device.

hash algorithm An algorithm that produces a fixed length character string from an input string such as a file.

hash rules Part of software restriction policies. A rule in software restriction policies that uses a hash to identify software.

hidden updates Updates you've asked Windows not to notify you about or to install automatically.

host firewall A firewall that can be run on individual hosts as protection against attacks originating from inside the local network, or from outside the network when perimeter defenses have failed.

host ID Identifies a host in a TCP/IP subnetting scheme.

I

image A file that contains the contents and structure of a data medium, such as a hard disk.

ImageX A command-line tool for administering WIM images.

inbound rule A Firewall rule applicable to incoming network traffic.

IntelliMirror A group of technologies that enables users' data and programs to follow them around a network.

Internet Explorer 7 (IE7) Program for browsing the Internet.

Internet Explorer add-ons Software components that extend the functionality of Internet Explorer.

Internet Explorer Compatibility Evaluator (IECE) Part of ACT 5.0. Identifies potential web application and website issues that occur due to the release of a new operating system.

Internet Explorer Protected Mode A mode the gives Internet Explorer the privileges it needs to browse the Internet while withholding privileges needed to silently install programs or modify sensitive system data. Available only on Windows Vista or later, running Internet Explorer 7 or later.

Internet Protocol Security (IPsec) A suite of protocols for securing communication between two TCP/IP hosts.

Inventory collector Compatibility evaluator that identifies installed applications and gathers system information.

IP address In IPv4, a 32-bit numeric address that identifies a TCP/IP host, such as a computer. In IPv6, IP addresses are expressed in hexadecimal and are 128 bits long, providing for a much larger address space.

Ipconfig A command-line utility for displaying and configuring TCP/IP client settings.

K

key exchange When two peers create a shared secret key across an unsecured network.

L

last writer wins Used in reference to the application of Group Policy settings. Last writer wins means that the last GPO to designate a configuration for a policy setting is the GPO that determines the configuration for that policy setting.

LCD monitor Liquid crystal display (LCD) monitors use liquid crystal technology to display pixels. They are very flat in physical dimension compared to traditional (CRT) monitors.

LoadState Part of USMT 3.0. Responsible for deploying profile data and settings to destination computers in a profile migration.

Local Group Policy objects (LGPO) Group Policy Objects stored on the local computer instead of in Active Directory. LGPOs are limited in scope to the local computer.

Local resources Used in reference to networking. Resources that exist on or are directly attached to the local computer.

local UserProfile location The default location for the loading and saving of data within a user profile.

loopback address The special IP address 127.0.0.1. This IP address represents the host no matter the host's actual IP address.

M

Management Point (MP) Advanced clients communicate with Systems Management Server Management Points to retrieve Advanced Client Policy and check for advertisements.

master computer The computer from which you capture a customized WIM image.

maximum resolution The highest screen resolution that your monitor and video card combination is able to display.

Microsoft Office Update A website that provides updates for all the programs in the Microsoft Office suite. This site overlaps with the Microsoft Update site, which also offers updates for Microsoft Office 2007, Microsoft Office 2003, and Microsoft Office XP.

Microsoft Update A website that provides updates for Microsoft Windows Vista, Microsoft Office, and other current Microsoft applications. It supports Windows Vista, Windows XP, Windows 2000 SP4 or later, and Windows Server 2003. It also provides updates for Microsoft Office 2007, Microsoft Office XP, Microsoft Office 2003, Microsoft SQL Server, and Microsoft Exchange Server.

Microsoft Windows User State Migration Tool (USMT) version 3.0 A tool for migrating profile data and settings from source workstations to destination workstations during large deployments of Windows XP and Windows Vista.

MigApp.xml Part of USMT 3.0. A configuration file used in configuring migration of application settings in profile migrations.

MigSys.xml Part of USMT 3.0. A configuration file used in configuring migration of system settings in profile migrations.

MigUser.xml Part of USMT 3.0. A configuration file used in configuring migration of user settings in profile migrations.

modularization Used in reference to the architecture of Windows Vista. A componentization of the Windows Vista operating system into distinct modules that work together to perform operating system functions.

native resolution The highest resolution that an LCD monitor is able to display without truncating pixels (removing pixels from images to mimic higher resolutions).

N

Net view A command-line tool for displaying the network resources on the local computer.

Network Access Protection (NAP) A technology that can restrict computers from connecting to a network if they do not meet minimum thresholds for security and system health.

network ID Identifies a network in a TCP/IP subnetting scheme.

network resources Resources that are available through the network.

network zone rules Part of software restriction policies. A rule in software restriction policies that uses a program's URL to identify software.

Non-Administrators LGPO An LGPO that applies only to non-administrators.

non-destructive imaging Non-destructive imaging enables you to partially apply an image without overwriting the target drive. This means that you can selectively install part of an image to an existing installation.

NOT A logical operation. In the context of subnetting, it is used to combine a subnet mask and IP address to determine the host ID and the network ID.

Nslookup A command-line tool for making DNS queries to a DNS server.

NTFS The file system that Windows Vista uses.

NTFS permissions The component of NTFS that controls user access. Also exerts control over files and folders.

O

octet Used in reference to IP addresses. One of four parts of an IPv4 IP address. Each octet contains is 8 bits in length.

organizational unit (OU) Containers in Active Directory that can contain other OUs and objects such as users and computers.

outbound rule A firewall rule applicable to outgoing network traffic.

P

path rules Part of software restriction policies. A rule in software restriction policies that uses a software file's location or its registry information to identify the software.

Pathping A command-line tool for tracing TCP/IP data from the local TCP/IP client to another TCP/IP client. Pathping offers statistics on how long the data takes to get to its destination along the path.

performance counters Used in reference to the Performance Monitor. Measurements of system state or activity, for example, CPU utilization as a percentage.

Performance Monitor A component of the Windows Reliability and Performance Monitor that focuses on system performance.

Phishing Filter Part of Internet Explorer. Attempts to detect phishing scams, which solicit personal information as an attempt at identity theft.

Ping A command-line tool for troubleshooting networking. Enables you to check connectivity between your TCP/IP client and another TCP/IP client.

pixels Single points in graphics images.

Plug and Play (PNP) A protocol that enables devices to communicate information about themselves to computers.

port rule Used in reference to Windows Firewall. A firewall rule based on what port is being used to communicate.

pre-defined rule Used in reference to Windows Firewall. A firewall rule based on pre-defined criteria.

principle of least privilege A principle that requires each subject in a system be granted the most restrictive set of privileges (or lowest clearance) needed for the performance of authorized tasks. The application of this principle limits the damage that can result from accident, error, or unauthorized use.

Private profile Part of Windows Firewall. Profiles in Windows Firewall enable different behavior depending on what type of network a computer is logged onto. The Private profile is used when a computer is connected to a private network behind a private gateway or router. Only a user with administrative privileges can designate a network as private.

privilege The right of an account, such as a user or group account, to perform various system-related operations on the local computer, such as shutting down the system, loading device drivers, or changing the system time.

Program Compatibility Assistant An application that sometimes intervenes when a program is not running correctly. Asks if you want to try running it as an administrator.

program rule Used in reference to Windows Firewall. A firewall rule based on which program is attempting to communicate.

public facing IP addresses IP addresses that are directly accessible from the Internet without being translated from another IP address space.

Public profile A profile in Vista that contains data that contains profile data applied to all users that log onto a workstation. This is the Vista version of the All Users profile in previous Windows operating systems.

Public profile Part of Windows Firewall. Profiles in Windows Firewall enable different behavior depending on what type of network a computer is logged onto. The Public profile is used when a computer is connected directly to an unidentified network in a public location. The Public profile is active when there is at least one public network or unidentified connection.

R

refresh rate How fast in hertz (Hz; number of times per second) the screen is redrawn.

registry path rules Part of software restriction policies. A rule in software restriction policies that uses the registry entry for a program to identify it.

Reliability Monitor A component of the Windows Reliability and Performance Monitor that focuses on system reliability.

Remote Assistance A technology in Windows operating systems that enables a technology professional or other user to connect to your computer remotely to assist you.

Reset Internet Explorer Settings (REIS) A feature in Internet Explorer 7 and later that enables you to reset many Internet Explorer settings to the default state simultaneously.

resolving Process of looking up a domain name with DNS to find out its IP address.

Restart Manager Limits the number of restarts needed after updates or installations by checking whether the part of the system that needs to be updated can be cleared and updated without affecting the system adversely. Part of Automatic Updating.

Resultant Set of Policy (RSoP) Snap-in that is used to see how multiple Group Policy objects affect various combinations of users and computers or to predict the effect of Group Policy settings on the network.

roaming profiles User profiles that are stored on a network share so that a user's profile can be loaded on any computer that can access the share.

routers A TCP/IP host that can route TCP/IP traffic between other TCP/IP hosts.

S

ScanState Part of USMT 3.0. Responsible for saving profile data and settings from source workstations in a profile migration.

schtasks.exe A command-line tool for configuring tasks in Task Scheduler.

scope Used in reference to GPOs. The set of objects to which the policies in a GPO apply.

scope of management (SOM) The Active Directory objects to which a Group Policy Object applies.

screen resolution Measurement of how many pixels horizontally by how many pixels vertically your screen displays.

Secure Desktop Part of UAC. A desktop that Windows Vista uses to alter the user interface to protect against malware fooling users into selecting an option that they do not mean to accept.

Security Configuration and Analysis Snap-in A tool used to analyze and deploy security settings.

security templates Used in reference to the Security Configuration and Analysis snap-in. A collection of security settings used by the Security Configuration and Analysis snap-in.

security zones A division of URL namespace for the purposes of applying security levels accordingly.

settings Used in reference to Task Scheduler. Execution options for tasks. For example, you can use settings to determine how many times a task is retried if it fails for some reason.

signed drivers Used in reference to Windows Vista. Drivers that have met the Designed for Windows Vista requirements and have been given a digital signature.

single instancing Used in reference to WIM images. The storing of identical files only once in a WIM image. The file is stored once, and metadata indicates how many instances there are in the original data and where they are located.

smart card A plastic card about the size of a credit card. A data smart card has electronic logic embedded in it in; for, smartcards with processing ability have a microprocessor. Smart cards are commonly used to store digital signatures, authenticate users, and store encryption keys to encrypt or decrypt data.

Software Explorer Part of Windows Defender. A tool that enables you to view detailed information about software that can affect privacy and security, and to control startup programs (programs that are started when you start Windows Vista).

software restriction policies (SRP) Group Policy settings that restrict the running of software.

Special permissions The permissions that NTFS uses to control user access. Also offers control over files and folders.

split token Part of UAC. Windows Vista implements a split token when you log on as an administrator, which means that you are issued two tokens: an administrator token (AT) and a standard user token (SUT). The AT is filtered to create the SUT by removing privileges. Tasks are started using the SUT, and you must explicitly elevate to use the AT if the task requires it.

spyware Typically malware or websites that attempt to gather data from you or your computer and send it across the Internet to a party with possible malicious intent.

Standard permissions Collections of special permissions grouped together to make administration of permissions easier.

standard user token (SUT) Part of UAC. The standard user token in a split token pair.

subnet masks A 4-octet number that looks like an IP address and divides IP addresses into network IDs and host IDs. Similar to IP addresses, subnet masks are composed of 4 octets. The most common values of the octets in a subnet mask are 255 and 0. An example of a subnet mask for the IP address 10.23.132.23 is 255.0.0.0.

subnets Subdivisions of TCP/IP networks created by subnetting with subnet masks.

subnetting Using subnet masks to partition a network into smaller networks called subnets.

subscription A paring of a collector computer and forwarding computers in an event forwarding scheme.

Sysmain.sdb A database containing a very large list of legacy applications that require administrator privileges to run correctly.

System Information tool A tool that provides a large amount of information on a system, including details on hardware resources, hardware components (from optical drives to ports and input devices), and the software environment (for example, drivers, print jobs, and running services).

T

task Used in reference to Task Scheduler. A task is an action combined with a trigger that instructs the action to execute.

task history Used in reference to Task Scheduler. Log entries for task successes, failures, and other task-related events.

Task Scheduler A Microsoft Management Console snap-in that administrators can use to schedule tasks according to a schedule, event occurrence, or change in the system state.

Terminal Services A set of services that enables you to access applications or data stored on a remote computer over a network connection.

Terminal Services Gateway server (TS Gateway server) A server that a Terminal Services user can connect to as a connection-point between the remote computer and the computer that the user wants to connect to.

token Contains information that identifies you to the computer (tokens are based on your security identifier, also called a SID) and details what privileges you have.

Top-Level Domain names (TLDs) The most broad level in the hierarchical structure of a fully qualified domain name. For example, .com, .gov, and .net.

TraceRt A command-line tool for tracing TCP/IP data from the local TCP/IP client to another TCP/IP client.

Transmission Control Protocol/Internet Protocol (TCP/IP) The most commonly used protocol for communication on computer networks. The network communications protocol that is the basis for the Internet.

transparency Used in reference to encryption. The extent to which the user does not notice that a file is encrypted.

triggers Used in reference to Task Scheduler. Criteria that when met cause the computer to start actions. For example, you can set a time each week to be a trigger.

Trusted Platform Module (TPM) A hardware component used to store cryptographic information, such as encryption keys, and to perform other security duties. BitLocker can use TPMs in its encryption scheme.

U

update compatibility evaluator (UCE) Part of ACT 5.0. Gathers information on application dependencies and can identify potential effects of Windows operating system security updates on applications.

User Account Control (UAC) Primarily a set of policies to reduce the exposure and attack surface of Windows Vista by requiring that all users run in standard user mode unless it is necessary to do otherwise. Essentially, User Account Control enforces the principle of least privilege.

User Account Control Compatibility Evaluator (UACCE) Part of ACT 5.0. Identifies potential compatibility issues due to permissions restrictions enforced by User Account Control (UAC).

user profile A collection of user data that partly dictates user settings and user experience when logged onto Windows.

user-specific LGPOs LGPOs that apply to a specific user.

V

virtual private network (VPN) A private network established within a public network (most frequently the Internet).

VPN server A server to which users can connect through the Internet to create a VPN.

W

Wi-Fi Protected Access (WPA) A wireless security protocol. WPA was designed to eliminate the known security flaws of WEP. Wireless devices and the access point use a pre-shared key (PSK) that can be either a 256-bit number or an alphanumeric password between 8 and 63 characters long.

Wi-Fi Protected Access 2 (WPA2) A wireless security protocol. WPA2 is currently the preferred security technology for enterprise wireless networks. It uses 802.1X-based authentication and Advanced Encryption Standard (AES) encryption. This ensures that the data is from who it says it is from, and that the data cannot be easily decrypted or altered. There are two versions of WPA2: WPA2-personal and WPA2-enterprise. WPA2-enterprise requires that a user authenticate on the network before wireless connectivity is granted.

Windows Automated Installation Kit (WAIK) A tool for deploying Windows Vista.

Windows Deployment Services (Windows DS) A set of services that enables you to deploy Windows Vista remotely using Windows PE and Windows DS Server.

Windows Diagnostic Infrastructure (WDI) A set of built-in monitoring tools, diagnostic logic, and solutions that help users and administrators diagnose and resolve computer problems

Windows Event Collector service A service that must be run on the collector computer in an event forwarding scheme.

Windows Firewall A host firewall offered by Microsoft (included with Windows Vista).

Windows Firewall Settings dialog box A configuration control panel for Windows Firewall.

Windows Imaging Format (WIM) image Microsoft's proprietary image file format for storing images of Windows operating systems.

Windows Installer (MSI) Windows Installer is a proprietary Microsoft system for installing applications on Windows operating systems. The file extension for Windows Installer packages is .msi.

Windows Network Diagnostics Part of the Windows Diagnostic Infrastructure (WDI). A tool that helps users and administrators solve networking issues.

Windows Preinstallation Environment (Windows PE) A very basic operating system used for installing Windows Vista and other Windows operating systems.

Windows Reliability and Performance Monitor A tool that enables you to monitor and analyze system performance and reliability. It is a combination of new technologies and the following legacy tools: Performance Logs and Alerts (PLA), Server Performance Advisor (SPA), and System Monitor.

Windows Remote Management service A service that must be run on both the collector computer and forwarder computers in an event forwarding scheme.

Windows Server Update Services 3.0 (WSUS) Administration console A console for administering Windows Server Update Services 3.0 (WSUS) that can be installed on any Windows computer in the domain.

Windows Server Update Services (WSUS) server A component of Windows Server Update Services 3.0 (WSUS) installed on a Windows server that enables administrators to manage and distribute updates by using the WSUS 3.0 Administration console.

Windows Server Update Services 3.0 (WSUS) Services that manage the distribution of updates to workstation computers and that enable you to track update deployment.

Windows Update A website that provides updates for current Windows operating systems (it therefore overlaps with Microsoft Update) and the following earlier versions of Windows: Windows 2000 SP2 or earlier, Windows Me, Windows 98, Windows 95, and Windows NT Workstation 4.0. It also provides updates for applications that come with Windows, such as Internet Explorer.

Windows Vista Capable PC Microsoft's designation for computers capable of running Windows Vista's core functions.

Windows Vista compatibility evaluator Part of ACT 5.0. Identifies miscellaneous issues related to compatibility with Windows Vista.

Windows Vista Hardware Assessment tool A tool for assessing hardware compatibility with Windows Vista.

Windows Vista Premium Ready PC Microsoft's designation for computers capable of running all or most of Windows Vista's functionality.

Windows Vista Upgrade Advisor A tool for evaluating the hardware and software of an individual system for compatibility with Windows Vista.

Wired Equivalent Policy (WEP) A wireless security protocol. It encrypts data between any device and its access point. It requires a WEP key, which you supply to the wireless devices that connect to the access point. The key can be either 60 bits long or 128 bits long (5 or 13 characters long). WEP has known vulnerabilities that enable hackers to crack it with retail hardware. WEP is not recommended for enterprise use.

wireless network profiles Contain connections to wireless networks.

X

xml control files Part of USMT 3.0. The set of files that controls ScanState and LoadState behavior in a profile migration.

Index